RETIREMENT SAVINGS PLANS

Design, Regulation, and Administration of Cash or Deferred Arrangements

RETIREMENT SAVINGS PLANS

Design, Regulation, and
Administration of Cash
or Deferred Arrangements

David A. Littell
Donald C. Cardamone
Wilhelm L. Gruszecki

JOHN WILEY & SONS, INC.

New York • Chichester • Brisbane • Toronto • Singapore

This publication is designed to provide accurate and authoritative information in regard to the subject matter covered. It is sold with the understanding that the publisher is not engaged in rendering legal, accounting, or other professional services. If legal advice or other expert assistance is required, the services of a competent professional person should be sought. *From a Declaration of Principles jointly adopted by a Committee of the American Bar Association and a Committee of Publishers.*

Library of Congress Cataloging-in-Publication Data

Littell, David A.
    Retirement savings plans : design, regulation, and administration of Cash or Deferred Arrangements / David A. Littell, Donald C. Cardamone, Wilhelm L. Gruszecki.
        p.   cm.
    Includes index.
    ISBN 0-471-57112-1
    1. Pension trusts—United States. 2. Pension trusts—Law and legislation—United States. 3. Deferred compensation—Law and legislation—United States. 4. Income tax—United States— Deductions—Retirement contributions. I. Cardamone, Donald C. II. Gruszecki, Wilhelm. III. Title.
HD7105.45.U6L57   1992
331.25'2—dc20   92-32666
                                                                      CIP

Printed in the United States of America

10 9 8 7 6 5 4 3 2 1

THE EMPLOYEE BENEFITS LIBRARY FROM WILEY LAW PUBLICATIONS

CANADIAN HANDBOOK OF FLEXIBLE BENEFITS
Hewitt Associates—Robert J. McKay, Editor

DRAFTING AND REVISING EMPLOYMENT HANDBOOKS
Kurt H. Decker and H. Thomas Felix II

EMPLOYEE BENEFITS CLAIMS LAW AND PRACTICE
Henry H. Perritt, Jr.

ERISA: A COMPREHENSIVE GUIDE
Martin Wald and David E. Kenty

ERISA CASE DIGEST (TWO VOLUMES)
Jaime Ruth Ebenstein and Mark E. Schmidtke

ERISA LITIGATION FORMBOOK
Jaime Ruth Ebenstein and Mark E. Schmidtke

FEDERAL REGULATION OF EMPLOYEE BENEFITS
James O. Castagnera and David A. Littell

FUNDAMENTALS OF FLEXIBLE COMPENSATION
Hewitt Associates—Dale L. Gifford and Christine Seltz, Editors

MANAGING ADA: THE COMPLETE COMPLIANCE GUIDE
Ari Cowan and Robert A. Naeve

MANAGING COBRA: THE COMPLETE COMPLIANCE GUIDE
Ari Cowan and Lee T. Paterson

PENSION PLAN TERMINATIONS
Edward Thomas Veal and Edward R. Mackiewicz

RETIREMENT SAVINGS PLANS: DESIGN, REGULATION, AND ADMINISTRATION
OF CASH OR DEFERRED ARRANGEMENTS
David A. Littell, Donald C. Cardamone, and Wilhelm L. Gruszecki

SUBSCRIPTION NOTICE

This Wiley product is updated on a periodic basis with supplements to reflect important changes in the subject matter. If you purchased this product directly from John Wiley & Sons, Inc., we have already recorded your subscription for this update service.

If, however, you purchased this product from a bookstore and wish to receive (1) the current update at no additional charge, and (2) future updates and revised or related volumes billed separately with a 30-day examination review, please send your name, company name (if applicable), address, and the title of the product to:

Supplement Department
John Wiley & Sons, Inc.
One Wiley Drive
Somerset, NJ 08875
1-800-225-5945

HOW TO USE THIS BOOK

This book comprises a complete review of the design, implementation, administration, and regulation of each of the types of employer-sponsored employee savings plans that an employer can establish. The book covers the following types of plans:

- 401(k) cash or deferral plans;
- 403(b) annuity plans;
- simplified employee pensions;
- nonqualified deferred compensation plans.

With regard to each of these plans, the book can be used in a number of ways:

- As a primer on employer-sponsored savings plans;
- As a reference on the federal regulation of each type of employee savings plan;
- As a guide to determining which type of plan is best suited for a particular employer;
- As a source of suggestions regarding the specific design features (or redesign) of each type of plan;
- As a tool to assist in the ongoing administration of the plan established;
- As a research source for sample forms.

Part II, which describes the legal implications and ramifications of all types of employer-sponsored employee savings plans, can be used to become familiar with each type of plan and to find references to specific rules. The materials are comprehensive and give in-depth coverage.

For the employer interested in establishing any of the plans discussed in this book, Part III proceeds through the determination of which type of plan is best for a particular employer, to address both the general and specific concerns involved with designing a plan. Part III will be equally useful to an employer considering making design changes.

Part IV identifies each of the tasks involved in the setup and ongoing administration of each type of plan, and discusses particular areas of concern and sensitivity.

The appendixes provide numerous plan documents, administrative forms, design worksheets, and other useful forms and documents.

D.A.L.
D.C.C.
W.L.G.

PREFACE

Today, more and more employers are offering their employees savings programs that provide an opportunity to save on a tax-preferential basis. The trend probably has many roots, but several reasons stand out more prominently than others. Money is tighter, for both public and private employers, and other types of retirement benefits are, in many cases, being limited or reduced.

Employers that are still very concerned about employees' financial readiness for retirement have the option of establishing savings plans that allow participants to save on a tax-preferential basis. The Internal Revenue Code's § 401(k) allows private, for-profit employers to sponsor plans to which employees can elect to contribute amounts that they would otherwise have received in cash on a tax-preferential basis. Small private employers have the option to adopt a somewhat simpler arrangement, referred to as a simplified employee pension (SEP). Public school systems, and most nonprofit employers, are allowed, under Code § 403(b), to sponsor a similar type of plan, referred to as a "403(b) annuity plan." Finally, employers looking for a more flexible arrangement can generally allow employee savings on a tax-preferential basis through nonqualified arrangements.

These employer-sponsored plans allow employees a relatively simple route to a regular pattern of savings. The employer can further encourage this savings process by matching employee savings. This "marriage" between employer and employee savings can be mutually very beneficial: it limits the employer's cost of providing retirement benefits and helps the employee to begin to save for retirement.

This book is intended as a guide for employers, and their advisers, that are thinking of establishing or have already implemented one of these employee savings plans. Employers and their advisers will find it to be a resource that goes beyond simply a restatement of the rules; it gives guidance regarding the design, implementation, and ongoing administration of available plans, and it offers an in-depth look at the design and implementation of employer-sponsored savings plans. For employers establishing or maintaining such a plan, this book will aid in all aspects of plan development.

September 1992

DAVID A. LITTELL
Bryn Mawr, Pennsylvania

DONALD C. CARDAMONE
Trevose, Pennsylvania

WILHELM L. GRUSZECKI
Lansdowne, Pennsylvania

ABOUT THE AUTHORS

David A. Littell is an Assistant Professor of Taxation at the American College in Bryn Mawr, Pennsylvania, concentrating on employee benefit law. He also speaks and writes on this subject and maintains a legal practice in Lansdowne, Pennsylvania. He is a co-author of *Federal Regulation of Employee Benefits*. Previously, he was employed by the law firm of Saul, Ewing, Remick & Saul, and at Paul A. Tanker and Associates, an employee benefit consulting firm. Mr. Littell received a J.D. degree from Boston University and a B.A. from Northwestern University.

Donald C. Cardamone is a Senior Consultant with Richard Gabriel Associates in Trevose, Pennsylvania. He specializes in design, installation, and administration of all types of retirement programs. He provides consulting advice for publicly and privately held corporations, nonprofit organizations, municipalities, and labor unions. He has more than 20 years' experience providing actuarial and employee benefits services. Mr. Cardamone received an M.B.A. in investment finance and a B.A. in mathematics from Temple University.

Wilhelm L. Gruszecki is a Participating Associate in the law firm of Pearlstine/Salkin Associates, Lansdowne, Pennsylvania. His practice is concentrated in the area of employee benefits and business law. He is admitted to the Pennsylvania Bar, the Federal District Court for Pennsylvania's Middle District, and the United States Supreme Court.

He received a B.A. degree from Dickinson College, a J.D. degree from Drake University Law School, and an LL.M. degree from Villanova University School of Law.

For Wilhelm M., Violet, Kimberly, Ashley,
and Matthew Gruszecki.

WLG

Thanks to Edward for all his support.

DAL

For all those I met along the way who provided
opportunities for professional and personal growth.

DCC

SUMMARY CONTENTS

DETAILED CONTENTS

PART I
OVERVIEW

CHAPTER 1

OVERVIEW OF CASH OR DEFERRED ARRANGEMENTS

§ 1.1   Why Offer a Cash or Deferred Arrangement?

More and more employers are choosing today to include as part of their employee benefit program a savings plan for employees. For example, a Department of Labor (DOL) report ("Trends in Pensions, 1992") shows a rapid increase in the number of plan participants in Code § 401k plans ("401(k) plans") in the 1980s. Participation grew from 4.4 million persons covered in 1983 to 15.5 million participants in 1987. There are many reasons for this trend, including the reasons described below.

An employer-sponsored plan can generally provide employees the opportunity to save on a tax-deferred basis. Employees can reduce their taxable income (for federal income tax purposes) by electing to defer a portion of their compensation until a later time. These amounts are segregated and earn interest on a pretax basis. The amount saved is not treated as taxable income until the time it is distributed. Deferral of taxation will generally result in a larger total sum saved for retirement.[1] Tax deferral is a central theme in employer savings plans. (The impact of tax deferral is discussed further in § **1.2.**)

Outside of the employer–employee relationship, the opportunity to save "pretax" dollars is quite limited. Employees (if they earn at least $2,000) may establish an individual retirement arrangement (IRA) and contribute up to $2,000 annually. The earnings on the amounts in the IRA are not taxed until distributed. In some circumstances, the contribution may be

---

[1] Note that the impact of tax deferral is dependent on several factors, including the current tax rate, the tax rate at the time the amount is included in taxable income, interest earnings on the investments, and the length of deferral.

deducted for federal tax purposes, which essentially means that the individual may save pretax dollars. However, if the individual, or his or her spouse, is a participant in most types of employer-sponsored retirement plans, the ability to take the tax deduction may be limited or eliminated.

> *Example:* A single person with earnings in excess of $35,000 will not be able to take any deduction for a contribution to an IRA.

Even in the case of an individual who would otherwise be able to take a $2,000 deduction, this limit is substantially lower than the annual pretax contribution limits in employer-sponsored plans.

> *Example:* An individual may make a pretax contribution to a § 403(b) annuity plan in the amount of $9,500 a year (subject to certain other limitations).

An employer-sponsored savings plan may provide employees with a method to "discipline" their savings by offering a savings mechanism on a pretax basis. Many individuals find saving through payroll deductions easier than saving in other environments.

Savings plans are often designed so that employee contributions are matched (to some extent) by employer contributions. In this way, the employer and employee share the expense of saving for retirement. This joint savings approach appears to be well received by employees; they seem to have more awareness (and maybe even appreciation) of the cost of the benefit program to the employer. More traditional retirement plans may cost the employer a great deal of money without employees understanding or appreciating the benefit.

An employee savings plan that includes employer matching is also a way to limit the employer's expense for providing retirement benefits by involving the employees.

As employee pretax savings plans become a benefit offered by many employers, an employer without such a program may be at a competitive disadvantage in attempting to attract and retain employees.

Commingled investment may result in greater investment returns than investing separately. Example, an employer plan with significant assets can negotiate a high rate of return in an investment contract (GIC).

§ 1.2   The Joys of Tax Deferral

There are many reasons for an employer to sponsor an employees savings plan. Tax deferral can often result in substantially larger accumulations of capital at retirement than saving on a posttax basis. With pretax savings, larger amounts are set aside to accumulate. They accumulate more rapidly than after-tax savings, because of the deferral of taxation of interest earnings. Just how much better off an individual will be, saving on a pretax basis, depends on the assumed rate of interest earnings that the individual will earn and the taxrate that will be paid at the time of distribution from the plan. The following example serves to demonstrate the impact of tax deferral on retirement savings.

Example: Sylvia is age 45, earns $42,000, and is looking to save for retirement (at age 65). She pays taxes at a combined state and federal rate of 30 percent. She thinks that she would like to save $2,000 a year, but she knows that she needs $28,000 to meet her costs of living. If she saves using a salary deferral election under a 401(k) plan, she will be able to save $2,000 a year and still have $28,000 of net income. However, she is concerned about having to pay income taxes later on the 401(k) accumulation. Sylvia's financial adviser tells her that she will be better off using the 401(k) approach than saving outside of the 401(k).

In support of the choice of the 401(k), the comparison in **Table 1–1** will be helpful. Assume that Sylvia's 30 percent combined federal and state tax rate will not change; that she will earn 10 percent (pretax) on her

Table 1–1

Comparison of 401(k) Plan and Personal Savings Alternative

	Personal Savings	401(k)
Current Year:		
Gross earnings	$42,000	$42,000
401(k) deferral	—	2,000
Taxable compensation	$42,000	$40,000
Federal and state taxes	12,600	12,000
Net pay	29,400	28,000
Living expenses	28,000	28,000
Personal savings for retirement	1,400	-0-
Immediate gain for IRA: $600 ($2,000 − $1,400)		
At Age 65:		
Interest earnings	7% aftertax	10% pretax
Savings accumulation (annual contribution + earnings)	$57,394	$114,550
Taxes on distribution	$ 0	34,365
Net cash for retirement	$57,394	$80,185

investments; and that at age 65 she will receive the entire distribution and pay taxes on it.

This simple comparison demonstrates the power of tax deferral. Under this set of assumptions, Sylvia will have $80,185 at retirement if she saves using the 401(k) plan, versus $57,394 if she does not.

It is important to understand that many variables will impact the results in the above example. Some of the most important factors are:

- If pretax savings are in a qualified plan, an individual who receives a single-sum distribution may be eligible for special tax treatment, which further increases the advantages of tax deferral.
- An individual can generally receive benefits in a stream of payments, which would result in a longer period of deferral and consequently in larger posttax savings.
- Generally, the longer the period of the deferral, the more pronounced the impact of saving within the tax-deferred environment.
- The advantage of deferral is enhanced if tax rates are lower (than the current rate) at the time distributions are made.
- The advantage of deferral is diminished if tax rates are higher (than the current rate) at the time distributions are made.

§ 1.3   The Defined-Contribution Approach

All of the plans discussed in this book use the individual account plan approach. Individual account plans that are qualified plans under the Internal Revenue Code ("the Code") § 401 are also referred to as defined-contribution plans. The similarity that all individual account plans have in common is that, as contributions are made to the plan by either the employer or the employee, the contribution is allocated to the account of an individual participant under the plan. In most of the plans discussed in this book, the contributions are made to a single funding vehicle, usually a trust. As amounts are contributed to the trust, they are allocated to participants' accounts. A participant "account" is a bookkeeping entry, one for each participant. The account identifies the portion of the trust attributable to each participant. All dollars held in the trust fund are allocated to a particular participant's account. The accounts of participants grow over time as additional contributions are made. In some situations, a participant who leaves the employer before completing a minimum amount of service will lose or "forfeit" some or all of his or her account. The concept of forfeiture is referred to as "vesting." When the necessary service has been completed, a participant is deemed to be "vested" in such amount. If forfeitures occur in a plan, the forfeitures are either allocated among other persons' accounts or used to reduce contributions.

In an individual account plan, the investment experience on amounts held in the fund will be allocated to participants' accounts. Therefore, if the investments earn interest, or if growth in the underlying investments occurs, individual accounts will grow. If there are any losses on the investments, participants will share in them as well. Sometimes, the administrative costs of operating the plan will be withdrawn from the fund, which also will reduce the value of participants' benefits. At other times, the employer will pay administrative costs directly from company funds. Interest experience and administrative expense are usually allocated pro rata, based on individual account balances in relation to the total account balances held under the plan.

The following Sections review the basic features of each type of individual account plan discussed in this book.

§ 1.4   401(k) Plans

Certain employer-sponsored retirement plans that receive special tax treatment under Code § 401 may include a provision allowing participants the option to choose between receiving current versus deferred compensation. These *cash or deferred arrangements* are referred to as "CODAs." A CODA can be provided as part of a profit-sharing plan or stock bonus plan (or, in some circumstances, a money purchase pension plan in effect since 1973). Under a CODA arrangement, an employee who is eligible to participate in the plan may elect to have amounts, which he or she would otherwise be entitled to receive as cash, contributed to the plan. The amounts are contributed to a trust and are allocated to the account of the employee. The trust is an irrevocable trust for the benefit of the participants (meaning that the trust assets are secured from the creditors of the employer). Trust fund assets are invested, and participants share in the investment experience. The investments are under the control of trustees. However, the participants are often given the option to choose to have assets held on their behalf invested in one of several investment options.

The amounts that an individual elects to defer under a CODA are generally excluded from the individual's taxable income for purposes of federal income taxes at the time the election is made, and will not be taxed until distributed from the plan.

Because a CODA is a "feature" of another type of plan, the plan may also contain other types of employer (and, possibly, employee) contributions. For instance, a plan may provide employer profit-sharing contributions, employer matching contributions, and employee aftertax contributions.

Amounts contributed to the plan on the behalf of the participants are taxed at the time of distribution, as in any other qualified retirement plan. This also means that, if certain eligibility requirements are met, the distribution may be subject to special "lump sum" tax treatment.

A dollar limit is imposed on the total amount of elective contributions an individual may exclude from gross income for any taxable year, under all cash or deferral elections. The dollar limit for 1992 is $8,728.

A mathematical test, known as the actual deferral percentage test ("ADP test"), begins by calculating the amount of money deferred into the plan by each eligible employee, expressed as a percentage of salary. Employees are divided into two groups, HCEs (highly compensated employees) and non-HCEs, for the nondiscrimination test. The average of the ADPs of the non-HCE group determines the maximum average ADPs of the HCE group.

In addition, many plans that contain CODAs also provide that sponsors must contribute a matching amount based on the employee's elective deferrals. The matching contributions are an incentive for a participant to make elective deferrals. In that way, matching contributions can improve the results of the ADP test, by bringing up the level of participation of the non-HCE group and allowing the HCE group the opportunity to make larger deferrals.

Because matching contributions are based on the amount of elected deferrals made by the participant, a nondiscrimination test also applies to these amounts. One other type of discretionary contribution often allowed in such plans is an employee after-tax contribution. After-tax contributions are added to the employer's matching contributions and the two amounts are tested together. This test is performed in a manner similar to the ADP test. Under this separate discrimination test, referred to as the actual contribution percentage test ("ACP test"), employer matching contributions and any employee after-tax contributions are added together in order to determine an individual's ACP. As with the ADP test, the ACPs of the non-HCE group are averaged together. This average ACP of the non-HCE group determines the maximum average ACP of the HCE group.

All employee deferrals (CODA contributions) and any investment experience thereon must be nonforfeitable at all times. Other accounts accrued under the plan may be subject to a vesting schedule, as allowed generally for qualified retirement plans.

Qualified plans can require, as a condition of participation, one year of service and attainment of age 21 (see **Chapter 3**).

The right to make elective deferrals under a CODA is subject to the general rule that the plan cannot discriminate in favor of highly compensated employees. This means that the CODA feature must be nondiscriminatory in amount and availability. A plan could not, for example, provide that only highly compensated employees can defer bonus payments, even if all employees have the right to defer regular compensation earned.

In a profit-sharing plan, distributions may be made upon termination of employment, death, disability, attainment of retirement age, completion of a stated number of years (the minimum period is two years after the contribution has been made), or the occurrence of a stated event. However, when a profit-sharing plan contains a cash or deferral arrangement, the cash or deferral portion (including interest experience thereon) of the individual's profit-sharing account is subject to special withdrawal limitations. Like the other portions of the profit-sharing account, the cash or deferral account can be withdrawn at termination of employment (for any reason, including retirement, death, and disability). Unlike other profit-sharing accounts, such amounts cannot be withdrawn while the employee is still employed (often referred to as an in-service distribution), unless the individual has attained age 59½ or has suffered a financial hardship. In order for an individual to receive an in-service distribution based on a financial hardship, the participant must demonstrate that he or she has suffered an immediate and heavy financial need, and that the withdrawal is necessary to meet that need.

§ 1.5   403(b) Annuity Plans

Code § 403(b) provides special tax treatment for tax-sheltered annuities bought for employees by public schools and certain tax-exempt organizations. As with qualified plans, the tax benefit of a tax-sheltered annuity is that the employee is allowed to postpone paying tax on the employer's contributions toward the annuity (and earnings on such contributions) until receipt of the annuity payment. The entities eligible to sponsor such plans are generally not required to pay federal income taxes, and, therefore, sponsoring entities do not receive (nor do they need) a tax deduction for premiums paid into the plan.

The term tax-sheltered annuity actually describes a broader range of funding vehicles than annuities alone. These vehicles may include investments in custodial accounts holding mutual fund shares or, in the special case of church plans, investments held in "retirement income accounts." Contributions to tax-sheltered annuities may be made by salary reduction agreements between the employees and their employer.

A § 403(b) program can only be sponsored by employers that are exempt from tax under Code § 501(c)(3) or are educational institutions of a state, political subdivision of a state, or an agency or instrumentality of either of the above. Tax-exempt organizations under Code § 501(c)(3) generally include organizations that are organized and operated exclusively for religious, charitable, scientific, public safety testing, literary, or educational purposes.

Employers may use 403(b) plans in a number of ways (a feature that makes them similar to profit-sharing plans). In addition to salary deferral arrangements, the plan may provide promised employer contributions on a schedule that provides additional retirement benefits for its employees. Typically, such plans provide contributions as a uniform percentage of compensation; also, the employer contribution can be stated as an employer match. If this is true, the ACP test described for 401(k) plans applies to the match. However, the ADP test does not apply.

Both 403(b) plans and 401(k) plans are subject to minimum coverage and minimum participation requirements.

A 403(b) plan also is an employee pension plan subject to the requirements of ERISA. (These requirements are described in **Chapter 5**.) Coverage under ERISA generally requires that the plan be in writing; that employees are given a summary plan description, and other information; and that the plan file annual reports. ERISA coverage also means that individuals will be held to be fiduciaries, and will be held to a higher standard of care when dealing with the plan. Some types of 403(b) plans are exempted from the ERISA requirements. These include government plans, and certain plans that are entirely funded with employee arrangements to defer income.

Amounts contributed under salary reduction are excludable from gross income (for federal tax purposes) subject to three separate limitations: (1) the employee's deferral amount cannot exceed $9,500; (2) the limitation cannot exceed the employees' exclusion allowance (discussed in § **6.13**); (3) the contribution cannot exceed the Code § 415 limits, which do not allow annual additions to exceed 25 percent of compensation or $30,000.

§ 1.6   Simplified Employee Pensions (SEPs)

Another type of plan that may maintain employee arrangements to defer income on a tax-preferred basis is a simplified employee pension (SEP) plan. As its name implies, this type of plan is simpler than a qualified retirement plan. The documentation, reporting, and disclosure requirements are less cumbersome than for a qualified plan. Another substantial difference is that the plan is funded with individual retirement arrangements (usually referred to as IRAs), not with a commingled trust fund for participants. On the other hand, some SEP requirements are not any less burdensome than under a qualified plan. Unfortunately, this is especially true for a SEP containing a pretax salary reduction feature. The salary reduction nondiscrimination requirements under a SEP are just as burdensome as under a qualified plan: annual nondiscrimination testing (similar to the requirements described in **Chapter 2**) must be performed.

Because contributions under a SEP are made to IRAs, each of the "qualification requirements" applicable to IRAs is applicable to a SEP. These are discussed fully herein. Generally, individual retirement arrangements are established by individuals as a method of saving for retirement on a tax-preferential basis. An individual may make annual contributions of up to $2,000. The entire contribution is deductible, unless the individual participates in an employer-sponsored qualified retirement plan, SEP, or 403(b) plan, in which case the deduction may be limited or unavailable. In some cases, individuals may also contribute to a plan on behalf of their spouse. Earnings in such plans are not taxed until distributed from the plan. There are two types of individual retirement arrangements: individual retirement accounts and individual retirement annuities. Both of these vehicles have to meet a number of specific qualification requirements in order for an individual to receive the tax advantages described above.

Generally, compared to a qualified plan, establishing and maintaining a SEP is somewhat less burdensome. However, in exchange for simplicity, the rules allow for substantially less flexibility in the design of the plan. The plan has to meet rigid vesting, coverage, nondiscrimination, contribution, and withdrawal requirements. The specific requirements of establishing a SEP are discussed below.

An employer may provide a salary reduction feature, in which participants may elect to defer current income, which is contributed to an IRA on a pretax basis. The rules governing such arrangements are very similar to the rules contained in Code § 401(k). Salary reduction amounts are subject to the same maximum dollar limitation ($8,728 in 1992) and a nondiscrimination test. State and local governments, and tax-exempt organizations, may not establish salary reduction SEPs.

To qualify as a salary reduction SEP, the following requirements must be met: (1) the employer must have fewer than 25 employees eligible to participate during the plan year; (2) not less than 50 percent of the eligible employees must elect to defer salary; and (3) the employer must comply with nondiscrimination testing.

A SEP arrangement, as an employee pension benefit plan, is subject to the provisions of ERISA described in **Chapter 5**. However, simplified reporting and disclosure requirements apply if the following prerequisites are met.

The employer must use, as the written instrument, an IRS-provided form referred to as Form 5305-SEP. The form must be completed without modifications. If other documents are used, a SEP can still meet the reporting and disclosure requirements if the plan meets specific disclosure requirements described in the Regulations. Generally, the requirements are that the plan administrator must provide to all participants an explanation of the specific provisions of the SEP, as well as notification of any amendments to the plan.

§ 1.7   Nonqualified Deferred Compensation Plans

These salary reduction programs, like the other plans discussed in this book, are methods for employees to save for retirement. Also, like the other plans, the programs are primarily driven by the hypothesis that more savings will occur if tax is deferred until later. Nonqualified deferred compensation may also be provided as supplemental compensation to participants on a deferred basis. Such supplemental plans, referred to as SERPs, can be designed to meet a number of objectives, such as rewarding excellence, encouraging long-term employment, or encouraging excellence through incentive arrangements. The two approaches can be combined by encouraging employee savings and providing matching contributions.

Employee elective deferred compensation can be provided through tax-qualified retirement plans containing a CODA or through nonqualified arrangements. Both qualified and nonqualified plans are generally established with the intent of attracting and retaining talented employees.

From the viewpoint of both the employer and the employees, tax-qualified plans offer certain advantages over nonqualified arrangements. Because contributions to a qualified plan are deductible at the time the contributions are made, the employer receives a deduction at the time the employee elective deferrals are contributed to the plan, regardless of when participants actually receive benefits. In a nonqualified plan, the employer's deduction generally does not occur until the employee actually receives the deferred income. Under both qualified and nonqualified arrangements, the employee is generally taxed at the time benefits are received from the plan, and therefore the tax benefits are the same from the employee's perspective. However, benefits are not as secure in a nonqualified plan. In a qualified plan, the amounts subject to elective deferral by the employee are contributed to an irrevocable trust, which must be used for the exclusive benefit of the participants. In a nonqualified plan, the benefits are often paid out of general corporate assets or out of a trust known as a rabbi trust; both are subject to the corporation's creditors.

However, qualified plans, SEPs, and 403(b) plans have significant limitations, especially when the company's goal is specifically to reward and retain executives. Each of the other plans requires broad-based participation and similar benefits for all participants. Participants have to be immediately "vested" in any elective deferrals or after-tax contributions, and employer-provided benefits must be vested within a specified number of years. Benefits must be distributed within prescribed time periods. The maximum amount of benefits provided by such plans is limited, to the extent that it may be considered insufficient to provide adequate retirement benefits for management personnel. Contributions have to be held in trust, to be used solely for the provision of benefits, and not for company use.

Generally, a nonqualified plan may only be maintained for a select group of management or highly compensated employees, in order for the plan to be exempt from the participation, vesting, funding, and fiduciary requirements found in the other plans.

Some employers simply make a promise to pay executive deferred compensation, without setting aside any funds. In the past, employers would sometimes purchase insurance contracts or annuities to make the payment; however, to avoid current taxation to the participant, an employer had to be both owner and beneficiary of a contract. This meant that the participant in the plan had no more right to those assets than to any other asset of the employer. The use of annuity contracts has become less attractive, in light of Code § 72(u), which taxes income on an annuity contract held by anyone other than a natural person as income to the contract owner.

Along with the increase of hostile takeovers has come an increased interest in securing the promise to pay deferred compensation. Several methods of securing the promise exist; however, in no case can the plan's assets be protected from the sponsor's creditors without losing tax deferral.

§ 1.8   Terminology

In the retirement planning industry, the savings plans discussed in this book are identified by several different names. Following the industry, in this book certain plan terms are used interchangeably. To eliminate confusion, please note the following:

- A qualified retirement plan that allows participants the right to defer salary on a pretax basis is referred to as a:

  —401(k) plan

  —plan containing a CODA.

- A plan for a nonprofit organization or public school system subject to the rules of Code § 403(b) is referred to as a:

  —403(b) annuity plan

  —tax-sheltered annuity plan

—403(b) tax-sheltered annuity

—403(b) plan.

- A simplified employee pension containing a salary deferral feature and subject to the requirements of Code § 408(k) is referred to as a:

  —SEP

  —salary reduction SEP.

- A nonqualified arrangement that contains a salary deferral feature is referred to as a:

  —nonqualified plan

  —nonqualified arrangement

  —nonqualified deferred compensation plan.

PART II

LEGAL REQUIREMENTS

CHAPTER 2

TAX RULES FOR
401(k) PLANS

§ 2.1 General

Section 401(k) of the Internal Revenue Code ("the Code") permits certain qualified retirement plans to include a cash or deferral arrangement (CODA). A CODA is an arrangement, provided as part of a profit-sharing plan or stock bonus plan (or, in some circumstances, a money-purchase pension plan or rural cooperative plan, as discussed in § 2.3 below), that permits an eligible employee to elect to have his or her employer contribute an amount which the individual would otherwise be entitled to receive as cash (an "elective contribution").[1] The amounts that an individual elects to defer under a CODA are generally excluded from the individual's taxable income for purposes of federal income taxes at the time the election is made, and will not be taxed until distributed from the plan.[2] Because a CODA is a "feature" of one of the various types of qualified plans, the plan may also contain other types of employer (and possibly employee) contributions. For instance, a plan may provide employer profit-sharing contributions, employer matching contributions, and employee after-tax contributions.

Code § 401(k) is the sole means by which an employee may elect to make contributions to a qualified employee retirement plan on a pre-federal-tax basis. This means that if a qualified plan effectively gives participants a choice between participating in a qualified plan or receiving cash benefits in lieu of participation, the plan will be subject to the provisions of Code § 401(k), regardless of whether the plan identifies itself as a plan with a CODA arrangement. Treasury Regulations have discussed this issue at length with regard to qualified plans of partnerships in which partners have traditionally determined their own level of participation in the plan. The Regulations confirm that plans of partnerships that give partners the opportunity to elect the level of their own participation in the

---

[1] I.R.C. § 401(k); Treas. Reg. § 1.401(k)-1.

[2] I.R.C. § 402.

plan will be subject to the requirements of Code § 401(k).[3] This issue is discussed further in § **2.4** below.

However, several types of plans that are not qualified plans do provide employees the right to elect to defer compensation on a pre-federal-tax basis. These arrangements, discussed later in the book, include: nonqualified plans (**Chapter 8**), § 403(b) plans (**Chapter 6**),and simplified employee pensions (SEPs) (**Chapter 7**).

Qualified plans that contain CODA arrangements are subject to special qualification rules under Code § 401(k); these rules must be met in order for employee elective deferrals to be treated on a pre-federal-tax basis. These special CODA requirements are the subject of this chapter. **Chapters 3** and **4** discuss the general rules that apply to all qualified retirement plans.

A cash or deferral arrangement can be either a one-time election to receive a specified sum (such as a bonus amount) in cash or contribute to a qualified plan, or an ongoing salary reduction agreement between an employee and employer under which a contribution is made to a plan only if the employee elects to reduce cash compensation or to forgo an increase in cash compensation. An election to defer can only be made with respect to amounts that the employee has not yet received.

When a participant makes an election to defer current compensation, the employer contributes the amount to a trust that forms part of the qualified plan. Technically, the contributions, for most qualified plan purposes, are treated as employer contributions and are subject to the rules generally applicable to other employer contributions (discussed in **Chapter 3**).

§ 2.2   Tax Treatment of CODAs

The amounts an individual elects to defer under a CODA are generally excluded from the individual's taxable income for purposes of federal income taxes at the time the election is made. To be eligible for the exclusion, amounts subject to the election cannot be "currently available" to the employee and the CODA has to be a qualified CODA as described in Code § 401(k). An amount is currently available if it has been paid to the employee or if the employee is able to receive it at his or her discretion, and if there is no significant limitation or restriction on the right to receive it. A significant limitation includes the limitation to receive the amount at a later date.

Consistent with the above taxation rule, elective contributions to a qualified CODA are not subject to income tax withholding to the extent that they are not includable in the employee's gross income.

---

[3] Treas. Reg. § 401(k)-1(a)(6).

Amounts contributed to the plan on behalf of the participant are taxed at the time of distribution, as in any other qualified retirement plan. This means that, if certain eligibility requirements are met, the distribution may be subject to special "lump sum" tax treatment.[4]

If the plan fails to meet the CODA requirements, the individual is taxed on the deferred amounts at the time the election to defer is made. This is the tax result, regardless of whether the election is made in the year prior to the year in which the amount is earned.[5] This rule is somewhat harsher than the general rules for taxing elective deferrals under a nonqualified arrangement, discussed in **Chapter 8**. A special rule provides that plans subject to collective bargaining, for plan years beginning before 1993, are not required to meet the actual deferral percentage test ("ADP Test") in order for participants to be eligible for the special tax treatment on elective deferrals. Also, as discussed in **§ 2.13**, special rules apply when the plan corrects excess contributions in the following plan year.

FICA Tax

Although elective deferrals under a CODA generally defer federal income tax, deferral amounts are not exempt from FICA (social security and medicare) and FUTA (unemployment) taxes. Both the individual and the employer are required to pay these taxes.[6]

State and Local Taxes

Most states and local governments follow the federal scheme of excluding amounts subject to elective deferrals in a CODA from income tax withholding rules and deferring income tax on such amounts until distributed from the plan. However, there are significant exceptions. Several states require payment of income tax on such amounts, and some localities that have a wage tax do not follow the federal scheme. It is important to determine, prior to establishing a CODA, whether state and/or local income tax withholding laws apply and whether such amounts are included in taxable income under such laws.

§ 2.3   Plans Containing CODAs

A qualified CODA may only be included as a part of a qualified plan that is a profit-sharing plan, a stock bonus plan, a pre-ERISA money-purchase

---

[4] I.R.C. § 402(e).

[5] Treas. Reg. §§ 1.401(k)-1(a)(5)(iii) and 1.402(a)-1(d)(1).

[6] I.R.C. §§ 3121(v)(1) and 3306(r)(1).

plan, or a rural electric cooperative plan. A pre-ERISA money purchase pension plan is a plan that was in existence on June 27, 1974, and on that date contained a salary reduction arrangement. A rural cooperative plan is a defined contribution plan sponsored by either a rural cooperative or a national association of such cooperatives. A rural cooperative is an organization engaged primarily in providing electric or telephone service on a mutual or cooperative basis and is exempt from tax under Code § 501(a).

Certain types of organizations are prohibited from sponsoring a plan containing a CODA. A plan sponsored by a state or local government or a tax-exempt organization cannot include a qualified CODA unless it is a part of a plan maintained by a rural cooperative. However, a "grandfathering" rule provides that a plan containing a CODA, if adopted by a state or local government before May 6, 1986, or if adopted by a tax-exempt organization prior to July 2, 1986, may continue to provide a cash or deferral election.[7]

§ 2.4 Plans of Partnerships

Partnerships, like corporations, may have plans that contain CODAs. These plans are subject to the same rules as corporate plans. CODA features contained in partnership plans create no special problems when the plan complies with the rules under Code § 401(k). However, problems may exist for partnership plans when the sponsor does not realize the plan is subject to Code § 401(k) rules. Traditionally, qualified plans of partnerships have allowed partners to choose their own level of participation in the plan. For example, a plan may have provided that participants receive a contribution of 10 percent of compensation, but may have given partners the option to choose to have a lower level of participation, or to choose not to participate at all. Treasury Regulations clarify that any arrangement that directly or indirectly permits individual partners to vary the amount of contributions made on their behalf will be subject to the CODA requirements of Code § 401(k).[8]

The Regulations do permit an exception for plans of partnerships that provide for a one-time irrevocable election, upon commencement of employment or initial eligibility under the plan, to have a specified amount or percentage of compensation (or, no amount) contributed by the employer throughout the employee's employment. This provision allows employees to elect different rates of employer contributions, without the arrangement being treated as a CODA. This exception also applies to plans sponsored by corporations or sole proprietorships.

---

[7] I.R.C. § 401(k)(4)(B); Treas. Reg. §§ 1.401(k)-1(e)(4)(i) and 1.401(k)-1(e)(4)(vi).

[8] Treas. Reg. § 401(k)-1(a)(6).

A separate issue for plans of partnerships relates to the timing of a partner's election to defer compensation. The general rule discussed in **§ 2.2** above states that amounts deferred are subject to income tax currently, if such amounts are "currently received." Under the partnership tax rules, a partner's distributive share of partnership income is determined as of the last day of the partnership's taxable year, and the partner is taxed on the distributive share in the partner's taxable year in which the partnership's taxable year ends, regardless of whether it is actually distributed. This means that, for a partner, an amount is currently received as of the last day of the plan year, and an election to defer income for a plan year cannot be made after such date. A transitional rule permitting a later election date applies to plan years beginning before October 15, 1991.

Another important concern for plans of partnerships is that the rules (indirectly) prohibit matching contributions to be made on behalf of a partner. This result occurs because the partnership tax rules require that amounts contributed on behalf of a partner in a defined-contribution plan must be deducted by that partner, and the Regulations under Code § 401(k) require that, if deductions for partnership matching contributions are allocated to the partner for whom they were made, the matching contribution is treated as an elective contribution. The Internal Revenue Service (IRS) is aware of the conflict and is considering a change in the deduction rules to eliminate this result. However, until such time as the conflict is resolved, a partnership plan may have a problem if the plan allocates matching contributions to partners.

§ 2.5   Dollar Limit on Elective Deferrals

A dollar limit is imposed on the total amount of elective contributions an employee may exclude from gross income for any taxable year under all cash or deferral elections. For this purpose, elective deferrals include elections under qualified plans, Code § 403(b) annuities, simplified employee pensions (SEPs), and certain retirement plans funded solely by employee contributions. The dollar limit, effective originally (in 1987) at $ 7,000, is adjusted annually for inflation.[9] The limits for the past several years are indicated in **Table 2–1**.

The dollar limitation is increased (but not above $9,500) to the extent that the individual has elective deferrals under a Code § 403(b) tax-sheltered annuity arrangement.

---

[9] I.R.C. § 402(g); Treas. Reg. § 1.402(g).

Table 2–1

Maximum Elective Deferrals

Year	Maximum Deferral
1987	$7,000
1988	7,313
1989	7,627
1990	7,979
1991	8,475
1992	8,728

Example: In 1992, an individual makes a $400 elective deferral under a Code § 403(b) plan. Assuming that the individual also defers the maximum amount in a qualified plan ($8,728 in 1992), the individual has not violated the maximum contribution amount because the total ($9,128) does not exceed the $9,500 limit. If, instead, the individual defers $4,000 under the Code § 403(b) plan, the maximum deferral under the qualified plan is $5,500 ($9,500 − $4,000).

The $9,500 dollar limit is not subject to cost-of-living increases. A catch-up exception to the $9,500 limit applies in limited circumstances, as described in § **6.12**.

The testing year for measuring whether deferrals exceed this limit is the individual's tax year. Almost all individuals are on a calendar tax year. The limit applies with respect to the aggregate amount of elective deferrals made, during the taxable year of the individual, under all of the plans in which the individual participates. For example, if an individual holds two jobs with unrelated employers and participates in CODA arrangements with both employers, the maximum deferral limit is applied aggregating all deferral elections. Similarly, an employee may change employers during the calendar year, making elective deferrals in both plans. Amounts exceeding the limit are referred to as "excess deferrals."

In addition to the dollar limit that applies to individuals, a separate qualification requirement applies to all qualified plans containing a CODA feature. Each plan must provide that elective deferrals on behalf of a participant under the plan—and under all other plans, contracts, or arrangements of the employer who maintains the plan—may not exceed the dollar limitation.[10] If an employee defers more than the dollar limitation in one or more plans of the employer or related employers, all plans may be

---

[10] I.R.C. § 401(a)(30).

disqualified. However, corrective distributions, discussed in § **2.6**, can prevent disqualification.

§ **2.6**   —Correcting Excess Deferrals

In some cases, an employee may defer more money in a calendar year than the annual dollar maximum ($8,728 in 1992, and indexed for inflation). This will most often occur if he or she worked for two unrelated employers in the same calendar year. The employee in such a case will suffer adverse tax consequences. Note that if the plans are of unrelated employers and the dollar limit is not exceeded in either plan separately, the resulting excess deferrals will not disqualify either plan. On the other hand, if the excess deferral occurs in one or more plans of an employer (including related employers), then excess deferrals may cause the plans to lose their tax preferential treatment (also referred to as "disqualification" of the plan). Both problems can be avoided if a "corrective distribution" is made.

Because the excess will most often occur when an individual is a participant in more than one plan, the first step in correcting an excess deferral is for the individual to allocate the amount of excess deferrals among the plans in which he or she is involved, and to notify each plan of such excess. Under the Code,[11] this notice must occur not later than March 1 of the following year. However, the Regulations apparently extend this date until April 15.[12] A plan can provide that such notice is unnecessary when the excess deferrals are made in one plan or in plans of related employers. A plan should include such waiver language, because excess deferrals in these cases could disqualify the plan(s). Otherwise, the plan would have to rely on the participants' coming forward before the "excess deferral" can be remedied.

An excess deferral can be made during the plan year as long as the amount has been identified as an excess distribution (using the methodology discussed in the previous paragraph) and the distribution is identified by the plan as being a correction of an excess deferral. The distribution of the excess deferral can also be made as late as the following April 15. If possible, it is better to return the excess before the year ends, to minimize paperwork for both employer and employee. In either case, an amount representing interest earned on the excess distribution must also be distributed. The methodology for determining the amount of interest to be distributed is similar to the methodology used for calculating interest on excess contributions, discussed in § **2.14**.

---

[11] I.R.C. § 402(g)(2)(A)(i).

[12] Treas. Reg. § 1.402(g)-1(e)-(2)(i).

If a plan does not satisfy the requirements of the ADP Test (see § **2.8**), the employer may distribute excess contributions to highly compensated employees or may recharacterize such contributions as after-tax employee contributions. If either event occurs, the plan may make a proportionate reduction in the amount of such individuals' excess deferrals.

Taxation of Excess Deferrals

An excess deferral will always be taxed to the employee in the year when the excess is made. If a corrective distribution is made, the amount of the distribution that is attributable to excess deferrals is not included as income in the year distributed. However, interest attributable to the excess deferral will be included in income for the year in which the distribution is made. Excise taxes on early distributions and certain large distributions do not apply to such distributions, and the distributions are not subject to other qualification requirements generally applicable to plan distributions. If corrective distributions are not made, then the individual will be subject to taxation when the excess distribution is finally made from the plan. The participant will then be subject to double taxation on such excess deferrals, once for the year in which the excess deferral was made, and a second time when the amount is distributed. In addition, if the corrective distribution is not made, the distribution (of such excess deferrals) can only occur in accordance with the special withdrawal rules discussed in §§ **2.16** and **2.17**.

§ 2.7 Nondiscrimination Testing—General

In a CODA, eligible participants have the right to elect to defer or not to defer current income. Congress decided that highly compensated employees (HCEs) should only be able to make deferral elections if there is substantial participation by the non-highly compensated employees (non-HCEs). This objective has been quantified through the use of a mathematical test that (1) compares the level of participation between these two groups of employees and (2) provides that the level of participation by the HCEs cannot exceed the level of participation by the non-HCEs by more than a certain amount.

The test, known as the actual deferral percentage test ("ADP Test"),[13] begins by calculating the amount of money deferred into the plan by each

---

[13] Throughout this chapter, the term "ADP Test" refers to the entire test that the Regulations refer to as the actual deferral percentage test. When referring to the deferral percentage of an individual (actual deferral percentage in the Regulations), "ADP" is

eligible employee, expressed as a percentage of salary, also referred to as the actual deferral percentage ("ADP"). Employees are divided into two groups, the HCEs and the non-HCEs, and the average of the ADPs of the non-HCE group determines the maximum average ADPs of the HCE group.

In addition, many plans that contain CODAs also provide that sponsors contribute a matching amount based on each employee's elective deferral. Such matching contributions are an incentive for an employee to make elective deferrals. Matching contributions can improve the results of the ADP Test by bringing up the level of participation of the non-HCE group and allowing the HCE group the opportunity to make larger deferrals.

Because matching contributions are based on the amount of elective deferrals made by the participant, the amount of contributions made to each individual participant will vary. To ensure that HCEs do not benefit significantly more than non-HCEs, matching contributions are subject to a separate nondiscrimination test referred to as the actual contribution percentage test ("ACP Test").[14]

Plans containing a CODA may allow participants to make additional contributions on an after-tax basis. If the plan provides for after-tax contributions, these amounts are also subject to the ACP Test. The ACP Test is performed in a manner similar to the ADP Test. Under this nondiscrimination test, employer matching contributions and any employee after-tax contributions are added together, in order to determine an individual's actual deferral percentage ("ACP"). As with the ADP Test, the ACPs of the non-HCE group are averaged together. This average ACP of the non-HCE group determines the maximum average ACP of the HCE group.

The ACP Test applies to any plan that contains employer matching and/or employee after-tax contributions. This means that (1) the test will not apply to all plans with CODAs, but only to those that contain employer matching or employee after-tax contributions, and (2) the ACP Test may apply to plans other than plans containing CODAs. The methodology for applying the ACP Test is contained in **§ 2.19**.

A third nondiscrimination test applies to a plan that is required to perform both the ADP Test and the ACP Test. This test, referred to as the multiple use test (MUT), is the subject of **§ 2.21**.

---

used. To identify the average of the deferral percentages of the HCE or the non-HCE group the term "average ADP" is used.

[14] Throughout this chapter, the term "ACP Test" refers to the entire test that the Regulations refer to as the actual contribution percentage test. When referring to the deferral percentage of an individual (actual contribution percentage in the Regulations), "ACP" is used. To identify the average of the deferral percentages of the HCE or the non-HCE group, the term "average ACP" is used.

Plans that are required to perform any or all of these nondiscrimination tests must contain plan provisions specifying that the nondiscrimination tests will be satisfied. The plan must maintain the records necessary to show satisfaction of the various nondiscrimination tests, and how the tests were administered.

§ 2.8   Nondiscrimination Testing for Elective Contributions

The first step in applying the nondiscrimination test for CODAs is to determine the actual deferral percentage (ADP). The ADP represents the amount of money deferred into the plan by each eligible employee, expressed as a percentage of salary.

Employees are divided into two groups for the nondiscrimination test, and the average of the ADPs of the non-HCE group determines the maximum average ADP of the HCE group. (The higher paid group in any company is referred to as the highly compensated employees (HCE) group; all other employees are referred to as the non-highly compensated employees (non-HCE) group.)

The test itself consists, first, of calculating the ADP for each employee who is eligible to participate in the plan. Next, the employees are divided into two groups (as explained above): the HCEs and the non-HCEs. In each group, the ADPs for each person are added together and the total is divided by the number of individuals in the group. The result is the average deferral percentage of the group.

To pass the test, the plan must meet one of these requirements:

- The average ADP of the HCE group cannot be more than 1.25 times the average ADP of the non-HCE group;
- The average ADP of the HCE group cannot be more than 2 times the average ADP of the non-HCE group, and the average ADP of the HCE group cannot be more than 2 percentage points higher than the average ADP of the non-HCE group. The second test is called the "2 times 2 percent" alternative test.[15]

This statement of the general rule may be easier to understand when presented in a format that applies the general rule to hypothetical average deferral percentages for the non-HCE group. **Table 2–2** indicates the maximum permissible average of the ADPs for the HCE group, for each corresponding ADP average of the non-HCE group.

---

[15] I.R.C. § 401(k)(3)(A)(ii); Treas. Reg. § 1.401(k)-1(b)(1)(ii).

Table 2–2

Summary of Nondiscrimination Test General Rule

Average ADP for Non-HCE Group	Maximum Average for HCE Group
Up to 2%	2 times ADP of non-HCE
2% to 8%	ADP of non-HCE plus 2%
8% and over	1.25 × ADP of non-HCE

To calculate the average ADP for each group, each employee who is eligible to participate in the plan must be considered, whether or not an actual deferral is made. The following example demonstrates how to calculate the average deferral percentages of a group of non-HCEs.

Example: Assume that the employer has a group of four non-HCEs eligible to participate in the plan:

- Employee Arthur earns $10,000 and defers $500; the ADP is $500/$10,000 = 5 percent ADP.
- Employee Barbara earns $20,000 and defers $2,000; the ADP is $2,000/$20,000 = 10 percent ADP.
- Employee Cathy earns $30,000 and elects to make no deferrals; the ADP is 0 percent.
- Employee Donald earns $40,000 and defers $2,500; the ADP is $2,500/$40,000 = 6.25 percent ADP.

The calculation of the average ADP for the non-HCE group is:

$$\frac{5\% + 10\% + 0\% + 6.25\%}{4} = \begin{array}{l} 5.31 \text{ percent average ADP} \\ \text{for the non-HCE group.} \end{array}$$

Based on the maximum deferral percentages in **Table 2–2**, the maximum average ADP for HCEs is 7.31 percent. To see whether the test has been satisfied, the average ADP for the HCE group must be calculated. Assume that the employer has two HCEs eligible to participate in the plan:

- Employee Eleanor earns $100,000 a year and defers $7,000; the ADP is $7,000/$100,000 = 7 percent ADP.
- Employee Frank, a 5 percent owner of the Company, earns $75,000 a year and defers $10,000; the ADP is $10,000/$75,000 = 13.3 percent ADP.

The calculation of the average ADP for the HCE group is:

$$\frac{7\% + 13.3\%}{2} = \begin{array}{l} 10.15 \text{ percent average ADP} \\ \text{for the HCE group.} \end{array}$$

The average ADP for the HCE group (10.15 percent) exceeds the maximum allowed under the test (7.31 percent).

As seen by the example, the mathematical application of the ADP Test is fairly simple. However, mistakes are often made, when performing the test, in (1) the determination of who is an HCE (discussed in **§ 2.11**); (2) the amount of compensation used for each participant (discussed in **§ 2.10**), and what amounts are considered elective deferrals. Each of these components of the test is quite complex and needs to be thoroughly understood before the test is performed. Another factor that can complicate the application of the test is if the employer has more than one plan containing a CODA (discussed in **§ 2.9**).

§ 2.9   —Aggregation and Disaggregation of CODAs

Some employers sponsor several plans containing CODAs, or an employer may sponsor one plan that contains multiple CODAs. Numerous aggregation rules apply to such situations. For purposes of discussion, it is important to understand that the term "employer" means all entities that are treated as one entity under the controlled group and affiliated service group rules contained in Code § 414 (see **§ 3.11** for further discussion).

The first aggregation rule is that, for any HCE who has made deferrals under more than one CODA of an employer, those deferrals are combined and the total is tested together for purposes of each plan. The only exception is when the plans are required to be disaggregated for purposes of the ADP Test, as described below.

Second, plans that are aggregated in order to satisfy the minimum coverage requirements of Code § 410(b) are treated as one plan for purposes of the CODA rules. Under the minimum coverage requirements, certain plans cannot be aggregated, under any circumstances, for purposes of applying the minimum coverage tests. If aggregation is not permitted, such plans will also have to be treated separately for purposes of the CODA nondiscrimination tests. This means that contributions to an employee stock ownership plan (ESOP) cannot be combined with contributions or allocations under a non-ESOP. It also means that a CODA covering both employees who are in a unit covered by a collective bargaining agreement and employees who are not in the bargaining unit has to be treated as two separate plans.

Under the general qualified plan rules, a plan can be broken up into component parts in order to satisfy the minimum coverage requirements of Code § 410(b). This "restructuring" is not allowed as a method of satisfying the ADP and ACP tests with a plan containing a CODA arrangement. In other words, a plan with one or more CODA arrangements cannot be divided in any way to satisfy the ADP or ACP. A separate rule requires that a single plan that has more than one CODA has to be treated as one arrangement, in order to satisfy the coverage requirements.

§ 2.10 —Definition of Compensation

To calculate the ADP and ACP, the participants' deferrals are divided by their "compensation." For purposes of this calculation, compensation includes those amounts paid to the participants that are included in gross income. At the employer's election, "compensation" can also include those amounts deferred under a CODA as well as amounts deferred under a Code § 125 cafeteria plan or a Code § 403(b) annuity program. Compensation may be computed based on the plan year, or based on compensation earned for the calendar year ending within the plan year. In no circumstances may compensation exceed the $200,000 limit contained in Code § 410(a)(17). (The $200,000 limit is indexed for inflation; for plan years beginning in 1992, the limit is $228,860.)[16]

When an employee is not eligible to participate in the plan for the entire year, the plan may elect (on a uniform basis) to treat as compensation only that amount earned after the individual became eligible to participate in the plan. Limiting compensation will generally have the effect of increasing individual ADP percentages, which, in most cases, is a desirable result.

§ 2.11 —Highly Compensated Employees

An employee is a highly compensated employee (HCE) for a plan year if, during the current year or the previous year, the employee:

- Was at any time a 5 percent owner of the employer;
- Received compensation from the employer in excess of $93,518 (for 1992, and indexed for inflation in subsequent years);
- Received compensation from the employer in excess of $62,345 (for 1992, and indexed for inflation in subsequent years) and was in the top paid group for the year (generally, the highest paid 20 percent of the employees, based on compensation paid during the year);
- Was at any time an officer and received compensation greater than 50 percent of the amount in effect under Code § 415(b)(1)(A) (this limit is $112,221 for 1992, and is indexed for inflation). If no officer earns

---

[16] I.R.C. § 401(a)(17).

more than the minimum compensation limit, the highest paid officer will also be considered an HCE.

An exception to the general rule applies to certain individuals who become HCEs for the first time during the current year. Such individuals will not be considered HCEs unless they are 5 percent owners or (in the case of individuals falling into any of the other three categories) they are one of the top 100 paid employees of the employer (including all entities required to be affiliated, under Code § 414; see **§ 3.11**).

An individual is a 5 percent owner if he or she owns *more than* 5 percent of the value of the outstanding stock of the corporation or stock possessing more than 5 percent of the total combined voting power of all stock of the corporation. If the entity is not a corporation, an individual is a 5 percent owner if he or she owns more than 5 percent of the capital or profits interest in the employer. In limited situations, ownership by related persons will be attributed to an individual in determining ownership.

Compensation, for purposes of determining who is an HCE, includes gross income (for federal income tax purposes) plus: any employee nontaxable contributions to a cafeteria plan, employee nontaxable deferral amounts to a § 401(k) plan, and similar pretax deferrals to SEPs and § 403(b) annuity plans.

Determining who is an officer is based on all "facts and circumstances," including the source of authority, the term of election or appointment, and the nature and extent of the duties involved. The determination is based on the individual's actual authority, not on whether the individual has or does not have a title. The rules further provide that a limited number of individuals will be considered officers of a particular entity. Generally, the number of officers is limited to 10 percent of the total number of employees. However, if the total number of employees is fewer than 30, the limit is 3 officers; if the total number of employees is more than 500, the limit is 50 officers.

For the third category of HCE, the identification of the "top paid group" is required. This is the highest paid 20 percent of all employees. To identify who is in the top paid group, the "determination group" must be defined. Employees of all entities that are required to be aggregated as part of an affiliated service group, a controlled group of corporations, or a leased work force are included, under Code § 414(b), (m), (n), and (o).

In identifying the determination group, the following employees can be disregarded: employees who have not completed 6 months of service; employees who normally work fewer than 17½ hours per week; employees who normally work during not more than 6 months of any year; employees who have not attained age 21; employees covered by a collective bargaining agreement, except to the extent otherwise provided in the

Regulations; and certain nonresident aliens. An employer may elect to count some or all of the excludable employees, as long as the count is done on a nondiscriminatory basis. Even if an employee can be excluded from the determination of the top paid group, he or she may still be considered an HCE under any of the other tests.

§ 2.12 —Family Aggregation

When determining the average ADP for the HCE group and the non-HCE group, the first step is to calculate the ACP for each individual. However, under the special family aggregation rules, several family members may be required to be treated as one individual for purposes of performing the ADP Test.[17] Family aggregation may apply if a plan with a CODA has eligible participants, including certain family members of HCEs who are 5 percent owners or who are among the 10 highest paid employees (during the current year). Family members include the employee's spouse and lineal descendants (children and grandchildren) or ascendants (parents and grandparents), and the spouses of any such lineal descendants or ascendants. When a family has to be aggregated, the elective deferrals as well as the compensation of each of the family members are aggregated and the whole family group is treated as one HCE under the ADP Test. If the plan sponsor makes additional "qualified contributions" that are treated as employee elective deferral contributions, then these amounts are aggregated as well. The $200,000 cap (as adjusted for inflation, $228,860 for 1992) on compensation also applies to the aggregated family group.

The family aggregation rule can have drastic effects on ADP testing. The following example demonstrates this point.

Example: Esther is an HCE because she owns 100 percent of her company and earns $250,000 a year. She makes elective deferrals in the amount of $7,500. Calculating her ADP separately, $7,500/$220,220 = 3.41 percent. Her husband, Will (who is not an officer of the company), is also a participant in the plan. Will earns $40,000 and defers $1,800. Separately, Will's ADP is $1,800/$40,000 = 4.5 percent. More importantly, if treated separately, Will is a non-HCE and will help increase the deferral percentage of the non-HCE group. However, Will and Esther must be aggregated and treated as one HCE under the family aggregation rules. Calculated together, their ADP is $9,300/$220,220 = 4.22 percent; the result is an increase in the average ADP for the HCE group and a decrease in the average ADP for the non-HCE group (assuming that the non-HCE average ADP was less than Will's 4.5 percent ADP).

---

[17] I.R.C. § 401(q); Treas. Reg. § 1.401(k)-1(g)(1)(ii)(B)(1).

This example demonstrates the importance of properly understanding and applying the family aggregation rule under the ADP Test. If the administrator is unaware of the rule and/or the familial relationships of plan participants, the test results can be inaccurate.

§ 2.13   —Aggregation of Deferrals and Other Contributions

If elective salary deferrals alone cannot meet the ADP Test, the employer may use other qualified employer contributions (either matching or nonelective) to help pass the ADP Test.[18] All or any part of such contributions can be treated as elective contributions for the ADP Test, as long as the contributions are "qualified" nonelective or matching employer contributions and specified nondiscrimination requirements are met with respect to the plan.

To be used in the ADP Test, employer contributions must be "qualified," which means that they must be fully vested (see § 2.15) and be subject to the special withdrawal restrictions that apply to CODAs (see §§ 2.15 and 2.16). Once contributions are so designated in the plan, the special CODA restrictions apply forever to the qualifying contributions, even if the money is not actually needed to pass the ADP Test.

In addition, the plan has to meet several nondiscrimination tests when qualified matching or nonelective contributions apply. First, all nonelective contributions that include qualified nonelective contributions must not discriminate in favor of highly compensated employees. Second, the nonelective contributions that exclude the qualified amounts must not discriminate in favor of highly compensated employees.

In application, a § 401(k) plan may contain a provision allowing, on a discretionary basis, additional "qualified contributions." Employers generally wait until the end of the plan year, perform a preliminary ADP Test, and then make qualified contributions as necessary to meet the ADP Test. Unless "qualified contributions" are necessary, they are generally not desirable, because they must be 100 percent vested. In order to pass the ADP Test, such qualifying contributions are often made only for non-HCEs. This result is not desirable: key management personnel will not receive a share of the contributions. If qualifying contributions are made over a period of time, they can serve as a disincentive to non-HCE elective participation in the plan. Employees will figure out that they will get additional employer contributions if they keep their own contribution level low.

---

[18] Treas. Reg. § 1.401(k)-1(b)(5).

To pass the ADP Test, contributions from another plan may even be aggregated with salary deferrals, but only if the two plans have the same plan year and the plans are allowed to be aggregated. Although it is not simple to change a plan year, some employers may find it worth the trouble to schedule all plans for the same plan year, to give themselves as much flexibility as possible in the future.

§ 2.14   —Correcting Excess Contributions

If the plan cannot pass the ADP Test, the employer has several options. If a preliminary ADP Test is performed prior to the end of the plan year, elective contributions by the HCE group can be limited for the remainder of the year, thereby eliminating the problem altogether. However, if the plan year ends and the plan has failed the ADP Test, several other options are available. One option, already discussed in **§ 2.13**, is for the employer to make qualified nonelective contributions and/or qualified matching contributions. This section describes the remaining two methods of correcting excess contributions. The first method is to recharacterize elective contributions as employee after-tax contributions; the second is to distribute excess contributions to the employees. A plan may use any of the three methods, alone or in combination, to correct the problem.

Generally, if a plan does not correct excess distributions within 2½ months after the plan year for which they were made, the employer is liable for a 10 percent penalty tax. The excise tax can be avoided, however, if the employer chooses to make qualifying contributions in the amount necessary to satisfy the ADP test, even if this is done more than 2½ months after the end of the plan year.[19] In any case, if the excess contributions are not corrected within a year after the close of the plan year, the plan will be disqualified for the plan year in which the excess contributions were made, as well as for all subsequent years in which the excess is not corrected.[20]

As discussed in **§ 2.8**, the ADP Test is performed comparing the average of the deferral percentages for both the HCE and non-HCE groups. If the average of the individual ADPs within the HCE group exceeds the maximum deferral percentage, excess contributions have occurred and the average for the entire HCE group has to be reduced to the maximum permissible level. The question at this point is: Which individuals within the HCE group will be deemed to have excess contributions that have to be

---

[19] I.R.C. § 4979; Treas. Reg. § 1.401(k)-1(f)(6)(i).

[20] I.R.C. § 401(q); Treas. Reg. § 1.401(k)-1(g)(1)(ii)(B)(1).

remedied? The Regulations provide a methodology for identifying which HCE contributions are to be considered excess contributions (correctable either by returning the excess or recharacterizing the excess).

Under the Regulations, the amount of excess contributions for an HCE for a plan year is the amount by which the employee's elective contributions must be reduced so that the employee's actual deferral ratio will equal the highest permitted actual deferral ratio under the plan.[21] To calculate the highest permitted actual deferral ratio under a plan, the actual deferral ratio of the HCE who has the highest actual deferral ratio is reduced by the amount required to cause the employee's actual deferral ratio to equal the ratio of the HCE with the next highest actual deferral ratio. If a lesser reduction would enable the arrangement to satisfy the actual deferral percentage test, the lesser reduction is made. This process must be repeated until the cash or deferral arrangement satisfies the actual deferral percentage test. The highest actual deferral ratio remaining under the plan after leveling is the highest permitted actual deferral ratio.[22]

The problem with this method is that, in most plans, the employees with the highest ADPs are not top executives, but employees at the bottom of the highly compensated group. The $220,000-a-year executive vice president who defers the maximum $8,465 has an ADP of only 3.84; the $70,000-a-year employee deferring the maximum has an ADP of 11.29. Therefore, individuals required to reduce contributions are not those with the highest salary and may not be the management personnel who are the most likely candidates for reduction.

Calculating Interest Earnings

A corrective distribution of an excess contribution must include the income allocable to that contribution. Income allocable includes the sum of the allocable gain or loss for the plan year and the allocable gain or loss for the period between the end of the plan year and the date of distribution (the "gap period").

A plan may use any reasonable method for computing the income allocable to excess contributions, as long as the method does not violate Code § 401(a)(4) and is used consistently for all participants and for all corrective distributions under the plan for a particular plan year.

The Regulations do provide one "alternative method" for allocating interest to the excess contributions. Under this method, the plan may

---

[21] Treas. Reg. § 1.401(k)-1(f)(6)(i).

[22] Treas. Reg. § 1.401(k)-1(f)(2).

allocate income to excess contributions by multiplying, by a fraction, the portion of income for the plan year (as well as income earned during the gap period, if the plan so desires) that is allocable to elective contributions and amounts treated as elective contributions (qualified nonelective and matching contributions). The numerator of the fraction is the excess contributions for the plan year; the denominator is the elective contribution account balance at the beginning of the plan year plus elective contributions made during the plan year. If the plan is using this method to calculate interest earned during the gap period as well, then elective contributions during the gap period are added to the denominator.

If the plan does not have frequent valuation dates, it may not be feasible to readily determine the interest earned during the gap period, and it will be difficult to apply the safe harbor method to determine gap-period interest attributable to the excess contributions. The Regulations recognize this possibility and provide a safe harbor for calculating gap-period interest. Under this method, income on excess contributions for the gap period is equal to 10 percent of the income allocable to excess contributions for the plan year (using the alternative method to calculate plan year interest earnings) multiplied by the number of calendar months that have elapsed prior to the correction.

A drawback of the interest calculation methods provided by the Regulations is that they calculate interest as if the excess contributions were in the plan for the entire plan year. This may result in a disproportionate amount of interest being credited for the excess contribution. Therefore, a plan may choose to adopt an alternative method for calculating interest.

Recharacterization

Excess contributions can remain in the plan if they are treated as employee after-tax contributions. The participant involved and the Internal Revenue Service must be notified of the recharacterization, and the administrator has to treat the amounts as after-tax contributions.[23] The latest date when the recharacterization can occur is 2½ months after the close of the plan year to which the recharacterization relates. Amounts can only be recharacterized in a plan that otherwise allows employee contributions, and the rules regarding maximum employee contributions under the plan must be observed.

Excess contributions recharacterized in this manner are includable in the employee's gross income on the earliest dates when any elective contribution made on behalf of the employee during the plan year would have

---

[23] Treas. Reg. § 1.401(k)-1(f)(3)(ii).

been received by the employee, had the employee originally elected to receive the amounts in cash.

Return of Excess

Another method of correcting excess contributions is to return them, along with allocable interest, to the HCE. For a distribution to correct an excess contribution, it must be designated as a distribution of an excess contribution. The distribution must be made after the close of the plan year in which the excess contribution related, but no later than 1 year after the close of the plan year. However, if the excess contributions are not distributed within 2½ months following the close of the plan year in which they arose, the 10 percent penalty tax of Code § 4979 will apply.

If an excess contribution is returned within 2½ months after the end of the plan year, it is included in the employee's taxable income as of the first date the employee could have received cash instead of deferring it into the plan.

As an illustration of this rule, consider the example of an employee who defers too much in a plan for the plan year beginning November 1, 1992 (and ending on October 31, 1993). Assume that the excess is returned on January 1, 1994 (within 2½ months after the end of the plan year). If the employee first made a deferral election as of November 31, 1992, the excess is included in income for the 1992 tax year (even though the amount is not distributed until 1994).

This rule can cause difficulty for the employees involved. If the plan year is a calendar year, the employer can minimize the problems for the employees by completing the nondiscrimination testing immediately after the end of the plan year and notifying the employees of the increase in taxable income for the previous year, prior to the time when the employees file their income taxes. However, if the employer waits until the end of the 2½-month period before returning the excess deferrals, employees who have filed their tax returns will have to file amended returns. This problem can be quite pronounced when the plan year is not the calendar year, as demonstrated in the above example, where the individual receiving a distribution on January 1, 1994, would have to go back and amend the 1992 tax return.

If the excess is returned more than 2½ months after the plan year, however, it will be included in the employee's current year income and can be handled with much less difficulty. This is considered to be a late distribution and the employer pays a 10 percent excise tax. Many employers will decide, however, that it is worth the penalty to avoid the need for employees to amend their tax returns for the prior year.

§ 2.15   Special Vesting and Participation Requirements

All employee elective deferrals (CODA contributions) and any investment experience thereon must be nonforfeitable at all times. Other accounts accrued under the plan may be subject to a vesting schedule as allowed generally for qualified retirement plans. However, as discussed in **§ 2.13** above, an employer may elect to have other employer contributions treated as elective contributions for purposes of the ADP Test, as long as such amounts are subject to the immediate vesting requirements discussed herein, as well as the special distribution rules discussed in **§§ 2.16** and **2.17** below.

Qualified plans can generally require, as conditions of participation, 1 year of service and attainment of age 21 (see **§ 3.5**). Plans that provide immediate 100 percent vesting can require 2 years of service. This special 2-year eligibility provision is not available to any plan that contains a CODA feature.[24]

The right to make elective deferrals under a CODA is subject to the general rule that the plan cannot discriminate in favor of highly compensated employees. This means that the CODA feature must be nondiscriminatory in amount and availability. A plan could not, for example, provide that only HCEs can defer bonus payments, even if all employees have the right to defer regular compensation earned.

§ 2.16   Special Withdrawal Rules

In a profit-sharing plan, distributions may be made upon termination of employment, death, disability, or attainment of retirement age; or after a stated number of years (the minimum period is 2 years after the contribution has been made); or upon the occurrence of a stated event. However, when a profit-sharing plan contains a cash or deferral election, the cash or deferral portion (including interest experience thereon) of the individual's profit-sharing account is subject to special withdrawal limitations. Similar to the other portion of the profit-sharing account, the cash or deferral account can be withdrawn at termination of employment (for any reason, including retirement, death, and disability). Unlike the other portion of the profit-sharing account, such amount cannot be withdrawn while the employee is still employed (often referred to as an in-service distribution) unless the individual has attained age 59½ or has suffered a financial hardship. Additionally, in-service distributions may occur (only in the

---

[24] I.R.C. § 401(k)(2)(D); Treas. Reg. § 1.401(k)-1(e)(5).

form of a single sum) if the plan is terminated and no successor plan is established, or if an employee becomes ineligible to participate in the plan because the plan sponsor sells the subsidiary (through a stock sale or a sale of substantially all of the subsidiary's assets) for which the employee works, and the employee becomes an employee of the purchaser.[25]

Although pre-ERISA money-purchase pension plans containing CODA elections are rare, it is important to note that a money-purchase pension plan may only allow distributions upon retirement, disability, death, or other termination of employment. This means that such a plan may not provide in-service distributions under any circumstances.

§ 2.17 —Hardship Withdrawals

For an individual to receive an in-service distribution based on a financial hardship, the participant must demonstrate that he or she has suffered an immediate and heavy financial need, and that the withdrawal is necessary to meet that need.[26]

Treasury Regulations provide both general guidance on how to meet these standards and "safe harbor" rules for determining whether a hardship has occurred. A plan may define hardship in any manner it desires, as long as the definition stays within the regulatory guidelines. However, if the plan sponsor is concerned about having some level of certainty that the plan's hardship withdrawal provisions conform with the Regulations, the sponsor will generally choose to use the "safe harbor" definition of hardship withdrawal.

Under the general guidelines, whether an individual has an immediate and heavy financial need must be determined on a case-by-case basis, considering all the facts and circumstances. For example, the need to pay funeral expenses of a family member would constitute an immediate and heavy financial need; a distribution for the purchase of a boat or television set would not.

The Regulations identify four types of distributions that will be "deemed" to constitute a hardship (without further investigation):

1. Expenses necessary for the participant, spouse, or dependent to obtain medical care;
2. Costs directly related to the purchase of a principal residence for the employee;

---

[25] I.R.C. § 401(k)(2)(B); Treas. Reg. § 1.401(k)-1(d)(1).

[26] Treas. Reg. § 1.401(k)-1(d)(2)(ii).

3. Payment of tuition and related educational fees for the next 12 months of postsecondary education for the participant, spouse, or dependents;

4. Payments necessary to prevent foreclosure or eviction from the employee's principal residence.

After a hardship event has been identified, under either the general rule or the safe harbor provisions, the participant still must demonstrate that a distribution is necessary to satisfy the financial need. Under general guidelines, the amount sought cannot exceed the amount of the financial need, and the need may not be satisfied from other resources that are reasonably available to the employee.

To prove that the employee has no other resources available to meet the financial hardship, the plan administrator may rely (if such reliance is reasonable) on the written statement of the employee that the need cannot reasonably be relieved through:

1. Reimbursement or compensation by insurance or any other source;

2. Reasonable liquidation of assets, including assets of the employee's spouse and minor children (assuming their liquidation would not create a hardship in itself);

3. Distributions or nontaxable loans from all retirement plans, including those sponsored by another employer;

4. Reasonable loans from banks or other commercial lenders;

5. Stopping elective deferrals and after-tax contributions to employer plans.

The plan administrator has to ask for documentation that the employee cannot meet the financial need from these or any other sources.

In the alternative, the Regulations provide that a distribution is "deemed to be on account of an immediate and heavy financial need" if "safe harbor" procedures are followed by the plan. The safe harbor requirements are satisfied if:

1. The amount of the distribution does not exceed the amount of the immediate and heavy financial need (including amounts necessary to pay any taxes that will be imposed upon distribution);

2. The employee has already taken all other distributions and nontaxable loans available from all plans sponsored by the employer;

3. All employer plans require a suspension period of at least a year after the hardship withdrawal, during which the employee cannot make salary deferrals or after-tax contributions;

4. All employer plans adjust the maximum salary deferral in the employee's next tax year to reflect the hardship withdrawal.

Example: If an employee defers $5,000 in 1990 and then takes a hardship withdrawal, the maximum deferral for 1991 will be reduced by the $5,000. With the limit for 1991 at $8,475, the maximum amount that such individual may defer in 1991 is $3,475.

Under the Regulations, a participant generally cannot make a hardship withdrawal of the entire amount of his or her account that is attributable to CODA elections. The general rule is that the distribution cannot include that portion of the cash or deferral account that is attributable to interest earnings. However, the plan may allow the amount distributed upon financial hardship to include interest earnings earned during plan years ending prior to July 1, 1989.

The special hardship withdrawal rules do not apply to accounts that are held under a profit-sharing plan and are not subject to cash or deferral elections. It is not unusual, for example, for a profit-sharing plan with a cash or deferral feature to allow more liberal in-service distributions on the accounts attributable to employee after-tax contributions or employer contributions.

§ 2.18   The Noncontingency Restriction

An employee's decision to make (or not make) elective deferrals generally cannot be contingent on receiving any other employer-provided benefit from the sponsoring employer.[27] This restriction generally applies to all employee benefits, whether they receive special tax treatment or not. For example, an employer cannot make salary increases or cash bonuses contingent on the employee's decision to make elective deferrals into the plan. Other examples of benefits that cannot be contingent on elective deferrals include vacation pay, benefits under a defined benefit plan, life insurance, stock options, dependent care assistance, and legal services plans.

There are a number of substantial exceptions to this rule. Most importantly, employer matching contributions may be contingent on the employee's making elective deferrals. Many plans with CODA features encourage employee participation through an employer matching feature. The way a matching feature generally works is that the employer promises to match employee elective deferrals, in whole or in part, with employer contributions. For example, the employer promises to contribute 50 cents for each dollar that the employee elects to defer.

---

[27] I.R.C. § 401(k)(2)(D); Treas. Reg. § 1.401(k)-1(e)(6)(i).

Another exception applies to situations where an employer sponsors a nonqualified plan of deferred compensation in addition to the qualified plan containing the cash or deferral election. In that case, the employer may prohibit employee elective deferrals in the nonqualified plan until the participant attains a particular level of employee elective deferrals in the qualified plan. If the employer sponsors a nonqualified "excess" plan (that is, a plan providing benefits in excess of the limits on benefits and contributions from qualified plans contained in Code § 415), eligibility for the excess plan may be affected by a participant's level of elective deferrals.

Additional exceptions apply as follows. The no-condition rule does not apply to benefits provided (in lieu of CODA deferrals), at the participant's election, under a Code § 125(d) cafeteria plan. Plan loans or plan distributions are not considered contingent on an employee's elective deferrals simply because availability is based on the participant's account balance. A benefit provided under a defined-benefit plan is "not contingent" if it is limited by the maximum contribution and benefit limits contained in Code § 415.

A limited exception applies when the qualified plan contains employee after-tax contributions. In that case, the CODA deferrals may reduce, dollar-for-dollar, allowable contributions under an after-tax feature. However, in other circumstances, the after-tax contributions cannot be contingent on CODA deferrals. For example, the plan cannot specify that after-tax contributions can be made only after a particular level of CODA deferrals have been made.

§ 2.19   Nondiscrimination Testing for Matching and After-Tax Contributions

A similar nondiscrimination test is applied to the sum of employer matching contributions and employee after-tax contributions.[28] In the context of a plan that contains a CODA, this test only has application if the plan allows for either employer matching and/or after-tax employee contributions.

This test is referred to as the actual contribution percentage test ("ACP Test") and is the exclusive method of determining whether matching and employee after-tax contributions have satisfied the nondiscrimination rule of Code § 401(a)(4). In other words, if the plan does not satisfy the ACP Test, the plan can lose its tax-qualified status.

The ACP Test is calculated using the same methodology described in § **2.8** above. For each employee eligible to participate, employer matching contributions and employee after-tax contributions for the plan year are added together. The actual contribution percentage for ACP is the total of

---

[28] I.R.C. § 401(m); Treas. Reg. § 1.401(m)-1.

the employer matching and employee after-tax contributions divided by the participant's compensation for the plan year. As in the ADP Test, the average of the ACPs of the non-HCE group is calculated and compared to the average of the ACPs of the HCE group. The same disparity allowed under the ADP Test also applies to the ACP Test:

- The average ACP of the HCE group cannot be more than 1.25 times the average ACP of the non-HCE group; or
- The average ACP of the HCE group cannot be more than 2 times the average ACP of the non-HCE group, and the average ACP of the HCE group cannot be more than 2 percentage points higher than the ACP of the non-HCE group.

Matching contributions are employer contributions made on account of a participant's election to make either after-tax contributions or a deferral under a qualified CODA. For a matching contribution to be credited for a particular plan year, the contributions must be allocated to the participant's account for that year and contributed by the employer within 1 year after the close of the plan year.[29] However, if matching contributions are treated as "qualified matching contributions," which are treated as elective contributions for purposes of the ADP test (see § 2.13), such amounts are not treated as matching contributions and will not be counted under the ACP test.

Employee after-tax contributions are taken into account for the plan year in which they are made. Under the ADP test, elective contributions may be recharacterized as employee after-tax contributions (see § 2.14). Such amounts have to be counted when performing the ACP test. The recharacterized amounts are treated as contributed in the plan year in which they are included in the employee's gross income.

When the plan is required to perform both the ADP Test and the ACP Test, in certain circumstances the plan must pass a third test, referred to as the multiple use test (MUT), discussed in § 2.21. If the plan can pass either the ADP Test or the ACP Test using the 1.25 test, then the MUT does not have to be performed. However, when the 2 times 2 percent test is relied on to pass both the ACP Test and the ADP Test, the MUT must also be satisfied.

If an employer makes "qualified nonelective contributions" (defined in the same manner as in § 2.13) all or a portion of those amounts can be counted as elective deferral amounts for purposes of performing the ADP Test. Similarly, under the ACP Test, all or a portion of qualified

---

[29] Treas. Reg. § 1.401(m)-1(f).

nonelective contributions can be treated as matching contributions for purposes of performing the ACP Test. The same qualified employer nonelective contributions can be counted under both the ADP and ACP Tests.

A portion of elective contributions can be treated as matching contributions for purposes of performing the ACP Test, as long as the employee elective contributions, including those treated as matching contributions, meet the requirements of the ADP Test, described in **§ 2.8**. The following example demonstrates the use of elective contributions to pass the ACP Test.

Example: A plan allows elective contributions and employee contributions (after-tax) only. The test results were as follows:

	ADP	ACP
HCEs	10%	10%
Non-HCEs	10%	6%

The plan fails the ACP Test because the average ACP of the HCE group exceeds 125 percent of the average ACP of the other employees, and exceeds the average ACP of the other employees by more than two percentage points. As long as the plan allows such recharacterization, the plan may decide to use elective contributions equal to 2 percent of the compensation of the non-HCE group in the ACP Test. The results of this recharacterization are:

	Average ADP	Average ACP
HCEs	10%	10%
Non-HCEs	8%	8%

After recharacterization, the average ACP of the HCE group is now 125 percent of that for non-HCEs. The average ADP of the HCEs similarly satisfies the 125 percent test after the recharacterization. The plan would also meet the requirements of the ACP Test if all elective contributions were used in the ACP Test. This is because the average ACP for the HCE group (20 percent) would be 125 percent of the average ACP for the non-HCE group (16 percent).

When performing the ACP Test, many of the same rules that govern ADP testing apply. Compensation used in the denominator of the ACP is determined under the same rules that apply to the ADP Test (see **§ 2.10**). The methodology for determining who qualifies as an HCE (see **§ 2.11**) and who must be aggregated into a single family group (see **§ 2.12**) is the same for both the ADP and the ACP Tests. The aggregation and disaggregation rules described in **§ 2.9** apply in essentially the same manner under the ACP Test.

§ 2.20 —Correcting Excess Aggregate Contributions

If the average ACP for the HCE group exceeds the maximum percentage, the plan will not be disqualified if the plan takes one of the permitted corrective measures. When the average test has not been satisfied, the HCE contributions in excess of the limit are referred to as excess aggregate amounts.

One method of correcting excess aggregate amounts is for the employer to make qualified employer contributions in the amount necessary to satisfy the ACP Test. These contributions are defined in the same manner as under the ADP Test (see **§ 2.13**).

In lieu of this solution, the employer's primary option is to return the excess aggregate amounts to the employee. The process of returning excess aggregate amounts is done on an employee-by-employee basis, much in the same manner as under the ADP Test. The methodology for determining which HCEs are considered to have excess aggregate contributions is the same as under the ADP Test, except that the methodology is applied to employee after-tax contributions and employer matching contributions. This means that HCEs with excess aggregate amounts are determined and interest earnings must then be added.

Such excess aggregate amounts, and interest attributable thereto, must be distributed within 12 months of the close of the plan year being tested. However, if the distribution is made more than 2½ months after the close of the plan year, the employer will be charged a 10 percent excise tax under Code § 4979.

Excess aggregate contributions that are returned are includable in the HCE's income, except to the extent that such amounts were already taxed. For example, if the excess is attributable to employee after-tax contributions, only that portion of the distribution attributable to interest earnings is treated as taxable income. If the distribution is made within 2½ months after the close of the plan year, the excess is taxed for the plan year for which the contributions were made. If the distribution is made later than this deadline, the distribution will be taxed in the year in which it is distributed. Such distributions are not subject to the excise tax charged on distributions before age 59½, nor are they subject to other requirements that generally apply to distributions from qualified plans.[30]

A major complication arises when the employer makes the decision to return excess aggregate contributions to HCEs. Excess amounts may be attributable to either employee after-tax contributions or matching

---

[30] I.R.C. § 4980A; I.R.C. § 401(m)(7); Treas. Reg. § 1.401(m)-1(e)(3).

contributions. The nature of matching contributions is that they reward participation by matching either pretax (CODA) contributions or posttax contributions. For example, assume that the match is based on after-tax contributions, and the employer determines that excess employee after-tax contributions will be distributed. In this case, the employer will not want the employee to retain the match nor will the employer want to distribute the match to the participant. (The match is based on the amount of the employee contribution).

The Regulations[31] limit the choice of methods available to remedy the excess aggregate contributions in such a situation. Certain methods of correction are specifically prohibited. First, the plan cannot solve the problem by not making matching contributions that are required under the terms of the plan. Second, the plan may not forfeit vested matching contributions. Third, excess aggregate contributions may not be allocated to a suspense account to be allocated in a subsequent year.

Finally, the Regulations provide that the method of returning excess aggregate contributions must meet the nondiscrimination requirements of Code § 401(a)(4). Assume the employer described above simply returns employee contributions, without changing the matching contributions. Using hypothetical facts, assume that an HCE earning $100,000 for the plan year has made employee after-tax contributions in the amount of $3,000 or 3 percent of compensation. Assume that the company match is 50 percent of the first 3 percent of employee contributions, or $1,500. Assume that $1,000 representing employee contributions is returned to the employee as excess aggregate contributions. If none of the match is returned, this HCE is now receiving a match of 75 percent of the employee contribution. In this situation, the affected HCE receives a matching contribution that is larger than the match for the non-highly compensated employees, and the plan will have a problem under Code § 401(a)(4).

The numerous limitations on methods of correcting matching contributions point out the necessity of careful planning. The best way to solve the problem is to avoid excess aggregate contributions. If such contributions do arise, and matching contributions are involved, a plan is allowed to forfeit matching contributions on those amounts that are not vested at the time the excess occurs. Other matching contributions that are distributed will simply constitute additional information. Because the individuals involved are generally the most highly compensated, providing additional income may not cause any special problems for the employer.

---

[31] Treas. Reg. § 1.401(m)-1(e)(1).

§ 2.21   The Multiple Use Test

The discussion above reviews the ADP Test, which must be performed on employee elective deferrals, and the ACP Test, which applies to plans that contain employee after-tax contributions and/or employer matching contributions. As described above, under each of these tests the basic test is the 1.25 test, and the alternative limitation is the 2 times 2 percent test.

Code § 401(m)(9)(B) authorizes the Treasury to issue Regulations as may be necessary to prevent the multiple use of the alternative limitation with respect to any highly compensated employee. The "alternative limitation" to which the Code is referring is the 2 times 2 percent test described above for both the ACP and the ADP tests. Regulations have in fact been issued to limit the multiple use of the alternative test.

These Regulations create a third test, which must be applied to the plan or plans of an employer if one or more HCEs of an employer are eligible to participate both in a CODA and in a plan to which employee contributions or matching contributions are made, and the plan or plans must rely on the alternative test (2 times 2 percent) in order to pass both the ADP and ACP Tests.[32]

Example: An employer maintains a profit-sharing plan with a CODA and employer matching contributions. Assume the following test results:

	ADP	ACP
HCEs	3.3%	2.0%
Non-HCEs	2.2%	1.6%

Given these facts, the plan relies on the alternative test to satisfy the ADP. The 3.3 HCE deferral percentage exceeds 1.25 multiplied by the 2.2 non-HCE deferral percentage ($1.25 \times 2.2 = 2.75$). However, 3.3 is not more than 2 percentage points higher than 2.2 and is not more than 200 percent of 2.2 ($2.2 \times 2 = 4.4$). The plan does not have to rely on the alternative test to satisfy the ACP Test. The 1.6 non-HCE deferral percentage multiplied by 1.25 does not exceed the 2.0 HCE deferral percentage ($1.25 \times 1.6 = 2.0$). Therefore, in this case, the plan does not have to satisfy the multiple use test.

If the plan or plans of the employer rely on the alternative to comply with both the ADP and the ACP Tests, then the HCE deferral percentage may be further limited if the plan does not satisfy the multiple use test. The multiple use test is applied as follows:

---

[32] Treas. Reg. § 1.401(m)-2.

1. A "multiple use" is deemed to have occurred (the test is failed) if the sum of the ADP and ACP of the HCE group exceeds an "aggregate limit."

2. The aggregate limit is calculated as the greater of (A) or (B):
    A. is the sum of:
    i. 1.25 multiplied by the greater of the non-HCE ADP or the non-HCE ACP and
    ii. Two percentage points plus the lesser of the non-HCE ADP or the rank-and-file ACP (in no event shall this amount exceed twice the lesser of the non-HCE ADP or the non-HCE ACP).
    B. is the sum of:
    i. 1.25 multiplied by the lesser of the non-HCE ADP or the HCE ACP, and
    ii. Two percentage points plus the greater of the non-HCE ADP or the HCE ACP (in no event shall this amount exceed twice the greater of the non-HCE ADP or the non-HCE ACP).

Example: Alpha Corporation maintains a 401(k) plan; the ADP for the HCE group is 7.0 percent and the ADP of the non-HCE group is 5.5 percent. The plan also contains employer matching contributions. The ACP for the HCE group is 4.5 and the ACP for the non-HCE group is 2.9. The plan will not satisfy the multiple use test if the sum (12.5) of the ADP (7.0) and the ACP (5.5) for the HCE group exceeds the aggregate limit.

The aggregate limit is the greater of (A) or (B) where:

(A) is the sum of:
   (i)   1.25 × 5.5 (the greater of 5.5 and 2.9) = 6.875 and
   (ii) Two percentage points plus 2.9 (the lesser of 2.9 and 5.5) = 4.9. (This does not exceed 2 × 2.9.)

   Total = 6.875 + 4.9 = 11.775.

(B) is the sum of:
   (i)   1.25 × 2.9 (the lesser of 2.9 or 5.5) = 3.625 and
   (ii) Two percentage points plus 5.5 = 7.5. (This does not exceed 5.5 × 2.)

   Total = 3.625 + 7.5 = 11.125.

This plan does not meet the multiple use test because the sum of the ADP and ACP for the HCE group (12.5) exceeds the aggregate limit (11.775).

For purposes of applying the MUT test, the same aggregation rules that govern the ADP and ACP Tests apply.

§ 2.22   Correction of Multiple Use

If a multiple use of the alternative limitation is present, the employer may elect to reduce either the average ADP or the average ACP of the HCE group in order to satisfy the MUT. If a reduction is made from amounts under the ADP Test, such excess amounts will be treated as excess contributions as that term is defined under the ADP rules, and will be subject to the allocation methodology, tax treatment, and other rules that apply to such excess contributions. Similarly, the amounts subject to the ACP Test are treated as the excess, and the excess amounts will be treated as excess aggregate contributions. If amounts are treated as excess contributions (under the ADP Test), the employer still has the option to recharacterize the contributions as employee after-tax contributions. If this method is elected, the plan must still pass the ACP Test and the MUT after recharacterization.

CHAPTER 3

GENERAL QUALIFIED PLAN REQUIREMENTS

§ 3.1   Overview

Chapter 1 introduced the types of qualified retirement plans that may contain CODA elections. **Chapter 2** covered the special rules that apply to those CODA elections. A CODA feature must be part of a profit-sharing plan, stock bonus plan, or pre-ERISA money-purchase pension plan. Each of these plans is a "qualified defined contribution plan" subject to the qualification requirements of Code § 401(a). Most qualification requirements are identical for all three types of plans. This chapter addresses these general "qualification" requirements. Each of the requirements discussed applies to all three types of plans unless otherwise identified. The primary differences among the different types of plans are discussed in the first part of the chapter.

One "qualification requirement" that is not discussed in this chapter is the minimum distribution requirement. This is discussed, along with the taxation of distribution rules, in **Chapter 4**.

§ 3.2   Plans Containing CODAs

Chapter 2 identified the types of plans that may contain CODAs. The specific "identity" of each type of plan is discussed below; a fourth type of plan, the thrift (or savings) plan, is also discussed. Technically, thrift plans are a type of profit-sharing plan. In operation, however, they work quite differently than a traditional program that allocates employer profit-sharing contributions among participant accounts. Thrift plans are discussed separately below.

Profit-Sharing Plans

A profit-sharing plan is a plan established and maintained by an employer allowing employees or their beneficiaries to participate in the profits of the employer's trade or business, pursuant to a definite formula for allocating contributions. The plan must specify the terms of distribution. The plan may allow distributions after a fixed number of years, the attainment of a stated age, or upon the prior occurrence of some event such as layoff, illness, disability, retirement, death, or severance of employment.[1] At one time, contributions could only be made if the employer had profits. However, today the employer may, if it so elects, make contributions regardless of whether the employer has current or accumulated earnings and profits.[2]

The heart of a profit-sharing plan is the method of allocating employer contributions among the participants. This formula must be definite and predetermined. This essential element ensures that participants can determine what benefits they are entitled to under the plan.

Thrift or Savings Plan

Thrift or savings plans are technically profit-sharing plans and are subject to the rules pertaining to a profit-sharing plan. Thrift plans, in some ways, are the predecessors of many of today's 401(k) plans. In a thrift plan, employee contributions are made on an after-tax basis, and employer contributions are generally made to match such contributions. Both employee and employer matching contributions are subject to the nondiscrimination tests described in Code § 401(m) (see **§ 2.19**). The after-tax employee contribution feature of many traditional thrift plans has been transformed to pretax CODAs. However, some thrift plans continue to allow participants the option to save on either a pre- or posttax basis. Participants sometimes elect to save on a posttax basis, so that they will not be subject to the withdrawal limitations that apply to CODA deferral arrangements (see **§§ 2.16** and **2.17**).

Money-Purchase Pension Plan

In a money-purchase pension plan, the employer's contribution must be definitely determinable. The employer makes an annual contribution, which is credited to individual bookkeeping accounts maintained on behalf of the participants. The benefit that a participant receives is based on the annual contributions credited to the individual's account and the investment experience attributable to the individual's account.

Because it is a pension plan, distribution of benefits may begin only upon the participant's retirement, death, disability, or other separation from service. A money-purchase pension plan is subject to minimum

---

[1] Treas. Reg. § 1.401-1(a)(2).

[2] I.R.C. § 401(a)(26).

funding requirements, and, if contributions are not made within the required time period, an excise tax for failure to meet the minimum funding standards may apply.[3]

The company's annual contribution is generally stated as a specified percentage of each participant's compensation. For example, the money-purchase contribution formula may provide that annual contributions will equal 10 percent of compensation for each participant. (The term money purchase arose because the participant's account is traditionally used to purchase an annuity that provides monthly retirement benefits.)

At one time, the definitely determinable benefit requirement meant that a money-purchase pension plan could not allocate employee forfeitures to other plan participants. Forfeitures could only be used to reduce employer contributions. However, for plan years beginning after 1986, a money-purchase plan may elect to allocate forfeitures among the participants.

Stock Bonus Plans

A stock bonus plan is similar to a profit-sharing plan in that employer contributions may be made on a discretionary basis, and contributions are allocated on a predetermined formula. Stock bonus plans differ from profit-sharing plans primarily in that benefits are distributable in stock.

§ 3.3   Formal Requirements

Every qualified plan must be established and maintained according to a written instrument. The written document must contain all of the formal requirements for qualification discussed herein. The plan document contains the provisions regarding eligibility, vesting, benefits provided under the plan, and timing and form of benefit payments.

The plan has to be sponsored either by an employer or an employee organization. To satisfy this requirement, the plan has to simply be established and maintained by the employer, even if all contributions are made by employees.[4]

All contributions have to be held in trust by one or more trustees. However, the trust requirement does not apply to assets of a plan that consist of insurance contracts or annuities or are held by insurance companies.

Each plan is subject to the exclusive benefit rule, which means that the plan must be operated for the exclusive benefit of participants and

---

[3] Treas. Reg. § 1.401-1(a)(2).

[4] Treas. Reg. § 1.401-1(a)(2).

beneficiaries. Exceptions to this rule (as they apply to defined-contribution plans) include the following:

1. Contributions may be returnable upon IRS denial of qualified plan status;
2. Contributions may be returned within 1 year of mistake in fact;
3. Contributions may be returned within 1 year of disallowance of the deduction.

Benefits under a qualified plan must be definitely determinable. In a defined-contribution plan that is a pension plan, this means that the contribution formula (promised annual contribution) must be clearly stated; in a profit-sharing plan, the plan must clearly identify how any employer contribution will be divided up among the participants. In either type of plan, the definitely determinable requirement does not prohibit the plan from either allocating forfeitures of nonvested benefits to other participants or using such forfeitures to decrease future contributions.

The plan has to meet the plan permanency requirement, a regulatory offshoot of the exclusive benefit rule. If the plan is not intended to be permanent, this constitutes evidence that the plan is for a reason other than providing benefits (for example, as a tax shelter). In operation, this rule is relevant only when a plan is terminated within a few years of inception. In such circumstances, the sponsor must demonstrate that the termination is a result of business necessity.

A general prohibition exists against assignment or alienation of benefits.[5] The rule applies except in the following circumstances:

Ten percent of benefit payments;
Collateral for plan loan;
Qualified domestic relations order.

Qualified Domestic Relations Order

A qualified domestic relations order (QDRO) is a domestic relations court order requiring a plan to pay all, or a portion, of the benefits owed to a plan participant to another person (called an "alternate payee").[6] A plan administrator who is presented with such an order may pay the alternate payee without violating the assignment or alienation of benefits provisions. However, if the order does not meet all of the requirements that make the order a QDRO, the administrator must not honor the court order.

---

[5] I.R.C. § 401(a)(13); Treas. Reg. § 1.401(a)-13.

[6] I.R.C. § 401(a)(13).

For an order to be considered a QDRO, the following requirements must be satisfied. First, the term domestic relations order means any judgment, decree, or order of a state domestic relations court that relates to the provision of child support, alimony payments, or marital property to a spouse, former spouse, child, or other dependent.[7]

The order must specify the plan subject to the order; the name and address of the participant and alternate payee; the amount or percentage of the benefit to be paid to the alternate payee; and the period (or number of payments) to which the order applies. The order cannot alter the form of benefit, timing of payment (except as described below), or amount of the benefit in requiring the plan administrator to make payments to one or more alternate payees. However, a QDRO may require payments to be made to the alternate payee beginning at the time when the participant attains the earliest retirement age described in the plan, even if the participant has not yet terminated employment. The term earliest retirement age is the earlier of (1) the earliest date when a participant is entitled to a distribution under the plan, or (2) the later of the date the participant attains age 50 or the earliest date on which the participant could begin receiving benefits under the plan if the participant were separated from service.

An alternate payee may be any spouse, former spouse, child, or other dependent of a participant. The rules also allow a QDRO to substitute a divorcing spouse for an individual's current spouse (spouse at the time payments begin), for purposes of the spousal benefit requirements (see **§ 3.23**).

The plan is required to meet certain procedures when processing a QDRO. First, when the plan administrator receives the order, the administrator must promptly notify the participant, and all alternate payees, of receipt of the notice and of the plan's procedures for determining whether the order meets qualification requirements. The determination must be made within a reasonable period of time, and notice of the determination must be given to the interested parties. During the time when the order is being evaluated, the plan administrator must separately account for the amounts that would be payable to the alternate payee, should the order later be determined to be a QDRO. If, within 18 months of the date on which the first payment would be required under the order, the order is found to be qualified, the payee is to be given the separately accounted-for amounts plus interest. If the order is found not to be a QDRO or if the issue is not resolved within the 18-month period, the administrator must pay the segregated amounts, plus interest, to the person who would be entitled to them, as if there had been no order. Any determination that the order is a QDRO, if made after the end of the 18-month period, is to be

---

[7] I.R.C. § 414(p).

given prospective effect only, that is, amounts that were payable before the determination are not to be paid to the payee.

§ 3.4   Obtaining an Advance Determination Letter

When an employer establishes, amends, or terminates a qualified retirement plan, the plan sponsor has the opportunity, on a voluntary basis, to submit the plan to the Internal Revenue Service. Many taxpayers take advantage of this procedure, and obtain an advance determination letter regarding the qualified status of the plan. When a new plan is established, the letter that the IRS will issue states that the language of the plan meets the qualification requirements of the IRC. However, the letter will not address ongoing qualification requirements, such as the plan's obligation to continue to meet the minimum coverage requirements and minimum participation requirements as well as the various nondiscrimination requirements.

There are several reasons to obtain an advance determination letter. One reason is that the letter gives the employer, the plan drafter, and the participants a level of comfort that the plan is qualified. The rules are complex, and the penalties for disqualification can be severe. Second, if by chance, the plan is missing a required provision, submitting the plan for qualification extends the period during which the plan can be retroactively amended to correct the insufficiency. If the plan is not submitted in a timely manner and the IRS identifies the problem upon audit of the plan in a subsequent year, the plan generally cannot be retroactively amended, and the plan may be disqualified for such years.

The procedures for submitting the plan for approval are updated periodically; currently, they are in flux because of the numerous changes made to recent tax laws.[8] Generally, a new plan will have been submitted to the IRS by the due date of the tax return (plus extensions) for the employer's tax year that ends with or within the first plan year.

The application for an advance determination letter should be filed with the "key district"[9] for the IRS district in which the employer's principal place of business is located. Participants must be given notice of the IRS submission and must be informed that the participants may comment to the IRS or to the U.S. Department of Labor within a specified period of time.

If the determination letter is denied (the IRS issues an adverse letter), the taxpayer may appeal the decision to the governing regional office, and, if needed, to the Washington offices of the Internal Revenue Service.

---

[8] Identify the rev. procs. regarding current submission programs.

[9] 9 key districts have been formed.

§ 3.5   Minimum Coverage Requirements

For a plan to be qualified, it has to meet minimum coverage requirements. These requirements can be complex, and various methods or strategies can be used in order to satisfy them.

Before discussing the details of the rules, an overview can be helpful. The rules basically require that a plan that covers individuals who are highly compensated employees (HCEs) (defined in the same manner as described in § **2.11**) must also cover a significant number of non-HCEs. The more HCEs (as a percentage of the total HCEs in the work force) who are covered under the plan, the larger the number of non-HCEs (also as a percentage of non-HCEs in the work force) that have to be covered. A plan that does not cover any HCEs does not have to be concerned about the minimum coverage requirements.

A plan will satisfy the minimum coverage requirements if the plan satisfies either a mathematical percentage test, referred to as the ratio test (see § **3.09**), or a more nebulous "average benefits" test, discussed in § **3.10**. Under the minimum coverage requirements, the work force used to determine whether the plan satisfies the test includes all employers that must be aggregated under the common control rules or the affiliated service rules contained in Code § 414(b), (c), (m), and (n), as discussed in § **3.11**. However, in some circumstances, the larger "employer" may be broken into several units if it can be demonstrated that each unit constitutes a "separate line of business," as discussed in § **3.13**. Certain union employees, employees under the age of 21, and individuals employed less than 1 year can be excluded from consideration when determining whether a plan meets the minimum coverage requirements (see § **3.07**). In some circumstances, plans that are essentially similar may be aggregated for determining whether the plan satisfies the minimum coverage requirements (see § **3.12**).

Under Code § 401(a)(6), a plan must satisfy the coverage requirements (regardless of the method of compliance chosen) at least one day in each quarter of the plan year.[10] The Treasury Regulations provide some additional flexibility by allowing testing to be done on an annual basis. Annual testing must be done on the last day of the plan year and must include all employees employed on any day during the plan year. The annual testing approach is the only method that may be used for plans containing CODAs; plans with matching employer contributions; and plans that use the fair cross-section average benefits test.[11]

A separate, additional coverage requirement, referred to as the minimum participation test, must also be satisfied by each qualified plan.

---

[10] I.R.C. § 401(a)(6).

[11] Treas. Reg. § 1.410(b)-8.

Under the minimum participation test, discussed in § **3.14**, the plan must cover an absolute minimum number of participants in order for the plan to remain qualified. The minimum number is not contingent on the number of HCEs covered, nor can the plan be aggregated with any other plan in determining whether the minimum participation test has been satisfied. However, a plan that does not cover any HCEs will not have to meet the minimum participation requirements. To remain qualified, a plan must meet the minimum coverage requirement as well as the minimum participation requirement.

§ 3.6   —Plans Subject to Special Rules

In some instances, a plan is not required to satisfy the minimum coverage requirements (or, in some cases, the minimum participation requirements) for a plan year. For instance, neither test must be satisfied if the plan benefits no highly compensated employees for the plan year.[12] As described further below, in a plan containing a CODA election, "benefiting" under the plan for a year means having the opportunity to make an elective deferral for the year.[13]

If all employees of an employer are HCEs, a plan sponsored by that employer is deemed to have automatically satisfied § 410(b).[14]

As described in the next section, employees subject to a collective bargaining agreement are generally excluded for purposes of Code § 410(b) testing. Similarly, a plan that solely benefits collectively bargained employees for a plan year is deemed to satisfy the minimum coverage requirements. When a plan covers employees in and outside of the collectively bargained unit, the plan is treated as two separate plans. The portion covering collectively bargained employees automatically satisfies § 410(b) and the remaining portion must satisfy either the ratio test or the average benefits test.[15]

The minimum coverage requirements do not apply to government plans, church plans, plans that have not, after September 2, 1974, provided for employer contributions, and plans established and maintained by certain tax-exempt societies, orders, or associations calling for no employer contributions.[16]

---

[12] I.R.C. § 410(b); Treas. Reg. § 1.410.

[13] Treas. Reg. § 1.410(b)-2(b)(6).

[14] Treas. Reg. § 1.410(b)-2(b)(5).

[15] Treas. Reg. § 1.410(b)-2(b)(7).

[16] I.R.C. § 410(c).

§ 3.7   —Excluded Employees

When determining whether a plan satisfies the minimum coverage test and the minimum participation test, certain employees can be disregarded entirely. This means that, if a plan does not cover any of the excluded employees, the plan will not be "penalized" for purposes of the coverage tests. In essence, the statute provides that certain short-term employees, employees under age 21, part-time employees, employees who negotiate through collective bargaining, and nonresident aliens receiving no earned income within the United States may be excluded from any qualified retirement plan.[17] This does not mean that a plan must cover all other nonexcluded employees; it simply means that all other nonexcluded employees have to be counted toward performing the coverage tests.

The collective bargaining exception applies to individuals who are part of a unit of employees covered by an agreement which the Secretary of Labor finds to be a collective bargaining agreement between employee representatives and one or more employers, as long as there is evidence that retirement benefits were the subject of good faith bargaining between the employee representatives and the employer or employers.[18]

Short-term (and part-time) employees who can be disregarded are those employees who have not earned a year of eligibility service. A special rule applies when the plan provides for immediate vesting. In this case, 2 years of eligibility service can be required. However, the 2-year requirement does not apply to eligibility for a CODA feature under a qualified plan.

Eligibility Service

An individual will be deemed to have earned a year of eligibility service when he or she is credited with 1,000 hours of service during the consecutive 12-month period measured from the individual's date of hire. The initial eligibility computation period must be the consecutive 12-month period beginning with the date the employee becomes an employee. After the first period, the plan may elect to change the computation period to the plan year. If this change is made, the second eligibility computation period will be the plan year beginning with or within the first eligibility computation period. This change in measurement period is made for administrative ease. However, the change may have significant implications if the plan has 2-year eligibility, because an employee will earn a year of eligibility service for each computation period in which 1,000 hours of work are completed.

---

[17] I.R.C. § 410(a).

[18] I.R.C. § 410(b)(3).

Example: A plan that has a calendar plan year, and 2-year eligibility, changes the eligibility computation period to the plan year after the first computation period. Joe began full-time employment (40 hours per week), beginning on December 1, 1991. As of December 31, 1992 (13 months later), Joe will have earned 2 years of eligibility service—one for the period from December 1, 1991, to November 30, 1992, and a second for the 1992 plan year.

In some circumstances, service that has been earned may be disregarded. The basic unit for making such determination is referred to as a "break in service." For participation purposes, a plan may provide that a 1-year break in service occurs when an employee is credited with fewer than 501 hours of service during an eligibility computation period. The circumstances in which service can be disregarded after a break in service is discussed later.

Hours of Service

For determining eligibility service, as well as vesting service and benefit service, the term "hours of service" means any hours for which an employee is, directly or indirectly, entitled to compensation either by reason of the performance of duties or for certain reasons unrelated to the performance of duties, such as vacation or sick leave.

A plan actually has substantial discretion in choosing the methods of crediting hours of service. The plan may elect from among numerous methods. If the plan elects to count the number of actual hours worked and the hours for which the employee is entitled to be paid, the hours have to be credited in the following three circumstances:

1. Credit must be given for hours for which an employee is paid, or entitled to payment, for the performance of duties for the employer.
2. Credit must also be given for periods for which an employee is paid, or entitled to payment, by the employer on account of a period during which no duties are performed (regardless of whether the employment relationship has terminated)—vacation, holiday, illness, incapacity, or leave of absence.[19]
3. Each hour for which backpay, irrespective of mitigation of damages, is awarded or agreed to by the employer must be credited. The same hours need not be counted twice under any of the three provisions.

If the plan sponsor does not want to be concerned with crediting service when work is not actually performed, the plan can elect one of two

---

[19] I.R.C. § 410(a)(3); Labor Reg. § 2530.200b-2(b).

alternatives that credit employees only for hours actually worked. Under both of these options, the hours under the second and third categories described above are ignored entirely. The cost of choosing one of these alternatives is that the total hours of service needed in order to earn a year of service are reduced. Under the first option, the plan credits the employee for all hours actually worked. The employee will be considered to have earned a year of service, under this alternative, if he or she logs 870 hours of actual hours worked (reduced from 1,000). The minimum number of hours of service needed to avoid a break in service is also reduced. No break will occur if the employee earns 435 hours of service (instead of 500).

The second "hours worked" alternative credits only those hours of service that are considered regular time. Nonregular hours (overtime) do not have to be credited. This method is simple and may ease administration considerably when employees work large amounts of overtime. Once again, the price of choosing this alternative method is that the number of hours needed in order to be credited with a year of service is further reduced. Under the regular hours method, the employee needs 750 hours of service to be credited with a year of service and 375 hours to avoid a break in service.

Another option is to credit service based on units of time. Four similar options are available. Under each, an employee works a single hour of service during a particular unit of time, and the employee is credited with a specified number of hours of service. Under any of the methods, a year of service is earned when 1,000 hours of service are credited. The appeal of these methods is that the employer only has to determine whether the individual worked during the specified time period and does not have to count the actual hours worked during the period. The price of such a method is that the number of hours credited will generally exceed the number of hours actually worked. Under each of these methods, if the employee works one hour of service during the specified time period, he or she will be credited with the following number of hours of service:

Specified time period	Hours Credited
One day	10 hours
One week	45
Half-month	95
Month	190
Single shift	8 (or regularly scheduled shift hours)

The shift equivalency is similar to the other methods in that the employee is credited with the whole shift if he or she works at least one hour of service during that shift. The number of hours credited, however, is based on the number of regularly scheduled hours in the shift. If the employer has some shifts that are scheduled for a longer time period than other shifts, both numbers can be used when determining hours of service.

An employer may also elect an equivalency based on earnings. Under this method, the employee's total earnings during a computation period are divided by the hourly pay rate during that period. If a plan elects this earnings equivalency, an individual will earn a year of service with 750 credited hours (instead of 1,000 hours) and a break in service will occur if fewer than 375 hours (versus 500 hours) are credited.

The final equivalency method described in the Regulations is referred to as the elapsed time method.[20] Under this method, the plan credits service based on the total period of time of employment. Employment is credited from the date of hire until a severance of employment. However, generally, if an individual returns to work within 12 months from the last date of employment, the service will be deemed to be continuous, for purposes of eligibility service.

Entering the Plan

Upon meeting the 1-year (or, in some cases, 2-year) service requirement and attaining age 21, the individual must become a participant on the first day of the following plan year, or within 6 months, if earlier. For instance, for a calendar-year plan, an employee who meets the age and service requirements on March 1 must become a participant by September 1. To simplify administration, many plans elect to have two "entry dates"—one on the first day of the plan year and one the first day of the seventh month of the plan year. The eligible employee becomes a participant on the next entry date after meeting the requirements. Other plan sponsors prefer a single entry date, in which case the minimum service requirement has to be reduced to less than one year to satisfy the 6-month entry date requirement. If an individual does not enter the plan by the 6-month deadline, he or she is counted as an employee not covered by the plan. In other words, the individual is no longer in the "excludable" category.

§ 3.8   —Covered under the Plan

Prior to determining whether a plan satisfies one of the coverage tests, it must be determined who is considered "covered" under the plan. The following example helps to identify the issue.

---

[20] Treas. Reg. § 1.410(a)-7.

Example: A calendar-year profit-sharing plan containing a CODA is testing on December 31 to see whether the minimum coverage requirements have been met. As described above, under the annual testing method, all employees working at any time during the year, regardless of whether they are employed on the last day of the year, are counted for testing. Arnold, a participant as of the first day of the year, left the plan on May 15, after working 100 hours of service. Arnold was not making elective deferrals into the plan and is not eligible for a profit-sharing allocation.

In the example, is Arnold considered a plan participant or an individual who is not covered by the plan? Under Code § 410(b), this plan is treated as two separate arrangements. Testing is done separately for the CODA portion of the plan and the profit-sharing portion of the plan. For purposes of the profit-sharing portion, the rules require (with several small exceptions) that an individual actually receive an allocation, in order to be considered a participant of the plan. Therefore, in the example, Arnold is not a plan participant (of the profit-sharing portion) for Code § 410(b) testing.

For purposes of the CODA portion of the plan, an employee is treated as benefiting if the employee is eligible to make elective deferrals under the plan. Therefore, in the example, Arnold is counted as a plan participant (of the CODA portion) for Code § 410(b) testing.

§ 3.9   —Ratio Percentage Test

To meet the "ratio" test, the percentage of non-HCEs who benefit under the plan must be at least 70 percent of the percentage of HCEs who benefit under the plan. As discussed above, for determining the number of employees for testing purposes, employees excluded under the minimum age and service requirements, nonresident aliens with no source of earned income in the United States, and employees covered under a collective bargaining agreement are all disregarded.

The definition of highly compensated employees (HCEs) is the same as in § 2.11. Briefly recapping, HCEs are individuals who, during the current year or previous year, are 5 percent owners; earn over $75,000 ($93,518 for 1992) a year; earn over $50,000 ($62,345 for 1992) a year and are in the top 20 percent of all active employees for such year; or are officers earning over 50 percent of the defined-benefit (50 percent of $112,221 for 1992) limit on annual benefits. Individuals, other than 5 percent owners, who do not meet any of these earnings tests in the previous year will not be HCEs unless they are among the top 100 paid employees for that year.

For purposes of the ratio test (as well as the fair cross-section test described below), an individual is considered as "benefiting" under the plan only if he or she accrues a benefit (in a defined-benefit plan) or if contributions or forfeitures are allocated to his or her account (in a defined-contribution plan).[21] An exception applies to a plan that benefits no one for a particular plan year. Another exception applies to plans that allow elective (pretax CODA) contributions and after-tax employee contributions and matching contributions subject to § 401(m). Under these arrangements, an employee "benefits" under the plan for the year if he or she is eligible currently to make such elective or after-tax contributions or to receive matching contributions.

§ 3.10   —Average Benefits Test

Under this test, the plan must satisfy both the nondiscriminatory classification test and the average benefit percentage test for the plan year. The nondiscriminatory classification test is satisfied if a "reasonable classification" is established and the classification is nondiscriminatory. The reasonable classification portion of the test requires that the eligibility requirements (specifying who qualifies for participation and who does not) must be stated using some objective means of classification, such as job classification, nature of compensation (salaried or hourly), or geographic location. Establishing eligibility criteria that name individuals who are excluded (or included) is not deemed to be a reasonable classification. For instance, a plan that states that salaried employees are eligible will generally constitute a reasonable classification; a plan that states that Ralph, George, and Peter are eligible will not be a reasonable classification.

The reasonable classification has to be nondiscriminatory. This requirement can be satisfied either by covering a safe-harbor percentage test or meeting a facts-and-circumstances test. The safe-harbor test is satisfied if the percentage of non-HCEs covered equals at least 50 percent of the HCEs covered under the plan. The 50 percent safe harbor is reduced by $3/4$ of 1 percent for each percentage that the non-HCE concentration percentage exceeds 60 percent. The non-HCE concentration percentage is the percentage of employees of an employer who are non-HCEs (not counting the "excludable employees"). For example, if 80 percent of the employees are non-HCEs, then the safe-harbor percentage is 35 percent. **Table 3–1** shows the safe harbors based on the non-HCE concentration.

The facts-and-circumstances test is satisfied if two conditions are met. First, the percentage of non-HCEs covered must equal or exceed 40 percent of the percentage of HCEs covered under the plan. This lower threshold is referred to as the "unsafe harbor." Similar to the safe harbor, the unsafe

---

[21] Treas. Reg. § 1.410(b)-3(b).

Table 3–1

Safe-Harbor and Unsafe-Harbor Percentage Limits

Non-HCE Concentration	Safe Harbor Percentage	Unsafe Harbor Percentage
0-60	50.00	40.00
61	49.25	39.25
62	48.50	38.50
63	47.75	37.75
64	47.00	37.0
65	46.25	36.25
66	45.50	35.50
67	44.75	34.75
68	44.00	34.00
69	43.25	33.25
70	42.50	32.50
71	41.75	31.75
72	41.00	31.00
73	40.25	30.25
74	39.50	29.50
75	38.75	28.75
76	38.00	28.00
77	37.25	27.25
78	36.50	26.50
79	35.75	25.75
80	35.00	25.00
81	34.25	24.25
82	33.50	23.50
83	32.75	22.75
84	32.00	22.00
85	31.25	21.75
86	30.50	20.50
87	29.75	19.75
88	29.00	19.00
89	28.25	18.25
90	27.50	17.50
91	26.75	16.75
92	26.00	16.00
93	25.25	15.25
94	24.50	14.50
95	23.75	13.75
96	23.00	13.00
97	22.25	12.25
98	21.50	11.50
99	20.75	10.75

harbor is reduced when the non-HCE concentration percentage exceeds 60 percent. **Table 3–1** shows both the safe-harbor and unsafe-harbor limits. Second, in a review of all the facts and circumstances, the classification must be proven nondiscriminatory. Relevant factors include the business reason for the classification, the percentage of employees covered under the plan, and whether the number of employees covered in each salary range is representative of the number of employees in each salary range of the employer's work force.

If a nondiscriminatory classification has been satisfied, the plan must also satisfy the requirements of the average benefits test. This is a fairly complex calculation, and is explained only generally herein.

A plan satisfies the average benefit percentage test for a plan year if and only if the average benefit percentage of the plan for the plan year is at least 70 percent. The average benefit percentage is determined by dividing the actual benefit percentage of the non-highly compensated employees in plans in the testing group for the testing period that includes the plan year by the actual benefit percentage of the highly compensated employees in plans in the testing group for the testing period.

The actual benefit percentage of a group is the average of the benefit percentages calculated for each individual. The amount of benefit used to calculate the benefit percentage does not count benefits attributable to employee contributions. The employer-provided benefits are determined by adding all benefits provided under employer contributions (including employee elective deferrals and forfeitures) from all qualified plans of the employer during the testing period. The benefit percentage can be determined by comparing either benefits or contributions. For example, if an individual is a participant in both a defined-benefit and a defined-contribution plan, the contribution to the defined-contribution plan may be translated into a monthly retirement benefit and added to the benefit provided by the defined-benefit plan; or, the present value of the defined-benefit plan benefit can be added to the contribution from the defined-contribution plan. The testing period includes the plan years ending with or within the same calendar year.

§ 3.11 —Aggregation of Employers and Employees

Code § 414 contains rules that require separate entities, in whole or in part, to be treated as a single employer for purposes of applying the qualification requirements discussed in **Chapters 2** through **4**. The aggregation of two or more employers will have the most impact on the qualified status of a retirement plan under the minimum coverage and minimum participation rules and under the top-heavy rules. In addition, aggregation can have a significant impact when applying the nondiscrimination test to benefit and contribution requirements, minimum vesting standards, and maximum benefit rules.

Code § 414 contains several aggregation rules that apply to a broad range of situations. These include the controlled group rules of Code § 414(b) and (c), which require aggregation when there is a significant amount of common ownership among two or more entities.

Code § 414(m) requires aggregation of two or more entities in three different circumstances. Each rule was enacted to stop perceived abuses. In all three situations, the perception was that business owners were dividing single organizations (and providing one product or service) into separate entities as a way to get around the minimum coverage requirements. One entity would then adopt a plan and the other would not. The rules were adopted to address three different types of avoidance schemes. What each rule has in common is that it requires the individuals of the separate employers to work together in performing a single service or providing a product to the public.

A similar rule contained in Code § 414(n) states that leased employees who provide services to a recipient on a full-time basis for more than a year are treated as employees of the recipient. Finally, Code § 414(o) provides that the Secretary of the Treasury may prescribe Regulations to prevent the avoidance of any employee benefit requirements through the use of separate organizations, employee leasing, or other arrangements. Proposed Regulations have introduced a number of different rules, under Code § 414(o). Affiliation rules, including those covering controlled groups, affiliated service groups, employee leasing, and § 414(o) affiliation, are discussed below.

Controlled Groups

The Code contains two separate "controlled group" rules that require aggregation of employers within common control. One pertains to corporations and one pertains to "trades and businesses," including partnerships, proprietorships, estates, and trusts. The rules are essentially similar and are discussed together herein, with any differences noted. The rules refer to three types of controlled groups: parent–subsidiary, brother–sister, and combined groups. In all three situations, if two or more entities are considered part of a controlled group, they have to be treated as a single employer for purposes of applying the qualified plan requirements.

A parent–subsidiary controlled group relationship exists whenever one entity (referred to as the "parent company") owns at least 80 percent of one (or more) other entities. Additional entities may be brought into the group if a chain of common ownership exists. Other entities included in the chain are entities that are at least 80 percent owned by one or more (in combination) of the other entities within the chain.

> *Example:* Corporation A owns 80 percent of Corporations B and C. Corporations B and C each own 40 percent of Corporation D. Because Corporation D is 80 percent owned by entities within the group, Corporation D is part of the parent–subsidiary controlled group that includes all four corporations.

A corporation will be deemed to have an 80 percent ownership of another entity if it owns either 80 percent of the entire value of all stock or 80 percent of the voting shares of that corporation.

A brother–sister controlled group exists whenever two or more entities have the same five (or fewer) owners who own 80 percent or more of each entity, and more than 50 percent of each entity, counting only "identical ownership."

Identical ownership is tested by counting each person's ownership to the extent that it is identical in each entity. For example, if an individual owns 10 percent of Corporation A and 20 percent of Corporation B, he or she has a 10 percent identical ownership interest with respect to each corporation. The identical ownership interests of each of the five (or fewer) individuals is added together to determine whether the 50 percent test has been satisfied, as shown for these fictitious shareholders:

Shareholder	Corporation X	Corporation Y	Identical Ownership
Joe	20%	12%	12%
Sally	60	14	14
Ralph	20	74	20
Total	100%	100%	46%

Under these assumed facts, the 80 percent ownership test has been met but the 50 percent identical ownership interest test has not been satisfied. Therefore, this group does not constitute a controlled group.

Under the 80 percent test, only those individuals who have some ownership interest in each entity may be counted toward determining common ownership. In another fictitious analysis, the results qualify, as follows:

Shareholder	Corporation A	Corporation B	Identical Ownership
Cindy	65%	65%	65%
George	35	0	0
David	0	35	0
Total	100%	100%	65%

Under these assumed facts, the 50 percent identical ownership test has been satisfied, but the 80 percent ownership test has not. Cindy is the only individual with ownership interests in each company, and she does not own 80 percent of both companies. As a result, no brother–sister relationship exists.

When determining an individual's ownership interest under the brother–sister controlled group rules, certain attribution rules will require that interests owned by others must be attributed to an individual. First, an individual will be deemed to own any interests owned by his or her spouse, with one narrow exception. Spousal attribution will not apply if:

- The individual owns no interest in his or her own name;
- The individual is not a director or employee and does not participate in the management of the spouse's organization;
- Not more than 50 percent of the entity's income stems from passive sources;
- The spouse's ownership interest is not subject to any conditions running in favor of the individual.

Second, an individual is deemed to own the stock owned by his or her children who have not attained age 21. Third, if an individual owns more than 50 percent of an entity, he or she is deemed to own any interests owned in that entity by his or her adult children, grandchildren, parents, and grandparents. Adopted children are treated the same as natural children under these rules.

An individual who owns 5 percent or more of an entity is deemed to own a proportionate part of any interests owned by the entity. Similar pass-through rules are applicable to estates and trusts.[22]

A combined group under common control consists of two related controlled groups. A combined group exists if an entity is both a common parent in a parent–subsidiary group and a member of a brother–sister group.

Affiliated Service Groups

In 1980, Congress enacted the first affiliated service group rules. Small business corporations had managed to separate management and rank-and-file employees into separate entities and avoid the controlled group rules. The "A-Org" and "B-Org" affiliation rules (see below) were enacted to eliminate the typical schemes that had been established to avoid the controlled group rules. In 1983, the management services affiliation rules

---

[22] I.R.C. § 1563(e)(3); Treas. Reg. § 1.414(c)-4(b)(3).

were established to eliminate another type of avoidance scheme that was not addressed in the 1980 legislation.

When analyzing any fact pattern to determine whether an affiliated service group exists, the individual must test whether, under the facts, any of the three types of affiliated service groups exist.

A-Org Type of Affiliation.   An A-Org affiliated group consists of a first service organization ("FSO"), and any other "service organization" ("A-Org") which (1) is a shareholder or partner in the FSO, and (2) regularly performs services for the FSO or is regularly associated with the FSO in performing services for third persons.

> *Example:* Ruth, an attorney, is incorporated, and her corporation is a partner in a law firm. Ruth and her corporation are regularly associated with the law firm in performing services for third persons. Considering the law firm as the FSO, Ruth's corporation is an A-Org because it is a partner in the law firm and is regularly associated with the law firm in performing services for third persons. Accordingly, Ruth's corporation and the law firm constitute an A-Org type of affiliated service group.

For purposes of testing A-Org (and B-Org) affiliation, a service organization is an organization for which capital is not a material income-producing factor. However, organizations in the fields of health, law, engineering, actuarial science, consulting, and insurance are automatically considered service organizations regardless of whether the organization is capital-intensive. For a corporation to be an FSO under the A-Org rules, the corporation has to be a professional service corporation, which is defined as a corporation that is organized under state law for the principal purpose of providing professional services and has at least one shareholder who is licensed or otherwise legally authorized to render the type of service for which the corporation is organized. "Professional services" means the services performed by accountants, actuaries, architects, attorneys, doctors (including a wide number of professional designations), dentists, engineers, psychologists, and veterinarians.[23] The Regulations state that the professional services corporation limitation is intended to limit the application of the A-Org rules; the A-Org rules could otherwise be applied to nonabusive situations.

Under the A-Org rules, the A-Org must "regularly perform services for" or be "regularly associated with" the FSO. Proposed Regulations indicate that such determination will be made after considering the specific facts and circumstances of each situation. Unfortunately, the Proposed

---

[23] Prop. Treas. Reg. § 1.414(m)-1(c).

Regulations give no additional guidance on how to make this crucial determination.

B-Org Type of Affiliation.   A B-Org type of affiliated group consists of a first service organization ("FSO") and any other organization ("B-Org") if (1) a significant portion of the B-Org's business is the performance of services for the FSO (or any A-Org related to the FSO), as long as such services are of a type "historically performed by employees," and (2) 10 percent or more of the B-Org is owned by highly compensated employees (HCEs) of the FSO.

> *Example:* George owns an employee benefit consulting firm and is also an HCE of an insurance company. A significant portion of the business of the consulting firm consists of assisting the insurance agency in developing employee benefit packages for sale to third persons and providing services to the insurance company in connection with employee benefit programs sold to other clients of the insurance agency. Thirty percent of the total gross receipts of the consulting firm represent gross receipts from the performance of these services for the insurance agency.
>
> Considering the insurance agency as an FSO, the consulting firm is a B-Org because a significant portion of the business of the consulting firm is the performance, for the insurance agency, of services of a type historically performed by an HCE of the insurance agency. Thus, the insurance agency and the consulting firm constitute an affiliated service group.

For purposes of testing under the B-Org rules, an FSO can be any service organization. The B-Org does not necessarily need to be a service agency, as long as the above described tests are satisfied. The "significant portion" test is satisfied if 10 percent or more of the B-Org's receipts are from providing services to the FSO.[24] Services are deemed to be of a type "historically performed by employees" in a particular service field if it was not unusual for such services to be performed by employees of organizations in that service field on December 13, 1980. Individuals are highly compensated employees as defined in Code § 414(q) (see **§ 2.11**).

A third type of affiliation is referred to as a "management service group." This type of affiliation is substantially different from the other types in that no common ownership is required and neither of the entities involved needs to be a "services organization." The management services rules were incorporated to prohibit employers from separating management from rank-and-file employees in order to avoid the qualified plan requirements.

---

[24] Prop. Treas. Reg. § 1.414(m)-2(c)(2).

A management services group consists of (1) an organization the "principal business" of which is performing "management functions" for one organization (or for one organization and other organizations "related" to that one organization), and (2) the one organization (and related organizations) for which such management functions are performed. The principal business of an organization is deemed to consist of management functions when more than 50 percent of the management company's gross receipts are from the performance of management functions for the recipient company.[25] Management functions generally include: "determining, implementing, or supervising" many business functions such as production, sales, marketing, compensation, product development, and any other management activity or service.

Unlike A-Org and B-Org affiliation, the Internal Revenue Code does not contain a "historically performed test" under the management services rules. However, the conference committee report, demonstrating legislative intent, indicates that affiliation should occur only when such management functions have been historically performed by employees. The Proposed Regulations, recognizing this requirement, state that only those management services that are historically performed by employees are treated as management services. Services are considered historically performed by employees if in a particular business field it was not unusual for management services of such type to be performed by employees on September 3, 1982. Notwithstanding the general rule, any management services that were actually performed by employees of that particular organization will be counted for the 5-year period after the employment relationship has been severed.

A complicating factor under the Proposed Regulations is that "management services" also are deemed to include professional services, if the professional services are of the type performed by the organization receiving the management services. These management services are not required to meet the "historically performed" test. This rule in the Proposed Regulations has been very disconcerting to the medical industry because many doctors who are regularly associated with hospitals (such as radiologists) operate not as employees of the hospital but as separate entities. Under this definition of management services, a physician group, such as a group of radiologists who earn more than 50 percent of their receipts from one hospital, may be considered affiliated with the hospital through the performance of "management services" for the hospital.

---

[25] Prop. Treas. Reg. § 1.414(m)-4(b).

Leased Employees.   A leased employee is a person who is not an employee of the recipient, but who provides services to the recipient under the following circumstances:

1. The services are provided pursuant to an agreement between the recipient and a leasing organization;
2. The services are provided on a substantially full-time basis for a period of at least 1 year;
3. The services are of a type historically performed, by employees, in the business field of the recipient.

An individual need not be an employee of a leasing organization. The "leasing relationship" can exist directly with the leased employee, which means that a self-employed individual can be treated as a leased employee.[26] The agreement between the recipient and the leasing organization need not be in writing. Services will be deemed "historically performed" by employees of the recipient if it was not unusual for such services to be performed by employees in that business field, in the United States, on September 30, 1982. Services will be deemed to be substantially full-time for a year if the individual is credited with 1,500 or more hours of services (fewer hours are required, in some cases, where employees generally work fewer than 40 hours a week).

Even an individual who is a leased employee (under the above conditions) will not be treated as an employee of the recipient if leased employees constitute no more than 20 percent of the recipient's non-highly compensated work force and the leasing entity maintains a safe-harbor plan. A safe-harbor plan must be a money purchase plan with a nonintegrated contribution rate of at least 10 percent of compensation and must provide for immediate eligibility and 100 percent immediate vesting.

Every recipient of nonemployee services is required to maintain sufficient records to determine whether an individual is a leased employee. An employer may be exempted from the record-keeping requirement, but only if all three of the following conditions are satisfied:

• All of the recipient's qualified plans must specifically provide that leased employees are not eligible to participate;
• No qualified plan of the recipient can be top-heavy;
• The number of leased persons providing services to the recipient during the plan year must be less than 5 percent of the number of employees

---

[26] Prop. Treas. Reg. § 1.414(n).

(excluding leased persons and highly compensated employees) covered by the recipient's qualified plans.

Code § 414(o) Affiliation. Under Code § 414(o), the Secretary of the Treasury is authorized to provide rules, in addition to the affiliated service group and leased employee rules, that are necessary to ensure that the employee benefit provisions are not circumvented through the use of separate organizations, employee leasing, or other arrangements. Under this Code provision, the IRS has issued Proposed Regulations that would require various types of aggregation of employees (or employers) under the following circumstances.[27]

1. *Leased owners.* Generally, this rule applies to any 5 percent (or more) owner who performs services for the organization (the recipient entity) in a capacity other than as an employee. When applicable, the leased owner's plan will be compared to that of the recipient organization. If the qualification requirements are not met, on a combined basis, the leased owner's plan will be disqualified.

2. *Leased managers.* This rule applies if more than 50 percent of an organization's management functions are performed by nonemployees. The rule applies in the same way as for a leased owner.

3. *Successive organizations in time.* If two or more organizations would be part of a controlled group but for the fact that they exist at different times, the qualification requirements applicable to controlled groups will be applied as though the organizations existed concurrently. For example, Code § 415 would be applied by aggregating the benefits under all of the plans.

4. *Inside corporate directors.* An individual who is an employee of an organization and, in addition, receives "self-employment income" for services as a director of that same organization, generally may not maintain a separate plan with respect to those director's fees.

5. *Five percent owners of service organizations.* An individual who is a 5 percent owner of more than one service organization must combine all benefits received from qualified plans issued by such organizations, in applying the maximum benefit limitations under Code § 415.

6. *Shared employees.* Individuals who are "shared employees" will be treated as if they are employees of each of the employers that share their services, for purposes of the qualified plan coverage rules. Shared employees are those employees who work for more than one employer at a common location, where the total hours of services of all employees performing a similar job for one of the employers is more than 1,000 hours.

---

[27] Prop. Treas. Reg. § 1.414(o)-1.

Example: Five doctors lease an office suite that interconnects with a common reception area. Each doctor is a sole proprietor. The doctors collectively employ five nurses who perform only nursing duties. Each nurse is considered to spend one-fifth of his or her time working for each doctor. With respect to each doctor, the total service during the calendar year exceeds 1,000 hours. All five of the nurses are shared employees with respect to each of the five doctors.

§ 3.12   —Aggregation of Plans

In some limited circumstances, two separate plans of an employer may be treated as one plan, for satisfying either the ratio percentage test or the nondiscriminatory classification test. If plans are aggregated, they must be treated as a single plan for all purposes under §§ 410(b) and 401(a)(4).

§ 3.13   —Separate Lines of Business

In order for a separate line of business (SLOB) to be treated separately, the following requirements must be satisfied. The line of business must:

- Be organized as a separate organizational unit within the employer;
- Be a separate profit center within the employer;
- Have its own separate employee work force;
- Have its own separate management;
- Have its own tangible assets.[28]

Once these requirements have been satisfied, the line of business must still demonstrate that it is a qualified SLOB. To be qualified, the SLOB must employ at least 50 employees who provide services exclusively to the SLOB, the IRS must be notified of the SLOB status, and the plan must satisfy the administrative scrutiny test by either meeting IRS approval or fulfilling one of the following safe harbors:

- The plan's coverage of HCEs cannot be less than 50 percent or more than 200 percent of its coverage of non-HCEs;
- The SLOB must be in a different industry from other lines of business, based on IRS industry codes;

---

[28] Treas. Reg. § 1.414(r)-1.

- The separate reportable industry segment must be defined in the Financial Accounting Standards Board's (FASB) Statement of Financial Accounting Standards No. 14;
- The level of benefits provided to employees of the SLOB must satisfy certain maximum or minimum benefit requirements.

§ 3.14   Minimum Participation Requirement

In addition to satisfying the minimum coverage requirements, each plan must satisfy the minimum participation requirement of Code § 401(a)(26). Under this rule, a plan must cover the lesser of 50 employees or 40 percent of all of the employer's employees. In counting the number of employees of the employer, employees who are not eligible because of the age and service requirements or who are part of a group covered by a collective bargaining agreement are not included. The effect of this rule is that employers with more than 125 employees cannot maintain a plan covering fewer than 50 participants; if the employer has fewer than 125 employees, then the 40 percent limit applies.

The minimum participation requirement was introduced by the Tax Reform Act of 1986 ("TRA 86"). For plan years beginning prior to 1989, under the minimum coverage requirements, an employer could establish several plans and treat them as one plan for purposes of the minimum coverage requirements, as long as the plans were "comparable." This was perceived as an abuse, and the minimum participation requirement was intended as a remedy. Now, even comparable plans cannot be added together to determine whether the plans meet the minimum participation requirement. This means that a small employer may never have more than two plans covering different employees (each must cover at least 40 percent of the employees), and each plan must cover the minimum required percentage.

In a defined-contribution plan, an individual is not treated as "covered" under the plan unless he or she receives an allocation. However, if no participants receive an allocation of either a contribution or forfeiture, the plan automatically meets the coverage requirements. A major exception to this rule applies to CODAs: eligibility to participate, alone, is treated as participation.

§ 3.15   Nondiscrimination in
Contributions or Benefits

A plan cannot discriminate in favor of the HCEs with regard to benefits or contributions. The requirements are satisfied if either the contributions or the benefits are nondiscriminatory. A plan will not be deemed to be discriminatory if contributions or benefits bear a uniform relationship to compensation.[29] For instance, if a profit-sharing plan allocates contributions based on an individual's compensation to total compensation earned by all participants, each participant will receive a contribution that is the same percentage of pay.

A plan is also not deemed to discriminate if the plan contains some disparity of contributions or benefits because of integration of social security. (See § **3.16**.)

Comprehensive regulations issued in September 1991 provided guidance as to the meaning of nondiscrimination in contribution and benefits requirements. These rules were at first intended to be effective for the plan year beginning in 1992, but the IRS delayed the effective date for such rules to the plan year beginning in 1993. The IRS appears to be reconsidering the Regulations and may change them. Therefore, the rules summarized herein may never become effective in the form described.

A plan can choose to satisfy the requirements by establishing that either benefits or contributions are nondiscriminatory. In a defined-contribution plan, the plan will generally attempt to demonstrate that contributions are nondiscriminatory. However, the plan may also translate the contributions into a benefit and then test the benefits against the nondiscrimination requirements. Only the nondiscrimination requirements applicable to testing contributions are discussed herein.

In order to understand the nondiscrimination requirements, a plan that contains a CODA must be broken into component parts. The application to the component parts is as follows:

- The portion of the plan attributable to CODA elections is tested for nondiscrimination solely through the testing in Code § 401(k) (see §§ **2.07** through **2.13**);
- The portion of the plan attributable to employer matching contributions and employee after-tax contributions is tested under the nondiscrimination test of Code § 401(m) (see § **2.19**);
- Any employer contribution under a profit-sharing feature (or pre-ERISA money purchase plan) will be subject to the tests described in this section.

The general rule is that the rate of contribution, stated as a percentage of compensation or as a stated dollar amount, for any HCE cannot exceed the rate of contribution for all non-HCEs. The rule is actually much more flexible than it sounds, because a plan that provides contributions at

---

[29] I.R.C. § 401(a)(5).

different rates for its employees may group the employees receiving contributions at each rate. If each grouping covers employees who meet the minimum coverage requirements (see §§ **3.09–3.10**) (disregarding the average benefits test), then the plan will satisfy the nondiscrimination test. Dividing the plan into component parts is not allowed under the Code § 401(k) or § 401(m) testing requirements. Testing is required on an annual basis.

A plan that satisfies one of the safe-harbor tests may avoid some or all of the annual testing requirements. To be exempt from all annual testing, a plan will be deemed to satisfy the requirements if the plan has:

- A uniform retirement age and allocation formula for all employees;
- A uniform vesting schedule and a uniform method of crediting service;
- A uniform allocation formula, meaning that contributions are allocated as a uniform percentage of compensation or the same dollar amount is allocated to all employees.

Another safe-harbor method allows for consideration of age and or service in the formula; however, the plan using this allocation method is required to do modified annual testing.[30]

The availability of benefits, rights, and features provided under a plan cannot discriminate in favor of highly compensated employees. Rights and features include all optional forms of benefit, ancillary benefits, and other rights and features available to any employee under the plan. A benefit, right, or feature must be "currently available" to a group of employees that satisfies the ratio percentage test (see § **3.09**) or the average benefits test (see § **3.10**). Generally, a benefit, right, or feature is currently available if the employee has met all preexisting conditions to receive such benefit. Certain age and service requirements are disregarded in making this determination.

§ 3.16 —Integration with Social Security Benefits

As described above, if the contribution allocated to each of the plan's participants is a uniform percentage of compensation, the plan is considered to comply with the nondiscrimination in contribution requirements. In addition, a plan will not be considered discriminatory if contributions are allocated in a way that provides for a higher contribution rate as a percentage of compensation, as long as certain disparity requirements are met.[31]

---

[30] Treas. Reg. § 1.401(a)(4)-2(b)(3).

[31] I.R.C. § 401(a)(5).

The rationale for allowing such disparity has to do with the way the social security system works. Private employers and employees are required to pay a tax on wages, called the FICA tax, which is used to provide retirement benefits, survivor benefits, disability benefits, and retiree medical benefits.

The FICA tax requires the employer to pay tax on wages earned, capped at a certain level; the cap amount is referred to as the taxable wage base. If an employee earns more than the taxable wage base, no employer contributions are made on the earnings above the cap. This means that the employer pays into the system more, as a percentage of compensation, for non-highly compensated employees.

> *Example:* An individual earns $40,000 in 1992. The employer portion of the tax is $2,480, or 6.2 percent of compensation. Another employee earns $100,000. The employer portion of the tax is $3,441, or 3.4 percent of compensation. From this perspective, the social security system discriminates against the highly compensated employees.

The disparity rules provide an opportunity for the employer to make up for the discrimination against the highly compensated.

For a defined-contribution plan to meet the disparity requirements, the plan must meet several criteria. The disparity must not exceed the maximum excess allowance, which is the lesser of (1) the base contribution percentage or (2) the greater of (a) 5.7 percentage points or (b) the percentage equal to the rate of social security tax (in effect for the year) attributable to old-age insurance.[32] The maximum excess allowance is determined by subtracting the base contribution percentage from the excess contribution percentage. The excess contribution percentage is that percentage of an employee's compensation contributed to the plan which is attributable to compensation in excess of the integration level. The base contribution percentage is that percentage of an employee's compensation contributed to the plan which is attributable to compensation not in excess of the integration level. Currently, the portion attributable to old-age insurance is less than 5.7 percent. The IRS is required to publish a new percentage at such time that it exceeds 5.7 percent.

The disparity for all employees under the plan must be uniform. To be uniform, the plan must use the same base contribution percentage and excess contribution percentage for all employees in the plan.[33] The integration level generally must equal the taxable wage base in effect at the beginning

---

[32] I.R.C. § 401(l).

[33] Treas. Reg. § 1.401(l)-2(a).

of the plan year. However, a lower amount may be chosen if the maximum 5.7 percent is adjusted, as follows:

Integration Level	Maximum Disparity Percentage
Taxable wage base (TWB)	5.7%
80% or more of TWB	5.4%
20% or more of TWB	4.7%
Less than 20% of TWB	5.7%

The following example demonstrates how the rules apply.

Example: The Alpha Corporation has an integrated money-purchase pension plan. Under the plan's formula, the corporation is required to make a contribution in the amount of 6 percent of total compensation and 5.7 percent of compensation in excess of the taxable wage base on the first day of the plan year. The plan satisfies the integration requirements because the excess contribution percentage is 11.7 percent (contribution percentage contributed on earnings in excess of the integration level) and the base contribution percentage is 6 percent (contribution percentage on earnings up to the integration level). An individual's contribution under such a plan is calculated as follows. Susan, a participant in the plan, has $100,000 of compensation. The contribution made on Susan's behalf for the plan year ending December 31, 1992, will be:

Contribution attributable to 6 percent of compensation	$6,000
Contribution attributable to compensation in excess of the taxable wage base ($100,000 − $55,500)	$2,536
Total contribution	$8,536

§ 3.17   Cap on Compensation

The nondiscrimination of contribution and benefit limitations discussed above is tested in connection with the limitation that annual compensation cannot exceed $200,000, indexed for inflation ($228,860 for 1992). Any compensation paid to an employee who is the spouse of or a child (under age 19) of a 5 percent owner or of one of the 10 employees who were paid the highest compensation during the year is treated as paid to the 5 percent owner or highly compensated employee.[34]

---

[34] I.R.C. § 401(a)(17).

§ 3.18   Maximum Contribution and Benefit Limits

Several different limits effectively determine the contribution and/or benefit amounts that a participant will receive from a qualified retirement plan. Code § 415(c) limits the annual contributions that can be allocated to a participant's account under a defined-contribution plan. The combined plan limits of Code § 415(e) may further limit annual additions, if the individual also participates in a qualified defined-benefit plan.

Indirectly, the maximum deductible amount that an employer may contribute to a plan limits the benefits that a participant may receive. This is especially true since passage of the Tax Reform Act of 1986, which introduced an excise tax that applies to any nondeductible contributions made to the plan. (These rules are discussed in the next section.)

Other indirect limitations on contributions and benefits are the 15 percent excise tax on certain large distributions and the 15 percent estate tax on excess accumulations (see **§§ 4.13–4.14**). The 15 percent excise tax on large distributions creates a 15 percent tax on annual distributions from IRA accounts, qualified plans, and § 403(b) annuity plans that exceed a threshold amount (currently, $150,000 in most cases). The estate tax similarly applies to large accumulations that still remain in these tax-preferred retirement plans at the individual's death. The excise taxes may discourage an individual from accumulating large amounts of benefits under such plans, and thus may indirectly limit plan benefits. These excise taxes have the most effect on individuals who can control the amount of benefits accruing on their behalf—usually, the owners of closely held companies, or self-employed professionals. Generally, however, because these excise taxes only apply to large distributions, they do not have any effect on most plan participants. How much these excise taxes will discourage an individual from accruing benefits under a plan is uncertain. The effect will depend on the individual's perception of future tax rates, the length of time when benefits will accrue before being distributed, and the individual's perception of the plan's interest earnings.

Annual Addition Limits under Code § 415

The limits contained in Code § 415 apply to all qualified defined-contribution plans, as well as Code § 403(b) annuity plans and SEPs. A plan must meet the Code § 415 limits at all times, to maintain its qualified status.

Of primary concern to a defined-contribution plan is the limit of Code § 415(c) regarding "annual additions" made to a participant's account.

The amount of additions that may be made to a participant's account for the "limitation year" may not exceed the lesser of $30,000 or 25 percent of the participant's compensation. Although the $30,000 limit is increased for inflation, it is currently frozen, until the maximum benefit dollar limitation for defined-benefit limits exceeds $120,000 (in 1992, it had reached $112,221). At that time, the $30,000 limit will remain at a quarter of the applicable limit for defined benefit plans.

The term "annual additions" includes all of the following:

- Employer contributions made to the participant's account;
- Forfeitures allocated to the participant's account;
- Employee contributions made by the participant.

Employee contributions do not include any rollover contributions but do include both voluntary and mandatory contributions. As described in § 2.07, employee elective deferrals under a CODA will be treated as employer contributions for purposes of the Code § 415 limit.

The 25 percent limitation is based on an individual's compensation, which includes the participant's wages, salary, fees for professional service, and any amounts received for personal services; earned income from sources outside the United States, whether or not excluded from gross income; amounts received under medical reimbursement of disability policies to the extent included in gross income; nondeductible reimbursements for moving expenses; the value of a nonqualified stock option to the extent includable in gross income in the year granted; and amounts includable in gross income under Code § 83(b).

Certain types of income received in connection with compensation are not includable: amounts paid by the employer to a plan of deferred compensation; amounts realized by the exercise of a nonqualified option or from disposition of stock acquired under a qualified or incentive stock option; and amounts that receive special tax benefits, such as premiums for group term insurance.

If a plan does not want to use this complex definition, it may elect several alternative methods of defining compensation. One definition for compensation is: all wages that are subject to income tax withholding, or, alternatively, wages as defined for purposes of the FICA tax, used to pay for social security benefits (disregarding the taxable wage base limitation).[35] After 1991, compensation may include only those amounts paid or made available to a participant within the limitation year.[36]

---

[35] Treas. Reg. § 1.415-2(d).

[36] Treas. Reg. § 1.415(2)(d).

This limitation applies in the aggregate to all defined contribution plans sponsored by the same employer. The term employer includes all employers that are required to be aggregated under the controlled group rules or the affiliated service group rules (see **§ 3.11**). In fact, a special and more stringent test applies for determining whether two or more employers are part of a controlled group of corporations or a controlled group of trades or businesses for purposes of Code § 415 only. Under the standard rule, a parent–subsidiary controlled group exists when the parent has at least 80 percent ownership of a subsidiary. However, for purposes of determining aggregation for purposes of the Code § 415 limits, common control exists with more than 50 percent common ownership.[37] (See **§ 3.11** for a complete discussion of the controlled group rules.)

To determine whether the annual limitation rules have been satisfied, the year taken into consideration is called the "limitation year." The limitation year may be any consecutive 12-month period. However, if the plan does not elect a limitation year in the plan document, the limitation year becomes the calendar year. In most cases, a plan that has a noncalendar plan year will want to choose the plan year as the limitation year, because records are normally kept on a plan-year basis.[38]

A plan that does not satisfy the limitation on benefits or contributions will be disqualified in the year the limitation is exceeded. If the employee maintains more than one plan, the Treasury Regulations prescribe the order in which one or more of the plans will be disqualified.[39]

Due to the harsh penalties associated with failure to meet Code § 415, the Treasury Regulations provide several methods that may be used to correct annual additions in excess of the limit. A defined-contribution plan may provide that excess annual additions attributable to employee contributions be returned and that excess amounts attributable to employer contributions be allocated and/or reallocated to the accounts of other participants in the plan or held in a suspense account for allocation in succeeding years.[40] The Treasury Regulations indicate that this relief may only be granted in limited circumstances, such as when the excess results from forfeitures, from a reasonable error in estimating compensation or in estimating employee deferrals under a CODA election, or from other reasonable factors as determined by the Commissioner.[41]

Before leaving this subject, it should be noted that the above rules, generally quite straightforward, may be somewhat complex to administer in

---

[37] I.R.C. § 415(h).

[38] Treas. Reg. § 1.415(d)(2)(b).

[39] Treas. Reg. § 1.415-9(b)(3).

[40] Treas. Reg. § 1.415-6(b)(6).

[41] Treas. Reg. § 1.415(6)(b)(6).

the case of a plan that contains a CODA. The major complication is that amounts deferred by participants are not defined as compensation for purposes of determining the 25 percent limit.

> *Example:* An individual earns a salary of $20,000 and wants to defer $5,000 (the individual is not entitled to any other contributions or forfeitures under the plan). At first glance, the annual additions appear to equal 25 percent of salary ($5,000/$20,000), which satisfies Code § 415. However, because the $5,000 deferral cannot be considered compensation for the Code § 415 limits, the annual additions have exceeded the limit ($5,000/$15,000).

Combined Plan Limits

An individual who participates in both a defined-benefit plan and a defined-contribution plan maintained by the same employer is generally allowed benefits in excess of each limit separately. However, the combined limit of Code § 415(e) does limit benefits to approximately 1.25 times the individual limits.

Because the combined limit is based partially on the defined benefit limit, this limit will be discussed briefly. The maximum annual benefit that may be paid under a defined-benefit plan is the lesser of 100 percent of the participant's average compensation for the three highest paid years, or $90,000. This dollar limit, adjusted annually for cost of living increases, is $112,221 in 1992. A minimum benefit of $10,000 a year can be received without regard to the 100 percent limitation, as long as an individual has never participated in an employer-sponsored defined-contribution plan. For purposes of the maximum limits, all defined-benefit plans are treated as one.

The annual benefit subject to the limit is expressed as a benefit payable annually in the form of a straight life annuity. Therefore, the limitation is adjusted actuarially, when the benefit is more valuable than a single life annuity. An exception is made when the benefit is payable in the form of a qualified joint and survivor annuity, in which case the annual benefit payment does not have to be reduced. Converting to forms of benefit other than the life annuity, an interest rate cannot be used if it is less than the lesser of 5 percent or the rate under the plan.

The maximum benefit limit is based on payments beginning at the individual's social security retirement age. If retirement begins earlier, the $90,000 dollar limit has to be actuarially reduced for benefits commencing before the social security age (using an interest rate assumption not less than the lesser of 5 percent or the rate under the plan). The reduction for early retirement applies in a different way for certain governmental plans, tax-exempt organization plans, merchant marine plans, and plans for airline pilots.

If payments begin later than social security retirement age, they may be actuarially increased to reflect the shorter payout period (the interest rate is not to exceed the lesser of 5 percent or the rate under the plan).

A further limit restricts the annual benefit as it relates to an employee who has fewer than 10 years of service with the employer. The applicable limit (either the dollar limit or the 100 percent limit) is multiplied by a fraction. When the applicable limit is the dollar limit, the numerator of the fraction is the number of years (or part thereof) of participation with the employer, and the denominator is 10 years. When the applicable limit is the 100 percent limit, the numerator of the fraction is the number of years (or part thereof) of service with the employer and the denominator remains 10. In other words, the 100 percent limit is reduced for less than 10 years of service, and the dollar limit is reduced for less than 10 years of participation.

The combined limit is a mathematical calculation based on the projected benefit that the participant will receive from the defined-benefit plan and a historical analysis of the annual additions made on behalf of the individual, in relation to the maximum allowed annual addition.

To calculate the defined-benefit fraction for any year, the numerator is the projected annual benefit of the participant under the plan and the denominator is the lesser of 1.25 times the dollar limit or 1.4 times the 100 percent limit.

Calculating the defined-contribution fraction is somewhat more complex. For any year, the numerator is the sum of all annual additions, and the denominator is the sum of the lesser of the following amounts, determined for each year: the product of 1.25 times the dollar limit or 1.4 times the 25 percent limit.[42]

The fractions may be altered when the plan is top-heavy, as described in **§ 3.25**.

The rules under Code § 415 have been lowered several times. With each change, a transition rule has provided that benefits accrued at the time of the change did not have to be reduced. These "grandfather" provisions have also been accompanied with specific methodology for adjusting the Code § 415(e) fraction so that the new limits are satisfied in a situation where the grandfather rule applies. One transition rule allows a participant to retain benefits accrued on May 6, 1986, the effective date of the Tax Reform Act of 1986. Another transition rule applied to changes brought about by the Tax Equity and Fiscal Responsibility Act of 1982 (TEFRA).

---

[42] I.R.C. § 415(e).

§ 3.19   —Maximum Deduction Limits

In a profit-sharing plan, the maximum annual contribution is 15 percent of the compensation paid to participants during the taxable year.[43] Compensation in excess of the $200,000 limit is not taken into account. Compensation includes base pay, bonuses, commissions, and overtime pay, and does not include contributions to a qualified plan (including elective deferrals under a CODA).[44] Contributions to two or more profit-sharing (or stock bonus) plans of an employer are aggregated for purposes of the 15 percent limit.

Amounts contributed in excess of the limits may be deducted in subsequent years. However, any nondeductible contributions are subject to a 10 percent excise tax, payable to the employer. The excise tax applies to any nondeductible contributions in a qualified plan as of the close of the employer's tax year. The tax is based on the sum of:

Amounts contributed in excess of the deductible amount for the current year plus

The total employee contributions for preceding years that were not allowable as a deduction, reduced by the amounts returned to the employer during the taxable year and the portion that became deductible for a preceding taxable year or for the current year.[45]

The "oldest" contributions carried forward from prior years are deducted first, with current contributions deducted subsequently.

§ 3.20   Vesting Requirements

In a defined-contribution plan, a participant's account grows with periodic contributions and investment earnings. However, a participant is not always entitled to receive the entire account balance as a benefit at the time of termination of employment. A plan will often require that the participant remain employed with the employer for a period of time before becoming "vested" in the account. Sometimes, the participant will become partially vested as his or her service increases ("graded vesting") or will become entirely vested at one time ("cliff vesting").

The rules of Code § 411(a) limit the amount of service that can be required before an individual may become vested in an account balance. The

---

[43] I.R.C. § 404(a)(3)(A).

[44] Rev. Rul. 80-145, 1980-1 C.B. 89.

[45] I.R.C. § 4972(c).

rules require that an individual must, at all times, be 100 percent vested in the account balance attributable to his or her own contributions. This rule applies equally to both pretax (CODA deferrals) and posttax contributions.

A participant also must be 100 percent vested if employment continues until what is referred to as the "normal" retirement age. Generally, this will be the normal retirement age as defined in the plan. The date for full vesting may never occur later than the latest of the participant's 65th birthday or the fifth anniversary of the date when a participant began participation in the plan.

If the plan contains employer contributions and a participant does not attain the normal retirement age, the employer contributions must "vest" within a specified period of time. The plan must contain a schedule clarifying the vesting provisions, and the schedule must vest participants at least as rapidly as one of the statutory vesting schedules. The statute contains two vesting schedules:

1. Five-year cliff vesting: The participant becomes fully vested at one time, after completion of five years of service;

2. Seven-year graded vesting: The participant becomes 20 percent vested after 3 years and earns an additional 20 percent for each additional year of service.

Example: An individual with an account balance of $5,000, $3,000 of which is attributable to employee contributions and $2,000 of which is attributable to employer contributions, terminates employment after 4 years of service. The plan provides that terminated employees are immediately entitled to receive their "vested account balance." If the plan provides 5-year cliff vesting, this individual will be entitled to the $3,000 employee contribution and no portion of the $2,000 employer contribution account. If, instead, the plan has 7-year graded vesting, the participant is still entitled to the $3,000 and, in addition, is entitled to 60 percent of $2,000, or $1,200.

A plan does not have to adopt one of these schedules, but its own schedule must vest the participant at least as rapidly as under one of them. There is one major exception to the statutory vesting requirements. Plans that are established under a collective bargaining agreement may use 10-year cliff vesting, allowing for full and immediate vesting only after 10 years of participation under the plan.

The rules clarify when a participant must be credited with a year of service, for purposes of the vesting requirements. A year of vesting must be credited when a participant earns 1,000 hours of service during a 12-month period. Hours of service are credited in the same manner as described in **§ 3.07**. The plan may identify any 12-month "vesting computation period" for purposes of determining vesting service, although it is most common for the plan to choose either the plan year or the 12-month period beginning on the participant's initial date of hire. If a plan changes its vesting computation period, participants must be credited for a year of service for each of the overlapping years (resulting in 2 years of vesting service in less than a 2-year period).

Generally, credit must be given for all service with the employer or with any affiliated employer (see § **3.11**), regardless of whether the employee is a participant in the plan. If the employer adopts a plan of a predecessor employer, service with the predecessor will also have to be credited. However, service for vesting computation periods ending prior to the attainment of age 18 may be disregarded. The employer can choose to disregard service of all employees occurring prior to the effective date of the plan.

When a participant separates from service prior to being 100 percent vested and subsequently returns to employment, the rules require all prebreak and postbreak service to be aggregated except under limited circumstances. Prebreak service may be disregarded until an individual comes back to work and completes a full year of service. If a participant is at least partially vested, all service is aggregated. If an individual who is 0 percent vested returns to employment before the number of consecutive one-year breaks in service (incurred during the break) has exceeded the greater of 5 or the number of prebreak years of service, then all prebreak service must be credited.

§ 3.21   Death Benefits—Incidental Requirement

Death benefits must be incidental to the principal purpose of the plan, which is to provide retirement benefits and deferred compensation to the employee.[46] Current contributions may be used to purchase life insurance protection where the amount is incidental or subordinate to the primary purpose of the plan in providing deferred compensation. An investment in ordinary life insurance is considered incidental if (1) the aggregate amount of premiums to be paid for insurance on a participant's life is at all times less than 50 percent of the aggregate of the contributions and forfeitures (without regard to trust earnings and capital gains and losses) that have been allocated to the participant, and (2) the plan requires the trustee, at or before the participant's retirement, to either (a) convert the policy into

---

[46] Treas. Reg. § 1.401-1(b)(1)(i) and (ii); Treas. Reg. § 1.403(a)-1(d).

cash or provide the participant with retirement income without life insurance protection, or (b) distribute the policy to the employee.[47]

For purposes of the 50 percent limitation, the actual premiums paid for
ordinary life policies are to be considered rather than the one-year term
premiums used for computing the taxable cost of death protection.

Term insurance does not satisfy the foregoing conditions because of
its lack of cash value. However, term insurance is sanctioned as long as
the amount of the premium does not exceed 25 percent of the total of the
funds allocated to the participant's account.[48]

The limitations on the purchase of life insurance protection do not apply
to voluntary employee contributions. If the plan permits, a contributing
participant may direct that any or all of his or her contributions be used to
purchase additional life insurance protection.[49]

§ 3.22   Other Distribution Requirements

To ensure that participants are entitled to receive benefits within a reasonable period of time after retirement, benefit payments must begin, unless
the participant consents to a later payment, no later than 60 days following
the close of the plan year in which the latest of the following events occurs:

• Attainment of age 65 or, if earlier, normal retirement age under the
  plan;
• The participant's 10th anniversary of participation in the plan;
• Separation from service.

§ 3.23   —Spousal Rights to Distributions

All qualified plans must conform with requirements under the Retirement
Equity Act of 1984, which gives the spouse of a plan participant certain
legal rights in the participant's plan benefit. Generally, unless expressly
waived by both the participant and spouse in accordance with strict rules,
all qualified plans must automatically provide the following forms of sur-
vivorship benefits for a spouse:

---

[47] Rev. Rul. 73-501, 1973-2 C.B. 127; Rev. Rul. 69-421, pt. 2(n)(2), 1969-1 C.B. 59; Rev.
   Rul. 54-51, 1954 C.B. 147, as amplified by Rev. Rul. 57-213, 1957-1 C.B. 157 and Rev.
   Rul. 60-85, 1960-1 C.B. 159.

[48] Rev. Rul. 61-164, 1961-2 C.B. 99.

[49] Rev. Rul. 69-408, 1969-2 C.B. 58.

- Qualified preretirement survivor annuity (QPSA) for the surviving spouse of a participant who dies before the annuity starting date;
- Qualified joint and survivor annuity (QJSA) for the participant and the spouse at the annuity starting date.

All pension plans (including defined-benefit, money-purchase, target-benefit, and cash-balance plans) must conform with these requirements. Other defined-contribution plans (including profit-sharing plans, stock bonus plans, and ESOPs) must conform unless *all* of the following requirements are met:

- The plan pays a death benefit in the amount of the participant's nonforfeitable (vested) benefit prior to death to the surviving spouse or to another designated beneficiary, with the spouse's consent;
- The participant has not elected to receive benefits in the form of a life annuity;
- If the qualified plan is a recipient of a direct plan-to-plan transfer from a plan subject to the spousal benefit rules, then the general rules must apply to the transferred benefits.

If these requirements are met, a participant does not need his or her spouse's consent to take postretirement benefits in some form other than a joint and survivor annuity.

The exception to the spousal benefit provisions can apply to profit-sharing plans and other savings plans—the plans that most typically contain CODAs. This means that such plans have an opportunity to avoid some paperwork, administrative detail, and even potential litigation by avoiding the spousal rules. However, in order to avoid such restrictions, the plan must adhere to the requirements contained in the exception.

As stated above, the QPSA has to be provided if the participant dies prior to the annuity's starting date; the QJSA applies on or after the annuity starting date. Generally, the annuity starting date can be thought of as the date when retirement benefits commence. However, the technical definition depends on the form of benefit payment. If the benefit is payable as an annuity, the annuity starting date is the first day of the first period for which an amount is payable as an annuity. For benefits payable in a form other than an annuity, the annuity starting date is the first day on which all events have occurred which entitle the participant to a distribution. The annuity starting date is determined without regard to any "auxiliary" disability benefit.[50]

---

[50] I.R.C. § 417(f)(2).

Assuming that a plan is subject to the spousal benefit requirements, the following sections further explain the required spousal benefits.

Qualified Preretirement Survivor Annuity (QPSA)

Once a participant has earned a vested interest in the plan benefit, the nonparticipant spouse acquires the right to a QPSA, payable in the event of the death of the participant before the participant begins to receive the retirement benefits (referred to as prior to the "annuity starting date"). The QPSA requirement applies whether or not the vested participant is employed at the time of death.

In the case of a defined-contribution plan, the amount of the QPSA must be not less than 50 percent of the participant's vested account balance as of the date of death. The vested account balance includes amounts that become vested on account of the participant's death and amounts payable from life insurance proceeds.[51] In a defined-contribution plan, the QPSA must be payable as a life annuity (purchased with 50 percent of the account balance) and the spouse must have the opportunity to elect to have payments begin within a reasonable time after the participant's death.[52]

The plan administrator must generally give the participant notice of the right to waive the QPSA beginning with the first day of the plan year during which the participant reaches age 32 and ending with the close of the plan year preceding the plan year in which the participant reaches age 35. For a participant hired after age 32, the notice period must be a reasonable period after hiring. If an individual terminates employment prior to the notice period, he or she must also be given notice of the opportunity to waive the benefit. The actual election period begins with the first day of the plan year in which the participant attains age 35 and ends on the date of the participant's death.

The plan does not have to give the participant the opportunity to waive the QPSA if the employer "fully subsidizes" the benefit. A QPSA is fully subsidized if the participant's failure to waive the benefit will not cause a reduction in any plan benefit with respect to the participant and would not create increased contributions by the participant.

Qualified Joint and Survivor Annuity (QJSA)

When a married participant survives to retirement (the time benefit payments begin, referred to as the "annuity starting date"), the required form

---

[51] I.R.C. § 417(c)(2); Treas. Reg. § 1.401(a)(20), Q-12(b).

[52] Treas. Reg. § 1.411(a)-20, Q-22.

of benefit is a qualified joint and survivor annuity (QJSA). Under the QJSA, a monthly benefit is paid to the participant for the duration of his or her life, and payments continue for the life of a spouse if he or she outlives the participant. The amount of the spousal survivor benefit cannot be less than 50 percent or more than 100 percent of the joint benefit.

The participant has to be given the right to waive the QJSA benefit, during the 90-day period prior to the annuity starting date. The plan administrator must give the participant notice of this election within a reasonable period prior to the annuity starting date, and the notice must contain complete information describing to the participant the right to waive the QJSA, the economic effect of such an election, and the spouse's rights under such an election. Any valid waiver has to be in writing, consented to, in writing, by the participant's spouse.

Spousal Consent

Elections to waive QPSA or QJSA benefits must be consented to by the participant's spouse. The spouse's consent does not have to be irrevocable, but the plan may require irrevocable waivers. The spousal consent is in favor of a particular beneficiary. If the participant wishes to choose a different beneficiary, a new spousal consent must be obtained.

Waivers for Loans

When a participant obtains a loan from a plan, the loan is most often secured with the participant's account balance. From the standpoint of the plan, this is adequate security because the plan can easily "foreclose" on the participant's vested account balance in case of a default on the loan balance.[53] However, from the standpoint of the participant's spouse, a loan default would reduce the participant's benefit from the plan, reducing the promised QPSA or QJSA that the spouse is otherwise entitled to receive.

To avoid such conflicts, the rules provide that a plan subject to the QJSA and QPSA requirements must obtain the spouse's consent at the time of a participant loan. The consent, in writing, must be obtained within 90 days

---

[53] It is not clear that all types of plans may foreclose on a defaulted plan loan at the time of the default. If the plan is a pension plan, this may violate the general prohibition against in-service distributions. Similarly, in a 401(k) plan, such a default could be an in-service distribution that does not constitute a hardship withdrawal, again causing problems. A default does not generally cause any difficulties from a profit-sharing account, as long as the distribution is made out of contributions that have accumulated in the plan for at least 2 years. In any circumstance, the account balance may be defaulted at the time a participant terminates employment.

from the commencement of the loan; it must acknowledge the effect of the loan and be witnessed by a plan representative or a notary public. The spousal consent requirements do not apply when the individual's account is not subject to the QJSA and QPSA requirements or if the total accrued benefit subject to security does not exceed $3,500. As discussed above, many profit-sharing plans and savings type plans are exempt from the QJSA and QPSA requirements and are therefore exempt from the spousal waiver consent requirement.

Rules pertaining to participant loan programs are discussed elsewhere in the book. In particular, **§ 4.11** discusses the maximum loan that can be made without creating a taxable event, and **§ 5.11** reviews the "qualification requirements" of all loan programs.

§ 3.24   Top-Heavy Requirements

Under Code § 416, qualified plans that have accumulated, for certain "key" employees, benefits that exceed 60 percent of the total accumulated benefits under the plan are required to provide minimum benefits and accelerated vesting. The top-heavy requirements must be met in order for a plan to remain qualified. A separate requirement provides that all plans, except certain collectively bargained plans that have no participants who are key employees, must contain, as part of the plan document, provisions that apply if the plan at any time becomes top-heavy. The rules apply to qualified retirement plans and to simplified employee pensions (SEPs). The top-heavy rules generally do not apply to a plan that the Secretary of Labor determines to be maintained pursuant to a collective bargaining agreement, if there is evidence that retirement benefits were the subject of good-faith bargaining.

To determine whether a defined-contribution plan is top-heavy for a particular plan year, the account balances of the "key employees" are compared to the total account balances of all participants as of the determination date. The plan is top-heavy if the value of the accounts of key employees exceeds 60 percent of the value of all employees' accounts. The determination date for the first year of a plan's existence is the last day of the plan year; for all other years, the determination date is the last day of the previous plan year. For example, the date for determining whether a plan is top-heavy for the plan year ending June 30, 1992 (assuming that this is not the plan's first year of operation), is June 30, 1991.

Several details have a significant impact on the top-heavy testing. First, in calculating the account balances, any distributions made during the current year and the four previous years are added back to the totals. In addition, if an individual changes status from key employee to non-key employee, his or her account balance is ignored entirely, for purposes of administering the test. These two rules generally stabilize test results; drastic changes over the years, from top-heavy to non-top-heavy status, are eliminated.

An individual who is a key employee is one who, at any time during the current plan year or in any of the four preceding plan years, is (or was):

- *An officer:* generally, an officer who earns more than 50 percent of the defined-benefit plan Code § 415 dollar limit for the year (50% of the limit in 1992 is $56,110.50). However, no more than 50 individuals, or, if fewer, 10 percent of the employees (but never fewer than 3), are considered officers under the rule. The term officer does not apply to individuals who have a title but do not have the responsibilities usually associated with an officer. Even though unincorporated entities do not have named officers, those individuals in key management positions will be treated as officers.

- *A top-10 owner:* includes those employees earning more than the defined-contribution plan Code § 415 dollar limit for the year ($30,000 for 1992) who own one of the 10 largest employee ownership interests (as a percentage of the company). However, an individual must have a minimum ownership percentage of the company of 5 percent to be considered a key employee under this category.

- *A 5 percent owner:* includes an employee who owns directly (or is attributed ownership under the rules) more than 5 percent of the value of the corporation's outstanding stock or stock possessing more than 5 percent of the total combined voting power of all stock of the corporation.

- *A 1 percent owner:* an employee who owns 1 percent or more of the employer and who receives annual compensation from the employer exceeding $150,000. In determining ownership, rules similar to those applying to 5 percent owners, stated above, apply.

One of the more confusing aspects of determining who is a key employee is factoring in how the aggregation rules contained in Code § 414(b), (c), (m), and (o) apply. (See the discussion in **§ 3.11**.) For purposes of determining who is a 5 percent or 1 percent owner, the attribution rules do not apply. However, the aggregation rules do apply for determining whether an individual earns $150,000 or more, is an officer, or is one of the top-10 owners.

When an employer (including all employers that are required to be aggregated under Code § 414(b), (c), (m), and (o)) maintains more than one qualified plan, the plans must be tested together as a group to determine whether the plans are top-heavy, if the plans are part of what is referred to as a required aggregation group. A required aggregation group includes all plans in which a key employee participates and any other plans that enable the plans covering key employees to pass the minimum coverage rules of Code § 410 or the nondiscrimination rule of Code § 401(a)(4).

When a required aggregation group exists, all plans in the group will be top-heavy if, in the aggregate, as of the determination date, the sum of (1) the account balances of the key employees and (2) the present value of the cumulative accrued benefits for key employees (in the case of any defined benefit plans) exceeds 60 percent of a similar sum for all employees. This is a simple calculation when each plan is a defined-contribution plan and all have the same plan year. The top-heavy percentage of each plan is calculated and the totals of the plans are added up as of the determination date. If the total account balances (from all plans in the group) of key employees exceed 60 percent of the account balances of all employees, all plans in the required aggregation group are top-heavy. If not, then none of the plans is top-heavy.

Testing becomes slightly more complex when the employer sponsors both defined-contribution plans and defined-benefit plans. Defined-benefit plans generally promise to provide monthly pensions to participants for life, beginning at normal retirement age. To calculate the present value of cumulative accrued benefits in a defined-benefit plan, the promised monthly retirement benefits that are due to the participant as of the determination date (referred to as the "accrued benefits") are translated to a single-sum value ("present value"). When the plans in the required aggregation group have different plan years, the top-heavy calculation is made separately for each plan as of the plan's determination date, and then aggregated by adding together the results for all plans using the determination dates falling within the same calendar year.

Apart from the required aggregation rules, plans can be added to the group for testing purposes on a voluntary basis, as long as the group as a whole continues to satisfy Code §§ 401(a)(4) and 410. This "permissive" aggregation allows the employer a choice between testing such a plan separately or adding the plan to the group, if that result will be useful.

Example: An employer has a plan that can be permissively aggregated to a required aggregation group (which includes two other plans). The plan that can be permissively aggregated, tested separately, is not top-heavy but the plans in the required aggregation group test out as top-heavy. The employer may choose to add the third plan to the aggregation group if the result changes the test results by making the entire group not top-heavy. If adding the third plan does not help the testing, then the employer would choose to test that plan separately, because it is not top-heavy when tested alone.

§ 3.25 —Special Requirements for
Top-Heavy Plans

A defined-contribution plan that is top-heavy must meet minimum contribution requirements (in a defined-benefit plan, minimum benefits must be provided). The minimum contribution is the lesser of 3 percent of compensation or the highest contribution (stated as a percentage of compensation) allocated to a key employee for a plan year. Therefore, if no employer contribution is allocated to a key employee, no minimum contribution is required. The minimum contribution must be provided only to those plan participants who are not key employees and who are employed as of the last day of the plan year. The minimum must be given to any participant, regardless of the number of hours of service he or she performed during the plan year.

Special Effect of Rules on 401(k) Plans

As discussed in **Chapter 2**, in plans that contain cash or deferral elections, employee elective deferrals are treated as employer contributions. Under the top-heavy rules, this means that an employer making no other contribution to the plan will still be required to provide the maximum top-heavy contribution if a key employee elects to defer 3 percent of compensation into the plan. The Treasury Regulations[54] clearly state that employee elective deferrals made by non-key employees cannot be counted as employer contributions for satisfying the top-heavy minimum contribution rules. This result is of special interest to the employer who wants to design a plan meant to only provide the employee with the opportunity to save on a pretax basis. If the plan is top-heavy, the employer may find itself in an unexpected position where it must make additional contributions to satisfy the top-heavy minimum requirements.

Special Vesting Requirements

All top-heavy plans must contain vesting schedules that are at least as favorable as:

Full vesting upon completion of 3 years of service, or

Twenty percent vesting after completion of 2 years of service plus an additional 20 percent for each additional year of service. An individual with 6 or more years of service must be fully vested.

---

[54] Treas. Reg. § 1.416-1 Q&A M-18 through M-20.

Effect on Code § 415

As discussed in **§ 3.19**, an individual who is a participant in both a defined-contribution and a defined-benefit plan is subject to special multiple plan limits under Code § 415(e). If such an individual participates in a plan that is top-heavy, the method of calculating the Code § 415(e) "fractions" changes. This results in a lower maximum contribution/benefit limitation for the participant. The lower limit always applies when the plan is "super-top-heavy." In a super-top-heavy plan, more than 90 percent of the account balances of the participants are for the benefit of key employees as of the determination date. In a plan that is simply top-heavy (and not super-top-heavy), the employer has a choice. The employer can elect to provide additional minimum benefits/contributions to the plan, in order to retain the higher Code § 415 limit, or can choose not to provide the additional minimums, in which case plan participants become subject to the lower limit. To satisfy the increased minimum contribution rule for defined-contribution plans, a 4 percent contribution is required instead of the usual 3 percent.

§ 3.26   Requirements upon Plan Termination

Upon the termination of a defined-contribution plan, all benefits must become fully vested. In addition, if the plan is partially terminated, affected employees will have to become fully vested in their benefits under the plan. At the time a plan terminates, the sponsor may request a determination letter (see **§ 3.04** for a discussion of determination letters) from the IRS, stating that the termination of the plan does not have an adverse effect on the plan.

§ 3.27   Unrelated Business Income

Notwithstanding tax-exempt status, a tax-exempt qualified retirement trust is taxed on the receipt of "unrelated business taxable income" (UBTI). The definition of UBTI includes income from any unrelated trade or business regularly carried on by the tax-exempt entity. However, this rule has a broad number of exceptions. First, UBTI excludes dividend or interest income. However, if such dividend or interest income is received from property that was acquired, in whole or in part, with proceeds from a debt financing that remains outstanding in the taxable year when the dividend or interest is included in income, a proportionate part of the dividend or interest income is treated as UBTI.

A second significant exemption to UBTI treatment covers rents from real property. A lease in which the amount of the rent depends in whole or in part on the income or profits derived by any person from the property leased will not be added to the rents for purposes of this exclusion. As with the interest exception, a proportionate amount of earnings will be taxed, if the rent-producing real estate is purchased through debt financing.

Regardless of this general rule, under another exception, a qualified retirement plan can generally purchase real estate on a debt-financed basis, without UBTI. The exemption is not available, however, if the property is subject to a sale–leaseback, or the property was acquired with seller financing, or the purchase price for the property is not fixed at the time of acquisition. This exception will also apply in the case of a partnership that purchases debt-financed real estate, as long as all of the partnerships are tax-exempt investors.

CHAPTER 4

TAXATION OF DISTRIBUTIONS AND MINIMUM DISTRIBUTIONS

§ 4.1 Minimum Distribution Requirements

Qualified retirement plans must provide that distributions from the plan will meet the minimum distribution requirements.[1] Generally, these rules require that distributions begin within a specific time period after a participant attains age 70½ or dies, if earlier. The rules that apply to IRAs (which include SEPs) and Code § 403(b) annuity plans are essentially the same.

The minimum distribution rules are designed to limit the amount of time that the payment of tax can be deferred on plan benefits. The primary reason for allowing the deferral of taxes in retirement plans is to encourage savings for retirement, although the rules permit a plan to provide death and other nonretirement benefits, so long as they are incidental to the primary purpose of the retirement plan. Therefore, the rules are designed to require that a significant portion of the benefits must be paid out during an individual's retirement years, with remaining "incidental death benefits" distributed within a limited period of time after death.

Generally, distributions have to begin by the first day of April following the year in which the participant attains age 70½. If the entire distribution is not made at that time, the individual's benefit must be distributed over the individual's and a beneficiary's joint expected lifetime, using a method described in the Regulations.[2]

The rules also require that the distribution of a death benefit to the participant's beneficiary must be made within a specified period of time after the participant's death. When the participant has begun to receive

---

[1] I.R.C. § 401(a)(9).

[2] Prop. Treas. Reg. § 1.409(a)(9)-1.

distributions prior to the time of death, any remaining benefit payable to beneficiaries must be paid at least as rapidly as during the participant's lifetime. If the benefit has not yet begun to be distributed at the time of the participant's death, the general rule is that the distribution has to be made within 5 years of the participant's death. However, payments may be made over the expected lifetime of any beneficiary as long as payments begin within 1 year of the participant's death. If the beneficiary is the participant's spouse, payment may begin even later.

If the minimum distributions are not made in a timely manner, in addition to the penalty of plan disqualification, the plan participant is required to pay a 50 percent excise tax on the amount of the shortfall between the amount actually distributed and the amount required to be distributed under the minimum distribution rules described above.[3] The Internal Revenue Service (IRS) is authorized to waive the 50 percent excise tax if the taxpayer establishes that the failure to make the minimum required distribution is due to reasonable error, and reasonable steps are being taken to remedy the shortfall.[4] The payment of tax is reported on Form 5329.

The two sections that follow describe the application of the minimum distribution rules in some detail.

§ 4.2 —Minimum Distributions at Age 70½

Under the minimum distribution rules, benefits must begin by the plan's required beginning date. This date is generally April 1 of the year following the calendar year in which the covered participant attains the age of 70½.

However, an exception applies to participants in government and church plans who remain employees after attainment of age 70½. For these employees, the required beginning date is the April 1 following the later of the calendar year in which the participant reaches age 70½ or the calendar year in which the participant retires.

A grandfathering rule applies to participants of qualified plans who attained age 70½ prior to 1988 and who are not 5 percent owners of the entity sponsoring the plan. The required beginning date for this group is the April 1 following the later of the year of attainment of age 70½ or the year in which the individual retires.[5]

If the individual is a 5 percent owner, the required beginning date is the April 1 of the first year following the later of (1) the year in which

---

[3] I.R.C. § 4974.

[4] I.R.C. § 4974(d).

[5] Prop. Treas. Reg. § 1.409(a)(9)-1, Q & A B(2)(b).

the participant reaches age 70½ or (2) the earlier of (a) the year in which the participant becomes a 5 percent owner or (b) the year in which the participant retires.[6] For this purpose, an individual is a 5 percent owner for a plan year if at any time during such year he or she is a 5 percent owner as determined under the top-heavy rules (see **§ 3.24**).

Although the first distribution can be delayed until April 1 following the required beginning date, the minimum distribution made on April 1 is for the previous year, referred to as the "first distribution year." If the distribution of the entire amount of the participant's benefit is not made at this time, a second distribution will have to be made for the second distribution year by December 31 of that same year. In other words, two distributions are required, one by April 1 and the second by December 31. The minimum distribution for each subsequent year must be made by December 31 of such year.

The minimum distribution is based on the amount of the participant's benefit. The participant's benefit in a defined-contribution plan, Code § 403(b) plan, or IRA is based on the participant's account balance. For defined-contribution plans and Code § 403(b) plans, the participant's benefit is the account balance as of the last valuation date in the calendar year immediately preceding the distribution year. In an IRA account, the benefit for a distribution year is the IRA account balance at the end of the previous calendar year.

The minimum distribution for a given distribution year is generally the participant's benefit divided by the applicable life expectancy (ALE). The minimum may be larger, however, if required under the minimum distribution incidental benefit (MDIB) rules described below. The applicable life expectancy is either the actuarial single or the actuarial joint life and last survivor expectancy period of the participant and his or her designated beneficiary. The initial ALE is determined by use of the expected return multiples in Tables V of VI of Treasury Regulations ("Regulations") § 1.72-9. These Regulations are also used for determining the exclusion ratio for the income taxation of annuities.

The ALE is determined initially by using the attained age of the participant and his or her beneficiary on their birthdays in the first distribution year. In subsequent years, the applicable life expectancy is determined in one of several ways, depending on whether the participant, the beneficiary, or both, recalculate life expectancy based on their attained ages.

When life expectancies are not recalculated, the ALE in subsequent years may be determined by reducing the initial ALE by one for each subsequent calendar year. If life expectancies are recalculated each year, however, the ALE in subsequent years is determined as discussed below. Recalculation of life expectancy typically will result in a larger ALE and,

---

[6] Prop. Treas. Reg. § 1.409(a)(9)-1, Q&A B(2)(c).

therefore, smaller required annual payments under the minimum distribution rules.

The amount of the minimum distribution is dependent on several factors. First, the rules distinguish between distributions of discretionary payments made on an annual basis, and payments of annuities. Annuity payments include payments made in nonincreasing amounts with a life contingency, a period certain payment, or both. A life contingency includes a life annuity on the participant's life and contingent annuities where payments continue to a beneficiary if the beneficiary outlives the participant. Period certain payments include payments made at least annually for a specified number of years. If the payment is made in other forms, the distribution is treated as a discretionary payment.

The second factor is the impact of the minimum distribution incidental benefit (MDIB) rules.[7] Generally, the MDIB is an alternative test that has to be satisfied in addition to the minimum distribution rules of Code § 401(a)(9). The intent of the MDIB rule is to ensure that death benefits are "incidental" by requiring that a substantial amount of the retirement distribution must be made over the lifetime of the participant. The MDIB requirements, however, generally do not apply when the beneficiary is the participant's spouse. Therefore, the minimum distribution may be different, depending on whether the beneficiary is or is not the participant's spouse. The MDIB requirements are applied differently to annuity distributions and discretionary payments.

The subsections below describe the minimum distribution rules for distributions made as annuities and as discretionary annual installments. A discussion of the MDIB rules concludes the section.

Annuity Payments

The amount of the distribution is dependent on the form of benefit being distributed from the plan. When the benefit is distributed in the form of a life annuity on the life of the participant or a contingent annuity (payments are made for the life of the participant and continuing for the life of a beneficiary if the participant predeceases the beneficiary), such a distribution will generally meet the minimum distribution requirements. The annuity payments must begin in the first distribution year, and payments must be made in nonincreasing amounts (unless subject to cost-of-living increases). An annuity payment that contains a period certain feature will also meet the requirements if the period does not exceed the joint life expectancy of the participant and beneficiary. However, payments of a joint

---

[7] Prop. Treas. Reg. § 1.409(a)(9)-2.

annuity or an annuity with period certain payments may be limited by the minimum distribution incidental benefit (MDIB) rules described below.

However, in the defined-contribution type plans that are discussed in this book, as well as in IRA accounts and Code § 403(b) plans, distributions are often not made in the form of an annuity; instead, benefits are made in discretionary installments. In these cases, the minimum benefit calculation is made for each distribution year using the method described below.

Discretionary Annual Payments

When a participant has a beneficiary other than a spouse and is receiving benefits in the form of discretionary installments, the distribution must be at least equal to that computed under the applicable life expectancy (ALE) method of the participant and his or her beneficiary. If the minimum distribution computed under the MDIB requirements is greater than the amount computed under the ALE method, however, then the amount computed under the MDIB rules is the required minimum distribution.

The minimum distribution under the ALE method is determined by dividing the ALE into the participant's benefit. The ALE is a factor derived from Tables V and VI in Regulations § 1.72-9. The factor is expressed as a multiple representing the individuals' joint and last survivor life expectancy at their attained ages. The initial calculation uses the participant's and the beneficiary's attained ages as of the calendar year of the first distribution year (generally, the year in which the participant attains age 70½). In a subsequent year, unless ages are recalculated, the ALE is calculated by simply subtracting 1 year from the previous ALE. When this method is used to calculate the ALE, the ALE becomes independent of whether either individual lives or dies. If both individuals live beyond the expected joint life expectancy, the entire distribution has to be made within the expected period. The same result exists if either or both of the individuals die within the expected period. Distributions may be continued to the beneficiary or contingent beneficiary using the same payout schedule.

The Proposed Regulations also provide that the life expectancy of the participant may be recalculated each year (as long as the plan provides for such elections). However, when the beneficiary is not the spouse, the beneficiary's life expectancy may not be recalculated. The result of recalculation is that the ALE will be reduced annually by less than 1 year, resulting in a smaller required distribution.

When only the participant's age is being recalculated, the methodology for calculating the ALE is as follows. For the first distribution year, the calculation of life expectancy is the same as described above. For the second year, the ALE is calculated using the actual age of the participant as of the last day of the second distribution year and the "adjusted age" of the beneficiary. The adjusted age of the beneficiary requires a two-step calculation. The starting point is the beneficiary's age in the first distribution year (generally, the year the participant attains age 70½). The beneficiary's ALE is calculated, based on this age, by consulting Table V in the Proposed Regulations for single life expectancy. In the next year, 1 year is removed from the ALE. The beneficiary's adjusted age is then calculated by using Table V in reverse, that is, by comparing the adjusted ALE to the comparable age (rounded up to the age at the next birthday). That age is the beneficiary's adjusted age for that year. The same process is used to recalculate life expectancies in all subsequent years.

When the beneficiary is the participant's spouse, then either or both lives can be recalculated in determining the ALE. If both lives are recalculated, the ALE is calculated using the actual age of each person in the distribution year, based on the Table VI ALE. If one life is recalculated (either the spouse's or the participant's), the methodology described above is used to calculate joint life expectancy.

Although recalculation results in smaller annual distributions while both individuals are alive, a penalty is assessed at death. When the participant's life is being recalculated, at the time of the participant's death, life expectancy in the subsequent year becomes zero. In effect, the joint and survivor ALE becomes the single life ALE of the beneficiary in the year subsequent to the participant's death.

If an individual has accrued benefits in several plans and/or IRAs, the minimum distribution rules apply to each plan separately. However, for distributions from IRAs and Code § 403(b) plans, the minimum required distribution calculated for each plan may be aggregated and the minimum may be taken from one IRA account or one Code § 403(b) plan.[8]

Minimum Distribution Incidental Benefit Rules

The minimum distribution incidental benefit (MDIB) rule is an alternative test that must be satisfied as well as the general rules discussed above. The effect of the MDIB rules is dependent on the form of distribution and on whether the beneficiary is a spouse or nonspouse. When the distribution is in the form of discretionary installment payments and the beneficiary is the spouse, the MDIB rules have no effect. The MDIB rules have the greatest effect when the beneficiary is a nonspouse and distributions are made in discretionary installments. Specifically, the required minimum

---

[8] IRS Notice 88-38.

distribution is equal to the greater of the amount calculated by using the covered participant's life expectancy or the alternative MDIB rules.

Under the alternative MDIB rules, the minimum distribution is calculated by dividing the individual's benefit by the applicable divisor. The applicable divisor is a factor derived from a table included in the Proposed Regulations and reproduced here as **Table 4–1**.

When the distribution is in the form of an annuity payment, the MDIB rules apply in a different manner. The rules have no impact when payment is made in the form of an annuity for the life of the participant, or for the joint life expectancy of the participant and his or her spouse, as long as the benefit paid to the spouse does not exceed the participant's benefit. However, in other forms of annuities and for nonspouse beneficiaries, the MDIB rules may result in a larger required minimum distribution than under the standard method. If the distribution is in the form of a period certain, with no life contingency, the period certain may not exceed the maximum period, which is also based on **Table 4–1**. If the payment is in the form of an annuity and the beneficiary is not the spouse, the amount of contingent benefit that can be paid to the beneficiary after the death of the participant may not exceed the amount indicated in another table contained

Table 4–1

Table for Determining Applicable Divisor for Installment Payments and Maximum Period Certain for Term Annuities

Age of Employee	Applicable Divisor	Age of Employee	Applicable Divisor	Age of Employee	Applicable Divisor
70	26.2	85	13.8	101	5.3
71	25.3	86	13.1	102	5.0
72	24.4	87	12.4	103	4.7
73	23.5	88	11.8	104	4.4
74	22.7	89	11.1	105	4.1
75	21.8	90	10.5	106	3.8
76	20.9	91	9.9	107	3.6
77	20.1	92	9.4	108	3.3
78	19.2	93	8.8	109	3.1
79	18.4	94	8.3	110	2.8
80	17.8	95	7.8	111	2.6
81	16.8	96	7.3	112	2.4
82	16.0	97	6.9	113	2.2
83	15.3	98	6.5	114	2.0
84	14.5	99	6.1	115	1.8
		100	5.7		

in the Regulations. The applicable percentage will be 100 percent when the beneficiary is not less than 10 years younger than the participant. The applicable percentage is somewhat reduced when the beneficiary is more than 10 years younger than the participant.

§ 4.3 —Preretirement Death Benefits

As referred to above, when payments have already begun prior to the participant's death, they are required to continue at least as rapidly after death. As described in § 4.2, the Proposed Regulations specify the maximum period of distribution after death when the participant has elected a methodology for satisfying the minimum distribution rules at the required beginning date. However, when benefit payments have not begun prior to the participant's death, a different rule applies for determining the maximum length of the distribution period.

The general rule is that distributions must be made within 5 years after the participant's death. This means that the participant's entire interest must be distributed as of December 31 of the calendar year in which occurs the fifth anniversary of the date the participant died.[9] However, the rule has significant exceptions, and the 5-year rule does not have effect if one of these exceptions is satisfied. A plan will satisfy the minimum distribution rules as long as distributions will satisfy the general rule or one of the exceptions. The plan may or may not give the participants a choice in the matter.

Two major exceptions apply to the 5-year rule. One applies when the beneficiary is a nonspouse and the other applies to spousal beneficiaries. In the case of nonspousal beneficiaries, the minimum distribution rule is also satisfied if the distribution is made over the lifetime or expected lifetime of the beneficiary, as long as the benefit begins by December 31 of the year that follows the year of death. When the beneficiary is the participant's spouse, the distribution may be made over the life of the spouse, as long as payments begin on or before the later of (a) December 31 of the calendar year immediately after the calendar year in which the participant died, or (b) December 31 of the calendar year immediately after the year in which the participant would have reached age 70½. However, if the spouse dies prior to the commencement of benefit payments, then benefits may be distributed to his or her beneficiary under the same rules that would apply to the participant.

---

[9] Prop. Treas. Reg. § 1.401(a)(9)-1, Q & A C(2).

§ 4.4 Taxation of Distributions—Generally

Of considerable importance to plan participants is how and when distributions from their retirement plans will be taxed. The taxation of the distribution depends primarily on two factors: the type of plan from which the benefit is being distributed, and whether tax has been previously paid on any portion of the benefits being distributed. Because the tax treatment is plan-specific, a summary of the rules governing each type of distribution is given below. Following this general discussion are: a detailed analysis of each of the taxation methods and a review of how benefits are taxed when a portion of the benefit has already been taxed.

Distributions from Qualified Plans

When a distribution is from a qualified plan, the amount of the distribution that has not been previously taxed is subject to federal income tax as ordinary income. An exception applies when the participant receives what is referred to as a lump-sum distribution, in which case the individual may be eligible to elect special averaging tax treatment. Persons born on or before January 1, 1936, may also elect to treat a portion of a lump-sum distribution attributable to pre-1974 participation in a plan as capital gains and as subject to a "grandfathered" 20 percent tax rate.

In most cases, if the individual receives at least 50 percent of the balance of the account, he or she will be able to roll such distribution into either another qualified plan or an IRA account, in order to defer tax until later.

Distributions from qualified plans are subject to the following special excise taxes:

1. In most circumstances, distributions received prior to age 59½ are subject to the 10 percent premature distribution tax (see § **4.10**).
2. Distributions of large amounts may also be subject to the 15 percent excise tax generally applicable to distributions that exceed $150,000 in one year (see § **4.13**).
3. Large accumulations sheltered in qualified plans may be subject to a separate additional 15 percent excess accumulation tax, payable by the participant's estate (see § **4.14**).

Distributions from SEPs

The primary difference between distributions from qualified plans and those from simplified employee pensions (SEPs) is that SEP distributions are never eligible for special lump-sum tax treatment or grandfathered capital gains treatment. Such distributions are always includable as ordinary income (to the extent not previously taxed for federal income tax purposes). Another difference is that amounts distributed from a SEP (always funded with IRAs) can only be rolled over into another IRA and not into a qualified plan.

Such distributions are also subject to the three excise taxes referred to above. Distributions from qualified plans, SEPs, non-SEP IRAs, and Code § 403(b) plans are all aggregated for purposes of determining whether the excise taxes on large distributions apply.

Distributions from Tax-Sheltered Annuities

Generally, distributions from Code § 403(b) plans are treated the same as distributions from SEPs. No special lump-sum tax treatment applies. Similar to the rule for an IRA/SEP, distributions may only be rolled into another Code § 403(b) plan or an IRA, and not into a qualified plan. All excise taxes apply as well. Neither IRA/SEP distributions or Code § 403(b) distributions may be rolled into a qualified plan, to ensure that the distribution does not later become eligible for lump-sum treatment.

Distributions from Nonqualified Plans

The taxation of distributions from nonqualified plans is substantially different from the taxation for distributions from the other three types of plans. This topic is covered in **Chapter 8**.

§ 4.5   Taxation of Periodic Payments

Periodic payments made from qualified plans, IRA accounts, and Code § 403(b) annuities are generally taxable as ordinary income.[10] However, if some of the participant's benefit under the plan is attributable to dollars in the plan that have already been subject to taxation, such as employee contributions and amounts attributable to term insurance premiums (commonly referred to as P.S. 58 costs), then a portion of each annuity payment will be exempt from tax, until the total nontaxable amount has been distributed.

The rules apply differently, based on whether an individual has begun to receive periodic payments as a retirement benefit (the "annuity starting

---

[10] I.R.C. § 72(a).

date" has already occurred) or whether an in-service, "preannuity start-ing date" distribution is being made.

Discussion of the rules that apply to amounts received as an annuity is followed here by discussion of amounts received that are not part of a stream of periodic payments made prior to the annuity starting date.

Taxation of Amounts Received as an Annuity

If the participant has an investment in the plan (cost basis), each annuity payment is multiplied by an exclusion ratio. The exclusion ratio is deter-mined by dividing the distributee's investment in the plan by the expected return from the annuity. The exclusion ratio is then multiplied by the amount of the distribution in order to determine the taxable and nontax-able amounts.

The first step in determining the exclusion ratio is to determine the par-ticipant's investment in the contract. This amount includes the total of em-ployee after-tax contributions. Also included is the total cost of life in-surance actually reported as taxable income on federal income tax returns filed by the participant (the P.S. 58 costs, as discussed in **§ 4.12**), but only if payment is received under the contract that provided the life insurance protection.[11] The following items are also added to the investment in the contract: (1) other employer contributions that have already been taxed to the participant, and (2) the amount of any loans included in income as taxable distributions (see **§ 4.11**). An alternate payee under a qualified domestic relations order (QDRO) (see **§ 4.15**) receives a proportionate part of the participant's investment in the plan.[12] The rules for determining the cost basis of a self-employed person are somewhat different; the pri-mary difference is that an owner-employee may not include P.S. 58 costs.[13]

The exclusion ratio may be computed under two methods provided in the Regulations.[14] The distributee may use the "regular method," or, if cer-tain conditions are met, a "safe harbor method" for making such determi-nation. Calculation of the regular exclusion ratio for single or joint and 100 percent survivor life annuities (without a refund or guarantee feature) is rather easily determined. The ratio is a fraction; the numerator is the in-vestment in the contract (cost basis) and the denominator is the expected benefits from the contract:

$$\text{Exclusion ratio} = \text{Cost basis/Expected benefits}$$

---

[11] Treas. Reg. § 1.72-16(b)(4).

[12] I.R.C. § 72(m)(10).

[13] I.R.C. 72(m)(2); Treas. Reg. § 1.72-16(b)(4).

[14] Treas. Reg. § 1.72.

In order to calculate the exclusion ratio, the expected benefit must be determined. The expected benefit is determined by multiplying the annual benefit payable under contract by the number of years in which the benefits are expected to be paid. This life expectancy in years is found in Table V (single life annuities) and Table VI (joint and survivor annuities) under Regulations § 1.72-9.

If payments are to be made quarterly, semiannually, or annually, an adjustment of the applicable life expectancy may be required when computing the expected return.

The exclusion ratio continues to apply until the cost basis is fully recovered. Payments received subsequently are taxable in full. If the participant dies before the cost basis is fully recovered, a deduction for the unrecovered basis is allowed on the final income tax return.

Example: Bert Shamus is scheduled to receive $12,000 per year in monthly installments of $1,000 from a qualified plan paid in the form of a life annuity. The payments will begin in the first month after his retirement. Bert is age 65 and has a life expectancy of 20 years (as determined in Table V of the Regulations). He has made after-tax contributions to the plan amounting to $20,000. Bert's exclusion is determined as follows:

Investment in contract = $ 20,000
Expected annual benefits = $ 12,000 × 20 years = $240,000
Exclusion ratio = $ 20,000
$240,000
= .083 (rounded to three places)

When Bert receives his first monthly benefit of $1,000, he will not have to pay taxes on $83 and will pay taxes on the remaining $917. The $83 portion of the payment is considered a return of Bert's previously taxed basis. If Bert is still receiving benefits after 20 years, all subsequent benefit payments will be taxable as ordinary income because he will be deemed to have recovered all of his nontaxable basis from the plan benefit.

The regular method is easy to apply when calculating exclusion ratios for single or joint and 100 percent survivor life annuities without a refund or guarantee feature, but can become quite involved if other types of annuity arrangements are used.

When an annuity is paid in the form of a contingent annuity and the contingent annuitant's ratio is less than 100 percent of the participant's benefit, the exclusion ratio is determined as follows. The benefit received is calculated by multiplying the periodic payment times the life expectancy of the participant. Added to this amount is the difference between the joint life expectancy of the participant and the beneficiary and the single life expectancy of the participant multiplied by the reduced periodic payment that the contingent beneficiary will receive upon the participant's death.

The second method of determining the amount to be distributed, referred to as the "safe harbor" method, is simpler to apply than the regular method. However, in order to use the safe harbor method, three conditions must be met:

1. The annuity payments must depend on the life of the distributee or the joint lives of the distributee and beneficiary;
2. The annuity payments must be made from a qualified plan or § 403(b) annuity (but not from a SEP or IRA);
3. The distributee must be under age 75 when annuity payments commence or, if the distributee is age 75 or older, payment may not be guaranteed for more than 5 years.

Under the safe harbor method, the participant's investment in the contract is calculated in the same manner as under the regular method. What is different is that the participant's expected total benefit is calculated by multiplying the monthly benefit due times a specified number of months, based on the attained age of the participant at the time the annuity is payable. The Regulations provide a guide for indicating the appropriate multiplier (see **Table 4–2**).

The exclusion ratio is then calculated in the same manner as under the regular method. The calculation is as follows:

$$\frac{\text{Investment}}{\text{Number of monthly payments}} = \frac{\text{Tax-free portion}}{\text{of monthly annuity}}$$

The decision whether to elect one method over the other depends on a number of factors, and the determination of which method results in the largest tax-free distribution is dependent on the specific facts involved. A distributee should make the calculation using both methods, prior to determining which method to elect.

Table 4–2

Number of Months for Safe Harbor Exclusion

Age of Distributee	Number of Payments
55 and under	300
56 to 60	260
61 to 65	240
66 to 70	170
71 and over	120

Distributions Prior to the Annuity Starting Date

When a plan allows for preretirement distributions, it is not atypical for a participant to receive an in-service distribution of a portion of the benefit in order to meet financial hardships or to pay for other expenses. Prior to 1987, if a participant had an "investment in their contract" (typically consisting of employee after-tax contributions), an amount up to the participant's investment could be withdrawn prior to the annuity starting date. The Tax Reform Act of 1986 (TRA 86) changed this rule, providing generally that all distributions are subject to the exclusion ratio method of determination. However, a grandfather provision allows participants to continue to withdraw amounts up to their investment in the contract attributable to contributions made prior to 1987, without incurring any tax. Other amounts are subject to the annuity distribution rules described above, with one notable exception. Generally, an individual may treat the employee after-tax contributions as a separate contract when determining the tax consequences of the distribution. This means the exclusion ratio is calculated with the numerator consisting of all employee contributions, and the denominator consisting of the value of the participant's benefit, based on employee contributions plus interest earnings. The denominator does not include other benefits provided under the plan.

§ 4.6 Lump-Sum Tax Treatment

Special tax treatment of lump-sum distributions is available under certain circumstances for distributions from qualified plans. Distributions from IRA accounts (including SEPs), Code § 403(b) annuity plans, and non-qualified plans will not qualify for special tax treatment.

TRA 86 revised the averaging rules for lump-sum distributions; the new rules are referred to as "5-year averaging."[15] However, the old rules, referred to as "10-year averaging," were grandfathered for certain older employees. Employees who receive a lump-sum distribution and who had attained age 50 on or before January 1, 1986, may elect either 5-year averaging or 10-year averaging, using 1986 tax rates.

For a distribution to be treated as a lump-sum distribution eligible for 5-year averaging, the following conditions need to be met:

1. The individual must have completed 5 years of participation in the plan.

2. The participant's entire "balance to the credit" must be distributed within one calendar year.

---

[15] I.R.C. § 402(e).

3.   The amount distributed must be payable upon death, attainment of at least age 59½, separation from service (does not apply to self-employed individuals), or disability (applies only to self-employed individuals).

4.   Lump-sum tax treatment may only be elected once in a lifetime.

5.   If a distribution of the balance to the credit of an employee would constitute a lump-sum distribution, then a distribution of the balance to the credit of an alternate payee under a qualified domestic relations order (QDRO) constitutes a lump-sum distribution. An alternate payee may include a spouse, former spouse, child, or other dependent of a participant.

The IRS has ruled that, for purposes of satisfying the 5-year requirement, years of participation earned while participating in a predecessor plan may be counted if the benefit from the predeccesor plan is transferred to the current plan.[16] The years do not count in the case of a rollover from the prior plan. For example, if an employee, after 2 years of participation in a plan, transfers the vested balance to the new employer's plan, the 5-year requirement will be satisfied after 3 additional years of service under the new plan. The 5-year requirement does not apply when a distribution is made to a beneficiary on account of the participant's death.[17]

An amount paid out well after termination of employment can still be considered payable on account of separation from service.[18] Similarly, if an individual terminates employment and payment does not occur until a subsequent plan termination, the distribution will still be on account of separation from service.[19] It is significant that a payout occasioned by the termination of the plan is not an event that will trigger eligibility for lump-sum treatment, although a participant may be eligible if the participant is age 59½ at the time of the distribution.

To qualify as a distribution within one calendar year, the distribution does not have to be made in a single payment but the complete balance must be distributed within one calendar year.

In determining whether the distribution represents the entire account balance or benefit, all pension plans maintained by the same employer are treated as a single plan, all profit-sharing plans are treated as a single plan, and all stock bonus plans are treated as a single plan. For example, if an employee is covered under a defined-benefit plan, a money-purchase

---

[16] Priv. Ltr. Rul. 8134110.

[17] Priv. Ltr. Rul. 8632049.

[18] Priv. Ltr. Rul. 9119045, 8820092, and 854116.

[19] Priv. Ltr. Rul. 8651078.

pension plan, and a profit-sharing plan, he or she may elect lump-sum treatment for a distribution of the entire balance in the money-purchase plan only if the entire balance in the money-purchase plan and the entire accrued benefit in the defined-benefit plan are distributed in the same year. However, he or she may elect lump-sum treatment for the distribution of the entire balance in the profit-sharing plan even if neither of the pension plan benefit balances is distributed within the same calendar year.

The balance to the credit does not include earnings or contributions that are allocated to the account after the original distribution to the employee. If an employee terminates service to the employer, the balance to the credit does not include nonvested amounts.[20] If a person has received a partial distribution of employee contributions to a plan, a distribution of the balance of the plan in a subsequent year will not qualify for lump-sum treatment.

The general approach for determining the tax owed under both the 5-year and 10-year averaging methods is to separate a lump-sum payment from the recipient's other taxable income and to tax this payment as if it had been received evenly over a 5- or 10-year period. The methodology for calculating the tax is similar for each approach.

The amount of tax is based on only the taxable portion of the distribution. Amounts that constitute an individual's investment in the contract will not be taxed. These items, discussed in detail in **§ 4.05**, generally include employee after-tax contributions and P.S. 58 costs, as well as other amounts that had been taxed previously.

With 5-year averaging, a minimum distribution allowance is subtracted from the taxable amount. The minimum distribution allowance is the lesser of $10,000 or one-half of the total taxable amount, reduced by 20 percent of the total taxable amount in excess of $20,000. If the taxable amount is $70,000 or more, the minimum distribution allowance does not apply. The taxable amount remaining (after the minimum distribution allowance) is divided by 5, and a separate tax, based on the single taxpayer rate without any deductions or exclusions, is determined on this portion. The tax determined in this manner is multiplied by 5.

Example: (using 1991 tax rates shown in **Table 4–3**):

Total taxable amount	$40,000
Less: Minimum distribution allowance	6,000
Balance	$34,000
1/5 of balance	$ 6,800
Tax on $6,800	$ 1,020
Tax (5 × $1,020)	$ 5,100

---

[20] I.R.C. § 402(e)(6)(A).

Table 4–3

Tax under 5-Year Averaging

Five-Year Averaging
(Lump-Sum Distributions in 1991)

If the adjusted total taxable amount is:

At Least	But Not Over	The Separate Tax Is	Plus This Percentage	Of the Excess Over
. . .	$ 20,000	0	7.5%	0
$ 20,000	70,000	$ 1,500	18.0	$ 20,000
$ 70,000	101,750	10,500	15.0	70,000
$101,750	246,500	15,262	28.0	101,750
$246,500	. . .	55,792	31.0	246,500

Table 4–4

Tax Using 10-Year Averaging

Ten-Year Averaging
(Using 1986 Tax Rates)

If the adjusted total taxable amount is:

At Least	But Not Over	The Separate Tax Is	Plus This Percentage	Of the Excess Over
. . .	$ 20,000	0	5.5%	0
$ 20,000	21,583	1,100	13.2	$ 20,000
21,583	30,583	1,309	14.4	21,583
30,583	49,417	2,605	16.8	30,583
49,417	67,417	5,769	18.0	49,417
67,417	70,000	9,009	19.2	67,417
70,000	91,700	9,505	16.0	70,000
91,700	114,400	12,977	18.0	91,700
114,400	137,100	17,063	20.0	114,400
137,100	171,600	21,603	23.0	137,100
171,600	228,800	29,538	26.0	171,600
228,800	286,000	44,410	30.0	228,800
286,000	343,200	61,570	34.0	286,000
343,200	423,000	81,018	38.0	343,200
423,000	571,900	111,342	42.0	423,000
571,900	857,900	173,880	48.0	571,900
857,900	. . .	311,160	50.0	857,900

Under the grandfather provision, anyone who attained age 50 before January 1, 1986, may elect either 5-year averaging or a 10-year income-averaging tax treatment. Unlike other individuals, persons eligible for the grandfathered amount may make the election to take 10-year averaging (or 5-year averaging) prior to age 59½ (as long as one of the other triggering events applies). The one-election rule still applies: only one election for special averaging treatment may be made, and the election must apply to all such distributions received in one year.

Several differences apply when calculating the grandfathered 10-year averaging. The most important difference is that 1986 tax rates apply. **Table 4–4** demonstrates the amount of tax using 10-year averaging at different amounts.

The net unrealized appreciation in the employer's stock that is included in a lump-sum distribution is excluded when computing the income tax on the distribution. (This provision is discussed more fully in § **4.7**.) Persons born before January 1, 1936, may also elect to treat the portion of a lump-sum distribution that is attributable to pre-1974 participation in a plan as capital gain. If a person elects capital-gain treatment, the existing capital gain—that is, the pre-1974 plan accruals—is taxed at a flat 20 percent rate. This provision is discussed more fully in § **4.8**.

§ 4.7   Taxation of Employer Securities

If a participant receives a lump-sum distribution (disregarding the 5-year participation requirement) either partially or entirely consisting of employer securities, the net unrealized appreciation in the employer's stock is not taxed at the time of the distribution.[21] Employer securities may include shares of a parent or subsidiary corporation. The net unrealized appreciation is the difference between the value of the stock when credited to the participant's account and its fair market value on the date of distribution.

The unrealized appreciation that is excluded from income is taxable as long-term capital gain to the recipient when the shares are sold, regardless of how long the stock is held after distribution. At the time the shares are sold, any appreciation in value in excess of the excluded unrealized appreciation is taxed as long- or short-term capital gain, depending on how long the stock is held after distribution.[22]

An individual also has the option to elect to disregard the deferral of unrealized appreciation, including such amount as part of the lump-sum treatment. This election may be appropriate if the recipient intends to hold the stock for only a short period of time and would receive a favorable tax

---

[21] I.R.C. § 402(e)(4)(J).

[22] Prop. Treas. Reg. § 1.402(a)-1(b).

rate under either 5- or 10-year income averaging. In contrast, if the recipient intends to hold the stock for a period of time, the tax deferral on the unrealized appreciation of the distributed stock may provide a significant benefit, especially if a preferential tax rate for capital gain is reinstated in the tax system.

The deferral of unrealized appreciation does not apply to distributions that are not lump-sum distributions, except to the extent that the employer securities are attributable to nondeductible employee contributions.

§ 4.8   Special Capital Gains Treatment

Persons born before January 1, 1936, may also elect to treat the portion of a lump-sum distribution that is attributable to pre-1974 participation in a plan as capital gain.[23] If a person elects capital gain treatment on that portion of the distribution, it will be taxed at a flat 20 percent rate. If the capital gain provision is elected, the capital gain portion of a lump-sum distribution is then excluded when the person calculates either the 5- or 10-year averaging tax. Therefore, the total tax payable on a lump-sum distribution when a person elects capital gain treatment for pre-1974 plan accruals is equal to 20 percent of the portion of the distribution attributable to the pre-1974 plan accruals plus the averaging tax on the remainder.

The capital gain portion of a lump sum is determined by multiplying the total taxable amount of the distribution by a fraction, the numerator of which is the number of months of active participation in the plan before January 1, 1974, and the denominator of which is the number of months of total active plan participation. For the pre-1974 period, participation for any portion of a calendar year is counted as 12 months of participation. For the period after 1973, actual months of participation are credited.

The distributee may only make one such election of capital gains treatment with respect to an employer[24] and the election to take capital gains counts as an individual's election for special averaging treatment (only one election for special averaging per person). However, an individual may elect capital gains treatment and forgo the special averaging.

§ 4.9   Rollovers

Certain types of distributions from qualified plans, IRAs, SEPs, and Code § 403(b) tax-deferred annuity plans may be rolled over tax-free to an IRA, if the rollover is completed within 60 days of the receipt of the

---

[23] Tax Reform Act of 1986 § 1122(h)(3).

[24] TAMRA 1988 § 1011A(b)(13).

distribution. Failure to complete the rollover within the 60-day period will subject the participant to income tax and, if applicable, the 10 percent early withdrawal penalty on the entire taxable portion of the distribution.

In some cases, the distribution may be rolled over to another plan of the same type—for example, from a qualified plan of one employer to another employer's qualified plan. In general, a rollover into another qualified plan may be preferable to a rollover into an IRA because the preferential tax treatment may be preserved with regard to 5-year or 10-year forward income averaging, capital gain treatment, and certain other features, such as loan provisions. IRAs, SEPs, and Code § 403(b) annuity plans are not eligible for 5-year or 10-year forward averaging treatment, and IRAs may not provide loans.

Conduit IRAs are IRAs that are used to hold qualified plan funds for ultimate transfer from one qualified plan to another, when an employee changes employers and the transfer to the recipient qualified plan cannot be completed within 60 days of the distribution from the distributing plan. When the transfer between two qualified plans can be completed within 60 days, it is generally more convenient to roll the funds directly from one plan to the other. The initial transfer from the qualified plan to the IRA is tax-free if completed within 60 days. The amount in the conduit IRA may subsequently be transferred tax-free to another plan, if the conduit IRA holds no assets other than those attributable to the distribution from the distributing qualified plan.

The rollover is important when a participant's plan does not allow for a distribution option that meets his or her needs (for example, the plan only provides for lump-sum distributions). In addition, rollovers are appropriate for other valid reasons; for example, the participant may desire to continue to defer taxes, but wants to gain greater control over the investments. Or, an individual may desire to avoid the penalty tax on early distributions.

The only distributions that can be rolled over are the following:

1. Total distributions, from a qualified plan or § 403(b) annuity plan, that are paid in a single taxable year of the participant upon (a) attainment of age 59½; (b) separation from service; (c) death; or (d) disability, in the case of a self-employed person. These amounts may be rolled over to either an IRA or another qualified plan.

2. Partial distributions, from a qualified plan or Code § 403(b) annuity plan, that represent at least 50 percent of the balance to the credit of the employee, are not part of a series of periodic payments, and are made on account of the employee's (a) death, (b) separation from service, (c) retirement, or (d) permanent disability. These distributions may only be rolled over to IRAs, not to qualified plans.

3. Total distributions, within a single taxable year, of the balance to the credit of an alternate payee pursuant to a qualified domestic relations order (QDRO). These amounts may only be rolled over to IRAs, not to qualified plans.

4. Total distributions of the participant's balance from IRAs (other than conduit IRAs) and SEPs. These amounts may only be rolled over to IRAs, not to qualified plans.

§ 4.10   Early Distribution Excise Tax

Generally, when an individual receives a distribution from a qualified plan, IRA account (which includes a SEP), or Code § 403(b) annuity plan prior to attaining age 59½, a 10 percent excise tax is imposed on the taxable amount of the distribution.[25] Only those amounts of a distribution includable in taxable income are subject to the 10 percent penalty tax. If, for example, the distribution includes employee after-tax contributions that are not taxed upon distribution, such amounts are not subject to the excise tax. Under no circumstance does this tax apply to distributions after the recipient has attained age 59½.

There are, however, a significant number of exceptions that prohibit application of the excise tax to pre-59½ distributions. The broadest exception is for distributions made from a qualified plan or a Code § 403(b) annuity plan when the participant separates from service after attainment of age 55. Such distributions are exempt from the tax.

Also excluded are payments made to a beneficiary or to an employee's estate on or after the participant's death. Similarly, payments attributable to an individual's disability are exempted, as are distributions made to cover deductible medical expenses under Code § 213, unless the distributions are made from an IRA.

In limited circumstances, dividend payments made from certain tax-credit employee stock ownership plans (ESOPs) are exempted. Payments made to an alternate payee pursuant to a qualified domestic relations order (QDRO) are not subject to the excise tax (see **§ 3.03** for discussion of QDROs).

Other exceptions to the early distribution excise tax apply to the types of corrective distributions under Code § 401(k) plans, discussed in **Chapter 2**. These include distributions on account of contributions that exceed the "$7,000 limit" (referred to as "excess contributions");[26] distributions made in order to comply with the nondiscrimination testing applicable to

---

[25] I.R.C. § 72(t).

[26] I.R.C. § 401(k)(8)(D).

employee elective deferrals (referred to as "excess elective deferrals");[27] and distributions made in order to comply with the nondiscrimination testing applicable to employee after-tax and employer matching contributions (referred to as "excess aggregate contributions").[28]

The final (but certainly not the least important) exception applies in the situation where a participant elects to receive a scheduled series of substantially equal periodic payments over his or her life (or life expectancy) or over the joint lives of the participant and a beneficiary. In order to qualify for this exception, several requirements must be satisfied. If the distribution is made from a qualified plan or a Code § 403(b) annuity plan, distributions may not begin until the employee separates from service. Payments must be made at least annually. If the stream of payments is altered prior to the later of attainment of age 59½ or 5 years from the date distributions have begun, the exemption will no longer apply. If the payments are altered, the individual must pay the excise tax that would have been imposed had the exception not applied, plus interest payments.

The IRS has offered some guidance as to how much has to be distributed on an annual basis in order to constitute "substantial equal payments."[29] Amounts are treated as distributed under "substantially equal payments" using any one of three alternative methods:

1. Any method that would be acceptable for complying with the minimum distribution rules (see §§ 4.1–4.3) for retirement payments.

2. The amortization method. The account balance is amortized over the plan participant's life expectancy (based on the life expectancy tables under the minimum distribution rules) and using a reasonable interest rate.

3. An annuity approach, in which the individual's account balance is divided by an annuity factor, which is the present value of $1 per year beginning at the taxpayer's age in the first distribution year and continuing throughout the taxpayer's life. Under this method, the calculation must be based on a reasonable interest rate and mortality factor.

§ 4.11   Taxation of Loans

Many qualified plans with a CODA contain loan provisions. Loans are an important feature from the perspective of the participants, because a

---

[27] I.R.C. § 402(g)(2)(C).

[28] I.R.C. § 401(m)(7).

[29] IRS Notice 89-25, Q-12; IRB 1989-12, 68.

loan provision gives the participant an opportunity to have access to accumulated benefits in the case of financial need. Accessibility provides comfort to participants faced with the decision of making a deferral election that will reduce current compensation. Loans are also valuable because amounts borrowed (within specified limits) are not taxable at the time the loans are made.

Although loans are especially important to plans with CODAs, any type of qualified plan or Code § 403(b) annuity plan may permit loans to plan participants and beneficiaries. In no case may IRAs and SEPs permit loans to participants or beneficiaries. A loan program under a qualified plan is subject to two separate sets of rules. First, a loan will be a "prohibited transaction" unless the loan program meets certain requirements. If a loan is a prohibited transaction, this has implications for the fiduciary responsibility requirements under ERISA[30] and may also trigger an excise tax under the Internal Revenue Code.[31] A participant loan will not be a prohibited transaction as long as the loan meets the requirements of the participant loan exemption. (The requirements of the exemption are discussed in detail in **§ 5.11**.) However, loans to certain individuals are never exempted from the prohibited transaction rules. These individuals include S corporation employees who are shareholders owning more than 5 percent in the corporation, and owner-employees (proprietors or partners owning more than 10 percent of an unincorporated business).

The second set of rules applies to the taxation of loans made to participants or beneficiaries. The general rule is that aggregate loans of up to one-half of the participant's vested interest ($50,000 loan maximum) are permitted without the loans being treated as taxable distributions. A minimum-loan rule allows a participant to borrow up to $10,000, even if this is more than one-half of the vested benefit. For example, a person having a vested benefit of $13,000 could still borrow up to $10,000, even though half of the vested benefit is only $6,500.

The maximum "aggregate amount" of all such loans is $50,000. This limitation is reduced by the highest outstanding balance of all loans to the participant during the one-year period prior to the date of the loan. For example, if a participant repays a $50,000 loan amount (principal payment) on September 1, he or she may not borrow again from the plan until September 1 of the following year. The limits apply to all loans in the aggregate from qualified plans, Code § 403(b) annuity plans, and Code § 457 plans of the employer. The employer includes all employers aggregated under the controlled group or affiliated service group rules (see **§ 3.11**).

---

[30] ERISA 406.

[31] I.R.C. § 4975.

The loans must be repaid in essentially equal installments, no less frequently than quarterly, and within 5 years. However, if the loan is used to acquire the participant's principal residence, a longer repayment term, similar to terms on conventional mortgages, is permitted.

Interest paid to the plan by the employee is not deductible for federal income tax purposes unless the loan is secured by the employee's principal residence. Even if the loan is secured by a home, interest deductions are not permitted if the loan is (1) to a key employee, as defined by the Code's rules for top-heavy plans (see **§ 3.24**) or (2) secured by an account balance in a Code § 401(k) or § 403(b) annuity plan attributable to salary deferral contributions.

The entire amount of a loan that does not satisfy the maximum period requirements is treated as a distribution from the plan and is subject to federal income tax.[32] Loans that exceed the dollar limitations are treated as in-service distributions to the extent that the amount exceeds the maximum dollar limits. The amount of the loan in excess of the limits is subject to taxation as ordinary income and will be subject to the 10 percent excise tax on early distributions if applicable to a particular individual (generally, if the individual is under age 59½). If a portion of a loan is treated as a taxable distribution, the taxable portion of the loan, when repaid, is treated as a nondeductible employee contribution that may be recovered tax-free at a later time.

In general, spouses of participants must give written consent before a loan may be granted from the plan, in order to comply with the rules giving spouses certain rights to a participant's plan benefit (see **§ 3.22**).

§ 4.12   Special Rules Applying to Death Benefits

Generally, a beneficiary receiving benefits from a qualified plan "stands in the shoes" of the participant and is taxed on the distribution in the same manner as the participant.[33] However, two special rules may allow the beneficiary to exempt a portion of the benefit from tax.

The first rule involves the $5,000 death benefit exclusion. Generally, a beneficiary who receives a single-sum benefit on account of the participant's death may exclude from gross income $5,000 of the amount received from the plan.[34] The exclusion does not apply, however, if the beneficiary is a survivor annuitant and the annuity had commenced prior to the

---

[32] I.R.C. § 72(p).

[33] Treas. Reg. § 1.402(a)-1(a)(5).

[34] I.R.C. § 101(b).

participant's death. If the benefit is paid in the form of periodic payments, the $5,000 exclusion is available only to the extent that the employee's benefit was nonvested prior to death.[35]

The life insurance exclusion is governed by the second rule. The exclusion of life insurance from the income tax, which is generally applicable outside of tax-sheltered plans, also applies if the death benefit is payable under a life insurance contract held by a qualified plan. The amount that is excluded is the pure insurance amount paid (the difference between the policy's face amount and its cash value).[36] To qualify for the exclusion, the insurance cost (P.S. 58 costs) must have been taxable to the employee or paid with after-tax employee contributions.[37]

The remaining amount, representing the cash value, is treated as a taxable distribution. If the benefit contains other amounts that were already taxed, the death beneficiary can reduce the taxable portion of the distribution by these amounts as well. Among these exclusions are: P.S. 58 costs; the $5,000 death benefit exclusion discussed above; employee after-tax contributions, and any other amounts representing the participant's investment in the contract. A death beneficiary, in many cases, may be allowed to elect special 5-year averaging tax treatment (see **§ 3.6**).

One other difference applies to death benefit distributions: benefits received as a death benefit are not subject to the excise tax on large distributions. The spouse may elect, however, to treat such amounts as subject to the excise tax, in exchange for avoiding the excess accumulation tax that would otherwise be payable by the participant's estate. The impact of these taxes is discussed in **§§ 4.13–4.14**.

§ 4.13   Taxation of Certain Large Distributions

The Tax Reform Act of 1986 created a 15 percent excise tax under Code § 4980A that applies to certain large distributions from retirement plans made during an individual's life and certain large accumulations remaining in such retirement vehicles at the participant's death. The taxes only apply to benefits earned under retirement plans that have received preferential tax treatment—qualified retirement plans, IRAs (which includes SEPs), and Code § 403(b) tax-deferred annuities. Of the types of plans covered in this book, only nonqualified plans are not subject to the tax.

The tax on distributions is a 15 percent tax on what are called "excess distributions." This tax is the subject of this section. However, the excise

---

[35] I.R.C. § 101(b).

[36] I.R.C. § 72(m).

[37] Treas. Reg. § 1.72-16(c)(4).

tax does not apply to distributions made to a beneficiary on account of a participant's death. Instead, an additional 15 percent excess accumulations tax will apply to "excess retirement accumulations" remaining in such tax-deferred retirement vehicles at the time of the participant's death. (The estate tax payable by the estate is the subject of the next section.)

The 15 percent excise tax is applicable to excess distributions. Excess distributions exist to the extent that the total of distributions received from certain retirement plans in any tax year exceeds the annual threshold amount. The annual threshold amount is the greater of (1) $150,000 or (2) $112,500, as indexed each year for inflation (in 1992, the indexed value is $140,276). The $150,000 threshold amount does not apply if an individual elects a special grandfather election described below.

In the case of a lump-sum distribution from a qualified retirement plan in which the individual elects 5- or 10-year averaging tax treatment, a special additional limit applies. The limit is five times the applicable annual exemption for regular distributions. For example, in 1992 the lump-sum exemption is $750,000 (five times the $150,000 annual exemption for regular distributions). The exemptions for regular distributions and for lump-sum distributions apply separately. For example, if an individual in 1992 receives a lump sum of $750,000 from a qualified plan and elects 5-year averaging treatment on such amount, and in the same year also withdraws $150,000 from an IRA account, no excise tax is assessed because neither threshold has been exceeded. However, any extra "unused" exemption for one type of distribution may not be used to shelter excess distributions of another type.

Generally, all distributions received by an individual from qualified retirement plans, annuity plans under Code § 403(a), individual retirement arrangements (which by definition include SEPs), and Code § 403(b) tax-sheltered annuity plans are counted toward determining whether any excess distributions have been made. However, certain amounts are excluded when determining whether the excess distribution tax applies. Among the amounts generally excluded are:

- Distributions payable at death (subject to the 15 percent excise tax on excess retirement accumulations, discussed in § **4.14** below);
- Distributions of the participant's after-tax investment in the plan;
- Distributions that are rolled over to an IRA or another qualified plan;
- Distributions to an alternate payee under a QDRO, but only if the payments are included in gross income by the alternate payee;
- Distributions of retirement annuities to the extent that the value is not includable in gross income at the time of distribution;

• Amounts that are distributed from a qualified retirement plan (or a SEP) and that are treated as excess deferrals or excess contributions (including income allocated to such amounts);
• Distributions of annuity contracts to the extent they are not includable in income at the time of the distribution.

One complicating factor under the excise tax rules is that individuals with an accrued benefit under all applicable plans of more than $562,500 on August 1, 1986, were allowed to make a grandfather election, "protecting" such amounts earned as of that date from the excise tax. The deadline for making the election has passed;[38] however, the effects of such an election have an ongoing significance and need to be discussed further. If a person made the grandfather election, the $150,000 exemption does not apply. Instead, the applicable annual exemption is $112,500 as indexed for inflation ($140,276 for 1992). In effect, persons who made the grandfather election risk exposing to the excise tax the amount of any distributions that are in excess of the $112,500 indexed annual exemption but less than $150,000. In return for giving up the use of the currently higher $150,000 annual exemption, taxpayers who made the election may reduce the amount subject to the excise tax each year by their grandfather recovery amount.

The grandfather recovery amount depends on the total amount that was grandfathered and on which of two methods these taxpayers have elected to use to compute the recovery amount. A person's original grandfather amount is equal to the total taxable balance in all of his or her qualified plans, IRAs, SEPs, and Code § 403(b) tax-deferred annuities as of August 1, 1986. Each year, as distributions are received, part or all of the distributions are sheltered for excise tax purposes by the person's grandfathered recovery amount, until the entire grandfather amount is depleted.

As noted above, persons making the grandfather election were permitted to select between two methods for computing the grandfather recovery amount. They are: the discretionary method and the attained age method. However, because the discretionary method provides for the election of two separate recovery rates, there are effectively three recovery methods.

Under the regular discretionary method, 10 percent of each distribution is considered a recovery of the remaining grandfathered amount. For example, if a person received a regular distribution of $155,000 in 1992, 10 percent ($15,500) of this amount would be considered a recovery of any

---

[38] Grandfather election could have been made on IRS Form 5329, filed along with the individual's tax return, for years prior to 1989.

remaining grandfather amount. Therefore only $139,500 would be subject to the excise tax, and no excise tax would be imposed because the threshold in 1992 is $140,276.

The grandfathered amount must be reduced by 10 percent of each distribution even if the recovery amount provides no tax shelter. For example, if a person receives a distribution of $80,000, $8,000 of the person's remaining grandfathered amount is used up even though the entire $80,000 distribution was sheltered by the annual exemption anyway. The advantage of the 10 percent discretionary method is primarily to preserve a large portion of the grandfathered amount for later use, either for a time when a large distribution is taken, or to shelter excess retirement accumulations at death (discussed in **§ 4.14** below). If a person is not in good health, for instance, preserving the grandfathered amount to shelter retirement accumulations at death may be an important objective.

A person who elects the discretionary recovery method may in any year choose to increase the recovery rate to 100 percent. Once the accelerated rate is chosen, however, the accelerated rate applies to all future years until the entire grandfathered amount is used up. Consequently, the accelerated discretionary recovery method will provide complete tax shelter for lifetime distributions that would otherwise be subject to the excise tax, but the grandfathered amount is used up more quickly. Because the remaining grandfathered amount is also used when determining the excise tax on excess retirement accumulations at death, choosing to accelerate the recovery rate to shelter lifetime distributions may increase a person's estate's exposure to the tax at death. Therefore, if and when to elect to accelerate the recovery rate is an important planning issue.

The alternative grandfathered recovery method is the attained age method. Under this approach, the amount of each distribution that is considered a recovery of the grandfathered amount (sheltered from the excise tax) is determined by multiplying the distribution by a fraction based on the individual's attained age. The attained age method is generally viewed as having no advantages over the discretionary method, and it is doubtful that many individuals elect this recovery method.

In some circumstances, it is possible that a distribution could be subject to the penalty tax on early withdrawals[39] and the 15 percent excise tax. In such circumstances, the 15 percent excise tax is reduced to the extent of the penalty for early withdrawal.

---

[39] I.R.C. § 72(t).

§ 4.14   —Excess Retirement Accumulations

In order to ensure that an individual does not avoid the excise tax by minimizing lifetime distributions (within the limits imposed by the uniform MDIB rules), a comparable 15 percent estate tax applies to excess retirement accumulations at death. This tax is imposed in addition to any federal estate or gift taxes and may not be offset by the lifetime unified credit or by any deductions, such as the marital deduction or deductions for charitable contributions. However, it is deductible when computing the federal estate tax.

If all of the decedent's retirement balances go to the surviving spouse, the surviving spouse may elect to treat the balances as his or her own for purposes of both excise taxes. In this case, the excise tax is not imposed on the excess retirement accumulations at the first death; however, such amounts as they are distributed to the spouse will be counted toward determining whether the excise tax on excess distributions applies to the spouse. If this election is made, such amounts are counted toward determining excess retirement accumulations at the spouse's later death. The decision of a spouse to defer the tax must be made carefully, in order to limit the effects of these two taxes.

Excess retirement accumulations are defined as the value of benefits remaining in covered retirement plans, at the time of an individual's death, that exceed the specified threshold. The threshold is determined by multiplying the applicable annual exemption (the $150,000 limit, or the $112,500 indexed limit, if applicable) by an annuity factor. The annuity factor is based on the individual's age at death and the interest rate and mortality assumptions for valuing life annuities, as provided in Regulations § 20.2031-7. For example, assuming the discount rate is 12 percent and the annual exemption is $150,000, the threshold amount for a person who is 60 years old at the time of death and has not made the grandfather election is $1,017,195. Because the life expectancy factors decline at advancing ages, the threshold amount is smaller for older persons. Therefore, for any given retirement balances, the excess accumulation and therefore the potential death excise tax will be greater as age increases.

If a person has made the grandfathered election, the threshold amount is computed using the inflation-indexed annual exemption in the year of death as the annual payment amount, not $150,000, if that is greater. This means that, until such time when the indexed amount exceeds $150,000, the threshold amount for an individual electing the grandfather election is lower than for someone who has not made the election. However, this disadvantage is offset by the fact that remaining grandfathered amounts are recovered at the time of death, which can reduce the excise tax due at death.

Similar to the rules for the 15 percent excise tax on excess distributions, certain amounts are excluded from the excise tax on excess accumulations. In addition to the exclusions mentioned above for excess distributions, amounts are excluded to the extent that the sum of such death benefits, plus other benefits payable with respect to the decedent, exceeds the total value of benefits payable immediately prior to death. Basically, this means that the portion of life insurance benefits "at risk," meaning the face value of the policy less the cash value of the policy, is not subject to the 15 percent death excise tax.

§ 4.15   Taxation of Payments under a QDRO

As described in **Chapter 3** (see § **3.23**), a state court with domestic relations jurisdiction may issue an order requiring the plan to give some or all of a participant's benefit payments to a spouse, former spouse, child, or other dependent of the participant, as long as the order is determined to be a qualified domestic relations order (QDRO). This section reviews the tax treatment of amounts paid out under a QDRO.

If the alternate payee is the participant's former spouse, the amount paid to such person under the QDRO is includable in the alternate payee's gross income.[40] However, distributions to nonspousal alternate payees are included in the gross income of the participant. Because the spousal alternate payee is required to pay taxes on amounts received, he or she may also share in recovery of the nontaxable portion of the participant's benefit (referred to as the "investment in the contract"; see § **4.5**). The investment in the contract is allocated ratably to the spouse, based on the amount paid to the spousal payee in relation to the total benefits to which the participant may be entitled under the plan.

For purposes of the lump-sum distribution rules (see § **4.6**), the participant who otherwise qualifies to elect lump-sum treatment will continue to be eligible for such election even if a portion of his or her benefit is payable to an alternate payee under a QDRO.[41] In addition, an alternate payee who is the spouse or former spouse of the participant is eligible to receive lump-sum tax treatment. The alternate payee is eligible if a distribution of the balance of the credit to the participant would constitute a lump-sum distribution *and* the alternate payee receives the balance to the credit of the alternate payee's entitlement under the QDRO.

A tax-free rollover rule generally applies to an alternate payee under the same circumstances as the participant. Apparently, a rollover is also

---

[40] I.R.C. § 402(a)(9).
[41] I.R.C. § 402(a)(1).

allowed by the alternate payee's beneficiary when the alternate payee dies before receiving a qualifying distribution.

§ 4.16   Income Tax Withholding

Distributions from employer plans of deferred compensation are required to withhold federal income taxes, unless the participant elects otherwise.[42] This rule applies to all types of plans discussed in this book: Code § 401(k) plans, nonqualified deferred compensation, Code § 403(b) plans, and SEPs. For applying the rule, plans are divided into two categories, periodic and nonperiodic distributions. Nonperiodic distributions are further divided into qualified total distributions and other kinds of nonperiodic distributions. Periodic payments are annuity payments to an employee or beneficiary, in the form of a life annuity, contingent annuity, annuity certain, or installment payments.

The tax rationale for withholding on periodic payments is that the payments are wages paid to the recipient as though the recipient is a married person with three additional exemptions. Amounts withheld are determined from a table issued by the IRS as a guide for withholding taxes from wages. If monthly payments are less than $450 ($5,400 annually), no withholding is required.

For nonperiodic payments, the rate of tax withheld is generally 10 percent of each payment. No withholding is required for annual distributions of less than $200. For qualified total distributions (those distributions eligible for lump-sum treatment; see **§ 4.6**), special tables are provided to determine the amount of tax to be withheld.

The plan administrator or payor is required to send, to every recipient of a distribution, a notice of the application of the withholding rules. Such individuals must be informed of the opportunity to elect not to have withholding apply, and the opportunity to revoke and renew such election at any time prior to payment. For periodic payments, notices have to be sent at some time during the 6 months prior to commencement of the payments for periodic distributions. Thereafter, notices have to be given annually. No notices are required for recipients who receive less than $5,400 per year in periodic payments. To those whose nonperiodic payment is $200 or more per year, a notice must be sent at, or prior to, the time each payment is made.

A payee who wishes to waive withholding must complete and file Form W-4P, which allows both elections to waive withholding, as well as an opportunity to change the amount withheld.

---

[42] I.R.C. § 3405.

CHAPTER 5

ERISA REQUIREMENTS

§ 5.1   General

Prior to the enactment of the Employee Retirement Income Security Act (ERISA), little federal regulation existed for pension plans outside of the tax laws, and state laws were incomplete, inconsistent, and generally ineffective. Similarly, regulation of other employee benefits (to the extent regulation existed at all) was left to such state statutes as wage payment and collection laws.

This all changed with the enactment of ERISA in 1974. The law was in response to numerous instances of pension fund mismanagement and abuse. Retired employees had their pension benefits reduced or terminated because their pension plan had been inadequately funded or depleted through mismanagement. In other instances, employees retiring after 20 years or more of service with an employer were ineligible for pensions because of complex and strict eligibility requirements.

ERISA was intended to prevent such abuses and to protect the interests of employees and their beneficiaries in pension plans. The Act, in response to the pension abuses, instituted minimum vesting requirements, minimum participation requirements, and minimum funding requirements for certain types of retirement plans, however, the Act does much more. Title I of ERISA establishes a comprehensive regulatory program for many types of benefit plans, including most plans that provide deferred compensation to employees and most types of health and welfare plans.

ERISA imposes standards of conduct and responsibility on plan fiduciaries (persons having authority or control over the management of the plan or over the investment of fund assets). It also requires that plan administrators disclose relevant financial information to employees and the government. The statute imposes various minimum standards with regard to the number of employees that must be covered under the plan, minimum standards for when benefits must vest, and minimum funding requirements for some types of plans. Finally, ERISA provides legal remedies to employees and their beneficiaries (as well as to the Department of Labor) in event of violations.

The goal of the Act is to ensure that employers (and employee organizations such as unions) that establish benefit plans clearly define the benefits provided under the plan, communicate the benefits under the plan to employees, and give employees the ability to force employers to provide promised benefits. However, ERISA *does not require* an employer to provide a pension plan, or any welfare benefits plan, for its employees.

An employer (or employee organization) planning to establish any type of employee benefit plan must be careful to determine whether such a plan will be governed by ERISA. If the plan is subject to ERISA, all relevant provisions must be met. Of special note to plans covered by ERISA are the annual reporting requirements, which, if not met, can subject an employer to fines of up to $1,000 a day.

ERISA requirements apply to most of the plans discussed in this book, with the exception of certain plans of deferred compensation, Code § 403(b) plans established by government employers, and Code § 403(b) annuity plans that are only funded with employee salary deferral elections. The reporting and disclosure requirements are vastly simplified in the case of Simplified Employee Pensions (SEPs) that meet minimum requirements. This chapter discusses plans that are subject to ERISA and reviews the requirements for such plans. The focus remains on the ERISA provisions that have the most relevance to plans that contain cash or deferral opportunities.

§ 5.2   Coverage under ERISA

Title I of ERISA generally applies to all employee benefit plans that are established or maintained by employers and/or employee organizations engaged in any industry or activity affecting interstate commerce. Employee benefit plans include pension plans and welfare plans.

Pension plans, as defined in ERISA, include any plan, fund, or program that provides retirement income to employees or results in a deferral of income by employees for periods extending to the termination of employment. This broad definition includes all of the types of plans that receive special tax treatment under Code § 401(a), including defined-benefit pension plans, money-purchase pension plans, target benefit plans, profit-sharing plans, thrift plans, stock bonus plans, and employee stock ownership plans (ESOPs). The definition also includes any other type of deferred compensation plan that is not specifically exempted from the coverage provisions. The term pension plan excludes severance pay plans as long as the plan pays benefits that are not contingent on an employee's retirement, the benefit does not exceed twice the participant's final salary, and the benefit is paid within 24 months of the termination of employment.

Although none of the plans discussed in this book is considered a welfare plan, ERISA does cover such plans. The terms "employee welfare benefit plan" and "welfare benefit plan" mean any plan, fund, or program heretofore or hereafter established or maintained by an employer or employee organization, or by both, to the extent that such plan, fund, or program was established or is maintained for the purpose of providing for its participants or their beneficiaries, through the purchase of insurance or otherwise, medical, surgical, or hospital care benefits; or benefits in the event of sickness, accident, disability, death, or unemployment; or vacation benefits; or apprenticeship or other training programs; or day-care centers, scholarship funds, or prepaid legal services.

Certain plans specifically exempted from the requirements of Title I include plans that are established by federal, state, or local governments as employers; plans covering employees of tax-exempt churches; plans maintained outside of the United States primarily for the benefit of nonresident aliens; and plans maintained solely for the purpose of complying with applicable workers' compensation, unemployment compensation, or disability insurance laws. An additional exception is contained in the Regulations, which define the term employee benefit plan. Plans that only cover individuals (and their spouses) who wholly own an incorporated or unincorporated business, and plans that only cover partners (and their spouses) of a partnership are deemed not to be employee benefit plans.

The Regulations also exclude specific plans from the definition of pension or welfare plan. The following employment practices are excluded:

Pay policies that pay employees a premium for services performed in other than normal circumstances, such as for overtime, holidays, or less desirable shifts;

Payment to employees from the employer's general funds when the employee is absent for medical reasons or for disability, or in other situations where the employee is absent from work for such reasons as vacation, military leave, jury duty, training, and sabbatical leave.

The discussion above does not exhaust the exemptions from the ERISA coverage requirements. Other relevant exceptions are covered within the descriptions of specific types of plans. Exceptions applicable to Code § 403(b) plans are treated in § **6.10**; nonqualified deferred compensation, in § **8.3**; and SEPs in § **7.7**.

There is significance under ERISA as to whether a plan is defined as an employee benefit welfare plan or an employee benefit pension plan. Under Title I of ERISA, both types of plans are subject to ERISA's fiduciary provisions, reporting and disclosure requirements, and judicial proceeding

rules. However, only pension benefit plans are subject to ERISA's participation, vesting, and minimum funding requirements.

§ 5.3   Fiduciary Responsibilities

One of the primary elements in the ERISA enforcement scheme is the
rules regulating fiduciaries. The rules specify that those persons exercising
discretionary authority over the management or assets of employee benefit
plans are considered "fiduciaries" and are subject to certain standards of
conduct in carrying out their responsibilities. If the fiduciaries fail to meet
those standards, they are personally liable for any losses that result. This
section identifies who is a fiduciary, what fiduciaries' responsibilities are,
and what is the extent of their liability. The rules contain various affirmative duties, as well as specific prohibited transactions.

§ 5.4   —Identifying the Fiduciaries

Fiduciaries include the following:

1. Individuals who exercise control with respect to the management of
   the plan or with respect to the management or disposition of plan
   assets;
2. Individuals who render investment advice for a fee;
3. Individuals who have discretionary authority in administration of the
   plan.

An investment adviser is an individual who renders advice regarding value
or regarding sale or purchase of securities and other property; has discretionary authority to purchase or sell investments or render investment advice on a regular basis; and renders advice that is the primary basis on
which investment decisions are made. Excluded are broker-dealers and
banks when they are acting on specific buy–sell instructions that describe
the specific security, price range, time period, and limits regarding the
amount of the sale.

The U.S. Department of Labor ("DOL") has indicated that rendering
legal, accounting, actuarial, or consulting services to an employee benefit
plan will not in itself render an individual a fiduciary. Such individual
would be a fiduciary only if acting in any of the three capacities referred
to above.

Certain individuals convicted of serious felonies are prohibited from being fiduciaries, officers, administrators, trustees, custodians, counsel,

agents, employees, consultants, or decision makers in any capacity or position of custody or control of plan assets of any employee benefit plan. An individual is prohibited from acting in any of the above capacities for 13 years after conviction of robbery, bribery, extortion, embezzlement, fraud, grand larceny, burglary, arson, a felony violation of federal or state law involving drugs, murder, rape, kidnapping, perjury, or assault with intent to kill.

A plan has to name a fiduciary and a trust has to name the trustees (or have the named fiduciary appointed by the trustees).[1] This rule is intended to avoid the possibility that the decision makers cannot be ascertained, thus avoiding responsibility. A plan instrument is considered to have identified a named fiduciary if the instrument clearly identifies one or more persons by name or title and combines the identification with a statement that such person or persons have authority to control and manage the operation of the plan. However, the better practice is to explicitly state that such person is the named fiduciary for purposes of ERISA.[2]

§ 5.5 —Affirmative Fiduciary Duties

ERISA establishes a number of affirmative duties that a fiduciary must satisfy. These duties include all of the following.

Exclusive Benefit

Fiduciaries are required to discharge their duties "solely in the interest of the participants and beneficiaries" for the exclusive purpose of providing benefits and defraying reasonable expenses.[3]

Prudence

Fiduciaries must act with the care, skill, prudence, and diligence (under prevailing circumstances) that a "prudent man," acting in a like capacity and familiar with such matters, would use in the conduct of an enterprise of a like character and with like aims.[4] DOL Regulations provide additional guidance under the prudent-man standard with respect to the investment of plan assets.[5] Under the DOL Regulations, a fiduciary must give

---

[1] ERISA § 402(a).

[2] 29 C.F.R. § 2509-75-5, FR-1.

[3] ERISA § 404(a)(1).

[4] ERISA § 404(a)(1)(B).

[5] 29 C.F.R. § 2550.404a.

"appropriate consideration" to facts and circumstances, given the scope of the fiduciary's duty, that the fiduciary knows or should know are relevant to the particular investment or investment course of action. Specifically, the fiduciary must consider the role the investment course of action plays in that portion of the plan's portfolio with respect to which the fiduciary has investment duties. The fiduciary must act in accordance with such information. Facts that should be given consideration in determining the portfolio's risk of loss and opportunity for gain include the composition with regard to diversification, liquidity, and current return of the portfolio relative to anticipated cash flow, and the projected return of the portfolio relative to the funding objectives of the plan.

Diversification of Investments

A fiduciary has a duty to diversify the investments of the plan so as to minimize the risk of large losses, unless, under the plan, it is clearly prudent not to do so.[6] The legislative history of ERISA indicates that the diversification requirement cannot be stated as a fixed percentage but depends on facts and circumstances of each investment. The following factors must be considered:

1. The purposes of the plan;
2. The amount of the plan's assets;
3. Financial and industrial conditions;
4. The type of investment, whether mortgages, bonds, shares of stock, or otherwise;
5. Distribution as to geographical location;
6. Distribution as to industries.[7]

In Accordance with Documents

Fiduciaries are required to operate the plan in accordance with the documents and instruments governing the plan.

§ 5.6   —Extent of Fiduciary Responsibility

Trustees are given the exclusive authority and discretion to manage and control the assets of the plan. Co-trustees manage assets together, unless a

---

[6] ERISA § 404(c).

[7] 1974 U.S. Code Cong. & Admin. News 4639, 5084.

specific agreement divides responsibility. An investment manager can be appointed, to relieve the trustees from liabilities. However, in all cases, an individual is responsible for the breach of a co-fiduciary when the individual participates in or conceals the breach of action or omission by the co-fiduciary, or fails in his or her own duty and thus allows the breach of the co-fiduciary, or has knowledge of the breach and does not make reasonable efforts to remedy.

ERISA § 410(c) provides that the plan, the fiduciary, or the company can purchase insurance to cover losses caused by a fiduciary's breach. In addition, the DOL has indicated that a company can "indemnify" a fiduciary against any losses to the same extent as if insurance had been purchased.

§ 5.7 —Individual Account Plan Exception

ERISA allows fiduciaries to limit their liability if individual participants are given discretion over the investment of trust assets held in their behalf. In the case of an individual account plan that provides for such investment direction, the fiduciaries are relieved of any liability for any losses caused by the exercise of participant investment direction.

This exception is especially important for Code § 401(k) plans that allow participants some choice with regard to the investment of the account held on their behalf. Generally, in this type of plan, each participant is free to pursue his or her own investment policy, within parameters. Such participant will not be considered a fiduciary (except with regard to the prohibited transaction rules and unrelated business income). Therefore, plans should prohibit investments that result in prohibited transactions or create unrelated business income.

Under the exception, if the trustee follows the participant's investment instructions, the trustee will not be liable for violations of the prudent-man rule or diversification requirement. The exception is met if the following requirements are satisfied:

1. The individual account plan provides an opportunity for a participant or beneficiary to exercise control over the assets in his or her account;
2. The individual has the opportunity to choose from a broad range of investment alternatives;
3. The participants have the opportunity to invest in (a) an interest-bearing deposit in a bank, with a high degree of liquidity and fully insured by the United States, or (b) a pooled investment fund, with assets consisting solely of cash and securities issued or guaranteed

by the United States, and with principal investment objectives that include a high level of current income consistent with the preservation of capital and a high degree of liquidity.

The term opportunity to control means a reasonable opportunity to give investment instructions to the fiduciary. It is permissible to limit the frequency of investment elections and to charge for the expenses incurred in making the elections.

The term broad range of investment alternatives means that the investment can materially affect the potential return and the degree of risk. The individual must also be given a minimum of choices from three diversified categories in which: each has a materially different risk; the aggregate portfolio is a balanced mix; and investing in two categories offers offsetting risks. The three categories must combine the following factors:

- A high level of income, while preserving capital in the long term;
- A capital appreciation;
- A high current income with preservation of capital and a high degree of liquidity.

Within each investment choice, assets must be diversified to minimize the risk of large losses. Functionally, when participants have small account balances, the use of "look-through investments" (such as mutual funds) may be required. Finally, individuals must be given sufficient information to make an informed investment decision.

The term exercise of control requires that the participants have true independence, and that no one is permitted to exercise undue influence on them.

If the investment options contain pooled investment funds, participants must have a choice among four funds, each having the following primary objectives:

- Generation of highest level of income consistent with the preservation of capital over the long term;
- Capital appreciation;
- Balance between capital appreciation and preservation of capital and generation of income;
- Generation of high level of current income consistent with the preservation of capital and a high degree of liquidity.

If the participant does not supply investment directions, the plan may have a written default provision as long as the default is an interest-bearing investment.

§ 5.8   Bonding Requirements

ERISA § 412 requires that every fiduciary and every other person who handles funds or other property of the plan must be bonded. Handling money means "physical contact" with the funds while having power to exercise control, power to transfer, power to disburse, power to sign checks, and all other responsibilities involving supervisory power. The type of bond is a "guarantee" called a surety bond: a third party agrees to pay to the plan any losses that occur to the plan because of fraud or dishonesty on the part of the plan official. The amount of the bond for a given plan year is fixed at the beginning of the plan year; it must be equal to 10 percent of the funds handled (calculated as of the last valuation date in the previous year). The minimum applicable bond amount is $1,000 and the maximum is $500,000. The amount handled may differ among individual fiduciaries, in accordance with the amount of money handled. The types of bonds that can be used include blanket bonds (covering all fiduciaries and those who handle assets), individual bonds (covering a named individual), or schedule bonds (covering by position, rather than by name). The bonds must be purchased from a corporate surety that holds a Certificate of Authority issued by the Secretary of the Treasury.

§ 5.9   Prohibited Transactions

Two broad categories of transactions are prohibited because they are deemed, by their nature, to be contrary to the interest of plan participants.[8] In the first category, a fiduciary is prohibited from causing the plan to engage in a transaction if the fiduciary knows or should know that such transaction constitutes a direct or indirect:

- Sale or exchange, or leasing, of any property between the plan and a party in interest;
- Lending of money or other extension of credit between the plan and a party in interest;
- Furnishing of goods, services, or facilities between the plan and a party in interest;
- Transfer to, or use by or for the benefit of, a party in interest, of any assets of the plan;
- Acquisition, on behalf of the plan, of any employer security or employer real property in violation of ERISA § 407(a).

---

[8] ERISA § 406.

Under ERISA § 407(a), a plan may not acquire or hold any employer security that is not a "qualifying employer security" or any employer real property that is not "qualifying employer real property." A qualifying employer security is an employer security consisting of stock or a marketable obligation. Qualifying employer real property is real property, and related personal property, leased to an employer of employees covered by the plan where a substantial number of the parcels are dispensed geographically and each parcel of real property and the improvements thereon are suitable (or adaptable without excessive cost) for more than one use.

A plan may not acquire any qualifying employer security or qualifying employer real property if, immediately after such acquisition, the aggregate fair market value of employer securities and employer real property held by the plan exceeds 10 percent of the fair market value of the assets of the plan. This limitation does not apply to eligible individual account plans. An eligible individual account plan is a profit-sharing, stock bonus, thrift, or savings plan, or an employee stock ownership plan, or a money-purchase plan that was in existence on the date ERISA was enacted and, on such date, invested primarily in qualifying employer securities. To qualify as an eligible account plan, the plan must explicitly provide for the acquisition and holding of qualifying employer real property or qualifying employer securities.

A party in interest is defined in ERISA § 407(a) as any of the following individuals;

1. Any fiduciary (including, but not limited to, any administrator, officer, trustee, or custodian), counsel, or employee of such employee benefit plan;

2. A person providing services to such plan;

3. An employer any of whose employees are covered by such plan;

4. An employee organization any of whose members are covered by such plan;

5. An owner, direct or indirect, of 50 percent or more of (a) the combined voting power of all classes of stock entitled to vote or the total value of shares of all classes of stock of a corporation; (b) the capital interest or the profits interest of a partnership; or (c) the beneficial interest of a trust or unincorporated enterprise that is an employer or an employee organization as described in item 1 or 2 of this list;

6. A relative of any individual described in items 1, 2, 3, or 5 of this list;

7. A corporation, partnership, trust, or estate of which 50 percent or more of (a) the combined voting power of all classes of stock entitled to vote or the total value of shares of all classes of stock of such

corporation, (b) the capital interest or profits interest of such partnership, or (c) the beneficial interest of such trust or estate, is owned directly or indirectly or is held by persons described in any of items 1 through 5 of this list;

8. An employee, officer, or director (or an individual having powers or responsibilities similar to those of officers or directors), or a 10 percent or more shareholder, directly or indirectly, of a person described in any of items 2 through 5, or item 7 of this list, or of the employee benefit plan; or a 10 percent or more partner or joint venturer of a person described in any of items 2 through 5, or item 7 of this list.

The second category of prohibited transactions involves self-dealing. The fiduciary is required with respect to a plan:

• Not to deal with the assets of the plan in his or her own interest or for his or her own account;
• Not to act, in an individual or any other capacity, in any transaction involving the plan, on behalf of a party whose interests are adverse to the interest of the plan or the interest of its participants or beneficiaries;
• Not to receive any consideration from his or her own personal account from any party dealing with such plan in connection with a transaction involving assets of the plan.

§ 5.10 —Exemptions

Because of the breadth of the prohibited transaction rules, many exceptions are provided. Exemptions come in several different forms: statutory, administrative, and individual. The statutory exemptions under ERISA include:

• Loans to parties in interest who are participants or beneficiaries of the plan, if certain conditions are met (this exception is described in more detail in § 5.11);
• Contracts or reasonable arrangements with parties in interest for office space or services necessary for the establishment or operation of the plan, if no more than reasonable compensation is paid;
• Loans to employee stock ownership plans, if specific conditions are met;
• A plan for bank employees investing in the bank's certificates of deposit;

- A plan for insurance company employees purchasing a life, health, or annuity contract from the insurance company;
- Provision of reasonable ancillary services by a bank or financial institution fiduciary;
- Exercise of a privilege to convert securities, if the plan receives adequate consideration pursuant to such conversion;
- Certain pooled fund transactions involving bonds, trust companies, and insurance companies;
- Distribution of assets in accordance with the terms of the plan and ERISA § 4404;
- Any transactions required or permitted under part I of subtitle E of Title IV;
- Merger of multiemployer plans, or transfer of assets or liabilities between multiemployer plans determined by the Pension Benefit Guarantee Corporation (PBGC) to meet the requirements of ERISA § 4231.

In addition to these exemptions, ERISA § 408(c) clarifies that the prohibited transaction rules do not prohibit any fiduciary from receiving benefits as a participant of a plan; receiving reasonable compensation for services rendered to the plan (full-time employees of the plan sponsor may not be paid) or receiving reimbursement for expenses incurred; and serving as fiduciary in addition to being an officer, employee, agent, or other representative of a party in interest.

A plan may acquire or sell qualifying securities from or to any party without violating the prohibited transaction rules if "adequate security" is paid, no commission is charged for the transaction, and the plan does not violate the 10 percent limitations. The DOL's Proposed Regulations provide some assistance in determining whether adequate consideration has been paid, in those situations where there is no established market for the securities. Fair market value of an asset must be established as of the transaction date of the asset.

ERISA § 408(a) allows the Secretary of Labor to grant certain administrative exemptions from the prohibited transaction rules. These exemptions can be individual in nature, or they may be "class" exemptions, which can be relied on by the general public. Class exemptions have almost the same impact as the statutory exemptions. In order to grant an administrative exemption, the Secretary of Labor must find that the exemption is:

1. Administratively feasible;
2. In the interests of the plan and its participants and beneficiaries;
3. Protective of the rights of the plan's participants and beneficiaries.

The Secretary of Labor has granted a large number of "class" exemptions since the enactment of ERISA. A prohibited transaction exemption only constitutes relief from the prohibited transaction rules and does not relieve a fiduciary from any other of the enumerated duties under ERISA.

If a plan or party in interest wants to engage in a transaction that appears to be a prohibited transaction, the party should first determine whether any statutory or administrative class exemptions apply. If not, the plan or party in interest may apply for a prohibited transaction exemption with the Department of Labor. The procedures for application for the exemption are set forth in Labor Regulations.[9]

§ 5.11   —Participant Loans

A fiduciary satisfying the exemption requirements under ERISA § 408 (b)(1) will be exempt from the prohibitions contained in ERISA § 406. This exemption is important to plans containing a cash or deferral arrangement because these plans are likely to provide loans to participants. Therefore, the exemption requirements are covered here in great detail. In addition to the ERISA requirements, participant loan programs are subject to the maximum loan limitations contained in Code § 72(p) (see **§ 4.11**).

Under ERISA, in order to meet the exemption from the prohibited transaction rules, all loans must:

- Be made available to all participants and beneficiaries on a reasonably equivalent basis;
- Not be made available to highly compensated employees in an amount greater than the amount available to other employees;
- Be made in accordance with specific provisions set forth in the plan;
- Bear a reasonable rate of interest;
- Be adequately secured.

DOL Regulations issued in 1989 offer further guidance as to the meaning of the statutory language.[10] Under the DOL Regulations, loans include any renewal or modification of an existing loan. Because loans are investments of the plan, they must meet the generally applicable fiduciary standards, which means that they must be prudently established and they must be administered for the exclusive benefit of participants and beneficiaries of the plan.

---

[9] Labor Reg. § 2570.32.
[10] DOL Reg. § 2550.408b.

Loans have to be made on a reasonably equivalent basis. A loan program cannot discriminate on the basis of race, color, religion, age, sex, or national origin. In determining who should receive a loan, only those factors considered in a commercial loan setting, such as creditworthiness, can be considered. Loans may not be offered on different terms to different applicants without valid economic justification. In general, after relevant facts and circumstances are reviewed, loans must not be unreasonably withheld from any participant and a large number of plan participants cannot be excluded from the loan program. However, a minimum loan amount can be established, as long as the minimum does not exceed $1,000.

One of the more controversial requirements relating to the "reasonable basis" rule is that loans must be available to all participants and beneficiaries. This is of concern to many plan sponsors, because a plan may have a significant number of participants and/or beneficiaries who are no longer employed at the company but continue to be owed benefits from the plan. Administering loans to such individuals is more difficult because repayment cannot be accomplished with payroll deduction, and communicating with such individuals is more difficult. However, the DOL Regulations do provide that loans may be offered on different terms than loans to active participants, if valid economic reasons for such differences exist. Subsequent to issuing the Regulations, the DOL issued Advisory Opinion 89-30A, which provides that loans only have to be made available to terminated participants and beneficiaries to the extent that those individuals continue to be parties in interest with respect to the plan (see **§ 5.9** for definition of parties in interest).

A loan program cannot make loans available to highly compensated employees in an amount greater than the amount available to other employees. Plan provisions imposing a maximum limitation stated either as a specific dollar amount or as a percentage of an individual's compensation will not violate this provision. Loan programs can limit loan amounts so that no portion of the loan is considered a distribution under Code § 72(p).

A loan must bear a reasonable rate of interest, to provide the plan with a return commensurate with the interest rates charged by persons in the business of lending money for loans that would be made under similar circumstances. Under this provision, interest rates cannot be limited by the state usury limit. To ease administration of a loan program where plan participants are located in a broad geographical area, the interest rate for such plans may use a national or regional rate of interest (or, if preferable, a rate based on geographical factors).

Loans must be adequately secured by something in addition to and supporting a promise to repay. The security pledged must be something that may be sold, foreclosed on, or otherwise disposed of, upon default of repayment of the loan. The value and liquidity of the security must be such that it may be reasonably anticipated that the plan will not suffer a loss of principal or interest as a result of the loan. A plan can use a participant's benefit for security, but only up to 50 percent of a participant's vested accrued benefit.

This may be a problem when a participant borrows 50 percent of his or her account balance and the loan is treated as a general asset of the trust. Assuming that the trust earns a lower rate of interest than the rate of interest specified in the loan agreement, over time, the security may become less valuable than the outstanding balance due on the loan. Because of this possibility, a plan using participant accounts as the only security should treat the loan as an individual investment election, where the borrower's account is solely credited with the loan interest.

The 50 percent account balance limit means that, if the plan makes a loan under the $10,000 minimum loan provision (meaning that the amount of the loan exceeds 50 percent of the individual's account balance), additional security beyond the individual's account balance would be required. A plan sponsor will probably choose not to make loans in excess of 50 percent of the individual's account balance, because most sponsors are reluctant to obtain security interests in other property.

Finally, a plan that offers a loan program must contain specific loan provisions that are made part of the plan—written into the plan itself or into a written instrument forming part of the plan, such as the summary plan description (SPD) or a loan manual. The document must set forth the identity of the person or positions authorized to administer the loan program; a procedure for applying for a loan; the basis on which loans are approved or denied; limitations on the amount and types of loans offered; the procedure for determining a reasonable rate of interest; the types of collateral that may be used to secure a loan; the events constituting default; and the steps that will be taken to preserve assets of the plan in the event of default.

§ 5.12   Reporting Requirements

ERISA § 104 requires employee benefit plans to file annual informational reports with the Department of Labor (DOL). The reports generally require disclosure of financial, actuarial, and other information. Because the Internal Revenue Service (IRS) and the Pension Benefit Guarantee Corporation (PBGC) (in the case of defined-benefit plans insured by that agency) also require annual reporting, a consolidated reporting system called the Form 5500 Series has been developed. The report, when appropriately filed with the IRS, meets the reporting requirements of all three agencies. The IRS forwards a copy of the report to the DOL, as well as to the PBGC, if applicable.

The annual report must be filed by the end of the seventh month follow-ing the close of the plan year. A plan may obtain a 2¹/₂-month extension by filing Form 5558 with the IRS prior to the deadline. In limited circum-stances, if a plan sponsor that is maintaining a plan with a plan year that matches the employer's tax year requests an extension for the corporate tax return, the plan sponsor may be entitled to an automatic 2¹/₂-month extension without filing Form 5558.

Who Files?

The actual filing requirement depends on the number of plan participants. A plan that has 100 or more participants at the beginning of the plan year must file Form 5500. Plans with fewer than 100 participants at the begin-ning of the plan year file Form 5500-C/R, which is substantially simpler than Form 5500. To simplify filing even further for small plans, the com-plete Form 5500-C/R only has to be completed every three years (begin-ning from the first year of operation); for intervening years, only the first two pages of the form must be completed. The complete form also has to be filed for the final year of the plan's operation.

A separate form, Form 5500-EZ, has been designed for plans that cover a small number of participants. Form 5500-EZ is filed by any plan cover-ing a single individual, or an individual and his or her spouse if they are sole owners of a business. Form 5500-EZ is also filed if a plan sponsored by a partnership only covers partners and their spouses, as long as the plan is not aggregated with another plan in order to satisfy the minimum cover-age requirements of Code § 410(b).

In addition to the appropriate form, attachments are required in specific instances. Each of the types of applicable attachments is discussed below:

- Schedule A. If any of the benefits under the plan are provided through insurance contracts, the annual report must include a Schedule A from each carrier involved, indicating: the premium charges, number of per-sons involved, and information regarding who receives commissions and the amount of the commissions.

- Schedule B. Applicable only to defined-benefit plans, this attachment is a report of the actuary regarding the funded status of the plan. Because defined-benefit plans may not contain CODAs, this attachment is not applicable for any of the plans discussed in this book.

- Annual report of the fiduciary. A voluntary filing, but it should be filed because it starts the running of the statute of limitations under Code § 6501.

- Financial statements. For any pension plan, the financial statement must include a statement of assets and liabilities and a statement of changes in net assets available for plan benefits, including revenue, expenses, and other changes.

- Accountant's audit and report. Plans with more than 100 or more participants at the beginning of the plan year must engage an independent public accountant to prepare a report. The primary subject of the report is the accountant's opinion as to whether the financial statements and schedules included in the annual report are presented fairly "in conformity with generally accepted accounting principles applied on a basis consistent with that of the preceding years." An accountant's report is not required when a statement is prepared and certified by a regulated bank or insurance carrier.

- Schedule SSA. This attachment must be included if any plan participant who separated from service in the prior plan year was entitled to a deferred vested benefit (that has not been paid).

Other Reporting Requirements

In addition to the annual report, a copy of the summary plan description (SPD) and the summary annual report (described below) must be filed with the Department of Labor.

§ 5.13 Disclosure Requirements

Annually, participants and beneficiaries receiving benefits under the plan must be furnished a summary annual report (SAR), which summarizes information contained in the annual report (Form Series 5500). The format for a SAR of a pension plan is prescribed by the DOL; a copy of the form that must be used is contained in **Appendix B.** The plan administrator simply fills in the applicable data and deletes any nonapplicable portion of the form.

Each participant covered under the plan, as well as each beneficiary receiving benefits under the plan, must receive a copy of the SAR on or before the last day of the ninth month after the close of the plan year. However, if the IRS has issued a 2½-month extension for filing the annual report, the deadline for distributing the SAR moves to 2 months after the annual report is filed.

In lieu of the standard SAR, a plan that files Form 5500R has several alternative options. The plan may distribute to all participants and beneficiaries receiving benefits either a copy of the Form 5500-R or a written notice stating that a copy of Form 5500-R will be furnished free of charge upon receipt of a written request. If the second option is elected, the notice must contain the name and address of the plan administrator to whom such requests may be directed. The notice may also be posted, in lieu of distribution, as long as copies are delivered to terminated employees and beneficiaries. Under any of the options discussed above, the plan is required to also furnish a standardized statement prescribed by the DOL. A copy of that statement is contained in **Appendix B.**

An additional requirement that applies to SARs is the foreign language requirement, which applies under the following circumstances:

- A plan covers fewer than 100 participants at the beginning of a plan year in which 25 percent or more of all plan participants are literate only in the same non-English language; or
- A plan covers 100 or more participants in which 500 or more participants, or 10 percent or more of all plan participants, whichever is less, are literate only in the same non-English language.

In these circumstances, the plan administrator must provide these participants with an English-language SAR that prominently displays a notice, in the non-English language common to these participants, offering them assistance.

Summary Plan Descriptions

Each participant in the plan, as well as beneficiaries entitled to receive benefits under the plan, must receive a summary plan description (SPD), a booklet that describes the major features of the plan. For new plans, the booklet must be distributed within 120 days after the date when the plan is adopted (or the effective date of the plan, if later). As new employees become participants in the plan, they are required to receive the SPD within 90 days of their entry into the plan. If the plan is amended in any material manner, participants must receive notice of this event through a notice referred to as a summary of material modification (SMM). This SMM must be distributed within 210 days after the close of the plan year in which the amendment was adopted. Finally, the SPD must be revised in its entirety (incorporating the changes described in the SMMs) every 5 years. However, if no amendments have been adopted, the SPD may be revised every 10 years.

The SPD must be written in a manner calculated to be easily understood by the participants. It must be comprehensive enough to apprise participants and beneficiaries of obligations and rights under the plan. The description must attempt to eliminate the use of technical jargon and should use examples to explain difficult concepts. For easy reading, the

SPD should use cross-references to other related sections and begin with a table of contents. The format must not hide or minimize restrictions or limitations under the plan.

Under a special foreign-language requirement, plans that have a substantial number of non-English-speaking participants must display a notice (in the foreign language) offering an opportunity for assistance to learn about the terms of the plan. The notice is required for plans with fewer than 100 participants if 25 percent or more of the participants speak the same (non-English) language. If the plan has 100 or more employees, the foreign-language notice requirement applies if the lesser of 10 percent or 500 participants speak the same (non-English) language.

SPDs for retirement plans are required to include the following information: the name and type of plan involved; the name and address of the employer, the plan administrator, *and* each trustee of the plan. If the plan is sponsored by an employee organization (such as a union), the name and address of the organization is required, as well as the name and address of the most significant contributing employer. A statement must be included indicating that a list of contributing employers is available upon request.

Other required plan information includes: the employer's (tax) identification number (EIN); the plan number; the type of administration used by the plan; the individual who is identified as the agent for service of process; and the plan year.

In addition to these general requirements, DOL Regulation § 2520.102 contains specific plan provisions that have to be discussed in the SPD. The plan's eligibility requirements and normal retirement age must be stated, as well as other conditions that must be met in order to receive benefits. Each of the benefits available under the plan must be summarized. The SPD must include: a description of the joint and survivor annuity provisions of the plan; a description of forfeitures or suspension of benefits; a statement that the plan is or is not insured by the Pension Benefit Guarantee Corporation; a description of how years of service under the plan are determined; a description of the claims procedure under the plan; and a description of the participant's rights under ERISA.

In addition to the DOL Regulations, the SPD must contain a description of what happens if the plan becomes top-heavy or if the plan is amended or terminated. One issue that has been litigated is whether the language of the SPD directly affects the rights of the participants under the plan. This is of concern if the language of the SPD describes benefits differently than the plan document. In at least one instance, a court has determined that the SPD does not affect the terms of the plan, as long as the SPD clearly indicates that the terms of the plan are contained entirely in the plan. Every SPD should include such a disclaimer.

§ 5.14   Administration and Enforcement of ERISA

ERISA's provisions and requirements are enforced by the DOL; the IRS enforces the minimum vesting and participation requirements and levies tax penalties for funding violations or prohibited transactions. Individual participants and beneficiaries may bring suit to enforce their rights under ERISA.

The Act provides criminal penalties for willful violations of the reporting and disclosure requirements. Persons who willfully violate those requirements are subject to a fine of not more than $35,000, or a prison term of up to 1 year, or both. Violations by corporate or union fiduciaries may be subject to a fine of up to $100,000.

Civil actions may be brought by a participant or beneficiary if the plan administrator fails to furnish requested materials on the plan. Civil suits may be brought to recover benefits due under the plan. Participants may collect penalties of up to $100 per day from an administrator who fails to provide, upon request, information to which the participant is entitled. In addition, the participant, as well as the Secretary of Labor, may bring actions to clarify rights to future benefits, to enjoin any violation of the Act or terms of the plan, and to obtain relief from a breach of fiduciary responsibilities.

The federal courts have exclusive jurisdiction over all actions brought under ERISA, except for actions by participants to recover benefits due them, to enforce their rights, or to clarify their rights to future benefits. State courts have concurrent jurisdiction with federal courts over these actions. Participants and beneficiaries are required to exhaust plan procedures and remedies before pursuing legal action. The following sections discuss further the typical causes of action that a participant or beneficiary may bring under ERISA.

§ 5.15   —Breach of Fiduciary Duty

ERISA allows a lawsuit by a participant, beneficiary, or another fiduciary for breach of fiduciary duty. Such suits are intended to protect the entire plan. This kind of lawsuit may be brought, for example, if the fiduciary improperly invests plan assets and the trust incurs losses.

Such a suit can also include nonfiduciaries, if they conspired with the fiduciaries to mismanage the funds in violation of ERISA. Accountants and lawyers who advise fund trustees sometimes get drawn into ERISA actions in this way.

§ 15.16 —Recovering Benefits and Enforcing Rights

Generally speaking, there are three situations in which a participant or beneficiary can bring a lawsuit:

- To try to recover benefits believed to be due under the terms of the plan;
- To enforce rights accorded to participants or beneficiaries under the plan;
- To clarify a right to future benefits under the plan.

A plan participant or beneficiary does not have to wait until an actual loss has been suffered. Such a person can go to court before the loss occurs, seeking a declaration of rights under the plan.

§ 5.17 —Failure of a Plan Administrator to Provide Information

To ensure that participants and beneficiaries are given information necessary to evaluate the benefits available under the plan (ideally, without having to bring suit), ERISA provides an incentive for employers and other plan administrators to comply with the disclosure provisions. The incentive is in the form of a discreet cause of action applicable when an administrator fails to respond to a request from a participant or beneficiary for information about the plan.

An administrator usually has 30 days from receipt of a proper request to mail out a response, or risks incurring a penalty of up to $100 per day. An individual officer or employee of the company can be held individually liable in the capacity of an administrator. The same holds true if an administrator fails or refuses to provide a statement of the individual participant's benefit rights under the plan. Administrators also must provide notice of material modifications of plans.

§ 5.18 —Equitable Relief under ERISA

A participant (or the Department of Labor) may request equitable relief under ERISA. For example, a participant may request a preliminary injunction to stop the plan trustee from continuing a course of action while the action is pending. To get this special relief early in the proceedings, the retiree's lawyer usually must convince the judge at a hearing that:

- The plaintiff-retiree is more likely than not to ultimately prevail in the lawsuit;
- The retiree will suffer greater harm, if the judge denies the preliminary order, than the corporation will suffer, if the injunction is granted;
- The retiree's remedy at law (i.e., getting dollars at the end of the case) won't be a sufficient remedy.

When a judge finds that this is the kind of injury the plaintiff will suffer, an injunction is likely and appropriate.

Participants and beneficiaries are not the only parties who can ask for a court order to preserve their ERISA rights. Other fiduciaries sometimes must, pursuant to their fiduciary duties, go to court to preserve the assets of a plan or to prevent a violation of the plan or of ERISA.

CHAPTER 6

TAX-SHELTERED ANNUITIES

§ 6.1   Overview

Tax-sheltered annuity programs are described in Code § 403(b), which provides special tax treatment for tax-sheltered annuities purchased for employees by public schools and certain tax-exempt organizations. Like that of qualified plans, the tax benefit of a tax-sheltered annuity is that an employee is allowed to postpone paying tax on the employer's contributions toward the annuity (and earnings on such contributions) until receipt of the annuity payment. The entities eligible to sponsor such plans are generally not required to pay federal income taxes, and therefore sponsoring entities do not receive (nor do they need) a tax deduction for premiums paid into the plan.

The term tax-sheltered annuity actually describes a broader range of funding vehicles than simply annuities. These vehicles may include investments in custodial accounts holding mutual fund shares or, in the special case of church plans, investments may be held in "retirement income accounts."

Tax-sheltered annuities are discussed in the context of this book because such programs may contain contributions that are made by a salary reduction agreement between employees and their employer.

§ 6.2   Eligible Sponsors

A Code § 403(b) program can only be sponsored by employers that are exempt from tax under Code § 501(c)(3) or are educational institutions of a state, political subdivision of a state, or agencies or instrumentalities of either of the above.[1] Tax-exempt organizations under Code § 501(c)(3)

---

[1] I.R.C. § 403(b); Treas. Reg. § 1.403(b)-1.

include entities organized and operated exclusively for religious, charitable, scientific, public safety testing, literary, or educational purposes; and entities organized and operated exclusively to encourage national or international amateur sports competition, or prevention of cruelty to children or animals. Such an organization can be a corporation, community chest, fund, or foundation.

A state or local government or any of its agencies or instrumentalities can be a qualified employer, but only with regard to employees who perform (or have performed) service, directly or indirectly, for an educational organization. An Indian tribal government is treated as a state government for this purpose. An educational organization is one that normally maintains a regular faculty and curriculum and normally has a regularly enrolled body of students in attendance at the place where its educational activities are regularly carried on. Government instrumentalities (other than public schools, described already) that are wholly owned state or municipal instrumentalities generally are not qualified employers. However, if the organization is a separate entity that is specifically tax-exempt because it is organized and operated only for the charitable purposes already stated, it is a qualified employer. A separately organized school, college, university, or hospital may qualify if it is not actively under a branch or department of a state or municipal government.

§ 6.3   Employee Status

Contributions to a Code § 403(b) annuity plan can only be made on behalf of individuals who are current, former, or retired employees of an eligible employer. This includes an employee at any level but does not include independent contractors. The determination of whether an individual is self-employed may be difficult, especially in the case of hospital-based physicians. Clergy members are generally considered self-employed for purposes of applying social security taxes, but are considered employees for purposes of Code § 403(b) plan participation.[2] In other cases, as a practical matter, if the employer pays social security taxes, an employee–employer relationship probably exists; if Social Security taxes are not paid, the necessary relationship generally does not exist.

§ 6.4   Funding Vehicles

Funding a Code § 403(b) annuity plan can be done by either purchasing an annuity contract from an insurance company or purchasing shares in a

---

[2] I.R.C. § 1402(c).

mutual fund. Neither the Code nor the Regulations define what type of annuity contracts can be provided. Therefore, contracts with a wide variety of features may be used. Contracts apparently may be single-premium or annual-premium; may provide for fixed or variable annuity payments; may begin immediately or provide deferred payments; and may be written either with or without a refund provision. Annuity contracts may contain "incidental life insurance protection."

Contracts may be individual annuity contracts owned by the employee or group annuity contracts with an insurer, as long as the contracts provide for separate accounts. Individual contracts can have an advantage over other types of plans, in that the accounts are portable to a new employer. The new employer may simply continue contributing to the same contract.

The term annuity contract, for purposes of Code § 403(b), also includes contributions to custodial accounts for the benefit of employees. These contributions are invested in regulated investment company stock, whether or not shares are redeemable. A regulated investment company is an issuer of securities registered with the Securities and Exchange Commission (SEC) under the Investment Company Act of 1940. The custodian must be a "bank," which includes credit unions and other organizations approved by the IRS.

When these types of custodial accounts are used, a special distribution rule applies. Distributions may not be paid or made available to employees prior to the time when the employee dies, attains age 59½, separates from service, becomes disabled, or, in the case of contributions made pursuant to a salary reduction agreement, encounters financial hardship. No clear definition of financial hardship has been identified. A hardship definition satisfying the hardship rules that apply to Code § 401(k) plans (see § 2.17) will most likely meet the requirement.

A third type of investment vehicle, called a retirement income account, may be used when the plan sponsor is a church, or a convention or association of churches, or a related organization principally engaged in the administration or funding of an arrangement providing benefits to employees of a church or convention or association of churches.[3] Retirement income accounts are individual account plans (or an individual account within a defined-benefit plan). Such plans are not subject to any restrictions regarding investments or custodianship.

§ 6.5   Life Insurance Protection

A contract used for funding a Code § 403(b) annuity plan may provide for a life insurance element, as long as the death benefit is "incidental." This

---

[3] I.R.C. § 403(b)(7).

term has essentially the same meaning as in the qualified plan context, described in § **3.21**. Generally, the policy is required to limit the death benefit to the larger of 100 times the projected monthly life annuity or the accumulated reserve. Alternatively, the amount used to pay premiums must, in the case of whole life protection, be less than 50 percent of accumulated employer contributions or, in the case of term insurance, less than 25 percent of accumulated employer contributions.

Providing life insurance protection in a Code § 403(b) annuity plan has the same tax consequences as in a qualified plan. The cost of providing such insurance protection is includable in the participant's income at the time the premium is paid. The amount subject to taxation is the amount of the death benefit minus the cash value of the contract at the end of the year. The amount includable is the cost of the term insurance portion (referred to as the P.S. 58 costs), as described in § **3.22**. The amounts subject to taxation are treated as employee contributions, increasing the employee's investment in the contract and lowering the amount of tax that will be paid upon distribution from the plan (see § **4.06**).

§ 6.6   Nonforfeitable and Nontransferable

An employee's rights under the contract must be "nonforfeitable." In the context of an annuity contract, this has a slightly different meaning than full vesting under a qualified plan with a vesting schedule. Without a trust, the employee's rights under the contract would appear to be nonforfeitable if ownership of the contract is vested solely in him or her. The same would appear to be true if there is some form of joint ownership of the contract, together with an agreement between employer and employee whereby the employee could not be deprived of benefits provided by annuity premiums previously paid, even though the employer could exercise control over the time of enjoyment of those benefits.

As a practical matter, it would appear that ownership ordinarily is vested solely in the employee, thus leaving him or her free of any restrictions or problems that might arise by virtue of insolvency or change of management of the employer. As sole owner of the contract, the employee is free to exercise any of his or her contractual rights—subject, of course, to restrictions on transferability. Thus, where an insurance company product is involved, the employee may be free to elect a reduced paid-up annuity, to exchange the contract for a reduced annuity with an earlier maturity date, to surrender the contract, or to borrow against its cash value from the insurer.

The IRS has indicated that, if a contribution is made by an employer to a Code § 403(b) plan as a result of a mistake of fact, the amount may be returned to the employee without violating the nonforfeitable provision.[4]

The contract also must be nontransferable.[5] This generally means that the contract cannot be assigned, discounted, or pledged as collateral for a loan or as security, or sold to anyone other than the insurance company. However, an assignment can be made to the insurance company as collateral for a loan. Loans from a Code § 403(b) annuity to a participant will not be a prohibited transaction under ERISA, if the loan program meets certain requirements (see **§ 5.11**). A loan will not result in a taxable distribution, if the loan terms and amounts remain within the same limits that apply to qualified plans (see **§ 4.11**).

§ 6.7   Distributions

Under current law, distributions from Code § 403(b) annuity plans must be made in accordance with the minimum distribution rules that apply to qualified plans. However, this rule was recently enacted, and an individual's benefit accrued as of December 31, 1986, is not subject to any specific restrictions on the timing of distributions.[6] This transition rule may not be that meaningful; plans will probably apply the minimum distribution rules on a uniform basis for administrative ease.

The substance of the minimum distribution rules is contained in **§§ 4.1–4.3**. Generally, these rules require payments of preretirement death benefits within a specified period of time, and require that retirement benefits must begin after an individual attains age 70½ and must be distributed over the individual's (and a beneficiary's) life or life expectancy. The incidental death benefit requirements also apply to Code § 403(b) annuity plans.

§ 6.8   Employer Contributions

Employers may use Code § 403(b) plans as a means of providing additional retirement benefits for their employees. Typically, such plans provide contributions as a uniform percentage of compensation; however, some flexibility is available in determining the allocation formula. When employer contributions are made, the nondiscrimination requirements of Code § 401(a)(4) will apply to the amount allocated to such contributions. (These rules are discussed in **§ 3.15**.) The minimum coverage and

---

[4] Gen. Couns. Mem. 38,992 (Sept. 7, 1982).

[5] I.R.C. § 401(g).

[6] P.L. 99-514, § 1852(a)(3)(C).

minimum participation requirements of Code §§ 401(a)(26) and 410(b) applicable to Code § 403(b) plans also mean that, if the plan has employer contributions, a broad number of employees have to be included in the plan (see **§§ 3.5–3.14** for a complete discussion of these subjects).

In some cases, additional employer contributions are made as matching contributions based on employee elections to deter compensation. If this is the case, the matching contributions must meet the nondiscrimination requirements of the Code § 401(m) test (discussed in **§ 2.19**).

§ 6.9   Parity with Qualified Plans

Beginning in 1989, many of the requirements that apply to qualified retirement plans apply to annuity plans as well. These are discussed in depth in **Chapter 3**; the requirements and cross-references are identified as follows:

* Nondiscrimination requirements in contributions and benefits of Code §§ 401(a)(4) and (5) (see **§ 3.15**);
* Minimum coverage requirements of Code § 410(b) (see **§§ 3.5–3.15**);
* Minimum participation rules of Code § 401(a)(26) (see **§ 3.14**);
* Nondiscrimination test on employer matching and employee after-tax contributions under Code § 401(m) (see **§ 2.19**);
* Survivor benefit requirements of Code §§ 401(a)(9) and 417 (see **§ 3.23**).

§ 6.10   Coverage under ERISA

A Code § 403(b) plan also is an employee pension plan subject to the requirements of ERISA, as described in **Chapter 5**. Coverage under ERISA generally requires that the plan be in writing; that employees be given a summary plan description (SPD) and other information; and that the plan file annual reports. ERISA coverage also means that individuals will be held to be fiduciaries, and will be held to a higher standard of care when dealing with the plan. The requirements of a plan covered under ERISA are discussed in depth in **Chapter 5**.

Some types of Code § 403(b) plans are exempted from the ERISA requirements. These include government plans and certain plans that are entirely funded with employee elections to defer income. More specifically, to meet the exemption, the plan must satisfy *all* of the following Code § 403(b) exemption requirements:[7]

---

[7] Labor Reg. § 2510.3-2.

1. Participation in the plan must be completely voluntary.

2. Rights under either the annuity or mutual fund account must be enforceable solely by the employee, or his or her authorized representative or beneficiary.

3. The employer must not receive consideration or compensation other than reasonable compensation to cover administrative expenses.

4. The employer may be involved in the plan only to the extent of the following activities:

   a. To permit vendors to publicize their products to employees;

   b. To request information concerning proposed funding media, products, and sponsors;

   c. To summarize or make comparisons among proposed products and services, to facilitate employee review;

   d. To collect and remit contributions as required by salary reduction agreements;

   e. To limit funding media or products available to employees, or to limit sponsors in such a manner that employees are given a reasonable choice;

   f. To hold, in the name of the employer, group annuity contracts covering its employees.

   g. To limit the number of products from which employees can choose, as long as the number and selection are designed to afford employees a reasonable choice in light of all relevant circumstances.

For purposes of item 4.g. above, the factors considered include, but are not necessarily limited to, the following: the number of employees affected; the number of contractors who have indicated interest in approaching employees; the variety of available products; the terms of the available arrangements; the administrative burdens and cost to the employer; and the possible interference with employees' performance as a result of direct solicitation by contractors.

A second important exclusion applies to government plans. A government plan is a program established and maintained by the federal or a state government or an agency, instrumentality, or political subdivision thereof. This definition will include public educational institutions. Looking at the government plan exception and the exception applying to plans paid for with elective salary deferrals, a substantial number of Code § 403(b) plans are exempt from the requirements of ERISA.

§ 6.11   Employee Elections to Defer Salary

Tax-sheltered annuity contracts must be purchased by an eligible employer, which means that the employer must pay the premiums. However, the premiums paid by the employer may either constitute additional compensation for the employee or may be indirectly paid by the employer as a reduction in salary. Amounts contributed under salary reduction are excludable from gross income (for federal tax purposes), subject to three separate limitations:

1. The employee's deferral amount cannot exceed $9,500 (see **§ 6.12**);
2. The limitation cannot exceed the employees' "exclusion allowance" (see **§ 6.13**);
3. The contribution cannot exceed the Code § 415 limits.

The agreement to defer salary must be legally binding and irrevocable, for amounts earned while the agreement is in effect. An individual cannot make more than one agreement with the same employer during a tax year. The exclusion will not apply to contributions under any further agreement made with the same employer during the same tax year. However, an individual can end the agreement for amounts not yet earned. A continuing salary reduction agreement entered into in an earlier tax year does not prevent the individual from entering into a new salary reduction agreement at any time during the current tax year.

Although the mathematical testing that applies to Code § 401(k) plans and SEPs does not apply to Code § 403(b) annuity plans, certain requirements do apply to elective deferrals. If one employee has the option to defer salary under a plan, all employees (regardless of age or service) of the employer must have the right to make salary deferrals on the same basis, unless such employees are covered under a Code § 457 plan, a Code § 401(k) plan, or another Code § 403(b) annuity plan.[8] In addition, the employer may not require a minimum contribution level, except that a de minimis contribution of $200 may be required.

When a plan (funded with annuity contracts) contains a salary deferral feature, contributions attributable to deferral election must be subject to special withdrawal provisions. Such amounts may not be distributed until the employee attains age 59½, separates from service, dies, becomes disabled, or becomes a hardship case. As discussed above, when the plan is funded with mutual fund shares, the special distribution requirements apply to all contribution amounts. The special distribution requirements do

---

[8] I.R.C. § 403(b)(12).

not prohibit an employer from making a distribution to a former spouse, pursuant to a qualified domestic relations order (QDRO) (see § **3.03**).

§ 6.12   —Maximum Deferral Limit

An individual covered by a single Code § 403(b) annuity plan may elect to defer up to $9,500 each tax year (almost always the calendar year). The limit will be increased for inflation, in the same manner as the $7,000 limit applicable to Code § 401(k) plans ($8,728 limit for 1992), when that limit exceeds $9,500. The limitation applies in the aggregate to all elective deferrals made under Code § 403(b) annuity plans, SEPs, and Code § 401(k) plans. For example, an individual deferring $4,000 in a Code § 403(b) plan will be able to defer a maximum of $5,500 under a Code § 401(k) arrangement.

A special "catchup" election allows certain older, long-service employees the opportunity to save amounts above the $9,500 limit at a time when they may be more financially capable of saving for retirement. Eligible for the catchup election are those individuals who have completed at least 15 years of service with an educational organization, hospital, home health service agency, health and welfare service agency, church, or convention or association of churches (or associated organization). The $9,500 limit is increased for such eligible individuals by the smallest of the following amounts:

- $3,000;
- $15,000, reduced by increases to the $9,500 limit the individual was allowed during earlier years because of this rule;
- $5,000 times the number of years of service for the organization, minus the total elective deferrals made under the plan for the individual during earlier years.

Tax Treatment of Excess Deferrals

If the total deferral amount is more than the limit for the year, the excess must be included in gross income for the year in which the contribution was made. The excess will be taxed a second time (at the time the amount is distributed from the plan), if the excess amount is not corrected through distribution by April 15th of the following year. A plan may, but is not required to, allow such distributions. If only one plan is involved and it permits such distributions, the individual must notify the plan by March 1, after the end of the tax year in which an excess was deferred. The plan must then pay out the excess, along with any income on that amount, by April 15. If more than one plan is involved, an individual may have the excess paid out of any of the plans that permit distributions, subject to the same time deadlines. The 10 percent early distribution excise tax does not apply to such corrective distributions.

Even if the individual takes out the excess, the amount still counts as having been contributed for satisfying or not satisfying the requirements the plan must meet regarding not discriminating in favor of highly compensated employees.

§ 6.13   —Exclusion Allowance

For contributions to be excludable from income at the time they are made, the contributions may not exceed the "exclusion allowance." The amount excludable is 20 percent of an employee's "includable compensation" times the number of years of service with the employer minus excludable contributions made for the employee by the employer in prior years. **Table 6–1** gives a step-by-step approach to determining the exclusion allowance.

Includable Compensation

The term includable compensation is the salary from the employer that is includable in gross income earned for the "most recent period"—the period that constitutes a full year of service. However, the period cannot end later than the close of the taxable year for which the exclusion allowance is being determined. For a full-time employee working a complete year, the most recent period is simply the compensation earned during the taxable year. However, the "most recent period" is more complex when the employee works part-time, because part-time service is credited for only a

Table 6–1

Exclusion Allowance Calculation

1. 20%	20%
2. Includable compensation for most recent period of service	
3. Years of service	
4. Line 1 × line 2 × line 3	
5. Minus amounts previously excludable	
6. Exclusion allowance (before reduction for any excess contributions)	

fraction of a year. Such fractional years are added together to create a full year. For example, if an individual works half-time for two consecutive tax years, compensation earned during the 2-year period is added together. The most recent period of service will include more than one tax year if the individual is a full-time employee who worked only part of the current year but worked in prior tax years.

Because includable compensation only includes gross income, amounts subject to salary reduction used to purchase the annuity on behalf of the employee are not treated as "includable compensation." This has an impact on the basic 20 percent limit because the limit is on the reduced compensation. For example, assume an individual has no previous years of service and no prior exclusions. The maximum contribution (salary reduction) that this individual can make is 20 percent × (gross salary less elective contributions to the plan). Expressed in mathematical terms, assuming x = contributions:

$$x = .2 \text{ (compensation } - x)$$

Solving for x:

$$x = .2 \text{ compensation } - .2x$$
$$1.2x = .2 \text{ compensation}$$
$$x = .2/1.2 \text{ compensation}$$
$$x = .166$$

In this instance, x (employee salary deferral contributions) cannot exceed 16.6 percent of gross compensation.

Years of Service

The individual's years of service are the total number of years the individual worked for the specific employer sponsoring the plan, determined as of the end of the tax year for which the exclusion allowance is being determined. Years of service include full years of full-time service as well as fractional years for full-time service for a portion of the year, and fractional years for part-time service. In no case will the number of years of service be less than 1.

The past service credit, which is incorporated in the exclusion allowance formula, in effect makes available to the employee the unused portions of exclusion allowances for previous years. Moreover, the credit is based on the assumption that the employee was earning his or her present salary in each of the previous years. Thus, the exclusion allowance of a long-time employee may greatly exceed 20 percent of his or her current compensation. This past service allowance may be prorated over future years of service if a level annual premium is desired. The following formula may be used to determine the maximum salary reduction for a level contribution under the regular exclusion allowance:

$$\text{Maximum level premium} = \frac{SY - 5(B + AF = QN)}{Y + 5F}$$

Where

  $S =$ current includable compensation before reduction of the proposed annuity but after salary reduction for qualified plan, state teachers' retirement system, or Code § 457 deferred compensation plan;

  $Y =$ total number of years of service from initial employment date to retirement;

  $B =$ sum of (1) employer contributions excluded from taxable income in previous years for an annuity and/or qualified pension plan, (2) excludable contributions to a Code § 457 deferred compensation plan by any employer in any previous tax year counted as a year of service, and (3) in tax years beginning after January 24, 1980, contributions in excess of the Code § 415 overall limits made in prior tax years beginning after January 24, 1980;

  $A =$ excludable employer contributions for a tax-sheltered annuity previously started and to be continued;

  $F =$ current year plus future years in which tax-sheltered annuity premium is to be paid;

  $Q =$ excludable employer contributions for a qualified pension plan or Code § 457 deferred compensation plan previously started and to be continued;

  $N =$ number of annual excludable contributions (Q) to be made, but not including any contribution to be made in the final year tax-sheltered annuity premium is to be paid.

The formula is based on the assumption that, as to contributions to plans other than tax-sheltered annuities, only contributions made in prior years reduce the exclusion allowance.

§ 6.14   —Code § 415 Limitations

The Code § 415 limitations that apply to qualified defined-contribution plans, discussed in § **3.19**, also apply to Code § 403(b) annuity plans. The annual amount that can be credited to a participant's account, including employer contributions, employee contributions, and forfeitures cannot exceed the lesser of 25 percent of the employee's compensation from the employer or $30,000.

To conform with the cumulative nature of the exclusion allowance applicable to Code § 403(b) annuity plans, several special rules under Code § 415 apply only to Code § 403(b) annuity plans. In a Code § 403(b) plan, a participant has the opportunity to elect from several alternative limitations. These are identified as follows:

1. An employee may elect not to have the 25 percent limit apply in the year he or she terminates employment. If this election is made, the exclusion allowance takes into account only 10 percent ending on the date of termination.

2. An employee may elect to replace the 25 percent limit for any year with the least of (a) $4,000 plus 25 percent of the includable compensation under Code § 403(b), (b) the exclusion allowance for the year, or (c) $15,000.

3. An employee may elect to have the exclusion from gross income for any year measured by the contribution limitation under Code § 415 instead of the exclusion allowance under Code § 403(b). This election changes the manner in which the Code § 403(b) annuity plan is aggregated with other plans.

4. An employee may elect to replace the Code § 415 limitation for a year with a limit of $10,000 until contributions subject to the election total $40,000.

Elections made under alternatives 1, 2, or 3 are irrevocable. An election under alternative 1, 2, or 3 precludes an individual from making an election under one of the other alternatives. An employee who elects alternative 1 may make such an election only once, and may not elect alternative 4 for the same year. These elections are not available to all employees who are eligible for tax-deferred annuities (TDAs). Alternatives 1, 2, and 3 are only available for employees of hospitals, health and welfare service agencies, educational organizations, home health service agencies, and certain church organizations. Alternative 4 is only available to employees of certain church organizations.

CHAPTER 7

SIMPLIFIED EMPLOYEE PENSIONS

§ 7.1 Overview

Another type of plan that may maintain employee elections to defer income on a tax-preferred basis is a simplified employee pension (SEP) plan.[1] As its name implies, this type of plan is simpler than a qualified retirement plan. The documentation, reporting, and disclosure requirements are less cumbersome than for a qualified plan. Another substantial difference is that the plan is not funded with a commingled trust fund for participants, but with individual retirement arrangements (usually referred to as IRAs). On the other hand, some SEP requirements are not any less burdensome than the requirements under a qualified plan. Unfortunately, this is especially true for a SEP containing a pretax salary reduction feature. The salary reduction nondiscrimination requirements under a SEP are just as burdensome as under a qualified plan; annual nondiscrimination testing (similar to the requirements described in **Chapter 2**) must be performed.

Because contributions under a SEP are made to IRAs, each of the "qualification requirements" applicable to IRAs is applicable to a SEP. These requirements are discussed fully herein. Generally, individual retirement arrangements are established by individuals as a method of saving for retirement on a tax-preferential basis. An individual may make annual contributions of up to $2,000. The entire contribution is deductible, unless the individual participates in an employer-sponsored qualified retirement plan, SEP, or Code § 403(b) plan, in which case the deduction may be limited or unavailable. Some individuals may also contribute to a plan on behalf of their spouse. Earnings in such plans are not taxed until distributed. There are two types of individual retirement arrangements: individual retirement accounts and individual retirement annuities. Both of these vehicles have

---

[1] I.R.C. § 408(k).

to meet a number of specific qualification requirements in order for an individual to receive the tax advantages described above.

In the case of a SEP, the employer makes the contributions on behalf of the participant, either as an additional benefit or under a pretax salary deferral election. The $2,000 annual contribution limit that normally applies to an individual establishing an IRA does not apply to either type of employer contribution. Such contributions are limited by the deduction limitations for employer contributions contained in Code § 404. The maximum deductible contribution is 15 percent of compensation. In addition to the employer contributions, the employee treats the employer-established IRA as if he or she had established the IRA, and makes additional contributions in the amount of $2,000 annually. As a participant in a SEP, the employer contributions may limit or eliminate the employee's opportunity to take a deduction for the contribution to the IRA.

Generally, a SEP is somewhat less burdensome to establish and maintain than a qualified plan. However, in exchange for simplicity, the rules allow for substantially less flexibility in the design of the plan. The plan has to meet rigid vesting, coverage, nondiscrimination, contribution, and withdrawal requirements. The specific requirements of establishing a SEP are discussed below.

§ 7.2   Individual Retirement Arrangements

The IRA must be established by a written instrument, under which all contributions must be in cash. When established by an individual, the contributions may not exceed $2,000 for any tax year, except as to certain qualifying rollover contributions. No assets of the account may be invested in insurance contracts. The individual's interest in his or her account balance must be nonforfeitable. The account's assets are not to be commingled with other property except in a common trust or investment fund with other IRA accounts or qualified plan assets. The trust must be created or established for the exclusive benefit of an individual or his or her beneficiaries. Assets of the account must be distributed as required under the minimum distribution requirements that also apply to qualified plans (see **§§ 4.1–4.3**).

An individual retirement account must be a trust or custodial account established in the United States for the exclusive benefit of the owner and beneficiaries. The trustee or custodian must be a bank, federally insured credit union, or "other person who demonstrates to the satisfaction of the Secretary [of the Treasury] that the manner in which such other person will administer the trust will be consistent with the requirements of Code § 408. An acceptable trustee may not be an individual, but can be a partnership or corporation that demonstrates that it has fiduciary ability, capacity to account for the interests of a large number of persons, fitness to handle retirement funds, ability to administer fiduciary powers, and adequate net worth.[2]

The written agreement requirement may be satisfied by completing IRS Form 5305 (for a trust agreement) or Form 5305-A (for a custodianship). Or, an individual may use a prototype agreement that has been approved by the IRS. If either of these documents is used, an individual is assured that contributions qualify as IRA contributions. A nonapproved instrument that meets all the qualification requirements is also acceptable; however, it is generally not advisable. Most IRA trustees and custodians have approved documents available.

§ 7.3   Individual Retirement Annuities

An individual retirement annuity is an annuity contract issued by an insurance company. The contract may not be transferable by the owner. Annual premiums may not be fixed and cannot exceed $2,000 for any individual; the aggregate premiums paid under all such contracts may not exceed $2,000 (unless purchased by the employer under a SEP). Refunds of any premiums for any year must be used by the end of the following calendar year for the payment of future premiums. Unlike an individual retirement account, the contract does not have to be held in trust.

Other rules are essentially similar to an individual retirement account. The individual's interest in his or her annuity must be nonforfeitable and the minimum distribution rules apply to such amounts. The contract has to be for the exclusive benefit of the purchaser and/or beneficiaries.

§ 7.4   Employer-Sponsored Individual Retirement Account

A separate funding arrangement that can qualify as an individual retirement arrangement is an employer or employee association sponsored trust that contains individual participant accounts.[3] The arrangement has essentially the same requirements as an individual retirement account (§ **7.2** above), except that the trust, in the case of an employer sponsor, must be for the exclusive benefit of the employees, and, in the case of a plan sponsored by an employee association, for the exclusive benefit of members or their beneficiaries.

Such an arrangement can operate in essentially the same manner as an individually sponsored arrangement, with the individual electing the

---

[2] Treas. Reg. § 1.408-2(b)(2).

[3] I.R.C. § 408(c).

amount of contributions (up to the lesser of earned income or $2,000). The sponsor simply acts as the administrator of the plan. These trusts may also act as the funding vehicle under a SEP. In this case, the employer must meet the requirements discussed below.

§ 7.5 SEP Qualification Requirements

SEPs are subject to a very different set of participation requirements than qualified retirement plans. The rules require that the employer make contributions for employees who have (1) attained age 21, (2) performed services for the employer for at least 3 of the immediately preceding 5 years, and (3) received a minimum of $300 (adjusted for cost-of-living increases; $374 for 1992) in compensation from the employer during the year. Compensation for these purposes is within the meaning of Code § 414(q)(7) from the employer.

The term employer includes all entities that must be aggregated under the controlled group and the affiliated service group rules (see **§ 3.11** for a complete discussion of these requirements). The term employee includes all employees, including leased employees, of the employer except for (1) union employees whose employee benefits have been the subject of good-faith collective bargaining, and (2) nonresident aliens with no U.S. income.

As stated above, individuals are eligible if they earn more than the minimum amount of compensation within the plan year. This means the plan may not exclude any employees who are not employed on the last day of the plan year (or mandate any other employment requirement). Employees cannot be required to meet any specific number-of-hours-of-employment requirement, in order to be included as participants.

A SEP may not discriminate in favor of highly compensated employees (HCEs; defined in **§ 2.11**). In general, a SEP is discriminatory unless it provides that contributions bear a uniform relationship to total compensation (or earned income, for a self-employed person). The IRS has ruled that where an employer contributes a stated amount per hour for each employee, the nondiscrimination test is satisfied.[4] The contribution percentage may vary annually. In other words, an employer may determine the amount of the contribution annually (as in a discretionary profit-sharing plan), as long as the contribution is allocated in a manner that allows each participant to receive a uniform percentage of salary. The allocation formula must be a definite written formula that specifies the manner in

---

[4] Priv. Ltr. Rul. 8824019.

which the allocation is computed and the requirements necessary for the participants to share in the allocation.[5]

Nevertheless, the employer may integrate its contribution with social security in the manner that is allowed for qualified defined-contribution plans (see **§ 3.16**). However, elective salary reduction contributions cannot be integrated with social security benefits. The uniform-relationship-to-compensation requirement does not apply to salary reduction amounts. Whether these amounts are considered nondiscriminatory is based solely on the special nondiscrimination requirements described below.

The term compensation is defined in Code § 414(s). As in the qualified plan rules, compensation is limited to the first $200,000 (increased for cost-of-living adjustments; $228,860 in 1992) of the employee's compensation.

SEPs differ substantially from qualified plans in that they may not place limitations on employee distributions from a plan. The plan may not condition employer contributions on the requirement that an employee not withdraw such contributions. Neither may the employer prohibit such withdrawals.

Because SEPs are funded with IRAs, the nonforfeitability requirements applying to IRAs apply to SEPs.

If a SEP is top-heavy (key employees hold more than 60 percent of the aggregate account balances allocated to all employees), then the employer must contribute to the IRA of nonkey employees the lesser of (1) 3 percent of compensation, or (2) the highest percentage of compensation contributed to a key employee's IRA. The top-heavy provisions apply in the same manner as to qualified plans, as discussed in depth in **§ 3.24**.

§ 7.6   Maximum Deductible Contribution

Employer contributions to a SEP are deductible, subject to the following limitations. Under the rules limiting deductions, a SEP can apparently be established only for either the calendar year or the sponsor's fiscal year. If the plan is on the calendar-year basis, a deduction may be taken for the tax year ending with or within the calendar year, as long as contributions are made by the due date of the tax return for the tax year to which the contribution relates (including extensions).[6] The maximum deductible contribution is 15 percent of compensation. If the plan is a calendar-year plan, compensation is measured taking into consideration compensation earned

---

[5] Prop. Treas. Reg. § 1.408-7.

[6] I.R.C. § 404(h)(1).

during the calendar year. If the plan is on a fiscal-year basis, then compensation is measured based on the fiscal plan year.

In the event that the employer's contribution exceeds the permitted deduction, the excess is carried over to succeeding taxable years in order of time, and remains subject to the 15 percent deduction limitation in such succeeding years. Nondeductible contributions are subject to the 10 percent excise tax described in § **3.19**.

Allocations to participants under a SEP are subject to the Code § 415 limits. A SEP is treated as a defined contribution plan for purposes of Code § 415. Therefore, the primary limit is that contributions to an employee's account may not exceed the lesser of $30,000 or 25 percent of compensation. (See § **3.18** for a complete discussion of the maximum contribution and benefit limitations contained in Code § 415.)

§ 7.7   —Salary Reduction SEPs

An employer may provide a salary reduction feature, in which participants may elect to defer current income, which is contributed to an IRA on a pretax basis. The rules governing such arrangements are very similar to the rules contained in Code § 401(k). Salary reduction amounts are subject to the same maximum dollar limitation ($8,728 in 1992) and a nondiscrimination test. As with Code § 401(k) contributions, employees' elective deferrals are characterized as employer contributions. State and local governments, and tax-exempt organizations, may not establish salary reduction SEPs.[7]

To qualify as a salary reduction SEP, the following requirements must be met:

1.   The employer must have fewer than 25 employees eligible to participate during the plan year;

2.   Not less than 50 percent of the eligible employees must elect to defer salary;

3.   The employer must comply with the nondiscrimination testing described below.[8]

The deferral percentage for each highly compensated employee may not exceed 125 percent of the average deferral percentage for all employees eligible to participate. The deferral percentage is the ratio of elective contributions to employee compensation (up to $200,000). In the event that

---

[7] I.R.C. § 408(k)(6)(E).

[8] I.R.C. § 408(k)(6)(A)(ii), (B), and (F).

the deferral percentage exceeds the amount generally applicable to excess contributions, the rules under Code § 401(k) apply.

Under Code § 401(k) (8), to correct excess contributions, such contributions (and income allocable to such contributions) must be distributed to the employee no later than the close of the tax year following the year of contribution.

If the employer does not distribute the excess contributions with $2\frac{1}{2}$ months after the end of the tax year, Code § 4979 imposes a 10 percent excise tax on the employer.

Code § 408(k) is silent on whether the Code § 72(t) 10 percent excise tax applies to excess contributions in this context. The legislative history indicates that, until the IRS issues Regulations to indicate otherwise, the excise tax will apply.

§ 7.8   ERISA Requirements

A SEP arrangement is an employee pension benefit plan and therefore is subject to the provisions of ERISA described in **Chapter 5**. However, simplified reporting and disclosure requirements apply if certain requirements are met.

The simplified reporting requirements can be met if the employer uses, as the written instrument, IRS Form 5305-SEP. The form must be completed without modifications. The modified reporting and disclosure requirements are as follows:

1.   At the time an individual becomes eligible to participate in a SEP, the sponsor must give the participant a copy of the completed contribution agreement, the general information and guidelines, and the questions and answers (see **Appendix C** for a sample Form 5305);

2.   Following the end of the calendar year, the administrator must notify each participant of the amount of contribution made to his or her IRA for the year;

3.   Participants must be notified of any restrictions regarding the choice of IRA or other restrictions or limitations under the plan.[9]

If other documents are used, a SEP can still meet the reporting and disclosure requirements if the plan meets specific disclosure requirements described in the Regulations.[10] Generally, the requirements are that the plan

---

[9] Labor Reg. § 2520.104-48.
[10] Labor Reg. § 2520.104-29.

administrator provide to all participants an explanation of the specific provisions of the SEP, as well as notification of any amendments to the plan. The administrator must also provide to participants additional general information about IRAs and SEPs (similar to the information contained in the questions and answers and general information in **Appendix C**).

If a plan complies with one of these alternative compliance measures, none of the other required reporting and disclosure requirements under ERISA must be satisfied. The requirements include filing Form 5500 annually distributing summary plan descriptions, and distributing summary annual reports.

CHAPTER 8

NONQUALIFIED DEFERRED COMPENSATION

§ 8.1 Nonqualified Deferred Compensation

This chapter primarily addresses employee elections to defer compensation under what are referred to as nonqualified plans. These salary reduction programs, like other plans discussed in this book, are methods of employee savings. Like the other plans, the programs are primarily driven by the hypothesis that more savings will occur if tax is deferred until later.

A second type of nonqualified deferred compensation provides employer-paid supplemental compensation to participants on a deferred basis. Such supplemental plans, referred to as SERPs, can be designed to meet a number of objectives, such as rewarding excellence, encouraging long-term employment, or encouraging excellence through incentive arrangements. Such plans can provide additional income after a stated time period, upon termination of employment, upon death or disability, or, as in the case of "golden parachutes," upon a change in ownership. The two approaches can be combined: employee savings can be encouraged by providing matching contributions.

Employee elective deferred compensation can be provided through tax-qualified retirement plans containing a CODA arrangement or through nonqualified arrangements. Both qualified and nonqualified plans are generally established with the intent of attracting and retaining talented employees.

From the viewpoint of both the employer and the employees, tax-qualified plans offer certain advantages over nonqualified arrangements. Because contributions to a qualified plan are deductible at the time the contribution is made, the employer receives a deduction at the time the employee elective deferrals are contributed to the plan, regardless of when participants actually receive benefits. In a nonqualified plan, the employer's deduction generally does not occur until the employee actually receives the deferred income. Under both qualified and nonqualified arrangements, the employee is generally taxed at the time benefits are

171

received from the plan, and therefore the tax benefits are the same from the employee's perspective. However, benefits are not as secure in a non-qualified plan. In a qualified plan, the amounts subject to elective deferral by the employee are contributed to an irrevocable trust that must be used for the exclusive benefit of the participants. In a nonqualified plan, the benefits are often paid out of general corporate assets, or out of a trust, known as a rabbi trust. Both are subject to creditors.

However, qualified plans have significant limitations, especially when the company's goal is specifically to reward and retain executives. The qualified plan rules[1] generally require broad-based participation and a similar level of benefits for all participants. Participants have to be immediately "vested" in any elective deferrals or after-tax contributions, and employer-provided benefits must be vested within a specified number of years. Benefits must be distributed within prescribed time periods. The maximum amount of benefits provided by such plans is limited to the extent that the benefits may be considered insufficient to provide adequate retirement benefits for management personnel.[2] Contributions have to be held in trust, to be used solely for the provision of benefits, and not for company use.

§ 8.2 —Objectives of Deferred Compensation

Nonqualified deferred compensation plans are designed to meet a broad range of objectives. One of the most common objectives is to shift income to a year in which an executive's marginal tax bracket is lower, because of either retirement or a bunching of compensation attributable to a large bonus payment. With this objective in mind, some plans are designed to allow participants to make elective deferrals. However, the reduced tax rates of the Tax Reform Act of 1986 (TRA 86), combined with the expectation that rates will increase in the future, may decrease interest in the benefits of deferring compensation.

Another goal is to encourage long-term employment. This can be accomplished by requiring some period of future service before the benefits will

---

[1] Tax rules pertaining to qualified plans are contained generally in I.R.C. §§ 401 through 417.

[2] For plan years beginning in 1991, the maximum annual benefit for any employee from all defined-benefit plans of the employer, expressed as a life annuity and beginning at social security retirement age, is $108,000. I.R.C. § 415(b). The maximum annual addition, which includes all employer contributions, forfeitures, and employee contributions, for any plan year, in all defined-contribution plans of an employer, is $30,000. I.R.C. § 415(c). Combined plan limits also apply if an employee participates in both defined-contribution and defined-benefit plans. I.R.C. § 415(e).

be considered "nonforfeitable" or "vested." Plans with vesting requirements are often referred to as "golden handcuffs" because they offer an
incentive only if employment is continuous. Deferred compensation plans
can be designed to yield retirement benefits that supplement those provided
under the employer's qualified plan. These types of plans have become
more common since the tax law changes in the mid-1980s, which lowered
the maximum benefits and contributions to plans,[3] provided new limitations on the maximum amount of compensation that can be considered for
determining benefits under a plan,[4] and added excise taxes on large benefits received from plans.[5]

Deferred compensation arrangements can also be used to enhance the
incentive for retirement for a certain group of individuals, or to soften the
blow of certain forced retirements. (Note that such arrangements are subject to the limitations of the Age Discrimination in Employment Act and
ERISA Title I.) Deferred compensation can also be used to reward performance by structuring the plan to pay only when certain performance
targets have been met. For example, the plan can be structured around stock
performance, such as in phantom stock plans or stock appreciation rights.

Deferred compensation can also be used to restore lost benefits to an
executive who has lost benefits from previous employment.

As discussed in **§ 6.15**, deferred compensation can also be used to protect management personnel in the event of a "hostile takeover" of the employer. These types of arrangements are commonly referred to as "golden
parachutes."

Both ERISA and federal income tax laws have an impact on the design
and administration of a nonqualified deferred compensation plan. The following sections describe these rules.

§ 8.3   Coverage under ERISA

As discussed above, the decision to establish a nonqualified plan of deferred compensation is often based on the sponsor's unwillingness to meet
the coverage, vesting, and funding requirements contained in Code §§ 401–
417. Because ERISA contains similar coverage, vesting, and funding requirements, plans designed to avoid the tax requirements for qualified plans
will also aim to avoid coverage under Title I of ERISA. This design

---

[3] Maximum benefit limits are discussed in note 2 *supra*. Effective generally on January
1, 1987, the maximum elective, pretax deferral that an employee can make is limited
to $7,000, with increases for inflation ($8,475 for 1991).

[4] I.R.C. § 401(a)17.

[5] I.R.C. § 4980.

requires careful planning; the coverage provisions of ERISA are broad and the exceptions to the coverage provisions are narrow. Following are the general coverage rules as they apply to nonqualified deferred compensation, and the applicable exceptions.

Title I of ERISA generally applies to all plans or programs maintained by an employer that provide for either retirement income to employees or deferral of income by employees for periods extending to the termination of covered employment or beyond.[6] This general rule appears to apply to most plans of deferred compensation.

However, one complete and several partial exemptions from Title I of ERISA may apply to nonqualified deferred compensation plans. Plans of deferred compensation that are completely exempt from Title I are unfunded "excess benefit plans."[7] Excess benefit plans are plans maintained by an employer solely for the purpose of providing benefits in excess of the limits on contributions and benefits imposed by Code § 415.[8]

Under Code § 415, a defined benefit pension plan may pay an annual benefit, beginning at the individual's social security retirement age, in the amount of the lesser of 100 percent of the high 3 years of average compensation, or $108,963 (for plan years beginning in 1991, and increased annually for cost-of-living increases). The maximum dollar limitation is reduced for less than 10 years of service with the employer. The maximum annual addition to all defined contribution plans under Code § 415 is the lesser of 25 percent of compensation or $30,000.

An excess benefit plan can be designed to provide benefits in excess of either limit, and therefore may resemble either a defined-benefit or defined-contribution plan. However, to qualify for the exemption, an excess benefit plan may not provide benefits in excess of other benefit limitations, such as the $200,000 cap on compensation considered under the plan.[9] Excess benefit plans do not have to limit participation to any particular group of participants in order to be eligible for the exemption.

To meet the requirements of the exemption, the excess benefit plan must be unfunded. Whether a plan is deemed to be funded or not can at times be a difficult question. (This issue is discussed at length below.) ERISA provides for a partial exemption for funded excess benefit plans. Funded excess benefit plans are subject to the reporting and disclosure requirements, fiduciary responsibility rules, and ERISA enforcement provisions, but are exempt from ERISA's participation, vesting, and funding rules.[10]

---

[6] ERISA § 3(2)(A)(i), 29 U.S.C.A. 1002(2)(A) (West Supp. 1991).

[7] ERISA § 3(36), 29 U.S.C.A. § 1002(36) (West Supp. 1991).

[8] *Id.*

[9] I.R.C. 401(a)(17).

[10] ERISA §§ 101(a); 201(7); 301(a)(9); 29 U.S.C.A. §§ 1003, 1051(7), 1081(a)(9) (West 1985 & West Supp. 1991).

This partial exemption is still quite meaningful, because a funded excess benefit plan will not be required to cover a broad base of the employee population.

Another partial exemption is for "top-hat" plans. Such plans are subject to the ERISA reporting requirements and enforcement provisions. Top-hat plans are exempt from the participation, vesting, funding, and fiduciary requirements. A top-hat plan is unfunded and is maintained by an employer "primarily for the purpose of providing deferred compensation for a select group of management or highly compensated employees . . . ."[11]

Unfortunately, no Regulations have been issued by the Department of Labor (DOL) to clarify exactly who, or how many employees, can constitute a "select group of management or highly compensated employees" under this definition. The DOL will not issue a ruling on this issue, determining instead that it involves a question of fact rather than law.[12] However, a recent DOL Advisory Opinion provides some indication of the DOL's current thinking on this issue. The DOL stated that the top-hat exemption of ERISA was enacted in recognition that certain individuals, by virtue of their position or compensation level, have the ability to control or effectively negotiate their deferred compensation and, therefore, do not need the protection of ERISA.[13] Apparently, the DOL's current focus is on the employees' "ability to influence" rather than the amount of an individual's compensation or title. The Advisory Opinion also indicates that the DOL rejects the view that the term primarily in the statute means that the plan may cover some employees other than management or highly compensated employees. The DOL's current position seems to be that this term simply modifies the type of benefits that may be provided under the plan.

Without further regulatory guidance, a plan sponsor may have difficulty determining exactly which employees may be covered under a top-hat plan. Until such guidance is issued, it may be prudent for deferred compensation plans to provide that, if subsequent Regulations indicate that a plan participant is not a qualified participant, such individual will be cashed out of the plan prior to the effective date of such Regulations.

The top-hat exemption only applies to an unfunded top-hat plan. In addition, as previously discussed, a funded excess benefit plan is only eligible for a partial ERISA exemption. The term unfunded is not defined in ERISA. The Conference Report to ERISA, alluding to the

---

[11] ERISA §§ 201(2), 301(a)(3), 401(a)(1), 29 U.S.C.A. §§ 1002(2)(A), 1051(2), 1081(a)(3), 1101(a)(1) (West 1985 and West Supp. 1991).

[12] ERISA Proc. 76-1, 41 Fed. Reg. 36,281 (Aug. 27, 1976).

[13] DOL Advisory Op. Ltr. 90-14A (May 8, 1990).

Table 8–1

Deferred Compensation Plans—ERISA Requirements

	Unfunded Excess Benefit Plan	Funded Excess Benefit Plan	Unfunded Top-Hat Plan
Participation	N/A	N/A	N/A
Vesting	N/A	N/A	N/A
Funding	N/A	N/A	N/A
Fiduciary	N/A	Yes	N/A
Enforcement	N/A	Yes	Yes
Reporting and disclosure	N/A	Yes	Notice only

top-hat exemption, cites a "phantom stock" or "shadow stock" plan as an example of an unfunded plan.[14]

The DOL, in Proposed Regulations issued in 1979, implied in its definition of plan assets that general assets of an employer may be considered plan assets when the employer has indicated to plan participants that such assets would be used only to pay plan benefits.[15] However, such language was dropped from the final plan asset Regulations, which were silent on the issue.[16] In a recent DOL Advisory Opinion, the DOL indicated that any determination of the "funded" status of a plan would be based on surrounding facts and circumstances, including the funded status of the arrangement under relevant non-ERISA law. Under the Internal Revenue Code, whether or not a plan is deemed to be "funded" has tax implications, which are discussed in § **8.4.** The DOL Advisory Opinion recognizes that how the issue is resolved under the Internal Revenue Code will be given substantial weight.[17] Until such time as DOL Regulations are issued, the only clear guidance on the issue is found in the relevant tax rules, which are discussed in depth in § **8.4.**

Table 8–1 summarizes the ERISA requirements for deferred compensation plans that have partial or complete exemptions from ERISA.

---

[14] H.R. Rep. No. 93-1280, 93rd Cong., 2d Sess. 2099 (1974).

[15] Prop. Labor Reg. §§ 2550.401b-1(a) (2) and (3) (Aug. 28, 1979; *amended* June 6, 1980; *withdrawn* January 2, 1985). *See also* Labor Reg. § 464.1 promulgated under Section 13 of Welfare and Pension Plans Disclosure Act of 1958.

[16] Labor Reg. § 2550.401b 1, 51 Fed. Reg. 41261 (Nov. 13, 1986).

[17] DOL Advisory Op. Ltr. 90-14A (May 8, 1990).

§ 8.4   Taxation to the Employee

When an employee earns, and is paid, cash compensation from an employer for services performed, the amount paid is taxable under Code § 61. When the employee is promised cash to be payable at a later date, the timing of taxation to the employee can be quite complex. Several basic tax principles apply in determining the time when taxation occurs.

To understand the taxation of deferred compensation, consider the example of an employer who makes a simple contractual promise to pay $5,000 in cash to the firm's president at the time of the president's termination of employment. Ordinarily, when the employee is a cash-basis taxpayer and the employer is not tax-exempt, an unsecured promise to pay an employee compensation at some later date does not result in taxable income to the employee until compensation is actually paid.[18] However, accelerated taxation can occur under several different theories. The employer-sponsor and/or the employer's tax adviser need to have a clear understanding of these rules, to ensure that the design of the plan meets the intended objectives. The various theories that can result in accelerated taxation include the constructive receipt doctrine, the economic benefit doctrine, and the application of Code §§ 83 and 402(b). Where the employer is a governmental entity or a nonprofit entity, Code § 457 could create immediate tax concerns. This provision is discussed separately in § 4.10.

§ 8.5   —Constructive Receipt

The first theory, the constructive receipt doctrine, began as common law but has now been codified in Code § 451 and the Regulations thereunder. Under Code § 451, a cash-basis taxpayer must generally recognize income when it is received. Under the Regulations, amounts are considered paid or made available to the employee without a substantial risk of forfeiture, even though the amounts have not been reduced to the participant's possession, if the amounts have been constructively received. Constructive receipt occurs in the taxable year during which it is credited to the employee's account, set apart for the employee, or otherwise made available so that the employee may draw it at any time, or could have drawn on it during the taxable year if notice of intention to withdraw had been given. However, income is not constructively received if the taxpayer's control of its receipt is subject to substantial limitations or restrictions.

---

[18] Rev. Rul. 60-31, 1960-1 C.B. 174, *modified by* Rev. Rul. 64-279, 1964-2 C.B. 121 and Rev. Rul. 70-435, 1970-2 C.B. 100.

The Internal Revenue Service's additional guidance on what types of substantial limitations or restrictions preclude constructive receipt includes the following: no constructive receipt results when interest income is credited on time deposit certificates that could be withdrawn only with penalties;[19] no constructive receipt results when an employee's right to surrender an annuity contract was subject to significant penalties.[20]

Constructive receipt problems can exist if distribution options under the plan are not carefully designed. For example, if the plan allows a participant at the time of retirement to choose between an installment option or a lump-sum benefit, a participant electing installment payments may be subject to taxation on the entire benefit owed at the time the election is made under the constructive receipt doctrine. This mistake is surprisingly easy to make because nonqualified plans are often designed to mirror provisions contained in the company's qualified plan. Qualified plans may offer such distribution options because they are not subject to the constructive receipt doctrine.

The constructive receipt doctrine should not result in taxation at the time contributions are "set aside" in a "rabbi trust" or "secular trust," as long as the benefits are subject to substantial limitations on the participant's right to receive the benefits (e.g., the benefits are not payable until termination of employment).

§ 8.6   —Economic Benefit

The economic benefit doctrine is similar but theoretically distinct from constructive receipt. Under the economic benefit doctrine, the creation by the obligor (employer) of a fund in which the taxpayer (employee) has vested rights will result in immediate inclusion by the taxpayer in the amount funded. A fund is created when an amount is irrevocably placed with a third party, and a taxpayer's interest in such fund is "vested" if it is nonforfeitable.[21]

The rationale underlying this theory relates to the irrevocable nature of the transfer of the funds, rather than the employee's ability to control the timing of the actual receipt of the benefits.[22] The economic benefit doctrine does not apply where the amounts involved are subject to the rights

---

[19] Rev. Rul. 80-157, 1980-1 C.B. 186.

[20] Rev. Rul. 68-482, 1968-2 C.B. 186.

[21] Gen. Couns. Mem. 39,230 (Jan. 20, 1984).

[22] *See* Sproull v. Commissioner, 16 T.C. 244 (1951), *aff'd per curiam,* 194 F.2d 541 (6th Cir. 1952); Frost v. Commissioner, 52 T.C. 89 (1969); Goldsmith v. United States, 586 F.2d 810 (1978); Jacuzzi v. Commissioner, 61 T.C. 262 (1973).

of the employer's creditors, such as in a rabbi trust, because no "fund" is created.[23]

However, in a secular trust, where a plan's assets can only be used to provide benefits to the participants, the economic benefit theory would result in taxation at the time the participant became vested in his or her benefit under the plan.

§ 8.7   —Other Statutory Provisions

Code § 83 represents, to some extent, a codification of the economic benefit doctrine in employment-related situations. The economic benefit doctrine is set forth in Code § 83 and Regulations § 1.83-3. Under Code § 83(a), if property is transferred in connection with the performance of services to any person other than the person for whom such services are performed, the difference between the market value of such property and the amount paid for such property shall be included in the gross income of the person who performed such services. Under Code § 83(a), the date for determining the "transfer," which fixes the date for calculating the market value, as well as determining the year in which the transferred amount will be included in gross income, is the date when the recipient receives the "economic benefit" of the property. This occurs ". . . at the first time the rights of the person having the beneficial interest in such property are transferable or are not subject to a substantial risk of forfeiture, whichever occurs earlier."

The Regulations further define these terms. The term property includes all real and personal property except money or an unfunded and unsecured promise to pay money in the future. However, the term also includes a beneficial interest in assets (including money) that are transferred or set aside from the claims of creditors—for example, contributed to a trust or escrow account.[24]

A substantial risk of forfeiture occurs when rights to transferred property are conditioned on future performance, or refrain from performance, of substantial services by any person, and the condition has not been satisfied. The determination is fact-specific and is made on a case-by-case basis.[25] An example of a condition based on refraining from performance of services is conformance with a noncompete clause.

The rights of a person in property are transferable if such person can transfer any interest in the property to any other person but only if the

---

[23] Casale v. Commissioner, 247 F.2d 440 (2nd Cir. 1957).

[24] Treas. Reg. § 1.83-3(e).

[25] Treas. Reg. § 1.83-3(c)(1).

rights of the transferee in the property are not subject to a substantial risk of forfeiture. Merely designating a beneficiary to receive property upon a person's death is not considered to constitute transferability.[26]

Code § 83 does not apply to contributions to the trust of a qualified plan.[27] It also should not apply to contributions made to a rabbi trust, if the funds remain subject to the claims of the employer's creditors.

The final rule that has to be examined with regard to nonqualified plans is Code § 402(b), which provides that contributions to a nonqualified employee's trust made by an employer shall be taxed to the employee in the manner provided under Code § 83, except that when measuring the value to be taxed, the "market value" is substituted with the "employee's interest in the trust."

Under these rules, amounts that are contributed to a secular trust, for the exclusive benefit of the participants, will result in taxable income to an employee in the year when the employee becomes vested in the benefits.

§ 8.8   —Employee Elections to Defer Income

Sections **8.4, 8.5**, and **8.6** addressed the general principles of taxation of deferred compensation plans. This section discusses how these tax principles apply when a nonqualified deferred compensation plan (of any type) allows for employees to elect to defer income that they could otherwise receive currently.

Employees' elections to defer income create concerns under the constructive receipt doctrine. A Private Letter Ruling can be requested to ensure that such a program does not create current income. Certain guidelines have been issued, in which minimum requirements for such elective deferral arrangements have been outlined. First, the election must be made before the beginning of the period for which the compensation is payable and before the compensation is earned.[28] Exceptions are generally made for new plans and newly eligible employees. The IRS will ordinarily allow employees to be afforded 30 days after the plan's effective date within which to elect to defer amounts earned after election.[29] Newly hired or newly eligible employees will often be permitted to elect, within 30 days after being hired or becoming eligible, to defer compensation earned after the election.[30]

---

[26] Treas. Reg. § 1.83-3(d).

[27] Treas. Reg. § 1.83-8(a).

[28] Rev. Proc. 71-19, 1971-1 C.B. 698.

[29] *See* Priv. Ltr. Rul. 8421063 (Feb. 21, 1984), 8418070 (Jan. 30, 1984), 8321051 (Feb. 18, 1983).

[30] *See* Priv. Ltr. Rul. 8637085 (June 16, 1986), 8602039 (Oct. 15, 1985), 8421063 (Feb. 21, 1984).

Second, subsequent elections, such as to elect the time or form of payment, may create a taxable event, unless the substantial forfeiture provisions remain in effect throughout the entire deferral period.[31] For example, if employees have the option, at the time they elect installment payments, to elect installment payments or a lump sum, and begin to receive such installments, the entire amount will be included in income at the time of the election. To avoid this problem, the plan should be designed so that any required elections are made at the time of deferral. However, some plans have received approval when they contained a hardship provision, as long as such withdrawals have been expressly limited to the amount necessary to meet the hardship need.[32]

§ 8.9   —Tax Consequences for the Employer

Code § 404(a)(5) establishes a "matching rule" under which an employer's deduction for nonqualified deferred compensation is deferred until the "amount attributable to the employer's contribution" is includable in the employee's gross income.[33]

The employer will be entitled to deduct its contributions to a rabbi trust only to the extent that the amounts are taxable to the participants. Moreover, a deduction is only allowed under a plan that benefits more than one executive, if a separate account is maintained for each executive.[34] The amount of the employer's deduction should be the entire amount included in the executive's income, not just the amount the employer contributed to the rabbi trust (i.e., the principal amount of the contribution, disregarding any income earned thereon). This result should occur because the original contribution was not a transfer of property to which Code § 402(b) or Code § 83 applies, so there never was a contribution to the trust.

Under a secular trust, the executive is taxed immediately on his or her benefit under the plan. This results in the employer's being able to deduct its contributions to the secular trust immediately, at least if a separate account is maintained for each executive.[35]

---

[31] Rev. Proc. 71-19, *supra* note 28.

[32] *See* Priv. Ltr. Rul. 8845007 (Aug. 11, 1988), 8746023 (Aug. 14, 1987); 8732005 (Apr. 29, 1987); Rev. Rul. 55-424, 1955-1 C.B. 42.

[33] Treas. Reg. § 1.404(a)-12.

[34] I.R.C. § 404(a)(5); Treas. Reg. § 1.4019(a)-13(b).

[35] I.R.C. § 404(a)(5).

§ 8.10   Special Tax Rules for Plans of Government and Tax-Exempt Entities

As discussed in § **8.3** above, nonqualified deferred compensation generally results in a deferral of income to the participant, as well as a deferral of the employer's tax deduction. Presumably, the deferral of the employer's deduction creates somewhat of a disincentive to provide inordinate amounts of deferred compensation. Conversely, tax-exempt employers not concerned with deductions would not have such a disincentive, and hypothetically would be more willing to agree to provide large sums of deferred compensation.

Out of this concern, Congress, in the Tax Reform Act of 1978, enacted Code § 457, which effectively limited the amount of compensation that could be deferred without incurring immediate taxation for certain tax-exempt employers. These provisions have been subsequently modified several times, and currently apply to nonqualified deferred compensation plans of state or local governments as well as organizations exempt from federal tax under Code § 501.[36] For this purpose, state or local government includes states, political subdivisions of a state, or any agency or instrumentality of either of them. Many types of nongovernmental organizations are exempt from tax under Code § 501. Many are nonprofit organizations established to provide services to their members or to meet some public or charitable purpose. However, churches, as defined in Code § 3121(w)(3)(A), are exempt from the rules of Code § 457.

Under Code § 457, a plan of deferred compensation, other than qualified plans under Code § 401 or annuity plans under Code § 403(b), sponsored by tax-exempt or governmental entities, may result in taxation at the time when deferred compensation is promised, except when amounts are deferred in an "eligible deferred compensation plan." If the deferred compensation plan does not qualify as an eligible plan, compensation deferred under the plan is included in the gross income of the participant or beneficiary in the first taxable year in which there is no substantial risk of forfeiture of the rights to such compensation.[37] Compensation is subject to a substantial risk of forfeiture if future service is required to secure rights to such compensation.[38]

---

[36] Generally effective for plans of tax-exempt organizations for taxable years beginning after December 31, 1986. In some cases, deferral agreements subsequent to this date are also exempt from I.R.C. § 457, if such later deferral elections were subject to an agreement in effect as of August 16, 1986, and such elections met several additional requirements. Tax Reform Act of 1986 § 1107(c)(3)(B).

[37] I.R.C. § 457(f)(1).

[38] I.R.C. § 457(f)(3)(B).

The taxation rules of Code § 457 seem to be the exclusive method for calculating the timing of taxable income to participants for plans sponsored by governmental and tax-exempt entities, except when the transaction results in a transfer of property under Code § 83 or contributions are made to a trust subject to the tax rules of Code § 402(b). Certain plans are not subject to the taxation rules of Code § 457. Bona fide vacation leave, sick leave, compensatory time, severance pay, disability pay, or death benefit plans are treated as plans not providing for the deferral of compensation.

If the rules and limitations of Code § 457 are met, meaning that the plan constitutes an "eligible plan of deferred compensation," amounts of compensation deferred under the plan, and any income attributable to the amount so deferred, are included in gross income for the taxable year in which the compensation or other income is paid or otherwise made available to the participant or to a beneficiary.[39]

A plan is an eligible deferred compensation plan if it is established and maintained by an eligible employer, as described above, and if the plan meets requirements relating to (1) who participates in the plan, (2) the maximum annual deferral allowed, (3) the timing of deferral agreements, (4) the timing of distributions, and (5) property rights.

The plan may cover as participants only those individuals who perform service for the employer, including independent contractors.[40] In the case of tax-exempt employers, participation must be limited to a select group of management or highly compensated executives.

The maximum amount that may be deferred under the plan for a given taxable year is the lesser of $7,500 or 33.3 percent of the participant's includable compensation.[41] However, a plan may allow for an increased "catch-up" limit during any of the 3 years prior to attainment of normal retirement age under the plan. The higher limit for those years is the lesser of $15,000 or the sum of the regular ceiling of $7,500 and the amount of the regular ceiling unused from prior taxable years.[42]

In addition, each individual is limited to a maximum aggregate deferral in all eligible plans, in the amount of $7,500 each taxable year.[43] In calculating the aggregate limit, amounts excluded from gross income under a tax-sheltered annuity program under Code § 403(b), and any amount that is excluded from gross income as an elective deferral under a qualified cash or deferred arrangement under Code § 402(a)(8) or a simplified employee

---

[39] I.R.C. § 457(a); Treas. Reg. § 1.457-1(a)(1).

[40] I.R.C. § 457(b)(1).

[41] I.R.C. § 457(b)(3).

[42] *Id.*

[43] I.R.C. 457(c)(1).

pension for the taxable year[44] are counted. The amounts included under a Code § 403(b) program include both elective deferred compensation and nonelective deferred compensation,[45] in cases where the Code § 457 plan is sponsored by the same employer who sponsored the Code § 457 plan.[46]

Under an eligible plan, amounts may be deferred for any calendar month, but only if an agreement to defer has been entered into before the beginning of the month. An exception is made for new employees who begin employment during the month and who enter the deferral agreement prior to the first day of employment.

The plan cannot provide for making amounts available prior to the calendar year in which the participant attains age 70½, separates from service, or is faced with "an unforeseeable emergency." Certain minimum distribution rules must be satisfied, particularly the minimum distribution rules of Code § 401(a)(9) for qualified plans (see §§ **4.1–4.3**). In addition, when distributions begin during the life of the participant, (1) amounts must begin in accordance with the times determined under Code § 401(a)(9)(G), (2) amounts payable over a period of more than one year can only be made in nonincreasing annual amounts, and (3) payments after the participant's death must be distributed at least as rapidly as the method in effect on the date of the participant's death. When distributions begin after the death of the participant, the entire amount must be paid within 15 years or, if the surviving spouse is the participant's beneficiary, the life expectancy of the surviving spouse.

Finally, an eligible plan must provide that all amounts deferred, and the income on the amounts deferred, remain property of the employer who sponsors the plan, subject to the claims of its general creditors.

§ 8.11   Securing the Promise

In some cases, the employer simply makes a promise to pay executive deferred compensation, without setting aside any funds. In the past, the employer would sometimes purchase insurance contracts or annuities to make the payment; however, to avoid current taxation to the participant, the employer had to be both owner and beneficiary of the contracts.[47] This meant that the participant in the plan would have no more right to those assets than to any other asset of the employer. In addition, the use of annuity contracts has become less attractive, in light of Code § 72(u), which taxes

---

[44] I.R.C. 457(c)(2).

[45] IRS Notice 87-13, Q & A 26.

[46] Treas. Reg. § 1.457-2(e)(1).

[47] Rev. Rul. 68-99, 1968-1 C.B. 193.

income on an annuity contract held by anyone other than a natural person as income to the contract owner.

Along with the increase of hostile takeovers has been an increased interest in securing the promise to pay deferred compensation. This trend may be further accelerated if, in the 1990s, nonqualified deferred compensation becomes the primary source of retirement benefits to executives. Several methods of securing the promise exist, and each has its own set of tax considerations, as introduced briefly above.

§ 8.12 —Surety Bonds

Another way for an employee to ensure receipt of deferred compensation is to obtain a third party that will guarantee payment of such deferred compensation if the employer defaults on the promise. It may be possible for the employee to purchase a surety bond from an insurance company, or, similarly, purchase a letter of credit, to guarantee payment upon default. This method is limited in its usefulness by the employee's ability to obtain such a bond at a reasonable price. This will be most difficult in the circumstances when the employee needs the most protection, that is, when the employer is in bad financial circumstances.

The Internal Revenue Service issued a Private Letter Ruling in 1984 indicating that such a guarantee would not result in constructive receipt of deferred compensation or the conferral of an economic benefit requiring immediate taxation to the employee. The arrangement that was approved was the purchase of a surety bond by an employee, which ran for a period of years and was renewable.[48] However, the IRS, out of concern about surety bonds and related similar arrangements, has suspended rulings on such matters. Based on the limitations in the marketplace on the availability of surety bonds, the uncertainty of the tax consequences of such arrangements, and the required cash outlay by the employee, such arrangements are very limited as a method for an employee to ensure receipt of promised deferred compensation.

§ 8.13 —Rabbi Trusts

One common vehicle is known as the "rabbi trust." This funding vehicle is generally an irrevocable grantor trust established by an employer to hold assets supporting deferred compensation obligations by the employer.

---

[48] Priv. Ltr. Rul. 8406012.

Assets held by the trust can be used only to pay the promised deferred compensation, except that assets may be "invaded" by creditors.

A properly constructed rabbi trust has the advantages of providing security to the participants that their benefits will be paid, without resulting in taxation to the participants at the time contributions are made to the trust. As discussed in the taxation section above, because rabbi trust assets are subject to claims of creditors, the Internal Revenue Service has determined that an "economic benefit" has not been conferred on the participants nor does the "constructive receipt" doctrine apply to such contributions. Therefore, the employee generally does not receive taxable income until the time when amounts are distributed from the trust. The employer is not entitled to receive a deduction for such contributions, and will only recieve a deduction at the time when benefits are distributed to participants. The deduction should reflect amounts attributable to both employer contributions and trust earnings. In addition, the employer is generally taxed on the income of the rabbi trust, prior to distribution, to the extent that it would have been taxed had it directly held the assets owned by the trust.

The Internal Revenue Service will issue Private Letter Rulings on whether the terms of a particular trust will result in current or deferred taxation to participants. In fact, the only way to be certain that the terms of a particular rabbi trust will not result in current taxation to participants is to obtain a Private Letter Ruling. However, rulings over the years have indicated certain guidelines that must be met in order to achieve tax deferral. These guidelines include the following.

Generally, the rulings allow a rabbi trust to put restrictions on when creditors can look to trust assets to satisfy claims. The rulings have allowed the rabbi trust to restrict claims by creditors to cases where the employer is insolvent. To protect the rights of creditors, the rulings have required the employer to notify the trustee of insolvency; benefits must be suspended at the time of insolvency. Trusts also must contain spendthrift provisions, requiring that benefits earned under the plan are not anticipated, alienated, sold, transferred, assigned, pledged, encumbered, garnished, attached, or subject to any charge or legal process. Finally, Private Letter Rulings are caveated, indicating that the ruling is not determinative on the issue of whether the trust results in the plan's being considered funded under Title I of ERISA.

Private Letter Rulings have also approved several features to rabbi trust agreements that an employer may wish to consider beneficial to participants. Several rulings have approved rabbi trusts that contain hardship withdrawal provisions.[49] In one case, the IRS specifically stated that "(a)

---

[49] Priv. Ltr. Rul. 8843045 (Aug. 3, 1988), 8844020 (Aug. 5, 1988).

participant's right to request a distribution from his or her account because of financial hardship [would] not cause the deferred amount to be includable" in the participant's gross income currently.[50] Recent Private Letter Rulings have approved a rabbi trust used in connection with a plan allowing participants to direct the investment of rabbi trust assets attributable to their account.[51]

§ 8.14   —Secular Trusts

Under a rabbi trust, the employee is not protected in the case of the employer's insolvency. If that risk is not acceptable to the employee, the employer may elect to maintain a plan of deferred compensation in which benefits are funded through contributions to an irrevocable trust. This type of funding arrangement provides the maximum protection to the participant; however, it has several limitations.

The major limitation is that such arrangements result in taxable income to the employee in the amount of the employee's interest in such a trust in the year in which employee's rights in the trust assets are no longer subject to a substantial risk of forfeiture.[52] Generally, the employer will be entitled to a deduction in the same amount for the same year.[53] A second limitation is that a plan funded with a secular trust will generally be deemed to be a funded plan under ERISA. Unless the plan is an excess plan, the plan will have to satisfy the minimum funding, coverage, and vesting requirements of ERISA. Regardless of these limitations, the tax changes of the Tax Reform Act of 1986 (TRA 86) have made the use of secular trusts more attractive. Prior to TRA 86, funding with a rabbi trust was the preferred method, because it avoided taxation to the employee until distribution of benefits. This desired tax result was based on several assumptions. First, at that time, the corporate income tax rate was generally lower than the individual tax rate, and therefore it was advantageous to keep the funds in the corporation subject to a lower tax rate. Another assumption was that the executive would be in a lower income tax bracket than currently, when he or she received the benefits (after retirement). Finally, the assumption was made that income tax rates would remain constant (or decrease).

---

[50] Priv. Ltr. Rul. 8952037 (Sept. 29, 1989).

[51] Priv. Ltr. Rul. 8952037 (Sept. 29, 1989), 8834015 (May 25, 1988), 8804023 (Oct. 30, 1987).

[52] I.R.C. 402(b); Treas. Reg. § 1.402(b)-1.

[53] I.R.C. § 404(a)(5); Treas. Reg. § 1.404(a)-12.

However, TRA 86 has changed the tax rules dramatically. First, the corporate income tax rate is 34 percent, which is higher than the individual tax rate of 28 percent, eliminating the effectiveness of retaining assets in the corporation. Second, many executives will be in the same 28 percent tax bracket at the time of retirement as they are currently. Third, many tax practitioners believe that it is inevitable that the income tax rates will rise, resulting in higher, now lower, taxes in the future. For these reasons, it may be more tax-effective (in the long run) for the amounts to be taxed to the executive currently.

If this is the case, the question remains: Why not simply pay more current compensation and let the executives fend for themselves? The choice is really up to the company, based on the needs and attitudes of its executives. The choice to establish the secular trust in lieu of current compensation may be based on a paternal concern for employees, a belief that the joint investment will result in a better return, a perception of employees as valuing the deferred compensation more than current compensation, or any other applicable reason.

PART III

PLAN DESIGN

CHAPTER 9

GENERAL DESIGN CONSIDERATIONS

§ 9.1 Introduction

The preceding Parts of this book have identified the various types of employee savings plans and the legal requirements that govern their existence. To one or more of these plans, an employee may contribute portions of annual salary in order to: defer current federal income taxes until the contribution is actually received, enjoy the benefits of the contributions' tax-free growth, and accumulate assets for retirement. The discussion in this chapter turns to plan design in general, which encompasses the consideration of those factors that influence an employer's decision to adopt an employee savings plan—specifically, to adopt a plan under Code § 401(k) ("401(k) plan") or Code § 403(b) ("403(b) annuity plan"); a salary reduction simplified employee pension (SEP); or a nonqualified pension plan. **Chapters 10** through **13** each discuss one of the four types of employee savings plans and the factors influencing the respective designs. **Part IV** (**Chapters 14** through **17**) will cover the topic of employee savings plan administration.

§ 9.2 Factors Influencing Adoption of an Employee Savings Plan

The fact of life confronting most people is that, as one reaches the recognized retirement years, roughly ages 55 to 70, the mental desire, the physical ability, and the employment opportunities to generate income through the sale of one's services to meet the cost of living all diminish. An obvious question arises: Where will these individuals obtain income to replace the income no longer earned through active employment? Fortunately, we are all the beneficiaries of scientific and technological advances that enable us to live longer; unfortunately, this longevity adds to the urgency of

191

finding a solution to the need for income generation in lengthening retirement years.

Three sources usually provide retirement income:

1. Benefits available under federal laws such as the Social Security Act; employers/self-employed and employed individuals contribute to a fund that is administered by the federal government;
2. Assets a person accumulates;
3. Benefits provided through employer-sponsored retirement plans.

This chapter is not intended to be an exhaustive discussion of the socioeconomic factors that have driven employers to assume the responsibility of meeting retired persons' income needs, but it may be observed that many employers have assumed such a responsibility, probably because of a combination of the following factors working together:

- Employees who have organized into collective bargaining units have negotiated retirement benefits, thereby establishing a standard compensation package for other organized and nonorganized employees in the employer's industry of geographic location.
- Federal tax laws have encouraged employers to adopt qualified retirement plans. Employers are permitted to immediately deduct against income their contributions to qualified retirement plans. Certain distributions from qualified retirement plans are eligible for favorable tax treatment. Accumulation of larger amounts has generally been permitted through an employer-sponsored qualified retirement plan (in contrast to the individual retirement account).
- Employers who offer retirement benefits may look more attractive to potential employees who are considering multiple employment opportunities. The benefit may also aid in retaining employees.
- When employers not only communicate but promote sponsorship of a plan to their employees and, through that promotion, tie the plan's existence to worker productivity, the retirement benefit can be used to reward employees for good service, thus adding to the overall success of the enterprise.

Employers initially assumed the responsibility of providing retirement benefits through the sponsorship of qualified defined-benefit pension plans that permitted them to accumulate assets on a favorable tax basis. The defined-benefit pension plan promises to provide its participants with a definitive and determinable benefit at retirement. The employer funds the defined-benefit plan based on actuarial computations of the amount of funding needed over the employee's career to provide the promised benefit at retirement. For example, such a plan may promise to pay, at a participant's normal retirement, a benefit equal to 1 percent of pay for each year of service, where pay is defined as the participant's average compensation during the entire period of employment by the plan sponsor or the period of participation in the plan.

A defined-benefit pension plan can be complex, expensive to administer, and difficult to communicate. The complexity arises from a number of fronts. Benefit costs and funding requirements may only be determined actuarially. Pension expense must be reported pursuant to the requirements of the Financial Accounting Standards Board's Statement of Financial Accounting Standards No. 87, "Employers Accounting for Pensions." Title IV of ERISA has created a statutory structure for ensuring certain levels of benefits promised by defined-benefit pension plans. Each employer must pay its allocated share of premiums to the Pension Benefit Guaranty Corporation (PBGC) to ensure not only its own employees' benefits, but those of every other employee who participates in a similarly covered defined-benefit pension plan. Proposed Regulations under Code § 401(a)(4) and provisions under Code § 412 have tightened the qualification requirements relating to what are permissible nondiscriminatory benefits and the funding of those benefits.

The costs of administering the defined-benefit pension plan are potentially the highest of any kind of retirement plan, in that the services of an actuary are required to assist the employer in the calculation of benefits and funding requirements and nondiscrimination rules pursuant to the requirements of the Code and ERISA.

Defined-benefit pension plans have also been criticized as being difficult to communicate to employees and not well appreciated by employees, who often do not spend their entire careers with a single employer. The focus of these employees is "How much am I entitled to today?" rather than "What am I promised when retirement age is reached?"

These factors have combined to influence employers to adopt alternative types of retirement plans of a defined-contribution nature: the services of an actuary are not required, and benefits are represented by the amount standing to the individual account of each participant. Defined-contribution plans include profit sharing, money purchase, or one or more of the employee savings plans discussed herein.

Employee savings plans are generally thought to have significant advantages over any other retirement plan alternative. Of these advantages, cost effectiveness is first on the list. Each employee savings plan is characterized by the employee's redirecting part of his or her compensation to the plan. No longer is the employer assuming the full burden of providing employees' retirement income. In contrast to the defined-benefit pension plan, the employer is freed from the complexities of benefit accounting, actuarial assumptions, and the insurance provisions of Title IV of ERISA that do not apply to defined-contribution plans. The cost to administer the plan is lower, in contrast to the defined-benefit pension plan. Although consulting services may be necessary to keep track of account balances and undertake discrimination testing in the context of the 401(k) plan and the salary reduction SEP, such costs should be less than the cost to retain an actuary to perform the actuarial functions associated with a defined-benefit type plan.

The employer should perceive the employee, now a partner in the business of accumulating retirement income, as taking a more active interest in understanding the retirement plan. In contrast to a promise of a retirement benefit under a defined-benefit type plan, the employee's benefit in an employee savings plan is represented by an account balance, which is easier for the employee to understand.

Employees are further attracted to employee savings plans because, under certain conditions, they afford accessibility to plan assets prior to retirement, albeit at a high federal tax cost.

An employee savings plan may also encourage participation by permitting employees to direct the investment of all or part of their account balances. The possible advantage to this approach is that it may afford a method under which the risk of potential fiduciary responsibility in the management of plan assets may be reduced. In early 1991, the Department of Labor (DOL) reissued Proposed Regulations under ERISA § 404(c) which, if properly followed, could result in reduced fiduciary liability with respect to those plan assets invested by an employee.[1] An opportunity for flexibility is also created. Each employee can develop his or her own investment strategy, in contrast to the defined-benefit plan (its primary concern is the promise, and then the investment) or other defined-contribution plans that do not offer participant direction of investment (the plan assets are invested without regard to individual investment considerations).

The flexibility of employee savings plans is further seen in each employee's ability to set a rate of contribution, subject to the annual contribution limits and the limits placed on the deferral rates of highly compensated employees. In contrast to the typical profit-sharing plan, where an employer contributes a straight percentage of compensation on behalf of all participants, the employer could increase compensation and let the employee decide what amount to defer to the employee savings plan.

---

[1] 54 Fed. Reg. 30520 (1991) (to be codified at 29 C.F.R. § 2550.404e-1, proposed Feb. 26, 1991).

In summary, employee savings plans provide, on their own, a good program to meet the objective of accumulating income for retirement years. These plans also are useful tools in conjunction with the more traditional defined-benefit pension plans once principally and traditionally offered to employees by their employers.

§ 9.3   —General Overview of Factors Influencing a Specific Plan

An employer who is considering the adoption of a specific employee savings plan is influenced by the legal requirements that apply to the respective types of plans; the characteristics, needs, and benefits philosophy of the business; and the economic environment in which the business operates. Working together, these factors influence the decision-making process to mold the type and terms of the particular employer-sponsored employee savings plan that the employer adopts.

§ 9.4   Legal Requirements: Influence on Plan Design

The previous chapters of this book have revealed that each type of employee savings plan must comply with the numerous requirements of the Internal Revenue Code and ERISA, in order to deliver its intended benefits. In a specific setting, one or more of these requirements may affect an employer's decision concerning whether to adopt an employee savings plan, what type to adopt, and/or what the terms will be. This section discusses the more significant legal requirements and their impact.

§ 9.5   —Specific Code Authorization Necessary for Adoption

Federal tax law specifically delineates which types of employers may adopt specific types of employee savings plans. An explanation of the various types of employers will be useful in this regard. Employers are distinguished by two characteristics, the first being the legal form of the employer. The principal legal forms include: sole proprietorship, partnership, corporation (for-profit and nonprofit), and governments (states, local municipalities, or subdivisions, instrumentalities, or agencies thereof). The second characteristic is whether the legal form is a non-tax-exempt or tax-exempt entity for federal income tax purposes.

A 401(k) plan may only be sponsored by a non-tax-exempt entity that is a sole proprietorship, a partnership, or a for-profit corporation. A 401(k) plan will not be treated as a qualified cash or deferred arrangement, if made a part of a plan maintained by a state or local government, or a political subdivision, agency, or instrumentality thereof, or by any organization that is exempt from federal income tax.

A 403(b) annuity plan may only be sponsored for an employee by two types of employers. The first type of employer is that described in Code § 501(c)(3); this type is exempt from tax under Code § 501(a). Employers of this type include the most common forms of tax-exempt entity—a corporation, community chest, fund, or foundation that is both organized and operated exclusively for religious, charitable, scientific, testing (for public safety), literacy, or educational purposes; for the prevention of cruelty to children or animals; or for promotion of amateur sports competition. The second type of employer, described in Code § 170(b)(1)(A)(ii), is a state or political subdivision, agency, or instrumentality thereof, which sponsors plans for employees who perform services for an educational organization. In general, these employers are public schools and state colleges and universities. A 403(b) annuity plan may not be sponsored by any other government whose employees are not performing services for an educational organization as described above or by a non-tax-exempt or tax-exempt entity.

A salary reduction SEP may be sponsored by non-tax-exempt entities, including sole proprietorships, partnerships, or for-profit corporations. The salary reduction SEP cannot be sponsored by a state, local government, or political subdivision, agency, or instrumentality thereof, or any organization that is exempt from federal income taxes.

Nonqualified pension plans may be sponsored by any employer (it would appear that a sole proprietor could not establish a nonqualified pension plan for himself or herself). However, if the employer is a state or its political subdivision or instrumentality, or any other organization exempt from federal income tax, the form that the nonqualified pension plan may take is limited to that described in Code § 457. Although tax-exempt nongovernmental entities may adopt nonqualified pension plans subject to Code § 457 for their employees, ERISA limits participation in Code § 457 plans to employees who are a select group of management or are highly compensated employees. Otherwise, ERISA would require that the plan be funded, which runs contrary to the requirements of Code § 457. **Section 13.1** discusses this issue in greater detail.

Table 9–1 summarizes the plans available for sponsorship by the various types of legal entities.

Thus, the legal form and the taxable status, for federal income tax purposes, of the entity desiring to sponsor a plan immediately dictates the

Table 9–1

Entities Permitted to Adopt Specific Types of Employee Savings Plans

Type of Employee Savings Plans	Entities That May Adopt
401(k) plan	Non-tax-exempt sole proprietorship, partnership, corporation
403(b) annuity plan	Entities described in Code § 501(c)(3) and exempt from tax under Code § 501(a); public schools of governments
Nonqualified pension plan	All entities, except it appears that a sole proprietor could not establish such a plan for himself or herself; governments and tax-exempt entities are subject to rules in Code § 457
Salary reduction SEP	Non-tax-exempt sole proprietorship, partnership, corporation; subject to 25-employee test

types of employee savings plans available to that entity to consider for adoption.

§ 9.6   —Holding of Employee Savings

The manner in which employee savings contributions are held and invested varies among the various types of employee savings plans. The Code requires that all employer contributions and employee salary deferral contributions to a 401(k) plan must be held in a trust, a custodial account, or a qualifying insurance contract. However, ERISA requires that the assets of an employee benefit plan must be held in trust by one or more trustees unless a specific statutory exception applies. The trustee(s) must either be named in the trust instrument or plan or appointed by a named fiduciary. Unless the trustee is an employee of the employer who is not permitted to receive compensation for services as a trustee under ERISA, trustee compensation must be addressed. The assets of the trust must be accounted for, valued periodically, and invested by the trustee, employer, or properly appointed and eligible investment manager. The investment thereof must be closely monitored so as to fulfill the fiduciary responsibilities imposed by ERISA. If the employer designs the plan to permit the participants to direct the investment of one or more of their account balances, this design will require establishing various funds from which the participant may select. Additional accounting functions must be generated, to maintain a proper record of each participant's investment in each fund and his or her transfers among funds.

Under a salary reduction SEP, the holding and investment of salary deferral contributions are less complicated than in the 401(k) plan. An individual retirement account or annuity with a bank, insurance company, or other qualified financial institution is established for each employee under the employee's name, to hold the contributions made pursuant to the employee's salary reduction election. Upon the employer's deposit of the contribution, the employee generally has control over when it is withdrawn and how it is invested. As with any other individual retirement account or annuity established by the employee, the entity with which the individual retirement account or annuity is established generally deals directly with the employee on matters of distribution and investment.

One type of 403(b) annuity plan, the salary deferral only (SDO) 403(b) annuity plan, which only permits employee salary deferral contributions on a voluntary basis, is similar to the individual retirement account or annuity. Upon the employer's deposit of the contribution, the employee generally assumes control of its disposition and investment, beginning with the selection of the insurance company or regulated investment company with which the employee elects to establish an annuity or account. The employer's responsibility with respect to the contribution is limited to the timely deposit of contributions. The SDO 403(b) annuity plan must be contrasted to the 403(b) annuity plan to which, in lieu of or in addition to voluntary employee salary deferral contributions, the sponsoring employer makes contributions as well. This plan, the employer 403(b) annuity plan, resembles plans subject to the requirements of Code § 401(a).

The federal tax law requires that the assets of a nonqualified pension plan must remain subject to the claims of the employer's creditors. Employers may not, therefore, establish trust or custodial accounts similar to those established for 401(k) plans, but may attempt to shelter nonqualified pension plan assets through "rabbi trusts" (see **§ 8.14**). However, employers customarily invest employee deferrals to a nonqualified pension plan in, or permit the employee to direct employee deferrals to a nonqualified pension plan to, investment accounts specifically established for that purpose under the employer's federal tax identification number. With the establishment of a segregated account, the employer and employee may more easily track the account balances of the participants. Administration of the nonqualified pension plan salary deferrals is thus somewhat more complex for the employer, in contrast to the salary-saving SEP or 403(b) annuity plan, in that the details of investment must be coordinated and the accounting for the investment must be properly undertaken.

§ 9.7 —Coverage Requirements

The requirements of Code § 410 (minimum coverage), § 401(a)(26) (minimum participation), and § 414(r) (separate lines of business) establish the number of employees that a 401(k) plan must permit to defer compensation in order to be and remain qualified. As discussed at length in **Chapter 3**. In addition, Code § 410 requires the 401(k) plan to meet the "ratio" test—the percentage of non-highly compensated employees who benefit under the plan must be at least 70 percent of the percentage of highly compensated employees who benefit—or the average benefit test, whose two components include a nondiscriminatory classification test and the average benefit percentage test. Code § 401(a)(26) requires that a plan must benefit at least the lesser of 50 employees or 40 percent of the employees of the employer. Code § 414(r) permits the application of these rules to what are called separate lines of businesses. Unless the 401(k) plan does not benefit any highly compensated employees, its design must specifically maneuver through these requirements.

Under SDO 403(b) annuity plans, all employees of an organization that sponsors this type of annuity plan (funded solely by salary deferral contributions) must be permitted to elect to have the employer make contributions of more than $200 pursuant to a salary reduction agreement, if any employee of the organization may elect to have the organization make such contributions. The employer 403(b) annuity plan is similar to the 401(k) plan, which is subject to Code §§ 401(a)26 and § 410(b).

Under a salary reduction SEP, participation must be extended to employees who have attained age 21, performed service for the employer during at least 3 of the immediately preceding 5 years, and received at least $300 in compensation (subject to adjustment). At least 50 percent of the eligible employees must defer, and the employer may not have more than 25 eligible employees during the preceding year or a salary reduction SEP may not be sponsored.

A nonqualified pension plan is subject to the participation requirements of ERISA; however, these requirements do not apply to certain types of nonqualified pension plans, an example of which is the ERISA-defined "top-hat" plan. As discussed at length in **§ 8.3**, a top-hat plan is an unfunded plan maintained by an employer primarily for the purpose of providing deferred compensation for a select group of management or highly compensated employees. With a top-hat plan, an employer may effectively give salary deferral options to the small group of employees. It may be noted that, because ERISA's requirements do not apply to governments, nonqualified pension plans of governments are exempt from ERISA, including ERISA's participation requirements.

As long as a nonqualified pension plan covers government employees, or is structured so as not to be considered an employee pension benefit plan covered by ERISA, an employer may avoid the strict coverage and participation requirements applicable to 401(k) and salary reduction SEPs, and may specifically select those employees whom it desires to make eligible to defer compensation through salary deferral.

§ 9.8 —Deductibility of Employee Savings

In the context of a non-tax-exempt employer, the timing of its deduction against gross income for the contribution to the employee savings plan may influence which employee savings plan is adopted. As discussed above, a non-tax-exempt employer is the only type of employer permitted to sponsor a 401(k) plan or salary reduction SEP. A non-tax-exempt employer is permitted to deduct employee savings contributions to a 401(k) plan in the tax year in which they are paid, if such tax year ends within or with the tax year of the trust with respect to which the trust is exempt under Code § 501(a). The rules with respect to SEPs provide that contributions are deductible, for calendar-year SEPs, for the taxable year with or within which the calendar year ends; or, if maintained on the basis of the taxable year of the employer, for such taxable year. For either type of employee savings plan, the employer may take the deduction almost coterminous with the contribution. The amount of the deduction taken as a result of contributions to a 401(k) plan or salary deferral SEP cannot exceed 15 percent of the compensation of the covered employees.

The 401(k) plan, salary reduction SEP deduction rules contrast significantly with the deductibility rules applicable to nonqualified pension plans, which prohibit the employer from deducting employee savings to a nonqualified pension plan against gross income until the year in which the contribution is includable in the gross income of the employee. That generally occurs at the time of the distribution to the employee. The total amount paid to the employee is deductible by the employer, subject to whether the amount paid constitutes reasonable compensation to the employee.

In the context of a 403(b) annuity plan and nonqualified pension plans subject to Code § 457, sponsoring employers that are exempt from federal taxation are not concerned with tax deductions. Whether an immediate deduction against gross income for the amount of the employee's salary deferral may be taken is irrelevant to the tax-exempt employer's plan design.

§ 9.9 —Amount of Employee Savings
Permitted Annually

Dollar limitations are imposed on the annual amounts that an employee may contribute to a 401(k) plan, 403(b) annuity plan, salary reduction

SEP, and nonqualified pension plan subject to Code § 457 in which the employee participates in a calendar year. Under the rules applicable to nonqualified pension plans exempt from the requirements of Code § 457, no such limitations are applicable.

The dollar limitations may tend to influence a non-tax-exempt employer to use a nonqualified pension plan as a supplemental or alternative method, to permit highly compensated employees to increase the amount of their annual deferral. Because the employee's savings contribution to a nonqualified pension plan subject to Code § 457 is specifically limited by law, employees of tax-exempt entities who are eligible to participate in a nonqualified pension plan subject to Code § 457 are not permitted the latitude available to employees of non-tax-exempt employers with respect to the amounts they may contribute to a nonqualified pension plan in a calendar year.

§ 9.10   —Top-Heavy Requirements

Code § 416 requires that employers who sponsor a 401(k) plan or salary reduction SEP must make minimum contributions on behalf of nonkey employees if the plan is top-heavy. In general, a plan is top-heavy if the aggregate accounts of key employees under the plan exceed 60 percent of the aggregate of the accounts of all employees under the plan. The top-heavy minimum contribution is the lesser of 3 percent of compensation or the percentage at which contributions are made under the plan for the year, for the key employee for whom such percentage is the highest. No amount of a nonkey employee's salary deferral will be credited toward the amount that the employer is obligated to pay in satisfaction of the minimum contribution to a top-heavy plan. The consequence of this rule is to place on employers who sponsor a 401(k) plan or salary reduction SEP the burden of making a top-heavy contribution to all nonkey employees.

For example, although eligible, some employees may decline the opportunity to make salary deferral contributions to the employer-sponsored 401(k) plan or salary reduction SEP, while at least one key employee makes salary deferrals in excess of 3 percent of compensation. Under such circumstances and pursuant to the top-heavy minimum contribution rules, the employer is obligated, at a minimum, to make a contribution to the accounts of all nonkey employees eligible to participate in an amount equal to 3 percent of their compensation. However, if the highest rate of a key employee's salary deferral is less than 3 percent, the amount of the employer's top-heavy minimum obligation would be reduced to the highest percentage deferred by any key employee. Even if the 401(k) plan has a matching feature wherein the employer matches the employee's salary deferral, the employer is not entitled to any credit against the top-heavy minimum for the amount of matching contributions it makes, unless the matching contributions are not needed to satisfy the discrimination test under Code § 401(m).

§ 9.11   —Tax Treatment of Plan Distributions

Distributions of benefits from an employee savings plan are generally taxable to the participant employee as ordinary income for federal tax purposes. The only exceptions to this rule are distributions from a 401(k) plan that may be eligible for lump-sum distribution tax treatment. As discussed in **§ 4.6**, lump-sum distribution tax treatment may reduce a participant's federal income tax liability on the 401(k) plan distribution. This special attribute, which may attach to the 401(k) plan distribution, is a significant factor that may influence an employer to adopt the 401(k) plan rather than the salary reduction SEP or nonqualified pension plan, under which any distributions are taxed as ordinary income.

In addition to federal income tax, the imposition, on employee savings plan distributions, of the 10 percent early distribution excise tax, 15 percent excise tax on excess accumulations and distributions, and 50 percent excise tax on failure to take a minimum annual distribution after attaining age 70½, varies depending on the employee savings plan's source of the distribution. Each of the foregoing taxes is applied to distributions under 401(k) plans, 403(b) annuity plans, and salary reduction SEPs. None of these excise taxes applies to distributions from nonqualified pension plans not subject to Code § 457. It appears that the 50 percent excise tax applies to nonqualified pension plans subject to Code § 457.

The last area of comparison involves determining which employee savings plans are subject to the minimum distribution requirements discussed in **§ 4.1**. Only nonqualified pension plan distributions not subject to Code § 457 are not subject to minimum distribution requirements.

§ 9.12   —In-Service Distributions

In-service distributions connote a distribution being made from an employee savings plan to an employee whose employment relationship with the employer-sponsor remains intact. The employee's accessibility to salary deferral contributions through an in-service distribution prior to the customary distribution events of termination of employment (death, disability, retirement or otherwise) is generally a consideration but is never a controlling factor in the sponsorship of an employee savings plan. Salary deferrals to a 401(k) plan, 403(b) annuity plan, and nonqualified pension plan subject to Code § 457 may be withdrawn, provided the conditions established by the applicable statute have been met. An in-service distribution may be made from a 401(k) plan if the employee has experienced a financial hardship. In a 403(b) annuity plan, the employee must establish hardship as a reason to obtain the distribution. The law governing 401(k) plans and 403(b) annuity plans prohibits, in general, any earnings attributable to salary deferrals from being withdrawn.

A nonqualified pension plan subject to Code § 457 may only permit in-service distributions under circumstances described as an "unforeseeable emergency." Any other access would potentially cause the full amount of the deferral to be includable in the employee's gross income for federal tax purposes.

In contrast to these types of employee savings plans, an employee's salary deferrals to a salary reduction SEP may be withdrawn without restriction. Excepting the withdrawals from any nonqualified pension plan, withdrawals prior to age 59½ from a 401(k) plan, 403(b) annuity plan, or salary reduction SEP are subject to the 10 percent excise tax on premature distributions. Thus, the employee is subject not only to federal income tax on the amounts withdrawn, but to an additional 10 percent excise tax. The excise tax may only be avoided if the 401(k) plan or 403(b) annuity plan permits a withdrawal in the form of a loan. Salary reduction SEPs and nonqualified pension plans subject to Code § 457 are prohibited from permitting loans.

§ 9.13 —Nondiscrimination Requirements

The amount that highly compensated employees may defer to a 401(k) plan or salary reduction SEP is subject to limits that are determined by the application of specific nondiscrimination rules. As discussed in **Chapter 2**, these include the "1.25 times test," the "2 times 2 percent alternative test," and the "multiple use test." These nondiscrimination rules control the amount of employee savings by highly compensated employees by connecting the limit to the amount of deferrals by non-highly compensated employees. The testing scheme of 401(k) plans is more complicated than that of salary reduction SEPs, where the highly compensated employee's deferral percentage cannot be more than 125 percent of the average of the deferral percentages for the year of all non-highly compensated employees. The simplicity does not benefit highly compensated employees, who are more restricted in the amount of their deferrals in the salary reduction SEP than if they were participants in a 401(k) plan, where the 2 times 2 percent alternative test would apply. The application of these discrimination tests is complex and potentially confusing, and adds to the expenses of plan administration. As currently structured, the tests make compliance uncertain and may require post-plan-year adjustments in the amounts of salary deferrals.

The amounts that employees may defer to a 403(b) annuity plan, non-qualified pension plan, and nonqualified pension plan subject to Code § 457 are not limited by the application of discrimination rules. Apparently, in these plans, Congress felt that the dollar limitation on the annual amount that an employee may defer was sufficient.

§ 9.14   —Plan Documentation

The complexity of plan documentation and the process of adoption vary significantly among the types of employee savings plans. The instrument that embodies the 401(k) plan must include a significant number of provisions to exhibit compliance with the qualification requirements of Code §§ 401(a) and 401(k). A formal trust document or custodial agreement must also be written, to establish the legal framework for the holding and investing of plan assets. There are at least three ways to satisfy the written document requirement: (1) an individually designed and drafted plan; (2) a volume submitter plan; or (3) a prototype plan. Sponsoring employers may adopt an individually designed and drafted 401(k) plan. The principal distinction is that the IRS has not seen the plan prior to the sponsor's submission of the plan to the IRS. In today's employee benefit marketplace, numerous vendors of 401(k) plans abound; banks, insurance companies, attorneys, accountants, and employee benefit consulting firms may offer volume submitter plans or standardized or nonstandardized prototype 401(k) plans to their clientele. Volume submitter and prototype plans have, prior to the employer's adoption, been submitted to the IRS for review and have been issued an opinion letter that the plan, as to form, complies with the requirements of Code § 401(a) and that the trust established therewith is exempt from federal income tax under Code § 501(a). The principal distinction between a volume submitter plan and a prototype plan is that the language of a volume submitter plan may, subsequent to the initial IRS review and issuance of an opinion letter, be modified to a limited extent to accommodate the needs of the sponsor. The language of a prototype plan may not be changed after the IRS has issued the plan an opinion letter.

The fundamental purposes of the 401(k) plan are: to permit the employer to obtain an immediate deduction for the employee's savings contribution; to enable the employee to effectively defer compensation without the deferral being subject to federal income tax; and to enable the employee to receive federal income tax deferral on the growth of the employee's savings contributions and, ultimately, favorable tax treatment on the distribution. The sponsoring employer, therefore, must have an immediate assurance that, as to form, the 401(k) plan complies with applicable law. The 401(k) plan must be covered by a favorable determination letter from the IRS, stating that the plan complies with Code § 401(a) and that the trust established therewith is exempt from tax under Code § 501(a).

In an individually designed 401(k) plan, volume submitter plan, and nonstandardized prototype 401(k) plan, the 401(k) plan should be submitted to the IRS on a timely basis, in order to receive a favorable determination letter that will be retroactive to the plan's effective date. There are standard prototype 401(k) plans that, under certain circumstances, need not be submitted to the IRS in order to receive the assurance of a favorable determination letter. As may be expected, the adoption of a volume submitter, nonstandard, or standardized prototype 401(k) plan reduces the cost of document preparation and user fees payable to the IRS for receipt of a favorable determination letter.

An employer adopts a 401(k) plan by execution of the written instrument embodying the plan and trust or custodial account prior to the date when employees will be permitted to defer portions of their compensation to the plan. Employers that are corporations will have the 401(k) plan adoption authorized by the corporation's board of directors, either by approval of the proposed plan for adoption or by authorization of one or more corporate officers to take such action as may be necessary to establish and maintain the 401(k) plan in accordance with the requirements of applicable law.

In contrast to the highly complex 401(k) plan, the salary reduction SEP falls on the less complex side of the spectrum. There are at least three ways in which an employer may embody the written agreement that is required to establish a salary reduction SEP: (1) IRS Form 5305A-SEP (rev. September 1990); (2) prototype SEP; or (3) individually designed SEP. These written agreements are discussed in greater detail in **Chapter 12**.

The 403(b) annuity plans also fall on the less complex side of the spectrum. An SDO 403(b) annuity plan has principally taken the form of either an individual annuity contract sold by an insurance company to the employee, or a custodial account, opened by the employee, at a regulated investment company. The employer's adoption is typically limited to entering into a salary reduction agreement with the employer and fulfilling that agreement by reducing salary and forwarding the reductions to the insurer or regulated investment company. The insurance company or regulated investment company has available for the employee and employer form plans and salary reduction agreements through which the plan may be adopted. Adoption is accomplished when the employer and employee execute the form plan and salary reduction agreement.

Employer 403(b) annuity plans customarily take the form of plans provided by insurance companies or regulated investment companies.

Adoption is accomplished by the employer's executing the forms presented by the funding vehicle sponsor.

The Code does not require an employer, insurance company, or custodian sponsoring a 403(b) annuity to approve of the form of the annuity contract or custodial agreement. However, because of the potentially high tax cost of failure to effectively defer compensation and earnings thereon from current federal income tax, adopting a 403(b) annuity plan that has been approved by the IRS (if rulings are available) is advisable.

Somewhat in the middle of the complexity spectrum are nonqualified pension plans and nonqualified pension plans subject to Code § 457. Because the legal requirements governing these types of plans are significantly less detailed than those found in § 401(k) plans, salary reduction SEPs, or 403(b) annuity plans, there are fewer legal considerations to address in the plan document. Nonetheless, care must be exercised in the drafting of nonqualified pension plans and nonqualified pension plans subject to Code § 457, to achieve the objective of deferring current income for federal income tax purposes until the events of distribution set forth in the plan. Adoption is accomplished by the employer's execution of the plan and the employee's execution of a salary reduction agreement.

In the case of a nonqualified pension plan subject to Code § 457, the Code permits the employer, which is a state or political subdivision thereof, to correct a plan provision if, upon review by the IRS, it is found not to be in compliance with the requirements of Code § 457. Similar to model and prototype salary reduction SEPs and 403(b) annuity plans, nonqualified pension plans and nonqualified pension plans subject to Code § 457 are not subject to submission to the IRS for a favorable determination letter. To this extent, the nonqualified pension plan is similar to model and prototype salary reduction SEPs and 403(b) annuity plans. However, it is recommended that the sponsor of a nonqualified pension plan or a nonqualified pension plan subject to Code § 457 consider the submission of such a plan to the IRS for a ruling on the tax effect of the plan. Whether the IRS will issue a ruling as to the tax effect of the plan must be determined by the submitter under the current Revenue Procedures of the IRS, which delineate the Code sections under which the IRS will issue a ruling.

§ 9.15 —Reporting and Disclosure

As discussed in **Chapter 5**, ERISA imposes various reporting and disclosure requirements on sponsors of "employee benefit plans," including "employee pension benefit plans" and "employee welfare benefit plans."

The focus here is on employee pension benefit plans, defined by ERISA as any plans, funds, or programs which were heretofore or are hereafter established or maintained by an employer or by an employee organization, or by both, to the extent that, by their expressed terms or as a result of surrounding circumstances, such plans, funds, or programs (1) provide retirement income to employees, or (2) results in a deferral of income by employees for periods extending to the termination of covered employment or beyond, regardless of the method of calculating the contributions made to the plans, the method of calculating the benefits under the plans, or the method of distributing benefits from the plans.

Using this definition, 401(k) plans, employer 403(b) annuity plans (if sponsored by a nongovernmental entity), salary reduction SEPs, nonqualified pension plans, and nonqualified pension plans subject to Code § 457 (excluding Code § 457 plans sponsored by a government) are employee pension benefit plans because they are established or maintained by an employer or an employee organization, or both, to provide retirement income or a deferral of income to periods extending beyond covered employment.

Sponsors of 401(k) plans are subject to the fullest extent of the reporting and disclosure requirements. Among the principal requirements are: annual reports (Form 5500 Series) must be sent to the IRS; summary annual reports must be distributed to the plan participants; plan participants must be given summary plan descriptions and a summary of material modifications (if applicable); and, upon a participant's written request (but not more often than once in a 12-month period), the participant must be given a personal benefit statement and, for inspection and copying, plan documents, the latest annual report, or other instruments under which the plan was established or is operated.

A sponsor of a 403(b) annuity plan, if it is a tax-exempt entity but not a state or its political subdivision or a church as described in ERISA §§ 4(b)(2) and 3(33), must also comply with the reporting and disclosure requirements of ERISA, if the 403(b) annuity plan is part of an employer-sponsored plan within the meaning of ERISA. Coming within ERISA's coverage are employer 403(b) annuity plans, described herein.

SDO 403(b) annuity plans are not subject to ERISA under certain circumstances. Department of Labor (DOL) Regulations provide that, if a program for the purchase of an annuity contract, described in Code § 403(b) pursuant to salary reduction agreements or agreements to forgo an increase in salary, meets certain requirements of the Code of Federal Regulations,[2] the program shall not be "established or maintained by an employer" as that phrase is used in the definition of an employee pension benefit

---

[2] Treas. Reg. § 1.403(b)-1(b)(3) (as amended in 1986).

plan and a pension plan. To qualify, the program must have the following characteristics:

1. Participation is completely voluntary for employees;

2. All rights under the annuity contract or custodial account are enforceable solely by the employee, by a beneficiary of such employee, or by any authorized representative of such employee or beneficiary;

3. The sole involvement of the employer, other than pursuant to item 2 above, is limited to any of the following:

   a. Permitting annuity contractors (which term includes any agent or broker who offers annuity contracts or who makes available custodial accounts within the meaning of Code § 403(b)(7) to publicize their products to employees;

   b. Requesting information concerning proposed funding media, products, or annuity contracts;

   c. Summarizing or otherwise compiling the information provided with respect to the proposed funding media or products that are made available, or the annuity contractors whose services are provided, in order to facilitate review and analysis by the employees;

   d. Collecting annuity or custodial account considerations as required by salary reduction agreements or by agreements to forgo salary increases, remitting such considerations to annuity contractors, and maintaining records of such consideration;

   e. Holding in the employer's name one or more group annuity contracts covering its employees;

   f. Limiting the funding media or products available to employees, or the annuity contractors who may approach employees, to a number and selection designed to afford employees a reasonable choice in light of all relevant circumstances. Relevant circumstances may include, but would not necessarily be limited to, the following types of factors:

      —Number of employees affected;

      —Number of contractors who have indicated interest in approaching employees;

      —Variety of available products;

      —Terms of available arrangements;

      —Administrative burdens and cost to the employer;

      —Possible interference with employee's performance, resulting from direct solicitation by contractor;

4. The employer receives no direct or indirect consideration or compensation, in cash or otherwise, beyond reasonable compensation to cover expenses properly and actually incurred by such employer in the performance of the employer's duties pursuant to the salary reduction agreements or agreements to forgo the salary increases described here.

For a 403(b) annuity plan that is in the form of a custodial account, the employer or custodian must file the annual return required by Code § 6058, and the custodian must report distributions to the IRS under Code § 6047. Whether the custodial account is part of an employer-sponsored plan may determine whether multiple annual returns are required for each custodial account.

Salary reduction SEPs are apparently subject to the reporting and disclosure requirements of ERISA. The sponsors of salary reduction SEPs who utilize IRS Form 5305A-SEP have available to them an alternative method of complying with the reporting and disclosure requirements of ERISA, set forth in the DOL Regulations.[3] This alternative method is discussed in greater detail in **Chapter 12**.

Nonqualified pension plans and nonqualified pension plans subject to Code § 457 (if adopted by a tax-exempt nongovernmental entity, excepting custom plans adopted by churches) are subject to ERISA reporting and disclosure. However, the DOL Regulations[4] establish an alternative method of compliance for unfunded pension plans maintained by an employer for a select group of management or highly compensated employees. The requirements of the alternative are met if a statement is filed with the Secretary of Labor that includes the name and address of the employer, the employer (tax) identification number (EIN) assigned by the IRS, a declaration that the employer maintains a plan or plans primarily for the purpose of providing deferred compensation for a select group of management or highly compensated employees, and a statement of the number of such plans and the number of employees in each, and provides plan documents to the Secretary of Labor upon request. Only one statement is required to be filed for each employer maintaining one or more plans in this category. This alternative method is only permitted if the benefits are paid as needed from the general assets of the employer or provided exclusively through insurance contracts or policies, the premiums of which are paid directly by the employer from its general assets and are issued by an insurance company or similar organization qualified to do business in the state.

---

[3] 29 C.F.R. § 2520.104-48 (1991).

[4] 29 C.F.R. § 2528.104-23 (1991).

§ 9.16 —Required Distributions

Chapter 4 discussed the requirements of Code § 401(a)(9), which requires distributions from 401(k) plans, 403(b) annuity plans, and salary reduction SEPs to begin at specific times measured from a participant's death or attaining age 70¹/₂. The failure to take minimum distributions may cause the imposition of the 50 percent excise tax unless waived by the IRS. Nonqualified pension plans subject to Code § 457 must comply with the requirements of Code § 401(a)(9) in addition to the requirements of Code § 457(d)(2)(B) and (C). Nonqualified pension plans are not subject to these minimum distribution rules.

§ 9.17 —Security of Plan Assets

With respect to the assets of the plan, which will pay plan benefits, 401(k) plans, 403(b) annuity plans, salary reduction SEPs, nonqualified pension plans, and nonqualified pension plans subject to Code § 457 provide varying levels of security to the plan participant. The sanctity of the assets from the participant's creditors will not be discussed herein, but, as to the sponsor's creditors, 401(k) plans and 403(b) annuity plans are not subject to the claims of the sponsor's creditors. Salary reduction SEP assets being held by the participant's individual retirement account are similarly not subject to the sponsor's creditors. However, with respect to nonqualified pension plans and nonqualified pension plans subject to Code § 457, the very nature of these plans requires that their plan assets be subject to the claims of the sponsor's creditors. As discussed in **Chapter 8**, sponsors of nonqualified pension plans must create devices to (1) satisfy the applicable tax rules to avoid current federal income taxation on the amounts of the employees' salary deferrals and (2) keep the plan assets away from the sponsor's creditors. In these types of plans, the participant relies on the financial strength of the sponsor to provide the promised benefit.

§ 9.18 —Spousal Rights in Plan Assets

Aside from considerations of state divorce and inheritance laws, the rights of an employee's surviving spouse and the amounts accumulated in an employee savings plan vary among the types of employee savings plans. Under the Retirement Equity Act of 1984 (which amended the Code and ERISA), as a matter of qualification under ERISA, a 401(k) plan must distribute a participant's benefit upon his or her death to his or her surviving spouse in the form of a qualified joint and survivor annuity (or qualified preretirement survivor annuity). A 401(k) plan need not provide the qualified joint and survivor annuity (or qualified preretirement survivor annuity) if it meets certain requirements. The principal requirement is that the plan must provide that the participant's benefit be payable in full, on the death of the participant, to the participant's surviving spouse or, if there is no surviving spouse or the surviving spouse consents to the naming of a beneficiary other than himself or herself, to a designated beneficiary. A 401(k) plan may define a spouse for this purpose as a person who has been married to the participant throughout the 1-year period ending on the earlier of the participant's annuity starting date or the date of the participant's death.

Employer 403(b) annuity plans, which are subject to ERISA, must provide the same joint and survivor annuity and qualified preretirement survivor annuity forms as are applicable to 401(k) plans.

Salary reduction SEPs, nonqualified pension plans, and nonqualified pension plans subject to Code § 457 are not required by the Code or ERISA to make an employee's spouse the automatic beneficiary of all or a portion of the employee's benefits in the plan. Thus, participants of these types of plans have full discretion, subject only to applicable state law, with respect to naming who should receive the plan benefits.

§ 9.19   Entity Characteristics, Needs, and Benefit Philosophy: Influence on Plan Design

Nature of Legal Existence

As discussed in § 9.2, the statutes creating the various employee salary plans make the nature of the sponsoring employer's legal existence the principal entity characteristic that influences plan design.

Employer Demographics

The number of employees employed by an employer is the next significant factor, but only in the context of the non-tax-exempt employer. It is unlikely that the number of employees affects a tax-exempt employer's decision to adopt a nonqualified pension plan subject to Code § 457 or an SDO 403(b) annuity plan, because no minimum participation requirements or maximum number of employee participants exist, in contrast, for example, to those that apply to a 401(k) plan, salary reduction SEP, or employer 403(b) annuity plan.

The number of employees employed by an employer first dictates whether the employer has the option to adopt a 401(k) or a salary reduction SEP. Salary reduction SEPs may not be sponsored by employers who have more than 25 employees who are eligible to participate (or would have been required to be eligible to participate if the pension was maintained) at any time during the preceding year. Thus, employers who employ 25 or fewer employees in the previous year are the only ones who have a choice between a 401(k) plan and a salary reduction SEP.

Interestingly, even though the employer may be precluded from adopting a salary reduction SEP, as the number of the employer's employees increases, the 401(k) plan design alternatives increase. An employer may be able to establish more than one 401(k) plan and still meet the requirements of Code §§ 410 and 401(a)(26). As discussed in **Chapter 3**, Code § 410 establishes a coverage test and Code § 401(a)(26) establishes a minimum participation test that each 401(k) plan must satisfy in order to be qualified. This may be advantageous to an employer that conducts its business from multiple locations and desires to treat each location differently from a benefits point of view.

Employers that are eligible for the benefits under Code § 414(r) have the broadest design alternatives available, in that separate 401(k) plans can be established even though the employees are employed by employers who must be aggregated for purposes of the qualified plan rules. The concern to keep track of compliance with Code § 410 would be eliminated. It is also observed that the more non-highly compensated employees an employer employs, the easier it may be to meet the 401(k) discrimination tests.

The number of employees employed by a closely held business has probably a more significant influence on plan design. The success of a 401(k) plan in the context of the closely held business depends on the non-highly compensated employees' achieving high levels of salary deferrals. As discussed in **Chapter 2**, 401(k) plans and salary reduction SEPs are subject to the discrimination tests found in Code §§ 401(k) and 408(k), respectively. It follows that sponsors with larger numbers of employees may be able to achieve a higher rate of non-highly compensated employee participation so as to permit the highly compensated employees to defer larger amounts of salary within the limits of the actual deferral percentage test (ADP Test). Further, as the number of employees increases, the employer may be able to design modest financial inducements to achieve higher rates of participation. The primary example is a small matching contribution or a matching contribution that is subject to a more stringent vesting schedule.

In addition to the number of employees, an employer's inclination to adopt a 401(k) plan or a salary reduction SEP may be influenced by the characteristics of its employees: the more likely the employees will defer to the plan, the more likely the highly compensated employees will be able to defer as well. Older employees tend to be more concerned with accumulating retirement income than their younger counterparts. Highly paid employees have more discretionary income for allocation to retirement needs whereas lower paid employees have less discretionary income and a greater concern with having access to their deferrals. Similarly, employees with children may have less discretionary income. Highly educated employees may have less difficulty in comprehending the functioning of the plan. Married employees may have second wage earners in their families, thus creating, for them, a larger amount of discretionary income to be used for retirement funding. This possibility brings into consideration again whether and to what extent the sponsor will have to design the 401(k) plan with financial inducements in order to entice participation. To attract plan participants, plan sponsors may have to contribute matching contributions and place them on a more rapid vesting schedule.

Employers with employees who are members of a collective bargaining unit that has negotiated the subject of employee benefits in good faith with the employer have a further influence on plan design. If such employees' benefits were negotiated, the employer, in designing the plan for the other noncollective bargaining unit employees, is free to disregard the bargaining-unit employees for most qualified plan purposes. Most of the lower-paid employees may be in the bargaining unit. This situation may be beneficial to the extent that the 401(k) plan would have good participation rates; most of its participants would be at salary levels where salary deferrals may be accommodated.

Entity's Financial Strength

The extent of an entity's financial strength generally does not dictate a choice among the employee savings plans available to it for adoption, especially if the plan will be principally funded by employee contributions. However, entities that have a sound financial foundation have additional considerations, such as whether to adopt or retain the other major type of retirement plan delivery system that is available, which is the defined-benefit pension plan. Richer and more stable companies, by virtue of these attributes, can consider the defined-benefit pension plan, especially if the plan is assigned to place the full funding obligation on the employer. Along these same lines, employers that fewer demands on their resources enjoy similar flexibility.

If the potential sponsoring entity is not a strong and stable company, employee savings plans with their greater cost-efficient and cost-sharing features will be attractive; the less financially sound enterprise may nonetheless be able to provide a retirement income accumulation vehicle to its employees.

Employer Needs

Non-tax-exempt and tax-exempt employers share common goals in deciding to sponsor a 401(k) plan, salary reduction SEP, 403(b) annuity plan, or nonqualified pension plan subject to Code § 457. The primary goal is to attract and retain qualified and dependable employees. Other than with respect to lower-paid employees who are generally more concerned with the amount of their cash wages and medical benefits, most employees may be attracted and retained by the retirement benefits that may be available to them. Employers that provide retirement benefits may have an easier time suggesting early retirement to older employees when economic conditions may require staff reductions. In contrast to the more costly and less understood defined-benefit pension plan, the employee savings plan provides a cost-effective manner through which to obtain these goals.

Employer Philosophy

Much has been written on how an employer's benefits philosophy may influence its retirement benefit plan choices. Two questions that are considered when developing an employer's benefit philosophy are: What percentage of total compensation should be allocated toward the accumulation of retirement income for the employees? To what extent should this allocation be placed in the vehicle that will guarantee a certain level of benefits for the employer's employees? Employers that have elected to attempt to guarantee a certain level of retirement benefits for their employees have been characterized as having a paternalistic approach, as compared to employers that are content with making an annual contribution and letting the employee run the risk that the contribution will grow to the extent necessary to provide the employee with a retirement benefit. Employers who have desired to guarantee benefits have generally sponsored defined-benefit type plans; others desiring to limit exposure to annual contributions have sponsored defined-contribution plans.

However, through the 1980s and now in the 1990s, numerous factors have been eroding the paternalistic attitude. Accounting and funding standards for defined-benefit pension plans have become more rigid. Premiums payable to the Pension Benefit Guaranty Corporation have increased. Governmental regulation has taken a more complex and intricate role through the proposals of Treasury Regulations under Code

§ 401(a)(4).[5] Employers are finding that employee savings plans are a more cost-effective method of assisting employees with their accumulation of retirement income and are in concert with the philosophy of employee cost sharing.

The decision by the nongovernmental tax-exempt employer to offer an SDO 403(b) annuity plan or nonqualified pension plan subject to Code § 457 is not difficult, because of the relative ease through which these plans are adopted and administered. An SDO 403(b) annuity plan and a nonqualified pension plan subject to Code § 457 are not as administratively intensive, are not subject to complex discrimination rules, and require less extensive reporting and disclosure requirements than may be found in 401(k) plans. These plans may also be used as a supplement to the more traditional types of retirement benefit plans, such as defined-benefit pension plans principally offered by the employer.

In the context of the non-tax-exempt employer, the decision to offer a 401(k) plan is more complicated because of the numerous factors associated with administering the plan, such as investment, discrimination testing, and reporting and disclosure. Rather than being an easily implemented add-on, as is the SDO 403(b) annuity plan or the nonqualified pension plan subject to Code § 457, the 401(k) plan must compete in the employer's mind with the other benefits to be offered to employees, such as medical insurance (insured or self-insured), replacement income (disability and/or death benefits), and retirement income delivered through such other plans as profit sharing, money purchase, and defined-benefit pension plans.

§ 9.20   Business Environment: Effect on Plan Design

The business environment in which an employer operates has a significant impact on whether the employer should adopt an employee savings plan and the design of that plan. Both non-tax-exempt and non-government tax-exempt employers are affected by the business environment, because both are competing to maintain economic viability and to attract employees from other employers. A short list of the business environmental factors must include:

1.   The benefit norms of the industry;
2.   The benefit norms of the geographical locality where the employer does business;

---

[5] Prop. Treas. Reg. § 1.401(a)(4), (1991).

3. The impact of benefits negotiated through collective bargaining agreements;

4. The number of business locations;

5. The number of potential employees in the work force from which the employer may select;

6. The amount of the employer's resources that may be allocable to an employee's savings plan without jeopardizing the competitive status and economic viability of the employer.

CHAPTER 10

DESIGN OF 401(k) CASH OR DEFERRED ARRANGEMENTS

§ 10.1 Types of Cash or Deferred Arrangements

There are two basic types of cash or deferred arrangements (CODAs) to consider when designing a 401(k) plan. The first is a cash option plan. Under this type of plan, the plan sponsor contributes an amount on behalf of each plan participant. The participant then elects to take some or all of the contribution in cash and directs that the difference, if any, be deposited into a qualified retirement plan.

The second type of CODA is a salary reduction plan. Under this type of plan, the participant elects to reduce the salary that is otherwise payable and directs the sponsor to deposit the amount of the reduction, on the participant's behalf, into a qualified retirement plan.

The cash option is usually employed where a profit-sharing plan is already in place and has a history of steady contributions year after year. A sponsor may, for instance, offer employees the option of taking some or all of the profit-sharing contribution as cash. The sponsor may use this offer as a strategy to reduce or forgo salary increases for a given year.

The salary reduction plan is by far the more prevalent form of CODA in use today. Salary reduction plans are generally used as stand-alone plans, as supplements to a primary pension or profit-sharing plan, or as the main components of thrift plans. This chapter covers design considerations in the salary savings type of 401(k) CODA.

§ 10.2 Stand-Alone Plans

A stand-alone plan is a plan established by a plan sponsor that allows employees to reduce their salaries and to contribute the amount of the reduction to a qualified retirement plan on a pretax basis. It is the sole plan covering the employees; the plan sponsor provides no other retirement benefits. The sponsor of a stand-alone plan provides a vehicle for its employees to save for retirement on a pretax basis through payroll deductions at work, but offers no other employee benefits.

An organization that cannot afford a comprehensive retirement program may find it strategically advantageous to establish a stand-alone CODA for its employees. It can provide a retirement savings fund that allows for a higher level of pretax contributions than in an individual retirement account (IRA). Thus, pretax retirement savings can be more attractive to the employee in the CODA than in the IRA. If the plan sponsor pays the administrative expenses, the employee can enjoy the higher savings rate and tax benefits without the burden of the expenses that may be incurred in some IRAs or other nonqualified personal savings vehicles. The stand-alone plan can be expanded and enhanced in the future, as the financial strength of the sponsor grows. The stand-alone plan enables an employer that otherwise could not afford to provide a traditional retirement plan to create a base program on which it can build for the future even as it provides an attractive pretax savings vehicle for its employees. **Table 10–1** contrasts the advantages offered by a 401(k) savings plan with the savings realized by an individual who prefers to maintain the spendable income level associated with after-tax personal savings.

§ 10.3   Supplemental Plans

Many employers sponsor retirement programs for the benefit of their employees. These can be traditional defined-benefit pension plans, money-purchase pension plans, and/or profit-sharing plans. These employers may find it attractive to offer employees a vehicle for supplementing their normal retirement income through the pretax salary savings of a 401(k) CODA. If an employer sponsors a traditional defined-benefit plan, money-purchase pension plan, or any other plan that is not generally classified as a profit-sharing plan under IRS rules, the employer must establish a second qualified plan in order to implement the supplemental 401(k) CODA. If the employer maintains a profit-sharing plan, it need only add a 401(k) CODA provision to the plan that is already in place, in order to provide supplemental pretax salary savings in its retirement program. The supplemental plan allows an employer to provide its employees with an appropriate retirement benefit which, along with social security, replaces a portion of the employees' work-life income lost at retirement. The plan also provides a convenient, cost-effective vehicle for employees to set aside a

Table 10–1

Comparison of 401(k) Savings to Other Vehicles

	401(k) CODA	IRA	Personal Savings
Current Spendable Income			
Annual earnings	$ 40,000	$ 40,000	$40,000
401(k) savings	2,794	0	0
IRA savings	0	2,000	0
Gross income	$ 37,206	$ 38,000	$40,000
Federal taxes	6,211	6,435	6,981
State taxes	1,040	1,040	1,040
FICA taxes	3,060	3,060	3,060
Personal savings	0	546	2,000
Spendable income	$ 26,919	$ 26,919	$26,919
Future Retirement Income			
Single sum at retirement	$189,930	$162,764	$98,197
Annual gross retirement income	$ 22,456	$ 19,244	$11,610
Estimated taxes	2,299	1,381	150
Annual net retirement income	$ 20,157	$ 17,863	$11,460

Bases of financial results:

1. Savings begin at age 40. Retirement is at age 65.
2. Individual is married and files separately with two exemptions and standard deduction.
3. Individual resides and works in the State of Pennsylvania.
4. Annual earnings, tax brackets, and investment returns are constant over the career of the individual.
5. Invested funds earn 7½ percent income compounded annually. Capital is converted to income based on the 1984 unisex pension mortality.
6. Individual bears no direct administrative expense under any vehicle.

portion of their retirement income through pretax salary savings. **Tables 10–2** and **10–3** illustrate how a supplemental savings program with annual employee contributions of 3% of pay can significantly increase retirement security. **Table 10–2** combines the savings plan with a traditional defined benefit plan. **Table 10–3** contains a money purchase pension plan and savings plan combination.

Table 10–2

Retirement Income from Supplemental 401(k) CODA—Defined Benefit Pension Plan

Final Earnings	Age Participation Begins	Retirement Income				Income Replacement Rates			
		Pension Plan	401(k) CODA	Social Security	Total	Pension Plan	401(k) CODA	Social Security	Total
$ 20,000	30	$ 7,000	$10,942	$ 9,091	$ 27,033	35.0%	54.7%	45.4%	135.1%
20,000	40	5,000	4,822	9,091	18,913	25.0	24.1	45.4	94.5
20,000	50	3,000	1,853	9,091	13,944	15.0	9.3	45.4	69.7
40,000	30	14,000	21,885	12,856	48,741	35.0	54.7	32.1	121.8
40,000	40	10,000	9,645	12,856	32,501	25.0	24.1	32.1	81.2
40,000	50	6,000	3,706	12,856	22,562	15.0	9.3	32.1	56.4
60,000	30	21,000	32,828	13,861	67,689	35.0	54.7	23.1	112.8
60,000	40	15,000	14,467	13,861	43,328	25.0	24.1	23.1	72.2
60,000	50	9,000	5,559	13,861	28,420	15.0	9.3	23.1	47.3
80,000	30	28,000	43,771	13,861	85,632	35.0	54.7	17.3	107.0
80,000	40	20,000	19,290	13,861	53,151	25.0	24.1	17.3	66.4
80,000	50	12,000	7,411	13,861	33,272	15.0	9.3	17.3	41.5
100,000	30	35,000	54,713	13,861	103,574	35.0	54.7	13.8	103.5
100,000	40	25,000	24,112	13,861	62,973	25.0	24.1	13.8	62.9
100,000	50	15,000	9,264	13,861	38,125	15.0	9.3	13.8	38.1

Bases of financial results:

1. Pension benefit is 1 percent of earnings times years of service. Retirement is at age 65 in the year 2000.
2. Funds accumulate at 7½ percent interest. Capital is converted to income based on 1984 unisex pension mortality.
3. Earnings and social security wage base are constant throughout the career.
4. Salary savings is 3 percent of gross earnings each year. Earnings are level throughout career.

Table 10-3

Retirement Income from Supplemental 401(k) CODA—Defined Contribution Plan

Final Earnings	Age Participation Begins	Retirement Income				Income Replacement Rates			
		Plan	401(k) CODA	Social Security	Total	Plan	401(k) CODA	Social Security	Total
$ 20,000	30	$18,236	$10,942	$ 9,091	$ 38,269	91.1%	54.7%	45.4%	191.3%
20,000	40	8,036	4,822	9,091	21,949	40.2	24.1	45.4	109.7
20,000	50	3,088	1,853	9,091	14,032	15.4	9.3	45.4	70.1
40,000	30	36,473	21,885	12,856	71,214	91.1	54.7	32.1	178.0
40,000	40	16,073	9,645	12,856	38,574	40.2	24.1	32.1	96.4
40,000	50	6,177	3,706	12,856	22,739	15.4	9.3	32.1	56.8
60,000	30	54,710	32,828	13,861	101,399	91.1	54.7	23.1	169.0
60,000	40	24,110	14,467	13,861	52,438	40.2	24.1	23.1	87.4
60,000	50	9,265	5,559	13,861	28,685	15.4	9.3	23.1	47.8
80,000	30	72,946	43,771	13,861	130,578	91.1	54.7	17.3	163.2
80,000	40	32,147	19,290	13,861	65,298	40.2	24.1	17.3	81.6
80,000	50	12,353	7,411	13,861	33,625	15.4	9.3	17.3	42.0
100,000	30	91,183	54,713	13,861	159,757	91.1	54.7	13.8	159.7
100,000	40	40,183	24,112	13,861	78,156	40.2	24.1	13.8	78.1
100,000	50	15,441	9,264	13,861	38,556	15.4	9.3	13.8	38.5

Bases of financial results:

1. Contribution is 5 percent of earnings for each year of service. Retirement is at age 65 in the year 2000.
2. Funds accumulate at 7½ percent interest. Capital is converted to income based on 1984 unisex pension mortality.
3. Earnings and social security wage base are constant throughout the career.
4. Salary savings is 3 percent of gross earnings each year. Earnings are level throughout career.

§ 10.4   Thrift Plans

A common practice today is to combine a thrift feature with the salary savings component of the 401(k) CODA. In the thrift feature, the plan sponsor agrees to match the savings of the employees to a certain extent; for example, the sponsor might agree to contribute $0.50 to the plan for each $1.00 that the employee saves.

The sponsor may limit the coverage of the match to a set level of savings, stated as a percentage of the gross earnings of the plan participants. The sponsor may, for example, limit the matching contribution to 6 percent of covered earnings, even though the employee can save much more than 6 percent of earnings each year.

Employees who save via 401(k) CODAs will thus benefit differently under various types of matching contribution formulas. **Table 10–4** illustrates the variances from plan to plan for employees earning $25,000 annually who are subject to different rates of saving and matching contribution formulas.

Limitations on the coverage for matching contributions are just as important as the matching percentage itself, in determining the level of benefits to be available through the match and in placing a budget ceiling on the contribution for the plan sponsor.

If an employer is considering a thrift feature in the 401(k) CODA, it may wish to calculate the maximum exposure to its benefit budget under the premise that all employees maximize their savings under the plan. A sponsor that has a $5,000,000 payroll, for example, and has no individual earning more than the maximum level of allowable covered earnings

Table 10–4

Variances in Matching Employer Contributions

Rate of Savings in Plan	Matching Limit per Dollar Saved/Matching Rate			
	$.25/4%	$.50/4%	$.25/6%	$.50/6%
2%	$125.00	$250.00	$125.00	$250.00
3	187.50	375.00	187.50	375.00
4	250.00	500.00	250.00	500.00
5	250.00	500.00	312.50	625.00
6	250.00	500.00	375.00	750.00
7	250.00	500.00	375.00	750.00
8	250.00	500.00	375.00	750.00
9	250.00	500.00	375.00	750.00
10	250.00	500.00	375.00	750.00

($228,860 for 1992) might assess its budget exposure, before incorporating the thrift feature into its plan, as shown in **Table 10–5**.

The employer then knows the matching contribution formula that represents the maximum exposure to the benefit budget. It can choose the formula that best fits its actual budget, adjusted for its best estimate of actual plan usage by employees.

Matching contributions can follow various other types of formulas and philosophies. Graded formulas are currently prevalent. Under a graded formula, the matching contribution rate varies at different levels of covered earnings. A typical graded formula might promise to provide $.50 for each $1.00 saved by the plan participant, up to 4 percent of covered earnings, plus $.25 for each $1.00 saved over 4 percent, but not more than 6 percent of covered earnings. This provides higher levels of salary savings incentives for the lower range of salary rates.

Matching contributions can also be made on a discretionary basis, like a profit-sharing plan. Under this approach, the plan sponsor sets a rate of matching contributions at year end, based on the operating results of the organization. In good years, the contribution may be high; in bad years, the contribution may be low. The rate of contribution is based on the profits of the organization each year. Employees know that if they work harder, contributing to favorable financial results for the organization, the contribution from the organization toward their retirement will be that much higher.

Many organizations that employ the profit-sharing feature typically provide a small guaranteed matching contribution during the year, in order to encourage plan participation. If the operating results warrant, a larger matching contribution is made at the close of the fiscal year. This device is meaningful for limiting budget exposure by committing to a small rate of match during the year, and then adding to that commitment at year end if the financial results are favorable.

The thrift feature is usually added to a 401(k) CODA in order to stimulate plan participation through the offer of an instant return on the

Table 10–5

Thrift Feature Budget Exposure

Rate of Match	Covered Earnings for Match			
	2%	4%	6%	8%
$ .25	$ 25,000	$ 50,000	$ 75,000	$100,000
.50	50,000	100,000	150,000	200,000
.75	75,000	150,000	225,000	300,000
1.00	100,000	200,000	300,000	400,000

participant's savings by way of the matching contributions. Matching contributions are also employed by plan sponsors who want to encourage employees to contribute to their own retirement program. Under this philosophy, an employer is committed to contribute toward an employee's funds for retirement but only if the employee is willing to save for retirement. The employer has the psychological benefit of knowing that the contributions of the organization are made on behalf of those who are concerned enough to save for their own retirement. (Under a traditional retirement program, this type of employee appreciation is difficult to gauge.) Finally, the thrift feature can be added as a profit-sharing incentive. Under this approach, incentives are given to create higher levels of operating results and thereby to save a greater amount for retirement; with good operating results, the rate of matching contribution can be maximized each year for the employees.

§ 10.5 Nondiscrimination Standards

According to federal rules, the employee salary deferrals and employer matching contributions must comply with certain nondiscrimination standards. Under the rules, employees are divided into two groups: highly compensated employees and non-highly compensated employees. The highly compensated employees for 1992 are those who are in one or more of these categories:

- Own 5 percent or more of the company;
- Earn $93,518 or more in compensation;
- Earn $63,345 or more in compensation and are among the 20 percent of employees who received the most compensation;
- Earn $56,111 or more in compensation and are officers of the company;
- Were in one or more of the above categories in the previous year.

The non-highly compensated employees are all the other employees of the organization.

Both the average of the employee deferrals as a percentage of compensation and the average of employer matching contributions as a percentage of compensation are computed separately for each group. The averages for highly compensated group can not exceed the percentage indicated in **Table 10–6**. As the table shows, the average for the highly compensated group is dependent upon the average of the non highly compensated average deferral percentage.

Similar relationships apply to average salary deferrals and matching contributions of the non-highly compensated employees that exceed 15

Table 10–6

Nondiscrimination Standards for 401(k) Plans

If the non-highly compensated employees defer salary or receive matching contributions on the average of:	Then the highly compensated employees can defer salary or receive matching contribution on average no higher than:
0%	0%
1	2
2	4
3	5
4	6
5	7
6	8
7	9
8	10
9	11¹/₄
10	12¹/₂
11	13³/₄
12	15
13	16¹/₄
14	17¹/₂
15	18³/₄

percent. A plan must comply with these and other related nondiscrimination rules, in order to preserve its tax qualification status with the federal government.

The salary savings test is known as the actual deferral percentage test ("ADP Test") and the matching contribution test is known as the actual contribution percentage test ("ACP Test"). Both salary savings and matching contributions must comply with these standards. In the stand-alone plans and supplemental plans, the average rates of savings for both the highly compensated employees and the non-highly compensated employees must meet the standards set forth in **Table 10–6**. In the thrift plan, both the salary savings and the matching contributions must comply with the nondiscrimination standards separately. In addition, the plan must comply with a third nondiscrimination standard known as the multiple use test.

Under the basic nondiscrimination standards, the maximum rate of salary savings or matching contributions for the highly compensated employees (HCEs) cannot exceed the average rate of savings for the non-highly compensated employees (non-HCEs) multiplied by 1.25. This formula applies when the average rate of savings or matching contributions is 8 percent or more for the non-HCEs. Below an average savings or matching contribution rate of 8 percent for the non-HCEs, the maximum average rate of savings or matching contributions is either a multiple of 2 or is 2 percent (the "2 times 2 percent alternatively," mentioned earlier) greater than that of the non-HCEs. This formula can be summarized as shown in **Table 10–7**.

Under the multiple use test, only one of the individual tests, ADP or ACP, can use the compliance formula for average rates of savings or contributions for the non-HCEs that applies below the 8 percent rate. The ADP and ACP Tests cannot be passed simultaneously by either the 2 times rule or the 2 percent plus rule. Put another way, at least one test must be passed by using the 1.25 times rule that normally applies to average rates of savings or matching contributions in excess of 8 percent for the non-HCEs.

The effect of the multiple use rule is to further limit the benefits of the HCEs relative to the level of the matching contributions in the plan and the rate of savings of the non-HCEs. **Table 10–8** illustrates, on average, the limitation on the HCEs imposed by the multiple use test.

Prescribed formulas are used to compute the multiple use limitations. The sum of the average rate of salary savings and the average rate of matching contributions to the HCEs cannot exceed the greater of:

1.25 times the ADP of the non-HCEs plus the lesser of 2 times the ACP of the non-HCEs and 2 percent plus the ACP of the non-HCEs;

1.25 times the ACP of the non-HCEs plus the lesser of 2 times the ADP of the non-HCEs and 2 percent plus the ADP of the non-HCEs.

Each of these non discrimination rules is discussed at length in **Chapter 2**.

Table 10–7

Salary Savings and Matching Contribution Maximums

Average Rate of Savings or Matching Contributions for Non-Highly Compensated Employees	Basis for Determining Maximum Rate of Savings and Matching Contributions for Highly Compensated Employees
0% to 2%	Multiply the rates of non-highly compensated employees by 2.
2% to 8%	Add 2% to the rates of the non-highly compensated employees.
8% and over	Multiply the rates of the non-highly compensated employees by 1.25.

Table 10–8

Maximum Average Salary Savings for Highly Compensated Employees Under Multiple Use Test

Average Salary Savings Rate for Non-Highly Compensated Employees	Rate of Employer Matching Contribution				
	0%	25%	50%	75%	100%
1%	2.00%	1.85%	1.75%	1.67%	1.62%
2	4.00	3.70	3.50	3.35	3.25
3	5.00	4.75	4.58	4.57	4.37
4	6.00	6.00	6.00	5.71	5.50
5	7.00	7.00	7.00	6.85	6.62
6	8.00	8.00	8.00	8.00	7.75
7	9.00	9.00	9.00	9.00	8.87
8	10.00	10.00	10.00	10.00	10.00
9	11.25	11.25	11.25	11.25	11.25
10	12.50	12.50	12.50	12.50	12.50

§ 10.6   Other Federal Rules

Several other federal rules impact directly on plan design considerations. These include but may not be limited to the following:

1. Coverage rules of Code § 410(b). In its most basic form, the percentage of non-HCEs covered in the plan relative to the percentage of HCEs covered in the plan must exceed 70 percent. Although there are other more complicated coverage compliance methods, this formulation is the best framework for cost-effective plan design and plan administration.

2. The maximum amount an employee can save each year is $8,728 (for 1992).

3. The overall maximum benefit allowable each year is 25 percent of net earnings, or up to $30,000 for each plan member.

4. The overall tax-deductible amount for a single 401(k) CODA, including profit sharing (if applicable), with no credit carryovers, is 15 percent of net covered earnings. In combination with a pension plan, the overall tax-deductible amount for both plans together is 25 percent of covered earnings.

5. The maximum annual benefit for each participant is further limited if the plan sponsor maintains another plan (defined benefit or defined contribution) in which the participants also participate.

6. The maximum covered earnings for a given individual is $228,860 per year, as of 1992.

7. Certain HCE family members—lineal descendants and ascendants, as well as spouses—are aggregated for the coverage and nondiscrimination tests.

8. Spouses of certain HCEs are aggregated in determining the applicability of the $228,860 limitation on annual covered earnings.

9. Fiduciary responsibilities can be transferred to employees if certain investments can be provided for direct selection by the employees.

10. Loan and in-service withdrawals can be permitted as long as the respective administrative restrictions are applied.

Although many other federal rules will affect the daily administration of the 401(k) program, the ten rules given above have the most direct impact on the program's design.

§ 10.7   Major Plan Design Issues

Many plan design issues must be addressed before the actual design can be created and the plan installed. These include:

1. Who should be eligible to participate in the plan? Who must be eligible? Can several different plans be sponsored?

2. Will the funds be trustee-directed or will employees direct their own investments?

3. If the funds are trustee-directed, what will be the investment mix?

4. If the funds are employee-directed, how many funds will be available? Which particular investment funds are to be used?

5. How often can participants change their elections? Can they change past accumulated funds as well as future investment funds?

6. Should there be a limit, other than that imposed by federal government rules, on salary savings by participants?

7. How often can employees revise their salary deferral amount? Can they stop altogether at any time? What are the requirements for resuming salary deferrals?

8. Will there be matching employer contributions? If so, how much will the company match? When will the matches be credited to employee

accounts? Will the matches be set by formula or will they vary with company operating results? Will employees be required to complete several years of service in order to obtain vested rights? If not, will the company make discretionary contributions for every plan member regardless of the salary deferral?

9. Will loans be permitted? If so, will there be a minimum amount for a depositor to qualify as a borrower? Will deferrals continue during the loan repayment period? Who will pay the loan expenses, the company or the employee?

10. Will hardship withdrawals be permitted? If so, who will pay the withdrawal expenses, the company or the employee? What will be the minimum qualifying amount in order for an employee to make a withdrawal?

11. How will the plan comply with the nondiscrimination requirements regarding the salary deferrals and matching contributions?

   a. Restrict deferral limits of HCEs?

   b. Return excess salary deferrals at year end to affected HCEs?

   c. Recharacterize salary deferrals to after-tax contributions?

   d. Contribute additional 100 percent vested amounts on behalf of the non-HCEs?

   e. Credit 100 percent vesting to matching or profit-sharing contributions on behalf of the non-HCEs for aggregation of benefits?

12. Who will bear the expenses of the Plan? The employer? The employee? Should the employer bear some expenses and the employee bear other expenses? Should a distinction be made among investment expenses, administrative expenses, consulting and other professional fees, and ad hoc expenses such as loans, withdrawals, and fund exchanges?

13. Who will function as trustee: individuals, a bank, or a trust company?

14. Who will provide record-keeping services and how will the record keeper interact with the payroll department, the investment manager, the plan sponsor, and the plan members?

15. How rapidly will individuals become vested in employer contributions?

16. Will there be ancillary benefits? What amount is payable upon death, disability, or separation from service of the plan participant?

17. What is the normal retirement age under the plan?

18. When are benefits payable to a plan member who separates from service prior to normal retirement? What forms of payment are to be available?

19. Will forfeitures supplement or reduce matching contributions?

20. What will be the structure of the underlying profit-sharing benefit, if any?

Although there are many considerations in the design of a 401(k) plan, the points given above form the foundation of the design. The rest of this chapter addresses each of these design considerations.

§ 10.8   Coverage in the Plan

A primary consideration is the group or groups that are to be covered by a plan or plans. If all employees are to be covered, then no analysis of the employee group need be made in order to ensure plan qualification.

If only selected groups of employees are to be covered, various stages of analysis must take place. For example, suppose an organization that is closely held by a few shareholders wishes to cover two companies out of a group of five that are under the control of some or all of the shareholders. The first step is to determine which companies are members of either a controlled group of companies or an affiliated service group. If there are five shareholders, 1 through 5, and five companies, A, Z, C, D, and E, then an analysis of the ownership would proceed from the following facts in order to determine the controlled group. The controlled group, if it is determined to exist, would be of the brother–sister type, based on the facts at hand. It is the desire of the shareholders to cover only companies A and Z.

Companies A, Z, C, and E are members of a brother–sister controlled group. This is because five—or fewer—shareholders own 80 percent or more of each of these companies collectively and the common interest of each shareholder in all four companies in the group totals 50 percent or more. (See **Table 10–9**.) Company D is not a member of the controlled group because the total common interest among the five shareholders is

Table 10–9

Ownership of Equity in Considered Company Group

Shareholders	Companies				
	A	Z	C	D	E
1	10%	25%	30%	5%	20%
2	20	25	20	5	20
3	40	25	20	5	10
4	15	25	10	40	20
5	15	25	20	40	30

only 40 percent, which is less than the 50 percent threshold for determination of the common interest in the companies. Therefore, companies A, Z, C, and E must be considered for coverage in the plan even though the organization wishes to cover only companies A and Z. At this point, one approach may be to establish separate lines of business for companies A and Z together and companies C and E separately. This procedure, however, is cumbersome and restrictive. It is thus best to avoid the line-of-business approach if at all possible.

The coverage in the plan must comply with one of the standards set forth in Code § 410(b). An analysis for compliance with the basic 70 percent ratio test would proceed from the information in **Table 10–10**.

Because the coverage ratio of 85.2 percent exceeds the 70.0 percent threshold, the coverage of companies A and Z is permitted under Code

Table 10–10

Analysis of Coverage of Highly Compensated and Non-Highly Compensated Employees

Employees	Companies					
	A	Z	A and Z	C	E	Total
Total employees	500	1,000	1,500	400	100	2,000
Employees excluded for minimum age and service requirements	20	80	100	30	10	140
Employees considered for coverage	480	920	1,400	470	90	1,960
Highly compensated employees in the group considered for coverage	100	200	300	50	20	370
Non-highly compensated employees in the group considered for coverage	380	720	1,100	420	70	1,590
Percentage of highly compensated employees covered	300 divided by 370 times 100 = 81.1%					
Percentage of non-highly compensated employee covered	1,100 divided by 1,590 times 100 = 69.1%					
Coverage ratio	69.1% divided by 81.1% times 100 = 85.2%					

§ 410(b). Indeed, because the coverage ratios for Company C and Company E would be 195.4 percent and 81.4 percent, respectively, each company could have in place its own unique plan. In the final analysis, one plan for Companies A and Z can be established, with separate plans for Companies C and E if desired.

§ 10.9   Participation in the Plan Benefits

Once the coverage is established, it is important to be able to project the number of those eligible to participate who will actually save, and the rates of earnings that they would be able to save each year. This information is required in order to ensure the financial viability of the plan in general, and the compliance with the nondiscrimination standards in particular.

If an organization so desires, it can conduct a preliminary survey of its employees to gauge the level of plan participation, the projected plan cash flows, ancillary plan features that should be incorporated into the design, and the status of the plan relative to the ADP, ACP, and multiple use nondiscrimination standards. **Appendix A.1** illustrates a brief sample survey form for distribution to employees and assessment of the likelihood of a successful plan and a meaningful plan design.

Interpretation of survey results can require some creativity. The survey in **Appendix A.1** was targeted to non-highly compensated employees through the use of a given identity code and to highly compensated employees through a second identity code. In this way, the analysis of the results of the survey could be conducted with respect to both groups.

Table 10–11 shows a response pattern that could arise from a group of employees from Companies A and Z (see **§ 10.9**) who are to be covered in the plan. These are hypothetical results based on a realistic process of analysis.

Based on the results of the survey, it is clear that the HCEs are willing, even eager, to participate in a 401(k) CODA without much incentive. This is typical of the attitude among this group of employees; they generally have the discretionary income for savings, are more likely to plan independently for their future, including their retirement needs, and have a basic understanding of the tax benefits of such a program. For them, matching contributions, a loan program, hardship withdrawal capabilities, and a range of investment options are plan features that simply add sweeteners to a program they find attractive in its basic form.

The non-HCEs, however, need the plan incentives in order to participate. A basic program, without any incentive features, would find 72 percent or more contributing 4 percent of their earnings (question 4). The average contribution would be about 2 percent of earnings for this group. With all

Table 10–11

Preliminary 401(k) Survey Results

Questions	Non-Highly Compensated Employees	Highly Compensated Employees	Totals
1. Do you currently contribute to an individual retirement account (IRA)?			
Yes	200 (66%)	200 (18%)	400 (29%)
No	80 (27)	800 (73)	880 (63)
No response	20 (7)	100 (9)	120 (8)
Totals	300 (100%)	1,100 (100%)	1,400 (100%)
2. Do you currently save for your own retirement by any means other than an IRA?			
Yes	120 (40%)	80 (4%)	200 (15%)
No	160 (53)	920 (87)	1,080 (77)
No response	20 (7)	100 (9)	120 (8)
Totals	300 (100%)	1,100 (100%)	1,400 (100%)
3. Would you like to save for your retirement through tax-deferred payroll deductions through the company?			
Yes	270 (90%)	400 (36%)	670 (48%)
No	10 (3)	600 (55)	610 (63)
No response	20 (7)	100 (9)	120 (8)
Totals	300 (100%)	1,100 (100%)	1,400 (100%)
4. Approximately what percentage of your pay would you contribute each pay period to a retirement savings plan at the company?			
0% to 2%	60 (20%)	750 (68%)	810 (58%)
2% to 4%	80 (26)	150 (14)	230 (16)
4% to 6%	100 (33)	70 (6)	170 (12)
6% to 8%	20 (7)	30 (3)	50 (4)
8% and over	20 (7)	0 (0)	20 (2)
No response	20 (7)	100 (9)	120 (8)
Totals	300 (100%)	1,100 (100%)	1,400 (100%)
5. Would you be more likely to participate in a retirement savings plan if the company also contributed to it?			
Not likely	5 (2%)	300 (27%)	305 (22%)
Likely	75 (25)	400 (37)	475 (34)
Extremely likely	200 (66)	300 (27)	500 (36)
No response	20 (7)	100 (9)	120 (8)
Totals	300 (100%)	1,100 (100%)	1,400 (100%)

6. If the company contributed on your behalf $.50 for each $1.00 you contributed, up to 6 percent of your pay, approximately how much of your pay would you contribute each pay period through pretax payroll deductions to a retirement savings plan at the company?

Table 10–11 *(Continued)*

Questions	Non-Highly Compensated Employees	Highly Compensated Employees	Totals
0% to 2%	50 (16%)	500 (46%)	550 (40%)
2% to 4%	70 (24)	200 (19)	270 (19)
4% to 6%	80 (27)	170 (15)	250 (18)
6% to 8%	50 (16)	80 (7)	130 (9)
8% and over	30 (10)	50 (4)	80 (6)
No response	20 (7)	100 (9)	120 (8)
Totals	200 (100%)	1,100 (100%)	1,400 (100%)

7. Would you be more likely to participate in a retirement savings plan if you knew you could have access to your savings, should you need them, by borrowing against your account?

Not likely	5 (2%)	280 (25%)	285 (20%)
Likely	70 (23)	410 (38)	480 (34)
Extremely likely	205 (68)	310 (28)	515 (38)
No response	20 (7)	100 (9)	120 (8)
Totals	300 (100%)	1,100 (100%)	1,400 (100%)

8. Would you be more likely to participate in a retirement savings plan if you had the opportunity to choose your own investments from among several types of funds?

Not likely	5 (2%)	250 (23%)	255 (18%)
Likely	20 (7)	350 (32)	370 (26)
Extremely likely	255 (84)	400 (36)	675 (48)
No response	20 (7)	100 (9)	120 (8)
Totals	300 (100%)	1,100 (100%)	1,400 (100%)

9. If the company matched your contributions up to 6 percent and you were able to borrow your funds and direct your own investments among several types of funds, what percentage of your pay would you contribute each pay period to a retirement savings plan at the company?

0% to 2%	40 (13%)	400 (36%)	440 (31%)
2% to 4%	80 (27)	250 (23)	330 (24)
4% to 6%	80 (27)	190 (18)	280 (20)
6% to 8%	40 (13)	100 (9)	140 (10)
8% and over	40 (13)	60 (5)	110 (7)
No respnse	20 (7)	100 (9)	120 (8)
Totals	300 (100%)	1,100 (100%)	1,400 (100%)

10. If you are married, does your spouse have the benefit of a salary savings plan at your spouse's place of employment?

Yes		200 (18%)	250 (18%)
No		370 (34)	460 (33)
N/A—Unmarried		180 (16)	220 (16)
N/A—Spouse works in home		250 (23)	350 (25)
No response		100 (9)	120 (8)
Totals		1,100 (100%)	1,400 (100%)

incentives, including matching contributions, a loan program, hardship withdrawals, and investment options, however, there is a significant shift in the propensity to contribute to the plan (question 9). The average contribution rate under this scenario is about 3.3 percent of covered earnings. The non-HCEs are saying in this survey that they would contribute 65 percent more to a salary savings plan that provides a full range of available incentives. What is more, 34 percent of the group have working spouses with no salary savings plan at their place of employment. This statistic provides significant potential for attracting salary savings from workers in two-income families, where the total household income could be at a level that would foster salary savings in the 401(k) plan.

The attitude of the non-HCEs, as reflected in the survey, is typically found among workers today. The incentives of the plan usually stimulate participation among this group. It is essential that they participate in significant numbers, in order to have a viable program and to enable the HCEs to save at the rates that they prefer.

§ 10.10 Basic Plan Structure

The services of any 401(k) CODA, whether a stand-alone, supplemental, or thrift type, depend on a high rate of plan participation by the employees. The savings incentives and their acceptance by the employees are important for promoting plan participation and satisfying the nondiscrimination requirements. The incentives available under each type of plan are summarized in **Table 10–12**.

All three plans can provide most of the incentives that are generally employed by plan sponsors in order to stimulate plan membership, especially among non-HCEs. The thrift plan, by its vague nature, provides the major incentive of a matching contribution from the plan sponsor.

If the basic retirement program of an organization is meaningful, then the supplemental plan should be successful, despite the fact that no matching contributions are available. This is especially true if all the other possible incentives are made available.

The stand-alone 401(k) CODA is the most difficult program with which to achieve successful participation. In certain organizations, like young professional firms, the stand-alone plan can be a success. It is usually important to promote the subtle advantages relating to taxes and expense savings among employees whose average income is relatively higher.

Based on the survey results of **Table 10–11**, the plan selected for Companies A and Z (see **§ 10.8**) will have the preliminary cash flow and nondiscrimination profit shown in **Table 10–13**.

Based on the results of the survey, a plan that has a $.50 matching contribution for each $1.00 saved, a loan program, hardship withdrawal

Table 10–12

Summary of Participation Incentives Available

Incentive	Stand-Alone Plans	Supplemental Plans	Thrift Plans
Current tax benefits	Yes	Yes	Yes
Future retirement income benefits	Yes	Yes	Yes
Investment options	Yes	Yes	Yes
Loan programs	Yes	Yes	Yes
Hardship withdrawals	Yes	Yes	Yes
Automatic matches	No	No	Yes
Discretionary matches	No	No	Yes
Employer-paid expenses	Yes	Yes	Yes
Additional employer-provided retirement income	No	Yes	Yes
Advanced distributions at service separation	Yes	Yes	Yes

Table 10–13

Survey Results on Plans Selected

Employees	Highly Compensated Employees	Non-Highly Compensated Employees	Total Employees
Number covered	300	1,100	1,400
Annual earnings	$24,000,000	$33,000,000	$57,000,000
Projected savings	1,100,000	1,090,000	2,190,000
Projected matches	550,000	545,000	1,095,000
Projected ADP	4.57%	3.28%	N/A
Projected ACP	2.28%	1.64%	N/A
Projected multiple use	6.85%	N/A	N/A
Maximum projected ADP	5.28%	N/A	N/A
Maximum projected ACP	3.28%	N/A	N/A
Maximum multiple use	7.33%	N/A	N/A

privileges, and participant investment options will be a successful plan. Annual contributions are projected to total $3,285,000, which represents about 5.2 percent of annual earnings.

The basic plan structure, then, consists of the following elements:

1. Selection of the appropriate plan type, based on its strategic mission within the sponsoring organization.
2. Projection of the plan funding, to determine the financial viability of the program and the budget requirements, and limitations, for the sponsor.
3. Development of appropriate savings incentives, to stimulate participation and maximize the chances of nondiscrimination compliance.

After the basic plan structure has been developed, the details of the plan provisions can be finalized, the plan budget can be created, and the administrative contracts can be reviewed.

§ 10.11   Major Plan Provisions

Before finalizing the details of the 401(k) CODA's features, it is best to formulate the other major plan provisions. The following sections discuss them in depth.

§ 10.12   —Eligibility

The group(s) of employees to be covered will have been determined in one of the first design phases.

At this point, the eligibility requirements for entry into the plan must be determined. Under federal rules, all employees in the covered group(s) who are age 21 and have given one year of service must be eligible to enter the plan within 6 months of the first day of the plan year following satisfaction of those requirements.

One year of service can be defined to be 1,000 hours of work performed within the eligibility computation period. The key to the actual structure of the eligibility rules is the definition of the plan entry date(s). The 1,000-hours requirement can only be imposed for eligibility purposes if one year in elapsed time is required and multiple entry dates are employed. **Table 10–14** lists examples of eligibility requirements that comply with the federal rules but may or may not use the restriction of 1,000 hours worked in a year.

Table 10–14

Sample Eligibility Requirements

Example	Minimum Age	Minimum Service	Minimum Hours	Entry Date(s)
1	21 years	12 months	1,000	First day of the plan year and a date 6 months thereafter.
2	20½ years	6 months	0	First day of the plan year following satisfaction of the requirements.
3	0 years	12 months	1,000	First day of the plan year and a date 6 months thereafter.
4	0 years	6 months	0	First day of the plan year following satisfaction of the requirements.
5	21 years	12 months	1,000	First day of the month following satisfaction of the requirements.

The eligibility requirements chosen hinge on three critical factors:

1. The extent to which the profile of the plan is important in attracting new employees;
2. The fraction of the work force that normally works 1,000 hours per year or less;
3. The administrative consideration in enrolling employees and in conducting the nondiscrimination tests.

It is important to promote the 401(k) plan in recruiting employees. The plan is an attractive benefit that enhances the competitive position of the firm in the labor market. What is more, once the new employee enters the plan, the individual will be inclined to save at a rate beneficial to the plan. It may be desirable to allow entry into the plan as quickly as possible after a new person joins the organization. Under these conditions, a short service requirement with immediate entry thereafter would be desirable. Many organizations, particularly those with stand-alone plans, allow entry into the plan shortly after hiring. Some organizations allow rapid entry into the 401(k) CODA portion of a supplemental or thrift plan but defer participation in the supplemental plan itself or the total thrift feature until a later date.

In some firms or industries, there may be a disproportionate number of employees who normally work fewer than 1,000 hours each year. Often considered part-time employees by the organization, they may have little incentive to save for their retirement under a plan, especially if they are young, entry-level workers. To exclude these workers, it may be best to require 12 months/1,000 hours of service before entry into the plan on one of the multiple entry dates.

Some organizations may prefer to limit enrollment to one or two dates per year. In this case, annual or semiannual entry dates may be preferable. For nondiscrimination testing, earnings as a participant are used to compute the rates. Using an annual entry day may ease the administrative burden because earnings of all plan members will be compiled on the same annual basis.

§ 10.13   —Normal Retirement Date

Each qualified retirement plan, including any 401(k) plan, must define a normal retirement date—the date on which full benefits are payable under the plan. The date is specifically related to a particular age. A typical plan provision might be: A plan member can retire on the first day of the month following attainment of the member's 65th birthday. The participant's normal retirement age would then be considered to be 65. Although the normal retirement age can be established, in general, at any age below 65, most organizations attempt to establish a retirement age that is considered to coincide with completion of a full career with the organization. Some organizations also require minimum service before retirement with benefits. Today, the most service that can be required is 5 years while a participant in the plan. Under this type of normal retirement formula, individuals can retire on the later of the first day of the month following the 65th birthday or the fifth anniversary of the date of plan participation. As will be seen in the following section on vesting, normal retirement dates in 401(k) plans are mostly formalities; benefits are usually paid immediately, at any time when employment of a participant terminates.

§ 10.14   —Vesting

Employees earn equity in their retirement accounts, based on their years of service with the plan sponsor, through the concept of vesting. **Section 3.20,** which reviews the federal rules for vesting in detail, summarizes the difference between the elapsed-time and the 1,000-hour methods for determining a year of service for vesting credit. In general, once a method is adopted, the federal rules allow two alternative vesting schemes that represent the least rapid schedules under which vesting can occur. **Table 10–15** compares the two alternatives.

In 401(k) CODA plans, all salary savings of the plan members are immediately 100 percent vested to the participants. If the participant separates from service with the organization before normal retirement age, the participant is always entitled to the salary savings accounts in the plan, adjusted for the gains or losses from income accumulated over the years, without regard to the years of service with the plan sponsor.

The employer contributions, or benefits, in the supplemental and thrift 401(k) CODAs are not under the vesting schedule of the salary savings accounts. The least rapid vesting schedules can be applied to the basic contributions, or benefits, in the supplemental plan and the matching employer contributions in the thrift plan. More rapid vesting can be employed, but the vested interest accumulated up to any one year must meet or exceed the vested percentage of one of the statutory minimum schedules. **Table 10–16** gives examples of vesting schedules that are more liberal than those permitted under the federal rules.

In the supplemental approach to 401(k) CODA plans, the schedule actually adopted for the employer contributions depends on the type of basic plan in operation; in the thrift approach, the schedule depends on the nature of the work force and the competition for labor.

Under the supplemental approach, if the underlying plan is a defined-benefit pension plan, then the vesting schedule of that plan can usually stand on its own merits and objectives, without regard to the supplemental 401(k) CODA. If the basic plan is a defined-contribution plan, however, it may be helpful to apply less restrictive vesting in the employer-provided

Table 10–15

Least Rapid Vesting Schedules

Years of Service	Alternative 1	Alternative 2
0	0%	0%
1	0	0
2	0	0
3	0	20
4	0	40
5	100	60
6	100	80
7 or more	100	100

Table 10–16

**Examples of Permitted Vesting Schedules in
Supplemental and Thrift Plans**

Years of Service	Schedule 1	Schedule 2	Schedule 3	Schedule 4
0	0	0	0	0
1	20	10	0	0
2	40	20	0	0
3	60	30	0	30
4	80	40	50	60
5	100	60	100	90
6	100	80	100	100
7 or more	100	100	100	100

benefits, in certain instances. Defined-contribution plans tend to be more easily understood by participants, more practicable than defined-benefit plans, and more certain for budgeting and costs. In industries where a mobile work force is an accepted condition, rapid vesting can be an enhancement that aids in the attraction of employees to the organization. In an organization or industry that requires longer-term stability of the work force, less rapid vesting can aid in the retention of employees.

These principles also apply to the vesting schedule to be adopted in a thrift plan. Vesting in matching employer contributions can be more or less rapid, based on the objectives of the sponsoring organization relative to its work force, its industry, and its own unique circumstances and budget. In addition, more rapid vesting can aid in increasing plan participation among new employees. Participants who are newcomers to an organization may be more inclined to use the salary savings program if they know that the employer's contribution will inure to them rapidly.

§ 10.15 —Withdrawal Benefits

If a participant separates from service prior to normal retirement age, the participant is entitled to certain withdrawal benefits. The benefits amount is the vested interest in the plan account(s) that has accumulated to the participant's credit during the years of participation in the plan. The participant's vested interest is 100 percent of the salary savings account, along with a fraction of the basic plan benefits in the supplemental program and the matching employer contribution in the thrift program. The balance of the funds credited to the employee is forfeited and provides benefits to the other members of the plan.

Under federal rules, the payment of these withdrawal benefits can be deferred to the later of:

1. The normal retirement date under the plan;
2. Age 65;
3. The tenth anniversary of participation in the plan.

Even though a plan member separates from service many years prior to normal retirement under the plan, benefit payments under the plan can be deferred all of those years until the normal retirement date is reached.

Employees view their salary savings under the 401(k) CODA as their own money, set aside for retirement in much the same way as the ordinary savings they may accumulate privately in a bank or other financial institution. Accessibility to the funds and portability of the funds are usually very important characteristics of the benefits among plan participants. Employees generally will not participate in a plan if they know that their benefits will be payable, not at separation from service, but only after they have achieved normal retirement age at a distant future time. Most 401(k) plans are designed to remedy this concern by permitting advance distributions: benefit payments are made at a time corresponding to the actual date of separation from service. Typically, advance distributions are made under the following types of administrative procedures:

1. Benefits are payable immediately on the day of separation.
2. Benefits are payable after the next valuation date following the separation from service.
3. Benefits are payable after the next valuation date following the occurrence of one (or several) break(s)-in-service.

The actual value of the benefits payable and the benefit payment timing policy can depend largely on the administrative systems tracking the benefits, as well as the philosophy of the organization.

Plans that are tracked through systems that provide daily values of plan accounts offer the plan sponsor the ability to pay benefits virtually immediately, at the market value, on the date of the distribution. Plans that are tracked through the use of separate financial institutions and record-keeping organizations usually conduct valuations on a less frequent basis (monthly, quarterly, semiannually, or annually). The long time constraints imposed by these methods of record keeping and valuation may force the plan sponsor to distribute benefits only after a valuation date has followed the separation from service. The benefit amount must be equal to the value established on that prior valuation date.

The nature of the plan investments themselves may have an impact on the benefit payout policy. A plan that permits, or has, only fixed-income investments takes little risk in deferring a payment to a subsequent valuation date. A plan that permits, or has, volatile investments may experience downturns in performance between a valuation date and a distribution date. This will create the effect of paying a benefit at a previously determined higher value and leaving the losses behind for allocation to the remaining plan members. The plan sponsor is clearly motivated in this investment context to distribute benefits on a valuation date. In the best of all worlds, daily valuations ensure that, whenever they occur, distributions are valued at market and gains and losses are accurately reflected in all accounts every day. The design of the distribution feature of the plan then depends on:

1. The distribution philosophy relative to the plan and the incentive for participants;
2. The valuation capabilities of the plan sponsor;
3. The notice of the investments.

See §§ **10.25** and **10.27** for a further discussion of investment and administrative policies.

§ 10.16   —Death Benefits

Upon the death of a married plan member, at least 50 percent of the vested interest of the member must be payable to the spouse, unless the spouse waives the right to this benefit. No death benefits are required for single plan members. At the death of a married plan member, only 50 percent of the vested accounts need be distributed to a surviving spouse; at the death of a single plan member, no benefits need be payable. The remaining funds, in either case, can be forfeited for the benefit of other plan members.

Under the 401(k) CODA, because the plan members have saved from their own salaries, it is essential that they know that their funds will be available to their heirs should the members die prematurely. Most 401(k) CODA plans provide that all salary savings accounts are payable at death to the named beneficiaries of both married and unmarried plan members. It is also prevalent today to provide the full value of all accounts as a death benefit in the defined-contribution supplemental plan and the thrift plan, regardless of the vested interest at the time of death. At the death of the plan member prior to retirement, most plans provide the full value of all accounts to the plan participants.

The plan rules for naming beneficiaries can vary, based on the flexibility the plan wishes to provide, possible administrative constraints, and the death benefit plan in the organization. For married plan members, there are several plan design options:

1. All death benefits payable to the spouse mandatorily. This eliminates the need for any elections or spousal consent to waiver of benefits.
2. The statutory minimum benefit payable to the spouse, with the participant designating a beneficiary(s) for the balance of the funds. This allows the participant to designate a beneficiary(s) and simultaneously eliminates the need to obtain a spousal consent to waiver.
3. Each participant may designate any beneficiary(s). Under this approach, the spouse must consent to the waiver of the death benefits and to the beneficiary(s) named by the plan member.

Unmarried plan members would always name a beneficiary(s). In light of this, and to satisfy the desire to provide flexibility for the plan members, most plans adopt the third option indicated above, allowing all plan members to name a beneficiary(s) for the full value of their accounts in the plan.

Some plans that have participant-directed investment options (see § 10.25) allow participants to supplement their preretirement death benefits through the purchase of life insurance. Plan members can earmark a fraction of their salary savings, along with a portion of the employer contributions, for a life insurance policy. Participants who choose this option designate a beneficiary(s) who would then typically receive the proceeds of the policy and the value of the other investment accounts at the death of the plan member.

Some plans provide that the full employer contribution for the year is payable to the deceased plan member's account, even if the participant died prior to a contribution allocation date (see § 10.16) and was technically not employed on that date.

Postretirement death benefits are dependent on the form of payment elected by the plan participant. (See § 10.15 for the forms of payment offered in a plan.) Most plan members elect single-sum payments, which means that the formal plan death benefits available cease at retirement.

§ 10.17 —Disability Benefits

There are no statutory requirements to provide disability benefits in a 401(k) CODA. If a plan member were to become totally and permanently disabled and were forced to separate from service, the withdrawal benefit would be payable. Some plans add to the withdrawal benefit payable, if the participant becomes permanently and totally disabled, by providing (1) full vesting and (2) a full allocation of the employer contribution for the year, despite the fact that the employee had separated from service prior to the allocation date. In the 401(k) arena, disability benefits have little impact. They have their greatest utility for plan members who have short service and partial vesting. Traditionally, disability benefits in retirement programs have been supplemental to basic benefits payable to those with longer service who have become totally and permanently disabled. Disability benefits in 401(k) plans are thus fringe benefits at best; they provide no meaningful additional retirement income to the group of employees most likely to be targeted for the benefits.

§ 10.18   —Other Provisions

Most other plan provisions that are incorporated into the design are statutory in nature and/or are common to all types of qualified retirement programs. These include but are not limited to the following provisions:

1. Benefits are limited to 25 percent of net annual earnings up to $30,000 each year.
2. Benefits payments must commence on the April 1 following the attainment of age 70½.
3. Covered earnings are limited to $228,860 (for 1992) as indexed by the IRS.
4. Salary deferrals are limited to $8,728 (for 1992) as indexed by the IRS.
5. Early retirement benefits can be provided but they have little significance in the context of a 401(k) CODA. Most plans do not incorporate a formal early retirement benefit because full vested rights are always payable after 5 or 7 years of service.
6. Rollover contributions from other qualified plans can be accepted. This provision would be incorporated into the plan at the option of the plan sponsor. It is another sweetener that can be added to a plan to encourage participation by new employees who were previously employed by another organization that provided a qualified retirement distribution.

All of these other plan provisions affect the operation of the 401(k) CODA plan.

§ 10.19   Matching Contributions

Matching contributions in the thrift plans can follow various formulas and schemes. (See § 10.4.) Typically, a plan sponsor will match at a certain rate, up to a proscribed percentage of earnings. Matching contributions can be graded to provide higher rates at lower savings levels. They can be capped with maximum dollar levels in lieu of a maximum percentage of covered earnings. In theory, they can be based on any variety of schemes that could be imagined. The plan must, however, comply with the nondiscrimination standards (see § 10.5) for the entire plan year.

Salary savings are typically withdrawn from the participants' earnings each payroll period. The savings are then deposited in the plan trust fund, usually within 31 days of the close of the month in which the salary savings were withdrawn.

Monthly contributions are usually made under one of these approaches:

1. They are deposited coincidentally with the deposits of the salary savings.
2. They are deposited at each allocation date, for plans with quarterly, semiannual, or annual allocations.
3. They are deposited at the final allocation date, regardless of the number of allocation dates that occur during the plan year.

When employees terminate employment with less than the 100 percent vested interest in matching contributions, the unvested value of the account is forfeited. The forfeited funds can then be used to provide benefits for other plan participants by either supplementing the matching contributions for the next year or reducing the deposit required by the employer to meet its obligation for the next year.

The plan rules for matching contributions and the benefits derived from them can vary, based on the objectives of the plan sponsor. (See **Table 10–17**.)

The characteristics of the matching contributions are thus the cornerstone of the design of thrift plans, not only in the concept itself but also in the mechanics of their delivery to the members of the plan.

§ 10.20   Loans

Participant loans can be included in the plan at the option of the plan sponsor. Employees are thought to be more likely to participate in a plan if they know they can have access to their funds should they need them.

Table 10–17

Characteristics of Matching Contributions Relative to Sponsor Objectives

Objective	Deposits	Flexibility	Forfeitures	Formula
1. Provide definite match each year at minimal cost without regard to visibility	Annually	1,000 hours and active on last day of the year	Reduce employee contributions	Proscribed
2. Provide definite match each year with high visibility to employees	Coincident with savings deposits	Employed on payroll withdrawal date	Reduce employer contributions	Proscribed
3. Provide pure profit salary incentive	Annually	1,000 hours and active on last day of the year	Supplement employer contribution	Discretionary
4. Provide profit-sharing incentive with minimum guaranteed highly visible match	Annually for profit sharing. Coincident with savings deposits for matching contribution.	1,000 hours and active on last day of the year for profit sharing. Employed on payroll withdrawal date for matching contribution.	Supplement employer contribution	Proscribed and discretionary
5. Provide visible match while minimizing cash flow outlays and plan costs	Each allocation period	Employed on allocation date	Reduce employer contribution	Proscribed

With the loan provision, employees can, within the federal rules, borrow from the plan the funds that they require, and repay the loan through additional payroll deductions. The loan provision thus offers additional incentives for plan participants.

In general, employees can borrow half of their vested interest in the plan, up to $50,000. (See § **4.11** and § **5.11** for complete details on loan rules.) This cap applies to loans secured by the employees' plan benefits. Up to $10,000 can be borrowed even when this amount exceeds half of the vested interest, if the plan is secured by an outside source. Indeed, up to $10,000 can be borrowed by a participant with no vested interest at all, as long as the loan is properly secured.

The loans must be repaid within 5 years, with at least quarterly installments. The 5-year requirement can be extended for the purchase of a principal residence. Plans will typically lend the equivalent of a one-half vested interest, up to $50,000, with repayments through payroll deductions, in order to simplify the administration of the plan.

The interest rate charged on the loan should reflect current market rates of interest. Typically, plans will set as their rates the prime rate of interest from their sponsor's commercial bank plus 100 or 200 basis points. The plan loan can thus be an attractive benefit to the employee. The employee can obtain a loan at a market rate of interest with none of the fees that are associated with loans from other institutions. In paying back the loan at the wholesale rate, the participant is earning a higher rate of interest on the retirement funds than could be earned at the retail rate. Plan loans can therefore (1) stimulate participation in the plan, (2) provide capital for the borrower at a competitive cost, and (3) generate a higher fixed-income yield in the participant's retirement funds.

§ 10.21   Hardship Withdrawals

Hardship withdrawals provide another means for plan participants to have access to their savings funds. (See § **2.17** for a complete discussion of the rules governing hardship withdrawals and the hardships that qualify for the withdrawals.) Allowing hardship withdrawals is considered yet another sweetener for the employees to participate in the plan. It is felt that, if employees know they have access to their funds in the event of one of the proscribed hardships, they may be more likely to participate in the plan.

Hardship withdrawals are more complicated to justify than loans, and the funds themselves may be subject to excise taxes upon withdrawal. Thus, a withdrawal for hardship will be subject to income tax and a 10 percent excise tax. The full use of the funds is not available, and retirement income is lost when hardship withdrawals take place. Plan loans are a much more attractive vehicle for providing plan participants with access to funds.

§ 10.22   Nondiscrimination Standards

The salary savings of the plan members and the matching contributions must be nondiscriminatory. (See **Chapter 2** for the full details on the definition of nondiscrimination in 401(k) CODAs and Code § 401(m) matching contributions.) To demonstrate compliance with the nondiscrimination standards, the salary savings must pass the actual deferral percentage test ("ADP Test") and the matching contributions must pass the actual contributions percentage test ("ACP test"). Both salary savings and matching contributions must pass these tests *and* the multiple use test (MUT), in order to comply with the nondiscrimination standards. If the plan fails the ADP Test for the year, then elective deferrals must be returned to the HCE in descending order of savings rates relative to annual earnings. (See § **2.14** for a complete description of the process by which salary savings are determined for return to the appropriate HCEs, to satisfy the ADP Test.) The returned elective deferrals and taxable income must be returned within 2½ months following the close of the plan year. This timing causes administrative burdens for the plan as well as great inconvenience for the HCEs who, in some cases, may be forced to recognize taxable income for federal and state purposes after they have filed their tax returns. If this were the case, the HCEs affected by the return of elective deferrals would be required to file amended tax returns with both the federal and state governments and to pay additional taxes due and any applicable penalties.

Similarly, if the plan fails the ACP Test, nonvested portions of the matching contributions for the HCEs are forfeited in descending order of matching contribution rates relative to annual earnings. Once the nonvested contributions are exhausted, the matching contributions themselves are distributed in descending order of the rate of contribution relative to annual earnings, until the ACP Test is satisfied. (See § **2.20** for a complete description of the process by which matching contributions are forfeited and returned to the HCEs in order to satisfy the ACP Test.) If the matching contributions must be returned to certain HCEs, the same administrative burdens fall on the plan. In addition, the same tax filing inconveniences fall on the HCEs as when elective deferrals are returned after failing the ADP Test.

Finally, failure of the multiple use test can again result in return of elective deferrals to and/or forfeitures of and return of matching contributions to certain HCEs. The same administrative and tax liability problems would be applicable in compliance with this test as well.

§ 10.23 —Compliance

To avoid these burdens and inconveniences associated with the return of contributions at year end, certain administrative policies can be incorporated into the design of the plan. Once it is known that the non-HCEs can be expected to save at a given average rate of annual earnings, several preemptive policies can be adopted to ensure that the plan complies with the nondiscrimination standards. Among these policies are the following:

1. Establish a maximum rate of savings in the plan that ensures compliance at year end.

2. Establish a maximum rate of savings for the plan for the HCEs only. This will allow the non-HCEs to save as much as they wish but will restrict the HCEs to a level that ensures compliance with the nondiscrimination standards at year end.

3. Create some flexibility, if the earnings of the HCEs are largely year-end bonuses. The organization can limit salary savings during the year to a small fraction of earnings for the HCEs, while monitoring the ADP, ACP, and multiple user profiles of the plan. The organization can then pay the bonuses before year end, allowing the HCEs to save as much as is tolerable under the actual results of the tests during the plan year.

4. Commit, on behalf of the non-HCEs, to contributions that have the characteristics of 401(k) elective deferrals or matching contributions (Code § 401(m)), to enable the plan to pass the ADP, ACP, and multiple use tests. (See § 2.5 for the description of elective deferrals and qualified nonelective contributions.)

5. Commit to contributions, on behalf of all employees, that will have the characteristics of 401(k) elective deferrals or Code § 401(m) matching contributions, to enable the plan to pass the ADP, ACP, and multiple use tests. (This approach is usually effective only where the average deferral rate of the non-HCEs is relatively high—8 percent or more.)

6. Convert what otherwise would have been discretionary profit-sharing plan contributions to qualified nonelective contributions, to enable the plan to pass the tests. Again, a high rate of elective deferral by the non-HCEs would be needed, for this approach to be effective.

7. Aggregate qualified matching contributions (matching contributions with the characteristics of 401(k) elective deferrals) with 401(k) salary savings in order to pass the ADP Test—and vice versa, to pass the ACP Test. Contributions can only be used for one test. In some circumstances, it may be effective to eliminate matching contributions for the HCEs and aggregate those of the non-HCEs in order to pass the ADP Test. The ACP Test is then passed by definition because the average rate of match would be technically 0 percent for both the HCEs and the non-HCEs.

8. Convert what otherwise might have been matching contributions to qualified matching contributions, to pass the tests. Usually, high

rates of salary savings among the non-HCEs are required, if the technique is to be effective.

9. Recharacterize elective deferrals of the HCEs as after-tax contributions. This saves the step of returning the funds to the affected HCEs, but it still leaves a tax liability for those participants. In addition, because the after-tax contributions must be included in the ACP Test, the recharacterized contributions may cause failure of this Code § 401(m) compliance standard.

10. Exclude some or all of the HCEs from the salary savings benefits of the plan in such a way that the ADP of the HCEs is reduced to a possible minimum or even to zero. This approach is effective especially in small and medium-size organizations and in organizations where the ratio of HCEs to total number of employees is small. The nonparticipating employees then can be covered, if the organization wishes, in a nonqualified retirement plan that either mirrors the 401(k) plan or provides even better executive retirement benefits.

A plan must be monitored every year for changes in its nondiscrimination profile. As changes occur, different administrative policies from among this group of ten can be utilized to ensure compliance and to avoid the problems associated with the return of contributions.

§ 10.24   Top-Heavy Plans

In general, a plan is top-heavy if 60 percent of the historical value of the plan benefits are on behalf of the key employees. (See § 3.24 for a discussion of top-heavy plans generally and for the definition of key employees.) Key employees and highly compensated employees are defined differently. In general, most organizations will have a different number of key employees, as compared to highly compensated employees.

If a 401(k) plan is top-heavy, then the contributions and forfeitures allocated to non-key employees must be at least as much as the maximum additions allocated to any key employee. The maximum allocation required is 3 percent of annual earnings. Salary deferrals of the key employees are includable in determining the maximum annual addition allocated to any one key employee. Salary deferrals of the non-key employees, however, are not includable in determining the annual addition that must be allocated to the non-key employees.

The result of this requirement is that, if a key employee saves 3 percent or more of salary in a 401(k) CODA, the organization must contribute at least 3 percent of earnings to each non-key employee in addition to any salary savings or matching contributions made on behalf of those non-key employees.

An organization with a top-heavy program has several approaches available, in satisfying the rules stated in the Code:

1. Make a contribution of at least 3 percent of earnings each year, on behalf of the non-key employees only, or on behalf of all employees. This will ensure compliance with the top-heavy requirements, so that the plan can operate smoothly. In addition, if the 3 percent contribution has the characteristics of a 401(k) elective deferral, it can be aggregated with the salary savings in order to pass the ADP Test. A 3 percent contribution to the non-key employees can thus ensure top-heavy compliance and possibly ADP Test passage simultaneously.

2. Exclude key employees from salary savings in the plan. This altogether eliminates the need for a minimum contribution for the non-key employees.

3. Exclude key employees from matching contributions in the plan. In some cases, excluding key employees from matching contributions will result in elimination of the ACP Test requirements. If so, the matching contributions of the non-key employees can be used to satisfy the top-heavy requirements. (Any contributions by the employee that are not used to satisfy the ACP Test can be used to satisfy the top-heavy requirements.) In this case, the organization need only provide the difference between the contribution actually made and 3 percent of annual earnings for each non-key employee.

In some instances, it is to the employer's advantage to contribute 4 percent, 5 percent, or 7½ percent of annual earnings for the non-key employees, in order to satisfy the top-heavy requirements. In instances where a defined-benefit plan also covers the plan participants, it may be beneficial to satisfy the top-heavy requirements through the second plan. This allows the 401(k) plan to operate smoothly without regard to the top-heavy minimum benefit requirements. At the same time, compliance is achieved in the defined-benefit plan.

§ 10.25   Investment Options

In general, plan investments can be directed by the trustee(s) or by the plan participants themselves. In a trustee-directed plan, the trustee, usually under the advice of an investment manager, structures the portfolio of the plan. It is the responsibility of the trustee, under this approach, to

maximize return and minimize risk. In a 401(k) plan, the plan participants view their salary savings as their own capital. They may tend to be
disgruntled and indeed shy away from plan participation if the portfolio
return to the plan and their accounts has a downward trend or even results
in investment losses. Trustees usually adopt conservative investment policies under these circumstances, in order to minimize the likelihood of
investment losses.

Some plan participants, on the other hand, may be willing to take some
risks in order to gain an opportunity for high investment returns. These
plan participants may be dissatisfied with a conservative approach to the
investment of their retirement savings. In either case, if employees perceive they have no control over the investment of their own savings, plan
membership may not be as high as it otherwise could be.

Typically, today's plan members are offered options to invest their
funds. When employees can choose from among several different types of
investments and make their own election, they will feel more secure about
the program and will be more willing to participate. Investment options
thus provide additional incentives for employees to participate, because
they allow the plan members themselves some control over the investment
portfolio.

The investment options provided to plan members should span the full
range of opportunities, from the fixed-return type of investment with
guaranteed opportunities of principal, to higher-risk investments that offer
greater return opportunities in the long run. The types of investments used
in these programs are summarized as follows:

- Certificates of deposit
- Common stocks
- Corporate bonds
- Government banks and notes
- Insurance contracts
- Pooled funds
- Real estate and real estate trusts.

The offerings themselves can be structured in several ways. They can be
self-developed, in which case the trustees choose investments in each prescribed category as new funds become available. Alternatively, they can
be offered through a product line provided by a bank, an insurance company, a brokerage firm, or a combination of all of these. Finally, a group of
pooled funds can be offered in combination with other investments and
other pooled funds, or through only a single family of pooled funds.

Pooled funds offer the trustees and the plan members the opportunity to participate in funds that are professionally managed; to subscribe to written, clearly stated investment objectives; and to enjoy the diversification associated with a large underlying investment base. Pooled funds provide an efficient means whereby several effective investment alternatives can be offered employees on a cost-effective basis.

Pooled funds are available through banks, brokerage firms, and insurance companies, which create their own diversified accounts with specific objectives. Mutual funds are also available through many open-ended and closed-ended investment companies.

A typical offering today might include a fixed return fund, with guaranteed principal; a growth mutual fund; and a balanced mutual fund. With selections such as these, each employee can develop a portfolio that suits his or her own risk tolerance, within the framework of the time left until retirement.

Investment options not only provide investors to participate for the employees but they also serve to shift some fiduciary responsibilities from the trustees to the plan members. The investment options must be structured so that participants can shift funds and otherwise exercise control over their investments at least four times a year. In addition, they must be offered a wide range of investments, consisting of at least three diversified categories of investments. Finally, information about the investments must be available to the employees at all times. (See § **5.7** for a full discussion of the Proposed Regulations of the U.S. Department of Labor regarding fiduciary relief under ERISA § 404(c).)

§ 10.26   Plan Expenses

Certain expenses will be incurred in designing, installing, and administering the 401(k) CODA. These expenses can be summarized as follows:

- Attorney's fees
- Consultant's fees
- Auditor's fees
- Administrative expenses
- Record-keeping expenses
- Investment fees
- Trustees' fees.

These fees can be consolidated through the use of a full service provided to design, install, and administer the plan, or they can be directed to individualized service providers and professional organizations.

Plan sponsors have three basic design options regarding the plan expenses: They can be fully paid by the employer, fully paid by the plan participants, or partially paid by the employer and the plan members. The extent to which any of these three alternatives is adopted depends on the strategic mission of the plan, the overall expenses of the plan, the structure of the expenses (consolidated versus diversified), the size of the plan in assets, the size of the plan in membership, and the nature of the expenses themselves (direct charges or indirect fees extracted from gross investment returns).

Generally, employer-paid plans provide an additional incentive for the employee to participate in the program; employers paying all programs do experience a higher level of participation. Investment expenses, by their very nature, can be passed on directly to the plan members. Banks, mutual funds, and insurance companies, for instance, have products in which fees are deducted from gross returns so that a net yield is credited to the plan and the participant. Many sponsors will bear the administrative expenses but will pass along the investment expenses to the plan members, either indirectly through the investment vehicle or directly as a charge to the participant's accounts.

Plans where employees pay all expenses ("pay-all plans") are rare but they do occur. Supplemental and thrift plans that cover a relatively high-earning population that needs little encouragement to understand the benefits and participate in the plan may be able to pass the charges on to the employees. This approach may be successful, for example, in a professional organization of engineers or lawyers that also sponsors an attractive employer-paid basic retirement plan.

§ 10.27   Administrative Framework

Certain operational features of the plan can add to its visibility and flexibility so that plan membership is enhanced. Among these features are:

1. Benefit statements. If employees are notified of the status of their accounts frequently, they should be more likely to save solely in the plan. For many plans today, the typical pattern is to send out quarterly statements. Few plans provide only annual statements.

2. Revised savings rates. Employees are usually given the opportunity to revise the rate or the amount of their salary savings on a proscribed basis. The typical approach is to allow revisions at the same frequency as the issuance of benefit statements. Quarterly statements will coincide, for instance, with a quarterly opportunity to revise the savings rate.

3.   Cessation of savings. Although a plan provides proscribed times to revise savings, it is usually a good idea to allow complete cessation at any time. This permits the participant the security of knowing that, if the money otherwise saved is needed for an emergency, the payroll deductions can be stopped.

4.   Revised investment mix. Typical practice is to allow employees to revise both their current and their future investment mixes on a schedule that is coincident with the benefit statement date. Individuals can exchange assets among funds once each quarter with quarterly statements, every 6 months with semiannual statements, and so forth.

This chapter has discussed the major issue of the design of 401(k) salary reduction CODAs. **Chapter 14** discusses the plan installation and annual administration of 401(k) CODAs.

CHAPTER 11

TAX-SHELTERED ANNUITY PLAN DESIGN

§ 11.1 Types of Tax-Sheltered Annuity Plans

Tax-sheltered annuity plans can be offered by nonprofit organizations described under Code § 501(c)(3). (See § **6.2** for a complete review of the types of organizations that can offer tax-sheltered annuity plans.) Like the 401(k) CODAs, there are stand-alone, supplemental, and thrift tax-sheltered annuity plans; they can have the same basic strategic missions as their 401(k) counterparts. The major difference is that a tax-sheltered annuity plan consists of an individual annuity contract for each employee, written by an insurance company under Code § 403(b), or an individual custodial account for each employee, created by a regulated investment company under Code § 403(b)(7). The 401(k) CODA is a qualified retirement plan under Code § 401(a); it covers a proscribed group of employees.

§ 11.2 Stand-Alone Plans

In a stand-alone plan, the nonprofit organization offers an array of investment opportunities for the employees, in order to help them provide for their own retirement. No other retirement vehicles are offered. In these plans, it is usually important to select service providers who manage investments for similar institutions. A university or a teaching hospital will often employ insurance companies and/or mutual fund companies that are service providers for other universities and teaching hospitals. In this way, the element of portability is added to the plan. When an employee separates from service at one such institution and joins another similar institution, the salary savings carried in those investment vehicles can be continued with the new employer. The stand-alone plan must cover all employees willing to save $200 or more each year. No other coverage rules and no other nondiscrimination rules apply.

§ 11.3 Supplemental Plans

The salary savings provided by the tax-sheltered annuity can be supplemental to a basic retirement program. The nonprofit organization can sponsor a Code § 401(a) defined-benefit pension plan or a defined-contribution plan that is structured in the same manner as a plan for a for-profit organization and is subject to the same federal rules under the Internal Revenue Code and ERISA. The annuity contracts are additional vehicles offered by the institution to afford employees expanded opportunities for retirement savings.

Tax-sheltered annuities are defined-contribution plans by their very nature. Some nonprofit organizations that wish to sponsor a basic plan will finance that plan through a tax-sheltered annuity. For example, an employer may wish to provide a 5 percent annual contribution through a money-purchase pension plan type of arrangement. The tax-sheltered annuity can be employed by depositing the annual 5 percent contribution on behalf of each plan participant into the tax-sheltered annuity contracts or custodial accounts established on behalf of each plan participant.

In the supplemental plan, where the program is financed by the tax-sheltered annuity, the basic plan is subject to the same coverage rules, participation standards, and nondiscrimination requirements that govern any plan that is to qualify under Code § 401(a). These plans are, in essence, subject to the same major coverage and operating requirements as a traditional retirement plan in the for-profit sector.

The advantages to using the tax-sheltered annuity plan as a financing vehicle for a basic retirement program are:

1. Plan documentation requirements are less stringent than in a traditional Code § 401(a) plan.

2. No submission to the IRS is needed for the offering institution.

3. Participants control their own investments and administrate their own accounts.

4. No benefit processing by the employer is required at retirement or separation from service.

5. The insurance company and regulated investment companies file the annual return/report for the tax-sheltered accounts. The offering organization need not file an annual return/report.

6. The administrative expenses are lessened in the tax-sheltered annuity context.

The major disadvantages, as seen by potential sponsors of basic retirement plans financed by a tax-sheltered annuity, are the very provisions that others might find advantageous. Tax-sheltered annuity contracts and custodial accounts are titled to the individual employees. As such, employees are always 100 percent vested in their own salary savings *and* the contribution made by the employer. An employer cannot require a prolonged length of service by the employee in order to achieve full vesting in the employer-provided accounts. Because the contracts and accounts are self-administrated and portable, employees can apply for withdrawals, take distributions, and apply for loans independently, without regard for any organizational policy. What one employer sees as an advantage can be viewed as a disadvantage by another employer.

Employers interested in ease of administration, provision of accelerated vesting, and portability of the plan for employees, can use the tax-sheltered annuity as the financing vehicle for the basic plan. Those interested in requiring longer-term vesting and applying uniform administrative policies and practices should install a traditional Code § 401(a) qualified retirement plan as their basic program. Finally, those organizations wishing to install a defined-benefit pension plan must create a Code § 401(a) qualified plan as the basic program.

§ 11.4 Thrift Plans

The tax-sheltered annuity plan can also be accompanied by a thrift feature. As with the 401(k) CODA, the employer can agree to match certain salary savings with an additional contribution. For example, the employer can provide $.50 for each $1.00 saved by the employee, up to a certain level—say, 6 percent—of covered earnings.

Because the matching contributions are nonelective contributions by the employer, they are subject to the coverage, participation, and nondiscrimination standards of Code § 401(a) qualified plans. In addition, they, like the matching contributions in the 401(k) CODA, must satisfy the actual contribution percentage test (ACP Test) of Code § 401(m). (See § **2.19** for a description of the ACP Test compliance parameters.)

The matching contributions can be financed through the tax-sheltered annuity contracts and/or custodial accounts. The employer simply determines the matching contributions and deposits them into the proper annuity contract and/or custodial accounts for each individual employee. Because they are employer contributions to a tax-sheltered annuity, they are subject to the same vesting requirements and other advantages (and disadvantages) of employer deposits into such vehicles, as described in § **11.3**.

As with the basic defined-contribution plan (see § **11.3**), if the employer, alternatively, wishes to extend the vesting period for matching contributions and to exert uniform administrative control on them, it can establish, under Code § 401(a), a second qualified retirement plan just to accumulate the matching contribution accounts. Such a plan would be subject to all the IRS and ERISA requirements as well as the administrative burdens associated with such a plan.

Employers interested in providing enhanced retirement benefits in conjunction with the employees' own commitment to salary savings, but with minimized administrative burdens, can provide matching contributions through the tax-sheltered annuity insurance contracts and/or custodial accounts. Employers wishing to provide the same enhancement through matching contributions, but desiring a requirement of longer service to achieve equity in plan contributions and to exercise administrative control, can install a Code § 401(a) plan to accumulate matching contribution accounts. In both cases, the employer will have the benefit of knowing that it is contributing on behalf of its employees who are, in turn, willing to save and committed to providing for their own retirement. The employer is thus providing benefits for employees who, it can feel fairly certain, will appreciate and value the benefit provided.

§ 11.5 Major Plan Features

The stand-alone, supplemental, and thrift tax-sheltered annuity plans have certain features in common. It is important to remember that a tax-sheltered annuity, an insurance policy or a custodial account is an individual contract titled to each employee covered in the program. Annuities and accounts are created by insurance companies and regulated investment companies, which obtain tax qualification for their contracts and products, for marketing to the public. They differ from Code § 401(a) retirement plans in that they are approved investment vehicles that can be offered by employers of certain nonprofit organizations. Generally, a traditional Code § 401(a) retirement plan is a unique program that is created for a group of employees within the framework of the federal government's rules and regulations.

§ 11.6 —Vesting

All contributions to tax-sheltered annuity plans are always and immediately 100 percent vested. There are no service requirements and there is no distinction among sources of funds. All employee salary savings and all employer nonelective contributions are completely vested to the employee at all times.

§ 11.7   —Limitations on Savings

The amount an employee may contribute is determined by a number of factors. Three limitations apply: the salary reduction (elective deferral) limitation, the exclusion allowance limitation, and the annual employer contribution limitation.

If the employer does not contribute to a Code § 403(b) plan for an employee, and the employee contributes to no other retirement plans, the employee may contribute up to $9,500 yearly, under the elective deferral or salary reduction limitation.

The $9,500 cap applies to the combined contributions made to all retirement plans in which the employee participates, including any Code § 457 plan, simplified employee pension (SEP) plan, or 401(k) plan to which the employee may also be contributing. The $9,500 cap does not include any IRA contributions or any employer contributions.

Under IRS rules, special catch-up provisions allow employees who have worked 15 or more years for an educational organization, a hospital, a home health service agency, a health and welfare service agency, or a church or church-related organization, to contribute greater amounts, in order to put more tax-deferred money aside for retirement. The amount that may be contributed over the $9,500 limit may be increased by the smallest of the following:

- $3,000;
- $10,000 minus the amount of all salary reduction contributions made in prior years under this provision; or
- $5,000 multiplied by the number of years of service with the organization, minus the total amount of salary reduction contributions in prior years.

The second limitation is the exclusion allowance. Contributions to the tax-sheltered annuity from all sources—salary savings and employer contributions—are included in the exclusion allowance. The exclusion allowance must fall within the following formula for a given year:

Where A = Gross income for the year;
    B = Salary reduction amount for the year;
    C = Years of service with the employer;
    D = Total of all contributions from previous years from all sources.

$$\text{Allowance} = (A - B) \times (C) \times (.20) - D$$

The third limitation is the annual employer contribution limitation. This is the same limitation described in **§ 3.18** as being applicable to all retirement programs. Contributions from all sources and all defined-contribution plans of the employer cannot exceed the lesser of 25 percent of taxable compensation (gross compensation less the salary savings) or $30,000 for any one year. This limit can be adjusted for some employees.

Employees of an educational organization, hospital, home health service agency, health and welfare service agency, church, or convention or association of churches, may be eligible to make one of three special elections. By using one of these special elections, greater amounts of contributions to tax-sheltered annuity accounts would be permitted than are otherwise allowed under the exclusion allowance limitation or the limitation on annual employer contributions. The three alternate limitations are as follows:

- Year of separation from service. This applies to the year in which the employee separates from service with the employer. The maximum amount of contributions that may be made to the plan for that year will be the lesser of:

  —$30,000; or

  —The exclusion allowance (defined earlier) in place of the 25 percent of employee's compensation limitation on employer contributions under the general rule.

- Any year limitation. This election may be made for any year. The employee can substitute, for the 25 percent of employee's compensation limitation, the least of the following:

  —$4,000 plus 25 percent of includable compensation for the tax year;

  —The exclusion allowance limitation for the tax year; or

  —$15,000.

- Overall limitation. In this election, the limitation on annual employer contributions and the exclusion allowance would be equal to the lesser of $30,000 or 25 percent of compensation for the tax year.

In summary, unless the employee meets one of the special provisions described above, the total contributions cannot exceed the least of:

- Elective deferral limitation;
- Exclusion allowance;
- Limitation on employer contributions.

Chapter 14 gives detailed examples of the limit determined for the year for given employees. The availability of the proper communication materials, simplified worksheets, and service provider assistance is a major factor in the selection of the companies permitted to offer the tax-sheltered annuity in the workplace. This, in turn, can affect the investment products available and, hence, the design of the program itself.

§ 11.8   —Loan and Withdrawal Programs

Loans and withdrawals are permitted in tax-sheltered annuities and custodial accounts. They are subject to the same rules as 401(k) CODA programs. As with any other features of these plans, the inclusion of loans and withdrawal provisions will depend on the products and contracts offered by the service providers. See **§§ 10.20** and **10.21** for the basic rules on loans and hardship withdrawals that can be incorporated into annuity contracts and custodial accounts.

§ 11.9   —Distributions and Portability

When a plan member separates from service, he or she continues to maintain the annuity contracts or custodial accounts titled to the individual. If the participant joins an organization that offers the same investment through the same service provider, the employee can simply resume the salary savings with the new employer. This is the portability dimension of the tax-sheltered annuity.

Some service providers predominate among certain classes of Code § 501(3)(c) organizations. Plan sponsors that wish to create a portable program should select service providers that offer their products and services in a wide range of similar institutions. Again, as with most aspects of the design of the program, the attractive features will depend on the selection of the service providers whose products contain those features.

Generally, tax-sheltered annuities can permit distributions at normal retirement under the contract or prior to retirement if an individual separates from service before that date, becomes disabled, or dies.

The tax-sheltered annuity can allow single-sum distributions and/or various forms of annuity payments from which the plan member can choose. Although these features are permitted, products of service providers will vary in the timing of benefit payments and the form of payment available. In designing the plan, service providers must be selected whose products contain the features desired in the program.

Distribution from tax-sheltered annuities are subject to the same rules as Code § 401(a) qualified plans and 401(k) CODAs. (See **Chapter 4** for a review of these rules.) There is a 10 percent excise tax on distributions made before age 59¹/₂, except in the following circumstances:

- Total and permanent disability of the employee;
- Medical expense incurred in excess of 7.5 percent of the adjusted gross income;
- An employee's separation from service with the employer, when the employee is at least age 55;
- A spread of distributions over the employee's life expectancy or over the joint life expectancy of the employee and the beneficiary;
- A rollover into another Code § 403(b) plan or into a rollover IRA;
- The death of the employee.

Minimum distributions must begin on the April 1 following the attainment of age 70¹/₂. (See **§ 4.2** for a description of the minimum distribution.) Finally, a 15 percent excise tax is imposed on distributions in excess of $150,000 per year.

§ 11.10   Investment Options and Service Providers

The most important aspect of the tax-sheltered annuity program is the investment options that will be offered to the employees. Insurance companies offer annuity contracts that provide traditional lifetime annuities in several optional forms at retirement. They can also provide separate accounts for investment, offering pooled investments in such instruments as stock funds, bond funds, income funds, growth funds, and combination funds.

Regulated investment companies offer a wide range of mutual funds within various types of investment objectives and portfolio mixes. Participants are usually permitted to apportion their investment in any combination they select, from among all of the funds that the company offers. The employee invests with the company, virtually on a personal basis, through the representative of the company that has been approved by the sponsoring organization to provide those services.

Selecting a service provider or providers is thus the cornerstone of the tax-sheltered annuity program. The service provider should be chosen for:

1.   Investment options and products that fit the philosophy of the program;

2. Access to the company representatives for inquiries, information, and plan transactions;

3. Assistance in the determination of the salary reduction limits and other administrative matters.

The selection of the insurance companies and/or regulated investment companies themselves creates the fundamental design of the program.

CHAPTER 12

SALARY REDUCTION SEP—DESIGN CONSIDERATIONS

§ 12.1 Overview

As discussed in **Chapter 7**, a salary reduction simplified employee pension (SEP) is a plan that permits employees to redirect a portion of their salaries into an individual retirement arrangement (IRA), in order to take advantage of the power of tax-deferred savings. A SEP is more advantageous than an individually sponsored IRA, in that the amount permitted to be contributed on a tax-favorable basis is higher. Contributions to a salary reduction SEP on behalf of each participant may be up to the lesser of 15 percent of compensation or $7,000 (as adjusted for increases in the cost of living; $8,728 in 1992). If the employer also maintains a SEP to which it makes nonelective contributions, these limits may be reduced. Where multiple plans are maintained, total contributions on behalf of an employee may not exceed the lesser of $30,000, as adjusted, or 15 percent of compensation. The salary deferral limit, currently at $8,728, is the cap that limits an employee's deferrals to all salary reduction SEPs, and 401(k) plans in the aggregate, regardless of the number of employers for which the employee works. In contrast, contributions to an IRA on behalf of one individual with the required amount of income are limited to $2,000 of adjusted annual gross income. The SEP contributions are made automatically through payroll deductions.

For non-tax-exempt entities that (1) have fewer than 25 employees eligible to participate during the plan year and (2) have at least 50 percent of the eligible employees willing to defer salary, the salary reduction SEP is a viable alternative to the 401(k) Plan. For these employers a SEP is the only other plan which; permits a current deduction for the contribution by the employer, segregates funds untouchable by the employer's creditors, and provides tax deferral on income generated from contributions.

Governmental and tax-exempt employers are not permitted to sponsor salary reduction SEPs. The salary reduction SEP is acknowledged as a low-administrative-cost method through which an employer can provide a retirement-type vehicle to its employees without incurring the higher cost of a 401(k) plan. A salary reduction SEP is principally funded solely by the employee's voluntary salary reductions, unless the employer desires to make additional contributions to non-salary-reduction SEP accounts.

§ 12.2 Plan Documentation

An employer that desires to sponsor a salary reduction SEP should execute the necessary documentation and disseminate the information to the employees prior to the plan's effective date. There are at least three alternatives whereby an employer can embody the written agreement required to establish a salary reduction SEP: (1) IRS Form 5305A-SEP, (2) a prototype SEP, or (3) an individually drafted SEP.

An employer may use IRS Form 5305A-SEP (revised, September 1990), provided that the employer:

- Does not maintain any other qualified retirement plan, except a Model SEP (Form 5305-SEP) or other SEP to which either elective or nonelective contributions are made;
- Has never maintained a defined-benefit plan;
- Does not have any eligible employees by or for whom IRAs have not been established;
- Does not have only highly compensated employees;
- Is not a member of an affiliated service group (as described in Code § 414(m)), a controlled group of corporations (as described in Code § 414(b)) or trade or businesses (as described in Code § 414(c)), or any other entity required to be aggregated with the employer under Code § 414(o), unless all eligible employees of all the members of such groups, trades, or businesses are eligible to make elective deferrals, and provided that, in the prior calendar year, there were never more than 25 employees eligible to participate in the SEP, in total, of all the members of such groups, trades, or businesses. The employer is not required to file Form 5305A-SEP with the IRS.

The IRA established by or on behalf of any employee must be a model IRA or a master or prototype IRA for which the IRS has issued a favorable opinion letter. Making the agreement on Form 5303A-SEP does not establish an employer IRA, as described under Code § 408(c).

The adoption of the model SEP embodied by IRS Form 5305-SEP is not completed until:

- IRAs have been established by or for all the employees eligible to participate in the salary deferral SEP;
- The employer has completed all the blanks on the Form 5305A-SEP;
- Copies of the Form 5305A-SEP, instructions, and questions and answers have been given to the employer's eligible employees.

Using a prototype SEP is the employer's second alternative to adopt a SEP. An employer may use a salary reduction SEP that has been approved by the IRS national office ("prototype SEP"), provided that the employer satisfies the eligibility criteria applied to the approved SEP. The approval of the IRS may only be relied on if (1) SEP contributions are made to an IRS model SEP (via filing of IRS Form 5305 or 5305A) or an IRS approved model or prototype IRA, and (2) contributions under the SEP do not (in combination with another SEP or any terminated, qualified, defined-benefit plan of the employer) fail to satisfy the requirements of Code § 415.

The IRS has permitted the following types of entities to secure approval for a prototype SEP: trade or professional organizations, banks, insured credit unions, regulated investment companies, investment advisers under contract with one or more regulated investment companies, principal underwriters that have principal underwriting contracts with one or more regulated investment companies, or other IRS-approved persons.

Drafting its own salary deferral SEP is the other alternative available to the employer to adopt a SEP. However, taking such a step is risky and is not recommended unless an IRS ruling is obtained or obtainable, stating that the SEP satisfies the requirements of Code § 408(k). Employers are usually confronted with this situation if the IRS model SEP or a prototype SEP, by its respective terms, prohibits an employer from adoption. This situation may occur, for example, if the employer's sponsorship of other qualified retirement plans creates issues concerning Code § 415, which limits the amount of benefits being accrued or the allocations to a participant's account.

Assuming that a prime motivating factor in adopting the salary reduction SEP is the low administrative cost, the documentation should be IRS Form 5305A-SEP or a prototype salary deferral SEP format, after the sponsor has obtained an IRS Opinion Letter stating that the prototype SEP meets Code requirements. It appears that the principal difference between these adoption methods is the fees or other requirements that may be imposed by the prototype plan sponsor versus using IRS Form 5305A-SEP where the employer should have to incur no documentation fees. Certain entities cannot adopt the salary reduction SEP (see § **9.2**).

Irrespective of which form the salary reduction SEP takes, no trust or custodial account is necessary because the establishment of the salary reduction SEP involves the employer's opening an IRA or requesting the employee to open an IRA to which the salary reduction contributions are to be made. Presumably, after the contributions have been made, they become subject to the investment control of the employee. To that extent, the employee has ultimate flexibility in selecting the investment vehicles in which to have the salary reductions invested. An employee who dislikes the investment vehicle offered by a particular IRA is, subject to the rules of Code § 408, able to roll over or, through trustee-to-trustee transfers, transfer such amounts to other IRAs.

§ 12.3   Reporting and Disclosure

Salary reduction SEPs are apparently subject to the reporting and disclosure requirements of ERISA. Sponsors of salary reduction SEPs who utilize IRS Form 5305A-SEP have available to them an alternative method of complying with the reporting and disclosure requirements of ERISA as set forth in U.S. Department of Labor (DOL) Regulations.[1] At the time when an employee becomes eligible to participate in the SEP (whether at the creation of the SEP or thereafter), the administrator of the SEP (generally, the employer establishing and maintaining the SEP) must furnish the employee with a copy of the completed and unmodified IRS Form 5305A-SEP used to create the SEP, including the completed contribution agreement, the general information guidelines, and the questions and answers.

Following the end of each calendar year, the administrator of the SEP is required to notify each participant in the SEP, in writing, of any employer contributions made under the contribution agreement to the participant's IRA (account or annuity) for that year.

If the employer establishing or maintaining the SEP selects, recommends, or in any other way influences employees to choose a particular IRA or type of IRA into which contributions under the SEP will be made, and if that IRA is subject to restrictions on a participant's ability to withdraw funds (other than restrictions imposed by the Code that apply to all IRAs), the administrator of the SEP is required to give each employee, in writing, at the time such employee becomes eligible to participate in the SEP, a clear explanation of those restrictions and a statement to the effect that other IRAs, into which rollovers or employee contributions may be made, may not be subject to such restrictions.

---

[1] 29 C.F.R. § 2520.104-48 (1991).

SEPs not established through IRS Form 5305A-SEP may nonetheless be able to afford sponsors a modified reporting and disclosure requirement.[2]

§ 12.4   Limited Design Alternatives

The Code's creation of the salary reduction SEP, a so-called simplified salary deferral plan, is at the cost of providing little flexibility to the employer in its design of the salary reduction SEP. First, salary reduction SEPs are only available to employers with 25 or fewer eligible employees at any time during the preceding year. Second, an employer may not sponsor a salary reduction SEP unless at least 50 percent of the employers eligible to participate make an election to defer salary. For example, if the employer has 24 employees, eligible to participate, then at least 2 of these employees would have to make an election to defer amounts of their salary to the SEP. Obtaining such participation may be difficult because the employer is not permitted to match salary deferral contributions, as would be possible under a 401(k) plan. Whether a salary reduction SEP is available for an employer to consider is immediately determined by this maximum employee test.

As discussed in **Chapter 7**, each employee who has attained age 21, has performed service for the employer during at least 3 of the immediately preceding 5 years, and receives at least $300 (indexed for inflation, $374 in 1992) in compensation for the year must be eligible to participate. Service is any work performed for the employer for any period of time. The advantage here is that eligibility is easily determined, in contrast to a 401(k) plan, which may require the counting of hours of service to determine whether an employee would be eligible to participate. The definition of employees includes employees of any member of an affiliated service group (as described in Code § 414(m)), a controlled group of corporations (as described in Code § 414(b)), trades or businesses (as described in Code § 414(c)), or any other entity required to be aggregated with the employer under Code § 414(o). Leased employees, within the meaning of Code § 414(n), of the affiliated employer must be permitted to make elective deferrals to the SEP.

The only identified sources of flexibility in actual plan design are found in:

* Reducing the plan's eligibility standards (age, service, compensation, and collective bargaining members);
* Limiting the amount of salary deferrals below the legal limits;

---

[2] 29 C.F.R. § 2528.104-49 (1991).

- Opening deferrals up to bonuses;
- Electing the accounting period to be used for the salary reduction SEP (either the calendar year or the employer's fiscal year may be used).

The marked disadvantage is that, in contrast to the 401(k) plan, the deferral percentage test for the salary reduction SEP is more restrictive than the actual deferral percentage test used in 401(k) plans. The deferral percentage for each highly compensated employee can be no more than 125 percent of the average deferral percentage of all other non-highly-compensated employees. The deferral percentage of each highly compensated employee must meet the deferral percentage test. In the 401(k) plan counterpart, each highly compensated participant's average deferral percentage is averaged with the others, to arrive at the average deferral percentage utilized in the test.

In summary, the current requirements with regard to salary reduction SEPs, which were enacted under the guise of simplicity, in fact make adoption more difficult than one would expect. Legislative proposals have attempted to address the salary reduction SEP shortcomings but none has yet been enacted into law.

CHAPTER 13

DEFERRED COMPENSATION—DESIGN CONSIDERATIONS

§ 13.1 Overview of Salary Reduction Nonqualified Plans

An employer may provide employees with the opportunity to defer receipt of taxable income under a nonqualified arrangement. Like the other types of plans discussed in this book, these plans are driven by the assumption that an employee will accumulate more savings at retirement through the deferral of taxes than if he or she saves on a posttax basis.

When an employer is looking for a savings plan that covers only key management personnel, a nonqualified arrangement is generally the only available option. A 401(k) plan, a 403(b) annuity plan, and a SEP all require broad-based participation and therefore cannot be used to cover a small group of management personnel. Therefore, nonqualified plans are an important tool for an employer looking to cover a limited number of employees.

Although nonqualified plans can be used to provide salary deferral elections for a small group of employees, only certain employees can be covered. For the plan to avoid the broad-based coverage requirements of ERISA, the plan must only cover "a select group of management or highly compensated employees" under the top-hat exemption. Unfortunately, as pointed out in § 8.3, there are no clear rules clarifying which employees are considered part of this group. (See § 8.3 for a complete discussion of this issue.) An employer establishing a nonqualified salary deferral plan should be careful to provide for the cashout of participants who would be ineligible under those regulations.

Nonqualified plans are tremendously flexible. As long as the plan is limited to the group of employees described above, the plan can be designed in almost any manner to meet the objectives of the employer, including designing different terms for different employees. One major exception to this rule applies to plan sponsors who are state or local governmental entities or are entities exempt from federal tax under Code § 501. In order for employees to participate in salary deferral elections that result in deferral of income taxes, plans of these employers are subject to the design constraints of Code § 457. The rules governing plans are discussed in **§ 8.3**, and the design considerations are discussed in **§§ 13.17–13.26**. This chapter discusses plans of private for-profit entities that are not subject to the limitations of Code § 457.

§ 13.2 Comparing Qualified and Nonqualified Deferred Compensation

One useful approach to determining whether an employer should establish a nonqualified plan is to compare and contrast nonqualified salary reduction plans with qualified 401(k) plans. Although an employer may establish and maintain both qualified and nonqualified salary deferral plans, reviewing the similarities is a good place to start when trying to determine whether a nonqualified plan is the appropriate type of plan.

Employee elective deferred compensation can be provided through tax-qualified retirement plans containing a CODA arrangement or through nonqualified arrangements. Both qualified and nonqualified plans are generally established with the intent of attracting and retaining talented employees.

From the viewpoint of both the employer and the employees, tax-qualified plans offer certain advantages over the nonqualified arrangements. Because contributions to a qualified plan are deductible at the time the contribution is made, the employer receives a deduction at the time the employee elective deferrals are contributed to the plan, regardless of when participants actually receive benefits. In a nonqualified plan, the employer' deduction generally does not occur until the employee actually receives the deferred income. However, the employer in most cases continues to have use of all corporate assets. Under both qualified and nonqualified arrangements, the employee is generally taxed at the time benefits from the plan are received, and therefore the tax benefits are the same from the employee's perspective. However, benefits are not as secure in a nonqualified plan. In a qualified plan, the amounts subject to elective deferral by the employee are contributed to an irrevocable trust, which must be used for the exclusive benefit of the participants. In a nonqualified plan, the benefits are often paid out of general corporate assets, or out of a trust, known as a rabbi trust, that is subject to the creditors. These advantages and disadvantages are summarized in the following sections.

Advantages of Qualified Plans

1. The employer receives a deduction at the time contributions are made to the plan.
2. Contributions to the plan (both additional employer contributions and salary reduction contributions) are not taxable to the employee until benefits are distributed.
3. Earnings on the assets held in trust are tax-exempt.
4. Lump-sum distributions made after age 59½ are eligible to be taxed under favorable 5-year or 10-year income-averaging rules.

Advantages of Nonqualified Plans

1. The sponsoring employer does not receive an income tax deduction at the time of the deferral, but the employer is also not required to set aside assets, meaning that the sponsor retains the opportunity to use corporate funds for other uses.
2. The employer's tax deduction is taken at the time of payout, and is based on the entire amount paid out to the employee, which may be substantially larger than in a qualified plan in which the deduction is based on the amount set aside to pay benefits.
3. Tremendous flexibility allows the employer to design the plan to exactly meet its objectives.
4. Because the plan may cover selected individuals, the employer can control the cost of the plan better than in a qualified plan.
5. Any forfeiture provision may be included in the plan.
6. Even executives can need help to force them to save. A payroll deduction nonqualified plan can (from both the employer's and employee's perspective) be a simple and inexpensive savings plan, unencumbered by a lot of rules and regulations.

Disadvantages of Qualified Plans

1. Rigid design limitations—most importantly, including requirements (discussed in **Chapters 2, 3**, and **4**) that the plan cover a broad range of participants—contain a prescribed vesting provision and generally provide the same level of benefits for all participants.
2. Contributions must be made to a trust and used solely to provide benefits to participants and pay the expenses of the plan.
3. Death benefits under the plan must be "incidental."

4. Small plans may be top-heavy, requiring additional employer contributions even in a plan that only contains employee elections to defer.

5. Expenses of administration include complex annual testing, employee communications, complex annual reporting, and the cost of obtaining an advance determination letter.

6. There are potential adverse tax consequences if the plan does not satisfy qualification requirements.

Disadvantages of Deferred Compensation

1. The employer's tax deduction is deferred. This has an economic cost (compared to making a contribution to a qualified plan), and it creates some level of uncertainty, because the deduction may not occur for many years. The employer does not know what its tax bracket will be, nor is it clear what the amount of the deduction will be.

2. From the employee's perspective, the greatest disadvantage is the lack of security. A portion of the individual's retirement security depends on the employer's financial ability and willingness to make the promised payments. The problem may be lessened through the use of a rabbi trust. The problem may or may not be a problem based on the financial soundness of the company.

3. Deferred compensation cannot generally be considered compensation under other qualified retirement plans. This means that other benefits could be adversely affected by the participant's decision to defer compensation under this plan.

§ 13.3   Overview of Tax and ERISA Requirements

Chapter 8 reviews in depth the federal tax and ERISA rules governing nonqualified deferred compensation. The purpose of this section is to review these rules as they specifically impact the design and implementation of a nonqualified plan.

Federal Tax Requirements

Ordinarily, when an employee receives an unsecured promise to receive compensation at some later date, the employee will not incur taxable income until the compensation is actually paid. However, several tax rules that could accelerate taxation have particular importance when discussing salary deferral type plans. Under the "constructive receipt doctrine," amounts are considered paid or made available (and included as taxable income for federal income tax purposes) even if such amounts have not been reduced to the participant's possession, if the amounts have been constructively received. Constructive receipt occurs in the taxable year during which compensation is credited to the employee's account, set apart for the employee, or otherwise made available so that the employee may draw on it at any time, or so that he or she could have drawn on it during the taxable year if notice of intention to withdraw had been given. However, income is not constructively received if the taxpayer's control of its receipt is subject to substantial limitations or restrictions. The constructive receipt doctrine can cause particular concern in a salary deferral plan, where the participant has the opportunity to receive the amount currently or defer receipt until a later time. For the plan to avoid such concerns, the guidelines for making such deferral elections to avoid constructive receipt should be followed, as discussed in § **8.5** and § **13.20**.

Constructive receipt problems can also exist if a plan has not been carefully designed to provide distribution options. For example, if the plan allows a participant at the time of retirement to choose between an installment option or a lump-sum benefit, a participant electing installment payments may be subject to taxation on the entire benefit owed at the time the election is made under the constructive receipt doctrine.

A similar tax consideration, but one that is theoretically distinct from constructive receipt, is the economic benefit doctrine. Under this doctrine, the creation by the obligor (employer) of a fund in which the taxpayer (employee) has vested rights will result in immediate inclusion by the taxpayer in the amount funded. A fund is created when an amount is irrevocably placed with a third party, and a taxpayer's interest in such a fund is "vested" if it is nonforfeitable. The economic benefit doctrine limits the employer's opportunity to finance or secure the promised benefits to participants without resulting in adverse tax consequences to the participants. Essentially, the doctrine means that any amounts set aside to pay the promise must be either maintained as general assets of the employer or held in a rabbi trust, where the assets are subject to the rights of the employer's creditors.

Although some deferred compensation plans are established using a secular trust (the plan's assets can only be used to provide benefits to the participants), under the economic benefit theory, taxation would result at the time the participant becomes vested in his or her benefit under the plan. This would generally defeat the purposes of a salary reduction plan, where the tax benefits drive the employee's election to defer compensation. As discussed below, if a plan is to avoid the broad coverage requirements of ERISA, the plan must be "unfunded" (see § **8.2**). Therefore, the plan cannot use a secular trust and still cover only the executives of a company.

Of concern are the tax implications of deferred compensation for the employer. Code § 404(a)(5) establishes a "matching rule" under which an employer's deduction for nonqualified deferred compensation is deferred until the "amount attributable to the employer's contribution" is includable in the employee's gross income. The amount of the employer's deduction should be the entire amount included in the executive's income, and not just the amount the employer set aside (i.e., the principal amount of any contribution, disregarding any income earned thereon).

ERISA

The decision to establish a nonqualified plan of deferred compensation is often based on the sponsor's unwillingness to meet the coverage, vesting, and funding requirements contained in Code §§ 401–417. Because ERISA contains similar coverage, vesting, and funding requirements, plans designed to avoid the tax requirements for qualified plans will also seek to avoid coverage under Title I of ERISA. In order to do so, a nonqualified salary deferral plan will have to meet one of the exceptions to the ERISA coverage requirements (see § **8.4**). The only exception available to the salary deferral plan is the top-hat exemption. Top-hat plans are not completely exempt from ERISA; however, the only requirement that they must meet is a simplified reporting requirement. (**Appendix C** contains a sample letter that meets the reporting requirements.) A top-hat plan must be unfunded and maintained by an employer "primarily for the purpose of providing deferred compensation for a select group of management or highly compensated employees . . .".[1] As discussed in § **8.4**, there is currently a great deal of uncertainty as to who may be covered under a top-hat plan. The top-hat exemption only applies to an unfunded top-hat plan. This means that, in the case of a salary deferral plan, if the plan seeks to cover a select group of employees, it must not use a secular trust in order to "fund" the promised benefits. A secular trust can defeat the purposes of the plan, because benefits would be taxable at the time of the distribution.

§ 13.4   Impact of Deferring Compensation on Plan Design

In a deferred compensation plan, participants are given the option to defer regular salary, bonuses, or future salary increases. In other words, money that they otherwise could have received is being deferred. From the employees' perspective, their own dollars are at risk (versus a supplemental

---

[1] ERISA §§ 201(2), 301(a)(3), 401(a)(1), 29 U.S.C.A. §§ 1002(2)(A), 1051(2), 1081(a) (3), 1101(a)(1) (West 1985 and West Supp. 1991).

employer-promised benefit)—a fact that impacts the design of the plan. For example, a nonqualified plan may have almost any type of forfeiture provision; however, it is unlikely that a forfeiture provision for voluntary salary deferrals would be acceptable to employees. Such a plan may be more likely than a supplemental plan (1) to actually set aside funds to provide the promised benefit and (2) to allow participants to direct the investment of the funds in their account.

§ 13.5   Why Should an Employee Elect to Defer?

Probably more than in other types of plans discussed in this book, non-qualified salary deferral plans are motivated by tax deferral. Although some plans may contain other incentives to defer, such as employer matching contributions, in many cases the only incentive is deferral of current taxable income. Therefore, before establishing this type of plan, both the employer and the executives must be convinced that, in today's tax environment, deferral of taxation makes sense.

In the early 1980s, nonqualified salary deferrals were becoming quite popular for executives. The thinking was that employees in the top income tax bracket (at that time, 50 percent) could defer taxation until after they retired, when they would be in a lower income tax bracket. In the years just prior to passage of the Tax Reform Act of 1986 (TRA 86), executives were aware that, in the political climate, tax rates might be dropping (which they in fact did). In this environment, it was much clearer to the executives that deferring income (and income tax treatment) was an intelligent choice.

Today, the top bracket is 31 percent. In 1992, for example, taxable income in excess of $51,900 is subject to the top 31 percent bracket. This means that executives are going to pay at least the same tax rate at the time of retirement, or possibly will pay tax at a significantly higher rate, if taxes go up. Given the current tax environment, the question is whether an executive would be better off paying taxes currently or under a nonqualified tax-deferred plan. Whether deferral is advantageous depends on the tax rate when funds are distributed, the length of the deferral, and the interest rate that deferred funds can earn.

To examine this issue, consider an executive who is looking to save for retirement. Assume that he or she has the choice to defer one dollar of salary under a deferral agreement, or take the dollar and invest it after paying taxes. Under the deferral arrangement, the entire dollar will be put aside. If the money were paid out currently, the executive would only have 69 cents (after paying the 31 percent federal income tax). The 31 cents is like an interest-free loan from the government. The question then becomes:

At what point will the interest earned on a certain interest-free loan be enough to offset the increase in taxes paid out due to the probable increased tax rate? **Table 13–1** sets forth the amount of time it will take to break even, taking into account various future tax rates and projected after-tax interest rates. Under the break-even analysis, if the employee has elected to defer for a time period longer than the break-even point, he or she is better off deferring taxes.

Although the TRA 86 federal tax law changes have somewhat reduced the efficacy of salary deferral, **Table 13–1** demonstrates that, under a range of assumptions, including substantial increases in the tax rate, tax deferral can still be a worthwhile choice. For example, assume that an individual defers $1.00, that funds are set aside and are earning 9 percent interest, and that the tax rate will be 45 percent at distribution. This individual will be better off deferring if the amount is not distributed until more than 4.32 years have elapsed.

Second, the TRA 86 changes have reduced the cost (to the employer) of providing nonqualified deferred compensation. When an employee elects to defer $1.00 of income, versus taking the amount in cash (assuming that the money is set aside), the employer loses the deduction that it would have received if the employee had elected cash. Prior to 1987, the maximum

Table 13–1

Impact of Increasing Tax Rates on Salary Deferral Elections

Current Tax Rate	31%	31%	31%	31%	31%
Projected Tax Rate	40	45	50	55	60
		Number of Years to Break Even			
4%	6.50	9.50	12.19	14.62	16.84
5	5.22	7.64	9.80	11.75	13.53
6	4.37	6.40	8.20	9.84	11.33
7	3.77	5.51	7.07	8.47	9.76
8	3.31	4.84	6.21	7.45	8.58
9	2.96	4.32	5.55	6.65	7.66
10	2.67	3.91	5.02	6.02	6.93
11	2.44	3.57	4.58	5.49	6.33
12	2.25	3.29	4.22	5.06	5.83

Assumptions:

1. Break-even analysis calculated as follows:

$$\text{Number of years} = \frac{\text{Natural log of (projected tax rate/current rate)}}{\text{Natural log of (1 + interest rate)}}$$

2. Calculation assumes interest is not taxed "inside" the deferred compensation plan.

corporate tax rate was 46 percent; today, the maximum corporate tax rate is 34 percent. From this perspective, providing $1.00 benefit (using the current tax rate) under a deferred compensation plan can cost the employer up to $1.51. This cost is ascertained by dividing 1 minus the current maximum corporate tax rate into $1 ($1/(1 - .34)$). Under previous law, the cost was $1.85 ($1/1 - .46$)), or 34 cents more for every dollar deferred. Therefore, the effect of the reduction in corporate tax rates has been to reduce the up-front cost of the plan by lowering the cost of deferring the eventual deduction.

Together, these two factors make nonqualified deferred compensation plans for executives viable both from the perspective of the employer and the employee.

§ 13.6   Primary Employer Objectives

Another factor that influences plan design of a nonqualified salary deferral plan is the motivating force behind the plan. In this regard, the employer generally will establish a nonqualified plan to meet one of the three general objectives described below.

Meeting the Minimum Coverage Requirements

As discussed in **Chapter 10**, one way to simplify the administration of a 401(k) plan is to carve out some, or all, of the HCEs from participation in the plan. If this is done, a nonqualified plan may be established for those highly compensated employees (HCEs) who have been excluded from the qualified plan. The sponsor may want to "mirror" the provisions of the 401(k) plan, or make the plan more attractive than the 401(k) plan for the non-highly compensated employees (non-HCEs). For example, if the 401(k) plan contains a matching employer contribution, the plan employer will probably want to include a similar or more attractive match in the nonqualified plan.

Providing Deferrals in Excess of the 401(k) Limits

Under a 401(k) plan, participants can generally defer up to $8,728 in 1992 (as long as this amount does not exceed any of the other applicable limits). Certain management personnel may want to defer larger amounts. This can be accomplished through a supplemental nonqualified plan. This arrangement may be ongoing or may apply only for those situations where compensation is expected to be exceptionally high for the period, and the employee wants to avoid current taxation on such large amounts of deferred compensation.

Providing Salary Deferral to Only a
Small Group of Employees

The employer may also not want to offer a salary deferral to a broad group of employees but, instead, may want to offer salary deferral for key management personnel. A 401(k) plan may seem like too heavy an administrative burden, or, given the particular demographics of the sponsor, the non-HCEs may not be interested in salary deferral. This may be true where the non-HCEs are particularly young or are at a low level of compensation. A nonqualified plan is much simpler and may meet the employer's needs.

§ 13.7   Specific Plan Provisions

The previous materials reviewed general concepts of nonqualified deferred compensation and discussed the circumstances in which the employer will want to establish such a plan. The rest of this chapter will identify specific features that should be considered when designing the plan.

§ 13.8   —Coverage

One of the first steps in designing any plan is determining who should be covered under the plan. As discussed above (and in **§ 8.3**), the legal restraints limit the potential employee population to "a select group of management or highly compensated employees." Determining who from this group is covered depends on the motivation for establishing the plan. In a nonqualified plan, the terms and conditions for each participant may be entirely different than for all other participants.

§ 13.9   —Matching Employer Contributions

One decision that an employer makes in designing the terms of the plan is whether to include employer contributions, which encourage employee participation to save under the program by "matching" employee elections to defer salary. In a 401(k) plan, inclusion of matching contributions is often driver by legal requirements. The nondiscrimination requirements of Code § 401(k) call for broad-based voluntary participation by the non-HCEs in order for the HCEs to have the opportunity to contribute to the plan. In a nonqualified plan, no such motivation exists, and the employer should include or exclude such a matching contribution based on the employer's objectives under the plan.

An employer considering a matching contribution should also be aware that the plan may have separate terms for each and every participant. A nonqualified program can be used to meet a number of objectives. For example, a match can be used as a method of profit sharing. If used in this way, the employer match would be designed to increase with the financial success of the company.

The employer may be interested in making the statement that savings for retirement is a joint obligation shared by the employee and employer, and that the employer will contribute only if the employee contributes as well.

A match may be motivated by the employer's interest in mirroring the compensation package of an employee hired away from another employer. For example, the employee may have participated in a 401(k) with a matching feature, at his or her previous employer. A match may be used to make up benefits lost when the participant changed jobs.

An employer match in a nonqualified plan has significant disadvantages when compared to contributions in other types of plans. If the employer sets aside the contribution in a rabbi trust, the assets can no longer be used by the company for its business purposes. However, the employer is not entitled to a deduction for the "contribution" to the plan, until such time that the amount is distributed from the plan.

§ 13.10 —Elections to Defer

Assuming that the goal is to defer taxation, the employer must be sure to meet the legal requirements necessary to avoid current taxation under the constructive receipt doctrine. An important design feature is the timing and form of election to defer salary. As described in § 8.8, in order for an employee to defer federal income taxes on the amount elected to defer, the election has to meet certain standards. If an employer wants absolute assurance that employees' salary deferral elections will not result in current taxation, the employer must apply for a Private Letter Ruling from the IRS. However, if the employer is willing to rely on guidance offered by past Private Letter Rulings,[2] the timing and form of election should be limited as follows:

---

[2] Under IRS procedures, a Private Letter Ruling can only be relied on by the particular taxpayer who asked for advice on a particular issue. Other taxpayers may not rely on a Private Letter Ruling as evidence of the IRS's official position on any particular issue.

1. Generally, the election to defer must be made before the period for which the compensation is payable, and before the compensation is earned.

2. Employees have 30 days after the time they enter the plan (new plan or initial eligibility) to elect deferrals.

§ 13.11   —Vesting

Because employees are making elections to defer salary otherwise available to them, in almost all cases, amounts attributable to participant deferral (and investment experience thereon) will be 100 percent vested at all times. However, unlike a 401(k) plan, this is not a legal requirement, and, in exceptional circumstances, the employer may want to provide for forfeitures. If the plan includes a matching contribution, virtually any forfeiture provision may be used. To encourage long service, the employer may require a specified number of years of employment, or may have complete vesting dependent on attainment of a retirement age. Another option is a graded vesting schedule providing for partial vesting after a specific number of years of service—for example, 20 percent vesting after 1 year, and an additional 20 percent for each additional year. To discourage certain behavior, forfeitures can occur when a specific event, such as violation of a noncompete provision or other improper behavior, becomes evident.

§ 13.12   —The Benefit Formula

In a salary reduction deferred compensation plan, the employer, in almost all cases, defines the promised benefit based on the defined-contribution approach. As discussed in **Chapter 1**, in a defined-contribution plan, the benefit is a function of the amount contributed to an account on behalf of an individual participant, plus (or minus) the investment experience on the amounts held in the account and less any administrative expenses paid out of the account. In a nonqualified plan, the plan sponsor is not required to actually set aside any specific funds with which to pay benefits. Even when amounts are set aside, they do not necessarily have to specifically match the promised benefit. Therefore, the sponsor has the flexibility either to operate an actual account approach (with the benefit promised as described above) or to use bookkeeping entries to identify contributions. In this instance, the employer has the option not to include an "interest credit" based on some external measure. Any number of methods of crediting interest can be used—a specific interest rate, or interest based on some external measure, such as a stock index or bond index, or various other measures. Another option is to base the interest on the average interest rate earned in another plan of the sponsor. For example, if the plan is designed to mirror a 401(k) plan, the rate of interest earned in the 401(k) plan can be used.

§ 13.13 —Distribution Options

A plan may allow for payment in a single sum or over a period of time after early termination or at normal retirement. However, with significant benefits, a single-sum payment will result in a large tax liability, which could negate the advantages of tax deferral. In a deferred compensation plan that promises to make payments based on an "account," the distribution options will generally be based on the amount of the account payable over a specific number of years, or a specific dollar amount, until the account is depleted. Annuity options were at one time a more viable option because the employer could purchase an annuity contract providing benefits, with the employee as the beneficiary. However, under current law, the employer is taxed on the inside buildup on the annuity contract. If the annuity is distributed to the participant, the participant will be required to take the entire value of the contract and will be taxed on the retirement benefit. Presumably, the employer could pay a life or contingent life annuity to the participant; however, this would change the nature of the promise to pay the amount accumulated in the participant's account.

The employer also has the option to allow payments at the time of early termination of employment or to require deferral until normal retirement. From the employee's standpoint, the terminee may want to postpone receipt until normal retirement, in order to avoid taxation during a time when he or she is still earning wages from another employer.

§ 13.14 Financing the Promise

A nonqualified plan is substantially different from the other types of plans discussed in this book, because there is no legal requirement that money be set aside to provide for the benefits promised under the plan. In fact, in a nonqualified plan, in order for the employee to defer income tax on the amount deferred, assets may not be set aside solely for the purpose of paying benefits. This gives the employer a great deal of flexibility as to how to meet the benefit obligations. At one end of the spectrum, the employer may decide not to set aside any funds from which to pay benefits. As benefits become due, payments are made out of the company's general assets. From the employer's perspective, this may be the best option: The employer can use all current assets for business opportunities, emergencies, or general operating costs. On the other hand, with no advance funding, the employer may not have adequate funding at the time benefits are due. If the employer does not set aside any funds to meet the obligation, the plan will have to operate using the "bookkeeping entry" approach described in the previous section, in which any credit for investment earnings is fictional, based on some assumed rate of interest which is either a stated amount or is floating with some external index.

A company's decision to finance or not to finance the promised benefits is partially based on the company's management philosophy and strategy. In many instances, it is a sound business practice to earmark funds for a pending liability. However, other factors will weigh in favor of prefinancing the deferred compensation agreement. One concern is the participant's need to feel secure about the employer's ability to meet its obligations. From this perspective, the participants will feel more secure if money is set aside (whether or not the money is held in a rabbi trust). Determining whether to finance the promise partially hinges on the plan design. For example, if the employer is establishing a plan that mirrors a 401(k) plan for the non-HCEs and allows participant investment election, the employer may want to establish a fund, credit interest in a manner based on the experience of the fund, and allow for participant investment election. If the employer is against setting aside funds, it is possible to allow "phantom" investment choices, in which the participant chooses a specific investment option, and interest is credited to a bookkeeping account based on the actual performance of the outside investment selected.

The other psychological factor in a salary deferral plan is that participants view salary deferrals as their money, and could be quite upset if the employer did not set the money aside in a separate fund.

§ 13.15   —Specific Investment Options

If the employer does decide to set aside funds from which to pay benefits, the next issue is what type of investments should be selected. When assets are held in a separate account in the name of the employer, or in a rabbi trust, trust income is taxable to the corporation. Therefore, there is an incentive to invest in tax-free or tax-deferred investments. Some common investment vehicles are described below.

Corporate-Owned Life Insurance

Life insurance policies on the employee's life, owned by and payable to the employer, can provide financing for the employer's obligation under nonqualified deferred compensation plans. With life insurance financing, the plan can provide a substantial death benefit even in the early years of the plan, which is of significant value to younger employees. One advantage of corporate-owned life insurance, over other investments, is that the inside buildup on the cash value of the policy is not taxable until the policy is surrendered.

The policy can be used in one of two ways. First, the policy can be surrendered at the time of the participant's retirement, and the cash value can be used to pay promised retirement benefits. Second, the company can pay the retirement benefits out of the company's general funds and hold the policy until the participant's death. At that time, the policy proceeds reimburse the employer. Death benefits have the additional advantage that the amount of the death benefit (which is the face value of the death benefit less the cash value of the contract) will be tax-free income to the corporation.

Tax-Free Investments

In a qualified plan, the assets held under the trust are not taxed to the trust. Therefore, it generally does not make sense to invest in tax-free investments. However, in a nonqualified plan, interest earnings on amounts set aside by the employer are treated as taxable income to the employer. Therefore, the employer may consider tax-free municipal bonds as an alternative investment option.

Other Investments

Many taxable investments will outperform tax-free investments, even after taxes are paid. Therefore, other types of investment may be used to finance nonqualified deferred compensation promises. The guidelines discussed in § **10.25** will also apply to nonqualified investments.

§ 13.16   Securing the Promise

As stated above, the employer may simply pay benefits out of the general assets of the company. For many reasons discussed above, in the case of a salary deferral plan, this option is unacceptable. The employer may also purchase insurance contracts or annuities to make the payment. However, to avoid current taxation to the participant, the employer has to be both owner and beneficiary of the contracts. This means that the participant in the plan has no more right to those assets than to any other asset of the employer. In addition, the use of annuity contracts has become less attractive, in light of Code § 72(u), which taxes income on an annuity contract held by anyone other than a natural person as income to the contract owner.

Along with the increase of hostile takeovers has come an escalated interest in securing the promise to pay deferred compensation. This trend may be further accelerated if, in the 1990s, nonqualified deferred compensation becomes the primary source of retirement benefits to executives. Several methods of securing the promise exist; each has its own set of tax considerations, and these have been introduced briefly above.

Reserve Account

One way, at least psychologically, for the employer to make the employee feel more secure is to establish an employer reserve account: The employer maintains an actual account invested in various types of securities. There is no trust, and funds are fully accessible to the employer and its creditors.

Similarly, the employer may establish an employer reserve account with employee investment direction. With this variation, the employee obtains greater security by having the right to "direct" (select) investments in the account. This right must be limited to a choice of a broad type of investment (equity, bonds, family of mutual funds, and so on) because the ability to choose specific investments may lead to constructive receipt by the employee.

Third-Party Guarantees

Another way for an employee to ensure receipt of deferred compensation is to obtain a third party that will guarantee payment of such deferred compensation if the employer defaults on the promise. It may be possible to purchase a surety bond from an insurance company, or, similarly, to purchase a letter of credit, to guarantee payment upon default.

This method is limited in its usefulness by the employee's ability to obtain such a bond at a reasonable price. This will be most difficult in circumstances when the employee needs the most protection, that is, when the employer is in bad financial circumstances. In addition, as discussed in § 8.12, there is some uncertainty regarding the tax consequences of surety bonds, and such purchases will require a cash outlay by the participant. For these reasons, other methods of securing the payment are often sought.

Rabbi Trusts

Another method of securing the promise is to establish a rabbi trust. This type of trust is set up to hold property used for financing a deferred-compensation plan, where the funds set aside are subject to the employer's creditors. The IRS has ruled that trusts designed in this way do not constitute formal funding in the tax sense.

This funding vehicle is generally an irrevocable grantor trust, which is established by an employer to hold assets supporting deferred compensation obligations by the employer. Assets held by the trust can be used only to pay the promised deferred compensation, except that assets may be "invaded" by creditors.

A properly constructed rabbi trust has the advantages of providing security to the participants that their benefits will be paid, without resulting in taxation to the participants at the time contributions are made to the trust. As discussed in the taxation section above, because rabbi trust assets are subject to claims of creditors, the IRS has determined that an "economic benefit" has not been conferred on the participants nor does the "constructive receipt" doctrine apply to such contributions. Therefore, the employee generally does not receive taxable income until the time amounts are distributed from the trust, and the employer receives a deduction at the time benefits are distributed to participants in an amount that reflects both employer contributions and trust earnings. In addition, the employer is generally taxed on the income of the rabbi trust, prior to distribution, to the extent that it would be taxed had it directly held the assets owned by the trust.

Generally, IRS Private Letter Rulings have defined permissible provisions in a rabbi trust. For example, a rabbi trust can put restrictions on when creditors can look to trust assets to satisfy claims. The rulings have allowed the rabbi trust to restrict claims by creditors to cases where the employer is insolvent. To protect the rights of creditors, the rulings have required the employer to notify the trustee of insolvency, and benefits are suspended at the time of insolvency.

To comply with the rulings, the trusts also must contain spendthrift provisions, requiring that benefits earned under the plan are not anticipated, alienated, sold, transferred, assigned, pledged, encumbered, garnished, attached, or subject to any charge or legal process.

Private Letter Rulings have also approved several features of rabbi trust agreements that an employer may wish to consider beneficial to participants. Several Private Letter Rulings have approved rabbi trusts that contain hardship withdrawal provisions.[3] In one case, the IRS specifically stated that "[a] participant's right to request a distribution from his or her account because of financial hardship [would] not cause the deferred amount to be includable" in the participant's gross income currently.[4] Recent Private Letter Rulings have approved a rabbi trust used in connection

---

[3] Priv. Ltr. Rul. 8843045 (Aug. 3, 1988); 8844020 (Aug. 5, 1988).

[4] Priv. Ltr. Rul. 8952037 (Sept. 29, 1989).

with a plan that allowed participants to direct the investment of rabbi trust assets attributable to their account.[5] These types of provisions are especially useful in a salary deferral type plan, where the employee is deferring his or her own salary. However, as discussed in **§ 8.13**, if an employer wants to have absolute certainty that the provisions will not create current taxation, the employer must request a Private Letter Ruling.

§ 13.17   Design of Code § 457 Plans

As discussed in **§ 8.10**, Code § 457 appears to be the exclusive method through which an employee of a governmental entity (and certain employees of tax-exempt entities) may effectively defer the inclusion of compensation for federal income tax purposes. The deferral is accomplished either through the "eligible deferred compensation plan" or the "ineligible deferred compensation plan," both of which are set forth in Code § 457. The focus of this section will be on "eligible deferred compensation plans," which are the more common type of plan utilized. The "ineligible deferred compensation plan" would not appear to be generally accepted by employees because of the highly negative requirement that any amounts deferred must be subject to a substantial risk of forfeiture.

One point that is worthy of discussion is that the limitation on the availability of Code § 457 to certain employees of tax-exempt entities is imposed by the requirements of ERISA. If ERISA applies to an "employee benefit pension plan," then the plan is subject to ERISA's funding, participation, vesting, reporting and disclosure, and fiduciary responsibility requirements. ERISA does not apply to plans sponsored by governmental entities, thus creating a high degree of flexibility in plan design for these types of entities. In contrast, ERISA generally applies to plans of tax-exempt entities, except that its provisions on participation, funding, and fiduciary requirements do not apply to a plan that is unfunded and is maintained by an employer primarily for the purpose of providing deferred compensation for a select group of management or highly compensated employees. Plans for these individuals are, in the terms of ERISA, "top-hat plans." Top-hat plans are subject to the reporting and disclosure requirements of ERISA, although U.S. Department of Labor Regulations establish alternative methods of compliance.

An alternative method of compliance is satisfied if the administrator files a statement with the Secretary of Labor that includes the name and address of the employer, the employer (tax) identification number (EIN) assigned by the IRS, a declaration that the employer maintains a plan or

---

[5] Priv. Ltr. Rul. 8952037 (Sept. 29, 1989); 8834015 (May 25, 1988); 8804023 (Oct. 30, 1987).

plans primarily for the purpose of providing deferred compensation for a select group of management or highly compensated employees, and a statement of the number of such plans and the number of employees in each period. If the Secretary of Labor requests, the plan docket must be provided.

§ 13.18   —Coverage Requirements

Code § 457 does not have any participation requirements, in contrast to qualified plans that are subject to Code § 410. The only time participation would be placed at issue is when the participation requirements of ERISA apply to the plan, but careful design would not cause the plan to extend to employees outside of the select group of management or to the HCE group. Thus, the employer may discriminate as to which employees it desires to include within the plan. A sponsoring entity may even expand coverage to include those who provide services as independent contractors.

§ 13.19   —Funding

The concept of funding generally means whether the assets of a plan intended to be used to pay plan benefits are segregated into an account or trust separate from the sponsor's assets and are not subject to the claims of the sponsor's creditors. Code § 457 requires that the plan be unfunded and that the amounts deferred remain, until made available to the participant or other beneficiary, solely the property and right of the employer, without being restricted to the provision of benefits under the plan and subject only to the claims of the employer's general creditors. Unfunded must be the standard, or ERISA requirements will arise; the top-hat plan must be unfunded as well.

When an entity is considering the adoption of an "eligible deferred compensation plan," the impact of the unfunded requirement on plan participation must be one of the initial considerations. Any employee who may elect to defer current compensation should have some concern regarding whether, when the time for payment occurs, the entity will have the financial resources to make good on the promise to pay deferred compensation. The financial circumstances of the sponsoring entity and the expected duration of existence must be considered. The principal governing bodies, such as states and local governments that have taxing powers and an expected unlimited existence, would appear to be these types of entities. The unfunded status of a Code § 457 plan would not be a significant negative, in contrast to specialized governmental bodies with limited power and to risky tax-exempt entities whose financial circumstances and expected duration are for a more questionable period.

A question associated with the concept of funding is: Who is in control of the amounts attributable to the deferral? Such amounts must be held in the name of the sponsoring employer. As to their investment, Treasury Regulations permit a plan to allow participants to direct, from among different modes under the plan, the investment of deferred amounts. With this regulatory authorization, the Code § 457 plan could be structured in a fashion similar to the 401(k) plan, 403(b) annuity plan, and salary reduction SEP, all of which offer their participants a wide variety of investment choices from which to select.

§ 13.20   —Maximum Permissible Deferrals

As explained in **§ 8.10**, the provisions of Code § 457 specifically limit the amount that may be deferred in any year, leaving little room for design alternatives. The plan could be written without the catch-up deferral, but there is little reason for not permitting such a provision to give the participant maximum deferral opportunities. Further, the employee is 100 percent vested at all times for the amount of his or her salary deferrals.

§ 13.21   —Benefit Forms

As explained in **§ 8.10**, in order to be considered an "eligible deferred compensation plan," the plan must provide that deferrals will not be made available to participants or beneficiaries earlier than: (1) the calendar year in which the participant attains age 70½; (2) when the participant is separated from service with the employer; or (3) when the participant is faced with an unforeseeable emergency. The statute is silent on what benefit forms the participant may elect and when the election must be made; the matter is left to Regulations.

The Treasury Regulations carve out certain benefit forms and elections which, if included in an "eligible deferred compensation plan," will not cause the entire amount deferred to be made available to the participant and, thus, to be currently includable as gross income for federal income tax purposes.

A plan may provide that, after the participant attains the normal retirement age under the plan (i.e., "normal retirement date," an optional date selected by the sponsor in the plan), the total amounts deferred under the plan will be paid to the participant in 120 substantially equal monthly installments beginning on the date 30 days after the normal retirement date, unless the participant elects, within the 90-day period ending on the normal retirement date, to receive a single lump sum. The single-sum payment is payable to the participant on the date when the first of the monthly payments would otherwise be payable to the participant.

If the plan permits the participant to accelerate installment payments, the full amount will be immediately includable in the participant's gross income period. The only exception to this rule would permit the participant to accelerate the payment of the amount remaining payable to the participant upon the occurrence of an unforeseeable emergency, as described in Treasury Regulations, and not in an amount exceeding that permitted by Treasury Regulations. In such circumstances, the right to accelerate does not cause the full amount to be immediately includable.

As to participants who separate from service before attaining the normal retirement age, a plan may provide that the total of the amounts deferred will be payable to the participant in a single-sum payment on the date 90 days after the date of the separation, unless, before the date 30 days after the separation, the participant irrevocably elects not to receive the payments until he or she attains the plan's normal retirement age, at which point he or she will have the elections available to such participants at that time. The plan could extend to the beneficiary the right to defer payment until the year in which the participant would have attained age 65. It is significant that any election must be made prior to the time when any payments commence and, once made, may not be revoked. The method of payment need not be chosen at that time and, if selected, may be revoked until the date 30 days preceding the date on which the payments are to commence.

In summary, an "eligible deferred compensation plan" may extend lump-sum or installment methods of payment subject to the requirements governing the timing of when the election of the benefit must be made, as discussed above. It further appears that, if the installment method is selected, limited access to the unpaid balance is given, except in the case of an unforeseen emergency.

§ 13.22 —Normal Retirement Age

A plan may specify any retirement age no later than age $70\frac{1}{2}$ and no earlier than the earliest age at which the participant has the right to retire under the state's basic pension plan without consent of the state and to receive immediate retirement benefits without actuarial or similar reduction because of retirement before some later specified age in the state's basic pension plan. The plan may further provide that, in the case of a participant who continues to work beyond the age specified in the two preceding sentences, the normal retirement age shall be that date or age designated by the participant. However, that date or age cannot be later than the mandatory retirement age provided by the state, or the date or age at which the participant separates from the service of the state. The Regulations provide that if no normal retirement age is specified, then the normal retirement age is the later of the latest normal retirement age specified in the basic pension plan of the state or age 65.

§ 13.23   —Unforeseeable Emergencies

Similar to the concept of hardship withdrawals in the 401(k) plan context, Code § 457 permits in-service distributions upon the occurrence of an unforeseeable emergency. This design alternative is available to the sponsor and, unless the administrative inconvenience of such provision is significant, it would appear advisable to give the participant withdrawal flexibility.

The Regulations define "unforeseeable" emergency as a severe financial hardship to the participant resulting from (1) a sudden and unexpected illness or accident of the participant or of a dependent (as defined in Code § 152(a)) of the participant, (2) a casualty to the participant's property, or (3) another similar extraordinary and unforeseeable circumstance arising as a result of events beyond the control of the participant. The Regulations acknowledge that the existence of an unforeseeable emergency depends on the facts and circumstances of each case, but they specifically exclude the need to send a participant's child to college or the desire to purchase a home.

The occurrence of an unforeseeable emergency does not permit the wholesale withdrawal of all amounts deferred. The payment may not be made to the extent that the hardship is or may be relieved: (1) by reimbursement or compensation by insurance or otherwise; (2) by liquidation of the participant's assets, to the extent the liquidation of such assets would not itself cause severe financial hardship, or (3) by cessation of deferrals under the plan.

Similar to hardship withdrawals from a 401(k) plan, withdrawals because of an unforeseen emergency must be permitted only to the extent reasonably needed to satisfy the need.

§ 13.24   —Plan Transfers

The plan may provide for the transfer amounts deferred by a former participant to another eligible plan of which the former participant has become a participant, provided certain conditions are met. These conditions include:

1. The entity sponsoring the plans must be located within the same state;

2. The plan receiving such amounts must provide for the acceptance of the amounts;

3. The plan must provide that, if the participant separates from service in order to accept employment with another such entity, payment will not commence upon separation from service, regardless of any other provision of the plan, and amounts previously deferred will automatically be transferred.

§ 13.25   —Establishment of Plan

The Code § 457 plan must be established through a written instrument setting forth the basic provisions of the Code. Other than attempting to secure a Private Letter Ruling from the IRS stating that the provisions of the Code § 457 plan are in compliance with applicable law, there is no separate submission procedure to satisfy oneself that the terms of the plan meet the requirements of applicable law, as is the case with qualified plans. However, in contrast to qualified plans, the Treasury Regulations do provide the governmental plan sponsor with some leeway with respect to meeting the requirements of the law: If a Code § 457 plan is not administered in accordance with the requirements, then the "eligible deferred compensation plan" will cease to be an eligible plan on the first day of the first plan year beginning more than 180 days after the date of written notification by the IRS that the requirements are not satisfied, unless the inconsistency is corrected before the first day of the plan year. Consequently, every effort should be taken to prepare a plan document that complies with Code § 457 but, to the extent that is requirements are not technically met, the regulatory grace period affords the governmental plan sponsor some degree of comfort.

§ 13.26   —Reporting and Disclosure

A Code § 457 plan sponsored by a governmental entity is not subject to the reporting and disclosure requirements of ERISA; plan documents need not be submitted to the participant and annual reporting need not be made to the participant and the IRS. If the plan is sponsored by a tax-exempt nongovernmental entity, the alternative reporting and disclosure requirements may be used as described above. However, no reason exists not to provide the participant with an accounting of the value of the account balance deferred in the Code § 457 plan on some regular basis, so as to keep the participant apprised of the status of the deferrals. In fact, taking such an approach would appear to foster good employer–employee relations.

PART IV

PLAN ADMINISTRATION

CHAPTER 14

ADMINISTRATION OF 401(k) CASH OR DEFERRED ARRANGEMENTS

§ 14.1 Plan Installation

After the plan is designed, the trustees are named, and the investment options have been determined, the plan itself is ready to be installed. To properly install a 401(k) CODA, careful planning is important and all of the events leading to the initiation of the plan must be coordinated and must follow the proper sequence.

§ 14.2 —The Budget

The first step is to review the budget for the initial year along with a projection for the next year or two. Both the anticipated monthly amount, if any, and the expenses that the employer is anticipating for administration should be carefully planned and budgeted.

§ 14.3 —The Action Plan

With the design and budget in hand, the employer can move on to creating a detailed plan of action for implementing the program. The action plan should list, for each event: the task itself, the sequence in which it occurs, the party or parties responsible for its completion, and the due date for finalizing the task. In general, the sequence of events should follow in this order:

1. Select service providers.
2. Adopt plan and trust agreement.
3. Create record-keeping–data base.

4. Coordinate payroll deduction process with record-keeping system.
5. Open investment vehicles to accept contributions.
6. Test all payroll and record-keeping systems.
7. Enroll employees.
8. Submit plan to IRS for approval of tax-exempt status (concurrent with steps 2 through 7).
9. Submit summary plan description (SPD) to U.S. Department of Labor (concurrent with steps 2 through 7).
10. Begin payroll deductions and salary savings deposits to investment funds.

The precise detail of each step will depend on: the number of service providers to be used; the degree to which the investment funds are self-developed and decentralized versus packaged products with centralized access; and the degree to which the payroll system can effectively interact with the plan record-keeping system. The more intricate and complicated these steps, the more tasks that should be included in the action plan. The responsible party(ies) and due dates for each step should be prominently noted. The plan may have to be revised several times before a final plan can be implemented.

§ 14.4 —Selecting Service Providers

In selecting the service providers for the plan, important factors to consider include:

1. The number of employees to be covered;
2. The number of operating locations to be included;
3. The size of the plan's annual cash flow and the projected asset accumulation over the new term;
4. The plan's expense budget and the extent to which the employees will bear some of the cost burdens;
5. The internal capabilities for data-processing and record-keeping systems;
6. The provisions of the benefit plan itself—plans with specialized and complicated provisions will generally require greater specialization in the creation of the plan and trust agreement;
7. The internal capability regarding benefit administration. Larger organizations with employee benefits staff can usually administer some of the program so that the sponsor needs less from the outside.

Many firms identify their needs in the various administrative areas and develop a request for proposal (RFP). In the RFP, the sponsoring organization requests from potential service providers information that specifically addresses the needs of their plan, and an estimate of the cost to provide the desired services. All proposals are systematically appraised and the project is then awarded to the service provider that demonstrates the capabilities to administer the program effectively at the best possible cost.

§ 14.5   —Plan and Trust Agreement

After the service providers have been selected, the governing instrument of the plan, the plan and trust agreement, should be drafted, approved by the board of directors, and adopted by the organization. The plan agreement summarizes all of the major plan provisions that have been designed into the program, as well as the various statutory provisions that are mandated under federal law and regulations. The trust agreement creates the vehicle whereby assets can be accumulated to plan benefit when they come due. It names the trustees and enumerates their duties and powers, along with the types of investments that they are permitted to make under the terms of the trust.

More complicated plan and trust agreements that are implementing plans for large, diverse organizations require professionally created, individually designed documents. These individually designed documents are generally more expensive to create, and their cost for receiving approval from the IRS for tax qualification is higher. The fees for submission of these documents to the IRS can be as high as $825.

Less complicated plan and trust provisions can usually be adopted through plans that are preapproved by the IRS; these are known as prototype plans. Sponsors of prototype plans can be banks, insurance companies, brokerage firms, trade associations, consulting firms, and administrative firms. These sponsors submit their plans in advance to the IRS, to obtain general approval on the major provisions of the plan and trust agreements. An employer who adopts a prototype plan has several options from which to choose in determining certain major provisions of the plans—eligibility, vesting, monthly contribution rates, limits on deferrals, and so forth. In most cases, the prototype plan as adopted by the employer sponsoring the 401(k) is then submitted to the IRS for tax qualification approval. The adoption of a prototype plan is usually much less expensive than an individually designed plan because most of the plan language is prewritten and preapproved. In addition, the IRS user fee is only $125 for review of a prototype plan.

Appendix A provides an example of a prototype plan and trust agreement that can be adopted by a sponsoring organization. It includes the resolution of the board of directors adopting the plan, and the adoption agreement whereby the variable plan provisions are specified for selection and possible adoption by the plan sponsor. It also individualizes the plan and trust agreement itself with prewritten, preapproved plan provisions, the details of the loan and hardship withdrawal programs, and a resolution of administrative policies for operation of the plan.

§ 14.6 —Record-Keeping Process

The next phase of the installation process is the alteration of the payroll system at the organization, in order to create payroll deductions, calculate the monthly contributions, and determine the apportionment of both of these sources of funds and the possible investment options that can be elected by each plan member. Coordination among the payroll system or outside payroll service provider, the sponsoring organization, the record keeper, and the investment funds is essential. To the extent that a single organization provides two or more of these services, tasks can be somewhat consolidated. The goal of the process is to create payroll records that provide at least this fundamental information for each plan member:

1. Name of participant;
2. Social security number;
3. Salary for the payroll period;
4. Elective deferral percentage of salary;
5. Elective deferral amount;
6. Employee monthly contribution;
7. Elective percentage for investments—Fund A, B, and so on;
8. Loan repayment amounts;
9. Other sources of funds (discretionary employer contribution, rollover deposits, after-tax employee contributions) and the applicable deposit amounts.

The employees' social security numbers are the key to coordinating data on all interacting systems. When the above information is processed after each payroll period, the amount of each contribution source and each investment fund apportionment will be determined for each participant. In addition, any loan repayments (which are technically fund exchanges among plan investment assets) made during the period are recorded and apportioned through a fund exchange to the elected plan investments for each applicable plan member. Totals by source, investment fund, and loan repayment can then be determined so that the proper remittance can be made to each investment fund.

These records are then accumulated throughout the valuation period. Payroll deductions are made, deposits are accumulated, and the corresponding records are maintained in an additive fashion. At the end of each valuation cycle (monthly, quarterly, semiannually, and so on), these totals for the cycle can be accumulated and combined with investment income and plan forfeitures to summarize all account activity for each participant and the total for the plan.

Again, it must be emphasized that the tasks of the record-keeping process will be delegated to certain individuals or service providers, depending on various factors regarding the capability of those service providers and the internal capabilities of the plan sponsor.

§ 14.7   —Investment Funds

In coordination with the record-keeping process, the investment funds should next be opened by the trustees to become part of the trust itself. A wide range of investment fund arrangements can be installed, depending on the provisions of the plan and the nature of the service providers selected. If the investment funds are independent of each other, the record-keeping system must be coordinated with their operation. Many investment service providers also offer record-keeping services. In a structure such as this, several processing and investment deposit steps can be consolidated, so that the record-keeping requirements of each payroll period correspond precisely to the actual placement of invested funds. Under both extremes— and any hybrid approach that can be developed—it is essential that the funds be properly created to accept plan deposits before employee enrollment begins.

§ 14.8   —Employee Enrollment

The employee enrollment should be preceded by group and/or individualized meetings to explain the program and investment options and should include effective communication materials that the employee can take home and review. The employee meeting groups should be as small as possible, so that each employee can feel a personalized interest in his or her welfare and can ask as many questions as needed. In very large organizations, videotaped presentations can be prepared for viewing by small groups of employees at various locations of the sponsor. Many organizations' middle managers or employee benefit staff can be sufficiently educated on the provisions of the program to answer questions after the videotape has been run. In smaller organizations, group meetings can be jointly conducted by the appropriate staff of the sponsoring organization. Typically, in these settings, representatives of the key service provider(s) are also present at the enrollment meetings to explain the program and to answer questions that may arise.

The basic material that should be included in an effective enrollment package includes, but may not be limited to:

1. Highlights of the overall program;
2. Detailed summary plan description that explains the provisions of the plan in colloquial language;
3. Personalized analysis of the current tax advantages of the plan for the employee, and the future retirement income potential the plan offers;
4. Enrollment material, including basic plan enrollment, beneficiary designations, investment elections, plan savings rate, and spousal consent to waiver.

Appendix A provides a basic format for the enrollment material that should be provided to each employee. Depending on the plan budget, these materials can be created more or less inexpensively. Generally speaking, the more attractive the enrollment package, the more general enthusiasm can be created. The result will be a higher level of individual plan participation.

To create a personalized analysis, it is necessary to collect the following information from each employee:

1. Participant's name;
2. Social security number;
3. IRS filing status;
4. Number of exemptions;
5. Spouse's income, if filing jointly;
6. State in which local taxes are paid.

Much of this information should be on file with the plan sponsor. Many service providers can collect this information and process it to create a personalized analysis for each individual. The analysis will show the advantages of the plan in terms of current tax saving and future retirement income.

§ 14.9   —IRS Submission

Concurrently with the installation of the record-keeping systems and plan enrollment, the plan and trust agreements should be submitted to the IRS for approval of the tax-exempt status of the plan. The following information must be forwarded to the region's IRS District Office for review, in order to obtain tax qualification determination for noncollectively bargained plans:

1. Cover letter, in duplicate, with receipt requested;
2. Copy of trust and plan agreement;
3. Form 5301 for individualized designed plans; Form 5307 for prototype plans—each with appropriate attachments;
4. Form 5302;
5. Copy of board of directors' resolution.

Appendix A provides a sample submission of a prototype plan under Form 5307, with cover letter and applicable forms. Acknowledgment of receipt of the material is requested through the signing and return of the duplicate of the cover letter. Return/receipt request can also accompany submission through certified mail provided by the U.S. Postal Service. Acknowledgment of receipt should be obtained when the submission is actually made to the federal government.

Finally, employees must be given (1) notice that the submission is occurring and (2) the right to comment on the filings with both the IRS and the U.S. Department of Labor (DOL). **Appendix A** provides a sample of such a notice to employees.

§ 14.10   —Labor Department Filing

The summary plan description (SPD), created for the enrollment of plan participants, is the employee booklet that summarizes the major provisions of the plan and the employee's legal rights under ERISA. Under the rulings of the DOL, the booklet must contain certain information and must be distributed to each plan member who enters the program. In addition, it must be kept up-to-date as the plan is amended and revised. (See § **5.13** for a description of the rules regarding SPDs.)

The SPD must be submitted to the DOL, where it is kept on file. **Appendix A** illustrates a sample SPD and a sample submission letter that covers the filing to the DOL. As with the IRS submission, duplicate letters are sent and a return acknowledgment is requested. Certified mail, return receipt requested, can be used to obtain acknowledgment of receipt of the SPD by the DOL.

§ 14.11   Annual Administration

The plan will be structured to provide periodic reports to management and to employees on an announced schedule (monthly, quarterly, semiannually, or annually). The reports indicate asset valuations, allocations of contributions, income, and forfeitures.

§ 14.12   —Financial Accounting

The first step in the periodic reporting process is to develop a financial accounting of plan assets as of the beginning and the end of the allocation period. Plan assets are almost universally valued at market for each individual investment held by the trust. A comprehensive balance sheet should list investment funds as assets and sources of funds as liabilities (plan benefits payable) as of both the beginning and the end of the allocation/reporting period. **Table 14–1** illustrates a sample balance sheet; the investment funds are listed as plan assets and the plan benefits, by source, as plan liabilities.

Table 14–1

Sample 401(k) Plan Balance Sheet

Investments	Market Value, March 31, 1991	Market Value, January 1, 1991
Assets:		
Growth fund	$ 100,000	$ 90,000
Fixed income fund	600,000	540,000
Balanced fund	400,000	370,000
Total assets	$1,100,000	$1,000,000
Liabilities:		
Employee salary savings	$ 730,000	$ 670,000
Employer matching contributions	370,000	330,000
Total Liabilities	$1,100,000	$1,000,000

Table 14–2

Sample 401(k) Sources and Uses of Funds

Sources of funds:		
Contributions		
Employee salary savings	$ 35,000	
Matching contributions	15,000	$ 50,000
Growth fund income		
Interest and dividends	0	
Appreciation (Depreciation)	(5,000)	(5,000)
Fixed income fund income		
Interest and dividends	35,000	
Appreciation (Depreciation)	0	35,000
Balanced fund income		
Interest and dividends	10,000	
Appreciation (Depreciation)	20,000	30,000
Total sources of funds		$110,000
Uses of funds:		
Benefits payments		$ 8,000
Plan expenses		2,000
Changes in net assets		
Market value on March 31, 1991	$1,100,000	
Market value on July 1, 1991	1,000,000	100,000
Total uses of funds		$110,000

The major transactions that have intervened during the period and have affected reconciliation of the beginning and ending balances should also be developed. These include contributions, income, benefit payments, expenses, and changes in the net value of plan assets. **Table 14–2** illustrates the types of transactions that should be recorded in order to reconcile financial activity for the period.

With this information, the allocation for the period can be made and reports can then be issued to management and the employees.

§ 14.13   —Periodic Allocations

When the financial statements are reported and the salary savings and matching contributions made during the period are recorded, the complete allocation can be performed. Most plans today employ dollar accounting procedures for completing the allocation. Under these procedures, the actual dollar contributions accredited to the employees during the allocation period are accumulated and the sum total is credited to each employee's account. The dollar investment earnings from all sources employed by the specific investment fund are then allocated to each plan member. The allocation is usually based on a pro rata share of the opening account balance, plus a weighted portion of the contribution for the period. The weighted factor applied to the contribution reflects the fact that contributions were being made during the period at uniform time intervals. Typically, 50 percent is utilized as the weighted factor when uniform contributions are made. With this method, then, one-half of the contribution made to the fund for the period is counted in the allocation base.

Table 14–3 illustrates the possible operation of such an allocation process for several participants in some of the available investment funds.

The process is repeated for all sources of funds within each investment fund for all employees; each participant then has several cells of account transactions. The total number of cells is the total sources of funds multiplied by the total number of possible investment options. A plan with two sources of funds and three investment options provides as many as six accounts for each plan participant.

Some plans today employ share accounting: all contributions, income, and dividends are converted immediately to shares in the appropriate investment fund, based on the published share price at the date of the specific

Table 14–3

Sample Income Allocation for a Single Investment Fund and Single Source of Funds

Fund totals:	
A. Total opening balance for fund	$100,000
B. Total contribution to fund	20,000
C. Allocation base (A + ((.5) × B))	110,000
D. Total income to fund	5,500
E. Allocation rate (D/C)	.0500
Participant A:	
F. Opening balance	2,000
G. Contributions this period	100
H. Allocation base (F + ((.5) × G))	2,050
I. Income allocation (E × H)	378
Participant B:	
J. Opening balance	8,000
K. Contributions this period	400
L. Allocation base (J + ((.5) × K))	8,200
M. Income allocation (E × L)	410

Table 14–4

Share Accounting for a Single Source and Single Investment Fund

Transaction	Dollar Amount	Share Price	Shares on Account
Beginning balance	$ 800	$10.00	80.000
First monthly contribution	150	10.50	94.286
Second monthly contribution	150	11.00	107.922
Third monthly contribution	150	11.50	120.965
Dividends	20	12.00	122.631
Ending balance	1,472	12.00	122.631

transaction. Unrealized appreciation is not directly allocated but is reflected in the share price at the end of the allocated period. The difference between this price and the price at the beginning of the period, as well as at the various contribution dates, is the income from the appreciations allocated. **Table 14–4** illustrates the concept for an allocated period. Each participant's account contains shares/net dollars.

This accounting would be created for each source and each investment fund for all employees in the plan.

Appendix A contains an abbreviated example of dollar accounting for several plan members in a sample management report.

§ 14.14 —Nondiscrimination Testing

The plan must be tested for nondiscrimination each year, in salary savings, matching contributions, and the combination of these in multiple use. The actual deferral percentage test (ADP Test) assesses 401(k) salary savings, and the actual contributions percentage test (ACP Test) assesses Code § 401(m) monthly employer and employee after-tax contributions. (See **Chapter 2** for a complete discussion of the rule and the mechanics of the tests.)

The nondiscrimination tests are naturally performed at year end to determine whether the plan complies with the standards for the plan year. The test should also be conducted on a projected basis during the year, in order to determine whether the plan will comply with the standards at year end. If it is determined that the plan is projected to pass all tests during the year, then no changes in the salary deferral rate of the highly compensated employees (HCEs) need be made during the remainder of the year. If it is determined that the tests will be failed by year end if the salary savings of the HCEs continue as is, then the salary savings for some or all of the HCEs must be scaled back or even eliminated for the rest of the year, in order to pass the test. **Table 14–5** illustrates a projected ADP Test conducted at midyear for a plan with a small group of HCEs, along with the suggested remedy for the balance of the year.

Employees A and B are scaled back to an annual rate of savings of 5 percent of gross earnings for the year, in order to pass the ADP Test. From midyear on, Employee A can save $800 ($4,000 is permitted; $3,200 has already been saved). Employee B can save $2,000 from midyear on ($5,000 is permitted; $3,000 has already been saved during the year).

In projecting earnings in the midyear test, it is important to know not only the annual rate of salary for each person being tested but also any additional earnings that can be expected from raises, bonuses, commissions, and other extra earnings.

If the plan has completed a year of operation without this midyear adjustment, then salary savings have to be returned to the HCEs in descending order of savings relative to actual earnings (see § 2.14). **Table 14–6** illustrates, for the same group, the salary savings that would have to be returned at year end in order to comply with the nondiscrimination standards.

If the midyear correction had not been made, $2,500 would have to be returned to Employee A at year end and $1,000 to Employee B at year end.

In conducting the nondiscrimination tests, either gross or net earnings can be used to test the HCEs and non-HCEs. The method used must be

Table 14–5

Midyear Correction to ADP Test

Employees	Savings to Date	Savings Rate	Projected Salary	Projected Savings	Revised Rate	Revised Savings
HCEs:						
A	$3,200	8.0%	$ 80,000	$6,400	5.0%	$4,000
B	3,000	6.0	100,000	6,000	5.0	5,000
C	2,400	4.0	120,000	4,800	4.0	4,800
D	1,400	4.0	70,000	2,800	4.0	2,800
E	1,350	3.0	90,000	2,700	3.0	2,700
F	1,650	3.0	110,000	3,300	3.0	3,300
HCE-ADP		4.7%			4.0%	
Non-HCEs:						
Non-HCE-ADP		2.2			2.2	
Maximum ADP for HCEs		4.2			4.2	

Table 14–6

Return of Salary Savings to Meet ADP Test

Employees	Annual Salary	Annual Savings	Savings Rate	Revised Rate	Revised Savings	Savings Returned
HCEs:						
A	$ 80,000	$6,400	8.0%	5.0%	$4,000	$2,400
B	100,000	6,000	6.0	5.0	5,000	1,000
C	120,000	4,800	4.0	4.0	4,800	0
D	70,000	2,800	4.0	4.0	2,800	0
E	90,000	2,700	3.0	3.0	2,700	0
F	110,000	3,300	3.0	3.0	3,300	0
HCE-ADP			4.7%	4.0%		
Non-HCEs:						
Non-HCE-ADP			2.2	2.2		
Maximizing ADP for HCEs			4.2	4.2		

specified and used consistently each year. In most cases, using gross earnings is the more effective approach to conducting the tests. **Table 14–7** illustrates that, on average, at low rates of savings for plan members, the ADP Test can be passed by using gross earnings but is failed by using net earnings.

In testing for nondiscrimination, the annual earnings used in the tests are limited to $228,860 (for 1992; indexed for inflation the amount generally tends to rise each year). An individual who earns $300,000 and saves $8,000 for a year has an ADP of 3.49 percent ($8,000 divided by $228,860 times 100), not 2.67 ($8,000 divided by $300,000 times 100).

Table 14–7

Earnings in the ADP Test

Employees	Gross Earnings	Net Earnings
ADP of non-HCEs	3.00%	3.09%
Maximum ADP for HCE	5.00	5.09
ADP of HCE	5.00	5.26
Results of ADP Test	Pass	Fail

Table 14–8

Family Aggregated ADP

Family Members (Employees' States)	Annual Earnings	Relationship to A	Salary Savings	Savings Rate
A (HCE)	$190,000	Top 10 paid	$ 8,000	4.20%
B (Non-HCE)	60,000	Spouse	3,000	5.00
C (Non-HCE)	30,000	Son, age 29	0	0.00
D (Non-HCE)	40,000	Daughter, age 30	2,000	2.50
Totals	$320,000		$13,000	4.50
ADP 1				
Salary of A + B	$228,860		$11,000	
Salary of C + D	70,000		2,000	
Totals	$298,860		$13,000	
ADP 1				4.34
ADP 2				
Salary of A + B	$228,860		$11,000	
Salary of D	40,000		2,000	
Totals	$268,860		$13,000	
ADP 2				4.83

The family members of 4 percent owners and the ten highest paid employees are aggregated in determining the ADP for that group. In addition, spouses and children under the age of 19 are further aggregated in imposing the maximum earnings limit used ($228,860 for 1992). Finally, the ADP for the family group that is used in the test is the higher of the ADP that is determined either with or without the family members who are highly compensated in their own right (see § **2.12**).

Table 14–8 illustrates the determination of the ADP for such an aggregate family group.

ADP 2 is used in the test because it is the higher of the two computed ADPs for this family group. Employee C is omitted altogether in the test. All these rules regarding early limits and family aggregation also apply when conducting the ACP and multiple use tests.

§ 14.15   —Top-Heavy Testing

Most large plans can avoid top-heavy testing each year because of their sheer size. Generally speaking, the number of employees who can be

Table 14–9

1992 Top-Heavy Determination

	Key Employees	Total Employees
All account balances	$550,000	$ 850,000
Distributions:		
1991	0	20,000
1990	0	30,000
1989	0	70,000
1988	0	15,000
1987	0	15,000
Total	$550,000	$1,000,000
Top-heavy ratio		55.5%
Top-heavy status		Negative

classified as key employees is limited in number; the larger the plan in terms of plan membership, the less likely that a plan is top-heavy.

For small plans, the top-heavy determination is usually made on the last day of the plan year. All account balances as of that date, including all contributions and forfeitures made during the plan, are considered, along with distributions made for each of the preceding 5 years. The total value for all plan members is determined, as is the total value for all key employees. The value of the key employees' accounts is divided by the value of the total accounts. If the result is greater than 60 percent, the plan is top-heavy for the next plan year. **Table 14–9** illustrates a basic top-heavy determination.

See **§§ 3.24** and **3.25** for the consequences of the top-heavy status in 401(k) CODAs. If the plan is not top-heavy for the next year, then it can operate without the top-heavy restraints for that year.

§ 14.16 —Management Reports

A full report on each allocation should be prepared for management and should contain the following information:

1. Employee data reconciliation;
2. Summary of account transactions by employee;
3. Results of the nondiscrimination tests;
4. Results of the top-heavy tests;

5. Financial reconciliation;
6. Analysis of plan with recommendations for action if needed.

Appendix B provides, in a brief sample format, a model report that presents all of the essentials required to be reviewed by management.

§ 14.17 —Employee Benefit Statements

A comprehensive benefit statement, provided to each employee after each allocation date, should contain the following information for each source of funds and each investment option:

1. Balance of account at the beginning of the period;
2. Contributions made during the period;
3. Investment income allocated during the period;
4. Forfeitures allocated during the period;
5. Loan repayments made during the period;
6. Fund employees made during the period;
7. Benefit distributions made during the period;
8. Expenses withdrawn during the period;
9. Vested balance of all accounts.

It is also helpful to recap certain plan information for the employee, including the social security number, the annual rate of elective deferrals, and the elected investment mix.

Appendix B provides a model employee benefit statement that creates source-of-fund transactions in which each individual investment option is detailed for the employee.

§ 14.18 —IRS Filings: Annual Return/Report

Each year an annual return/report on the plan must be filed with the IRS. The report must be filed within 7 months of the close of the plan year. The annual return/report is filed on Form 5500-C/R for plans with fewer than 100 participants and on Form 5500 for plans with more than 100 participants. In addition, plans with over 100 participants must provide schedules of assets and the results of an audit conducted by a certified public accountant.

Several schedules may be attached when the annual return/report is filed. Depending on the size of the plan and other factors, the most prevalent forms are:

1. Schedule A—Insurance Information
2. Schedule D—Fiduciary Information
3. Schedule SSA—Deferred Payment Information
4. Schedule C—Trustee Information

Appendix B illustrates a sample Form 5500-C/R with attachments for filing with the IRS.

The IRS will grant an extension of up to 2½ months, for filing the letter after the original deadline. Form 5558 must be filed prior to the filing date, in order to receive approval for the 2½ month extension of time. Approval Form 5558 must be included with Form 5500 or Form 5500-C/R when it is actually filed for the year with the IRS.

A summary annual report that condenses the information on the annual return/report must be distributed to all plan members within 2 months following the deadline for the filing of Form 5500 or Form 5500-C/R, including extensions. **Appendix B** provides a sample summary annual report that must be distributed to all plan members each year.

§ 14.19   Benefit Administration

The other important aspect of managing a 401(k) CODA is the administration of the benefits themselves: monitoring the limitations on benefits to each plan member, providing the loans and hardship withdrawals, processing fund exchanges, paying plan benefits when they come due, and providing the proper tax reports to the IRS.

§ 14.20   —Benefit Limitations

The annual benefits in a 401(k) CODA are limited; that is, both the salary savings amounts permitted under federal rules and the overall contributions made on behalf of a plan member are subject to limitations each year. In addition, if the sponsoring organization maintains a defined-benefit plan that covers the same plan members, the accumulated contributions and forfeitures in the 401(k), in combination with the benefits payable from the defined-benefit plan, are subject to an overall limitation. The overall salary savings permitted to one individual is $8,728 for 1992. **Table 14–10** lists the annual salary limits since the imposition of the limitations in 1987.

Prior to 1987, the salary savings were limited to the extent that they met the criterion for the overall limits on benefits and contributions in retirement programs. The salary deferral limit has increased historically, since

Table 14–10

Salary Savings Limits in 401(k) CODAs

Year	Limitation
1987	$7,000
1988	7,313
1989	7,627
1990	7,979
1991	8,475
1992	8,728

its inception, by approximately 4.7 percent per year. At this historical rate of increase, the salary savings limitation should surpass $10,000 per year in 1955.

The overall addition limit for a given year is 25 percent of net taxable earnings up to $30,000. The annual additions include both contributions and forfeitures from all defined-contribution plans, plus other sources of funds in the 401(k) CODA.

Table 14–11 illustrates the imposition of these limits on an individual who defers a high portion of earnings in a generous plan with matching contributions and a pure discretionary profit-sharing plan.

In this example, the total annual addition for the participant just satisfies the overall limitation for the year. The discretionary profit-sharing plan contribution was 4 percent of gross earnings, and the monthly employer contribution was $.50 for each $1.00 contributed, up to 6 percent of covered earnings. If the plan sponsor had contributed 5 percent of earnings ($3,010) and the plan participant had saved additional salary (say, $8,400), then the benefits from the employer contributions would have been capped in such a way as to limit the overall addition to $13,000 (rather than $13,516). In effect, high-salary savings in this situation results in scaled-back employer-provided benefits. These limitation problems should be monitored by the plan administrators so that the limits are not exceeded and the plan members maximize their employer-provided contributions and benefits.

If the employer maintains a defined-benefit plan, there is an additional limitation on the overall benefits that can be provided through both programs in combination. Annual additions in the 401(k) plan and other defined-contribution plans are recorded historically over the career of the plan member and added together. Similarly, the annual limitations that apply throughout the individual's entire career with the sponsoring organization are also recorded.

Table 14–11

Annual Addition Limitation in 401(k) CODA

Component of Annual Addition	Meeting Limitation Requirements	Exceeding Limitation Requirements
A. Salary savings	$ 8,200	$ 8,400
B. Employer matching contributions	1,806	1,806
C. Profit-sharing contributions	2,408	3,010
D. Profit-sharing forfeitures	300	300
E. Total annual addition (A + B + C)	$12,714	$13,516

Annual Net Taxable Earnings	Earnings Amounts	
F. Gross earnings	$60,200	$60,200
G. Salary savings	8,200	8,200
H. Net earnings (F − H)	$52,000	$ 5,200
I. Annual addition as a percentage of net earnings ((E/H) × 100)	24.4%	26.0%
J. Annual addition limitation (H × .25)	$13,000	$13,000
K. Scaled-back employer contributions or forfeitures	0	$ 516

If the individual is subject to the salary limitation in a given year (25 percent of net earnings), that limit is multiplied by 1.4. If the individual is subject to the dollar limitation in a given year ($30,000 for 1992), that limit is multiplied by 1.25. The pension benefit is divided by the limitation to form the defined-benefit fraction.

The sum of the defined-contribution fraction and the defined-benefit fraction must be equal to or less than 1.0. (It should be noted that, in top-heavy plans, the 1.25 adjustment factor used in the adjusted limit calculations of both fractions is reduced to 1.00. Relief from this restriction can be obtained, however, if the top-heavy ratio is less than 90 percent and the program sponsor provided increased minimum benefits to the plan's key employees.) **Table 14–12** illustrates the operation of the multiple plan limits rule.

An individual retiring after a full career with $630,000 in annual additions and $33,750 per year pension satisfies the multiple plan limits and can receive the benefits earned from both plans. If the individual were entitled to a larger pension benefit ($77,250 per year), however, the

Table 14-12

Multiple Plan Limits at Retirement

	Meeting Limitation Requirements	Exceeding Limitation Requirements
A. Historical sum of all annual additions	$630,000	$630,000
B. Historical sum of all adjusted limits	$900,000	$900,000
C. Defined-contribution fraction (A/B)	.7000	.7000
D. Annual pension benefit	$ 33,750	$ 47,250
E. Defined-benefit adjusted limit	$135,000	$135,000
F. Defined-benefit fraction (D/F)	.2500	.35000
G. Multiple plan fraction (C + F)	.9500	1.0500
H. Scaled-back defined benefit	$ 0	$ 6,750

defined benefit itself would be required to be scaled back (by $6,750 per year) in order for the multiple plan factor to add to 1.00 and for the rule to be satisfied. The individual in this position would receive benefits associated with $630,000 in annual additions and an annual pension benefit of $40,500.

Plans are designed and written to specify which benefit is scaled back in order to comply with the multiple plan limit rule. It is generally good practice to scale back the defined-benefit plan benefits, because these benefits are not allocated to actual accounts as under a defined-contribution plan. The defined-contribution plan benefits must be allocated to the participant's account in each applicable year. A contribution not made cannot be made up in future years. Defined benefits, on the other hand, always have the flexibility for future adjustment.

In certain programs, the 401(k) CODA is supplemental to the defined-benefit plan, which is the basic retirement plan of the organization. What is more, in a closely held organization, the senior officials tend to be the older plan participants whose multiple plan fractions tend to exceed the 1.0 limitation. Annual benefit accruals in a defined-benefit pension plan can be valued much higher than $30,000 each year. In a situation such as this, the participating executives should forgo 401(k) plan participation and accrue benefits in the defined-benefit plan. These pension benefits are more valuable than the 401(k) contribution, and represent a larger benefit to the executive than the defined-contribution benefits. In addition, by forgoing participation in the 401(k) plan, the executive reduces the impact of the ADP and ACP Tests in the 401(k) plan on the remaining, younger HCEs so that they may be entitled to additional pretax salary savings. This situation should be monitored administratively. If a plan member's multiple plan fraction is projected to exceed the 1.0 limitation and the individual is an older participant, it may be best for the individual to accrue more valuable pension benefits rather than participate in the 401(k) plan.

§ 14.21 —Loan Administration

Most plans permit loans up to limits allowed under federal rules; these loans can be secured by the vested interest in the plan. In general, the loan limit is one-half the vested interest up to $50,000.

The individual should apply for the loan in compliance with the rules of the loan program (see **§ 5.11**). The participant agrees to repay the loan through payroll deductions and signs a promissory note acknowledging the obligation to repay the loan at the specified rate of interest over a period of not more than 5 years. (The term of the loan can be extended beyond 5 years for purchase of a primary residence.)

An amortization schedule spreads repayments of the loan over the 5-year period through payroll deductions. The mode of the payment in the amortization schedule coincides with the mode of the payroll delivery in the organization (for example, biweekly, weekly, monthly, or semi-monthly). Copies of all the loan documents, including the amortization schedule, are retained by the trustees and given to the participant. The loan amount itself is withdrawn from the plan assets and delivered to the participant. The source(s) and the investment fund(s) from which the loan amount is to be withdrawn should be specified. Usually, plans establish a hierarchy of sources for withdrawal (for example, salary savings first, monthly contributions next, and so on). The investment funds can be withdrawn (1) in the same proportion as the participant elected to invest, (2) by some arbitrary method that allows certain discretion, or (3) through a hierarchy of funds.

Once the loan is established, it is recorded administratively as another investment option for the participant, within the source(s) from which it was made. The transaction of distributing the loan amount is recorded as a fund exchange from the elected investment account to the loan account. If there are no participant-directed investments in the plan, the loan is recorded as a general investment of the trust whose interest earnings are commingled with the trust earnings for allocation to the participants.

When the repayments are made, they are usually redeposited into the funds as elected by the employee for the salary savings. Repayments are apportioned among investments in the same manner as elected salary savings.

The repayments are recorded administratively as a fund exchange from the loan account to the investment fund accounts elected by the employee. Payments exchanging out of the loan account equal the deposits exchanging into the investment accounts.

§ 14.22   —Hardship Withdrawals

Hardship withdraws from 401(k) CODAs are permitted (see § 2.17 and the rules governing these withdrawals). The plan participant first applies for the hardship withdrawal. If the participant qualifies for the withdrawal and the trustees approve the application, the distributions of the funds can proceed. **Appendix B** gives a checklist of steps to cover and sample withdrawal documents.

The source of the funds and the investment funds from which the withdrawal will come should be specified. Only actual salary savings can be withdrawn from any source that includes elective deferrals as funds contributed in lieu of deferrals to satisfy the ADP Test or multiple use test. Investment earnings cannot be withdrawn from these accounts.

Withdrawals from other sources and investment accounts are usually limited to the vested interest in these accounts. Withdrawals cannot be made from these other accounts unless the funds have been on deposit for at least 2 years and the individual has participated in the plan for at least 5 years. Tracking the remaining vested interest in these accounts becomes administratively cumbersome if the plan member is partially vested. For this and other policy reasons, organizations may wish to limit withdrawals to sources of funds that are 100 percent vested.

See §§ 2.16 and 2.17 for a review of the safe-harbor in-service withdrawal rules that can be adopted by plans. In light of the fact that, under these parameters, all loans must be exhausted before in-service withdrawals can commence, it may be advisable to simply include a generous loan program in the plan design and forgo the use of in-service withdrawals.

Once the in-service, hardship withdrawal requirements have been satisfied by the participant, the distribution can be made. The funds can be withdrawn from the investment in proportion to the elected apportionment, through a prescribed hierarchy or through discretionary choice of the plan participant. The participant should also elect to have or to forgo income tax withholding.

At year end, the participant receives an IRS Form 1099-R reporting the taxable income to the plan participant. The participant pays the applicable federal income tax on the distribution. If the individual is younger than

59$\frac{1}{2}$ years of age, an additional 10 percent excise tax will be charged by the IRS. That excise tax is reported on Form 5329 and attached to the participant's individual tax return.

§ 14.23   —Fund Exchanges

Plan members are usually given the opportunity to revise their investment mix at various times throughout the year. These revisions can be made in conjunction with the issuance of the participant benefit statements. Quarterly statements imply quarterly changes, semiannual statements imply semiannual changes, and so forth. The changes in the accumulated accounts are accomplished through fund exchanges among the available investment options. The changes in future investment apportionments are accomplished through the simple redirection of the deposits in accordance with the new elections. Most loans require that all sources must be revised simultaneously, although plans can permit the selection of fund sources for revision. Most plans require the revisions to apply to future deposits as well as past accumulation; plans can permit the rearrangement of one but not the other. **Table 14–13** illustrates an example of fund exchanges that could take place within one source for a participant who revised the investment mix as indicated.

Plan members are usually required to request fund exchanges in writing, by completing a form designed for that purpose. Most plans require that the plan member specify a new portfolio mix, from which the exchanges are determined. Plans can, however, allow participants to indicate exact dollar amounts for exchange between funds. In these plans, participants specify that certain amounts are to be exchanged out of certain accounts, reapportioned, and then directed into the newly indicated accounts.

Table 14–13

Fund Exchanges within a Single Source of Funds

Investment Fund	Old Investment Mix		Fund Exchanges	New Investment Mix	
	Election	Amount		Election	Amount
A	50%	$ 5,200	$(2,700)	25%	$ 2,500
B	0	0	2,500	25	2,500
C	50	4,800	(2,300)	25	2,500
D	0	0	2,500	25	2,500
Total	100%	$10,000	$ 0	100%	$10,000

§ 14.24 —Benefit Distributions

Benefits are payable from 401(k) CODAs when individuals attain the retirement age under the plan. A common normal retirement age is 65, although some plans may permit earlier retirement. Most plans provide for the immediate payment of benefits when an individual separates from service prior to attaining normal retirement age. In addition, plans provide that benefits are payable if the plan member dies or becomes totally and permanently disabled.

The accounts of the plan members are aggregated as a single sum; plans usually distribute the plan benefits in that form. Although other plan payment options can be made available, most plans provide for, and most employers want to receive, the single sum of capital accumulated in the account. Single-sum distributions from pure 401(k) CODAs can be elected by married plan participants without spousal consent to waiver of any contingent benefits.

If a plan were to include optional forms of payment, they would usually consist of periodic distributions of the plan account over a specified number of years. The plan might offer, for example, monthly, quarterly, or annual payments over a period of 1, 15, or 20 years. All retirement funds would thus be exhausted when the payout period is completed.

If a plan were to offer annuities, it would be in the context of assisting the employee in the purchase of such an annuity from a recommended insurance company. The plan itself would not pay such an annuity but rather would purchase one, or assist in purchasing one, on behalf of the plan member.

By far the most prevalent form of payment is the single sum at retirement, separation from service, death, or disability. When a plan participant retires or separates from service, an application for the single sum should be completed. The individual should elect or decline withholding of federal income tax. A distribution, consisting of the benefit settlement along with a notice that informs the participant of the tax implications of the distribution, should then be made to the plan member. At the end of the year, the plan member is sent an IRS Form 1099-R that reports the taxable income to the IRS and to the plan member. **Appendix B** illustrates a typical set of distribution materials that can be used to process 401(k) plan benefits at retirement or at separation from service on the (most prevalent) single-sum basis choice.

The distribution can always be rolled over into an individual retirement account (IRA) until the former plan member attains age 70½. The participant continues to defer taxes on the distribution until payment commences and earns tax-deferred income in the IRA.

If the plan participant is younger than age 59½ and elects to take the plan distribution rather than roll it over to an IRA, the participant must pay federal income taxes on it at the applicable rate and a 10 percent excise tax. If the plan member is in a 31 percent federal tax bracket, 41 percent of the benefit distribution will be paid over to the IRS.

If the plan participant is over 59½, there is no income tax. If the former participant was age 55 or older on January 1, 1992, he or she could elect 5- or 10-year income averaging of the single-sum distribution, provided that the plan member had participated in the plan for 5 years or more. In the future, individuals who were not age 55 on January 1, 1992, but who received distributions after age 59½ may elect 10-year averaging, but not 5-year averaging, if they so desire. **Table 14–14** illustrates a comparison of the federal income tax on single sums under 5- and 10-year averaging methods, based on 1991 tax rates.

Single-sum distributions that qualify for 10-year or 5-year averaging are defined to be lump-sum distributions under the Code. Ten-year averaging is more advantageous for lump sums under $425,000. Five-year averaging is more advantageous for lump sums in excess of $425,000.

Table 14–14

Comparison of 5- and 10-Year Income Averaging

Lump Sum Amount	5-year Averaging		10-Year Averaging	
	Tax	Rate	Tax	Rate
$ 10,000	$ 750	7.5%	$ 550	5.5%
20,000	1,500	7.5	1,100	5.5
30,000	3,300	11.0	2,521	8.5
40,000	5,100	12.8	4,187	10.5
50,000	6,900	13.8	5,897	11.8
60,000	8,700	14.5	7,674	12.8
70,000	10,500	15.0	9,505	13.6
100,000	15,000	15.0	14,471	14.5
150,000	28,772	19.2	24,570	16.4
200,000	42,773	21.4	36,922	18.5
300,000	72,377	24.1	66,360	22.1
400,000	103,377	25.8	102,602	25.7
425,000	111,127	26.1	112,182	26.4
450,000	118,878	26.4	122,680	27.3
500,000	134,378	26.9	143,682	28.7

If a participant receives a large single sum, he or she should be aware that there is a 15 percent excise tax on excess distributions. (See **§ 4.13** for a full review of the rules on excess distributions.) In general, distributions over $150,000 are subject to the excise tax. If the distribution qualifies as a lump sum and 5- or 10-year averaging is elected, the amounts over $750,000 are subject to the 15 percent excise tax.

Benefits must be distributed by the April 1 following the year in which a participant attains age $70\frac{1}{2}$. The minimum benefit to be distributed is the amount that reflects the amortization of the plan accounts over the life expectancy of the participant or the life expectancy of the participant and the participant's spouse.

CHAPTER 15

ADMINISTRATION OF TAX-SHELTERED ANNUITY PLANS

§ 15.1   Selection of Service Providers

The most important aspect of a tax-sheltered annuity program is the selection of the service providers. At the outset, the sponsor should decide how many service providers it is willing to employ and which service providers offer the desired investment options, flexibility, and administrative services.

In searching for service providers, many employers will identify specific needs and evaluate prospective companies by their abilities to meet those needs. The areas to review include but are not limited to the following:

Guaranteed funds

Does the provider offer investments with guaranteed rates of return and guaranteed principal? What types of general investments back these fixed-return funds?

Pooled funds

Does the provider offer pooled investment funds with varying objectives and degrees of risk? For example:

- Growth funds;
- Income funds;
- Balanced funds;
- Government security funds;
- Guaranteed investment contract funds;
- Funds with a combination of objectives;
- Funds with special objectives.

Return risk profile

Does the service provider offer various pooled funds whose underlying securities range from high quality and low risk in a given fund to high risk and high return in other funds?

Forms of benefit payments

What forms of payment of benefits are available? For example:

- Single-sum payments;
- Guaranteed annuities for the life of the plan participant;
- Guaranteed annuities for the life of the plan participants, with death benefits payable to a spouse or named beneficiary;
- Fixed payout over a selected number of years.

Sales charges

Are there sales expenses associated with the purchase of a contract? Do these sales expenses recur every year? What are the sales expenses?

Management fees

Are there ongoing direct management fees? How often are they applied? How are they applied and what are they?

Performance history

What is the recent investment performance history of each fixed-return fund and each pooled fund that the service provider is proposing to offer? It is usually best to review the 1-year (or the three most recent 1-year periods), 3-year, 5-year, and 10-year compounded annual rates of return that $1 invested at the beginning of the period would have yielded at the end of the period of performance.

Withdrawal Penalties

What are the contractual penalties for premature withdrawal of funds? Many contracts impose penalties for the first 5 to 10 years for withdrawal of funds from the contractual arrangement.

Market value adjustment

Is there a market value adjustment for single-sum withdrawals from the fixed returned fund?

Fund Accumulation

The net theoretical accumulation in each investment fund should be calculated for 1-, 3-, 5-, 10-, and 25-year periods. Using a yield rate that reflects the performance history, deduct the expenses charged each year and determine the accumulated account balance that $1 invested at the beginning of the period would yield at the end of the period.

Fund exchange fees

Are there fees for exchanges of funds from one investment provided by the service provider to another investment offered in the same tax-sheltered annuity contract? What are the fund exchange fees?

Marketing representatives

How many marketing representatives will be available to review the products with the employees? Where are they located? What is their accessibility?

Employee meetings

Will the marketing representatives meet with each employee individually, if needed, at the initial enrollment and after the initial enrollment?

Product information

Does the service provider distribute clear, helpful marketing and enrollment material?

Technical representatives

How many technical representatives will be available to assist employees? Where are they located? How accessible are they?

Technical support

Do the technical representatives assist in the determination of the exclusion allowance and the overall employer limit on contributions? Do the technical representatives provide advice to the employees on making any special election with regard to the contribution limitations?

Administrative fees

Are there any special fees associated with technical assistance provided by the representatives of the service provider?

References

What are the references of the service provider? It is best to speak directly with officials of similar organizations that are offering the contracts and products of the prospective service provider. What is the employee utilization of those services and products at the referral organization? What is the level of employees' satisfaction with the investment performance as well as with the marketing and technical support?

Many larger organizations will formalize these items into a request for proposal (RFP). The RFP invites details on the important offerings of each service provider, along with sample contracts, brochures, and application forms. Once all of the responses to the RFP have been collected, many organizations will formally score each RFP through a predetermined system that reflects the importance of each item to the sponsor and the quality of the response given by each prospective service provider.

After the scores are compiled, the top several prospective providers may be asked to submit final offers. When the final offers are judged, the service providers can be engaged.

§ 15.2 Record-Keeping Process

After the service providers have been selected, the employer should establish the payroll deduction process. The employer need only identify, for each employee, the amount that is to be deducted from the periodic paycheck and deposited in the accounts of the service providers that the employee has elected to use. If, for example, the employer engages three service providers, then the payroll deduction process must account for three possible investment elections for each employee.

The employer then produces, for each service provider, a listing of all employees who are depositing funds for that period, along with their periodic investment amounts. Each service provider then apportions the investment for each employee among the appropriate funds, according to the elections that were made. In summary, the employer simply reports the deposit for each employee to each service provider. Each service provider directs each employee deposit to the individually selected investment funds.

§ 15.3 Employee Enrollment

Representatives of the service providers should meet with employees, either in groups or individually, to review their products and enroll the participants. Most service providers offer marketing material that includes an application form on which the employee can specify the amount of the salary savings deduction and the specific investment funds chosen for investment.

The employer collects the applications, records the proper payroll deduction amount, and forwards the applications to the appropriate service providers. The service providers then open individual accounts for the employees so that salary savings can begin for each plan participant.

§ 15.4 Employer Contributions

If the tax-sheltered annuity program includes employer contributions, the employees must elect the service provider and the investment funds to which contributions are to be directed. In many cases, especially in thrift plans, the selection of the service providers and the investment funds can coincide with the salary savings elections. This avoids the complications associated with multiple elections and simplifies the computation of the apportionment of the matching contributions among the service providers. As with the 401(k) CODA, matching contributions can be made coincident with the salary savings or at the end of the year.

If the employer also makes pension contributions to the tax-sheltered annuity plan, it is important to enroll those employees who elect not to reduce their salaries and save for retirement through the program. These employees should complete the applications for the service providers to which they wish to direct their employer contributions. Typically, these pension contributions are made once each year and are apportioned among the service providers and investment funds as elected by the employees. These employer contributions can, however, be made more often, if the employer so desires.

§ 15.5   Limitations on Contributions

Chapter 11 has detailed the three limitations on salary savings through the tax-sheltered annuity program: (1) annual deferral limit, (2) exclusion allowance, and (3) overall employer limitation. In most instances, it is the employee's responsibility to monitor these limits and contribute the proper tax-deferred amount. Employers and service providers, however, usually provide assistance to employers so that they can determine the proper limitation and maximize the benefits of the tax-sheltered annuity.

Table 15–1 illustrates the salary savings limit that an employee might calculate for a plan to which the employer gives 5 percent of gross earnings as a pension contribution each year.

According to the calculation, the employee can save $5,000, in addition to the contributions anticipated to be made by the employer. This calculation should be made at the beginning of every year so that the employee can be assured that the salary savings to be made for the year fall properly within the proscribed limits.

The salary deferral limit can be increased from $9,500 each year to as much as $12,500 for employees who have worked 15 years or more for certain types of organizations. (See **Chapter 11** for the list of these organizations.) **Table 15–2** illustrates a calculation that an employee might make regarding qualification for the extended salary deferral limit.

This individual can save $12,000 in the year in question, as long as this amount falls within the exclusion allowance and overall employer limitations. For those employees who deferred little or nothing in the past, the salary deferral limit can be extended by as much as $3,000 in a given year.

Table 15–1

Tax-Sheltered Annuity Limit Calculation

I. Salary deferral limit	$ 9,500
II. Exclusion allowance	
A. Gross annual earnings	$50,000
B. Year of prior service	5
C. 20% exclusion factor	.20
D. Employer contribution this year	$ 2,500
E. Total of all past contributions	$37,500
F. Numerator $((A \times B \times C) - (D + E))$	$10,000
G. Denominator $(1 + (B \times C))$	2
H. Exclusive allowance (F/G)	$ 5,000
III. Overall employer limitation	
A. Gross annual earnings	$50,000
B. 20%	.20
C. Employer contributions this year from all plans	$ 2,500
D. 80%	.80
E. 25% of earnings limitation $((A \times B) - (C \times D))$	$ 8,000
F. Annual dollar limitation	$30,000
G. Overall employer limitation (lesser of E and F)	$ 8,000
IV. TSA salary deferral limit (Least of I, II.H, and III.G)	$ 5,000

The total increments that an employee can accumulate over a career is $15,000. When this level of increments is reached, the $9,500 deferral limit will apply.

Finally, in order to take advantage of the extended deferral limits, past salary savings amounts should have averaged less than approximately $5,000 each year. If an employee's average deferred salary is significantly in excess of this amount, no salary savings increment will be available.

In computing the salary deferral limitation for the year, the employee in the example would simply replace the $9,500 component in **Table 15–1** with $12,000. The limit would remain at $5,000 for the year, but no additional deferrals would be credited against the overall $15,000 limit in accumulated incremental deferrals.

The overall employer limitation can be increased under certain circumstances. (See **Chapter 11** for a complete summary of the rules and the circumstances.) **Table 15–3** illustrates the extended overall limit when an employee elects to separate from service.

This employee would continue to be restricted to the $5,000 savings in the year of separation from service, because the exclusion allowance is below the calculated employee limit. This election is effective for those

Table 15–2

Extended Salary Deferral Limit

I. $3,000 limit	$ 3,000
II. $15,000 limit	
A. $15,000	$15,000
B. Salary reduction increments from this provision	
from all prior years	$12,500
C. Limitation (A − B)	$ 2,500
III. $5,000 limit	
A. $5,000	$5,000
B. Years of service with the organization	15
C. $5,000 for all service (A × B)	$75,000
D. Salary reductions from all prior years	$40,000
E. Limitation (C − D)	$35,000
IV. Additional permitted salary deferral (least of I, II.C, and III.E)	$ 2,500
V. Basic salary deferral limit	$ 9,500
VI. Extended salary deferral limits (IV + V)	$12,000

employees who have saved relatively little in the past. If the exclusion allowance is high, they can defer more than 25 percent of net earnings (the standard earnings limit in the overall employee limitation), up to $30,000 (the normal dollar limitation), in the year of separation from service. This provision allows the employee to catch up at separation from service but not to defer more than the tax-sheltered annuity exclusion allowance up to $30,000.

Another limit extension option is available for election by the employees for every year that substitutes for the standard overall employer limit. **Table 15–4** illustrates its applications (see **Chapter 11** for a description of the limit).

Table 15–3

Overall Limit in Year of Separation from Service

A. Dollar limitation	$30,000
B. Exclusion allowance (see II.H, in **Table 15–1**)	$ 5,000
C. Limit (lesser of A and B)	$ 5,000

Table 15–4

Overall Limit Election for Any Year

I. $4,000 limit	
A. $3,200	$ 3,000
B. Gross earnings	$50,000
C. 20%	.20
D. Limitation (A + (B × C))	$13,200
II. Exclusion allowances (see **Table 15–1**)	$ 5,000
III. $15,000 limit	$15,000
IV. Overall limitation	
(Least of I.D, II, and III)	$ 5,000

The employee of **Table 15–1** would continue to be limited by the exclusion allowance and would not elect overall limitation. Individuals with relatively low earnings who deferred little or no salary in the past can take effective advantage of this limitation. If these employees wish to contribute more than 25 percent of includable compensation up to the exclusion allowance, they should elect these overall employee limitations.

The special elections allow certain individuals to recover lost opportunities to contribute to the plan. Under all elections and limitations, however, employees can never defer salary in excess of the tax-sheltered annuity exclusion allowance.

§ 15.6   Benefit Statements

Benefit statements are usually provided directly to the employees from the service providers. Typically, the service providers will record the addresses of the plan members and issue statements of account directly to them. Naturally, the statement format will vary among providers. Employers are usually furnished with summary reports for their records. Employer involvement in the production and delivery of the statements is usually minimal in tax-sheltered annuity programs.

§ 15.7   Benefit Administration

Many aspects of benefit administration are transacted between the employee and the service provider directly. In some instances, the employer will act as a conduit, in order to assist employees in the benefit administration process.

If an employee wishes to revise the rate of savings or the investment elections, the employer must record the revisions for payroll deductions. Many other transactions, such as fund exchanges and benefit claims, can be administered directly through the service provider.

Employers can offer their employees attractive programs that require minimal internal administration.

CHAPTER 16

ADMINISTRATION OF SALARY REDUCTION SEPS

§ 16.1 Plan Installation

As discussed in **Chapter 12**, salary reduction SEPs currently have limited application. Therefore, before establishing such a plan, an employer must carefully consider whether this type of plan is appropriate for the organization. When this decision is made and the plan design process is complete, the plan installation process begins.

The employer can then create a detailed plan of action for implementing the program. The action plan should list, for each event, the task itself, the sequence in which it occurs, the party or parties responsible for its completion, and the due date for finalizing the task. In general, the sequence of events should follow in this order:

1. Select the service providers;
2. Adopt plan document;
3. Adopt underlying individual retirement arrangements (IRAs);
4. Create record-keeping data base;
5. Open coordinated payroll deduction process with record-keeping system;
6. Test all payroll and record-keeping systems;
7. Distribute enrollment–disclosure materials
8. Enroll employees;
9. Begin payroll deductions and salary savings deposits to IRAs.

§ 16.2 —Selecting Service Providers

Many employers will consider a SEP at the suggestion of a service provider, who can then become the focal point in the whole design and setup process. Employers should take the time to interview more than one service provider, in order to get different perspectives and be sure they are getting what they want.

The main reason for an employer to choose a SEP is simplicity. This goal will be defeated if the employer cannot obtain "full service" from one service provider. In other words, the SEP service provider should be able to do at least the following:

1.   Provide a standardized, IRS-approved SEP document, and employee disclosure information;
2.   Maintain eligibility as an IRA trustee or custodian and be able to provide a standardized, IRS-approved IRA agreement;
3.   Offer a range of reasonable investment options;
4.   Offer technical assistance regarding plan setup and administration;
5.   Provide periodic IRA statements to participants.

The sponsor should strongly consider finding a service provider that can perform the annual administrative tasks; with a SEP, these will include an annual nondiscrimination testing and top-heavy testing.

§ 16.3   —The Plan Document

Generally, an employer will adopt either a prototype plan approved by the IRS (which can be provided through most service providers) or will file Form 5305A-SEP. Copies of this form and instructions are reproduced in **Appendix D**. A SEP has to be adopted prior to the due date of the employer's tax return. If the IRS form or an approved prototype is adopted, the document does not have to be sent to the IRS or any other government agency.

The IRS-provided Form 5305A-SEP does not allow the employer the opportunity to make an additional contribution that is allocated on an integrated basis. If the employer wants an integrated form, the document must be custom-designed. Furthermore, Form 5305A-SEP cannot be used if the employer (1) currently maintains a qualified plan or (2) maintained a qualified defined-benefit plan at any time in the past, and that plan covered one or more of the employees to be covered under the SEP. Other qualifying conditions for use of Form 5305A-SEP are discussed in **§ 7.8**.

If Form 5305A-SEP cannot be used, the sponsor may substitute an approved prototype plan or have the plan custom-designed. A custom-designed plan is not a good idea: it defeats the goals of simplicity and administrative cost savings that SEPs generally offer. Not only would the employer have to pay for the documentation, but the plan would not be eligible for the simplified reporting and disclosure requirements. The plan would have to file annual reports, and a summary plan description (SPD) would have to be prepared.

Many service providers sponsor prototype SEP documents that have been approved by the IRS. These are a viable alternative to Form 5305A-SEP, as long as one of the documents is available to the employer. The only limitation of a prototype plan is that only the design options indicated by the choices that appear in the prototype plan are available.

§ 16.4   —Individual Retirement Arrangements

Underlying IRAs have to be established for each participating employee. These can follow the IRS's standardized form (Form 5305), or an IRS-approved prototype arrangement can be adopted.

§ 16.5   —The Record-Keeping Process

The next phase of the installation process is the alteration of the payroll system at the organization in order to create payroll deductions, calculate the monthly employer contributions, and determine the apportionment of both of these sources of funds and the possible investment options that can be elected by each plan member. Coordination among the payroll system or outside payroll service provider, the sponsoring organization, the record keeper, and the investment funds is essential. To the extent that a single organization provides two or more of these services, tasks can be somewhat consolidated. The goal of the process is to create payroll records that provide at least this fundamental information for each plan member:

1. Name of participant;
2. Social security number of participant;
3. Salary for the payroll period;
4. Elective deferral percentage of salary;
5. Elective deferral amount;
6. Employee monthly contribution;
7. Elective percentage for investments (within the individual IRA)—Fund A, Fund B, and so on;
8. Other sources of funds (discretionary employer contribution, rollover deposits, after-tax employee contributions) and the applicable deposit amounts.

The participant's social security number is the key to coordination of all the interacting systems. When the above information is processed after each payroll period, the amount of each contribution source and each investment fund apportionment will be determined for each participant. Totals by source and by IRA investment fund can then be determined so that the proper remittance can be made to each investment fund within the IRAs.

These records are then accumulated throughout the valuation period. Payroll deductions are made, deposits are accumulated, and the corresponding records are maintained in an additive fashion. In this way, the total account activity is maintained at the end of each year. Contributions and investment experience are recorded separately, so that top-heavy testing and nondiscrimination testing can be completed.

§ 16.6 —Employee Disclosure Information and Enrollment

The employee enrollment should include group and/or individualized meetings to explain the program, the investment options, and the communication materials that the employee can take home and review. If possible, the in-house contact person, as well as representatives of the service provider(s), should be present at the enrollment meetings to explain the program and answer questions that may arise.

To meet the legal alternative reporting requirements for IRAs, certain information has to be disclosed to participants. When the sponsor has used Form 5305A-SEP, each participant must receive:

* The completed Form 5305A-SEP;
* The general information guidelines (found in the instructions to Form 3505A-SEP);
* Questions and answers (found in the instructions to Form 3505A-SEP).

Similar requirements apply when an IRS-approved prototype plan is used.

Regardless of the legal requirements, the materials must be able to effectively accomplish the following:

* Highlight the overall program;
* Explain the details of the program in colloquial language;
* Communicate the personalized effect on individuals who choose to participate;

- Deliver enrollment material that clarifies basic plan enrollment, beneficiary designations, investment elections, and plan savings rate.

§ 16.7   —Government Filings

As long as the sponsor adopts the plan using Form 5305A-SEP or an IRS-approved prototype plan, the plan does not have to be submitted to the IRS for approval. An individually designed SEP is submitted to the IRS; however, as discussed above, a custom-designed SEP defeats the reasons for adopting a SEP in the first place.

§ 16.8   Annual Administration

The plan will be structured to provide periodic reports to management and to employees (monthly, quarterly, semiannually, or annually). Because contributions are made directly to IRA accounts, statements to the employees will be made periodically directly from the IRA sponsor. Management reports and the required nondiscrimination and top-heavy testing will be done on an annual basis.

§ 16.9   —Nondiscrimination Testing

The nondiscrimination requirements that apply to a SEP were discussed in § 7.8. The rules are generally harsher but less complex than under a 401(k) plan. To maintain a salary reduction SEP, the administrator must be sure that:

- The number of participants does not exceed the maximum limit of 25 participants;
- At least 50 percent of the participants make salary reduction agreements.

In addition, the administrator must make sure that no highly compensated employee (HCE) defers more than 125 percent of the average deferral amount of all non-HCEs. As with a 401(k) plan, any excess contributions can be returned to HCEs within a limited period of time. However, the administrator should do preliminary testing, to be sure that the plan satisfies the test limitations. If it does not, the deferral amounts of the HCEs should be limited for the rest of the year, to keep the plan within the requirements.

§ 16.10   —Maximum Contribution Limits

In addition to the nondiscrimination requirements, the administrator must make sure that the contributions do not exceed other applicable limits. These limits include:

- A maximum deferral amount ($8,728 for 1992);
- A maximum deductible employer contribution limit (15 percent of covered compensation);
- Code § 415 limits.

These limits apply in the same manner as under a 401(k) plan; the administrative issues are the same as discussed in § **14.20**.

§ 16.11   —Top-Heavy Testing

The top-heavy determination date is usually the last day of the plan year. All account balances as of that date, including all contributions and forfeitures made during the plan, are considered, along with distributions made for each of the preceding 5 years. The total value for all plan members and for all key employees is determined. The value of the key employees' accounts is divided by the value of the total accounts. If the result is greater than 60 percent, the plan is top-heavy for the next plan year.

Table 16–1 illustrates a basic top-heavy determination.

Table 16–1

1992 Top-Heavy Determination

	Key Employees	Total Employees
All account balances	$550,000	$ 850,000
Distributions:		
1991	0	20,000
1990	0	30,000
1989	0	70,000
1988	0	15,000
1987	0	15,000
Total	$550,000	$1,000,000
Top-heavy ratio		55.5%
Top-heavy status		Negative

See § **3.24** for the consequences of the top-heavy status in SEP arrangements. If the plan is not top-heavy for the next year, then it can operate without the top-heavy restraints for that next year.

§ 16.12   —Employee Benefit Statements

Periodic statements indicating the contributions made, the investment experience, and the total account balance should be distributed. Although annual statements are not required by law, employees who are not informed regularly as to their benefits are less likely to appreciate the benefit program.

To meet the alternative reporting and disclosure requirements (discussed in § **16.6**), the employer must disclose on an annual basis the total amount of employer contributions under the plan for the previous calendar year.

§ 16.13   —Annual Reports/IRS Filings

As long as the alternative reporting requirements are satisfied, the plan does not have to file an annual Form 5500s. The only ongoing administrative requirement is an annual notice of employer contributions made to the IRA on behalf of the employee by the employer.

§ 16.14   —Management Reports

A full report should be prepared for management, containing the following information on each allocation:

1. Employee data reconciliation;
2. Summary of account transactions by employee;
3. Results of the nondiscrimination tests;
4. Results of the top-heavy tests;
5. Financial reconciliation;
6. Analysis of plan, with recommendations for action if needed.

§ 16.15   Benefit Administration

One of the advantages of a SEP program is that benefit distributions do not require any difficult processing. Plans are not allowed to limit withdrawals, and the event is generally handled directly between the IRA sponsor and the participant. The IRA sponsor (and not the employer) must complete any required government filings, when a distribution is made. The IRA sponsor must also notify the plan administrator of the distribution, because the distribution will affect the top-heavy testing.

CHAPTER 17

ADMINISTRATION OF NONQUALIFIED PLANS

§ 17.1 Plan Setup

When a decision has been made to establish a nonqualified plan, the setup process can begin. In almost all cases, to meet stated objectives, the non-qualified deferred compensation plan will be an unfunded top-hat plan that meets the partial exemption from ERISA requirements (see **§ 8.2**). Meeting the exemption requirements keeps the administration very simple and creates the desired tax results. Because almost all plans will (or should be) top-hat plans, this chapter discusses only the administration of un-funded top-hat plans.

Implementation of the plan should begin with a detailed plan of action. The action plan should list, for each event, the task itself, the sequence in which it occurs, the party or parties responsible for its completion, and the due date for finalizing the task. In general, the sequence of events should follow in this order:

1. Select service providers;
2. Adopt plan document;
3. Adopt rabbi trust (if applicable);
4. Create record-keeping data base;
5. Coordinate payroll deduction process with record-keeping system;
6. Test all payroll and record-keeping systems;
7. Distribute enrollment materials;
8. Enroll employees;
9. Begin payroll deductions and salary savings deposits to IRAs.

§ 17.2 —Selecting Service Providers

A nonqualified plan is simple to administer, and the ongoing administration may easily be handled in-house. In the setup phase, an attorney should be involved to draft employment agreements, plan documents, and rabbi trust documents. If a rabbi trust is used, the employer will need a trustee and one or more sources for investments. If the plan simply earmarks an account for funding of the promised benefits, investment will be generally be handled by the individual who invests other liquid assets of the corporation.

The attorney chosen should be familiar with nonqualified deferred compensation arrangements. The attorney is important primarily in making sure that the plan stays within the unfunded top-hat exemption requirements.

§ 17.3 —Plan Documents

In a nonqualified arrangement that is not subject to ERISA (which is generally the case), no formal plan document is required. The arrangement can be established simply by drafting individual employment contracts with the parties involved. If a number of employees will be participating and the terms and conditions of their deferral agreement are the same, it may be simpler to draft a single plan document. **Appendix C** includes a sample plan document.

§ 17.4 —Rabbi Trust

If money is set aside in a rabbi trust, the trust document must be established and the trustee chosen. The trustee or trustees may be a corporate trustee, such as a bank, or one or more individuals. If individuals are chosen, assuming that they are employees of the company, the company may want to purchase insurance to cover their expenses, in case they are sued by plan participants. The insurance would cover all expenses (including legal fees) for negligent acts. A sample rabbi trust is included in **Appendix C**.

To be certain that the rabbi trust does not result in any adverse tax consequences to the participant, the employer has to make a request to the IRS for a Private Letter Ruling. A Private Letter Ruling request has an $800 filing fee, plus the legal expenses of preparing the submission. The IRS has granted a significant number of Private Letter Rulings on specific rabbi trusts, and an employer may decide to draft language similar to a trust that has been approved previously. However, it is important to understand that, under IRS procedures, a Private Letter Ruling that has been issued to another taxpayer has no authority with regard to any other taxpayer. Even if the IRS has previously approved individual language, the position taken could change subsequently.

§ 17.5   —Government Filings

Nonqualified salary deferral plans are, in almost all cases, designed to meet the ERISA top-hat exception (see § 8.2). Top-hat plans are exempt from most ERISA requirements; however, they are not exempt from the reporting and disclosure provisions of ERISA. A plan may satisfy all reporting and notice requirements by conforming with the alternative method of reporting and disclosure found in the U.S. Department of Labor (DOL) Regulations.[1] Appendix C includes a sample of a letter to the Department of Labor, containing the required disclosure. The notice must be filed with the DOL within 120 days after the later of the date when the plan is established or the date when the plan becomes effective.

Complying with alternative reporting requirements means that no annual reports or specific notices to the participants will be required.

§ 17.6   The Record-Keeping Process

The next phase of the installation process is the alteration of the payroll system at the organization in order to create payroll deductions and calculate monthly employer contributions (if any are provided). If deferred amounts are held in an investment account, apportionment of both of these sources of funds and of the possible investment options that can be elected by each plan member is required. Coordination between the employer and the sponsors of the investment funds is essential. The goal of the process is to create payroll records that provide at least this fundamental information for each plan member:

1.   Name of participant;
2.   Social security number of participant;
3.   Salary for the payroll period;
4.   Elective deferral percentage of salary;
5.   Elective deferral amount;

---

[1] 29 C.F.R. § 2520.104.23.

6.   Employee monthly contribution;
7.   Elective percentage for investments (assuming funds are set aside);
8.   Other sources of funds.

The participant's social security number is the key to coordination of the interacting systems. When the above information is processed after each payroll period, the amount of each contribution source and each investment fund apportionment will be determined for each participant. Totals by source and by investment fund can then be determined so that the proper remittance can be made to each investment fund.

These records are then accumulated throughout the valuation period. Payroll deductions are made, deposits are accumulated, and the corresponding records are maintained in an additive fashion. In this way, the total account activity is maintained at the end of each year.

§ 17.7   Annual Administration

The plan will be structured to provide periodic reports to management and to employees (monthly, quarterly, semiannually, or annually). Because contributions are made directly to IRA accounts, periodic statements to the employees will originate directly from the IRA sponsor. Management reports, and the required nondiscrimination and top-heavy testing, will be done on an annual basis.

§ 17.8   —FICA and FUTA Taxes

The taxation of deferred compensation for social security and federal unemployment purposes is substantially different from the federal income tax treatment. Amounts under such plans must be withheld on the later of either (1) the time when the employee performs the services that earn the salary to be reduced or (2) the time when the employee is no longer subject to a "substantial risk of forfeiture" (when the employee can no longer lose the amounts being deferred). Because few of these plans subject participants to a risk of losing their earnings, FICA and FUTA taxes will, in most cases, be taken out in the year when the deferred dollars are earned. Many individuals who are eligible for such plans have already paid the maximum social security taxes.

Amounts received under the plan will not be subject to withholding in the employee's postretirement years. Amounts received generally will not reduce the social security benefits that the individual is eligible to receive.

§ 17.9   —Taxable Income

If any money is set aside in a separate account or in a rabbi trust, the earnings are treated as taxable income and must be included on the employer's corporate tax return.

§ 17.10   —Benefit Statements

Periodic statements indicating the contributions made, the investment experience (or bookkeeping interest credits), and the total account balance should be calculated and distributed. Although annual statements are not required by law, employees who are not informed regularly as to their benefits are less likely to appreciate the benefit program.

§ 17.11   —Management Reports

A full report should be prepared for management, containing the following information on each allocation:

1. Employee data reconciliation;
2. Summary of account transactions by employee;
3. Financial reconciliation;
4. Analysis of plan, with recommendations for action if needed.

§ 17.12   Benefit Administration

One of the advantages of nonqualified programs is that benefit distributions do not require any difficult processing. The election regarding the timing of the distributions is made generally at the same time as the election to defer. The distribution is treated as ordinary income.

APPENDIX A

401(k) CODA DESIGN AND INSTALLATION MATERIAL

§ A.1 Retirement Plan Survey

ALPHA OMEGA Organization

Your Company is considering the establishment of a retirement savings plan for you. The plan would allow you to save your retirement through pre-tax payroll deductions. Your funds would accumulate with investment earnings year after year also on a pre-tax basis. When you leave employment your retirement savings would be distributed to you for continued savings for your retirement, immediate use or the provision of retirement income. When you use your funds for retirement they begin to be taxed but usually on a very favorable basis.

Before your Company establishes the plan we wish to check the enthusiasm among our employees for such a plan. In order for the retirement savings plan to be a success, it is important that employees actively support the program and take advantage of its financial benefits. Please take a few minutes to answer the following set of questions regarding your participation in a new salary savings program. Circle the response that best applies to you:

1. Do you currently contribute to an individual retirement account (IRA)?

Yes   No

2. Do you currently save for your own retirement by any means other than an IRA?

Yes   No

3. Would you like to save for your retirement through tax-deferred payroll deductions through the company?

Yes   No

4. Approximately what percentage of your pay would you contribute each pay period to a retirement savings plan at the company?

0%   1%   2%   3%   4%   5%   6%   7%   8%   9%   10%   More

5. Would you be more likely to participate in a retirement savings plan if the company also contributed to it?

    Not Likely   Likely   Extremely Likely

6. If the company contributed on your behalf $.50 for each $1.00 you contributed, up to 6 percent of your pay, approximately how much of your pay would you contribute each pay period through pretax payroll deductions to a retirement savings plan at the company?

    0%   1%   2%   3%   4%   5%   6%   7%   8%   9%   10%   More

7. Would you be more likely to participate in a retirement savings plan if you knew you could have access to your savings, should you need them, by borrowing against your account?

    Not Likely   Likely   Extremely Likely

8. Would you be more likely to participate in a retirement savings plan if you had the opportunity to choose your own investments from among several types of funds?

    Not Likely   Likely   Extremely Likely

9. If the company matched your contributions up to 6 percent and you were able to borrow your funds and direct your own investments among several types of funds, what percentage of your pay would you contribute each pay period to a retirement savings plan at the company?

    0%   1%   2%   3%   4%   5%   6%   7%   8%   9%   10%   More

10. If there are other features of a retirement savings plan that would encourage you to participate, or, if you have any comment on the proposed plan, use the space below.

    _____

    _____

    _____

    _____

11. If you are married, does your spouse have the benefit of a salary savings plan at your spouse's place of employment?

    Yes   No   N/A Unmarried   N/A Spouse Works In Home

Please complete your survey form and return it to the Director of Human Resources by March 12, 1992. It is important that your answers be as precise as you can make them and that you return your form by the date indicated.

Name: _____

§ A.2 Resolution of Board of Directors for Adoption of Retirement Savings Plan and Trust

On February 12, 1989 the following resolutions to adopt Alpha Omega Organization Retirement Savings Plan and Trust were duly adopted by unanimous consent of the Board of Directors of Alpha Omega Organization and that such resolutions have not been modified or rescinded as of the date hereof:

RESOLVED, that the form of Plan presented to this meeting is a Cash or Deferred Profit Sharing Plan as authorized under Internal Revenue Code Sections 401(a), 401(k), 402(g), and other Code Sections.

RESOLVED, that the form of Alpha Omega Organization Retirement Savings Plan and Trust presented to this meeting is hereby adopted and approved and that the proper officers of the Employer are hereby authorized and directed to execute and deliver to the Plan Administrator one or more counterparts of the Plan.

RESOLVED, that, the Plan Year shall be for a 12 month period beginning on January 1, and ending on December 31 of each year.

RESOLVED, that, for purposes of the limitations on contributions and benefits under the Plan as prescribed by Internal Revenue Code Section 415, the Limitation Year shall be for a 12 month period beginning on January 1 to December 31 of each year.

RESOLVED, that, prior to the due date (including extensions) of the Employer's federal income tax return for each of it fiscal years hereafter, the Employer shall contribute to the Plan amounts sufficient to meet its obligation under the Cash or Deferred Profit Sharing Plan for each such fiscal year in such amount as the Board of Directors determines. The Treasurer of the Corporation is empowered and directed to pay such contribution to the Trustee of the Plan in cash or property, in accordance with the terms of the Plan Document and shall notify the Plan Administrator as to which fiscal year said contributions shall be applied.

RESOLVED, that the proper officers of the Employer shall act as soon as possible to notify employees of the Employer of the adoption of the Plan and Trust by delivering to each employee a copy of the summary plan description of the Plan in the form of the Summary Plan Description presented to this meeting, which form is hereby approved.

The undersigned further certifies that attached hereto as Exhibits A, B, and C respectively are true copies of Alpha Omega Organization Retirement Savings Plan and Trust Document, Summary Plan Description and Adoption Agreement approved and adopted in the above resolutions.

Secretary

Date

§ A.3   Adoption Agreement

Richard Gabriel Associates Regional Prototype
Non-Standardized Cash or Deferred Profit
Sharing Plan and Trust

The RICHARD GABRIEL ASSOCIATES Regional Prototype Non-Standardized Cash or Deferred Profit Sharing Plan and Trust ("the Plan and Trust") is hereby adopted by Alpha Omega Organization (hereinafter "the Employer") effective as of January 1, 1989 ("the Effective Date"). The Plan and Trust as applicable to the Employer shall be known as: Alpha Omega Organization Retirement Savings Plan and Trust.

( ) a. The Plan and Trust is an amendment of a preexisting Plan which was originally effective as of _____/_____/_____.

( ) b. The Plan and Trust is a restatement of a preexisting Plan which was originally effective as of _____/_____/_____.

* * * Caution * * *
Failure to Fill Out the Adoption Agreement Properly
May Result in Disqualification of the Plan

PART I. The following identifying information pertains to the Employer and the Plan and Trust:

1. Employer Address : 1492 Atlantic Avenue
   Columbus, PA 18950-1990

2. Employer Telephone : 215-987-2341

3. Employer Tax ID : 23-0980981

4. Employer Fiscal Year : January 1 to December 31

5. Three Digit Plan Number : 003

6. Plan ID Number : 23-0980981

7. Trust ID Number : 23-1207321

8. Plan Fiscal Year (must be 12 consecutive mos.) : January 1 to December 31

9. Short Initial Plan Year : N/A

10. Plan Agent : Alpha Omega Organization
    1492 Atlantic Avenue
    Columbus, PA 18950-1990

11. Plan Administrator : Retirement Committee
    c/o Alpha Omega Organization
    1492 Atlantic Avenue
    Columbus, PA 18950-1990

12. Plan Administrator : 23-0009991
    ID Number

13. Plan Trustees : Faithful Fidelity Bank and Trust
    1776 Pennsylvania Boulevard
    Philadelphia, PA 19090-0090

14. IRS Determination : N/A
    Letter Date

15. IRS File Folder Number : N/A

16. Legal Organization of Employer:
    ( ) a. Sole Proprietorship
    ( ) b. Partnership
    (X) c. C Corporation
    ( ) d. Not for Profit Corporation
    ( ) e. S Corporation
    ( ) f. Other—Explain:

17. Business Code : 9999

18. Other Members of a Controlled Group or Affiliated Service Group:

    (If any, each member should sign Adoption Agreement or otherwise
    satisfy applicable participation requirements.)

PART II. The Plan contains certain predetermined design features intended to provide the statutory requirement or most commonly adopted
feature but permits the selection of alternative features. If an Employer
desires to retain the predetermined design feature, select the provision
designated Plan Provision. If an alternative design feature is desired, select the appropriate provision. Unless specifically provided to the contrary,
only one selection may be made for each design category. Section references are to relevant Plan Sections. Defined terms have the meanings provided in the Plan.

A. Eligibility and Service Provisions

 1. Eligible Employees—Section 1.2.22 provides that all employees, in-
    cluding employees of certain related businesses and leased employees
    are eligible except for certain union members and non-resident aliens.
    (Specify all applicable)
    ( ) a. Plan Provision
    ( ) b. Include members of collective bargaining unit
    (X) c. Exclude self-employed persons
    (X) d. Exclude Employees not employed by the Employer
    ( ) e. Exclude commissioned Employees
    ( ) f. Exclude hourly Employees
    ( ) g. Exclude salaried Employees

( ) h. Other—Specify. (Cannot discriminate in favor of Highly Compensated Employees).

2. Eligibility Requirements (See Section 2.1.1)—An Employee is eligible to receive an allocation of Non-Elective Contributions if he satisfies the following requirements during the Eligibility Computation Period. (Specify as many as are applicable):

( ) a. Date of hire, i.e., no age or service required (no other choices may be selected)

(X) b. Minimum Age of 21 years (Not to exceed 21, partial years may be used)

(X) c. Minimum of 24 months of service (Cannot require more than 24 months, or more than 12 months if full vesting after not more than 2 Years of Service is not selected; if periods other than whole years are selected an Employee cannot be required to complete any specified number of Hours of Service to receive credit for the fractional year)

(X) d. 1,000 Hours of Service required (cannot exceed 1000)

( ) e. Employed on _____/_____/_____. (For new plans only, select an additional option if this provision is selected)

3. For the purposes of having Elective Contributions made on the Employee's behalf, Section 2.1.1 provides that, unless the Employer specifies otherwise in the Adoption Agreement, an Employee must complete 1000 Hours of Service during the Eligibility Computation Period. For these purposes, an Employee is eligible if he satisfies the following requirements: (Specify all applicable)

( ) a. Date of hire, i.e., no age or service requirement (No other choices may be selected)

(X) b. Minimum Age of 21 years (Not to exceed 21, partial years may be specified)

(X) c. Minimum of 12 months of service (Not to exceed 12, if other than full years are selected hours may not be specified)

(X) d. 1,000 Hours of Service required (cannot exceed 1000)

( ) e. Employed on _____/_____/_____. (For new plans only, select an additional option if this provision is selected)

4. Matching Eligibility Requirements (See Section 2.1.1)—An Employee is eligible to receive an allocation of Matching Contributions if he satisfies the following requirements during the Eligibility Computation Period. (Specify all applicable):

( ) a. Date of hire, i.e., no age or service required (No other choices may be selected)

(X) b. Minimum Age of 21 years (Not to exceed 21, partial years may be used)

(X) c. Minimum of 12 months of service (Cannot require more than 24 months, or more than 12 months if full vesting after not more than 2 Years of Service is not selected; if periods other than whole years are selected an Employee cannot be required to complete any specified number of Hours of Service to receive credit for the fractional year)

(X) d. 1,000 Hours of Service required (cannot exceed 1000)

( ) e. Employed on _____/_____/_____. (For new plans only, select an additional option if this provision is selected)

5. Eligibility Computation Period—Section 1.2.21 provides that the eligibility computation period begins on the date of hire and the subsequent periods commence on each annual anniversary of such date. (Select one)

( ) a. Plan Provision

(X) b. If an Employee fails to satisfy the eligibility requirements during the initial eligibility computation period, the eligibility computation period shall be the Plan Year beginning with the first Plan Year commencing prior to the first anniversary of the employment commencement date.

NOTE: The Eligibility Computation Period and the Break in Service computation period for purposes of eligibility to participate must be the same.

6. Hour of Service—Section 1.2.33 provides that service will be credited on the basis of actual hours for which the employee is paid or entitled to payment. If records of actual hours are not maintained, credit is given on the basis of: (Select one)

(X) a. Plan Provision—Records are maintained

( ) b. Days Worked—An Employee will be credited with 10 Hours of Service if he is credited with at least 1 Hour of Service during the day

( ) c. Weeks Worked—An Employee will be credited with 45 Hours of Service if he is credited with at least 1 Hour of Service during the week

( ) d. Semi-Monthly Payroll Period—An Employee will be credited with 95 Hours of Service if he is credited with at least 1 Hour of Service during the payroll period

( ) e. Months worked—An Employee will be credited with 190 Hours of Service if he is credited with at least 1 Hour of Service during the month

7. Entry Date—Section 2.1.2 provides that an Employee who satisfies any eligibility requirements enters the Plan on the Entry Date. For this purpose the Entry Date is the: (Select one)

( ) a. First day of next Plan Year or _____ months (Not to exceed 6) after satisfying the eligibility requirements, if earlier

( ) b. First day of _____ month (Not more than 6 after satisfying eligibility requirements or the first day of the next Plan Year, if earlier

( ) c. Date of satisfying the eligibility requirements

( ) d. First day of Plan Year in which the eligibility requirements are satisfied

( ) e. First day of Plan Year nearest to the date the eligibility requirements are satisfied

(X) f. Semiannual—(X) first of ( ) last day of 6 month periods, beginning with first of Plan Year, coincident with or after satisfying eligibility requirements

( ) g. Quarterly—( ) first or ( ) last day of 3 month periods, beginning with first of Plan Year, coincident with or after satisfying eligibility requirements

( ) h. Monthly—( ) first or ( ) last day of each month of the Plan Year, coincident with or after satisfying eligibility requirements

NOTE: The Entry Date should be coordinated with the Compensation measuring period.

8. Break in Service—Section 1.2.8 provides that a Break in Service occurs if an Employee fails to complete more than 500 hours of service during the applicable computation period. (Select one)

(X) a. Plan Provision

( ) b. A Break will occur if the Employee fails to complete more than _____ (Not to exceed 500) Hours of Service

9. Break in Service Computation Period—For the purpose of determining a Break in Service Section 1.2.8 provides that the Employer may select the break computation period. For eligibility to participate, the break computation period is (Select one):

(X) a. The Plan Year

( ) b. The Eligibility Computation Period

For vesting purposes, the break computation period is (Select one):

(X) a. The Plan Year

( ) b. The Eligibility Computation Period

NOTE: The computation period for measuring Years of Service and Breaks in Service for vesting purposes must be the same.

B. Dating Provisions

1. Anniversary Date—Section 1.2.5 provides that the Anniversary Date is the last day of the Plan Year unless another date is specified. (Select one)

(X) a. Plan Provision—No other date is specified.
( ) b. The first day of the Plan Year.
( ) c. Other—Specify. (Must be at least annually)

2. Valuation Date—Section 1.2.62 provides that the Valuation Date is the Anniversary Date and any other date specified. (Select one)

( ) a. Plan Provision—No other date is specified.
( ) b. Semiannually on the last day of each 6 month period beginning with the first of the Plan Year
(X) c. Quarterly on the last day of each 3 month period beginning with the first of the Plan Year
( ) d. Monthly on the last day of each month of the Plan Year
( ) e. Other—Specify. (Must be at least annually)

3. Normal Retirement Date—Section 1.2.44 permits the adoption of a Normal Retirement Date. (Select one)

( ) a. Date Normal Retirement Age is attained
( ) b. First day of month in which Normal Retirement Age is attained
( ) c. First day of month nearest date Normal Retirement Age is attained
(X) d. First day of month coincident with or next following the date Normal Retirement Age is attained
( ) e. Anniversary Date nearest date Normal Retirement Age is attained
( ) f. Anniversary Date coincident with or next following date Normal Retirement Age is attained

4. Normal Retirement Age—For each Participant the Normal Retirement Age is:

( ) a. Age _____ (not to exceed 65)
(X) b. The later of age 65 (not to exceed 65) or the 5th (not to exceed the fifth (5th)) anniversary of the participation commencement date, if later. The participation commencement date is the first day of the Plan Year in which a Participant commenced participation in the Plan.

5. Early Retirement Date—See Section 1.2.16: (Select one)

(X) a. The Plan does not provide an early retirement date
( ) b. The actual date the Participant attains the Early Retirement Age
( ) c. The Anniversary Date coincident with or next following the date the Participant attains the Early Retirement Age
( ) d. The Valuation Date coincident with or next following the date the Participant attains the Early Retirement Age
( ) e. The last day of the month coincident with or next following the date the Participant attains the Early Retirement Age

( ) f. Other—Specify. (Cannot discriminate in favor of Highly Compensated Employees)

6. Early Retirement Age: (Select all applicable)

( ) a. Age _____ (not to exceed 65)
( ) b. _____ Years of Service
( ) c. _____ Years of Service while a Participant
( ) d. _____ years prior to the Normal Retirement Age

NOTE: Cannot discriminate in favor of Highly Compensated Employees.

C. Compensation

1. Compensation—See Section 1.2.10. For purposes of the Plan a Participant's compensation is based on the Limitation Year and shall: (Select all applicable)

(X) a. Statutory: Include all compensation paid
(X) b. Include compensation which is not includable in gross income by reason of Code 125, 402(a)(8), 402(h)(1)(B) or 403 (b)
( ) c. Exclude compensation which is for overtime
( ) d. Exclude compensation which is for commissions
( ) e. Exclude compensation which is for discretionary bonuses
( ) f. Exclude compensation which is for all bonuses
( ) g. Exclude compensation which is for taxable employee benefits
( ) h. Exclude compensation in excess of $_____
( ) i. Other exclusion—Specify. (Cannot discriminate in favor of Highly Compensated Employees)

NOTE: Exclusions are permissible if the Plan is not integrated with Social Security. Exclusions may cause the Plan to be impermissibly discriminatory.

2. For the initial year of participation, include Compensation from: (Select one)

( ) a. Entry Date as a Participant
(X) b. First day of the Plan Year

NOTE: Option a. may only be selected for plan years beginning before the later of January 1, 1992 or the date which is 60 days after publication of final regulations requiring compensation for the entire year to be taken into account. The Compensation taken into account should be coordinated with the Entry Date.

D. Contribution and Allocation

1. Non-Elective Contribution Formula—The Employer's Non-Elective contribution to the Plan shall be: (Select one)

( ) a. Discretionary, out of profits

(X) b. Discretionary, but not limited to profits

( ) c. _____% of each Participant's Compensation.

2. Allocation Method—The Employer contribution is allocated to Participants: (Select one)

(X) a. Proportionate to Salary. Based upon each Participant's Compensation in proportion to the Compensation of all Participants.

( ) b. Integrated with Social Security. Based each Year on each Participant's Compensation to the extent of a base contribution percentage multiplied by the Participant's Compensation plus the lesser of 5.7% or the base contribution percentage multiplied by the Participant's Compensation in excess of the Social Security Integration Level and any remainder is allocated based upon each Participant's Compensation in proportion to the Compensation of all Participants.

The Social Security Integration Level is equal to:

( ) c. The Social Security Wage Base in effect as of the first day of the Plan Year.

( ) d. $_____ (Not to exceed the Social Security Wage Base in effect as of the first day of the Plan Year).

( ) e. _____% (Not to exceed 100) of the Social Security Wage Base in effect as of the first day of the Plan Year.

( ) f. The greater of $10,000 or 20% of the Social Security Wage Base in effect as of the first day of the Plan Year.

NOTE: The Employer Contribution allocable to Compensation in excess of the Social Security Integration Level (SSIL) may not exceed 5.4% if the SSIL is more than 80% but less than 100% of the Social Security Wage Base (SSWB), and may not exceed 4.3% if the SSIL is greater than 20% of the SSWB, but not more than 80% of the SSWB, and greater than $10,000.

3. Requirement to Share in Non-Elective Contribution Allocation. In order to share in the allocation of the Employer's Non-Elective Contribution a Participant: (Select all applicable)

( ) a. Is eligible regardless of Hours of Service if the Employee dies during the Plan Year

( ) b. Is eligible regardless of Hours of Service if the Employee retires during the Plan Year

( ) c. Is eligible regardless of Hours of Service if the Employee becomes totally disabled during the Plan Year

(X) d. Must complete 1,000 (May not require in excess of 1000) Hours of Service during Plan Year

(X) e. Must be employed at Plan Year end

4. Requirement to Share in Matching Contribution Allocation—In order to share in the allocation of the Employer's Matching Contribution a Participant: (Select all applicable)

    (X) a. Is eligible regardless of Hours of Service if the Employee dies during the Plan Year

    (X) b. Is eligible regardless of Hours of Service if the Employee retires during the Plan Year

    (X) c. Is eligible regardless of Hours of Service if the Employee becomes totally disabled during the Plan Year

    ( ) d. Must complete _____ (May not require in excess of 1000) Hours of Service during Plan Year

    ( ) e. Must be employed at Plan Year end

5. Matching Contributions—The Matching Contribution by the Employer for the Plan Year in accordance with Section 2.2.1(b) is: (Select one, but if b. is selected also select one of c. through g. for purposes of allocation)

    ( ) a. Not applicable—Matching Contributions are not permitted

    ( ) b. Discretionary each Plan Year

    (X) c. Equal to 50 percent of the Elective Contributions made on behalf of a Participant

    ( ) d. Graded based on the dollar amount of the Elective Contribution of each Participant as follows:

    _____% of the first $_____ plus
    _____% of the next $_____ plus
    _____% of the next $_____ plus
    _____% of the next $_____.

    ( ) e. Graded based on the percentage of compensation of the Elective Contribution of each Participant as follows:

    _____% of the first _____% plus
    _____% of the next _____% plus
    _____% of the next _____% plus
    _____% of the next _____%.

    ( ) f. Graded based on the dollar amount of the Elective Contribution of each Participant as follows:

    _____% if contribution is $_____ or more;
    _____% if contribution is $_____ or more;
    _____% if contribution is $_____ or more;
    _____% if contribution is $_____ or more.

    ( ) g. Graded based on the percentage of compensation of the Elective Contribution of each Participant as follows:

    _____% if contribution is _____% or more
    _____% if contribution is _____% or more

_____% if contribution is _____% or more
_____% if contribution is _____% or more

NOTE: Graded percentages entered in d. through g. must decrease as percentage or amount of compensation increases.

6. Matching Contribution Allocation Date—Matching Contributions are allocated as of the Anniversary Date unless an alternate date is selected. For the purposes of this Plan the Matching Contribution is allocated as of: (Select one)

( ) a. Plan Provision—the Anniversary Date.
( ) b. the next Valuation Date.
(X) c. Other—Specify. (Must be allocated at least annually)
        allocated when elective deferrals are allocated

7. Limitations on Matching Contributions—The Employer shall not make Matching Contributions: (Select all applicable)

(X) a. with respect to Elective Contributions in excess of 6 percent of a Participant's Compensation
( ) b. in excess of $_____ for any Participant
( ) c. to Key Employees

8. Allocation of Qualified Non-Elective Contributions—(Select all applicable)

( ) a. Qualified Non-Elective Contributions are not permitted.
(X) b. Qualified Non-Elective Contributions shall be made in the Employer's discretion.

Qualified Non-Elective Contributions shall be made:
( ) c. On behalf of all Participants.
( ) d. Solely on behalf of Participants who are not Highly Compensated Employees.
(X) e. Solely on behalf of Participants who are not Highly Compensated Employees to the extent necessary to satisfy the ACP test or the ADP test.

Qualified Non-Elective Contributions shall be allocated:
(X) f. In proportion to a Participant's Compensation.
( ) g. As a uniform dollar amount.

9. Limitation Year—Section 1.2.38 provides that the Limitation Year for purposes of the limitations imposed by IRC Section 415 is the Plan Year. (Select one)

(X) a. Plan Provision
( ) b. Calendar year coinciding with or ending within the Plan Year

NOTE: Compensation is based on the Limitation Year and should be coordinated with the Entry Date.

E. Vesting Provisions

1. Years of Service—Section 1.2.64 provides that a Year of Service is any Plan Year (including years prior to the effective date) in which at least 1000 Hours of Service are performed. It also includes the eligibility computation period during which the employee completes the eligibility requirements which overlaps Plan Years if 1000 Hours of Service are not performed in at least one Plan Year. (Select all applicable)

   (X) a. Plan Provision
   ( ) b. Use Eligibility Computation Period in lieu of Plan Year
   ( ) c. Use _____ in lieu of 1000 Hours of Service (Not to exceed 1000 hours)

2. Excluded Years—Section 1.2.64 provides that all Years of Service are taken into account.
   (X) a. Plan Provision—Include all Years of Service
   ( ) b. Exclude Plan Years prior to age 18
   ( ) c. Exclude Plan Years prior to adoption of plan or predecessor plan. Date of adoption: _____/_____/_____

3. Vesting Schedule—Section 2.4.2(f) provides that benefits will vest in accordance with the method specified in the Adoption Agreement.

   Employer Accounts:
   ( ) a. At the rate of 20% each year after 3 Years of Service. (20% vested in third year)
   ( ) b. At the rate of 20% each year after 2 Years of Service. (20% vested in the second year)
   (X) c. 100% vesting upon participation.
   ( ) d. 100% vesting after _____ Year(s) of Service (Not to exceed 5)
   ( ) e. 100% vesting at Early Retirement Date (Must also select another alternative)
   ( ) f. Other: (Optional vesting schedule must be at least as favorable as a. or d.)

Year(s) of Service	Percent Vesting
Less than 1	_____
1 but less than 2	_____
2 but less than 3	_____
3 but less than 4	_____
4 but less than 5	_____
5 but less than 6	_____
6 but less than 7	_____
7 or more	_____

Matching Accounts:
( )　a. At the rate of 20% each year after 3 Years of Service. (20% vested in third year)
( )　b. At the rate of 20% each year after 2 Years of Service. (20% vested in second year)
( )　c. 100% vesting upon participation.
( )　d. 100% vesting after _____ Year(s) of Service (Not to exceed 5)
( )　e. 100% vesting at Early Retirement Date (Must also select another alternative)
(X)　f. Other: (Optional vesting schedule must be at least as favorable as a. or d.)

Year(s) of Service	Percent Vesting
Less than 1	0
1 but less than 2	0
2 but less than 3	50
3 but less than 4	75
4 but less than 5	100
5 but less than 6	100
6 but less than 7	100
7 or More	100

4. Top-Heavy Vesting Schedule—Section 2.7.1(b) provides that if the Plan becomes Top Heavy, unless the Employer specifies otherwise, vesting will be at a rate of 20% per year beginning with the second Year of Service.

Employer Accounts:
( )　a. Plan Provision
( )　b. 100% vested after _____ Year(s) of Service (Not to exceed 3)
( )　c. Other: (Optional vesting schedule must be at least as favorable as a. or b.)

Year(s) of Service	Percent Vesting
Less than 1	_____
1 but less than 2	_____
2 but less than 3	_____
3 but less than 4	_____
4 but less than 5	_____
5 but less than 6	_____
6 or More	_____

Matching Accounts:

( )　a. Plan Provision
( )　b. 100% vested after _____ Year(s) of Service (Not to exceed 3)

(X) c. Other: (Optional vesting schedule must be at least as favorable as a. or b.)

Year(s) of Service	Percent Vesting
Less than 1	0
1 but less than 2	20
2 but less than 3	50
3 but less than 4	75
4 but less than 5	100
5 but less than 6	100
6 or More	100

5. Re-employment—Section 2.4.4 provides that Years of Service completed after a Break in Service are not counted for purposes of increasing the vested percentage attributable to service before the Break unless reemployed within 5 years.

(X) a. Plan Provision
( ) b. Count all service after the Break

6. Distribution Date—Subject to the necessity of obtaining the consent of a Participant and spouse, Section 2.4.5 provides that if the Participant is not fully vested, the Distribution Date is postponed until the last day of the 5th consecutive Plan Year in which the Participant incurs a Break in Service.

( ) a. Plan Provision
( ) b. The Distribution Date is advanced to the last day of the Plan Year in which the Participant incurs a Break in Service.
(X) c. The Distribution Date is advanced to the last day of the Plan Year following termination of employment without regard to Break in Service.
( ) d. The Distribution Date is advanced to the Plan Year following the Year in which termination of employment occurs without regard to Break in Service.

7. Forfeitures—Section 2.4.6 provides that forfeitures are allocated as of the last day of the Plan Year in which the Participant's entire interest is distributed from the Plan.

(X) a. Plan Provision.
( ) b. Allocate in Plan Year of 5th consecutive Break in Service.
( ) c. Not applicable—All benefits are fully vested.

8. Forfeitures shall be reallocated to participants:

(X) a. In the same manner as Non-Elective Contributions.
( ) b. In proportion to participant's Compensation (Non-integrated plans only).

9. Forfeitures shall be applied to: (Select all applicable)

( ) a. Supplement Matching Contributions
(X) b. Reduce Matching Contributions
( ) c. Reduce Qualified Non-Elective Contributions
(X) d. Supplement Non-Elective Contributions
( ) e. Reduce Non-Elective Contributions

10. Restoration of Forfeitures—If a Participant is entitled to a restoration of a forfeiture, the amount to be restored shall be restored by:

( ) a. An additional contribution by the Employer specifically allocated to the Participant's Account.
(X) b. Allocating other forfeitures arising in the year of restoration to the Participant's Account.

F. CODA Limitation Provisions

1. Actual Deferral Percentages—Qualified Non-Elective Contributions may be taken into account for purposes of calculating the ADP-Actual Deferral Percentages. For purposes of the ADP test in Section 2.6.1, the amount taken into account shall be:

( ) a. All Qualified Non-Elective Contributions.
(X) b. The Qualified Non-Elective Contributions that are needed to meet the ADP test.

2. Average Contribution Percentage—The amount of Elective Deferrals and Qualified Non-Elective Contributions taken into account as contribution percentage amounts for the purpose of calculating the ACP-Average Contribution Percentage, subject to such other requirements as may be prescribed by the Secretary of the Treasury, shall be: (select a., b. or c. and d., e. or f.)

( ) a. All such Elective Deferrals.
(X) b. Only those Elective Deferrals that are needed to meet the Average Contribution Percentage test.
( ) c. Elective Deferrals are not to be included in the ACP test.
( ) d. All such Qualified Non-Elective contributions.
(X) e. Only those Qualified Non-Elective Contributions that are needed to meet the Average Contribution Percentage test.
( ) f. Qualified Non-Elective Contributions are not to be included in the ACP test.

3. Excess Aggregate Contributions—Forfeitures of Excess Aggregate Contributions pursuant to Section 2.6.7 shall be:

(X) a. applied to reduce Employer contributions.
( ) b. allocated, after all other forfeitures under the Plan, to each Participant's Matching Contribution Account in the ratio

which each Participant's Compensation for the Plan Year bears to the total Compensation of all Participants for the Plan Year. Such forfeitures will not be allocated to the Account of any Highly Compensated Employee.

G. Distribution Provisions

1. Form of Distributions—Section 2.5.2 provides that the Employer may elect to permit Plan distributions to be made in the form of: (Select all applicable)

(X) a. Lump sum without regard to amount.

( ) b. Lump sum but not to exceed $_____.

( ) c. Installments over _____ years payable: (Select one or more)

    ( ) c.1. annually

    ( ) c.2. quarterly

    ( ) c.3. monthly

( ) d. An annuity for not more than _____ years

( ) e. An annuity for the life of: (Select one or more)

    ( ) e.1. the Participant

    ( ) e.2. the Participant and spouse

    ( ) e.3. the Participant and a designated beneficiary

( ) f. An annuity for _____ years certain and thereafter for the life of: (Select one or more)

    ( ) f.1. the Participant

    ( ) f.2. the Participant and spouse

    ( ) f.3. the Participant and a designated beneficiary

( ) g. An annuity for a period certain selected by the Participant that is less than the life of: (Select one or more)

    ( ) g.1. the Participant

    ( ) g.2. the Participant and spouse

    ( ) g.3. the Participant and a designated beneficiary

NOTE: Any number of options may be selected. Once selected, however, any option may not thereafter be eliminated.

If an annuity option of life or longer is selected Qualified Joint and Survivor Annuity provisions are required.

2. Survivor Annuity Percentage—If a Joint and Survivor Annuity is payable, Section 1.2.35 provides that the normal survivor annuity is 50% of the amount payable during the joint lives of the participant and spouse, unless the Employer elects a different percentage (Select one):

( ) a. Plan Provision—50%

( ) b. Other Percentage—____% (Note less than 50% nor more than 100%)

3. Time of Distribution—Section 2.5.1(b) provides that distributions are deferred to Participants who resign or are discharged prior to retirement until the retirement date. Section 2.5.4 also provides that an employer may elect to permit distributions in advance of such date.

( ) a. Plan Provision without advance distribution election.
(X) b. Permit advance distributions per Section 2.5.4.

4. Hardship Distributions—Section 2.5.5 provides that an Employer may permit distributions to Participants while employed in the event of financial hardship as specified in the Plan:

(X) a. Hardship distributions are permitted.
( ) b. Hardship distributions are not permitted.

Hardship Distributions may only be made for Elective Deferrals and earnings accrued thereon as of December 31, 1988. Subject to such limitation, Hardship Distributions may be taken from:

( ) c. all of Participant's Accounts.
(X) d. only the Participant's Account balances attributable to the following accounts:

       ( ) d.1. Employer Account
       ( ) d.2. Qualified Non-Elective Contribution Account
       (X) d.3. Elective Contribution Account
       ( ) d.4. Matching Account
       ( ) d.5. Segregated Account
       ( ) d.6. Voluntary Account

5. In Service Distributions—Section 2.5.6 provides that an Employer may permit distributions to fully vested Participants over the age of $59\frac{1}{2}$ prior to termination of employment if the amounts withdrawn have been allocated to the Participant for two (2) or more years or the Participant has been a Participant for at least five (5) years. (Select all applicable)

( ) a. Plan Provision.
( ) b. Require that amounts have been allocated for _____ years. (Must be at least 2)
( ) c. Require participation for at least _____ years. (Must be at least 5)
(X) d. In Service Distributions are not permitted.

6. Qualified Domestic Relations Orders—Section 3.12.9 provides that the Employer may elect to permit distributions to an alternate payee pursuant to the terms of a qualified domestic relations order even if the Participant continues to be employed. (Select one)

(X) a. Distributions to an alternate payee are not permitted while the Participant continues to be employed.

( ) b. Distributions to an alternate payee are permitted while the Participant continues to be employed.

H. Other Administrative Provisions

1. Earnings—Section 3.1.2 permits the Employer to specify the manner in which earnings are allocated to Participants who receive distributions on any date other than a Valuation Date. Select any of the following:

   ( ) a. Earnings will be credited solely as of the immediately preceding Valuation Date.

   (X) b. Actual earnings will be credited to the date of distribution.

   ( ) c. Earnings will be credited solely as of the immediately preceding Valuation Date if distribution is within _____ days of such Valuation Date and will be credited to date of distribution otherwise.

   ( ) d. Earnings will be credited to the date of distribution based upon an estimate of earnings equal to _____% annually.

   ( ) e. Earnings will be credited to the date of distribution based upon an estimate of earnings equal to the average rate of earnings during the preceding

       ( ) e.1. Valuation Period.

       ( ) e.2. Plan Year.

       ( ) e.3. _____ Valuation Periods.

2. Loans—Section 3.7.1 provides that the Employer may elect to permit loans to Participants and Beneficiaries in accordance with a participant loan program adopted by the Trustee.

   (X) a. Loan are permitted.

   ( ) b. Loans are not permitted.

3. Investment Control—Section 3.6.5 provides that the Employer may elect to permit Participants to control the investment of their Accounts.

   ( ) a. Participants may not control their investments.

   ( ) b. Participants may control the investment of their Accounts if fully vested in the Account.

   ( ) c. Participants may control the investment of their Accounts to the extent vested.

   (X) d. Participants may control their investments without regard to their vested interest.

   ( ) e. Participants may control their investments solely with respect to amounts attributable to: (Select all applicable)

       ( ) e.1. Non-Elective Contributions

       ( ) e.2. Qualified Non-Elective Contributions

       ( ) e.3. Elective Contributions

( )   e.4.   Matching Contributions
( )   e.5.   Voluntary Contributions

4. The interest rate used to establish the Present Value of Accrued Benefits in order to calculate the top heavy ratio under IRC Section 416 shall be _____% and the mortality tables used shall be _____. (Applies only if you also have a Defined Benefit plan)

5. Valuation Date—For purposes of computing the top-heavy ratio, the Valuation Date is (Select one):

( ) a. the first day of Plan Year.
(X) b. the last day of the Plan Year.
( ) c. Other—Specify. _____/_____ (Must be at least annually)

6. Single Plan Minimum Top-Heavy Allocation—For purposes of minimum top-heavy allocations, contributions and forfeitures equal to the following percentage of each non-Key Employee's compensation will be allocated to the Employee's account when the Plan is top-heavy (Select one):

(X) a. 3% or the highest percentage allocated to any Key Employee if less.
( ) b. _____% (Must be at least 3).

7. Multiple Plans Provision—The Employer which maintains or ever maintained another qualified defined benefit plan or welfare benefit fund or individual medical account in which any participant in the Plan is, was or could become a participant adds the following optional provision which it deems necessary to satisfy Section 415 or 416 of the Code because of the required aggregation of multiple plans: (Select one)

(X) a. Not applicable.
( ) b. A minimum contribution allocation of 5% of each Non-Key Participant's total compensation shall be provided in a defined contribution plan of the Employer.
( ) c. A minimum contribution allocation of 7.5% of each Non-Key Participant's total compensation shall be provided in a defined contribution plan of the Employer.
( ) d. Other—Specify.

NOTE: The method selected must preclude Employer discretion and the Employer must obtain a determination letter in order to continue reliance on the Plan's qualified status.

8. Multiple Defined Contribution Plans—If the Participant is covered under another qualified defined contribution plan maintained by the Employer, other than a master or prototype plan: (Select one)

(X) a. Not applicable.

( ) b. The provisions of this Plan limiting annual additions will apply as if the other plan is a master or prototype plan.

( ) c. Other—Specify.

NOTE: Specify the method under which the plans will limit total annual additions to the maximum permissible amount, and will properly reduce any excess amounts in a manner that precludes Employer discretion.

9. Top Heavy Duplications—The Employer who maintains two or more Defined Contribution plans makes the following election:

(X) a. Not applicable.

( ) b. A minimum non-integrated contribution of 3% of each Non-Key Participant's Compensation shall be provided by:

    ( ) b.1. this Plan.

    ( ) b.2. the following defined contribution plan:

_____

( ) c. Other—Specify.

NOTE: The method selected must preclude Employer discretion and avoid inadvertent omissions, including any adjustments required under Code Section 415(e). The Employer must obtain a determination letter in order to continue reliance on the Plan's qualified status.

10. Compensation Definition. For purposes of calculating an Employee's compensation pursuant to Section 3.2.1(h), relating to limitations on contributions and benefits, Compensation means all of each Participant's

( ) a. Section 3121(a) wages.

( ) b. Section 3401(a) wages.

(X) c. Section 415 safe harbor compensation.

The name, address and telephone number of the Plan Sponsor is:

RICHARD GABRIEL ASSOCIATES
ONE NESHAMINY INTERPLEX, SUITE 102
TREVOSE, PA 19053
(215)638-1700

The Plan Sponsor will inform the Employer of any amendments made to the Plan or of the discontinuance or abandonment of the Plan.

NOTE: An employer may not rely on an opinion letter issued by the National Office of the Internal Revenue Service as evidence that the plan as adopted is qualified under Section 401 of the Internal Revenue Code. In order to obtain reliance with respect to plan qualification, the employer must apply to the appropriate key district for a determination letter.

This Adoption Agreement may be used only in conjunction with the RICHARD GABRIEL ASSOCIATES Regional Prototype Non-Standardized Cash or Deferred Profit Sharing Plan and Trust No. 06, Revised 08/30/90.

* * *

The Employer and Trustee hereby adopt the Plan and Trust as evidenced by the foregoing Adoption Agreement on this _____ day of _____, 19____.

<table>
<tr><td>_____</td><td></td><td>_____</td></tr>
<tr><td>. Employer</td><td></td><td>Trustee</td></tr>
<tr><td>By: _____</td><td></td><td></td></tr>
<tr><td>Title</td><td></td><td></td></tr>
<tr><td></td><td></td><td>_____</td></tr>
<tr><td></td><td></td><td>Trustee</td></tr>
<tr><td>_____</td><td></td><td></td></tr>
<tr><td>Affiliate Employer</td><td></td><td></td></tr>
<tr><td>By: _____</td><td></td><td>_____</td></tr>
<tr><td>Title</td><td></td><td>Trustee</td></tr>
</table>

§ A.4 Plan and Trust Agreement

Non-Standardized Cash or Deferred
Profit Sharing Plan and Trust

I N D E X

Thanks to DATAIR Employees Benefit Systems and Richard Gabriel Associates for permission to reproduce in this Appendix the prototype 401(k) plan and trust that they sponsor.

PART I

ARTICLE I
INTRODUCTION

1.1.1   Creation and Title. The parties hereby create a Plan and Trust to be known by the name set forth in the Adoption Agreement.

1.1.2   Effective Date. The provisions of this Plan and Trust shall be effective as of the Effective Date set forth in the Adoption Agreement.

1.1.3   Purpose. This Plan and Trust is established for the purpose of providing retirement benefits to eligible employees in accordance with the Plan and the Adoption Agreement and to enable eligible Employees to supplement their retirement by electing to have the Employer contribute amounts to the Plan and Trust in lieu of payments to such Employees in cash. The Plan and Trust are intended to satisfy the provisions of Section 401(k) of the Internal Revenue Code of 1986, as amended.

ARTICLE II
DEFINITIONS

As used in this Plan and the Adoption Agreement, the following terms shall have the following meanings:

1.2.1 "Account": The Employer Account, Controlled Account, Elective Contribution Account, Matching Account, Qualified Non-Elective Contribution Account, Voluntary Account or Segregated Account of a Participant, as the context requires, established and maintained for accounting purposes.

1.2.2 "ACP": The average contribution percentage determined in accordance with the provisions of Part II, Article VI.

1.2.3 "Act": The Employee Retirement Income Security Act of 1974, as amended from time to time.

1.2.4 "ADP": The actual deferral percentage determined in accordance with the provisions of Part II, Article VI.

1.2.5 "Anniversary Date": Unless otherwise specified in the Adoption Agreement, the last day of each Plan Year.

1.2.6 "Beneficiary": The person or persons entitled hereunder to receive the benefits which may be payable upon or after a Participant's death.

1.2.7 "Board of Directors": The board of directors of an incorporated Employer.

1.2.8 "Break in Service": The failure of a Participant to complete more than five hundred (500) Hours of Service during any 12 consecutive month computation period, beginning with a Participant's first computation period after becoming a Participant. The computation period shall be specified by the Employer in the Adoption Agreement. A Year of Service and a Break in Service for vesting purposes shall be measured on the same computation period.

1.2.9 "Code": The Internal Revenue Code of 1986, as amended from time to time.

1.2.10 "Compensation": Unless otherwise specified in the Adoption Agreement, all of a Participant's (a) W-2 compensation or (b) compensation as that term is defined in Section 415(c)(3) of the Code (or Earned Income in the case of a self-employed individual) which is actually paid to the Participant by the Employer during the applicable period specified by the Employer in the Adoption Agreement (or, if no period is specified, during the Plan Year); provided that if specified by the Employer in the Adoption Agreement, compensation shall also include any amount which is contributed by the Employer pursuant to a salary reduction agreement and which is not includible in the gross income of the Employee under Sections 125, 402(a)(8), 402(h) or 403(b) of the Code; provided further that for years beginning after December 31, 1988, the annual gross compensation taken into account for purposes of the Plan shall not exceed $200,000, as such amount may be adjusted by the Secretary of the Treasury at the same time and in the same manner as under Section 415(d) of the Code, except that the dollar increase in effect on January 1 of any calendar year is effective for years beginning in such calendar year and the first adjustment to the $200,000 limitation is effected on January 1, 1990. If a plan determines compensation on a period of time that contains less than twelve (12) calendar months, then the annual compensation limit is an amount equal to the annual compensation limit for the calendar year in which the compensation period begins multiplied by the ratio obtained by dividing the number of full months in the period by 12. For purposes of this dollar limitation, the rules of Section 414(q)(6) of the Code requiring the aggregation of the compensation of family members shall apply, except that in applying such rules, the term "family" shall include only the spouse of the Participant and any lineal descendants of the Participant who have not attained age nineteen (19) before the close of the year. If, as a result of the application of such rules the adjusted $200,000 limitation is exceeded, then (except for purposes of determining the portion of compensation up to the Social Security Integration Level if this Plan provides for permitted disparity), the limitation shall be prorated among the affected individuals in proportion to each such individual's compensation as determined under this Section prior to the application of this limitation. If compensation for any prior plan year is taken into account in determining an employee's contributions or benefits for the current year, the compensation for such prior year is subject to the applicable annual compensation limit in effect for that prior year. For this purpose, for years beginning before January 1, 1990, the applicable annual compensation limit is $200,000.

1.2.11 "Controlled Account": An account established and maintained for a Participant to account for his interest in a Controlled Fund over which he exercises investment control.

1.2.12 "Controlled Fund": Assets held in the name of the Trustee which have been segregated pursuant to an election made by a Participant to exercise investment control with respect to such assets.

1.2.13 "Distributable Benefit": The benefit to which a Participant is entitled following termination of his employment.

1.2.14 "Distribution Date": The date as of which the Distributable Benefit of a Participant is determined.

1.2.15 "Early Retirement Age": The age specified as the Early Retirement Age, if any, in the Adoption Agreement.

1.2.16 "Early Retirement Date": The date specified as the Early Retirement Date, if any, in the Adoption Agreement.

1.2.17 "Earned Income": The net earnings from self-employment in the trade or business with respect to which the Plan is established for which personal services of the Participant are a material income-producing factor. Net earnings shall be determined without regard to items not included in gross income and the deductions allocable to such items but, in the case of taxable years beginning after 1989, with regard to the deduction allowed by Section 164(f) of the Code. Net earnings shall be reduced by contributions to a qualified plan to the extent deductible under Section 404 of the Code.

1.2.18 "Elective Contribution Account": An Account established and maintained for a Participant to account for the Elective Contributions made on his behalf.

1.2.19 "Elective Contribution": A contribution to the Plan by the Employer on behalf of an electing Employee.

1.2.20 "Elective Deferrals": Any Employer contributions made to the Plan at the election of the Participant, in lieu of cash compensation, including contributions made pursuant to a salary reduction agreement or other deferral mechanism. With respect to any taxable year, a Participant's Elective Deferral is the sum of all Employer contributions made on behalf of the Participant pursuant to an election to defer under any qualified CODA as described in Section 401(k) of the Code, any simplified employee pension cash or deferred arrangement as described in Section 402(h)(1)(B), any eligible deferred compensation plan under Section 457, any plan as described under Section 501(c)(18), and any employer contributions made on the behalf of a participant for the purchase of an annuity contract under Section 403(b) pursuant to a salary reduction agreement.

1.2.21 "Eligibility Computation Period": For purposes of determining Years of Service and Breaks in Service for purposes of eligibility, the initial eligibility computation period is the twelve (12) consecutive month period beginning with the employment commencement date on which the Employee first renders an Hour of Service for the Employer, and unless otherwise specified in the Adoption Agreement, the subsequent eligibility computation periods are each subsequent twelve (12) consecutive month period commencing on the first anniversary of such employment commencement date.

If in accordance with the election in the Adoption Agreement, the subsequent periods commence with the first Plan Year which commences prior to the first anniversary of the Employee's employment commencement date, an Employee who is credited with 1,000 Hours of Service in both the initial eligibility computation period and the first Plan Year which commences prior to the first anniversary of the Employee's initial eligibility computation period shall be credited with two (2) years of service for purposes of eligibility to participate.

1.2.22 "Employee": A person who is currently or hereafter employed by the Employer, or by any other employer aggregated under Section 414(b), (c), (m) or (o) of the Code and the regulations thereunder, including a Leased Employee subject to Section 414(n) of the Code and a self-employed owner of an unincorporated Employer but excluding (a) an independent contractor; (b) an employee who is a non-resident alien deriving no earned income from the Employer which constitutes income from sources within the United States; and (c) employees who are included in the unit of employees covered by a collective bargaining agreement, provided that retirement benefits were the subject of good faith negotiations.

1.2.23 "Employer": The Employer that is a party to this Plan, or any of its successors or assigns which adopt the Plan; provided, however, that no mere change in the identity, form or organization of the Employer shall affect its status under the Plan in any manner, and, if the name of the Employer is hereafter changed, a corresponding change shall be deemed to have been made in the name of the Plan and references herein to the Employer shall be deemed to refer to the Employer as it is then known.

1.2.24 "Employer Account": An account established and maintained for a Participant for accounting purposes to which his share of Employer contributions and forfeitures are added.

1.2.25 "Entry Date": The date or dates specified as the Entry Date in the Adoption Agreement.

1.2.26 "Excess Aggregate Contributions": With respect to any Plan Year, the excess of:

(a) The aggregate contribution percentage amounts taken into account in computing the numerator of the contribution percentage actually made on behalf of Highly Compensated Employees for such Plan Year, over

(b) The maximum contribution percentage amounts permitted by the ACP test (determined by reducing contributions made on behalf of Highly Compensated Employees in order of their contribution percentages beginning with the highest of such percentages).

Such determination shall be made after first determining Excess Elective Deferrals and then determining Excess Contributions.

1.2.27 "Excess Contributions": With respect to any Plan Year, the excess of:

(a) The aggregate amount of Employer Contributions actually taken into account in computing the ADP of Highly Compensated Employees for such Plan Year, over

(b) The maximum amount of such contributions permitted by the ADP test (determined by reducing contributions made on behalf of Highly Compensated Employees in order of the ADPs, beginning with the highest of such percentages.

1.2.28 "Excess Elective Deferrals": Those Elective Deferrals that are includible in a Participant's gross income under Section 402(g) of the Code to the extent such participant's Elective Deferrals for a taxable year exceed the dollar limitation under such Code section. Excess Elective Deferrals shall be treated as annual additions under the Plan.

1.2.29 "Excessive Annual Addition": The portion of the allocation of contributions and forfeitures that cannot be added to a Participant's Accounts due to the limitations on annual additions contained in the Plan.

1.2.30 "Family": The spouse and lineal ascendants or descendants of an Employee and the spouses of such lineal ascendants and descendants.

1.2.31 "Fiduciary": The Plan Administrator, the Trustee and any other person who has discretionary authority or control in the management of the Plan or the disposition of Trust assets.

1.2.32 "Highly Compensated Employee": A highly compensated active employee and a highly compensated former employee. A highly compensated active employee includes: any Employee who performs service for the Employer during the determination year and who, during the look-back year: (i) received compensation from the Employer in excess of $75,000 (as adjusted pursuant to Section 415(d) of the Code); (ii) received compensation from the Employer in excess of $50,000 (as adjusted pursuant to Section 415(d) of the Code) and was a member of the top-paid group for such year; or (iii) was an officer of the Employer and received compensation during such year that is greater than 50 percent of the dollar limitation as in effect under Section 415(b)(1)(A) of the Code. The term highly compensated employee also includes: (i) employees who are both described in the preceding sentence if the term "determination year" is substituted for the term "look-back year" and the employee is one of the 100 employees who received the most compensation from the Employer during the determination year; and (ii) employees who are 5 percent owners at any time during the look-back year or determination year.

If no officer has satisfied the compensation requirement of (iii) above during either a determination year or look-back year, the highest paid officer for such year shall be treated as a highly compensated employee.

For this purpose, the determination year shall be the Plan Year. The look-back year shall be the twelve-month period immediately preceding the determination year.

A highly compensated former employee includes any employee who separated from service (or was deemed to have separated) prior to the determination year, performs no service for the employer during the determination year, and was a highly compensated active employee for either the separation year or any determination year ending on or after the employee's 55th birthday.

If an Employee is, during a Plan Year or the preceding Plan Year, a family member of either a 5 percent owner who is an active or former employee or a Highly Compensated Employee who is one of the 10 most highly compensated employees ranked on the basis of compensation paid by the Employer during such year, then the family member and the 5 percent owner or top-ten highly compensated employee shall be aggregated. In such case, the family member and 5 percent owner or top-ten highly compensated employee shall be treated as a single employee receiving compensation and plan contributions or benefits equal to the sum of such compensation and contributions or benefits of the family member and 5 percent owner or top-ten highly compensated employee. For purposes of this section, family member includes the spouse, lineal ascendants and descendants of the employee or former employee and the spouses of such lineal ascendants and descendants.

The determination of who is a highly compensated employee, including the determination of the number and identity of employees in the top-paid group, the top 100 employees, the number of employees treated as officers and the compensation that is considered, will be made in accordance with Section 414(q) of the Code and the regulations thereunder.

1.2.33 "Hour of Service": An hour for which (a) the Employee is paid, or entitled to payment by the Employer for the performance of duties, (b) the Employee is paid or entitled to payment by the Employer during which no duties are performed (irrespective of whether the employment relationship has terminated) due to vacation, holiday, illness, incapacity (including disability), layoff, jury duty, military duty or leave of absence, or (c) back pay, irrespective of mitigation of damages, has been either awarded or agreed to by the Employer. Hours of Service shall be credited to the Employee under (a), above, for the period in which the duties are performed, under (b), above, in the period in which the period during which no duties are performed occurs, beginning with the first Hour of Service to which the payment relates, and under (c), above, for the period to which the award or agreement pertains rather than the period in which the award, agreement or payment is made; provided, however, that Hours of Service shall not be credited under both (a) and (b), above, as the case may be, and under (c) above. Notwithstanding the preceding sentences, (i) no more than five hundred one (501) Hours of Service shall be credited under (b), above, on account of any single continuous period during which the Employee performs no duties whether or not such period occurs in a single computation period, (ii) no Hours of Service shall be credited to the Employee by reason of a payment made or due under a plan maintained solely for the purpose of complying with applicable worker's compensation, or unemployment compensation or disability insurance laws, and (iii) no Hours of Service shall be credited by reason of a payment which solely reimburses an employee for medical or medically related expenses incurred by the Employee. The determination of Hours of Service for reasons other than the performance of duties and the crediting of Hours of Service to computation periods shall be made in accord with the provisions of Labor Regulation Sections 2530.200b-2(b) and (c) which are incorporated herein by reference.

Solely for the purposes of determining whether an Employee has incurred a Break in Service, an Employee shall be credited with the number of Hours of Service which would otherwise have been credited to such individual but for the absence or in any case in which such Hours cannot be determined with eight (8) Hours of Service for any day that the Employee is absent from work by reason of the Employee's pregnancy, the birth of a child of the Employee, the placement of a child with the Employee in connection with the adoption of such child by the Employee or for purposes of caring for such child for a period beginning immediately following such birth or placement. Such Hours of Service shall be credited only in the Plan Year in which the absence from work begins if the Employee would be prevented from incurring a Break in Service in such Plan Year solely because credit is given for such period of absence and, in any other case, in the immediately following computation period. Notwithstanding the foregoing, no credit shall be given for such service unless the Employee furnishes to the Plan Administrator information to establish that the absence from work is for the reasons indicated and the number of days for which there was such an absence.

In the event the Employer does not maintain records of the actual hours for which an Employee is paid or entitled to payment, credit for service shall be given in accordance with the method selected in the Adoption Agreement.

Service with another business entity that is, along with the Employer, a member of a controlled group of corporations, an affiliated service group or trades or businesses under common control, as defined in the applicable sections of the Code, or which is otherwise required to be aggregated with the Employer pursuant to Section 414(o) of the Code and the regulations issued thereunder shall be treated as service for the Employer. Hours of Service shall be credited for any individual considered an employee for purposes of this Plan under Section 414(n) or Section 414(o) of the Code and the regulations issued thereunder.

Except to the extent inconsistent with regulations issued by the Secretary of the Treasury, service for a predecessor to the Employer, whether as an employee of self-employed person, shall be treated as service for the Employer. If the Employer maintains the plan of a predecessor employer, service with such predecessor shall be treated as service for the Employer.

1.2.34   "Insurer": Any insurance company which has issued a Life Insurance Policy.

1.2.35   "Joint and Survivor Annuity": An immediate annuity for the life of the Participant with a survivor annuity for the life of the spouse which is not less than fifty (50%) percent and not more than one hundred (100%) percent of the amount of the annuity which is payable during the joint lives of the participant and the spouse and which is the amount of benefit which can be purchased with the Participant's vested Account balances. The percentage of the survivor annuity under the Plan shall be fifty (50%) percent unless a different percentage is elected by the Employer in the Adoption Agreement.

1.2.36   "Leased Employee": Any person (other than an employee of the recipient) who pursuant to an agreement between the recipient and any other person has performed services for the recipient (or for the recipient and related persons determined in accordance with Section 414(n)(6) of the Code) on a substantially full time basis for a period of at least one (1) year and such services are of a type historically performed by employees in the business field of the recipient employer; provided that any such person shall not be taken into account if (a) such person is covered by a money purchase pension plan providing (i) a nonintegrated employer contribution rate of at least ten (10%) percent of compensation, as defined in Section 415(c)(3) of the Code, but including amounts contributed by the employer pursuant to a salary reduction agreement which are excludable from the person's gross income under Sections 125, 402(a)(8), 402(h) or 403(b) of the Code; (ii) immediate participation; and (iii) full and immediate vesting; and (b) leased employees do not constitute more than twenty (20%) percent of the workforce of the recipient who are not Highly Compensated Employees. Contributions or benefits provided a leased employee by the leasing organization which are attributable to services performed for the recipient employer shall be treated as provided by the recipient employer.

1.2.37   "Life Insurance Policy": A life insurance, annuity or endowment policy or contract which is owned by the Trust and is on the life of a Participant.

1.2.38   "Limitation Year": Unless otherwise specified in the Adoption Agreement, the Plan Year; provided that all qualified plans maintained by the Employer must use the same Limitation Year.

1.2.39   "Mass Submitter": DATAIR Employee Benefit Systems, Inc.

1.2.40   "Matching Account": An Account established and maintained for a Participant for accounting purposes to which his share of Matching Contributions are added.

1.2.41   "Matching Contribution": A contribution to the Plan by the Employer which matches in whole or in part an Elective Contribution on behalf of an electing Employee.

1.2.42   "Non-Elective Contribution": A contribution to the Plan or any other Related Plan by the Employer which is neither a Qualified Non-Elective Contribution, a Matching Contribution nor an Elective Contribution.

1.2.43   "Normal Retirement Age": The earlier of the date specified as the Normal Retirement Age in the Adoption Agreement or the mandatory retirement age enforced by the Employer.

1.2.44   "Normal Retirement Date": The date specified in the Adoption Agreement as the Normal Retirement Date.

1.2.45   "Owner-Employee": An individual who is a sole proprietor or who is a partner owning more than ten percent (10%) of either the capital or profits interest of the partnership.

1.2.46   "Participant": Any eligible Employee who becomes entitled to participate in the Plan.

1.2.47   "Plan": The profit sharing plan for Employees as set forth in this Agreement and the Adoption Agreement, together with any amendments or supplements thereto.

1.2.48   "Plan Administrator": The person, persons or entity appointed by the Employer to administer the Plan, or, if the Employer fails to make such appointment, the Employer.

1.2.49   "Plan Sponsor": The Plan Sponsor specified in the Adoption Agreement.

1.2.50   "Plan Year" or "Year": The 12 consecutive month period designated by the Employer in the Adoption Agreement.

1.2.51   "Preretirement Survivor Annuity": a survivor annuity for the life of the surviving spouse of the Participant under which

(a) the payments to the surviving spouse are not less than the amounts which would be payable under a Joint and Survivor Annuity (or the actuarial equivalent thereof) if—

(i)   in the case of a Participant who dies after the date on which the Participant attained the earliest retirement age under the Plan on which he could elect to receive retirement benefits, such Participant had retired with an immediate Joint and Survivor Annuity on the day before the Participant's date of death; or

(ii)   in the case of a Participant who dies on or before such date, such Participant had separated from service on the date of death (except that a Participant who had actually separated from service prior to death shall be treated as separating on the actual date of separation), survived to the earliest retirement age, retired with an immediate Joint and Survivor Annuity at the earliest retirement age and died on the day after the day on which such Participant would have attained the earliest retirement age; and

(b) The earliest period for which the surviving spouse may receive a payment under such annuity is not later than the month in which the Participant would have attained the earliest retirement age under the Plan; and

(c) Any security interest held by the Plan by reason of a loan outstanding to the Participant for which a valid spousal consent has been obtained, if necessary, shall be taken into account.

1.2.52   "Qualified Non-Elective Contribution": A contribution to the Plan by the Employer which is neither a Matching Contribution nor an Elective Contribution, is one hundred percent (100%) vested and nonforfeitable when made, which a Participant may not elect to have paid in cash instead of being contributed to the Plan and which may not be distributed from the Plan prior to the termination of employment or death of the Participant, attainment of age 59-$\frac{1}{2}$ by the Participant or termination of the Plan without establishment of a successor plan.

1.2.53   "Qualified Non-Elective Contribution Account": An Account established and maintained for a Participant to account for the Qualified Non-Elective Contributions made on his behalf.

1.2.54   "Qualifying Employer Securities or Real Property": Securities or real property of the Employer which the Trustee may acquire and hold pursuant to the applicable provisions of the Code and the Act.

1.2.55   "Related Plan": Any other defined contribution plan, separate account of a key employee providing post-retirement medical benefits of a welfare benefit fund or individual medical account which is part of a pension or annuity plan, as defined in the applicable sections of the Code, maintained by the Employer or by any other business entity that is, along with the Employer, a member of a controlled group of corporations, an affiliated service group or trades or businesses under common control, as defined in Sections 414(b), (c) or (m) of the Code or which is otherwise required to be taken into account under Section 414(o) of the Code and the regulations issued thereunder which provides an annual addition during any Limitation Year.

1.2.56 "Segregated Account": An Account established and maintained for a Participant to account for his interest in a Segregated Fund.

1.2.57 "Segregated Fund": Assets held in the name of the Trustee which have been segregated from the Trust Fund in accordance with any of the provisions of the Plan.

1.2.58 "Self-Employed Individual": An individual who has Earned Income for the taxable year from the trade or business for which the Plan is established or who would have had Earned Income but for the fact that the trade or business had no net profits for the taxable year.

1.2.59 "Social Security Integration Level": The amount specified in the Adoption Agreement but not in excess of the maximum amount of earnings which may be considered "wages" under Section 3121(a)(1) of the Code, or corresponding future provisions of the Code, as in effect on the first day of the Plan Year for which allocations of Employer contributions and forfeitures are made (referred to as the Social Security Wage Base). The Social Security Integration Level shall be deemed to be the full amount of such Social Security Integration Level, even though a Participant's Compensation may include less than a full year's compensation because of either his participation commencing after the first day of the Plan Year or his service terminating prior to the end of the Plan Year.

1.2.60 "Trust Fund": All money and property of every kind and character held by the Trustee pursuant to the Plan, excluding assets held in Segregated Funds and Controlled Funds.

1.2.61 "Trustee": The persons, corporations, associations or combination of them who shall at the time be acting as such from time to time hereunder.

1.2.62 "Valuation Date": The Anniversary Date and such other date or dates specified as the Valuation Date in the Adoption Agreement.

1.2.63 "Voluntary Account": An Account established and maintained for a Participant for accounting purposes to which his voluntary Employee contributions made prior to Plan Years beginning after 1986 have been added.

1.2.64 "Year of Service": A Year of Service is a 12-consecutive month period (computation period) during which the employee completes at least 1,000 hours of service.

PART II

ARTICLE I
PARTICIPATION

2.1.1   Eligibility Requirements. Each Employee shall become eligible to participate in this Plan and receive an allocation of Non-Elective Contributions upon satisfying the eligibility requirements set forth in the Adoption Agreement. Unless otherwise specified in the Adoption Agreement, an Employee shall become eligible to have Elective Contributions and any other contributions made on the Employee's behalf upon completing 1000 Hours of Service during the Eligibility Computation Period.

2.1.2   Commencement of Participation. An eligible Employee shall become a Participant in the Plan on the Entry Date selected in the Adoption Agreement.

2.1.3   Participation upon Re-Employment. A Participant whose employment terminates and who is subsequently re-employed shall re-enter the Plan as a Participant immediately on the date of his re-employment. In the event that an Employee completes the eligibility requirements set forth in the Adoption Agreement, his employment terminates prior to becoming a Participant and he is subsequently re-employed, such Employee shall be deemed to have met the eligibility requirements as of the date of his re-employment and shall become a Participant on the date of his re-employment; provided, however, that if he is re-employed prior to the date he would have become a Participant if his employment had not terminated, he shall become a Participant as of the date he would have become a Participant if his employment had not terminated. Any other Employee whose employment terminates and who is subsequently reemployed shall become a Participant in accordance with the provisions of Sections 2.1.1 and 2.1.2.

2.1.4   Termination of Participation. An Employee who has become a Participant shall remain a Participant until the entire amount of his Distributable Benefit is distributed to him or his Beneficiary in the event of death.

2.1.5   Employer's Determination. In the event any question shall arise as to the eligibility of any person to become a Participant or the commencement of participation, the Employer shall determine such question and the Employer's decision shall be conclusive and binding, except to the extent of a claimant's right to appeal the denial of a claim.

2.1.6   Omission of Eligible Employee. If an Employee who should be included as a Participant in the Plan is erroneously omitted and discovery of the omission is made after the contribution by the Employer is made and allocated, the Employer shall make an additional contribution on behalf of the omitted Employee in the amount which the Employer would have contributed on his behalf had he not been omitted.

2.1.7   Inclusion of Ineligible Participant. If any person is erroneously included as a Participant in the Plan and discovery of the erroneous inclusion is made after the contribution by the Employer is made and allocated, the Employer may elect to treat the amount contributed on behalf of the ineligible person plus any earnings thereon as a forfeiture for the Plan Year in which the discovery is made and apply such amount in the manner specified in the Adoption Agreement.

2.1.8   Election Not to Participate. Notwithstanding anything contained in the Plan to the contrary, an Employee may elect with the approval of the Employer not to participate in the Plan if the tax-exempt status of the Plan is not jeopardized by the election. The Employee shall sign such documents as may be reasonably required by the Employer to evidence the election. If it is subsequently determined that the tax-exempt status of the Plan has been jeopardized, the Employer may elect to treat such Employee as having been erroneously omitted. An Employee may revoke the election only with respect to any subsequent Plan Year by written notice of revocation to the Employer prior to the end of the Plan Year for which the revocation is effective.

2.1.9   Existing Participants. An Employee who, on the Effective Date, was a Participant under the provisions of the Plan as in effect immediately prior to the Effective Date shall be a Participant on the Effective Date and the provisions of Sections 2.1.1 and 2.1.2, pertaining to participation, shall not be applicable to such Employee. The rights of a Participant whose employment terminated prior to the Effective Date shall be determined under the provisions of the Plan as in effect at the time of such termination.

2.1.10   Change in Status. If any Participant continues in the employ of the Employer or an affiliate for which service is required to be taken into account but ceases to be an Employee for any reason (such as becoming covered by a collective bargaining agreement unless the collective bargaining agreement otherwise provides) the Participant shall continue to be a Participant until the entire amount of his benefit is distributed but the individual shall be deemed not to have completed any "Years of Service" for purposes of Article V ("Benefits") during the period that the Participant is not an Employee for such reason. Such Participant shall continue to receive credit for Years of Service completed during the period for purposes of determining his vested and nonforfeitable interest in his Accounts. In the event that the individual subsequently again becomes a member of an eligible class of employees, the individual shall participate immediately upon the date of such change in status. If such Participant incurs a Break in Service and is subsequently reemployed, eligibility to participate shall be determined in accordance with Section 2.1.3. In the event that an individual who is not a member of an eligible class of employees becomes a member of an eligible class, the individual shall participate immediately if such individual has satisfied the eligibility requirements and would have otherwise previously become a participant.

ARTICLE II
CONTRIBUTIONS

2.2.1   Employer Contributions.

(a) Amount of Non-Elective Contribution. The Employer shall contribute to the Trust Fund each Plan Year such amount as a Non-Elective Contribution as the Employer may determine.

(b) Amount of Matching Contribution. Subject to applicable limitations provided by the Plan, the Employer shall contribute to the Trust Fund each Plan Year with respect to the amount of Elective Contributions on behalf of each electing Employee a Matching Contribution determined in the manner set forth in the Adoption Agreement.

(c) Amount of Qualified Non-Elective Contribution. The Employer shall contribute to the Trust Fund each Plan Year such amount as a Qualified Non-Elective Contribution as the Employer may determine. In addition, in lieu of distributing Excess Contributions or Excess Aggregate Contributions as provided in Article VI, below, and to the extent elected by the Employer in the Adoption Agreement, the Employer may make Qualified Non-Elective Contributions on behalf of Employees who are not Highly Compensated Employees that are sufficient to satisfy either the ADP test or the ACP test, or both, pursuant to regulations under the Code.

(d) Limitation. The contribution for any Plan Year by the Employer shall not exceed the maximum amount deductible from the Employer's income for such Year for federal income tax purposes under the applicable sections of the Code.

(e) Time of Contribution. All contributions by the Employer shall be delivered to the Trustee not later than the date fixed by law for the filing of the Employer's federal income tax return for the Year for which such contribution is made (including any extensions of time granted by the Internal Revenue Service for filing such return).

(f) Determination of Amount to be Final. The determination by the Employer as to the amount to be contributed by the Employer hereunder shall be in all respects final, binding, and conclusive on all persons or parties having or claiming any rights under this agreement or under the Plan and Trust created hereby. Under no circumstances and in no event shall any Participant, Beneficiary, or other person or party have any right to examine the books or records of the Employer.

(g) Rights of Trustee as to Contributions. The Trustee shall have no duty to report any contribution to be made or to determine whether contributions delivered to the Trustee by the Employer comply with the provisions of this Agreement. The Trustee shall be accountable only for funds actually received by the Trustee.

2.2.2   Elective Contributions by the Employer on Behalf of Electing Employees.

(a) Amount of Contribution. Each Employee may elect to have the Employer contribute to the Trust on his behalf for any Plan Year during which he is a Participant such amounts expressed either in dollars or in whole percentages of his Compensation as he may elect which would otherwise be payable by the Employer as Compensation (but not to exceed the dollar limitation provided by Section 402(g) of the Code as in effect at the beginning of the taxable year); provided that the Employer may impose reasonable limitations in a uniform, nondiscriminatory manner on the amounts which may be so contributed in order to satisfy applicable legal requirements and to assure the deductibility of amounts contributed by the Employer to the Plan and any other qualified plan of deferred compensation.

(b) Election. The Plan Administrator shall determine the manner in which a Participant may elect to have Elective Contributions made to the Plan on his behalf. The Plan Administrator shall establish reasonable periods during which the election may be made, modified or revoked. Unless the Plan Administrator establishes another period during which the election may be made, modified or revoked, any such election may be made, modified or revoked during the first and last months of the Plan Year. An election by an Employee may not be made retroactively and once made shall remain in effect until modified or terminated.

(c) Payment of Contribution. Elective Contributions shall be remitted by the Employer within a reasonable period after such amount would have otherwise been payable to the Participant. The Employer shall designate, in accordance with the Participant's election, the Plan Year to which any such contributions which are made after the end of the Plan Year pertain.

(d) Segregated Fund. Unless an Elective Contribution on behalf of a Participant is received by the Trustee within the time prescribed by the Plan Administrator prior to a Valuation Date, the Trustee shall establish a Segregated Fund with respect to such contribution. The funds contained in such Segregated Fund shall be transferred to the Trust Fund in accordance with the instructions of the Plan Administrator and such transfer shall be deemed to have been made as of such next succeeding Valuation Date. If an Elective Contribution on behalf of a Participant is received by the Trustee within the period prescribed by the Plan Administrator, such contribution shall be added to the Trust Fund. Notwithstanding the foregoing, if the Trust Fund is invested in such a manner that the Trustee can determine, with a reasonable degree of certainty, that portion of the adjustment to fair market value which is attributable to Elective Contributions received by the Trustee other than within such period, then the Trustee shall add any such Elective Contributions to the Trust Fund at the time the Trustee receives such Elective Contributions.

(e) Hardship Distributions. An Employee may not have Elective Contributions made on his or her behalf for the taxable year following the taxable year of a hardship distribution in excess of the applicable limit under Section 402(g) of the Code for such taxable year less the amount of the Employee's Elective Deferrals for the taxable year of the hardship distribution.

2.2.3   Employee Contributions.

(a) Amount of Contribution. An Employee is neither required nor permitted to contribute to the Plan for any Plan Year beginning after the Plan Year in which the prototype Plan is adopted by the Employer. Employee contributions for Plan Years beginning after 1986 shall be limited so as to meet the nondiscriminatory test of Section 401(m) of the Code. The Plan Administrator shall not accept deductible employee contributions attributable to any Plan Year.

(b) Withdrawal of Contributions. In accordance with the provisions of the Plan as in effect prior to Plan Years beginning after 1986, all or any portion of an Employee's contributions may be withdrawn by giving to the Plan Administrator written notice of any proposed withdrawal. The Plan Administrator may adopt such procedures with respect to such withdrawals as may be necessary or appropriate. The Trustee shall distribute any such withdrawal to the Participant in accordance with the procedures adopted by the Plan Administrator. Such withdrawals shall not include any interest or other increment earned on such contributions. No forfeitures shall occur as a result of withdrawal of an Employee's contributions. Notwithstanding the foregoing, a withdrawal of an Employee's contributions must be consented to in writing by the Participant's spouse.

2.2.4   Return of Contributions. Non-Elective and Matching Contributions shall be returned to the Employer in the following instances:

(a) If a Qualified Non-Elective, Non-Elective or Matching Contribution is made by the Employer by mistake of fact, then the contribution shall be returned within one year after its payment upon the Employer's written request.

(b) If a Qualified Non-Elective, Non-Elective or Matching Contribution is conditioned on initial qualification of the Plan under the applicable sections of the Code, and the Commissioner of Internal Revenue determines that the Plan does not qualify, then the contribution made incident to the initial qualification by the Employer shall be returned within one year after the date of denial of initial qualification of the Plan; provided that the application for initial qualification is made by the time prescribed by law for filing the Employer's tax return for the taxable year in which the Plan is adopted, or such later date as the Secretary of the Treasury may prescribe.

(c) Each Qualified Non-Elective, Non-Elective and Matching Contribution is conditioned upon the deductibility of the contribution under the applicable sections of the Code and to the extent of a disallowance of the deduction for part or all of the contribution, the contribution shall be returned within one year after such disallowance upon the Employer's written request.

ARTICLE III
ALLOCATIONS

2.3.1   Non-Elective Contributions. As of each Anniversary Date, the Non-Elective Contributions made by the Employer with respect to the preceding Plan Year, and forfeitures, shall be allocated among the Employer Accounts of Participants during the Plan Year in the manner set forth in the Adoption Agreement.

2.3.2   Matching Contributions. Unless otherwise specified in the Adoption Agreement, as of each Anniversary Date, the Matching Contribution made by the Employer with respect to the preceding Plan Year, and forfeitures, shall be allocated to the Matching Accounts of Participants for whom Elective Contributions were made in amounts proportionate to such Elective Contributions subject to the limitations specified in the Adoption Agreement.

2.3.3   Elective Contributions. The Elective Contributions by the Employer on behalf of an electing Employee shall be allocated to the Elective Contribution Account of such electing Employee as of the Anniversary Date of the Plan Year to which the Elective Contribution pertains.

2.3.4   Qualified Non-Elective Contributions. The Qualified Non-Elective Contributions made by the Employer with respect to the preceding

Plan Year shall be allocated to the Qualified Elective Contribution Account of Participants during the Plan Year in the manner specified in the Adoption Agreement.

2.3.5   Limitation. The allocation of Employer contributions must satisfy the requirements of Section 416 of the Code regardless of how the Adoption Agreement is completed. Neither Elective Contributions nor Matching Contributions may be taken into account for the purpose of satisfying the minimum top-heavy contribution requirement imposed by Section 416.

2.3.6   Minimum Allocation. In the event the Plan becomes a Top-Heavy Plan during any Plan Year, the provisions of Section 2.7.1(a) shall apply.

2.3.7   Fail-Safe Allocation. Notwithstanding any provision of the Plan or Adoption Agreement to the contrary, for Plan Years beginning after December 31, 1989, if the Plan would otherwise fail to satisfy the requirements of Section 401(a)(26), 410(b)(1) or 410(b)(2)(A)(i) of the Code and the regulations thereunder because Employer contributions have not been allocated to a sufficient number or percentage of Participants for the Plan Year, an additional contribution shall be made by the Employer and shall be allocated to the Employer Accounts of affected Participants subject to the following provisions:

(a) The Participants eligible to share in the allocation of the Employer's contribution shall be expanded to include the minimum number of Participants who are not otherwise eligible to the extent necessary to satisfy the applicable test under the relevant Section of the Code. The specific Participant who shall become eligible are those Participants who are actively employed on the last day of the Plan Year who have completed the greatest number of Hours of Service during the Plan Year.

(b) If the applicable test is still not satisfied, the Participants eligible to share in the allocation shall be further expanded to include the minimum number of Participants who are not employed on the last day of the Plan Year as are necessary to satisfy the applicable test. The specific Participants who shall become eligible are those Participants who have completed the greatest number of Hours of Service during the Plan Year.

(c) A Participant's accrued benefit shall not be reduced by any reallocation of amounts that have previously been allocated. To the extent necessary, the Employer shall make an additional contribution equal to the amount such affected Participants would have received if they had originally shared in the allocations without regard to the deductibility of the contribution. Any adjustment to the allocations pursuant to this paragraph shall be considered a retroactive amendment adopted by the last day of the Plan Year.

ARTICLE IV
BENEFITS

2.4.1   Distributable Benefit. At such time that the employment of a Participant terminates for any reason, he or his Beneficiary shall be entitled to a benefit equal to the vested and nonforfeitable interest in his Accounts as of the Distribution Date. Such Accounts shall include the allocable share of contributions and forfeitures, if any, which may be allocated to said Accounts as of such Distribution Date and shall be determined after making the adjustments for which provision is made in the Plan.

2.4.2   Vesting. A Participant shall at all times be one hundred percent (100%) vested and have a nonforfeitable interest in his Elective Contribution Account, Qualified Non-Elective Contribution Account, Voluntary Account and Segregated Account. The vested and nonforfeitable interest of the Participant in his Controlled Account shall be determined by reference to the Account from which the funds were originally transferred. The vested and nonforfeitable interest in a Participant's Employer Account and Matching Account shall be determined as hereinafter provided.

(a) Normal Retirement. If a Participant terminates employment at his Normal Retirement Age, he shall be one hundred percent (100%) vested and have a nonforfeitable interest in his Employer Account and Matching Account.

(b) Deferred Retirement. If a Participant continues in active employment following his Normal Retirement Age, he shall continue to participate under the Plan. From and after his Normal Retirement Age, he shall be one hundred percent (100%) vested and have a nonforfeitable interest in his Employer Account and Matching Account.

(c) Disability. If the employment of a Participant is terminated prior to his Normal Retirement Age as a result of a medically determinable physical or mental impairment which may be expected to result in death or to last for a continuous period of not less than twelve (12) months and which renders him incapable of performing his duties, he shall be one hundred percent (100%) vested and have a nonforfeitable interest in his Employer Account and Matching Account. All determinations in connection with the permanence and degree of such disability shall be made by the Plan Administrator in a uniform, nondiscriminatory manner on the basis of medical evidence.

(d) Death. In the event of the death of a Participant, he shall be one hundred percent (100%) vested and have a nonforfeitable interest in his Employer Account and Matching Account.

(e) Termination of Plan. In the event of termination of the Plan (including termination resulting from a complete discontinuance of contributions by the Employer), each Participant shall be one hundred percent (100%) vested and have a nonforfeitable interest in his Employer Account and Matching Account. In the event of a partial termination of the Plan, each Participant with respect to whom such partial termination has occurred shall be one hundred percent (100%) vested and have a nonforfeitable interest in his Employer Account and Matching Account.

(f) Early Retirement, Resignation or Discharge. If the employment of a Participant terminates by reason of early retirement, resignation or discharge prior to his Normal Retirement Age, he shall be vested and have a nonforfeitable interest in a percentage of his Employer Account and Matching Account determined by, except as provided below, taking into account all of his Years of Service as of such termination date in accordance with the schedule set forth in the Adoption Agreement.

2.4.3   Leave of Absence. A temporary cessation from active employment with the Employer pursuant to an authorized leave of absence in accordance with the nondiscriminatory policy of the Employer, whether occasioned by illness, military service or any other reason shall not be treated as either a termination of employment or a Break in Service provided that the Employee returns to employment prior to the end of the authorized leave of absence.

2.4.4   Re-Employment. Unless otherwise elected by the Employer in the Adoption Agreement, in the case of a Participant who has five (5) or more consecutive Breaks in Service, all Years of Service after such Breaks in Service shall be disregarded for the purposes of vesting the employer-derived account balance that accrued before such breaks, but both pre-break and post-break service shall count for the purposes of vesting the employer-derived account balance that accrues after such breaks. Both accounts shall share in the earnings and losses of the Trust Fund. In the case of a Participant who does not have five (5) consecutive Breaks in Service, both the pre-break and post-break service shall count in vesting both the pre-break and post-break employer-derived account balance.

2.4.5   Distribution Date. The Distribution Date shall be determined as hereinafter provided.

(a) Less Than 100% Vested. Except as otherwise specified in the Adoption Agreement, if the employment of a Participant terminates and the Participant has less than a one hundred percent (100%) vested and nonforfeitable interest in his Employer Account or Matching Account as of the date of such termination, then the Distribution Date shall be the last day of the fifth (5th) successive Plan Year during each of which he incurs a Break in Service as a result of the termination of his employment, provided that he is not re-employed on the last day of such Plan Year.

(b) Termination of Plan. In the event of termination of the Plan (including termination resulting from a complete discontinuance of contributions by the Employer), the Distribution Date shall be the date of such termination. In the event of a partial termination of the Plan, as to each Participant with respect to whom such partial termination has occurred, the Distribution Date shall be the Anniversary Date coinciding with or immediately following the date of such partial termination.

(c) Other. Except as provided in subsections (a) and (b) above, the Distribution Date shall be the Anniversary Date coinciding with or next following the termination of employment of the Participant.

2.4.6   Forfeitures. If an Employee terminates service, and the value of the Employees' vested account balance derived from employer and employee contributions is not greater than $3,500 and the Employee receives a distribution of the value of the entire vested portion of such account balance, the nonvested portion shall be treated as a forfeiture as of the last day of the Plan Year in which the Participant's entire vested interest is distributed from the Plan. If the value of an Employee's vested account balance is zero, the Employee shall be deemed to have received a distribution of such vested account balance. A participant's vested account balance shall not include accumulated deductible employee contributions within the meaning of Section 72(o)(5)(B) of the Code for plan years beginning prior to January 1, 1989.

If an employee terminates service, and elects, in accordance with the requirements of Section 2.5.2(a), to receive the value of the employee's vested account balance, the nonvested portion shall be treated as a forfeiture. If the employee elects to have distributed less than the entire vested portion of the account balance derived from employer contributions, the part of the nonvested portion that will be treated as a forfeiture is the total nonvested portion multiplied by a fraction, the numerator of which is the amount of the distribution attributable to employer contributions and the denominator of which is the total value of the vested employer derived account balance.

If an Employee receives a distribution and the Employee resumes employment covered under the Plan, the Employee's employer-derived account balance shall be restored to the amount on the date of distribution if the Employee repays to the plan the full amount of the distribution attributable to Employer contributions before the earlier of 5 years after the first date on which the Participant is subsequently re-employed by the Employer, or the date the Participant incurs five (5) consecutive Breaks in Service following the date of the distribution. If an Employee is deemed to receive a distribution pursuant to this section, and the Employee resumes employment covered under the Plan before the date the Participant incurs five (5) consecutive Breaks in Service, upon the reemployment of such Employee, the employer-derived account balance of the Employee will be restored to the amount on the date of such deemed distribution.

Unless otherwise elected in the Adoption Agreement, such forfeiture shall be allocated in the same manner as a contribution by the Employer for the Year in which said forfeiture occurred. Notwithstanding any provision herein to the contrary, forfeitures resulting from contributions by an Employer shall not be reallocated for the benefit of another adopting Employer.

If a Participant is re-employed following a Break in Service and is entitled to restoration of any amount of his Accounts which was forfeited as a result of such Break in Service, such amount shall be restored in the manner specified in the Adoption Agreement.

ARTICLE V
DISTRIBUTIONS

2.5.1   Commencement of Distribution.

(a) Immediate Distribution. If the employment of a Participant is terminated for any reason other than resignation or discharge prior to either his Early Retirement Date or his Normal Retirement Date, distribution of his Distributable Benefit shall begin in accordance with the Participant's election at any time after the earlier of the date determined under subsection (b) below or within a reasonable period after the Distribution Date as of which his Distributable Benefit is determined; provided that, if he has not incurred a Break in Service, he is not re-employed prior to the date of the commencement of distributions.

(b) Deferred Distribution. Unless the Employer elects in the Adoption Agreement to permit the Employee to elect earlier commencement, if the employment of a Participant is terminated by reason of resignation or discharge prior to either his Early Retirement Date or his Normal Retirement Date, distribution of his Distributable Benefit shall be deferred and commenced unless the Participant elects to further defer distribution on the sixtieth (60th) day after the close of the later of the following Plan Years:

(i)   The Plan Year during which the Participant attains the earlier of age sixty-five (65) or the Normal Retirement Age;

(ii) The Plan Year during which the tenth (10th) anniversary of the commencement of the Participant's participation in the Plan occurs; or

(iii) The Plan Year during which the Participant terminates service with the Employer.

If, however, the Employer selects an Early Retirement Date in the Adoption Agreement, a Participant who terminates employment before satisfying the age requirement for early retirement but has satisfied any service requirement shall be entitled to a distribution of his Distributable Benefit in accordance with subsection (a) above upon attaining such age.

If distribution is so deferred, unless otherwise determined by the Trustee, the Trustee shall transfer the Distributable Benefit to a Segregated Fund from which distribution shall thereafter be made. Such transfer shall be made as of the Distribution Date. Notwithstanding the foregoing, the failure of a Participant and spouse to consent to a distribution while a benefit is immediately distributable, within the meaning of Section 2.5.2(j), shall be deemed to be an election to defer commencement of payment of any benefit sufficient to satisfy this section.

(c) Required Distribution. Notwithstanding anything herein to the contrary, unless the Participant has made an appropriate election by December 31, 1983 to defer distribution which has not been revoked or modified, the Participant's benefit shall be distributed to the Participant not later than April 1 of the calendar year following the calendar year in which he attains age $70^{1}/_2$ (the required beginning date) or shall be distributed, commencing not later than April 1 of such calendar year in accordance with regulations prescribed by the Secretary of the Treasury over a period not extending beyond the life expectancy of the Participant or the life expectancy of the Participant and a beneficiary designated by the Participant. The amount required to be distributed for each calendar year, beginning with distributions for the first distribution calendar year, must at least equal the quotient obtained by dividing the Participant's benefit by the applicable life expectancy. Unless otherwise elected by the Participant (or spouse, if distributions begin after death and the spouse is the designated beneficiary) by the time distributions are required to begin, the life expectancy of the Participant and the Participant's spouse shall be recalculated annually. Other than for a life annuity, such election shall be irrevocable as to the Participant or spouse and shall apply to all subsequent years. The life expectancy of a non-spouse beneficiary may not be recalculated. Life expectancy and joint and last survivor expectancy shall be computed by use of the expected return multiples in Tables V and VI of Section 1.72-9 of the Treasury Regulations. For calendar years beginning after December 31, 1988, the amount to be distributed each year, beginning with distributions for the first distribution calendar year shall not be less than the quotient obtained by dividing the Participant's benefit by the lesser of (1) the applicable life expectancy or (2) if the Participant's spouse is not the designated beneficiary, the applicable divisor then determined from the table set forth in Q&A-4 of Section 1.401(a)(9)-2 of the proposed regulations. Distributions after the death of the Participant shall be distributed using the applicable life expectancy as the relevant divisor without regard to Proposed Regulations Section 1.401(a)(9)-2. The minimum distribution for subsequent calendar years, including the minimum distribution for the distribution calendar year in which the Participant's required beginning date occurs, must be made on or before December 31 of that distribution calendar year.

(d) Distribution After Death. Unless the Participant has made an appropriate election by December 31, 1983 to extend the period of distribution after his death and the election has not been revoked or modified, the following provisions shall apply. If distribution of the Participant's benefit has begun and the Participant dies before his entire benefit has been distributed to him, the remaining portion of such benefit shall be distributed at least as rapidly as under the method of distribution being used as of the date of the Participant's death.

If the Participant dies before the distribution of his benefit has begun, the entire interest of the Participant shall be distributed by December 31 of the calendar year containing the fifth (5th) anniversary of the death of such Participant, provided that if any portion of the Participant's benefit is payable to or for the benefit of a designated beneficiary and such portion is to be distributed in accordance with regulations issued by the Secretary of the Treasury over the life of, or over a period not extending beyond the life expectancy of such designated beneficiary, such distributions shall begin not later than December 31 of the calendar year immediately following the calendar year of the Participant's death or such later date as may be provided by regulations issued by the Secretary of the Treasury. If the designated beneficiary is the surviving spouse of the Participant the date on which the distributions are required to begin shall not be earlier than the later of December 31 of the calendar year immediately following the calendar year in which the Participant had died and December 31 of the calendar year in which the Participant would have attained age 70$\frac{1}{2}$. If the surviving spouse thereafter dies before the distributions to such spouse begin and any benefit is payable to a contingent beneficiary, the date on which distributions are required to begin shall be determined as if the surviving spouse were the Participant.

If the Participant has not specified the manner in which benefits are payable by the time of his or her death, the Participant's designated beneficiary must elect the method of distribution no later than the earlier of (1) December 31 of the calendar year in which distributions would be required to begin under this section, or (2) December 31 of the calendar year which contains the fifth anniversary of the date of death of the Participant. If the Participant has no designated beneficiary, or if the designated beneficiary does not elect a method of distribution, distribution of the Participant's entire interest must be completed by December 31 of the calendar year containing the fifth anniversary of the Participant's death.

(e) Payments to Children. In accordance with regulations issued by the Secretary of the Treasury, any amount paid to a child shall be treated as if it had been paid to the surviving spouse if such amount shall become payable to the surviving spouse upon such child reaching majority (or other designated event permitted under such regulations).

(f) Incidental Death Benefit Distributions. Any distribution required by the rules applicable to incidental death benefits shall be treated as a distribution required by this Section. All distributions required under this Section shall be determined and made in accordance with the proposed regulations under Section 401(a)(9) of the Code, including the minimum distribution incidental benefit requirement of Section 1.401(a)(9)-2 of the proposed regulations.

(g) Distributions. For the purposes of this section, distribution of a Participant's interest is considered to begin on the Participant's required beginning date or the date distribution is required to begin to the surviving spouse. If distribution in the form of an annuity irrevocably commences to the Participant before the required beginning date, the date distribution is considered to begin is the date distribution actually commences.

(h) Definitions.

(1) Applicable life expectancy. The life expectancy (or joint and last survivor expectancy) calculated using the attained age of the Participant (or designated beneficiary) as of the Participant's (or designated beneficiary's) birthday in the applicable calendar year reduced by one for each calendar year which has elapsed since the date life expectancy was first calculated. If life expectancy is being recalculated, the applicable life expectancy shall be the life expectancy as so recalculated. The applicable calendar year shall be the first distribution calendar year, and if life expectancy is being recalculated such succeeding calendar year.

(2) Designated beneficiary. The individual who is designated as the beneficiary under the Plan in accordance with Section 401(a)(9) and the proposed regulations thereunder.

(3) Distribution calendar year. A calendar year for which a minimum distribution is required. For distributions beginning before the Participant's death, the first distribution calendar year is the calendar year immediately preceding the calendar year which contains the Participant's required beginning date. For distributions beginning after the Participant's death, the first distribution calendar year is the calendar year in which distributions are required to begin.

(4) Participant's benefit.

(i) The account balance as of the last valuation date in the calendar year immediately preceding the distribution calendar year (valuation calendar year) increased by the amount of any contributions or forfeitures allocated to the account balance as of dates in the valuation calendar year after the valuation date and decreased by distributions made in the valuation calendar year after the valuation date.

(ii) Exception for second distribution calendar year. For purposes of paragraph (i) above, if any portion of the minimum distribution for the first distribution calendar year is made in the second distribution calendar year on or before the required beginning date, the amount of the minimum distribution made in the second distribution calendar year shall be treated as if it had been made in the immediately preceding distribution calendar year.

(5) Required beginning date.

(i) General rule. The required beginning date of a Participant is the first day of April of the calendar year following the calendar year in which the Participant attains age $70^{1}/_{2}$.

(ii) Transitional rules. The required beginning date of a Participant who attains age $70^{1}/_{2}$ before January 1, 1988, shall be determined in accordance with (I) or (II) below:

(I) Non-5-percent owners. The required beginning date of a Participant who is not a 5-percent owner is the first day of April of the calendar year following the calendar year in which the later of retirement or attainment of age $70^{1}/_{2}$ occurs.

(II) 5-percent owners. The required beginning date of a Participant who is a 5-percent owner during any year beginning after December 31, 1979, is the first day of April following the later of:

(A) the calendar year in which the Participant attains age 70½, or

(B) the earlier of the calendar year with or within which ends the Plan Year in which the Participant becomes a 5-percent owner, or the calendar year in which the Participant retires.

The required beginning date of a Participant who is not a 5-percent owner who attains age 70½ during 1988 and who has not retired as of January 1, 1989, is April 1, 1990.

(iii) 5-percent owner. A Participant is treated as a 5-percent owner for purposes of this section if such Participant is a 5-percent owner as defined in Section 416(i) of the Code (determined in accordance with Section 416 but without regard to whether the Plan is top-heavy) at any time during the Plan Year ending with or within the calendar year in which such owner attains age 66½ or any subsequent Plan Year.

(iv) Once distributions have begun to a 5-percent owner under this section, they must continue to be distributed, even if the Participant ceases to be a 5-percent owner in a subsequent year.

(i) Transitional rule.

(1) Notwithstanding the other requirements of this Section and subject to the requirements of Section 2.5.2, distribution on behalf of any employee, including a 5-percent owner, may be made in accordance with all of the following requirements (regardless of when such distribution commences):

(a) The distribution by the trust is one which would not have disqualified such trust under Section 401(a)(9) of the Internal Revenue Code as in effect prior to amendment by the Deficit Reduction Act of 1984.

(b) The distribution is in accordance with a method of distribution designated by the employee whose interest in the trust is being distributed or, if the employee is deceased, by a beneficiary of such employee.

(c) Such designation was in writing, was signed by the employee or the beneficiary, and was made before January 1, 1984.

2.5.2   Method of Distribution. Subject to the provisions of Section 2.5.1 above and any security interest in a loan from the Plan for which any necessary spousal consent has been obtained (to the extent such security interest is used as repayment of the loan), distribution shall be made by one of the following methods, as determined in accordance with the election of the Participant (or in the case of death, his Beneficiary) with such spousal consents as may be required by law in any of the following methods which are designated by the Employer in the Adoption Agreement:

(a) In a single distribution; provided that if the Employer has applied a consistent policy since the first Plan Year beginning after 1988, the Employer may require a Participant who is a Highly Compensated Employee or who is otherwise entitled to receive a lump sum distribution in excess of $25,000.00 to execute a covenant not to compete with the Employer which shall provide that the Participant agrees that he shall not solicit the business of any person or entity doing business with the Employer at any time within the twelve month period prior to the date of termination of his employment and, in addition, shall not engage in any business, whether as a sole proprietor, partner, joint venturer, shareholder, employee, independent contractor, agent or otherwise, which is in competition with the business of the Employer for a period not exceeding two (2) years from the date of such distribution within fifty (50) miles of the principal offices of the Employer or containing such alternative provisions as determined by the Employer.

(b) In substantially equal annual, quarterly or monthly installments over a period of more than one year but which does not exceed the period designated in the Adoption Agreement, as selected by the Participant, plus accrued net income. If distribution is to be so made in installments, the Trustee shall cause the undistributed portion of the Distributable Benefit to be transferred to a Segregated Fund, from which installment payments shall thereafter be withdrawn from time to time.

(c) By the purchase and delivery of a single premium, nontransferable, fully refundable, annuity policy issued by a legal reserve life insurance company providing for payments over such period as may be designated in the Adoption Agreement as selected by the Participant; provided, however, unless the Employer has designated a life annuity distribution option in the Adoption Agreement, in the event of distribution of such an annuity policy to a Participant, such duration shall be for a fixed duration which is less than the Participant's life expectancy as of the annuity starting date. The refund feature under such annuity policy following the death of the Participant shall inure to the benefit of the person or persons designated by the Participant as his Beneficiary.

(d) Any alternative method of equivalent value contained in the Plan at any time on or after the first day of the first Plan Year beginning after 1988 to which the Participant consents.

(e) Annuity Payments

(1) Requirement of Annuity Payment

In the event that the Employer designates a life annuity distribution option in the Adoption Agreement or the Plan contained such an option at any time on or after the first day of the first Plan Year beginning after 1988, as of such date, except as otherwise provided herein, (i) a married Participant's vested Account balance shall be provided in the form of a Joint and Survivor Annuity, (ii) in the case of a married Participant who dies before the annuity starting date and has a surviving spouse, a Preretirement Survivor Annuity shall be provided to such surviving spouse and (iii) an unmarried Participant's vested Account balance shall be paid in the form of a life annuity.

A Participant's vested Account balance is the aggregate value of the Participant's vested account balances derived from employer and employee contributions (including rollovers), whether vested before or upon death, including the proceeds of insurance contracts, if any, on the Participant's life. The provisions hereof shall apply to a Participant who is vested in amounts attributable to employer contributions, employee contributions (or both) at the time of death or distribution.

The Participant may elect to have such annuity distributed upon attainment of the earliest retirement age under the Plan. A surviving spouse may elect to have such annuity distributed within the ninety (90) day period commencing on the date of the Participant's death.

(2) Election to Waive Annuity Payment

A Participant may elect at any time during the applicable election period to waive the Joint and Survivor Annuity form of benefit or the Preretirement Survivor Annuity form of benefit (or both) and may revoke any such election at any time during the applicable election period.

(3) Spouse Consent Required

An election to waive any annuity form of benefit shall not take effect unless the spouse of the Participant consents in writing to the election, such election designates a specific beneficiary, including any class of beneficiaries or contingent beneficiaries, or, solely in the case of a waiver of a Joint and Survivor Annuity, a form of benefits which may not be changed without spousal consent (or the consent of the spouse expressly permits designations by the Participant without any requirement of further consent by the spouse), and the spouse's consent acknowledges the effect of such election and is witnessed by a Plan representative or a notary public, or it is established to the satisfaction of the Plan Administrator that such consent cannot be obtained because there is no spouse or because the spouse cannot be located. A spouse may not revoke the consent without the approval of the Participant.

Any consent by a spouse obtained under this provision (or establishment that the consent of a spouse may not be obtained) shall be effective only with respect to such spouse. A consent that permits designations by the Participant without any requirement of further consent by such spouse must acknowledge that the spouse has the right to limit consent to a specific beneficiary, and a specific form of benefit where applicable, and that the spouse voluntarily elects to relinquish either or both of such rights. A revocation of a prior waiver may be made by a Participant without the consent of the spouse at any time before the commencement of benefits. The number of revocations shall not be limited. No consent obtained under this provision shall be valid unless the Participant has received notice as provided in subsection (4) below.

(4) Written Explanations

The Plan Administrator shall provide each Participant no less than 30 days and no more than 90 days before the annuity starting date a written explanation of—

(a) the terms and conditions of a Joint and Survivor Annuity;

(b) the Participant's right to make and the effect of an election to waive the Joint and Survivor Annuity form of benefit;

(c) the rights of the Participant's spouse to consent to a Participant's election;

(d) the right to make and the effect of a revocation of an election.

The Plan Administrator shall provide to each Participant within the applicable period a written explanation of a Preretirement Survivor Annuity comparable to that provided with respect to a Joint and Survivor Annuity.

(5) Applicable Period

The applicable period means with respect to a Participant, whichever of the following periods ends last:

(a) The period beginning with the first day of the Plan Year in which the Participant attains age 32 and ending with the close of the Plan Year preceding the Plan Year in which the Participant attains age 35.

(b) A reasonable period ending after the individual becomes a Participant.

(c) A reasonable period ending after the Plan ceases to fully subsidize costs.

(d) A reasonable period ending after Section 401(a)(11) of the Code first applies to the Participant.

(e) A reasonable period ending after separation from service in case of a Participant who separates before attaining age 35.

For purposes of applying the foregoing, a reasonable period ending after the enumerated events described in (ii), (iii) and (iv) is the end of the two-year period beginning one year prior to the date the applicable event occurs and ending one year after that date. In the case of a Participant who separates from service before the Plan Year in which age 35 is attained, notice shall be provided within the two-year period beginning prior to separation and ending one year after separation. If such a Participant thereafter returns to employment with the Employer, the applicable period for such Participant shall be redetermined.

(6) Applicable Election Period

The applicable election period means—

(a) in the case of an election to waive a Joint and Survivor Annuity, the ninety (90) day period ending on the annuity starting date; and

(b) in the case of an election to waive a Preretirement Survivor Annuity, the period which begins on the first day of the Plan Year in which the Participant attains age thirty-five (35) and ends on the date of the Participant's death; provided that in the case of a Participant who is separated from service, such period shall not begin later than the date of such separation from service.

A Participant who will not yet attain age 35 as of the end of any current Plan Year may make a special qualified election to waive the Preretirement Survivor Annuity for the period beginning on the date of such election and ending on the first day of the Plan Year in which the Participant will attain age 35. Such election shall not be valid unless the Participant receives a written explanation of the Preretirement Survivor Annuity in such terms as are comparable to the explanation required under subsection (4). Preretirement Survivor Annuity coverage will be automatically reinstated as of the first day of the Plan Year in which the Participant attains age 35. Any new waiver on or after such date shall be subject to the full requirements of this section.

(7)   Annuity Starting Date

The annuity starting date means the first day of the first period for which an amount is payable as an annuity or any other form.

(8)   Marriage Requirement

Notwithstanding the foregoing, the benefits under the Plan shall not be provided in the form of a Joint and Survivor Annuity or a Preretirement Survivor Annuity unless the Participant and his spouse have been married throughout the one (1) year period ending on the earlier of the Participant's annuity starting date or the date of the Participant's death. If a Participant marries within one (1) year before the annuity starting date and the Participant and his spouse in such marriage have been married for at least a one (1) year period ending on or before the date of the Participant's death, the Participant and such spouse shall be treated as having been married throughout the required period. A former spouse shall be treated as the spouse or surviving spouse and a current spouse will not be treated as the spouse or surviving spouse to the extent provided under a qualified domestic relations order as described in Section 414(p) of the Code.

(f) Terms of Annuity Contracts. Any annuity contract distributed from the Plan must be nontransferable. The terms of any annuity contract purchased and distributed by the Plan to a Participant or spouse shall comply with the requirements of the Plan. If the Participant's benefit is distributed in the form of an annuity purchased from an insurance company, distributions thereunder shall be made in accordance with the requirements of Section 401(a)(9) of the Code and the proposed regulations thereunder.

(g) Incidental Death Benefits. For calendar years beginning before January 1, 1989, if the Participant's spouse is not the designated Beneficiary, the method of distribution selected must assure that at least fifty (50%) percent of the present value of the amount available for distribution is paid within the life expectancy of the Participant.

(h) Consents. If the value of a Participant's vested account balance derived from Employer and Employee contributions does not exceed (and at the time of any prior distribution did not exceed) $3,500, the consent of the Participant and spouse (or where either has died, the survivor) must consent to any distribution of such account balance. The consent shall be obtained in writing within the 90 day period ending on the annuity starting date. Neither the consent of the Participant nor the Participant's spouse shall be required to the extent that a distribution is required to satisfy Section 401(a)(9) or Section 415 of the Code. In addition, upon termination of the Plan if the Plan does not offer an annuity option (purchased from a commercial provider), the Participant's account balance in the Plan may, without the Participant's consent, be distributed to the Participant or transferred to another defined contribution plan (other than an employee stock ownership plan as defined in Section 4975(e)(7) of the Code) within the same controlled group.

(i) Zero Benefits. If the value of the Participant's vested and nonforfeitable interest in the Plan at the time of his termination of employment is zero, the Participant shall be deemed to have received a distribution of such interest.

(j) Restrictions on Immediate Distributions. The Plan Administrator shall notify the Participant and the Participant's spouse of the right to defer any distribution until the Participant's account balance in the Plan is no longer immediately distributable. Such notification shall include a general description of the material features and an explanation of the relative values of the optional forms of benefit available under the Plan in a manner that would satisfy the notice requirements of Section 417(a)(3) of the Code and shall be provided no less than 30 days and no more than 90 days prior to the annuity starting date. Notwithstanding the foregoing, only the Participant need consent to the commencement of a distribution in the form of a qualified joint and survivor annuity while the Participant's account balance in the Plan is immediately distributable. Furthermore, if payment in the form of a qualified joint and survivor annuity is not required with respect to the Participant pursuant to the Plan, only the Participant need consent to the distribution of an account balance that is immediately distributable. The Participant's account balance is immediately distributable if any part of the Participant's account balance could be distributed to the Participant (or surviving spouse) before the Participant attains (or would have attained if not deceased) the later of age 62 or the Normal Retirement Age.

(k) Transitional Rules.

(1) Any living Participant not receiving benefits on August 23, 1984, who would otherwise not receive the benefits prescribed by the previous sections of the article must be given the opportunity to elect to have the prior sections of this article apply if such Participant is credited with at least one hour of service under this Plan or a predecessor plan in a Plan Year beginning on or after January 1, 1976, and such Participant has at least 10 years of vesting service when he or she separated from service.

(2) Any living Participant not receiving benefits on August 23, 1984, who was credited with at least one hour of service under this Plan or a predecessor plan on or after September 2, 1974, and who is not otherwise credited with any service in a Plan Year beginning on or after January 1, 1976, must be given the opportunity to have his or her benefits paid in accordance with Section (4) below.

(3) The respective opportunities to elect (as described above) must be afforded to the appropriate Participants during the period commencing on August 23, 1984, and ending on the date benefits would otherwise commence to said Participants.

(4) Any Participant who has elected pursuant to Section (2) above and any Participant who does not elect under Section (1) or who meets the requirements of Section (1) except that such Participant does not have at least 10 years of vesting service when he or she separates from service, shall have his or her benefits distributed in accordance with all of the following requirements if benefits would have been payable in the form of a life annuity:

(i) Automatic joint and survivor annuity. If benefits in the form of a life annuity become payable to a married Participant who:

(1) begins to receive payments under the Plan on or after normal retirement age; or

(2) dies on or after normal retirement age while still working for the Employer; or

(3) begins to receive payments on or after the qualified early retirement age; or

(4) separates from service on or after attaining normal retirement age (or the qualified early retirement age) and after satisfying the eligibility requirements for the payment of benefits under the plan and thereafter dies before beginning to receive such benefits;

then such benefits will be received under this Plan in the form of a qualified joint and survivor annuity, unless the Participant has elected otherwise during the election period. The election period must begin at least 6 months before the Participant attains qualified early retirement age and end not more than 90 days before the commencement of benefits. Any election hereunder will be in writing and may be changed by the Participant at any time.

(ii) Election of early survivor annuity. A Participant who is employed after attaining the qualified early retirement age will be given the opportunity to elect, during the election period, to have a survivor annuity payable on death. If the Participant elects the survivor annuity, payments under such annuity must not be less than the payments which would have been made to the spouse under the qualified joint and survivor annuity if the Participant had retired on the day before his or her death. Any election under this provision will be in writing and may be changed by the Participant at any time. The election period begins on the later of (1) the 90th day before the Participant attains the qualified early retirement age, or (2) the date on which participation begins, and ends on the date the Participant terminates employment.

(iii) For purposes of this Section (4):

(1) Qualified early retirement age is the later of:

(i) the earliest date, under the Plan, on which the Participant may elect to receive retirement benefits,

(ii)   the first day of the 120th month beginning before the Participant reaches normal retirement age, or

(iii) the date the Participant begins participation.

(2) Qualified joint and survivor annuity is an
annuity for the life of the Participant with a survivor
annuity for the life of the spouse as otherwise described in the Plan.

2.5.3   Nature of Distributions. The nature of the distribution of a
Participant's Distributable Benefit shall be as hereinafter provided.

(a) Trust Fund and Segregated Funds. Subject to the Joint and
Survivor Annuity requirements, except as provided in subsection (b)
with regard to Life Insurance Policies, distribution of a Participant's
Distributable Benefit shall consist of cash or property, or an annuity
contract as provided in Section 5.2 above.

(b) Insurance Policies. In the event that the Trustee has purchased Life Insurance Policies on the life of the Participant, the values
and benefits available with respect to each such Policy shall be distributed as follows:

(i)   If the Participant's employment terminates for any
reason other than death, then the Trustee shall either surrender
the Life Insurance Policy for its available cash value and distribute the proceeds as provided in subsection (a) above or, at
the election of the Participant, distribute the Life Insurance
Policy to the Participant, provided the Participant has a vested
and nonforfeitable interest in his Accounts in an amount at least
equal to the cash value thereof.

(ii) If the Participant's employment terminates by reason
of death, the beneficiary designated by the Participant in accordance with the terms of the Plan shall be entitled to receive
from the Trustee the full amount of the proceeds thereof.

The Trustee shall apply for and be the owner of any Policies purchased
under the terms of the Plan. The Policies must provide that the proceeds
are payable to the Trustee subject to the Trustee's obligation to pay over
the proceeds to the designated Beneficiary. Under no circumstances shall
the trust retain any part of the proceeds. In the event of any conflict between the terms of the Plan and the terms of any Policies purchased hereunder, the Plan provisions shall control.

2.5.4   Advance Distributions. If the Employer elects in the Adoption Agreement to permit advance distribution to a Participant or his

Beneficiary after his employment has terminated and before he is otherwise entitled to distribution of his Distributable Benefit, the Trustee upon the request of the Participant or Beneficiary shall make advance distributions to him or to his Beneficiary. The aggregate of such an advance distribution shall not exceed the sum of the vested and nonforfeitable interest in the Participant's Accounts.

If the Employer elects in the Adoption Agreement to forfeit nonvested amounts immediately upon distribution of the Employee's entire vested account balance on termination of service, an Employee who terminates service and elects to receive the value of the Employee's vested account balance shall forfeit the nonvested portion. If the Employee elects to have distributed less than the entire vested portion of the account balance derived from Employer contributions, the part of the nonvested portion that is treated as a forfeiture is the total nonvested portion multiplied by a fraction, the numerator of which is the amount of the distribution attributable to Employer contributions and the denominator of which is the total value of the vested Employer derived account balance.

Except as provided in the preceding paragraph, if a Participant receives a distribution which reduces the balance in his Employer Account when he has less than a one hundred percent (100%) vested and nonforfeitable interest in the Account, the amount, if any, of the Participant's vested and nonforfeitable interest in the undistributed balance of said Account on his Accrual Date shall be transferred to a Segregated Account and shall not be less than an amount ("X") determined by the formula: $X = P$ $(AB + (R \times D)) - (R \times D)$. For purposes of applying the formula: P is the vested percentage at the relevant time; AB is the account balance at the relevant time; and D is the amount of the distribution; and R is the ratio of the account balance at the relevant time to the account balance after distribution.

A Participant who receives a distribution of an amount deducted from his Employer Account when he has less than a one hundred percent (100%) vested and nonforfeitable interest in his Employer Account and who subsequently again becomes an Employee may repay the full amount of such distribution before he incurs five (5) consecutive Breaks in Service following the date of the distribution; provided, however, that in the event of repayment neither the Trust nor the Employer shall be liable for any federal or state income tax resulting from the distribution and the Participant shall indemnify and hold harmless the Trust and the Employer for and from any such liability. In the event of such repayment, the Employer Account of the Participant shall be credited with the full amount of such repayment and the previously undistributed balance. In the event the Participant fails to repay the full amount of such distribution within the time permitted for repayment, the non-vested and forfeitable portion of the previously undistributed balance of his Employer Account which had been transferred to a Segregated Account shall be deemed a forfeiture as of the last day of such period. If a Participant is deemed to receive a distribution because his vested and nonforfeitable interest at the time of his termination of employment is zero and the Participant resumes employment covered under the Plan before the date the Participant incurs five (5) consecutive Breaks in Service, upon the reemployment of such Participant, the employer-derived account balance of the Participant shall be restored to the amount on the date of the deemed distribution.

2.5.5   Hardship Distributions. If the Employer elects in the Adoption Agreement to permit hardship distributions, a Participant may request a distribution from the Plan as a result of immediate and heavy financial needs of the Participant to the extent that the distribution is necessary to satisfy such financial needs. Hardship distributions are subject to the spousal consent requirements contained in Sections 401(a)(11) and 417 of the Code. The determination of whether a Participant has an immediate and heavy financial need shall be made by the Plan Administrator on the basis of all relevant facts and circumstances. A distribution shall be deemed to be made on account of an immediate and heavy financial need if the distribution is on account of:

(a) Deductible medical expenses described in Section 213(d) of the Code incurred by the Participant, his spouse or dependents;

(b) Purchase (excluding mortgage payments) of a principal residence for the Participant;

(c) Payment of tuition for the next semester or quarter of post-secondary education for the Participant, his spouse, children or dependents; or

(d) The need to prevent the eviction of the Participant from his principal residence or foreclosure on the mortgage of the Participant's principal residence.

A distribution shall be considered as necessary to satisfy an immediate and heavy financial need of the Participant only if:

(a) The Participant has obtained all distributions, other than hardship distributions, and all nontaxable loans under all plans maintained by the Employer;

(b) All plans maintained by the Employer provide that the Participant's elective Deferrals and employee contributions shall be suspended for twelve (12) months after the receipt of the hardship distribution;

(c) The distribution is not in excess of the amount of an immediate and heavy financial need; and

(d) All plans maintained by the Employer provide that the Participant may not make Elective Deferrals for the Participant's taxable year immediately following the taxable year of the hardship distribution in excess of the applicable limit under Section 402(g) of the Code for such taxable year less the amount of such Participant's Elective Deferrals for the taxable year less the amount of such Participant's Elective Deferrals for the taxable year of the hardship distribution.

In the event of such distribution, when a Participant is less than one hundred percent (100%) vested in his Employer Account or Matching Account, the vested interest in the Employer Account or Matching Account shall thereafter be determined in accordance with Section 2.5.4 of the Plan.

2.5.6   In Service Distributions. If the Employer elects in the Adoption Agreement to permit distributions to a Participant after attaining age 59½ but prior to his termination of employment, a Participant shall be entitled to receive a distribution of all or a part of his interest in the Plan upon filing a written request with the Plan Administrator; provided that no distribution shall be made unless the interest of the Participant in the Account from which the distribution is to be made is fully vested and nonforfeitable and the balance in the Account to be distributed has accumulated for at least two (2) years or the individual has been a Participant for five (5) or more Plan Years.

ARTICLE VI
SPECIAL CODA LIMITATIONS

2.6.1   Limitation on Deferral Percentage for Highly Compensated Employees. Notwithstanding any provision herein to the contrary, the actual deferral percentage for all Highly Compensated Employees for each Plan Year must not exceed the actual deferral percentage for all other Employees eligible to participate by more than the greater of:

(a) the actual deferral percentage of such other Employees multiplied by 1.25; or

(b) the actual deferral percentage of such other Employees multiplied by 2.0, but in no event more than two (2) percentage points greater than the actual deferral percentage of such other Employees.

For purposes hereof, the actual deferral percentages for a Plan Year for all Highly Compensated Employees and for all other Employees respectively are the averages of the ratios, calculated separately for each Employee in the respective group, of the amount of Employer Contributions and Qualified Non-Elective Contributions paid under the Plan on behalf of each such Employee for such Plan Year including Excess Elective Deferrals to the Employee's Compensation for such Plan Year (whether or not the Employee was a Participant for the entire Plan Year) but excluding Elective Deferrals that are taken into account in the Contribution Percentage test (provided the ADP test is satisfied both with and without exclusion of those Elective Deferrals). An Employee who would be a Participant but for the failure to have Elective Contributions made on his behalf shall be treated as a Participant on whose behalf no Elective Contributions are made. For purposes of calculating the actual deferral percentages of Highly Compensated Employees who are 5 percent owners or among the ten most highly paid Employees, Elective Contributions and Qualified Non-Elective Contributions on behalf of a member of the Family of such Highly Compensated Employees shall be taken into account and Compensation of such Employees shall include the Elective Deferrals and Qualified Non-Elective Contributions and Compensation for the Plan Year of members of his Family (as determined in Section 414(q)(6) of the Code). A member of the Family of such Highly Compensated Employees shall be disregarded as a separate Employee in determining the actual deferral percentage both for Participants who are Highly Compensated Employees and for all other Employees.

For purposes of determining the actual deferral percentage test, Elective Contributions and Qualified Non-Elective Contributions must be made before the last day of the twelve month period immediately following the Plan Year to which the contributions relate.

The Employer shall maintain records sufficient to demonstrate satisfaction of the actual deferral percentage test and the amount of Qualified Non-Elective Contributions used in such test.

The determination and treatment of the actual deferral percentage amounts of any Participant shall satisfy such other requirements as may be prescribed by the Secretary of the Treasury.

2.6.2   Multiple Plan Limitations.

(a) The actual deferral percentage for any Participant who is a Highly Compensated Employee for the Plan Year and who is eligible to have Elective Contributions (and Qualified Non-Elective Contributions if treated as Elective Deferrals for purposes of the actual deferral percentage test) allocated to his or her Accounts under two or more arrangements described in Section 401(k) of the Code, that are maintained by the Employer, shall be determined as if such Elective Deferrals (and, if applicable, such Qualified Non-Elective Contributions) were made under a single arrangement. If a Highly Compensated

Employee participates in two or more cash or deferred arrangements that have different Plan Years, all cash or deferred arrangements ending with or within the same calendar year shall be treated as a single arrangement.

(b) In the event that this Plan satisfies the requirements of Section 401(k), 401(a)(4) or 410(b) of the Code only if aggregated with one or more other plans, or if one or more other plans satisfy the requirements of such sections of the Code only if aggregated with this Plan, then this section shall be applied by determining the actual deferral percentage of Employees as if all such plans were a single plan. For Plan Years beginning after December 31, 1989, plans may be aggregated in order to satisfy Section 401(k) of the Code only if they have the same Plan Year.

2.6.3   Limitation on Matching Contributions. Notwithstanding any provision herein to the contrary, the average contribution percentage for all Highly Compensated Employees for each Plan Year must not exceed the average contribution percentage for all other Employees eligible to participate by more than the greater of:

(a) the average contribution percentage of such other Employees multiplied by 1.25; or

(b) the average contribution percentage of such other Employees multiplied by 2.0, but in no event more than two (2) percentage points greater than the average contribution percentage of such other Employees.

For purposes hereof, the average contribution percentages for a Plan Year for all Highly Compensated Employees and for all other Employees respectively are the averages of the ratios, calculated separately for each Employee in the respective group, of the amount of Matching Contributions paid under the Plan on behalf of each such Employee for such Plan Year, to the Employee's Compensation for such Plan Year whether or not the Employee was a Participant for the entire Plan Year. Such contribution percentage amounts shall include forfeitures of Excess Aggregate Contributions or Matching Contributions allocated to the Participant's Accounts which shall be taken into account in the Plan Year in which such forfeiture is allocated. If so elected in the Adoption Agreement, the Employer may include Qualified Non-Elective Contributions in the contribution percentage amounts. The Employer may also elect to use Elective Deferrals in the contribution percentage amounts so long as the ADP test is met before the Elective Deferrals are used in the ACP test and continues to be met following the exclusion of those Elective Deferrals that are used to meet the ACP test. If an Elective Contribution or other contribution by an Employee is required as a condition of participation in the Plan, any

Employee who would be a Participant if such Employee made such a contribution shall be treated as an eligible Participant on behalf of whom no such contributions are made.

The Employer shall maintain records sufficient to demonstrate satisfaction of the average contribution percentage test and the amount of Qualified Non-Elective Contributions used in such test.

The determination and treatment of the contribution percentage of any Participant shall satisfy such other requirements as may be prescribed by the Secretary of the Treasury.

2.6.4   Special Rules.

(a) Multiple Use: If one or more Highly Compensated Employees participate in both a CODA and a plan subject to the ACP test maintained by the Employer and the sum of the ADP and ACP of those Highly Compensated Employees subject to either or both tests exceeds the Aggregate Limit, then the ACP of those Highly Compensated Employees who also participate in a CODA shall be reduced (beginning with such Highly Compensated Employee whose ACP is the highest) so that the limit is not exceeded. The amount by which each Highly Compensated Employee's contribution percentage amounts is reduced shall be treated as an Excess Aggregate Contribution. The ADP and ACP of the Highly Compensated Employees are determined after any corrections required to meet the ADP and ACP tests. Multiple use does not occur if either the ADP or ACP of the Highly Compensated Employees does not exceed 1.25 multiplied by the ADP and ACP of the Employees who are not Highly Compensated Employees.

(b) The contribution percentage for any Participant who is a Highly Compensated Employee and who is eligible to have contribution percentage amounts allocated to his or her Accounts under two or more plans described in Section 401(a) of the Code, or arrangements described in Section 401(k) of the Code that are maintained by the Employer, shall be determined as if the total of such contribution percentage amounts was made under each plan. If a Highly Compensated Employee participates in two or more cash or deferred arrangements that have different plan years, all cash or deferred arrangements ending with or within the same calendar year shall be treated as a single arrangement.

(c) In the event that this Plan satisfies the requirements of Sections 401(m), 401(a)(4) or 410(b) of the Code only if aggregated with one or more other plans, or if one or more other plans satisfy the requirements of such Sections of the Code only if aggregated with this plan, then this section shall be applied by determining the contribution percentages of Employees as if all such plans were a single plan. For Plan Years beginning after December 31, 1989, plans may be aggregated in order to satisfy Section 401(m) of the Code only if they have the same Plan Year.

(d) For purposes of determining the contribution percentage of a Participant who is a five-percent owner or one of the ten most highly-paid Highly Compensated Employees, the contribution percentage amounts and Compensation of such Participant shall include the contribution percentage amounts and Compensation for the Plan Year of members of the Family of such Highly Compensated Employees. Family members, with respect to Highly Compensated Employees, shall be disregarded as separate employees in determining the contribution percentage both for Participants who are Highly Compensated Employees and for all other Employees.

(e) For purposes of determining the contribution percentage test, Employee Contributions are considered to have been made in the Plan Year in which contributed to the trust. Matching Contributions and Qualified Non-Elective Contributions shall be considered made for a Plan Year if made no later than the end of the twelve month period beginning of the day after the close of the Plan Year.

2.6.5   Distribution of Excess Elective Deferrals. A Participant may assign to the Plan any Excess Elective Deferrals made during a taxable year of the Participant by notifying the Plan Administrator on or before March 15 of each calendar year of the amount of the Excess Elective Deferrals to be assigned to the Plan.

Notwithstanding any other provision of the Plan, Excess Elective Deferrals, plus any income and minus any loss allocable thereto, shall be distributed no later than April 15 to any Participant to whose account Excess Elective Deferrals were assigned for the preceding year and who claims Excess Elective Deferrals for such taxable year.

Excess Elective Deferrals shall be adjusted for any income or loss up to the date of distribution. The income or loss allocable to Excess Elective Deferrals is the sum of: (1) income or loss allocable to the Participant's elective deferrals for the taxable year multiplied by a fraction, the numerator of which is such Participant's Excess Elective Deferrals for the year and the denominator is the Participant's Account balance attributable to Elective Deferrals without regard to any income or loss occurring during such taxable year; and (2) ten percent of the amount determined under (1) multiplied by the number of whole calendar months between the end of the Participant's taxable year and the date of distribution, counting the month of distribution if distribution occurs after the 15th of such month.

2.6.6   Distribution of Excess Contributions. Notwithstanding any other provision of this Plan, Excess Contributions, plus any income and minus any loss allocable thereto, shall be distributed no later than the last day of each Plan Year to Participants to whose Accounts such Excess Contributions were allocated for the preceding Plan Year. If such excess amounts are distributed more than 2-$\frac{1}{2}$ months after the last day of the Plan Year in which such excess amounts arose, a ten (10) percent excise tax will be imposed on the Employer maintaining the Plan with respect to such amounts. Such distributions shall be made to Highly Compensated Employees on the basis of the respective portions of the Excess Contributions attributable to each of such Employees. Excess Contributions shall be allocated to Participants who are subject to the family member aggregation rules of Section 414(q)(6) of the Code in the manner prescribed by the regulations.

Excess Contributions shall be adjusted for any income or loss up to the date of distribution. The income or loss allocable to Excess Contributions is the sum of: (1) income or loss allocable to the Participant's Elective Contribution Account and the Qualified Non-Elective contributions, if applicable, for the Plan Year multiplied by a fraction, the numerator of which is such Participant's Excess Contributions for the year and the denominator is the Participant's Account balance attributable to Elective Contributions (and Qualified Non-Elective Contributions, if any of such contributions are included in the ADP test) without regard to any income or loss occurring during such Plan Year; and (2) ten percent of the amount determined under (1) multiplied by the number of whole calendar months between the end of the Plan Year and the date of distribution, counting the month of distribution if distribution occurs after the 15th of such month.

Excess Contributions shall be distributed from the Participant's Elective Contribution Account in proportion to the Participant's Elective Deferrals for the Plan Year. Excess Contributions attributable to Qualified Non-Elective Contributions shall be distributed from the Participant's Employer Account only to the extent that such Excess Contributions exceed the balance in the Participant's Elective Contribution Account.

2.6.7   Distribution of Excess Aggregate Contributions. Notwithstanding any other provision of this Plan, Excess Aggregate Contributions, plus any income and minus any loss allocable thereto, shall be forfeited, if forfeitable, or if not forfeitable, distributed no later than the last day of each Plan Year to Participants to whose accounts such Excess Aggregate Contributions were allocated for the preceding Plan Year. Excess Aggregate Contributions shall be allocated to Participants who are subject to the family member aggregation rules of Section 414(q)(6) of the Code in the manner prescribed by the regulations. If such Excess Aggregate Contributions are distributed more than 2-$\frac{1}{2}$ months after the last day of the Plan Year in which such excess amounts arose, a ten (10) percent excise tax will be imposed on the Employer maintaining the Plan with respect to those amounts.

Excess Aggregate Contributions shall be adjusted for any income or loss up to the date of distribution. The income or loss allocable to Excess Aggregate Contributions is the sum of: (1) income or loss allocable to the Participant's Voluntary Account, Matching Account (if any, and if all amounts therein are not used in the ADP test) and, if applicable, Elective Contribution Account for the Plan Year multiplied by a fraction, the numerator of which is such Participant's Excess Aggregate Contributions for the year and the denominator is the Participant's Account balance(s) attributable to contribution percentage amounts without regard to any income or loss occurring during such Plan Year; and (2) ten percent of the amount determined under (1) multiplied by the number of whole calendar months between the end of the Plan Year and the date of distribution, counting the month of distribution if distribution occurs after the 15th of such month.

Forfeitures of Excess Aggregate Contributions may either be reallocated to the accounts of Employees who are not Highly Compensated Employees or applied to reduce Employer Contributions, as elected by the Employer in the Adoption Agreement.

Excess Aggregate Contributions shall be forfeited, if forfeitable or distributed on a pro-rata basis from the Participant's Matching Account and Voluntary Account (and, if applicable, the Participant's Elective Contribution Account).

2.6.8   Limitation on Distributions. Except as otherwise provided in this Article, Elective Deferrals and Qualified Non-Elective Contributions and income allocable thereto are not distributable to a Participant or his or her Beneficiary in accordance with such Participant's or Beneficiary's election prior to separation from service, death or disability.

2.6.9   Limitation on Elective Deferrals. No Participant shall be permitted to have Elective Deferrals made under this Plan, or any other qualified plan maintained by the Employer, during any taxable year, in excess of the dollar limitation contained in Section 402(g) of the Code in effect at the beginning of such taxable year.

ARTICLE VII
CONTINGENT TOP-HEAVY PROVISIONS

2.7.1   Top-Heavy Requirements. If the Plan becomes a Top-Heavy Plan during any Plan Year, the following provisions shall supersede any conflicting provisions in the Plan or Adoption Agreement and apply for such Plan Year:

(a) Except as otherwise provided below, the Employer contributions and forfeitures allocated on behalf of any Participant who is not a Key Employee shall not be less than the lesser of three percent of such Participant's Compensation or in the case where the Employer has no defined benefit plan which designates this plan to satisfy Section 401 of the Code, the largest percentage of Employer contributions and forfeitures, as a percentage of the first $200,000 of the Key Employee's compensation, allocated on behalf of any Key Employee for that year. The minimum allocation is determined without regard to any Social Security contribution. This minimum allocation shall be made even though, under other plan provisions, the Participant would not otherwise be entitled to receive an allocation, or would have received a lesser allocation for the year because of (i) the Participant's failure to complete 1,000 Hours of Service (or any equivalent provided in the plan), or (ii) the Participant's failure to make mandatory employee contributions to the plan, or (iii) compensation less than a stated amount.

For purposes of computing the minimum allocation, Compensation shall mean a Participant's W-2 compensation, calculated in the manner provided in Section 1.2.10 of the Plan and the Adoption Agreement.

The minimum allocation provided above shall not apply to any Participant who was not employed by the Employer on the last day of the Plan Year.

The minimum allocation provided above shall not apply to any Participant to the extent the Participant is covered under any other plan or plans of the Employer and Employer has provided in the Adoption Agreement that the minimum allocation or benefit requirement applicable to top-heavy plans will be met in the other plan or plans.

(b) The vested and nonforfeitable interest of each Participant shall be equal to the percentage determined under the vesting schedule specified in the Adoption Agreement if the Plan becomes a Top-Heavy Plan, or if no vesting schedule is specified, the percentage determined under the following schedule:

Years of Service	Percentage
Less than 2	0%
2	20%
3	40%
4	60%
5	80%
6 or more	100%

The top-heavy minimum vesting schedule applies to all benefits within the meaning of Section 411(a)(7) of the Code, except those attributable to employee contributions, including benefits accrued before the effective date of Section 416 of the Code and benefits accrued before the Plan becomes top-heavy.

If the Plan ceases to be a Top-Heavy Plan, the vesting which occurs while the Plan is a Top-Heavy Plan shall not be cutback. Any minimum allocation required (to the extent required to be nonforfeitable under Section 416(b)) may not be forfeited under Section 411(a)(3)(B) or (D) of the Code.

2.7.2   Top-Heavy Definitions. The following terms, as used in this Plan, shall have the following meaning:

(a) "Key Employee": An Employee or former employee who, at any time during the Determination Period is either:

(i)   an officer of the Employer having an Annual Compensation greater than fifty (50%) percent of the amount in effect under Section 415(b)(1)(A) of the Code;

(ii) an owner (or a person considered an owner under Section 318 of the Code) of one of the ten largest interests in the Employer if such individual's Annual Compensation from the Employer is more than the limitation in effect under Section 415(c)(1)(A) of the Code;

(iii) any person who owns directly or indirectly more than five (5%) percent of the outstanding stock of the Employer or stock possessing more than five (5%) percent of the total combined voting power of all stock of the Employer or, in the case of an unincorporated Employer, the capital or profits interest in the Employer;

(iv) any person who owns directly or indirectly more than one (1%) percent of the outstanding stock of the Employer or stock possessing more than one (1%) percent of the total combined voting power of all stock of the Employer or, in the case of an unincorporated Employer, the capital or profits interest in the Employer and having an Annual Compensation from the Employer of more than $150,000; or

(v) any beneficiary of a Key Employee.

The determination of who is a Key Employee shall be made in accordance with Section 416(i)(1) of the Code and the regulations thereunder.

(b) "Aggregation Group": Each qualified retirement plan of the Employer in which a Key Employee is a participant and each other qualified retirement plan of the Employer which enables any plan in which a Key Employee is a participant to meet the requirements of Section 401(a)(4) or Section 410 of the Code.

(c) "Annual Compensation": Compensation as defined in Section 415(c)(3) of the Code, but including amounts contributed by the

Employer pursuant to a salary reduction agreement which are excludible from the Employee's gross income under Section 125, Section 402(a)(8), Section 402(h) or Section 403(b) of the Code.

(d) "Top-Heavy Plan": For any Plan Year beginning after December 31, 1983, the plan is top-heavy if any of the following conditions exists:

(i) If the top-heavy ratio for the plan exceeds 60 percent and the plan is not part of any required aggregation group or permissive aggregation group of plans.

(ii) If the plan is a part of a required aggregation group of plans but not part of a permissive aggregation group and the top-heavy ratio for the group of plans exceeds 60 percent.

(iii) If the plan is a part of a required aggregation group and part of a permissive aggregation group of plans and the top-heavy ratio for the permissive aggregation group exceeds 60 percent.

(e) "Top-Heavy Ratio":

(i) If the Employer maintains one or more defined contribution plans (including any simplified employee pension plan) and the Employer has not maintained any defined benefit plan which during the 5-year period ending on the Determination Date(s) has or has had accrued benefits, the top-heavy ratio for this plan alone or for the required or permissive aggregation group as appropriate is a fraction, the numerator of which is the sum of the account balances of all Key Employees as of the Determination Date(s) (including any part of any account balance distributed in the 5-year period ending on the Determination Date(s)), and the denominator of which is the sum of all account balances (including any part of any account balance distributed in the 5-year period ending on the Determination Date(s)), both computed in accordance with Section 416 of the Code and the regulations thereunder. Both the numerator and denominator of the top-heavy ratio are increased to reflect any contribution not actually made as of the Determination Date, but which is required to be taken into account on that date under Section 416 of the Code and the regulations thereunder.

(ii) If the Employer maintains one or more defined contribution plans (including any simplified employee pension plan) and the Employer maintains or has maintained one or more defined benefit plans which during the 5-year period ending on the Determination Date(s) has or has had any accrued benefits, the top-heavy ratio for any required or permissive aggregation group as appropriate is a fraction, the numerator of which is the sum of account balances under the aggregated defined contribution plan or plans for all Key Employees, determined in accordance with (i) above, and the present value of accrued benefits under the aggregated defined benefit plan or plans for all Key Employees as of the Determination Date(s), and the denominator of which is the sum of the account balances under the aggregated defined contribution plan or plans for all Participants, determined in accordance with (i) above, and the present value of accrued benefits under the defined benefit plan or plans for all Participants as of the Determination Date(s), all determined in accordance with Section 416 of the Code and the regulations thereunder. The accrued benefits under a defined benefit plan in both the numerator and denominator of the top-heavy ratio are increased for any distribution of an accrued benefit made in the five-year period ending on the Determination Date.

(iii) For purposes of (i) and (ii) above, the value of account balances and the present value of accrued benefits will be determined as of the most recent valuation date that falls within or ends with the 12-month period ending on the Determination Date, except as provided in Section 416 of the Code and the regulations thereunder for the first and second Plan Years of a defined benefit plan. The account balances and accrued benefits of a Participant (1) who is not a Key Employee but was a Key Employee in a prior year, or (2) who has not been credited with at least one hour of service with any Employer maintaining the plan at any time during the 5-year period ending on the Determination Date will be disregarded. The calculation of the top-heavy ratio, and the extent to which distributions, rollovers, and transfers are taken into account will be made in accordance with Section 416 of the Code and the regulations thereunder. Deductible employee contributions will not be taken into account for purposes of computing the top-heavy ratio. When aggregating plans, the value of account balances and accrued benefits will be calculated with reference to the Determination Dates that fall within the same calendar year.

The accrued benefit of a Participant other than a Key Employee shall be determined under (a) the method, if any, that uniformly applies for accrual purposes under all defined benefit plans maintained by the Employer, or (b) if there is no such method, as if such benefit accrued not more rapidly than the slowest accrual rate permitted under the fractional rule of Section 411(b)(1)(C) of the Code.

(f) "Permissive Aggregation Group": The required aggregation group of plans plus any other plan or plans of the Employer which, when considered as a group with the required aggregation group, would continue to satisfy the requirements of Sections 401(a)(4) and 410 of the Code.

(g) "Required Aggregation Group":

(i)   Each qualified plan of the Employer in which at least one Key Employee participates or participated at any time during the Determination Period (regardless of whether the plan has terminated).

(ii) Any other qualified plan of the Employer which enables a plan described in (i) to meet the requirements of Sections 401(a)(4) or 410 of the Code.

(h) "Determination Date": For any plan year subsequent to the first plan year, the last day of the preceding plan year. For the first plan year of the plan, the last day of that year.

(i) "Valuation Date": The date elected by the Employer in the Adoption Agreement as of which account balances or accrued benefits are valued for purposes of calculating the top-heavy ratio.

(j) "Present Value": Present value shall be based only on the interest and mortality rates specified in the Adoption Agreement.

(k) "Determination Period": The Plan Year containing the Determination Date and the four (4) preceding Plan Years.

PART III

ARTICLE I
ACCOUNTING

3.1.1   Accounts. All income, profits, recoveries, contributions and any and all monies, securities and properties of any kind at any time received or held by the Trustee shall be held as a commingled Trust Fund, except to the extent such assets are transferred to a Segregated Fund or Controlled Fund. For accounting purposes, the Plan Administrator shall establish and maintain certain Accounts for each Participant. An Employer Account shall be established and maintained for each Participant to which shall be added the Participant's share of Non-Elective Contributions and forfeitures. A Matching Account shall be established and maintained for each Participant to which shall be added the Participant's share of Matching Contributions and forfeitures. A Qualified Non-Elective Contribution Account shall be established and maintained for each Participant to which shall be added the Participant's share of Qualified Non-Elective Contributions. If a Participant has previously made voluntary nondeductible employee contributions, the Plan Administrator shall establish and maintain a Voluntary Account for the Participant. If, in accordance with any of the provisions of the Plan, assets are either deposited initially or transferred to a Segregated Fund for the benefit of a Participant, the Plan Administrator shall establish and maintain a Segregated Account for the Participant. If a Participant elects to exercise investment control over all or a portion of his Accounts, the Plan Administrator shall establish and maintain a Controlled Account for the Participant.

3.1.2   Adjustments. As of each Valuation Date, each Participant's Accounts shall be adjusted in the following order and manner.

(a) Distributions. Any distribution made to or on behalf of a Participant since the last preceding Valuation Date shall be deducted from the Participant's Account from which the distribution was made.

(b) Insurance Premiums. Payments made since the last preceding Valuation Date for Life Insurance Policies on the life of a Participant (including without limitation payments of premiums and interest on policy loans) shall be deducted from the Account of the Participant from which the payment was made.

(c) Adjustment to Fair Market Value. The value of all monies, securities and other property in the Trust Fund, excluding Life Insurance Policies, shall be appraised by the Trustee at the then fair market value. In determining such value, all income and contributions, if any, received by the Trustee from the Employer or Participants on account of such Year calculated under the method of accounting of the Trust shall be included and there shall be deducted all expenses determined in accordance with the method of accounting adopted by the Plan Administrator.

If the total net value of the Trust Fund so determined exceeds (or is less than) the total amount in the affected Accounts of all Participants, the excess (or deficiency) shall be added to (or deducted from) the respective Accounts of all Participants in the ratio that each such Participant's Account bears to the total amount in all such Accounts.

(d) Adjustment of Segregated and Controlled Accounts. The value of all monies, securities and other property in each Participant's Segregated Account or Controlled Account, if any, but exclusive of Life Insurance Policies, shall be appraised by the Trustee at the then fair market value. In determining such value, all income calculated under the method of accounting of the Trust shall be included and all expenses shall be deducted.

If the total net value of a Participant's Segregated Account or Controlled Account, as the case may be, so determined exceeds (or is less than) the previous balance in such Account, the excess (or deficiency) shall be added to (or deducted from) the Participant's respective Account.

(e) Insurance Dividends. Dividends or credits received since the last preceding Valuation Date on any Life Insurance Policy on the life of a Participant shall be added to the Account of the Participant from which the premiums for such Life Insurance Policy have been paid.

(f) Contributions and Forfeitures. Each Participant's Account shall be increased by that portion of the contribution and forfeitures which is allocated to him.

(g) Transfers to Segregated or Controlled Funds. To the extent that funds in the Trust Fund attributable to a Participant's Accounts were transferred since the last preceding Valuation Date or are to be transferred to either a Segregated Fund or Controlled Fund pursuant to any of the provisions of the Plan, the Account from which the funds were transferred shall be decreased and the Account to which the funds were transferred shall be increased.

(h) Transfers From Segregated or Controlled Funds. To the extent that funds are transferred from a Segregated Fund and/or Controlled Fund of a Participant to the Trust Fund pursuant to any of the provisions of the Plan, the Account from which the funds were transferred shall be decreased and the Account to which the funds were transferred shall be increased.

(i) Time of Adjustments. Every adjustment to be made pursuant to this Section shall be considered as having been made as of the applicable Valuation Date regardless of the actual dates of entries, receipt by the Trustee of contributions by the Participant or the Employer for such Year, or the transfers of funds to or from Controlled Funds or Segregated Funds. The Trustee's determination as to valuation of trust assets and charges or credits to the individual Accounts of the respective Participants shall be conclusive and binding on all persons. If funds are transferred from the Trust Fund to a Controlled Fund as of any date other than a Valuation Date pursuant to the terms of the Plan, the adjustment to be made pursuant to this Section shall be made as of the date as of which such transfer is made, as if such date is a Valuation Date.

If any Participant receives a distribution pursuant to the terms of the Plan as of any date other than a Valuation Date, then the adjustments to be made pursuant to this Section shall be made in the manner specified in the Adoption Agreement.

ARTICLE II
LIMITATIONS

3.2.1   Limitations on Annual Additions. If the Participant does not participate in, and has never participated in another qualified plan maintained by the Employer or a welfare benefit fund as defined in Section 419(e) of the Code maintained by the Employer, or an individual medical account, as defined in Section 415(l)(2) of the Code, maintained by the Employer, which provides an annual addition, subject to the adjustments hereinafter set forth, the amount of annual additions which may be credited to a Participant's Accounts during any Limitation Year shall in no event exceed the lesser of (a) thirty thousand dollars ($30,000.00) or, if greater, one-fourth of the dollar limitation in effect under Section 415(b)(1)(A) of the Code as in effect for the Limitation Year or (b) twenty-five percent (25%) of the Participant's Compensation for the Plan Year. The compensation limitation referred to in (b) shall not apply to any contribution for medical benefits (within the meaning of Section 401(h) or Section 419A(f)(2) of the Code) which is otherwise treated as an annual addition under Section 415(l)(1) or 419A(d)(2) of the Code. If the Employer contribution that would otherwise be contributed or allocated to the Participant's Account would cause the annual additions for the Limitation Year to exceed the maximum permissible amount, the amount contributed or allocated shall be reduced so that the annual additions for the Limitation Year shall equal the maximum permissible amount. For these purposes, the maximum permissible amount is the maximum annual additions permitted on behalf of a Participant.

(a) Annual Additions. The term "annual additions" shall mean the sum of the following amounts credited to a Participant's Accounts for the Limitation Year;

(i)   Employer contributions;

(ii)   Employee contributions;

(iii) Forfeitures;

(iv) Amounts allocated after March 31, 1984, to an individual medical account, as defined in Section 415(l)(2) of the Code, which is part of a pension or annuity plan maintained by the Employer and amounts derived from contributions paid or accrued after December 31, 1985, in taxable years ending after such date, which are attributable to post-retirement medical benefits, allocated to the separate account of a key employee, as defined in Section 419A(d)(3) of the Code, under a welfare benefit fund as defined in Section 419(e) of the Code maintained by the Employer; and

(v) Excess Elective Deferrals, Excess Contributions and Excess Aggregate Contributions.

Any excess amounts applied under subsections (b) and (c) below to reduce Employer contributions are considered annual additions for such Limitation Year.

(b) Excessive Annual Additions. Prior to determining a Participant's actual Compensation for a Limitation Year, the Employer may determine the maximum permissible Annual Addition for the Participant on the basis of a reasonable estimation of the Participant's Compensation for the Limitation Year, uniformly determined for all Participant's similarly situated. As soon as is administratively feasible after the end of the Limitation Year, the maximum permissible amount for the Limitation Year shall be determined on the basis of the Participant's actual Compensation for the Limitation Year. Any Excessive Annual Addition attributable to nondeductible voluntary employee contributions made by a Participant to the extent they reduce the excess amount shall be returned to the Participant before any other adjustments are made.

If an excess amount still exists, and the Participant is covered by the Plan at the end of the Limitation Year, the excess amount in the Participant's Account shall be used to reduce Employer contributions (including any allocation of forfeitures) for such Participant in the next Limitation Year, and each succeeding Limitation Year, if necessary. If an excess amount still exists, and the Participant is not covered by the Plan at the end of a Limitation Year, the excess amount shall be held unallocated in a suspense account. The suspense account shall be applied to reduce future Employer contributions for all remaining Participants in the next Limitation Year, and each succeeding Limitation Year, if necessary.

If a suspense account is in existence at any time during a particular Limitation Year, all amounts in the suspense account must be allocated and reallocated to Participants' Accounts before any Employer or any Employee contributions may be made to the Plan for that Limitation Year. Excess amounts may not be distributed to Participants or former Participants. If a suspense account is in existence at any time during a Limitation Year, it shall not participate in the allocation of the Trust's investment gains and losses.

(c) Participation in Certain Other Plans. If in addition to this Plan, the Participant is covered under another qualified regional prototype defined contribution plan maintained by the Employer, a welfare benefit fund, as defined in Section 419(e) of the code maintained by the Employer, or an individual medical account, as defined in Section 415(l)(2) of the Code, maintained by the Employer, which provides an

Annual Addition during any Limitation Year, the annual additions which may be credited to a Participant's account under this Plan for any such Limitation Year shall not exceed the maximum permissible amount reduced by the Annual Additions credited to a Participant's Account under the other plans and welfare benefit funds for the same Limitation Year. If the Annual Additions with respect to the Participant under other defined contribution plans and welfare benefit funds maintained by the Employer are less than the maximum permissible amount and the Employer contribution that would otherwise be contributed or allocated to the Participant's Account under this Plan would cause the Annual Additions for the Limitation Year to exceed this limitation, the amount contributed or allocated shall be reduced so that the Annual Additions under all such plans and funds for the Limitation Year shall equal the maximum permissible amount. If the Annual Additions with respect to the Participant under such other defined contribution plans and welfare benefit funds in the aggregate are equal to or greater than the maximum permissible amount, no amount will be contributed or allocated to the Participant's Account under this Plan for the Limitation Year.

Prior to determining the Participant's actual Compensation for the Limitation Year, the Employer may determine the maximum permissible amount for a Participant in the manner described in subsection (b) above. As soon as is administratively feasible after the end of the Limitation Year, the maximum permissible amount for the Limitation Year shall be determined on the basis of the Participant's actual Compensation for the Limitation Year.

If a Participant's Annual Additions under this Plan and such other plans would result in an excess amount for a Limitation Year, the excess amount shall be deemed to consist of the Annual Additions last allocated, except that Annual Additions attributable to a welfare benefit fund or individual medical account will be deemed to have been allocated first regardless of the actual allocation date.

If the excess amount was allocated to a Participant on an allocation date of this Plan which coincides with an allocation date of another plan, the excess amount attributed to this Plan will be the product of:

(i) the total excess amount allocated as of such date, times

(ii) the ratio of (I) the Annual Additions allocated to the Participant for the Limitation Year as of such date under this Plan to (II) the total Annual Additions allocated to the Participant for the Limitation Year as of such date under this and all the other qualified regional prototype defined contribution plans. Any excess amount attributed to this Plan will be disposed in the manner described in subsection (b), above

If the Participant is covered under another qualified defined contribution plan maintained by the Employer which is not a regional prototype plan, Annual Additions which may be credited to the Participant's Account under this Plan for any Limitation Year shall be limited as provided above as though the other plan were a regional prototype plan unless the Employer specifies other limitations in the Adoption Agreement.

For purposes hereof, the excess amount is the excess of the Participant's annual additions for the Limitation Year over the maximum permissible amount and a regional prototype plan is a plan the form of which is the subject of a favorable opinion letter from the Internal Revenue Service.

If the Employer maintains, or at any time maintained, a qualified defined benefit plan covering any Participant in this Plan, the sum of the Participant's defined benefit plan fraction and defined contribution plan fraction will not exceed 1.0 in any Limitation Year. The Annual Additions which may be credited to the Participant's account under this Plan for any Limitation Year shall be limited in the manner specified in the Adoption Agreement.

(d) Combined Plan Limitation. In the event that a Participant in this Plan participates in a defined benefit plan (as defined in the applicable sections of the Code) maintained by the Employer, the sum of the "defined benefit plan fraction" plus the "defined contribution plan fraction" shall at no time exceed 1.0. Except to the extent that applicable law permits greater amounts to be provided on behalf of a Participant, in which event such law is hereby incorporated by reference, the foregoing fractions are defined as follows. The "defined benefit plan fraction" for any year is a fraction (i) the numerator of which is the projected annual benefit of the Participant under all the defined benefit plans (whether or not terminated) maintained by the Employer (determined as of the close of the year), and (ii) the denominator of which is the lesser of (A) the product of 1.25 multiplied by the dollar limitation determined for the Limitation Year under Sections 415(b) and (d) of the Code, or (B) the product of 1.4 multiplied by one hundred (100%) percent of the Participant's average compensation for the three (3) consecutive Years of Service with the Employer that produces the highest average, including any adjustments under Section 415(b) of the Code. Notwithstanding the above, if the Participant was a Participant as of the first day of the first Limitation Year beginning after December 31, 1986, in one or more defined benefit plans maintained by the Employer which were in existence on May 6, 1986, the denominator of this fraction shall not be less than 125 percent of the sum of the annual benefits under such plans which the Participant had accrued as of the close of the last Limitation Year beginning before January 1, 1987, disregarding any changes in the terms and conditions of the Plan after May 5, 1986. The preceding sentence applies only if the defined benefit plans individually and in the aggregate satisfied the requirements of Section 415 for all Limitation Years beginning before January 1, 1987. The "defined contribution fraction" for any year is a fraction (i) the numerator of which is the sum of the annual additions to the Participant's accounts under all defined contribution plans (whether or not terminated) maintained by the Employer for the current and all prior Limitation Years, including the annual additions attributable to the Participant's nondeductible employee contributions to all defined benefit plans, whether or not terminated, maintained by the Employer, and the annual additions attributable to all welfare benefit funds and individual medical accounts (as defined in Sections 419(e) and 415(l)(2) of the Code) maintained by the Employer, and (ii) the denominator of which is the sum of the lesser of the following amounts determined for the current year and all prior limitation years of service with the Employer, regardless of whether a defined contribution plan was maintained by the Employer: (A) the product of 1.25 multiplied by the dollar limitation determined under Sections 415(b) and (d) of the Code in effect under Section 415(c)(1)(A) of the Code, or (B) thirty-five (35%) percent of the Participant's compensation from the Employer for such plan year. If the Employee was a Participant as of the end of the first day of the first Limitation Year beginning after December 31, 1986, in one or more defined contribution plans maintained by the Employer which were in existence on May 6, 1986, the numerator of this fraction will be adjusted if the sum of this fraction and the defined benefit fraction would otherwise exceed 1.0 under the terms of this Plan. Under the adjustment, an amount equal to the product of (1) the excess of the sum of the fractions over 1.0 times (2) the denominator of this fraction, shall be permanently subtracted from the numerator of this fraction. The adjustment is calculated using the fractions as they would be computed as of the end of the last Limitation Year beginning before January 1, 1987, and disregarding any changes in the terms and conditions of the Plan made after May 5, 1986, but using the Section 415 limitation applicable to the first Limitation Year beginning on or after January 1, 1987.

The annual addition for any Limitation Year beginning before January 1, 1987, shall not be recomputed to treat all employee contributions as annual additions.

The projected annual benefits under a defined benefit plan is the annual retirement benefit (adjusted to an actuarially equivalent straight life annuity if such benefit is expressed in a form other than a straight life annuity) or qualified joint and survivor annuity to which the Participant would be entitled under the terms of the Plan assuming the Participant continues employment until normal retirement age under the plan (or current age, if later), and the Participant's compensation for the current Limitation Year and all other relevant factors used to determine benefits under the Plan remain constant for all future Limitation Years.

(e) Special Transition Rule for Defined Contribution Fraction. At the election of the Plan Administrator, in applying the provisions of subsection (d) above with respect to the defined contribution plan fraction for any year ending after December 31, 1982, the amount taken into account for the denominator for each Participant for all years ending before January 1, 1983 shall be an amount equal to the product of the amount of the denominator determined under subsection (d) above for the year ending in 1982, multiplied by the "transition fraction." The "transition fraction" is a fraction (i) the numerator of which is the lesser of (A) $51,875 or (B) 1.4 multiplied by twenty-five (25%) percent of the Participant's compensation for the year ending in 1981, and (ii) the denominator of which is the lesser of (A) $41,500 or (B) twenty-five (25%) percent of the Participant's compensation for the year ending in 1981.

(f) Special Transition Rule for Excess Benefits. Provided that the Plan satisfied the requirements of Section 415 of the Code for the last Plan Year beginning before January 1, 1983, an amount shall be subtracted from the numerator of the defined contribution plan fraction (not exceeding such numerator) so that the sum of the defined benefit plan fraction and the defined contribution fraction computed in accordance with Section 415(e)(l) of the Code (as amended by the Tax Equity and Fiscal Responsibility Act of 1982) does not exceed 1.0 for such year, in accordance with regulations issued by the Secretary of the Treasury pursuant to the applicable provisions of the Code.

(g) Employer. For purposes of this Section, employer shall mean the Employer that adopts this Plan and all members of a group of employers which constitutes a controlled group of corporations or trades or businesses under common control (as defined in Sections 414(b) and (c) of the Code, as modified by Section 415(h) of the Code), or an affiliated service group (as defined in Section 414(m) of the Code) of which the adopting employer is a part and any other entity required to be aggregated with the Employer under Section 414(o) of the Code and the regulations issued thereunder.

(h) Compensation. For purposes of this Section as elected in the Adoption Agreement by the Employer, Compensation shall mean all of a Participant's:

(i) Section 3121 Wages. Wages as defined in Section 3121(a) of the Code for purposes of calculating social security taxes, but determined without regard to the wage base limitation in Section 3121(a)(1), the limitations on the exclusions from wages in Section 3121(a)(5)(C) and (D) for elective contributions and payments by reason of salary reduction agreements, the special rules in Section 3121(v), any rules that limit covered employment based on the type or location of an employee's employer and any rules that limit the remuneration included in wages based on familial relationship or based on the nature or location of the employment or the services performed (such as the exceptions to the definition of employment in Section 3121(b)(1) through (20) of the Code).

(ii) Section 3401(a) Wages. Wages as defined in Section 3401(a) of the Code for the purposes of income tax withholding at the source but determined without regard to any rules that limit the remuneration included in wages based on the nature or location of the employment or the services performed (such as the exception for agricultural labor in Section 3401(a)(2) of the Code).

(iii) Section 415 Safe-harbor Compensation. Wages, salaries and fees for professional services and other amounts received for personal services actually rendered in the course of employment for the Employer (including but not limited to commissions paid salesmen, compensation for services on the basis of a percentage of profits, commissions on insurance premiums, tips, bonuses, fringe benefits, reimbursements and expense allowances), but excluding:

(I) Employer contributions to a plan of deferred compensation which are not includible in the Employee's gross income for the taxable year in which contributed, or employer contributions under a simplified employee pension plan to the extent such contributions are deductible by the Employee or any distributions from a plan of deferred compensation;

(II) Amounts realized from the exercise of a non-qualified stock option or when restricted stock or property held by the Employee is no longer subject to a substantial risk of forfeiture or becomes freely transferable.

(III) Amounts realized from the sale, exchange or other disposition of stock acquired under an incentive stock option; and

(IV) Other amounts which received special tax benefits or contributions made by the Employer (whether or not under a salary reduction agreement) towards the purchase of an annuity described in Section 403(b) of the Code (whether or not the amounts are actually excludible from the gross income of the Employee).

For any self-employed individual, compensation shall mean earned income. For Limitation Years beginning after December 31, 1991, for purposes of applying the limitations of this Article, Compensation for a Limitation Year is the Compensation actually paid or includible in gross income during such Limitation Year.

(i) Short Limitation Year. If the Limitation Year is amended to a different twelve (12) consecutive month period, the new Limitation Year must begin within the Limitation Year in which the amendment is made. If a short Limitation Year is created because of an amendment changing the Limitation Year to a different twelve (12) consecutive month period, the maximum annual addition shall not exceed the defined contribution dollar limitation determined in accordance with Section 415(c)(1)(A) of the Code then in effect multiplied by a fraction, the numerator of which is the number of months in the short Limitation Year and the denominator of which is twelve (12).

3.2.2   Controlled Businesses. If this plan provides contributions or benefits for one or more owner-employees who control both the business for which this plan is established and one or more other trades or businesses, this plan and the plan established for other trades or businesses must, when looked at as a single plan, satisfy Sections 401(a) and (d) for the employees of this and all other trades or businesses.

If the plan provides contributions or benefits for one or more owner-employees who control one or more other trades or businesses, the employees of the other trades or businesses must be included in a plan which satisfies sections 401(a) and (d) and which provides contributions and benefits not less favorable than provided for owner-employees under this plan.

If an individual is covered as an owner-employee under the plans of two or more trades or businesses which are not controlled and the individual controls a trade or business, then the contributions or benefits of the employees under the plan of the trades or businesses which are controlled must be as favorable as those provided for him under the most favorable plan of the trade or business which is not controlled.

For purposes of the preceding paragraphs, an owner-employee, or two or more owner-employees, will be considered to control a trade or business if the owner-employee, or two or more owner-employees together:

(a) own the entire interest in an unincorporated trade or business, or

(b) in the case of a partnership, own more than 50 percent of either the capital interest or the profits interest in the partnership.

For purposes of the preceding sentence, an owner-employee, or two or more owner-employees shall be treated as owning any interest in a partnership which is owned, directly or indirectly, by a partnership which such owner-employee, or such two or more owner-employees, are considered to control within the meaning of the preceding sentence.

ARTICLE III
FIDUCIARIES

3.3.1   Standard of Conduct. The duties and responsibilities of the Plan Administrator and the Trustee with respect to the Plan shall be discharged (a) in a non-discriminatory manner; (b) for the exclusive benefit of Participants and their Beneficiaries; (c) by defraying the reasonable expenses of administering the Plan; (d) with the care, skill, prudence, and diligence under the circumstances then prevailing that a prudent man acting in a like capacity and familiar with such matters would use in the conduct of an enterprise of a like character and with like aims; (e) by diversifying the investments of the Plan so as to minimize the risk of large losses, unless under the circumstances it is clearly prudent not to do so; and (f) in accordance with the documents and instruments governing the Plan insofar as such documents and instruments are consistent with the provisions of the Act.

3.3.2   Individual Fiduciaries. At any time that a group of individuals is acting as Plan Administrator or Trustee, the number of such persons who shall act in such capacity from time to time shall be determined by the Employer. Such persons shall be appointed by the Employer and may or may not be Participants or Employees of the Employer. Any action taken by a group of individuals acting as either Plan Administrator or Trustee shall be taken at the direction of a majority of such persons, or, if the number of such persons is two (2), by unanimous consent.

3.3.3   Disqualification from Service. No person shall be permitted to serve as a Fiduciary, custodian, counsel, agent or employee of the Plan or as a consultant to the Plan who has been convicted of any of the criminal offenses specified in the Act.

3.3.4   Bonding. Except as otherwise permitted by law, each Fiduciary or person who handles funds or other property or assets of the Plan shall be bonded in accordance with the requirements of the Act.

3.3.5   Prior Acts. No Fiduciary shall be liable for any acts occurring prior to the period of time during which the Fiduciary was actually serving in such capacity with respect to the Plan.

3.3.6   Insurance and Indemnity. The Employer may purchase or cause the Trustee to purchase and keep current as an authorized expense liability insurance for the Plan, its Fiduciaries, and any other person to whom any financial or other administrative responsibility with respect to the Plan and Trust is allocated or delegated, from and against any and all liabilities, costs and expenses incurred by such persons as a result of any act or omission to act in connection with the performance of the duties, responsibilities and obligations under the Plan and under the Act; provided that any such insurance policy purchased with Plan assets permits subrogation by the Insurer against the Fiduciary in the case of breach by such Fiduciary. Unless otherwise determined and communicated to affected parties by the Employer, the Employer shall indemnify and hold harmless each such person, other than a corporate trustee, for and from any such liabilities, costs and expenses which are not covered by any such insurance, except to the extent that any such liabilities, costs or expenses are judicially determined to be due to the gross negligence or willful misconduct of such person. No Plan assets may be used for any such indemnification.

3.3.7   Expenses. Expenses incurred by the Plan Administrator or the Trustee in the administration of the Plan and the Trust, including fees for legal services rendered, such compensation to the Trustee as may be agreed upon in writing from time to time between the Employer and the Trustee, and all other proper charges and expenses of the Plan Administrator or the Trustee and of their agents and counsel shall be paid by the Employer, or at its election at any time or from time to time, may be charged against the assets of the Trust, but until so paid shall constitute a charge upon the assets of the Trust. All taxes of any and all kinds whatsoever which may be levied or assessed under existing or future laws upon the assets of the Trust or the income thereof shall be paid from such assets. Notwithstanding the foregoing, no compensation shall be paid to any Employee for services rendered under the Plan and Trust as a Trustee.

3.3.8   Agents, Accountants and Legal Counsel. The Plan Administrator shall have authority to employ suitable agents, custodians, investment counsel, accountants and legal counsel who may, but need not be, legal counsel for the Employer. The Plan Administrator and the Trustee shall be fully protected in acting upon the advice of such persons. The Trustee shall at no time be obliged to institute any legal action or to become a party to any legal action unless the Trustee has been indemnified to the Trustee's satisfaction for any fees, costs and expenses to be incurred in connection therewith.

3.3.9   Investment Manager. The Employer may employ as an investment manager or managers to manage all or any part of the Trust Fund any (i) investment advisor registered under the Investment Advisors Act of 1940; (ii) bank as defined in said Act; or (iii) insurance company qualified to perform investment management services in more than one state. Any investment manager shall have all powers of the Trustee in the management of such part of the Trust Fund, including the power to acquire or dispose of assets. In the event an investment manager is so appointed, the Trustee shall not be liable for the acts or omissions of such investment manager or be under any obligation to invest or otherwise manage that part of the Trust Fund which is subject to the management of the investment manager. The Employer shall notify the Trustee in writing of any appointment of an investment manager, and shall provide the Trustee with the investment manager's written acknowledgment that it is a fiduciary with respect to the Plan.

3.3.10   Finality of Decisions or Acts. Except for the right of a Participant or Beneficiary to appeal the denial of a claim, any decision or action of the Plan Administrator or the Trustee made or done in good faith upon any matter within the scope of authority and discretion of the Plan Administrator or the Trustee shall be final and binding upon all persons. In the event of judicial review of actions taken by any Fiduciary within the scope of his duties in accordance with the terms of the Plan and Trust, such actions shall be upheld unless determined to have been arbitrary and capricious.

3.3.11   Certain Custodial Accounts and Contracts. The term "Trustee" as used herein will also include a person holding the assets of a custodial account, an annuity contract or other contract which is treated as a qualified trust pursuant to Section 401(f) of the Code and references to the Trust Fund shall be construed to apply to such custodial account, annuity contract or other contract.

ARTICLE IV
PLAN ADMINISTRATOR

3.4.1   Administration of Plan. The Plan Administrator shall be designated by the Employer from time to time. The primary responsibility of the Plan Administrator is to administer the Plan for the exclusive benefit of the Participants and their Beneficiaries, subject to the specific terms of the Plan. The Plan Administrator shall administer the Plan and shall construe and determine all questions of interpretation or policy in a manner consistent with the Plan and the Adoption Agreement. The Plan Administrator may correct any defect, supply any omission, or reconcile any inconsistency in such manner and to such extent as he shall deem necessary or advisable to carry out the purpose of the Plan; provided, however, that any interpretation or construction shall be done in a nondiscriminatory manner and shall be consistent with the intent that the Plan shall continue to be a qualified Plan pursuant to the Code, and shall comply with the terms of the Act. The Plan Administrator shall have all powers necessary or appropriate to accomplish his duties under the Plan.

(a) The Plan Administrator shall be charged with the duties of the general administration of the Plan, including but not limited to the following:

(1) To determine all questions relating to the eligibility of an Employee to participate in the Plan or to remain a Participant hereunder.

(2) To compute, certify and direct the Trustee with respect to the amount and kind of benefits to which any Participant shall be entitled hereunder.

(3) To authorize and direct the Trustee with respect to all disbursements from the Trust Fund.

(4) To maintain all the necessary records for the administration of the Plan.

(5) To interpret the provisions of the Plan and to make and publish rules and regulations for the Plan as the Plan Administrator may deem reasonably necessary for the proper and efficient administration of the Plan and consistent with its terms.

(6) To select the insurer to provide any Life Insurance Policy to be purchased for any Participant hereunder.

(7) To advise the Trustee regarding the short and long-term liquidity needs of the Plan in order that the Trustee might direct its investment accordingly.

(8) To advise, counsel and assist any Participant regarding any rights, benefits or elections available under the Plan.

(b) The Plan Administrator shall also be responsible for preparing and filing such annual disclosure reports and tax forms as may be required from time to time by the Secretary of Labor, the Secretary of the Treasury or other governmental authorities.

(c) Whenever it is determined by the Plan Administrator to be in the best interest of the Plan and its Participants or Beneficiaries, the Plan Administrator may request such variances, deferrals, extensions, or exemptions or make such elections for the Plan as may be available under the law.

(d) The Plan Administrator shall be responsible for procuring bonding for all persons dealing with the Plan or its assets as may be required by law.

(e) In the event this Plan is required to file reports or pay premiums to the Pension Benefit Guaranty Corporation, the Plan Administrator shall have the duty to prepare and make such filings, to pay any premiums required, whether for basic or contingent liability coverage, and shall be charged with the responsibility of notifying all necessary parties of such events and under such circumstances as may be required by law.

3.4.2   Disclosure Requirements. Every Participant covered under the Plan and every Beneficiary receiving benefits under the Plan shall receive from the Plan Administrator a summary plan description, and such other information as may be required by law or by the terms of the Plan.

3.4.3   Information Generally Available. The Plan Administrator shall make copies of this Plan and Trust, the Adoption Agreement, the summary plan description, latest annual report, Life Insurance Policies, or other instruments under which the Plan was established or is operated available for examination by any Participant or Beneficiary in the principal office of the Plan Administrator and such other locations as may be necessary to make such information reasonably accessible to all interested parties. Subject to a reasonable charge to defray the cost of furnishing such copies, the Plan Administrator shall, upon written request to any Participant or Beneficiary, furnish a copy of any of the above documents to the respective party.

3.4.4   Statement of Accrued Benefit. Upon written request to the Plan Administrator once during any twelve (12) month period, a Participant or Beneficiary shall be furnished with a written statement, based on the latest available information, of his then vested accrued benefit and the earliest date upon which the same will become fully vested and nonforfeitable. The statement shall also include a notice to the Participant of any benefits which are forfeitable if the Participant dies before a certain date.

3.4.5   Explanation of Rollover Treatment. The Plan Administrator shall, when making a distribution eligible for rollover treatment, provide a written explanation to the recipient of the provisions under which such distribution will not be subject to tax if transferred to an eligible retirement plan within sixty (60) days after the date on which the recipient received the distribution and, if applicable, the provisions of law pertaining to the tax treatment of lump sum distributions.

ARTICLE V
TRUSTEE

3.5.1   Acceptance of Trust. The Trustee, by joining in the execution of the Adoption Agreement to the Plan, agrees to act in accordance with the express terms and conditions hereof.

3.5.2   Trustee Capacity—Co-Trustees. The Trustee may be a bank, trust company or other corporation possessing trust powers under applicable state or federal law or one or more individuals or any combination thereof. When there are two or more Trustees, they may allocate specific responsibilities, obligations or duties among themselves by their written agreement. An executed copy of such written agreement shall be delivered to and retained by the Plan Administrator.

3.5.3   Resignation, Removal, and Successors. Any Trustee may resign at any time by delivering to the Employer a written notice of resignation to take effect at a date specified therein, which shall not be less than thirty (30) days after the delivery thereof; the Employer may waive such notice. The Trustee may be removed by the Employer with or without cause, by tendering to the Trustee a written notice of removal to take effect at a date specified therein. Upon such removal or resignation of a Trustee, the Employer shall either appoint a successor Trustee who shall have the same powers and duties as those conferred upon the resigning or discharged Trustee, or, if a group of individuals is acting as Trustee, determine that a successor shall not be appointed and the number of Trustees shall be reduced by one (1).

3.5.4   Consultations. The Trustee shall be entitled to advice of counsel, which may be counsel for the Plan or the Employer, in any case in which the Trustee shall deem such advice necessary. The Trustee shall not be liable for any action taken or omitted in good faith reliance upon the advice of such counsel. With the exception of those powers and duties specifically allocated to the Trustee by the express terms of the Plan, it shall not be the responsibility of the Trustee to interpret the terms of the Plan and the Trustee may request, and is entitled to receive, guidance and written direction from the Plan Administrator on any point requiring construction or interpretation of the Plan documents.

3.5.5   Rights, Powers and Duties. The rights, powers and duties of the Trustee shall be as follows:

(a) The Trustee shall be responsible for the safekeeping of the assets of the Trust Fund in accordance with the provisions of the Plan and any amendments hereto. The duties of the Trustee under the Plan shall be determined solely by the express provisions hereof and no other further duties or responsibilities shall be implied. Subject to the terms of this Plan, the Trustee shall be fully protected and shall incur no liability in acting in reliance upon the written instructions or directions of the Employer, the Plan Administrator, a duly designated investment manager, or any other named Fiduciary.

(b) The Trustee shall have all powers necessary or convenient for the orderly and efficient performance of its duties hereunder, including but not limited to those specified in this Section. The Trustee shall have the power generally to do all acts, whether or not expressly authorized, which the Trustee in the exercise of its fiduciary responsibility may deem necessary or desirable for the protection of the Trust Fund and the assets thereof.

(c) The Trustee shall have the power to collect and receive any and all monies and other property due hereunder and to give full discharge and release therefor; to settle, compromise or submit to arbitration any claims, debts or damages due to or owing to or from the Trust Fund; to commence or defend suits or legal proceedings wherever, in the Trustee's judgment, any interest of the Trust Fund requires it; and to represent the Trust Fund in all suits or legal proceedings in any court of law or equity or before any other body or tribunal.

(d) The Trustee shall cause any Life Insurance Policies or assets of the Trust Fund to be registered in its name as Trustee and shall be authorized to exercise any and all ownership rights regarding these assets, subject to the terms of the Plan.

(e) The Trustee may temporarily hold cash balances and shall be entitled to deposit any funds received in a bank account in the name of the Trust Fund in any bank selected by the Trustee, including the banking department of a corporate Trustee, if any, pending disposition of such funds in accordance with the Plan. Any such deposit may be made with or without interest.

(f) The Trustee shall pay the premiums and other charges due and payable at any time on any Life Insurance Policies as it may be directed by the Plan Administrator, provided funds for such payments are then available in the Trust. The Trustee shall be responsible only for such funds and Life Insurance Policies as shall actually be received by it as Trustee hereunder, and shall have no obligation to make payments other than from such funds and cash values of Life Insurance Policies.

(g) If the whole or any part of the Trust Fund shall become liable for the payment of any estate, inheritance, income or other tax which the Trustee shall be required to pay, the Trustee shall have full power and authority to pay such tax out of any monies or other property in its hands for the account of the person whose interest hereunder is so liable. Prior to making any payment, the Trustee may require such releases or other documents from any lawful taxing authority as it shall deem necessary. The Trustee shall not be liable for any nonpayment of tax when it distributes an interest hereunder on instructions from the Plan Administrator.

(h) The Trustee shall keep a full, accurate and detailed record of all transactions of the Trust which the Employer and the Plan Administrator shall have the right to examine at any time during the Trustee's regular business hours. As of the close of each Plan Year, the Trustee shall furnish the Plan Administrator with a statement of account setting forth all receipts, disbursements and other transactions effected by the Trustee during the year. The Plan Administrator shall promptly notify the Trustee in writing of his approval or disapproval of the account. The Plan Administrator's failure to disapprove the account within sixty (60) days after receipt shall be considered an approval. Except as otherwise required by law, the approval by the Plan Administrator shall be binding as to all matters embraced in any statement to the same extent as if the account of the Trustee had been settled by judgment or decree of a court of competent jurisdiction under which the Trustee, Employer and all persons having or claiming any interest in the Trust Fund were parties; provided, however, that the Trustee may have its account judicially settled if it so desires.

(i) The Trustee is hereby authorized to execute all necessary receipts and releases to any parties concerned; and shall be under a duty, upon being advised by the Plan Administrator that the proceeds of any Life Insurance Policies are payable, to give reasonable assistance to the Beneficiary designated therein in collecting such sums as may appear to be due.

(j) If, at any time, as the result of the death of the Participant there shall be a dispute as to the person to whom payment or delivery of monies or property should be made by the Trustee, or regarding any action to be taken by the Trustee, the Trustee may postpone such payment, delivery or action, retaining the funds or property involved, until such dispute shall have been resolved in a court of competent jurisdiction or the Trustee shall have been indemnified to its satisfaction or until it has received written direction from the Plan Administrator.

(k) Anything in this instrument to the contrary notwithstanding, the Trustee shall have no duty or responsibility with respect to the determination of matters pertaining to the eligibility of any Employee to become or remain a Participant hereunder, the amount of benefit to which any Participant or Beneficiary shall be entitled hereunder, or the size and type of any Life Insurance Policy to be purchased from any Insurer for any Participant hereunder; all such responsibilities being vested in the Plan Administrator.

3.5.6   Trustee Indemnification. The Employer shall indemnify and hold harmless the Trustee for and from the assertion or occurrence of any liability to a Participant or Beneficiary for any action taken or omitted by the Trustee pursuant to any written direction to the Trustee from the Employer or the Plan Administrator. Such indemnification obligation of the Employer shall not be applicable to the extent that any such liability is covered by insurance.

3.5.7   Changes in Trustee Authority. If a successor Trustee is appointed, neither an Insurer nor any other person who has previously had dealings with the Trustee shall be chargeable with knowledge of such appointment or such change until furnished with notice thereof. Until such notice, the Insurer and any other such party shall be fully protected in relying on any action taken or signature presented which would have been proper in accordance with that information previously received.

ARTICLE VI
TRUST ASSETS

3.6.1   Trustee Exclusive Owner. All assets held by the Trustee, whether in the Trust Fund or Segregated Funds, shall be owned exclusively by the Trustee and no Participant or Beneficiary shall have any individual ownership thereof. Participants and their Beneficiaries shall share in the assets of the Trust, its net earnings, profits and losses, only as provided in this Plan.

3.6.2   Investments. The Trustee shall invest and reinvest the Trust Fund without distinction between income or principal in one or more of the following ways as the Trustee shall from time to time determine:

(a) The Trustee may invest the Trust Fund or any portion thereof in obligations issued or guaranteed by the United States of America or of any instrumentalities thereof, or in other bonds, notes, debentures, mortgages, preferred or common stocks, options to buy or sell stocks or other securities, mutual fund shares, limited partnership interests, commodities, or in such other property, real or personal, as the Trustee shall determine.

(b) The Trustee may cause the Trust Fund or any portion thereof to be invested in a common trust fund established and maintained by a national bank for the collective investment of fiduciary funds, providing such common trust fund is a qualified trust under the applicable section of the Code, or corresponding provisions of future federal internal revenue laws and is exempt from income tax under the applicable section of the Code. In the event any assets of the Trust Fund are invested in such a common trust fund, the Declaration of Trust creating such common trust fund, as it may be amended from time to time, shall be incorporated into this Plan by reference and made a part hereof.

(c) The Trustee may deposit any portion of the Trust Fund in savings accounts in federally insured banks or savings and loan associations or invest in certificates of deposit issued by any such bank or savings and loan association. The Trustee may, without liability for interest, retain any portion of the Trust Fund in cash balances pending investment thereof or payment of expenses.

(d) The Trustee may buy and sell put and call options, covered or uncovered, engage in spreads, straddles, ratio writing and other forms of options trading, including sales of options against convertible bonds, and sales of Standard & Poor futures contracts, and trade in and maintain a brokerage account on a cash or margin basis.

(e) The Trustee may invest any portion or all of the assets of the Trust Fund which are attributable to the vested and nonforfeitable interest in the Accounts of a Participant in the purchase of group or individual Life Insurance Policies issued on the life of and for the benefit of the Participant with the consent of the Participant, subject to the following conditions:

(i) The aggregate premiums paid for ordinary whole Life Insurance Policies with both nondecreasing death benefits and nonincreasing premiums on the life of any Participant shall not at any time exceed forty-nine percent (49%) of the aggregate amount of Employer contributions which have been allocated to the Accounts of such Participant.

(ii) The aggregate Premiums paid for Life Insurance Policies on the life of any Participant which are either term, universal or any other contracts which are not ordinary whole life Policies shall not at any time exceed twenty-five percent (25%) of the aggregate amount of Employer contributions which have been allocated to the Accounts of such Participant.

(iii) The sum of one-half of the aggregate premiums for ordinary whole Life Insurance Policies and all premiums for other Life Insurance Policies shall not at any time exceed twenty-five percent (25%) of the aggregate amount of Employer contributions which have been allocated to the Accounts of such Participant.

(f) The Trustee may invest the Trust Fund or any portion thereof to acquire or hold Qualifying Employer Securities or Real Property, provided that the portion so invested shall not exceed the amount allowed as an investment under the Act.

3.6.3   Administration of Trust Assets. Subject to the limitations herein expressly set forth, the Trustee shall have the following powers and authority in connection with the administration of the assets of the Trust:

(a) To hold and administer all contributions made by the Employer to the Trust Fund and all income or other property derived therefrom as a single Trust Fund, except as otherwise provided in the Plan.

(b) To manage, control, sell, convey, exchange, petition, divide, subdivide, improve, repair, grant options, sell upon deferred payments, lease without limit as determined for any purpose, compromise, arbitrate or otherwise settle claims in favor of or against the Trust Fund, institute, compromise and defend actions and proceedings, and to take any other action necessary or desirable in connection with the administration of the Trust Fund.

(c) To vote any stock, bonds, or other securities of any corporation or other issuer; otherwise consent to or request any action on the part of any such corporation or other issuer; to give general or special proxies or powers of attorney, with or without power of substitution; to participate in any reorganization, recapitalization, consolidation, merger or similar transaction with respect to such securities; to deposit such stocks or other securities in any voting trusts, or with any protective or like committee, or with the trustee, or with the depositories designated thereby; to exercise any subscription rights and conversion privileges or other options and to make any payments incidental thereto; and generally to do all such acts, execute all such instruments, take all such proceedings and exercise all such rights, powers and privileges with respect to the stock or other securities or property constituting the Trust Fund as if the Trustee were the absolute owner thereof.

(d) To apply for and procure, at the election of any Participant, Life Insurance Policies on the life of the Participant; to exercise whatever rights and privileges may be granted to the Trustee under such Policies, and to cash in, receive and collect such Policies or the proceeds therefrom as and when entitled to do so under the provisions thereof;

(e) To make, execute, acknowledge and deliver any and all documents of transfer and conveyance and any and all other instruments that may be necessary or appropriate to carry out the powers herein granted;

(f) To register any investment held in the Trust in the Trustee's own name or in the name of a nominee and to hold any investment in bearer form, but the books and records of the Trustee shall at all times show that all such investments are part of the Trust;

(g) To borrow money for the purposes of the Plan in such amounts and upon such terms and conditions as the Trustee deems appropriate;

(h) To commingle the assets of the Trust Fund with the assets of other similar trusts which are exempt from income tax, whether sponsored by the Employer, an affiliate of the Employer or an unrelated employer, provided that the books and records of the Trustee shall at all times show the portion of the commingled assets which are part of the Trust; and

(i) To do all acts whether or not expressly authorized which the Trustee may deem necessary or proper for the protection of the property held hereunder.

3.6.4   Segregated Funds. Unless otherwise determined by the Trustee to be prudent, the Trustee shall invest and reinvest each Segregated Fund without distinction between income or principal in one or more appropriately identified interest-bearing accounts or certificates of deposit in the name of the Trustee and subject solely to the dominion of the Trustee in a banking institution (which may or may not be the Trustee, if the Trustee is a banking institution) or savings and loan association. Any such account or certificate shall bear interest at a rate not less than the rate of interest currently being paid upon regular savings accounts by that banking corporation principally situated in the community in which the Employer has its principal business location, which has capital, surplus and undivided profits exceeding those of any other bank so situated. Such accounts shall be held for the benefit of the Participant for whom such Segregated Fund is established in accordance with the terms of the Plan and the Segregated Account of the Participant shall be credited with any interest earned in connection with such accounts. If the Trustee determines that an alternative investment is appropriate, the Trustee may invest the Segregated Fund in any manner permitted with respect to the Trust Fund and such Segregated Fund shall be credited with the net income or loss or net appreciation or depreciation in value of such investments. No Segregated Fund shall share in any Employer contributions or forfeitures, any net income or loss from, or net appreciation or depreciation in value of, any investments of the Trust Fund, or any allocation for which provision is made in this Plan which is not specifically attributable to the Segregated Fund.

3.6.5   Investment Control Option. If the Employer elects in the Adoption Agreement to permit Participants to direct the investment of their Accounts, each Participant may elect to have transferred to a Controlled Fund and exercise investment control with respect to funds in the Trust Fund which do not exceed the balances in his Accounts. To the extent that the balance in the Participant's Account with respect to which a transfer is to be made includes his share of an Employer contribution which has not been received by the Trustee, such transfer shall not be made until such contribution is received by the Trustee. In addition to the foregoing election, each Participant who has a Segregated Fund may elect to have transferred to a Controlled Fund any portion or all of such Segregated Fund. Funds so transferred to a Controlled Fund on behalf of the Participant shall be thereafter invested by the Trustee in such bonds, notes, debentures, commodities, mortgages, equipment trust certificates, investment trust certificates, preferred or common stocks, partnership interests, life insurance policies, including universal life insurance policies, or in such other property, real or personal (other than collectibles), wherever situated, as the Participant shall direct from time to time in writing; provided, however, that the Participant may not direct the Trustee to make loans to himself, nor to make loans to the Employer; and provided further that the Trustee may limit the investment alternatives available to the Participant in a uniform and nondiscriminatory manner but taking into account whether the interest of the Participant is fully vested and nonforfeitable. Any such election shall be made by the Participant giving notice thereof to the Trustee as the Trustee deems necessary and such notice shall specify the amount of such funds to be transferred and the Account from which the transfer is to be made. Any such election with respect to a Segregated Fund shall be made by the Participant giving the Trustee notice as the Trustee deems necessary and such notice shall specify the date the transfer is to take place and the amount of funds to be transferred. Any such election shall be at the absolute discretion of the individual Participant and shall be binding upon the Trustee. Upon any such election being made, the amount of such funds to be transferred shall be deducted from his Account as appropriate and added to a Controlled Account of the Participant. All dividends and interest thereafter received with respect to such transferred funds, as well as any appreciation or depreciation in his investments, shall be added to or deducted from his Controlled Account.

If a Participant wishes to make such an election to transfer funds from the Trust Fund to a Controlled Fund as of a date other than a Valuation Date, the Trustee may defer such transfer until the next succeeding Valuation Date or, in the Trustee's discretion, make such transfer, provided that the Trustee determines that the nature of the assets in the Trust Fund is such that it is feasible and practical to make, as of the date of such transfer, the adjustments to Participants' Accounts for which provision is made in the Plan, as if such date is a Valuation Date.

The Trustee shall not have any investment responsibility with respect to a Participant's Controlled Fund. In the event that a Participant elects to have any such funds transferred to a Controlled Fund and invested in particular securities or assets pursuant to this Section, the Trustee shall not be liable for any loss or damage resulting from the investment decision of the Participant. As of any Valuation Date, the Participant may elect to have all or any portion of any cash contained in his Controlled Fund transferred back to the Trust Fund, in which case such cash shall be invested by the Trustee together with other assets held in the Trust Fund. Any such election shall be made by giving notice thereof to the Trustee as the Trustee deems necessary, and the notice shall specify the amount of cash to be transferred.

As of the said Valuation Date, the amount of such funds to be so transferred which is attributable to the balance in the Participant's Controlled Account shall be deducted from such Account and added to the appropriate Account of the Participant.

ARTICLE VII
LOANS

3.7.1   Authorization. If the Employer elects in the Adoption Agreement to permit loans to Participants or Beneficiaries, the Trustee shall establish a participant loan program in compliance with Labor Regulation 2550.408b. The terms of such participant loan program shall be in writing and shall constitute part of the Plan. Such terms shall include:

(a) The identity of the person or positions authorized to administer the participant loan program;

(b) A procedure for applying for loans;

(c) The basis on which loans will be approved or denied;

(d) Limitations (if any) on the types and amount of loans offered;

(e) The procedure under the program for determining a reasonable rate of interest;

(f) The types of collateral which may secure a participant loan; and

(g) The events constituting default and the steps that will be taken to preserve plan assets in the event of default.

3.7.2   Spousal Consent. A Participant must obtain the written consent of his spouse, if any, to the use of the Participant's interest in the Plan as security for the loan within ninety (90) days before the date on which the loan is to be so secured. A new consent must be obtained whenever the amount of the loan is increased or if the loan is renegotiated, extended, renewed or otherwise revised. The form of the consent must acknowledge the effect of such consent and be witnessed by a Plan representative or a notary public but shall be deemed to meet any such requirements relating to the consent of any subsequent spouse. Such consent shall thereafter be binding with respect to the consenting spouse or any subsequent spouse with respect to that loan.

If a valid spousal consent has been obtained, then notwithstanding any other provision of the Plan, the portion of the Participant's vested Account balance used as a security interest held by the Plan by reason of a loan outstanding to the Participant shall be taken into account for purposes of determining the amount of the Account balance payable at the time of death or distribution but only if the reduction is used as repayment of the loan. If less than the entire amount of the Participant's vested Account balance (determined without regard to the preceding sentence) is payable to the surviving spouse, the Account balance shall be adjusted by first reducing the vested Account balance by the amount of the security used as repayment of the loan and then determining the benefit payable to the surviving spouse.

3.7.3 Limitations. Except to the extent provided in the participant loan program, in no event shall the amount loaned to any Participant or Beneficiary exceed the lesser of (a) fifty thousand dollars ($50,000.00) (reduced by the excess, if any, of the highest outstanding balance of loans from the Plan) during the one year period ending on the day before the date on which the loan was made over the outstanding balance of loans from the Plan on the date on which such loan was made) or (b) one-half of the sum of the vested and nonforfeitable interest in his Accounts, determined as of the Valuation Date coinciding with or immediately preceding such loan. For the purposes hereof, all loans from all plans of the Employer and other members of a group of employers described in Sections 414(b), (c), (m) and (o) of the Code shall be aggregated. All loans must be adequately secured and bear a reasonable interest rate. In the event of a default foreclosure on the note evidencing the loan and attachment of the security shall not occur until a distributable event occurs.

3.7.4 Availability. Loans, if any, must be available to all Participants and Beneficiaries without regard to any individual's race, color, religion, sex, age or national origin. Loans shall be made available to all Participants and Beneficiaries and loans shall not be made available to Highly Compensated Employees in an amount greater than the amount made available to other employees.

3.7.5 Prohibitions. A loan shall not be made to a five (5%) percent or greater shareholder-employee of an S corporation, an owner of more than ten (10%) percent of either the capital interest or the profits interest of an unincorporated Employer, a family member (as defined in Section 267(c)(4) of the Code) of such persons, or a corporation controlled by such persons through the ownership, directly or indirectly, of fifty (50%) percent or more of the total voting power or value of all shares of all classes of stock of the corporation, unless an exemption for the loan is obtained pursuant to Section 408 of the Act.

ARTICLE VIII
BENEFICIARIES

3.8.1   Designation of Beneficiaries. Each Participant shall have the right to designate a Beneficiary or Beneficiaries and contingent or successive Beneficiaries to receive any benefits provided by this Plan which become payable upon the Participant's death. The Beneficiaries may be changed at any time or times by the filing of a new designation with the Plan Administrator, and the most recent designation shall govern. Notwithstanding the foregoing and subject to the provisions of Section 2.5.2(e)(3), the designated Beneficiary shall be the surviving spouse of the Participant, unless such surviving spouse consents in writing to an alternate designation and the terms of such consent acknowledge the effect of such alternate designation and the consent is witnessed by a representative of the Plan or by a notary public. A spouse may not revoke the consent without the approval of the Participant. The designation of a Beneficiary other than the spouse of the Participant or a form of benefits with the consent of such spouse may not be changed without the consent of such spouse and any consent must acknowledge the specific non-spouse Beneficiary, including any class of Beneficiaries or any contingent Beneficiaries.

3.8.2   Absence or Death of Beneficiaries. If a Participant dies without having a beneficiary designation then in force, or if all of the Beneficiaries designated by a Participant predecease him, his Beneficiary shall be his surviving spouse, or if none, his surviving children, equally, or if none, such other heirs or the executor or administrator of his estate as the Plan Administrator shall select.

If a Participant dies survived by Beneficiaries designated by him and if all such surviving Beneficiaries thereafter die before complete distribution of such deceased Participant's interest, the estate of the last of such designated Beneficiaries to survive shall be deemed to be the Beneficiary of the undistributed portion of such interest.

ARTICLE IX
CLAIMS

3.9.1   Claim Procedure. Any Participant or Beneficiary who is entitled to a payment of a benefit for which provision is made in this Plan shall file a written claim with the Plan Administrator on such forms as shall be furnished to him by the Plan Administrator and shall furnish such evidence of entitlement to benefits as the Plan Administrator may reasonably require. The Plan Administrator shall notify the Participant or Beneficiary in writing as to the amount of benefit to which he is entitled, the duration of such benefit, the time the benefit is to commence and other pertinent information concerning his benefit. If a claim for benefit is denied by the Plan Administrator, in whole or in part, the Plan Administrator shall provide adequate notice in writing to the Participant or Beneficiary whose claim for benefit has been denied within ninety (90) days after receipt of the claim unless special circumstances require an extension of time for processing the claim. If such an extension of time for processing is required, written notice indicating the special circumstances and the date by which a final decision is expected to be rendered shall be furnished to the Participant or Beneficiary. In no event shall the period of extension exceed one hundred eighty (180) days after receipt of the claim. The notice of denial of the claim shall set forth (a) the specific reason or reasons for the denial; (b) specific reference to pertinent Plan provisions on which the denial is based; (c) a description of any additional material or information necessary for the claimant to perfect the claim and an explanation of why such material or information is necessary; and (d) a statement that any appeal of the denial must be made by giving to the Plan Administrator, within sixty (60) days after receipt of the notice of the denial, written notice of such appeal, such notice to include a full description of the pertinent issues and basis of the claim. The Participant or Beneficiary (or his duly authorized representative) may review pertinent documents and submit issues and comments in writing to the Plan Administrator. If the Participant or Beneficiary fails to appeal such action to the Plan Administrator in writing within the prescribed period of time, the Plan Administrator's adverse determination shall be final, binding and conclusive.

3.9.2   Appeal. If the Plan Administrator receives from a Participant or a Beneficiary, within the prescribed period of time, a notice of an appeal of the denial of a claim for benefit, such notice and all relevant materials shall immediately be submitted to the Employer. The Employer may hold a hearing or otherwise ascertain such facts as it deems necessary and shall render a decision which shall be binding upon both parties. The decision of the Employer shall be made within sixty (60) days after the receipt by the Plan Administrator of the notice of appeal, unless special circumstances require an extension of time for processing, in which case a decision of the Employer shall be rendered as soon as possible but not later than one hundred twenty (120) days after receipt of the request for review. If such an extension of time is required, written notice of the extension shall be furnished to the claimant prior to the commencement of the extension. The decision of the Employer shall be in writing, shall include specific reasons for the decision, written in a manner calculated to be understood by the claimant, as well as specific references to the pertinent Plan provisions on which the decision is based and shall be promptly furnished to the claimant.

ARTICLE X
AMENDMENT AND TERMINATION

3.10.1   Right to Amend.

(a) The Employer may at any time or times amend the Plan and the provisions of the Adoption Agreement, in whole or in part. Subject to subsection (b), an Employer that amends the Plan shall no longer participate in this prototype plan and shall be considered to have an individually designed plan.

(b) The Employer may change the choice of options in the Adoption Agreement, add overriding language in the Adoption Agreement when such language is necessary to satisfy Section 415 or 416 of the Code because of the required aggregation of multiple plans and add certain model amendments published by the Internal Revenue Service which specifically provide that their adoption shall not cause the Plan to be treated as individually designed. An Employer that amends the Plan for any other reason, including a waiver of the minimum funding requirements under Section 412(d) of the Code, shall no longer participate in this prototype plan and shall be considered to have an individually designed plan.

3.10.2   Manner of Amending. Each amendment of this Plan shall be made by delivery to the Trustee of a copy of the resolution of the Employer which sets forth such amendment.

3.10.3   Limitations on Amendments. No amendment shall be made to this Plan which shall:

(a) Directly or indirectly operate to give the Employer any interest whatsoever in the assets of the Trust or to deprive any Participant or Beneficiary of his vested and nonforfeitable interest in the assets of the Trust as then constituted, or cause any part of the income or corpus of the Trust to be used for, or diverted to purposes other than the exclusive benefit of Employees or their Beneficiaries;

(b) Increase the duties or liabilities of the Trustee without the Trustee's prior written consent;

(c) Change the vesting schedule under the Plan if the nonforfeitable percentage of the accrued benefit derived from Employer contributions (determined as of the later of the date such amendment is adopted or the date such amendment becomes effective) of any

Participant is less than such nonforfeitable percentage computed without regard to such amendment; or

(d) Reduce the accrued benefit of a Participant within the meaning of Section 411(d)(6) of the Code, except to the extent permitted under Section 412(c)(8) of the Code. An amendment which has the effect of decreasing a Participant's account balance or eliminating an optional form of benefit with respect to benefits attributable to service before the amendment shall be treated as reducing an accrued benefit.

If a Plan amendment changes the vesting schedule or the Plan is amended in any way that directly or indirectly affects the computation of the Participant's nonforfeitable percentage, each Participant who has completed three (3) or, in the case of Participants who do not have at least one (1) Hour of Service in any Plan Year beginning after 1988, five (5) or more Years of Service may elect within a reasonable period after the adoption of such amendment to have his nonforfeitable percentage computed without regard to such amendment or change. The period during which the election may be made shall commence with the date the amendment is adopted or deemed to be made and shall end on the latest of sixty (60) days after:

(i)   the amendment is adopted;

(ii) the amendment becomes effective; or

(iii) the Participant is issued written notice of the amendment by the Employer or Plan Administrator.

3.10.4   Voluntary Termination. The Employer may terminate the Plan at any time by delivering to the Trustee an instrument in writing which designates such termination. Following termination of the Plan, the Trust will continue until the Distributable Benefit of each Participant has been distributed.

3.10.5   Involuntary Termination. The Plan shall terminate if (a) the Employer is dissolved or adjudicated bankrupt or insolvent in appropriate proceedings, or if a general assignment is made by the Employer for the benefit of creditors, or (b) the Employer loses its identity by consolidation or merger into one or more corporations or organizations, unless within ninety (90) days after such consolidation or merger, such corporations or organizations elect to continue the Plan.

3.10.6   Withdrawal by Employer. The Employer may withdraw from participation under the Plan without terminating the Trust upon making a transfer of the Trust assets to another Plan which shall be deemed to constitute an amendment in its entirety of the Trust.

3.10.7   Powers Pending Final Distribution. Until final distribution of the assets of the Trust, the Plan Administrator and Trustee shall continue to have all the powers provided under this Plan as are necessary for the orderly administration, liquidation and distribution of the assets of the Trust.

3.10.8   Delegation to Sponsor. The Employer expressly delegates authority to the Plan Sponsor the right to amend any part of the Plan on its behalf to the extent necessary to preserve the qualified status of the Plan. For purposes of amendments by the Plan Sponsor, the Mass Submitter shall be recognized as the agent of the Plan Sponsor. If the Plan Sponsor does not adopt the amendments made by the Mass Submitter, the Plan shall no longer be identical to or a minor modifier of the mass submitter plan. The Plan Sponsor shall submit a copy of the amendment to each Employer who has adopted the Plan after first having received a ruling or favorable determination from the Internal Revenue Service that the Plan as amended satisfies the applicable requirements of the Code. The Employer may revoke the authority of the Plan Sponsor to amend the Plan on its behalf by written notice to the Plan Sponsor of such revocation.

ARTICLE XI
PORTABILITY

3.11.1   Continuance by Successor. In the event of the dissolution, consolidation or merger of the Employer, or the sale by the Employer of its assets, the resulting successor person or persons, firm or corporations may continue this Plan by (a) adopting the Plan by appropriate resolution; (b) appointing a new Trustee as though the Trustee (including all members of a group of individuals acting as Trustee) had resigned; and (c) executing a proper agreement with the new Trustee. In such event, each Participant in this Plan shall have an interest in the Plan after the dissolution, consolidation, merger, or sale of assets, at least equal to the interest which he had in the Plan immediately before the dissolution, consolidation, merger or sale of assets. Any Participants who do not accept a position with such successor within a reasonable time shall be deemed to be terminated. If, within ninety (90) days from the effective date of such dissolution, consolidation, merger, or sale of assets, such successor does not adopt this Plan, as provided herein, the Plan shall automatically be terminated and deemed to be an involuntary termination.

3.11.2   Merger with Other Plan. In the event of the merger or consolidation with, or transfer of assets or liabilities to, any other deferred compensation plan and trust, each Participant shall have an interest in such other plan which is equal to or greater than the interest which he had in this Plan immediately before such merger, consolidation or transfer, and if such other plan thereafter terminates, each Participant shall be entitled to a Distributable Benefit which is equal to or greater than the Distributable Benefit to which he would have been entitled immediately before such merger, consolidation or transfer if this Plan had then been terminated.

3.11.3 Transfer from Other Plans. The Employer may cause all or any of the assets held in connection with any other plan or trust which is maintained by the Employer for the benefit of its employees and satisfies the applicable requirements of the Code relating to qualified plans and trusts to be transferred to the Trustee, whether such transfer is made pursuant to a merger or consolidation of this Plan with such other plan or trust or for any other allowable purpose. In addition, the Employer, in its discretion, may permit rollover to the Trustee of assets held for the benefit of an Employee in a conduit Individual Retirement Account, a terminated plan of the Employer, or any other plan or trust which is maintained by some other employer for the benefit of its employees and satisfies the applicable requirements of the Code relating to qualified plans and trusts. Any such assets so transferred to the Trustee shall be accompanied by written instructions from the employer, or the trustee, custodian or individual holding such assets, setting forth the name of each Employee for whose benefit such assets have been transferred and showing separately the respective contributions by the employer and by the Employee and the current value of the assets attributable thereto. Upon receipt by the Trustee of such assets, the Trustee shall place such assets in a Segregated Fund for the Participant and the Employee shall be deemed to be one hundred percent (100%) vested and have a nonforfeitable interest in any such assets. Notwithstanding any provisions herein to the contrary, unless the Plan provides a life annuity distribution option or the Participant and his spouse have signed a written waiver of their rights to the annuity options in a form which satisfies the waiver requirements of Section 417 of the Code, the Plan shall not be a direct or indirect transferee of a defined benefit pension plan, money purchase pension plan, target benefit pension plan, stock bonus or profit sharing plan which is subject to the survivor annuity requirements of Section 401(a)(11) and Section 417 of the Code.

3.11.4 Transfer to Other Plans. The Trustee, upon written direction by the Employer, shall transfer some or all of the assets held under the Trust to another plan or trust of the Employer meeting the requirements of the Code relating to qualified plans and trusts, whether such transfer is made pursuant to a merger or consolidation of this Plan with such other plan or trust or for any other allowable purpose. In addition, upon the termination of employment of any Participant and receipt by the Plan Administrator of a request in writing, the Participant may request that any distribution from the Trust to which he is entitled shall be transferred to an Individual Retirement Account, an Individual Retirement Annuity, or any other plan or trust which is maintained by some other employer for the benefit of its employees and satisfies the applicable requirements of the Code relating to qualified plans and trusts. Upon receipt of any such written request, the Plan Administrator shall cause the Trustee to transfer the assets so directed and, as appropriate, shall direct the Insurer to transfer to the new trustee any applicable insurance policies issued by it.

ARTICLE XII
MISCELLANEOUS

3.12.1   No Reversion to Employer. Except as specifically provided in the Plan, no part of the corpus or income of the Trust shall revert to the Employer or be used for, or diverted to purposes other than for the exclusive benefit of Participants and their Beneficiaries.

3.12.2   Employer Actions. Any action by the Employer pursuant to the provisions of the Plan shall be evidenced by appropriate resolution or by written instrument executed by any person authorized by the Employer to take such action.

3.12.3   Execution of Receipts and Releases. Any payment to any person eligible to receive benefits under this Plan, in accordance with the provisions of the Plan, shall, to the extent thereof, be in full satisfaction of all claims hereunder. The Plan Administrator may require such person, as a condition precedent to such payment, to execute a receipt and release therefor in such form as he shall determine.

3.12.4   Rights of Participants Limited. Neither the creation of this Plan and Trust nor anything contained in this Plan or the Adoption Agreement shall be construed as giving any Participant, Beneficiary or Employee any equity or other interest in the assets, business or affairs of the Employer, or the right to complain about any action taken by or about any policy adopted or pursued by, the Employer, or as giving any Employee the right to be retained in the service of the Employer; and all Employees shall remain subject to discharge to the same extent as if the Plan had never been executed. Prior to the time that distributions are made in conformity with the provisions of the Plan, neither the Participants, nor their spouses, Beneficiaries, heirs-at-law, or legal representatives shall receive or be entitled to receive cash or any other thing of current exchangeable value, from either the Employer or the Trustee as a result of the Plan or the Trust.

3.12.5   Persons Dealing with Trustee Protected. No person dealing with the Trustee shall be required or entitled to see to the application of any money paid or property delivered to the Trustee, or determine whether or not the Trustee is acting pursuant to the authorities granted to the

Trustee hereunder or to authorizations or directions herein required. The certificate of the Trustee that the Trustee is acting in accordance with the Plan shall protect any person relying thereon.

3.12.6 Protection of the Insurer. An Insurer shall not be responsible for the validity of the Plan or Trust and shall have no responsibility for action taken or not taken by the Trustee, for determining the propriety of accepting premium payments or other contributions, for making payments in accordance with the direction of the Trustee, or for the application of such payments. The Insurer shall be fully protected in dealing with any representative of the Employer or any one of a group of individuals acting as Trustee. Until written notice of a change of Trustee has been received by an Insurer at its home office, the Insurer shall be fully protected in dealing with any party acting as Trustee according to the latest information received by the Insurer at its home office.

3.12.7 No Responsibility for Act of Insurer. Neither the Employer, the Plan Administrator nor the Trustee shall be responsible for any of the following, nor shall they be liable for instituting action in connection with:

(a) The validity of policies or policy provisions;

(b) Failure or refusal by the Insurer to provide benefits under a policy;

(c) An act by a person which may render a policy invalid or unenforceable; or

(d) Inability to perform or delay in performing an act, which inability or delay is occasioned by a provision of a policy or a restriction imposed by the Insurer.

3.12.8 Inalienability. The right of any Participant or his Beneficiary in any distribution hereunder or to any separate Account shall not be subject to alienation, assignment or transfer, voluntarily or involuntarily, by operation of law or otherwise, except as may be expressly permitted herein. No Participant shall assign, transfer, or dispose of such right nor shall any such right be subjected to attachment, execution, garnishment, sequestration, or other legal, equitable or other process. The preceding shall also apply to the creation, assignment, or recognition of a right to any benefit payable with respect to a Participant pursuant to a domestic relations order, unless such order is determined to be a qualified domestic relations order, as defined in Section 414(p) of the Code, or any domestic relations order entered before January 1, 1985.

In the event a Participant's benefits are attached by order of any court, the Plan Administrator may bring an action for a declaratory judgment in a court of competent jurisdiction to determine the proper recipient of the benefits to be paid by the Plan. During the pendency of the action, the Plan Administrator shall cause any benefits payable to be paid to the court for distribution by the court as it considers appropriate.

3.12.9   Domestic Relations Orders. The Plan Administrator shall adhere to the terms of any judgment, decree or order (including approval of a property settlement agreement) which relates to the provision of child support, alimony payments, or marital property rights to a spouse, former spouse, child or other dependent of a Participant and is made pursuant to a state domestic relations law (including a community property law) and which creates or recognizes the existence of an alternate payee's right to, or assigns to an alternate payee the right to, receive all or a portion of the benefits payable with respect to a Participant.

Any such domestic relations order must clearly specify the name and last known mailing address of the Participant and the name and mailing address of each alternate payee covered by the order, the amount or percentage of the Participant's benefit to be paid by the Plan to each such alternate payee, or the manner in which such amount or percentage is to be determined, the number of payments or period to which such order applies, and each plan to which such order applies.

Any such domestic relations order shall not require the Plan to provide any type or form of benefit, or any option not otherwise provided under the Plan, to provide increased benefits (determined on the basis of actuarial value) or the payment of benefits to an alternate payee which are required to be paid to another alternate payee under another order previously determined to be a qualified domestic relations order. Notwithstanding the foregoing sentence, a domestic relations order may require the payment of benefits to an alternate payee before the Participant has separated from service on or after the date on which the Participant attains or would have attained the earliest retirement age under the Plan as if the Participant had retired on the date on which such payment is to begin under such order (but taking into account only the present value of the benefits actually accrued and not taking into account the present value of any Employer subsidy for early retirement) and in any form in which such benefits may be paid under the Plan to the Participant (other than the form of a joint and survivor annuity with respect to the alternate payee and his or her subsequent spouse). The interest rate assumption used in determining the present value shall be five (5%) percent. For these purposes, the earliest retirement age under the Plan means the earlier of: (a) the date on which the Participant is entitled to a distribution under the Plan, or (b) the later of the date the Participant attains age 50, or the earliest date on which the Participant could begin receiving benefits under the Plan if the Participant separated from service.

If the Employer so elects in the Adoption Agreement, distributions may be made to an alternate payee even though the Participant may not receive a distribution because he continues to be employed by the Employer.

To the extent provided in the qualified domestic relations order, the former spouse of a Participant shall be treated as a surviving spouse of such Participant for purposes of Sections 401(a)(11) and 417 of the Code (and any spouse of the Participant shall not be treated as a spouse of the Participant for such purposes) and if married for at least one (1) year, the surviving former spouse shall be treated as meeting the requirements of Section 417(d) of the Code.

The Plan Administrator shall promptly notify the Participant and each alternative payee of the receipt of a domestic relations order by the Plan and the Plan's procedures for determining the qualified status of domestic relations orders. Within a reasonable period after receipt of a domestic relations order, the Plan Administrator shall determine whether such order is a qualified domestic relations order and shall notify the Participant and each alternate payee of such determination. If the Participant or any affected alternate payee disagrees with the determinations of the Plan Administrator, the disagreeing party shall be treated as a claimant and the claims procedure of the Plan shall be followed. The Plan Administrator may bring an action for a declaratory judgment in a court of competent jurisdiction to determine the proper recipient of the benefits to be paid by the Plan.

During any period in which the issue of whether a domestic relations order is a qualified domestic relations order is being determined (by the Plan Administrator, by a court of competent jurisdiction or otherwise), the Plan Administrator shall separately account for the amounts which would have been payable to the alternate payee during such period if the order had been determined to be a qualified domestic relations order. If, within the eighteen (18) month period beginning on the date on which the first payment would be required to be made under the domestic relations order, the order (or modification thereof) is determined to be a qualified domestic relations order, the Plan Administrator shall pay the segregated amounts, including any interest thereon, to the person or persons entitled thereto. If within such eighteen (18) month period it is determined that the order is not a qualified domestic relations order or the issue as to whether such order is a qualified domestic relations order is not resolved, then the Plan Administrator shall pay the segregated amounts, including any interest thereon, to the person or persons who would have been entitled to such amounts if there had been no order. Any determination that an order is a qualified domestic relations order which is made after the close of the eighteen (18) month period shall be applied prospectively only.

3.12.10 Authorization to Withhold Taxes. The Trustee is authorized in accordance with applicable law to withhold from distribution to any payee such sums as may be necessary to cover federal and state taxes which may be due with respect to such distributions.

3.12.11 Missing Persons. If the Trustee mails by registered or certified mail, postage prepaid, to the last known address of a Participant or Beneficiary, a notification that the Participant or Beneficiary is entitled to a distribution and if (a) the notification is returned by the post office because the addressee cannot be located at such address and if neither the Employer, the Plan Administrator nor the Trustee shall have any knowledge of the whereabouts of such Participant or Beneficiary within three (3) years from the date such notification was mailed, or (b) within three (3) years after such notification was mailed to such Participant or Beneficiary, he does not respond thereto by informing the Trustee of his whereabouts, the ultimate disposition of the then undistributed balance of the Distributable Benefit of such Participant or Beneficiary shall be determined in accordance with the then applicable Federal laws, rules and regulations. If any portion of the Distributable Benefit is forfeited because the Participant or Beneficiary cannot be found, such portion shall be reinstated if a claim is made by the Participant or Beneficiary.

3.12.12 Notices. Any notice or direction to be given in accordance with the Plan shall be deemed to have been effectively given if hand delivered to the recipient or sent by certified mail, return receipt requested, to the recipient at the recipient's last known address. At any time that a group of individuals is acting as Trustee, notice to the Trustee may be given by giving notice to any one or more of such individuals.

3.12.13 Governing Law. The provisions of this Plan shall be construed, administered and enforced in accordance with the provisions of the Act and, to the extent applicable, the laws of the state in which the Employer has its principal place of business. All contributions to the Trust shall be deemed to take place in such state.

3.12.14 Severability of Provisions. In the event that any provision of this Plan shall be held to be illegal, invalid or unenforceable for any reason, said illegality, invalidity or unenforceability shall not affect the remaining provisions, but shall be fully severable and the Plan shall be construed and enforced as if said illegal, invalid or unenforceable provisions had never been inserted herein.

3.12.15 Gender and Number. Whenever appropriate, words used in the singular shall include the plural, and the masculine gender shall include the feminine gender.

3.12.16 Binding Effect. The Plan and Adoption Agreement, and all actions and decisions hereunder, shall be binding upon the heirs, executors, administrators, successors and assigns of any and all parties hereto and Participants, present and future.

3.12.17 Qualification under Internal Revenue Laws. The Employer intends that the Trust qualify under the applicable provisions of the Code. Until advised to the contrary, the Trustee may assume that the Trust is so qualified and is entitled to tax exemption under the Code. If the Plan of the Employer fails to attain or retain qualification, the Plan of the Employer shall no longer participate in this prototype and shall be considered an individually designed plan.

§ A.5 —Resolution of the Retirement Committee

ALPHA OMEGA Organization
Retirement Savings Plan and Trust

In accordance with the terms of the Alpha Omega Organization Retirement Savings Plan and Trust, the Retirement Committee has established the following plan rules:

1. Participants may defer from 1% to 15% of compensation in whole percentage increments.

2. a) Participants may choose to direct their accounts among the following investments:
    - Fixed Guaranteed Fund
    - Balanced Return Fund
    - Growth Fund
    - Global Fund

    b) Participants shall direct their investments between these options in 5% increments.

    c) Participants who decline to direct their accounts shall be deemed to have elected 100% investment in the fixed return fund.

    d) Participants may change the direction of new contributions as of January 1, April 1, July 1 or October 1 of each year.

    e) Participants may transfer existing accounts between funds on January 1 of each year.

3. Re-enrollments will occur one per year calendar quarter. Participants may revise their rate of salary deferral effective January 1, April 1, July 1 or October 1.

4. Participants may cease salary deferrals altogether at any time. Participants who voluntarily suspend contributions may begin contributing again as of the second quarter (January 1, April 1, July 1 or October 1) following the quarter in which deferrals were suspended.

5. No rollover or voluntary after-tax contributions will be accepted.

RETIREMENT COMMITTEE

BY: _____

TITLE: _____

DATE: _____

§ A.6 —Participant Loan Program

Pursuant to the terms of Alpha Omega Organization Retirement Savings Plan and Trust the Trustee has adopted a participant loan program as part of such Plan and Trust. The program is intended to comply with Labor Regulation 2550.408b-1. Loans will be made pursuant to the terms of the Plan and Trust and the following provisions of this Participant Loan Program.

A. Administration of Program

The following person ("the Loan Administrator") is responsible for the administration of the loan program. All loan requests and other inquiries should be delivered to:

Retirement Committee
c/o Alpha Omega Organization
1492 Atlantic Avenue
Columbus, PA 18950-1990
215-987-2341

B. Application Procedure

1. Obtain and complete a loan application on forms provided by the Loan Administrator.

2. Submit the completed loan application to the Loan Administrator at least 15 days before the date the loan is to be made.

3. Loan applications will be reviewed by the Loan Administrator for completeness. Incomplete applications will be returned to the applicant for completion.

4. Approved loans will be processed on the last day of each month.

C. Basis for Approvals

Loans are available to all participants and, in the event of a participant's death, his or her beneficiaries without regard to any individual's race, color, religion, sex, age or national origin. Each application
will be reviewed on a nondiscriminatory basis but will be assessed on
the applicant's credit worthiness, financial need, and the purpose and
terms of the loan. An individual may be denied future loans if he or
she defaulted on any previous loan. A loan will not be made to a five
(5%) percent or greater shareholder-employee of an S corporation, an
owner of more than ten (10%) percent of either the capital interest or
the profits interest of an unincorporated Employer, or a family member (as defined in Section 267(c)(4) of the Code) of such persons,
unless an exemption for the loan is obtained pursuant to Section 408
of the Act.

D. Limitations

1. Limitations on Types of Loans

Subject to the limitations on the amount of any loan, loans will be
approved if the loan proceeds are to be used for any reason without limitation.

2. Limitations on Amounts of Loans

—The minimum amount of any loan is $1,000.

—The maximum amount of any loan is the lesser of $50,000 or
50% of the vested interest of the participant in the Plan. The
$50,000 maximum amount will be reduced by the participant's
highest outstanding loan balance in the previous twelve months,
even if amounts have been repaid.

—The maximum amount of any loan is $50,000.

—The balance of outstanding loans to a single participant may
not exceed $50,000.

E. Interest

The interest rate will be determined from time to time by the Trustee
with the intention of providing the Plan with a return commensurate
with the interest rates charged by persons in the business of lending
money for loans which would be made under similar circumstances.

Until otherwise determined by the Trustee, the interest rate will be
the prime rate of interest charged by Faith Fidelity Bank and Trust as
of the last day of the preceding calendar quarter, plus 2 percent.

The rate of interest will be constant throughout the term of the loan.

F. Collateral or Other Security

All loans must be adequately secured. No more than 50 percent of
the present value of a participant's vested interest in the Plan may be

considered by the Plan as security for the outstanding balance of all Plan loans made to the participant. If the interest of the participant in the Plan is to be used as security for a Plan loan, the written consent of the participant's spouse, if any, must be obtained within 90 days before the date on which the loan is to be so secured. A new consent must be obtained whenever the amount of the loan is increased or if the loan is renegotiated, extended, renewed or otherwise revised. The form of the consent must acknowledge the effect of such consent and be witnessed by a Plan representative or a notary public.

The Trustee will accept other collateral as security for the loan, such as a lien on real estate, marketable securities, savings accounts or other assets, provided that the Trustee determines that in the event of default, the collateral to be sold, foreclosed upon or otherwise disposed of has such value and liquidity that it may reasonably be anticipated that loss of principal or interest will not result from the loan.

G. Repayment Terms

All loans are required to be repaid within 5 years of the loan unless the purpose of the loan is to acquire a dwelling unit which is to be used within a reasonable time as the principal residence of the participant.

Loans are to be repaid on the basis of substantially level amortization with payments not less frequently than quarterly over the term of the loan.

H. Default

A loan is in default when a scheduled installment payment is 90 days late. If payment has not been made within 30 days of the installment due date, the Loan Administrator will notify the participant in writing that payment is due within 30 days of the date of the notification. If payment is not received within such stipulated time period, the following will take place:

1. The delinquent installment will be considered to be in default as of the date the last payment was due.

2. At the discretion of the Trustee exercised in a uniform and nondiscriminatory manner, the loan will be renegotiated and payments will be made through payroll withholding. If the loan is not renegotiated in a manner acceptable to the Trustee, if permitted in the Plan, the loan will be deemed an in-service withdrawal. Such withdrawal will be subject to personal income and possible penalty taxes. Form W-2P will be timely issued to the participant and the IRS showing such withdrawal.

3. If the participant fails to make provisions for repayment reasonably acceptable to the Trustee, at the election of the Trustee, exercised

in a uniform and nondiscriminatory manner, the remaining principal and interest on the loan shall be declared due and payable as of the date the last payment was due.

4. The amount of any uncured default will be considered as having been received in a taxable event, subject to personal income and penalty taxes. Such tax consequences do not affect the participant's obligation to repay the loan. Form W-2P will be timely issued to the Participant and the IRS; however, the loan will not be charged against the Participant's vested account balance until he or she terminates service, retires, dies, becomes disabled, or reaches the earliest date distribution is permitted under the Plan.

5. To the extent necessary, any other collateral pledged as additional security will be foreclosed upon.

§ A.7 —Hardship Withdrawal Program

Pursuant to the terms of ALPHA OMEGA ORGANIZATION RETIREMENT PLAN AND TRUST, the Trustee has adopted a hardship withdrawal program as part of such Plan and Trust. Hardship Withdrawals will be made pursuant to the terms of the Plan and Trust and the following provisions of this Hardship Withdrawal Program.

A. Administration of Program

The following person ("the Hardship Withdrawal Administrator") is responsible for the administration of the hardship withdrawal program. All requests for hardship withdrawals and other inquiries should be delivered to:

Retirement Committee
c/o Alpha Omega Organization
1492 Atlantic Avenue
Columbus, OH 18950-1990

B. Application Procedure

1. Obtain and complete a hardship withdrawal forms package provided by the Hardship Withdrawal Administrator.

2. Submit the completed forms package to the Hardship Withdrawal Administrator at least 30 days before the date the hardship withdrawal is to be made.

3. Applications for Hardship Withdrawals will be reviewed by the Hardship Withdrawal Administrator for completeness. Incomplete applications will be returned to the applicant for completion.

4. Approved hardship withdrawals will be processed on the first day of each month.

C. Basis for Approvals

In order to qualify for a hardship withdrawal, you must have no other resources or savings to take care of the immediate financial need. Under special rules permitted by the IRS you will be considered not to have sufficient resources to meet the immediate financial need, but only if:

1. the hardship distribution amount is not in excess of the immediate financial need including any amounts necessary to pay any federal, state, or local income taxes or penalties reasonably anticipated to result from the distribution;

2. you have already obtained all non-taxable loans and all distributions (other than a hardship distribution) available from any plan maintained by the Employer;

3. you agree not to make salary reduction and voluntary contributions to the plan and all other plans maintained by the Employer for a 12-month period after you receive the hardship distribution;

4. you agree to reduce the amount of salary reduction contributions for the calendar year following the calendar year in which you receive the hardship distribution by the amount of salary reduction contributions which you made in the year you received the hardship distribution; and

5. you agree to continue to make any loan payments currently through payroll deduction for the remainder of the loan.

The entire amount you withdraw will generally be subject to current Federal Income taxation. If you are under age 59-$\frac{1}{2}$ at the time of the distribution, there may also be an additional income tax because of your age at the time of distribution. You should consult your personal tax adviser as to the tax consequences of any distribution you contemplate before filing the application.

If you wish to apply for a hardship distribution, you should complete an application which the Administrator will provide.

D. Limitations on Hardship Withdrawals

—The minimum amount of any withdrawal is $500.

—Hardship Withdrawals are limited to the participant's salary reduction account excluding income or gains earned on the contributions.

The following expenses will be deemed to constitute an immediate and heavy financial need:

1. medical expenses incurred by the employee, the employee's spouse or dependents. These must be medical expenses described in Section 213 of the Internal Revenue Code;

2. the cost of purchasing a principal residence for the employee (excluding mortgage payments thereon);

3. the cost of tuition for the next 12 months of post-secondary education for the employee, the employee's spouse or dependents (excluding room, board, books, fees or other expenses); or

4. the amount needed to prevent the eviction of the employee from his principal residence or foreclosure of a mortgage on the principal residence.

§ A.8 —Administrative Policies

In accordance with the terms of the Alpha Omega Organization Retirement Savings Plan and Trust, the Retirement Committee has established the following plan rules:

1. Participants may defer from 1% to 15% of compensation in whole percentage increments.

2. a) Participants may choose to direct their accounts among the following investments:
   - Fixed Guaranteed Fund
   - Balanced Return Fund
   - Growth Fund
   - Global Fund

   b) Participants shall direct their investments between these options in 5% increments.

   c) Participants who decline to direct their accounts shall be deemed to have elected 100% investment in the fixed return fund.

   d) Participants may change the direction of new contributions as of January 1, April 1, July 1 or October 1 of each year.

   e) Participants may transfer existing accounts between funds on January 1 of each year.

3. Re-enrollments will occur one per year calendar quarter. Participants may revise their rate of salary deferral effective January 1, April 1, July 1 or October 1.

4. Participants may cease salary deferrals altogether at any time. Participants who voluntarily suspend contributions may begin contributing again as of the second quarter (January 1, April 1, July 1 or October 1) following the quarter in which deferrals were suspended.

5. No rollover or voluntary after-tax contributions will be accepted.

§ A.9   Enrollment Forms

§ A.10   —Enrollment and
Beneficiary Designation

ALPHA OMEGA Organization
Retirement Savings Plan and Trust

Participant's Name: _____

Address: _____

City: _____ State: _____ Zip Code: _____

Date of Employment: ___/___/____ Employment Location: _____

Date of Birth: ___/___/____ Social Security Number: ____-___-____

Marital Status: _____ single _____ married

PART 1—PRIMARY BENEFICIARY (BENEFICIARIES)

I name the following as the Primary Beneficiary to receive any benefits payable upon my death in the proportions indicated:

1. Name: _____ Relationship: _____

   Address: _____

   Percentage of total benefit to be paid to this person _____%

2. Name: _____ Relationship: _____

   Address: _____

   Percentage of total benefit to be paid to this person _____%

3. Name: _____ Relationship: _____

   Address: _____

   Percentage of total benefit to be paid to this person _____%

If I have named more than one Primary Beneficiary, and if at least one, but fewer than all, of those Primary Beneficiaries survive me, I direct that the death benefit be divided among my surviving Primary Beneficiaries in the ratio established by the percentages indicated. If the percentages do not add up to 100%, the benefit payable shall be allocated by the ratio of the percentages.

PART 2—SECONDARY BENEFICIARY

In the event that I survive the person designated in Part 1, I hereby direct that any amount which becomes payable by reason of my death be (Check one):

_____ Paid to my estate

_____ Paid to the following individual or if that person did not survive me, then to my estate

Name: _____ Relationship: _____

Address: _____

The execution of this form and delivery thereof to the Plan Administrator revokes all prior beneficiary designations that I have made.

Date: _____   _____
                                                          Signature

Witness:

_____

SPOUSAL CONSENT IS REQUIRED IF YOU ARE MARRIED AND DESIGNATE AN ALTERNATE BENEFICIARY.

§ A.11 —Spouse's Consent to Beneficiary Designation and Waiver of Benefits

ALPHA OMEGA Organization
Retirement Savings Plan and Trust

Participant _____ Social Security Number _____
Spouse _____ Beneficiary _____

I hereby consent to the designation by my spouse of the Beneficiary elected on the Enrollment and Beneficiary Designation Form as indicated above to receive benefits payable under the Alpha Omega Organization Retirement Savings Plan and Trust (the "Plan") reason of my spouse's death. These benefits may be paid in any form permitted under the Plan to my spouse's designated Beneficiary.

In granting this consent, I understand that I am waiving (giving up) any right I might have to any benefit under the Plan in the event of my spouse's death, except to the extent that my spouse may name me specifically as a Beneficiary herein. I also understand that, had I not granted this consent, I would have had a right protected by law (subject to the provisions of any applicable qualified domestic relations order in favor of another person) to benefits payable in the event of the death of my spouse if my spouse dies while married to me.

This consent and waiver is my free and voluntary act. I understand that I CAN NOT REVOKE this consent, and that, by executing this consent, I am voluntarily relinquishing my right to limit this consent to a specific form of benefits.

Retirement Committee   Participant's Spouse
(Plan Administrator)

By _____   By _____
        Signature   Signature

_____   _____
        Date   Date

§ A.12 —Investment Election

ALPHA OMEGA Organization
Retirement Savings Plan and Trust

This form is to be used to authorize contributions to the Savings Program and to specify how your account is to be invested. Please print the required information, sign the form and return it to the Retirement Committee.

Participant Information

Name: _____

Social Security Number: _____

Election Information

_____ Initial Election
_____ Change of Election

Salary Savings Election

As a Participant in the Alpha Omega Organization Retirement Savings Plan and Trust, I understand the Plan permits me to save for my retirement reducing my compensation. The amount by which I elect to reduce my compensation shall be withheld from my paycheck and paid by Alpha Omega Organization to the Plan on my behalf.

The Plan permits me to reduce my compensation by up to 15%.

_____ I hereby elect to reduce my salary by _____%.
_____ I do not wish to defer salary.

Withholding Authorization

This election authorizes Alpha Omega Organization to withhold this amount from my paycheck, and shall remain in effect until I revoke this election in writing, or change my election percentage in writing, in accordance with a policy established by the Retirement Committee.

Investment Election

I hereby direct the Trustee to invest my salary savings amount and any company contributions in increments of 5% (5%, 10%, etc.) as follows:

Fixed Guaranteed Return Fund	_____%
Growth Fund	_____%
Balanced Fund	_____%
Global Fund	_____%
Total Salary Savings	__100__ %

Signature: _____ Date: _____

§ A.13 Summary Plan Description

Effective Date: January 1, 1989
Table of Contents

Article

Article I
Introduction

In order to recognize the hard work and good efforts of its employees, your Employer has established a 401(k) Salary Deferral Plan for the exclusive benefit of all eligible employees and their beneficiaries. The Plan allows eligible employees to defer part of their income on a tax-favored basis into the Plan. The contributions which you make to the Plan as 401(k) salary deferrals are also called "salary reduction" contributions because your current taxable income is reduced for every dollar you deposit into the Plan.

Also, the money in the Plan grows tax free until your retirement. However, you must pay taxes when the money is paid out, unless it is transferred to another retirement plan or an IRA. You may also be eligible for benefits in the event of your death, total disability or other termination of your employment with the Employer. This Plan is subject to the provisions of the Employee Retirement Income Security Act of 1974 (ERISA).

This Summary Plan Description is a brief description of your Plan and your rights and benefits under the Plan. This Summary Plan Description is not meant to interpret or change the provisions of your Plan. A copy of your Plan is on file at your Employer's office and may be read by you, your beneficiaries, or your legal representatives at any reasonable time. If you have any questions regarding either your Plan or this Summary Plan Description, you should ask your Plan Administrator. If any discrepancies exist between this Summary Plan Description and the actual provisions of the Plan, the Plan shall govern.

Article II
General Information about Your Plan

Plan Name:	Alpha Omega Organization Retirement Savings Plan and Trust
Employer:	Alpha Omega Organization 1492 Atlantic Avenue Columbus, PA 18950-1990 215-987-2341
Employer I.D. No.:	23-0980981
Plan Number:	003
Type of Plan:	Cash or Deferred Arrangement (401k Plan)
Administration Type:	Self Administered

Plan Administrator:	Retirement Committee c/o Alpha Omega Organization 1492 Atlantic Avenue Columbus, PA 18950-1990 215-987-2341
Legal Agent:	Alpha Omega Organization 1492 Atlantic Avenue Columbus, PA 18950-1990 215-987-2341
Trustees:	Faithful Fidelity Bank and Trust
Trustees Address:	1776 Pennsylvania Boulevard Philadelphia, PA 19090-0090 215-345-9800
Plan Year:	January 1 to December 31
Limitation Year:	January 1 to December 31
Anniversary Date:	December 31

Article III
Participation in Your Plan

Before you become a Participant in the Plan, there are certain eligibility and participation requirements which you must meet. These requirements are explained in this section.

Eligible Employees:

All of your Employer's employees are considered Eligible Employees and may participate in the Plan, once they meet the Eligibility and Participation Requirements except members of a collective bargaining unit, self-employed persons, and nonresident aliens.

Eligibility Requirements:

You will be eligible to participate in the Plan after you have attained age 21, completed 24 months of service, and been credited with 1000 Hours of Service during the eligibility computation period.

The "eligibility computation period" is the 12 month period that begins with the date you were hired. If you don't meet the service requirements during the first year following your date of hire, the eligibility computation period becomes the Plan Year. You may then meet the requirements during any Plan Year.

Entry Dates:

Participation in the Plan can begin only on an Entry Date. Your first Entry Date will be the earlier of the first day of the Plan Year, or the first day of the month six months later, July 1st, coincident with or following the satisfaction of the Eligibility requirements.

Rehired Employees:

If you had satisfied the Eligibility requirements before you terminated employment, you will become a Participant immediately on the date you are rehired, if your rehire date is on or after your first Entry Date, as defined above. Otherwise, you will be eligible to participate on the next Entry Date.

If you had not yet satisfied the Eligibility requirements at the time you terminated employment, you must meet the Eligibility requirements as if you were a new employee.

Article IV
Employee Contributions

Your 401(k) Salary Deferral Plan offers you special tax advantages and incentives to participate. First, every dollar you put into the Plan reduces your income currently subject to Federal Income Tax. Thus, your deposits into the 401(k) Plan are often called "salary reductions." (However, you must still pay Social Security Taxes on your gross wages.)

Although you will have to pay income tax when you withdraw money from the Plan, you may be able to defer taxes on a withdrawal by depositing the funds into another Plan or an Individual Retirement Account (IRA). Because you defer paying taxes until you receive payments from the Plan, 401(k) contributions are sometimes called "salary deferrals."

The following chart illustrates the advantage of making deposits into the 401(k) Plan (saving on a tax-deferred basis) rather than saving on an after-tax basis such as a bank passbook savings account or a money market fund.

	401(k) Plan Tax-Deferred Savings	Passbook After-Tax Savings
Gross Wages	$20,000	$20,000
401(k) Deposit	1,000	N/A
Taxable Wages	19,000	20,000
Estimated Taxes (25%)	4,750	5,000
Passbook Deposit	N/A	1,000
Net Take-home Pay	$14,250	$14,000

In our example, net take-home pay (after paying taxes and after saving $1,000) is $250 greater when the savings are deposited into the 401(k)

Plan, rather than an after-tax savings program like a money market or bank passbook account. Saving $1,000 in the 401(k) Plan only "cost" our example person $750 in take-home pay.

This is only a rough illustration of the advantages of tax-deferred savings. Please discuss your situation with your tax advisor.

Tax-Free Accumulation:

Another big advantage your Plan offers is tax-deferred accumulation of the earnings on your investments. All the earnings on the money you contribute to your account compounds tax free. You pay taxes on this money only when you retire or take distributions for some other reason, such as death or becoming totally disabled. If you put your money into a savings account you are required to pay income taxes on the interest each year. Thus, by contributing to your 401(k) Savings Plan, you'll have more money available at retirement.

Salary Reduction Agreement:

To be eligible to enroll in the salary reduction portion of the Plan you must have attained age 21, completed 12 months of service, and be credited with 1,000 Hours of Service.

In order to enroll (or to refuse enrollment), your Employer will ask you to complete a Salary Reduction Agreement. It is here that you tell your Employer how much of your income you wish to defer to your Plan.

There are limits placed on the amount you can defer into this Plan. Your salary deferrals cannot exceed a maximum dollar amount determined by the Federal Government each year. For 1991, that amount is $8,475. Generally, if your total deferrals from all cash or deferred arrangements for a calendar year exceed the dollar amount set by the government, the excess must be included in your income for the year. The IRS also requires that the combined contribution by you and your Employer to your accounts not exceed the lesser of $30,000 or 25% of your pay. Your Employer may also place restrictions on the amount you may defer in order to meet IRS requirements.

Your Employer will deduct the amount you've elected from your paycheck in accordance with procedures established by your Employer.

Restrictions:

In order to provide tax-advantaged savings, the Plan must place restrictions on withdrawals from the Plan. Article X describes the circumstances under which you may withdraw 401(k) deposits from the Plan.

Election Not to Defer:

You may decide that you do not wish to make salary reduction contributions on your first Entry Date. The Plan Administrator will explain the procedures for delayed enrollment in the salary reduction portion of the Plan, if you decide to enroll at a later date.

Excess Deferrals:

If you participate in two or more deferred compensation plans (which include 401(k), Simplified Employee Pensions and 403(b) plans), your total deferrals to all plans could exceed IRS limits for the year. To avoid paying additional excise taxes if excess contributions have to be returned, you may want to designate which plan is to return any excess contributions to you.

If you elect to have this Plan return any excess, you should notify the Plan Administrator so that the excess can be returned to you, along with any earnings, before April 15.

Article V
Employer Contributions

Your Employer may make contributions to the Plan, in addition to your salary deferral 401(k) contributions. Your Employer may make matching contributions, non-elective or discretionary contributions and required minimum contributions, under the Top-Heavy rules (see Article XII) or other legal requirements.

Matching Contributions:

In order to be eligible for matching contributions, you must be making 401(k) contributions to the Plan. You must also have attained age 21, completed 12 months of service, and be credited with 1,000 Hours of Service.

The amount of the match depends on your 401(k) contributions. Your Employer will provide a matching contribution of 50 cents for every dollar you invest in the Plan.

Your employer will make matching contributions only on the first 6% of compensation deposited as elective contributions. Amounts deferred over 6% are not matched. allocated to you with each pay period as you save a portion of your salary.

Non-Elective or Discretionary Contributions:

In order to be eligible for discretionary Employer contributions, you must have attained age 21, completed 24 months of service and completed 1,000 Hours of Service.

In order to receive an allocation of discretionary Employer contributions, you must have worked 1,000 hours during the Plan Year, and be employed on the last day of the Plan Year. You do not have to make 401(k) contributions in order to receive a discretionary contribution.

The amount of the discretionary contribution is set by the Employer each year.

Your share of the non-elective/discretionary contribution is based on the relationship of your compensation to the total compensation for all Participants. For example, if your compensation is $20,000 and if the total compensation is $1,000,000, your share would be 2% of the total discretionary contribution. In our example, if the discretionary contribution was $30,000, your share would be:

$$\$30,000 \times (\$20,000/\$1,000,000) = \$600 \text{ or}$$
$$\$30,000 \times .02 \ (2\%) = \$600)$$

Other Required Contributions:

In certain situations, your Employer may be required to make additional contributions to the Plan. If the Plan is Top-Heavy (see Article XII) or if highly paid participants contribute a higher percentage of pay to the Plan than other participants, your Employer may have to take corrective action. This action could result in either a reduction in the contributions for the highly compensated participants or an additional Employer contribution.

Article VI
Vesting

The term "vesting" refers to the percentage of your Employer contribution account(s) that you are entitled to receive in the event of your termination of employment.

You are always 100% vested in the Employer discretionary account. Whenever you leave employment, you will be entitled to a distribution of the full value of your Employer discretionary account. If you terminate employment before you meet the requirements for retirement (see Article X), the distribution from the Employer matching account will be limited to the vested portion. Your vesting percentage grows with your Years of Service. Article VII explains how Years of Service are credited.

Vesting Schedule for Matching Employer Account:

Years of Service	Percent Vested
Less than 1	0%
1 but less than 2	0%
2 but less than 3	50%
3 but less than 4	75%
4 or more	100%

You will also become 100% vested at Normal Retirement, if you become disabled or if you die. Refer to Article X for information on retirement, disability or death.

In the event the Plan should become 'top-heavy', a faster vesting schedule will apply for the matching account. See Article XII for an explanation of the top-heavy rules.

Top-Heavy Vesting Schedule for the Matching Account:

Years of Service	Percent Vested
Less than 1	0%
1 but less than 2	20%
2 but less than 3	50%
3 but less than 4	75%
4 or more	100%

Article VII
Service Rules

Year of Service:

You will earn a Year of Service for vesting if you are credited with 1,000 Hours of Service during a Plan Year. However, if you are credited with 1,000 hours during your first year of employment, you'll earn a Year of Service. You cannot earn more than one year of service credit during any Plan Year, though.

If you terminate employment and are later rehired by the Employer, your Years of Service after reemployment may be added to the Years of Service you had accumulated when you left. In order for the two periods of service to be added together, you must return to work within 5 years of your termination date.

Hours of Service:

You are credited with the actual number of hours you work and for hours for which you are paid, but are not at work such as paid vacation or paid sick leave.

Break In Service Rules:

When you fail to complete at least 501 hours during the Plan Year, you incur a break in service. Thus, in any year in which you work less than 501 hours (approximately 3 months), you will incur a break in service.

However, in certain circumstances, your Plan is required to credit you with 501 hours, even though you didn't actually work 501 hours. This is primarily if you take time off to have, adopt or care for a child for a period immediately following the birth or adoption. You will receive this credit only for the purpose of determining whether you have incurred a break in service and not for receiving additional credit for a contribution or for vesting.

Article VIII
Compensation

Throughout this Summary Plan Description, the words "compensation" and "pay" are used to define contribution amounts. "Pay" or "Compensation" means the total wages paid to you by your Employer for the Plan Year.

Compensation includes all other deferred compensation which is not includible in your gross taxable income, such as your 401(k) contributions.

In no event shall compensation in excess of $200,000 (as adjusted for changes in the Consumer Price Index: $222,220 for 1991) be taken into account for any Participant in this Plan.

Your compensation for the first Plan Year in which you participate shall be your compensation from the Employer for the full Plan Year.

Article IX
Participants' Accounts

Under the 401(k) Savings Plan, the money you deposit and any Employer contributions are placed into investment accounts, which are credited with gains and losses at each Valuation Date. The Valuation Date for your 401(k) Plan occurs quarterly, on the last day of every three month period during the Plan Year.

Separate accounts are set up for each different type of money: 401(k) deposits, matching and discretionary contributions because there are different Plan and IRS rules for each type of contribution.

Forfeitures:

In addition to contributions, the Employer matching account and Employer discretionary contribution account are credited with forfeitures if they occur. "Forfeitures" are amounts which could not be paid to terminated participants because they were not 100% vested when they separated from service with the Employer.

Rollover and Voluntary Accounts:

Your Plan may allow employees who had retirement accounts with a previous Employer to transfer the previous account balance to your Plan. This is a segregated "Rollover" account and it is always 100% vested. In order to avoid taxes on your "Rollover" money, you must transfer the money from your old plan to this Plan within 60 days after receiving the money.

Also, your prior Plan (if any) may have allowed you to make voluntary after-tax contributions to your Plan. (You can no longer do this under this

Plan.) If you elected to make voluntary contributions under the prior Plan, you also have a "Voluntary" account.

Investments:

Your Plan offers several investment options and you may instruct the Trustees how you would like to invest the funds in your 401(k), matching, Employer discretionary and other Employer contribution accounts.

If you choose not to select how your accounts are invested, the Trustee will invest them for you. The Trustees are fiduciaries of the Plan, which means that they have a responsibility to you to invest the Plan assets prudently.

Contact your Plan Administrator for information concerning the investment options which are currently available.

Crediting Your Accounts with Gain or Loss:

Each investment account is credited with investment gain or loss as of each Valuation Date. Earnings or losses are allocated on the basis of the ratio your account balance bears to the total account balances of all participants in the same investment. You are then credited with that percentage of earnings or losses.

Article X
Distributions and Benefits under Your Plan

Distributions from your salary deferral accounts are not permitted prior to your Retirement Date, EXCEPT in the event of:

(a) death;

(b) disability;

(c) termination of employment; or

(d) reasons of proven financial hardship resulting from accident or sickness to you or your dependents; financial hardship resulting from establishing or keeping your place of residence, provided funds are not available to you from any other financial resources.

NOTE: Hardship withdrawals from your 401(k) salary deferral accounts will be limited to those funds deferred under the Plan. Income or earnings on your deferrals are not eligible for hardship distribution.

Normal Retirement Benefits:

The Normal Retirement Age for the Plan is the later of age 65 or your age on the 5th anniversary of your participation in the Plan.

Your Normal Retirement Date is the first day of the month coincident with or next following the date you reach Normal Retirement Age.

At your Normal Retirement Date, you will be entitled to 100% of your account balance. Payment of your benefits will begin as soon as practicable after you've retired. (See Article XI, Benefit Payment Options.)

Late Retirement Benefits:

If you decide to work past your Normal Retirement Date, you can defer payment of your benefits until your Retirement Date. Payment of your Retirement benefits will commence as soon as practicable following your late retirement date.

Death Benefits:

Should you die before retirement, your spouse or beneficiary will be entitled to 100% of your account balance plus proceeds from Life Insurance Contracts, if any.

If you are married at the time of your death, your spouse will be the beneficiary of your death benefits, unless you otherwise elect in writing on a form to be furnished to you by the Plan Administrator. IF YOU WISH TO DESIGNATE A BENEFICIARY OTHER THAN YOUR SPOUSE AS YOUR BENEFICIARY, YOUR SPOUSE MUST CONSENT TO WAIVE HIS/HER RIGHT TO RECEIVE DEATH BENEFITS UNDER THE PLAN. YOUR SPOUSE'S CONSENT MUST BE IN WRITING AND WITNESSED BY A NOTARY OR A PLAN REPRESENTATIVE.

If your spouse has consented to a valid waiver of any rights to the death benefit; or your spouse cannot be located; or you are single at the time of your death, then your death benefit will be paid to any beneficiary you may chose. The Plan Administrator will supply you with a beneficiary designation form.

Since your spouse has certain rights under your Plan, you should immediately inform the Plan Administrator of any changes in your marital status.

Disability Benefits:

Should you become permanently disabled while a Participant under this Plan, you will receive 100% of your account balance. "Disability" means a medically determinable physical or mental impairment which may be expected to result in death or to last at least a year and which renders you incapable of performing your duties with your Employer. A determination of disability will be made by the Plan Administrator in a uniform, nondiscriminatory manner on the basis of medical evidence.

If it is determined you are disabled, your payments will begin on or before the Anniversary Date following the date you were determined to be disabled.

Benefits upon Termination:

If your employment is terminated for any reason other than those set out above, you will only be entitled to that portion of your Employer accounts in which you are vested. (You are always entitled to 100% of the account balance of any Salary Reduction or Voluntary contribution money you contributed to your Plan.)

"Vesting" refers to the percentage of your account balance you are entitled to at any point in time. For each year you remain a Participant in the Plan, you become vested with a higher percentage of your Employer account balance. (See Vesting, Article VI.)

If your benefit is over $3,500, you may at your option, and with your spouse's consent, request the Plan Administrator to distribute your benefit to you before your retirement date. However, your distribution date will be the last day of the Plan Year after you terminate employment.

If your benefit is $3,500 or less, the Plan Administrator may distribute your benefit early. No spousal consent is needed for distributions of $3,500 or less.

Distributions Due to a Domestic Relations Order:

In general, contributions made by you or your Employer for your retirement are not subject to alienation. This means they cannot be sold, used as collateral for a loan, given away or otherwise transferred. They are not subject to the claims of your creditors. However, they may be subject to claims under a Qualified Domestic Relations Order (QDRO).

The Administrator may be required by law to recognize obligations you incur as a result of court ordered child support or alimony payments. The Administrator must honor a "Qualified Domestic Relations Order" which is defined as a decree or order issued by a court that obligates you to pay child support or alimony, or otherwise allocates a portion of your assets in the Plan to your spouse, child or other dependent. If a QDRO is received by the Administrator, all or portions of your benefits may be used to satisfy the obligation. It is the Plan Administrator's responsibility to determine the validity of a QDRO.

Taxation of Distributions:

The benefits you receive from the Plan will be subject to ordinary income tax in the year in which you receive the payment, unless you defer taxation by a "rollover" of your distribution into another qualified plan or an IRA. Also, in certain circumstances, your tax may be reduced by special tax treatment such as "5-year forward averaging."

In addition to ordinary income tax, you may be subject to a 10% tax penalty if you receive a "premature" distribution. If you receive a distribution upon terminating employment before age 55 and you don't receive the payment as a life annuity, you will be subject to the 10% penalty, unless you "rollover" your payment. If you take a hardship withdrawal before age 59½, the withdrawal will usually be subject to the 10% penalty. But, there is no penalty for payments due to your death or disability.

As the rules concerning "rollovers" and the taxation of benefits are complex, please consult your tax advisor before making a withdrawal or requesting a distribution from the Plan. The Plan Administrator will provide you with a brief explanation of the rules concerning "rollovers," if you request a distribution which is eligible for a "rollover."

Article XI
Benefit Payment Options

There is one form of payment under your Plan. Your distribution will be in the form of a lump-sum distribution of your total account balances, or you may select an alternate form of payment, if permitted under your Plan, at the time of your distribution. Consult your Plan Administrator for other options of payment.

The Plan Administrator may delay payment to you for a reasonable time for administrative convenience. However, unless you choose to defer receipt of your distribution, the Plan must begin your payments within 60 days after the close of the Plan Year following the latest of:

(a) the date on which you reached your Normal Retirement Age;
(b) the 10th anniversary of the year in which you became a Participant in the Plan; or
(c) the date you terminated employment with the Employer.

In any event, the law requires that your distributions begin no later than April 1 of the year following the date you reach age 70½ (the date six months after your 70th birthday).

Article XII
Top-Heavy Rules

A Plan becomes Top-Heavy when the total of the Key Employees' account balances make up 60% or more of the total of all account balances in the Plan. Key Employees are certain highly compensated officers or owners/shareholders.

If your Plan is Top-Heavy, Plan participants who are not "key" must receive a minimum contribution. This minimum contribution is the smaller of the percentage of pay contributed by the Employer to Key Employees, or 3% of your compensation. If the Employer contribution allocated to your account for the Top-Heavy year is equal to or more than this minimum contribution, no additional Employer contribution would be needed to meet the Top-Heavy rules.

Also, the vesting schedule which applies to the matching contributions changes if your Plan becomes Top-Heavy. Vesting is discussed in Article VI.

Article XIII
Miscellaneous

Protection of Benefits:

Your Plan benefits are not subject to claims, indebtedness, execution, garnishment or other similar legal or equitable process. Also, you cannot voluntarily (or involuntarily) assign your benefits under this Plan.

Loans:

You are allowed to borrow a percentage of your vested benefits. There are special circumstances that apply before you can borrow from your Plan. The Plan Administrator will provide you with the "Loan Procedure" which explains the loan provisions in detail.

Amendment and Termination:

The Employer has reserved the right to amend or terminate your Plan. However, no amendment can take away any benefits you have already earned. If your Plan is terminated, you will be entitled to the full amount in your account as of the date of termination, regardless of the percent you are vested at the time of termination.

Pension Benefit Guaranty Corporation:

The Pension Benefit Guaranty Corporation (PBGC) provides plan termination insurance for defined benefit pension plans. In your 401(k) Plan (a defined contribution plan), all of the contributions and investment earnings are allocated to Participants' accounts. PBGC insurance is not needed and does not apply.

Claims:

When you request a distribution of all or any part of your account, you will contact the Plan Administrator who will provide you with the proper forms to make your claim for benefits.

Your claim for benefits will be given a full and fair review. However, if your claim is denied, in whole or in part, the Plan Administrator will notify you of the denial within 90 days of date your claim for benefits was received, unless special circumstances delay the notification. If a delay occurs, you will be given a written notice of the reason for the delay and a date by which a final decision will be given (not more than 180 days after the receipt of your claim).

Notification of a denial of claims will include:

(a) the specific reason(s) for the denial,

(b) reference(s) to the Plan provision(s) on which the denial is based,

(c) a description of any additional material necessary to correct your claim and an explanation of why the material is necessary, and

(d) an explanation of the steps to follow to appeal the denial, including notification that you (or your beneficiary) must file your appeal within 60 days of the date you receive the denial notice.

If you or your beneficiary do not file an appeal within the 60-day period, the denial will stand. If you do file an appeal within the 60 days, your Employer will review the facts and hold hearings, if necessary, in order to reach a final decision. Your Employer's decision will be made within 60 days of receipt of the notice of your appeal, unless an extension is needed due to special circumstances. In any event, your Employer will make a decision within 120 days of the receipt of your appeal.

Article XIV, STATEMENT OF ERISA RIGHTS, describes the protection you have under ERISA and the steps you can take to enforce these rights.

Article XIV
Statement of ERISA Rights

As a participant in Alpha Omega Organization Retirement Savings Plan and Trust you are entitled to certain rights and protections under the Employee Retirement Income Security Act of 1974 (ERISA). ERISA provides that all Plan participants shall be entitled to:

(a) examine, without charge, at the Plan Administrator's office copies of all documents filed by the Plan with the U.S. Department of Labor, such as detailed annual reports and Plan descriptions,

(b) obtain copies of all Plan documents and other Plan information upon written request to the Plan Administrator (the Administrator may make a reasonable charge for the copies),

(c) obtain a statement telling you whether you have a right to receive a retirement benefit at Normal Retirement Age and if so, what your benefits would be at Normal Retirement Age if you stop working under the Plan now. If you do not have a right to a benefit, the statement will tell you how many more years you have to work to get a right to a benefit. This statement must be requested in writing and is not required to be given more than once a year. The Plan must provide a statement free of charge.

In addition to creating rights for Plan participants, ERISA imposes duties upon the people who are responsible for the operation of the employee benefit plan. The people who operate your Plan, called "fiduciaries" of the Plan, have a duty to do so prudently and in the interest of you and other Plan participants and beneficiaries. No one, including your Employer may fire you or otherwise discriminate against you in any way to prevent you from obtaining a retirement benefit or exercising your rights under ERISA.

If your claim for a retirement benefit is denied in whole or in part you must receive a written explanation of the reason for the denial. You have the right to have the Plan review and reconsider your claim.

Under ERISA, there are steps you can take to enforce the above rights. For instance, if you request materials from the Plan and do not receive them within 30 days, you may file suit in a federal court. In such a case, the court may require the Plan Administrator to provide the materials and pay you up to $100 a day until you receive the materials, unless the materials were not sent because of reasons beyond the control of the administrator.

If you have a claim for benefits which is denied or ignored, in whole or in part, you may file suit in a state or federal court.

If it should happen that Plan fiduciaries misuse the Plan's money, or if you are discriminated against for asserting your rights, you may seek assistance from the U.S. Department of Labor, or you may file suit in a federal court. The court will decide who should pay court costs and legal fees. If you are successful the court may order the person you have sued to pay these costs and fees. If you lose, the court may order you to pay these costs and fees, for example, if it finds your claim is frivolous.

If you have any questions about your rights under ERISA, you should contact the nearest Area Office of the U.S. Management Services Administration, Department of Labor.

401(k) ADMINISTRATIVE MATERIAL

§ B.1   Management Report

**ALPHA OMEGA Organization
Retirement Savings Plan
Allocation Report
December 31, 1990**

§ B.2   —Letter to Trustees

February 14, 1991

Trustees
Alpha Omega Organization Retirement Savings Plan
c/o Alpha Omega Organization
19 West Harrison Street
Philadelphia, PA 19111

Re: Retirement Savings Plan
      December 31, 1990 Allocation

Dear Trustees:

This report presents the results of the December 31, 1990 allocation of the Alpha Omega Corporation Retirement Savings Plan. Contributions of $26,628.00 were made for the plan year. This represented 7.1% of earnings covered in the Plan. Of this, $18,072.00 (4.8% of covered earnings) were participant salary savings and $8,556.00 (2.3% of covered earnings) were Alpha Omega Organization's matching contributions.

Forfeitures of $1,450.05 of matching contributions were allocated in proportion to the actual matching contributions for the year. This increased

---

Thanks to Richard Gabriel Associates for permission to reproduce the administrative forms in this Appendix.

the effective match for the year by 17.0%. Each plan member received an effective match of approximately $.58 for each $1.00 saved.

The annualized rate of investment return in each fund, and the overall plan investment mix at the end of the plan year are summarized as follows:

Investment Fund	Annualized Return	Percent of Assets
Fixed Return Fund	8.9%	29.9%
Balanced Fund	9.3%	23.0%
Growth Fund	10.4%	24.0%
Global Fund	7.7%	18.6%
Participant Loans	9.0%	4.5%
Total	9.2%	100.0%

The plan is in compliance for 1990 with the nondiscrimination standards for salary savings plans set forth by the federal government. Section IV of the report illustrates in detail the manner in which the required three (3) nondiscrimination tests were passed for 1990, demonstrating compliance with federal rulings.

The Top Heavy Ratio for the plan is 38.9%. Since this is below the 60.0% benchmark the plan is not Top Heavy for 1991.

The Fidelity Bond Coverage of $25,000 is sufficient for the 1991 plan year. This level of coverage should be adequate for the next several plan years.

> Very truly yours,
>
> RICHARD GABRIEL ASSOCIATES
>
> Donald C. Cardamone

Table of Contents

§ B.3 —Plan Specifications

PLAN SPECIFICATIONS
ALPHA OMEGA ORGANIZATION
RETIREMENT SAVINGS PLAN
FOR THE PLAN YEAR 01/01/90 THROUGH 12/31/90

TYPE OF ENTITY   Corporation

DATES   Effective - 01/01/87 Valuation - 12/31/90 Eligibility - 12/31/90 Year-end - 12/31/90

                  Period beginning - 01/01/90 and ending - 12/31/90

ELIGIBILITY   Minimum age- 21   Months of service- 12 Terminees do NOT get cont.
                  Age at last birthday.

                  HOURS REQUIRED FOR
                  Eligibility - 1000   Contribution - Active: 1000 Terminee: 1000   Vesting - 1000

                  PLAN ENTRY - January 1 or July 1 immediately following satisfaction of eligibility
                               requirements .

RETIREMENT   NORMAL - First of month coincident with or following attainment of age 65, and
                           completion of 5 years of participation.

                  EARLY - No provisions.

CONTRIBUTION   EMPLOYER - $0.00 allocated salary proportion.

                  SALARY REDUCTION - At participant's discretion.
                                     Maximum contribution for calendar year - $7,979.00

                  EMPLOYEE REQUIRED -- None.

                  EMPLOYEE VOLUNTARY -- None.

                  MATCHING -- Employer will match 50.000% of the aggregate SALARY REDUCTION
                              contribution. To the extent aggregate contribution does not exceed
                              6.000% of compensation.

                  LIMITS - Max percent of compensation - 25.000%   Maximum dollar amount - $30,000.00
                           Maximum deductible employer contribution is 15% of total considered compensation.

VESTING   EMPLOYER - 3-7 year.
                  Year   1   2   3   4   5   6   7
                  Pct   0   0   20   40   60   80 100
                  MATCHING - 3-7 year.
                  Year   1   2   3   4   5   6   7
                  Pct   0   0   20   40   60   80 100
                  Service is calculated using all years of service.

NORMAL FORM   Lump Sum Payment

PRE-RETIREMENT
  DEATH BENEFIT   Value Of Account Balances.

§ B.4 —Employee Census

EMPLOYEE CENSUS
ALPHA OMEGA ORGANIZATION
RETIREMENT SAVINGS PLAN
FOR THE PLAN YEAR 01/01/90 THROUGH 12/31/90

EMPLOYEE POS	PERCENT OWNER	PS	FS	PA	AA	RA	SEX	BIRTH	HIRE	PART	RETIRE	COMPENSATION	HOURS WORKED	STATUS
1	Dennis A. Adams													
P		11	15	46	50	65	M	08/09/40	01/01/80	01/01/87	09/01/05	$96,000.00	*	ACTIVE
2	Mary R. Brown													
O		11	9	51	55	65	F	02/08/35	01/01/80	01/01/87	03/01/00	$30,000.00	*	ACTIVE
3	Deborah S. Carter													
O		16	24	36	40	65	F	03/08/50	01/01/75	01/01/87	04/01/15	$28,800.00	*	ACTIVE
4	Robert F. Doyle													
O		8	29	32	36	65	M	08/07/54	12/31/82	01/01/87	09/01/19	$24,000.00	*	ACTIVE
5	Paul D. Earley													
O		3	35	27	30	65	M	03/14/60	09/08/86	01/01/88	04/01/25	$30,000.00		INACTIVE
*****	-- (terminated 12/30/89, BIS, forfeit 12/31/90)													
6	William A. Finch													
O		13	26	35	39	65	M	11/20/51	05/07/78	01/01/87	12/01/16	$48,000.00	*	ACTIVE
7	Theresa M. Gallagher													
O		3	36	27	28	65	F	02/03/62	10/01/88	01/01/90	03/01/27	$21,600.00	*	NEW-ACTIVE
8	Arthur W. Hamilton													
O		16	17	44	48	65	M	06/18/42	07/01/75	01/01/87	07/01/07	$48,000.00	*	ACTIVE
9	Martin D. Ingles													
O		10	33	28	32	65	M	09/30/58	08/11/80	01/01/87	10/01/23	$36,000.00	*	ACTIVE
10	Regina S. Jackson													
P		11	24	37	41	65	F	09/08/49	02/08/80	01/01/87	10/01/14	$60,000.00	*	ACTIVE

ACTIVE EMPLOYEES:	9	FULLY VESTED: 8	ACTIVE TOTAL COMPENSATION: $392,400.00
INACTIVE EMPLOYEES:	1	PARTIALLY VESTED: 1	INACTIVE TOTAL COMPENSATION: $30,000.00
INELIGIBLE EMPLOYEES:	0	NON VESTED: 0	INELIGIBLE TOTAL COMPENSATION: $0.00
TOTAL EMPLOYEES:	10		TOTAL COMPENSATION: $422,400.00

CONSIDERED COMPENSATION: $392,400.00

* EMPLOYEE WORKED MORE THAN MINIMUM HOURS REQUIRED FOR CONTRIBUTION

§ B.5 —Account Balance Statement

LIMIT ON DEDUCTIBLE CONTRIBUTIONS
ALPHA OMEGA ORGANIZATION
RETIREMENT SAVINGS PLAN
FOR THE PLAN YEAR 01/01/90 THROUGH 12/31/90

```
ELIGIBLE COMPENSATION.......................................      $392,400.00

SALARY REDUCTION CONTRIBUTION (401(k))......................       $18,072.00

TOTAL PARTICIPATING PAYROLL.................................      $374,328.00


EMPLOYER CONTRIBUTION.......................................            $0.00

SALARY REDUCTION CONTRIBUTION...............................       $18,072.00

MATCHING CONTRIBUTION.......................................        $8,556.00

OTHER EMPLOYER CONTRIBUTION.................................            $0.00

TOTAL EMPLOYER CONTRIBUTION.................................       $26,628.00


CONTRIBUTION AS PERCENT OF PARTICIPATING PAYROLL............            7.11%


15% OF PAYROLL.............................................        $56,149.20


CONTRIBUTION LIMITATION CARRYFORWARD FROM PRIOR YEAR........            $0.00


CONTRIBUTION LIMITATION CARRYFORWARD FOR NEXT YEAR..........            $0.00
```

```
*********************************************************
*                                                       *
*        ************************************           *
*        CONTRIBUTION PASSES DEDUCTIBILITY TEST          *
*        ************************************           *
*                                                       *
*********************************************************
```

ACCOUNT BALANCE STATEMENT
ALPHA OMEGA ORGANIZATION
RETIREMENT SAVINGS PLAN
FOR THE PLAN YEAR 01/01/90 THROUGH 12/31/90

SOURCE OF FUNDS	BEGINNING BALANCE	GAIN (LOSS)	FUND CONTRIBUTION	FORFEITURES ALLOCATED	ADJUSTMENTS	ENDING BALANCE	-----VESTED----- PCT	AMOUNT
Employee: 1 Dennis A. Adams								
SALARY REDUCTION								
1 FIXED RETURN	5,875.72	581.43	1,344.00	N/A	0.00	7,801.15	100	7,801.15
2 BALANCED	3,925.83	491.15	2,688.00	N/A	0.00	7,104.98	100	7,104.98
3 GROWTH	4,541.80	542.75	1,344.00	N/A	0.00	6,428.55	100	6,428.55
4 GLOBAL	3,362.45	309.44	1,344.00	N/A	0.00	5,015.89	100	5,015.89
5 LOAN	0.00	0.00	0.00	N/A	0.00	0.00	100	0.00
Subtotal:	$17,705.80	$1,924.77	$6,720.00	$0.00	$0.00	$26,350.57		$26,350.57
EMPLOYER MATCHING								
6 FIXED RETURN	2,801.25	274.33	576.00	97.62	0.00	3,749.20	100	3,749.20
7 BALANCED	1,825.63	223.83	1,152.00	195.24	0.00	3,396.70	100	3,396.70
8 GROWTH	2,132.97	252.02	576.00	97.62	0.00	3,058.61	100	3,058.61
9 GLOBAL	1,542.62	140.41	576.00	97.62	0.00	2,356.65	100	2,356.65
10 LOAN	0.00	0.00	0.00	0.00	0.00	0.00	100	0.00
Subtotal:	$8,302.47	$890.59	$2,880.00	$488.10	$0.00	$12,561.16		$12,561.16
Employee total:	$26,008.27	$2,815.36	$9,600.00	$488.10	$0.00	$38,911.73		$38,911.73
Employee: 2 Mary R. Brown								
SALARY REDUCTION								
1 FIXED RETURN	1,836.15	183.03	450.00	N/A	0.00	2,469.18	100	2,469.18
2 BALANCED	1,226.82	135.31	450.00	N/A	0.00	1,812.13	100	1,812.13
3 GROWTH	1,419.32	171.17	450.00	N/A	0.00	2,040.49	100	2,040.49
4 GLOBAL	1,050.77	97.85	450.00	N/A	0.00	1,598.62	100	1,598.62
5 LOAN	0.00	0.00	0.00	N/A	0.00	0.00	100	0.00
Subtotal:	$5,533.06	$587.36	$1,800.00	$0.00	$0.00	$7,920.42		$7,920.42
EMPLOYER MATCHING								
6 FIXED RETURN	875.38	87.72	225.00	38.13	0.00	1,226.23	100	1,226.23
7 BALANCED	570.51	63.66	225.00	38.13	0.00	897.30	100	897.30
8 GROWTH	666.56	81.10	225.00	38.13	0.00	1,010.79	100	1,010.79
9 GLOBAL	482.07	45.60	225.00	38.14	0.00	790.81	100	790.81
10 LOAN	0.00	0.00	0.00	0.00	0.00	0.00	100	0.00
Subtotal:	$2,594.52	$278.08	$900.00	$152.53	$0.00	$3,925.13		$3,925.13
Employee total:	$8,127.58	$865.44	$2,700.00	$152.53	$0.00	$11,845.55		$11,845.55
Employee: 3 Deborah S. Carter								
SALARY REDUCTION								
1 FIXED RETURN	1,762.71	175.71	432.00	N/A	0.00	2,370.42	100	2,370.42
2 BALANCED	1,177.74	119.83	216.00	N/A	0.00	1,513.57	100	1,513.57
3 GROWTH	1,362.54	148.59	129.60	N/A	0.00	1,640.73	100	1,640.73
4 GLOBAL	1,008.73	80.68	86.40	N/A	0.00	1,175.81	100	1,175.81
5 LOAN	0.00	0.00	0.00	N/A	0.00	0.00	100	0.00
Subtotal:	$5,311.72	$524.81	$864.00	$0.00	$0.00	$6,700.53		$6,700.53
EMPLOYER MATCHING								
6 FIXED RETURN	840.38	84.22	216.00	36.61	0.00	1,177.21	100	1,177.21
7 BALANCED	547.69	56.08	108.00	18.30	0.00	730.07	100	730.07
8 GROWTH	639.89	69.99	64.80	10.98	0.00	785.66	100	785.66
9 GLOBAL	462.79	37.15	43.20	7.32	0.00	550.46	100	550.46
10 LOAN	0.00	0.00	0.00	0.00	0.00	0.00	100	0.00
Subtotal:	$2,490.75	$247.44	$432.00	$73.21	$0.00	$3,243.40		$3,243.40
Employee total:	$7,802.47	$772.25	$1,296.00	$73.21	$0.00	$9,943.93		$9,943.93

SOURCE OF FUNDS	BEGINNING BALANCE	GAIN (LOSS)	FUND CONTRIBUTION	FORFEITURES ALLOCATED	ADJUSTMENTS	ENDING BALANCE	VESTED PCT	VESTED AMOUNT
Employee: 4 Robert F. Doyle								
SALARY REDUCTION								
1 FIXED RETURN	1,468.92	90.48	600.00	N/A	1,500.00-	659.40	100	659.40
2 BALANCED	981.46	83.08	120.00	N/A	300.00-	884.54	100	884.54
3 GROWTH	1,135.46	108.83	120.00	N/A	300.00-	1,064.29	100	1,064.29
4 GLOBAL	840.61	43.77	360.00	N/A	900.00-	344.38	100	344.38
5 LOAN	0.00	0.00	0.00	N/A	3,000.00	3,000.00	100	3,000.00
Subtotal:	$4,426.45	$326.16	$1,200.00	$0.00	$0.00	$5,952.61		$5,952.61
EMPLOYER MATCHING								
6 FIXED RETURN	700.31	75.51	300.00	50.85	0.00	1,126.67	100	1,126.67
7 BALANCED	456.41	45.33	60.00	10.17	0.00	571.91	100	571.91
8 GROWTH	533.24	58.63	60.00	10.17	0.00	662.04	100	662.04
9 GLOBAL	385.66	36.48	180.00	30.50	0.00	632.64	100	632.64
10 LOAN	0.00	0.00	0.00	0.00	0.00	0.00	100	0.00
Subtotal:	$2,075.62	$215.95	$600.00	$101.69	$0.00	$2,993.26		$2,993.26
Employee total:	$6,502.07	$542.11	$1,800.00	$101.69	$0.00	$8,945.87		$8,945.87
Employee: 5 Paul D. Earley -- (terminated 12/30/89, BIS, forfeit 12/31/90 - paid this period)								
SALARY REDUCTION								
1 FIXED RETURN	1,101.71	97.83	0.00	N/A	1,199.54-	0.00	100	0.00
2 BALANCED	852.60	79.46	0.00	N/A	932.06-	0.00	100	0.00
3 GROWTH	855.49	89.06	0.00	N/A	944.55-	0.00	100	0.00
4 GLOBAL	858.38	65.84	0.00	N/A	924.22-	0.00	100	0.00
5 LOAN	0.00	0.00	0.00	N/A	0.00	0.00	100	0.00
Subtotal:	$3,668.18	$332.19	$0.00	$0.00	$4,000.37-	$0.00		$0.00
EMPLOYER MATCHING								
6 FIXED RETURN	508.16	45.12	0.00	442.62-	110.66-	0.00	20	0.00
7 BALANCED	383.40	35.73	0.00	335.30-	83.83-	0.00	20	0.00
8 GROWTH	384.63	40.04	0.00	339.74-	84.93-	0.00	20	0.00
9 GLOBAL	385.88	29.60	0.00	332.39-	83.09-	0.00	20	0.00
10 LOAN	0.00	0.00	0.00	0.00	0.00	0.00	20	0.00
Subtotal:	$1,662.07	$150.49	$0.00	$1,450.05-	$362.51-	$0.00		$0.00
Employee total:	$5,330.25	$482.68	$0.00	$1,450.05-	$4,362.88-	$0.00		$0.00
Employee: 6 William A. Finch								
SALARY REDUCTION								
1 FIXED RETURN	2,937.86	250.02	480.00	N/A	724.63-	2,943.25	100	2,943.25
2 BALANCED	1,962.91	216.98	480.00	N/A	250.32	2,910.21	100	2,910.21
3 GROWTH	2,270.91	258.38	480.00	N/A	57.68-	2,951.61	100	2,951.61
4 GLOBAL	1,681.22	167.76	480.00	N/A	531.99	2,860.97	100	2,860.97
5 LOAN	0.00	0.00	0.00	N/A	0.00	0.00	100	0.00
Subtotal:	$8,852.90	$893.14	$1,920.00	$0.00	$0.00	$11,666.04		$11,666.04
EMPLOYER MATCHING								
6 FIXED RETURN	1,400.61	118.92	240.00	40.68	362.80-	1,437.41	100	1,437.41
7 BALANCED	912.82	102.08	240.00	40.68	124.99	1,420.57	100	1,420.57
8 GROWTH	1,066.49	122.02	240.00	40.68	28.68-	1,440.51	100	1,440.51
9 GLOBAL	771.31	78.58	240.00	40.66	266.49	1,397.04	100	1,397.04
10 LOAN	0.00	0.00	0.00	0.00	0.00	0.00	100	0.00
Subtotal:	$4,151.23	$421.60	$960.00	$162.70	$0.00	$5,695.53		$5,695.53
Employee total:	$13,004.13	$1,314.74	$2,880.00	$162.70	$0.00	$17,361.57		$17,361.57
Employee: 7 Theresa M. Gallagher								
SALARY REDUCTION								
1 FIXED RETURN	0.00	11.51	259.20	N/A	0.00	270.71	100	270.71
2 BALANCED	0.00	6.04	129.60	N/A	0.00	135.64	100	135.64
3 GROWTH	0.00	6.75	129.60	N/A	0.00	136.35	100	136.35
4 GLOBAL	0.00	4.97	129.60	N/A	0.00	134.57	100	134.57
5 LOAN	0.00	0.00	0.00	N/A	0.00	0.00	100	0.00
Subtotal:	$0.00	$29.27	$648.00	$0.00	$0.00	$677.27		$677.27

SOURCE OF FUNDS	BEGINNING BALANCE	GAIN (LOSS)	FUND CONTRIBUTION	FORFEITURES ALLOCATED	ADJUSTMENTS	ENDING BALANCE	-----VESTED----- PCT	AMOUNT
EMPLOYER MATCHING								
6 FIXED RETURN	0.00	5.75	129.60	21.96	0.00	157.31	20	31.46
7 BALANCED	0.00	3.02	64.80	10.98	0.00	78.80	20	15.76
8 GROWTH	0.00	3.37	64.80	10.98	0.00	79.15	20	15.83
9 GLOBAL	0.00	2.49	64.80	10.99	0.00	78.28	20	15.66
10 LOAN	0.00	0.00	0.00	0.00	0.00	0.00	20	0.00
Subtotal:	$0.00	$14.63	$324.00	$54.91	$0.00	$393.54		$78.71
Employee total:	$0.00	$43.90	$972.00	$54.91	$0.00	$1,070.81		$755.98
Employee: 8 Arthur W. Hamilton								
SALARY REDUCTION								
1 FIXED RETURN	2,106.63	211.16	288.00	N/A	254.54	2,860.33	100	2,860.33
2 BALANCED	716.07	104.66	432.00	N/A	381.81	1,634.54	100	1,634.54
3 GROWTH	608.25	119.80	576.00	N/A	509.08	1,813.13	100	1,813.13
4 GLOBAL	1,265.80	107.49	144.00	N/A	127.27	1,644.56	100	1,644.56
5 LOAN	4,156.15	376.58	0.00	N/A	1,272.70-	3,260.03	100	3,260.03
Subtotal:	$8,852.90	$919.69	$1,440.00	$0.00	$0.00	$11,212.59		$11,212.59
EMPLOYER MATCHING								
6 FIXED RETURN	1,400.61	130.77	144.00	24.40	0.00	1,699.78	100	1,699.78
7 BALANCED	912.82	95.14	216.00	36.61	0.00	1,260.57	100	1,260.57
8 GROWTH	1,066.49	126.01	288.00	48.81	0.00	1,529.31	100	1,529.31
9 GLOBAL	771.31	61.92	72.00	12.20	0.00	917.43	100	917.43
10 LOAN	0.00	0.00	0.00	0.00	0.00	0.00	100	0.00
Subtotal:	$4,151.23	$413.84	$720.00	$122.02	$0.00	$5,407.09		$5,407.09
Employee total:	$13,004.13	$1,333.53	$2,160.00	$122.02	$0.00	$16,619.68		$16,619.68
Employee: 9 Martin D. Ingles								
SALARY REDUCTION								
1 FIXED RETURN	2,203.40	175.24	540.00	N/A	1,000.00-	1,918.64	100	1,918.64
2 BALANCED	1,472.18	130.78	162.00	N/A	300.00-	1,464.96	100	1,464.96
3 GROWTH	1,703.18	172.51	108.00	N/A	200.00-	1,783.69	100	1,783.69
4 GLOBAL	1,260.92	87.89	270.00	N/A	500.00-	1,118.81	100	1,118.81
5 LOAN	0.00	0.00	0.00	N/A	0.00	0.00	100	0.00
Subtotal:	$6,639.68	$566.42	$1,080.00	$0.00	$2,000.00-	$6,286.10		$6,286.10
EMPLOYER MATCHING								
6 FIXED RETURN	1,050.47	105.27	270.00	45.76	0.00	1,471.50	100	1,471.50
7 BALANCED	684.61	67.58	81.00	13.73	0.00	846.92	100	846.92
8 GROWTH	799.86	86.08	54.00	9.15	0.00	949.09	100	949.09
9 GLOBAL	578.48	49.55	135.00	22.88	0.00	785.91	100	785.91
10 LOAN	0.00	0.00	0.00	0.00	0.00	0.00	100	0.00
Subtotal:	$3,113.42	$308.48	$540.00	$91.52	$0.00	$4,053.42		$4,053.42
Employee total:	$9,753.10	$874.90	$1,620.00	$91.52	$2,000.00-	$10,339.52		$10,339.52
Employee: 10 Regina S. Jackson								
SALARY REDUCTION								
1 FIXED RETURN	3,672.32	368.73	960.00	N/A	0.00	5,001.05	100	5,001.05
2 BALANCED	2,453.64	251.05	480.00	N/A	0.00	3,184.69	100	3,184.69
3 GROWTH	2,838.64	320.49	480.00	N/A	0.00	3,639.13	100	3,639.13
4 GLOBAL	2,101.53	179.60	480.00	N/A	0.00	2,761.13	100	2,761.13
5 LOAN	0.00	0.00	0.00	N/A	0.00	0.00	100	0.00
Subtotal:	$11,066.13	$1,119.87	$2,400.00	$0.00	$0.00	$14,586.00		$14,586.00
EMPLOYER MATCHING								
6 FIXED RETURN	1,750.77	176.78	480.00	81.35	0.00	2,488.90	100	2,488.90
7 BALANCED	1,141.02	117.53	240.00	40.67	0.00	1,539.22	100	1,539.22
8 GROWTH	1,333.10	151.27	240.00	40.67	0.00	1,765.04	100	1,765.04
9 GLOBAL	964.14	83.15	240.00	40.68	0.00	1,327.97	100	1,327.97
10 LOAN	0.00	0.00	0.00	0.00	0.00	0.00	100	0.00
Subtotal:	$5,189.03	$528.73	$1,200.00	$203.37	$0.00	$7,121.13		$7,121.13
Employee total:	$16,255.16	$1,648.60	$3,600.00	$203.37	$0.00	$21,707.13		$21,707.13

SOURCE OF FUNDS	BEGINNING BALANCE	GAIN (LOSS)	FUND CONTRIBUTION	FORFEITURES ALLOCATED	ADJUSTMENTS	ENDING BALANCE	VESTED PCT	VESTED AMOUNT
TOTALS FOR EACH ACCOUNT								
SALARY REDUCTION								
1 FIXED RETURN	$22,965.42	$2,145.14	$5,353.20	N/A	$4,169.63-	$26,294.13		$26,294.13
2 BALANCED	$14,769.25	$1,618.34	$5,157.60	N/A	$899.93-	$20,645.26		$20,645.26
3 GROWTH	$16,735.59	$1,938.33	$3,817.20	N/A	$993.15-	$21,497.97		$21,497.97
4 GLOBAL	$13,430.41	$1,145.29	$3,744.00	N/A	$1,664.96-	$16,654.74		$16,654.74
5 LOAN	$4,156.15	$376.58	$0.00	N/A	$1,727.30	$6,260.03		$6,260.03
Total:	$72,056.82	$7,223.68	$18,072.00	$0.00	$6,000.37-	$91,352.13		$91,352.13
EMPLOYER MATCHING								
6 FIXED RETURN	$11,327.94	$1,104.39	$2,580.60	$5.26-	$473.46-	$14,534.21		$14,408.36
7 BALANCED	$7,434.91	$809.98	$2,386.80	$69.21	$41.16	$10,742.06		$10,679.02
8 GROWTH	$8,623.23	$990.53	$1,812.60	$32.55-	$113.61-	$11,280.20		$11,216.88
9 GLOBAL	$6,344.26	$564.93	$1,776.00	$31.40-	$183.40	$8,837.19		$8,774.57
10 LOAN	$0.00	$0.00	$0.00	$0.00	$0.00	$0.00		$0.00
Total:	$33,730.34	$3,469.83	$8,556.00	$0.00	$362.51-	$45,393.66		$45,078.83
GRAND TOTALS:	$105,787.16	$10,693.51	$26,628.00	$0.00	$6,362.88-	$136,745.79		$136,430.96

```
Matching -
   Forfeitures Allocated:                          $1,450.05
   Forfeitures NOT Allocated:                          $0.00
```

ADJUSTMENTS TO ACCOUNT BALANCE STATEMENT
ALPHA OMEGA ORGANIZATION
RETIREMENT SAVINGS PLAN
FOR THE PLAN YEAR 01/01/90 THROUGH 12/31/90

SOURCE OF FUNDS	TRANSFERS	EXPENSES/ADJ	WITHDRAWALS	VESTED PAYMENTS	TOTAL ADJUSTMENTS
EMPLOYEE 4 Robert F. Doyle					
FIXED RETURN	1,500.00-	0.00	0.00	0.00	1,500.00-
BALANCED	300.00-	0.00	0.00	0.00	300.00-
GROWTH	300.00-	0.00	0.00	0.00	300.00-
GLOBAL	900.00-	0.00	0.00	0.00	900.00-
LOAN	3,000.00	0.00	0.00	0.00	3,000.00
SUBTOTALS:	$0.00	$0.00	$0.00	$0.00	$0.00
EMPLOYEE 5 Paul D. Earley					
FIXED RETURN	0.00	0.00	0.00	1,199.54	1,199.54-
BALANCED	0.00	0.00	0.00	932.06	932.06-
GROWTH	0.00	0.00	0.00	944.55	944.55-
GLOBAL	0.00	0.00	0.00	924.22	924.22-
FIXED RETURN	0.00	0.00	0.00	110.66	110.66-
BALANCED	0.00	0.00	0.00	83.83	83.83-
GROWTH	0.00	0.00	0.00	84.93	84.93-
GLOBAL	0.00	0.00	0.00	83.09	83.09-
SUBTOTALS:	$0.00	$0.00	$0.00	$4,362.88	$4,362.88-

SOURCE OF FUNDS	TRANSFERS	EXPENSES/ADJ	WITHDRAWALS	VESTED PAYMENTS	TOTAL ADJUSTMENTS
EMPLOYEE 6 William A. Finch					
FIXED RETURN	724.63-	0.00	0.00	0.00	724.63-
BALANCED	250.32	0.00	0.00	0.00	250.32
GROWTH	57.68-	0.00	0.00	0.00	57.68-
GLOBAL	531.99	0.00	0.00	0.00	531.99
FIXED RETURN	362.80-	0.00	0.00	0.00	362.80-
BALANCED	124.99	0.00	0.00	0.00	124.99
GROWTH	28.68-	0.00	0.00	0.00	28.68-
GLOBAL	266.49	0.00	0.00	0.00	266.49
SUBTOTALS:	$0.00	$0.00	$0.00	$0.00	$0.00
EMPLOYEE 8 Arthur W. Hamilton					
FIXED RETURN	254.54	0.00	0.00	0.00	254.54
BALANCED	381.81	0.00	0.00	0.00	381.81
GROWTH	509.08	0.00	0.00	0.00	509.08
GLOBAL	127.27	0.00	0.00	0.00	127.27
LOAN	1,272.70-	0.00	0.00	0.00	1,272.70-
SUBTOTALS:	$0.00	$0.00	$0.00	$0.00	$0.00
EMPLOYEE 9 Martin D. Ingles					
FIXED RETURN	0.00	0.00	1,000.00	0.00	1,000.00-
BALANCED	0.00	0.00	300.00	0.00	300.00-
GROWTH	0.00	0.00	200.00	0.00	200.00-
GLOBAL	0.00	0.00	500.00	0.00	500.00-
SUBTOTALS:	$0.00	$0.00	$2,000.00	$0.00	$2,000.00-
FIXED RETURN	1,970.09-	0.00	1,000.00	1,199.54	4,169.63-
BALANCED	332.13	0.00	300.00	932.06	899.93-
GROWTH	151.40	0.00	200.00	944.55	993.15-
GLOBAL	240.74-	0.00	500.00	924.22	1,664.96-
LOAN	1,727.30	0.00	0.00	0.00	1,727.30
FIXED RETURN	362.80-	0.00	0.00	110.66	473.46-
BALANCED	124.99	0.00	0.00	83.83	41.16
GROWTH	28.68-	0.00	0.00	84.93	113.61-
GLOBAL	266.49	0.00	0.00	83.09	183.40
GRAND TOTALS:	$0.00	$0.00	$2,000.00	$4,362.88	$6,362.88-

§ B.6 —Nondiscrimination Test

401(k) DISCRIMINATION TEST FOR
ALPHA OMEGA ORGANIZATION
RETIREMENT SAVINGS PLAN
FOR THE PLAN YEAR 01/01/90 THROUGH 12/31/90

```
********************************************************
  ***  D I S C R I M I N A T I O N   T E S T   P A S S E D   ***
********************************************************
```

```
************************************************************************************
*                                                                                  *
*                                        AVERAGE            AVERAGE                 *
*                       NUMBER OF        DEFERRAL        CONTRIBUTION               *
*                      PARTICIPANTS     PERCENTAGE        PERCENTAGE                *
*                                                                                  *
*  NON-HIGHLY COMPENSATED      7           3.86%            1.93%                   *
*                                                                                  *
*  HIGHLY COMPENSATED          2           5.50%            2.50%                   *
*                                                                                  *
************************************************************************************
*                                                                                  *
*                        401(k)           401(m)            401(m)                  *
*                       DEFERRAL       CONTRIBUTION      MULTIPLE USE               *
*                      (ADP) TEST       (ACP) TEST           TEST                   *
*                                                                                  *
*  MAXIMUM AVERAGE PERCENTAGE   5.86%       3.86%            8.68%                  *
*                                                                                  *
*  ACTUAL AVERAGE PERCENTAGE    5.50%       2.50%            8.00%                  *
*                                                                                  *
*                        PASSED           PASSED            PASSED                  *
*                                                                                  *
************************************************************************************
```

Types of contribution included in this test: SALARY REDUCTION, OTHER EMPLOYER

---EMPLOYEE---		HIGHLY	CONSIDERED		DEFERRAL
NUMBER	NAME	COMPENSATED	COMPENSATION	CONTRIBUTION	PERCENT

```
******************************************** HIGHLY COMPENSATED ********************************************
```

1	Dennis A. Adams				
		1	96,000.00	6,720.00	7.00
10	Regina S. Jackson				
		1	60,000.00	2,400.00	4.00
HIGHLY COMPENSATED:			156,000.00	9,120.00	11.00

```
******************************************** NON-HIGHLY COMPENSATED ********************************************
```

2	Mary R. Brown				
			30,000.00	1,800.00	6.00
3	Deborah S. Carter				
			28,800.00	432.00	1.50
4	Robert F. Doyle				
			24,000.00	600.00	2.50

---EMPLOYEE---		HIGHLY	CONSIDERED		CONTRIBUTION
NUMBER	NAME	COMPENSATED	COMPENSATION	CONTRIBUTION	PERCENT
6	William A. Finch				
			48,000.00	960.00	2.00
7	Theresa M. Gallagher				
			21,600.00	324.00	1.50
8	Arthur W. Hamilton				
			48,000.00	720.00	1.50
9	Martin D. Ingles				
			36,000.00	540.00	1.50
NON-HIGHLY COMP.:			236,400.00	4,476.00	13.50
GRAND TOTALS:			392,400.00	8,556.00	18.50

401(m) DISCRIMINATION TEST FOR
ALPHA OMEGA ORGANIZATION
RETIREMENT SAVINGS PLAN
FOR THE PLAN YEAR 01/01/90 THROUGH 12/31/90

```
*******************************************************
***   D I S C R I M I N A T I O N   T E S T   P A S S E D   ***
*******************************************************
```

	NUMBER OF PARTICIPANTS	AVERAGE DEFERRAL PERCENTAGE	AVERAGE CONTRIBUTION PERCENTAGE
NON-HIGHLY COMPENSATED	7	3.86%	1.93%
HIGHLY COMPENSATED	2	5.50%	2.50%

	401(k) DEFERRAL (ADP) TEST	401(m) CONTRIBUTION (ACP) TEST	401(m) MULTIPLE USE TEST
MAXIMUM AVERAGE PERCENTAGE	5.86%	3.86%	8.68%
ACTUAL AVERAGE PERCENTAGE	5.50%	2.50%	8.00%
	PASSED	PASSED	PASSED

Types of contribution included in this test: MATCHING

---EMPLOYEE---		HIGHLY	CONSIDERED		CONTRIBUTION
NUMBER	NAME	COMPENSATED	COMPENSATION	CONTRIBUTION	PERCENT

```
************************************* HIGHLY COMPENSATED *************************************
```

---EMPLOYEE---		HIGHLY	CONSIDERED		CONTRIBUTION
NUMBER	NAME	COMPENSATED	COMPENSATION	CONTRIBUTION	PERCENT
1	Dennis A. Adams				
		1	96,000.00	2,880.00	3.00
10	Regina S. Jackson				
		1	60,000.00	1,200.00	2.00
HIGHLY COMPENSATED:			156,000.00	4,080.00	5.00

---EMPLOYEE---		HIGHLY	CONSIDERED		DEFERRAL
NUMBER	NAME	COMPENSATED	COMPENSATION	CONTRIBUTION	PERCENT

```
************************************** NON-HIGHLY COMPENSATED **************************************
```

NUMBER	NAME	HIGHLY COMPENSATED	CONSIDERED COMPENSATION	CONTRIBUTION	DEFERRAL PERCENT
2	Mary R. Brown		30,000.00	900.00	3.00
3	Deborah S. Carter		28,800.00	864.00	3.00
4	Robert F. Doyle		24,000.00	1,200.00	5.00
6	William A. Finch		48,000.00	1,920.00	4.00
7	Theresa M. Gallagher		21,600.00	648.00	3.00
8	Arthur W. Hamilton		48,000.00	1,440.00	3.00
9	Martin D. Ingles		36,000.00	1,080.00	3.00
NON-HIGHLY COMP.:			236,400.00	8,952.00	27.00
GRAND TOTALS:			392,400.00	18,072.00	38.00

§ B.7   —Top-Heavy Test

TOP-HEAVY TEST
ALPHA OMEGA ORGANIZATION
RETIREMENT SAVINGS PLAN
FOR THE PLAN YEAR 01/01/90 THROUGH 12/31/90

```
******************************** T O P — H E A V Y  T E S T ********************************
```

```
****************************************
*  PLAN IS NOT TOP-HEAVY NEXT YEAR  *
*     IRC 416 (g) (1) (a) (ii)      *
****************************************
```

EMPLOYEE CLASSIFICATION	NUMBER IN CLASS	PRIOR DISTRIBUTIONS	CURRENT YEAR BALANCE	TOTAL	PERCENT OF TOTAL
KEY EMPLOYEES:	2	0.00	60,618.86	$60,618.86	38.9
NON-KEY EMPLOYEES:	8	18,952.88	76,126.93	$95,079.81	61.1
TOTALS:	10	18,952.88	136,745.79	$155,698.67	100.0

§ B.8 —Financial Summary

Balance Sheet
December 31, 1990

Investment	December 31, 1990 Market Value	December 31, 1989 Market Value
Assets		
Fixed Return Fund	$ 40,828.34	$ 34,293.36
Balanced Fund	31,387.32	22,204.16
Growth Fund	32,778.17	25,358.82
Global Fund	25,491.93	19,774.67
Participant Loans	6,260.03	4,156.15
Total Assets	$136,745.79	$105,787.16
Liabilities		
Salary Savings Account Balances	$ 91,352.13	$ 72,056.82
Matching Contribution Account Balances	45,393.66	33,730.34
Total Liabilities	$136,745.79	$105,787.16

Income Statement
January 1, 1990 through December 31, 1990

Receipts

Employer Contributions		
Salary Savings	$ 18,072.00	
Matching Contributions	26,628.00	$26,628.00
Net Investment Income		
Fixed Return Fund	3,249.53	
Balanced Fund	2,428.32	
Growth Fund	2,928.86	
Global Fund	1,710.22	
Participant Loans	376.58	10,693.51
Total Receipts		$37,321.51

Disbursements

Benefit Payments		$ 4,362.88
Hardship Withdrawals		2,000.00
Net Addition to Assets		
Market Value of Assets on December 31, 1990	$ 136,745.79	
Market Value of Assets on January 1, 1990	(105,787.16)	30,958.63
Total Disbursements		$37,321.51

§ B.9 —Annual Federal Returns

1990 ANNUAL FEDERAL RETURN

Returns Enclosed

The following forms are enclosed for filing with the Internal Revenue Service:

- Form 5500-C/R
- Schedule A
- Schedule P

Form 5500-C/R is to be signed and dated by a senior official of the organization on the lines denoted by "Signature of Employer/Plan Sponsor," and on the line below denoted by "Signature of Plan Administrator." Print the name of the individual(s) signing on the lines so indicated.

Schedule P should be signed and dated at mid-page by the plan Trustee on the line denoted by "Signature of Fiduciary."

Filing Deadline

The signed and dated annual returns should be forwarded by return/receipt mail no later than *July 31, 1991,* to:

Internal Revenue Service Center
Holtsville, NY 00501

Retain the mail receipt along with a copy of the signed returns with the records of the plan.

Form **5500–C/R**	**Return/Report of Employee Benefit Plan**	OMB No. 1210–0016
Department of the Treasury Internal Revenue Service Department of Labor, Pension and Welfare Benefits Administration Pension Benefit Guaranty Corporation	**(With fewer than 100 participants)** **This form is required to be filed under sections 104 and 4065 of the Employee Retirement Income Security Act of 1974 and sections 6039D, 6047(e), 6057(b), and 6058(a) of the Internal Revenue Code, referred to as the Code.** ►See separate instructions.	**1990** **This Form is Open to Public Inspection**

For the calendar plan year 1990 or fiscal plan year beginning   1 / 1   ,1990, and ending 12 / 31 ,19 90

You must check either box (5) or (6), whichever is applicable. See instructions. | For IRS Use Only

A If (1) through (4) do not apply to this year's return/report, leave the boxes unmarked. This return/report is: | EP–ID

(1) ☐ the first return/report filed for the plan (complete all information);

(2) ☐ an amended return/report;

(3) ☐ the final return/report filed for the plan; or

(4) ☐ a short plan year return/report (less than 12 months).

(5) **Form 5500–C filer check here.** . . . . ☒
(Complete only pages 1 and 3 through 6.)

(6) **Form 5500–R filer check here.** . . . . ☐
(Complete only pages 1 and 2. Detach pages 3 through 6 before filing.) If you checked box (1) or (3), you must file a Form 5500–C.

Information in 1a through 6b is used to identify your employee benefit plan. Check it for accuracy and make any necessary corrections. Also complete any incomplete items in 1a through 6b. This page must accompany your completed return/report.

B IF YOU MADE ANY CHANGES TO THE PREPRINTED INFORMATION OR FILLED IN ANY INCOMPLETE INFORMATION IN 1a THROUGH 6b BELOW, CHECK HERE . . . . ► ☐

C If your plan year changed since the last return/report, check this box . . . . ► ☐

1a Name and address of plan sponsor (employer, if for a single employer plan) (Address should include room or suite no.)

Alpha Omega Organization
19 West Harrison Street
Philadelphia, PA 19111

1b Employer identification number
23–9823600

1c Sponsor's telephone number
(215) 420–8100

1d Business code (see instructions, page 18)
9900

1e CUSIP issuer number

2a Name and address of plan administrator (if same as plan sponsor, enter "Same")
SAME

2b Administrator's employer identification no.

2c Administrator's telephone number

3 If you are not filing a page one with the historical plan information preprinted and the name and EIN of the plan sponsor or plan administrator is different than that on the last return/report filed for this plan, enter the information from the last return/report in **a** and/or **b** and complete **c**.

a Sponsor _____ EIN _____ Plan number __001

b Administrator _____ EIN _____

c If **a** indicates a change in the sponsor's name and EIN, is this a change in sponsorship only? (See instruction 3c for definition of sponsorship.) Enter "Yes" or "No."

4 Plan entity code (Enter only one code from the instructions for line 4 on page 8.) ►A

5a(1) Name of plan ►Alpha Omega Organization Retirement Savings Plan

5b Effective date of plan (mo., day, yr.)
1/ 1/87

5c Enter three-digit plan number ► 001

(2) Does this plan cover self-employed individuals? (Enter "Yes" or "No.") ► No

6a(1) Welfare benefit plan (Enter the applicable codes from page 8 of the instructions in the boxes.)

(2) If you entered a code M, N, or O, is the plan funded? ► . . . . ☐Yes ☐No

6b Pension benefit plan (Enter the applicable pension codes from page 9 of the instructions.) ► 2A

Be sure to include all required schedules and attachments. This page must accompany your completed return/report.

Under penalties of perjury and other penalties set forth in the instructions, I declare that I have examined this return/report, including accompanying schedules and statements, and to the best of my knowledge and belief it is true, correct, and complete.

Signature of employer/plan sponsor ► _____ Date ► _____
Type or print name of individual signing for employer/plan sponsor _____
Signature of plan administrator ► _____ Date ► _____
Type or print name of individual signing for plan administrator _____

For Paperwork Reduction Act Notice, see page 1 of the instructions.   Form **5500–C/R** (1990)

Form 5500-C/R (1990)   Page **3**

6c Other plan features: (if you check box **(1)** or **(2)**, attach Schedule E (Form 5500)): **(1)** ☐ ESOP

		Yes	No
(2) ☐ Leveraged ESOP **(3)** ☒ Participant-directed account plan			
(4) ☐ Pension plan maintained outside the United States **(5)** ☐ Master trust (see instructions)			
(6) ☐ 103-12 investment entity (see instructions) **(7)** ☐ Common/Collective trust **(8)** ☐ Pooled separate account			

----

d Single-employer plans enter the tax year end of the employer in which this plan year ends ▶ Month 12 Day 31 Year 90			
e Is the employer a member of an affiliated service group?	6e		X
f Does this plan contain a cash or deferred arrangement described in Code section 401(k)?	6f	X	
7a Total participants: **(1)** At the beginning of plan year ___10___ **(2)** At the end of plan year ___9___			
b Enter number of participants with account balances at the end of the plan year ___9___			
c (1) Were any participants in the pension benefit plan separated from service with a deferred vested benefit for which a Schedule SSA (Form 5500) is required to be attached?	7c(1)		X
(2) If "Yes," enter the number of separated participants required to be reported ▶			
8a Was this plan amended in this plan year or any prior plan year?	8a	X	
b If **a** is "Yes," enter the date the most recent amendment was adopted ▶ Month 12 Day 1 Year 90			
If the date in **b** is in the plan year for which this return/report is filed, complete **c** through **f**.			
c Did any amendment during the current plan year result in the retroactive reduction of accrued benefits for any participant?	8c		X
d Did any amendment during the current plan year provide former employees with an additional allocation or accrual this year?	8d		X
e During this plan year, did any amendment change the information contained in the latest summary plan description or summary description of modifications available at the time of the amendment?	8e	X	
f If **e** is "Yes," has a summary plan description or summary description of modifications that reflects the plan amendments referred to in **e** been furnished to participants and filed with the Department of Labor?	8f	X	
9a Was this plan terminated during this plan year or any prior plan year? If "Yes," enter year ▶ _____	9a		X
b Were all plan assets either distributed to participants or beneficiaries, transferred to another plan, or brought under the control of PBGC?	9b		
c Was a resolution to terminate this plan adopted during this plan year or any prior plan year?	9c		
d If **a** or **c** is "Yes," have you received a favorable determination letter from IRS for the termination?	9d		
e If **d** is "No," has a determination letter been requested from IRS?	9e		
f If **a** or **c** is "Yes," have participants and beneficiaries been notified of the termination or the proposed termination?	9f		
g If **a** is "Yes," and the plan is covered by PBGC, is the plan continuing to file a PBGC Form 1 and pay premiums until the end of the plan year in which assets are distributed or brought under the control of PBGC?	9g		
h During this plan year, did any trust assets revert to the employer for which the Code section 4980 excise tax is due?	9h		
I If **h** is "Yes," enter the amount of tax paid with your Form 5330 ▶			
10a Was this plan merged or consolidated into another plan(s), or were assets or liabilities transferred to another plan(s) since the end of the plan year covered by the last return/report Form 5500 or 5500-C which was filed for this plan (or during this plan year if this is the initial return/report)?	10a		X

If "Yes," identify the other plan(s):   **c** Employer identification number(s)   **d** Plan number(s)

b Name of plan(s) ▶ _____ _____ _____

e Has Form 5310 been filed?		☐ Yes	☒ No
11 Enter the plan funding arrangement code from page 13 of the instructions ▶ 2	**12** Enter the plan benefit arrangement code from page 13 of the instructions ▶ 2	Yes	No
13 Is this a plan established or maintained pursuant to one or more collective bargaining agreements?		13	X
14 If any benefits are provided by an insurance company, insurance service, or similar organization, enter the number of Schedules A (Form 5500), Insurance Information, that are attached, if none, enter "-0-" ▶ 1			

Welfare Plans Do Not complete Items 15 Through 28. Skip To Item 29. Fringe Benefit Plans Complete 22h and 22m.

		Yes	No
15a	If this is a defined benefit plan subject to the minimum funding standards for this plan year, is Schedule B (Form 5500) required to be attached? **15a**		
	If "Yes," attach Schedule B (Form 5500).		
b	If this is a defined contribution plan, i.e., money purchase or target benefit, is it subject to the minimum funding standards (if a waiver was granted, see instructions)? **15b**		
	If "Yes," complete (1), (2), and (3) below:		
	(1) Amount of employer contribution required for the plan year under Code section 412 . **15b(1)** $		
	(2) Amount of contribution paid by the employer for the plan year . . . . **15b(2)** $		
	Enter date of last payment by employer ▶ Month _ _ _ _ _ Day _ _ _ _ Year_ _ _ _ _ _		
	(3) If (1) is greater than (2), subtract (2) from (1) and enter the funding deficiency here.		
	Otherwise, enter zero. (If you have a funding deficiency, file Form 5330.) . . . . **15b(3)** $		
16	Has the plan been top-heavy at any time beginning with the 1984 plan year? **16**		X
17	Has the annual compensation of each participant taken into account under the plan been limited to $200,000 (as adjusted for cost of living)? **17**	X	
18a	If the plan distributed any annuity contracts this year, did these contracts contain a requirement that the spouse consent before any distributions under the contract are made in a form other than a qualified joint and survivor annuity? **18a**		X
b	Did the plan make distributions to participants or beneficiaries in a form other than a qualified joint and survivor annuity (a life annuity if a single person) or qualified preretirement survivor annuity (exclude deferred annuity contracts)? **18b**	X	
c	Did the plan make distributions or loans to married participants and beneficiaries without the required consent of the participant's spouse? **18c**		X
d	Upon plan amendment or termination, do the accrued benefits of every participant include the subsidized benefits that the participant may become entitled to receive subsequent to the plan amendment or termination? **18d**	X	
19	Were distributions made in accordance with the requirements of Code sections 411(a)(11) and 417(e)? (See instructions.) . **19**	X	
20	Have any contributions been made or benefits accrued in excess of the Code section 415 limits, as amended by the Tax Reform Act of 1986? **20**		X
21	Has the plan made the required distributions in 1990 under Code section 401(a)(9)? **21**	X	
22a	Does the employer apply the separate line of business rules of Code section 414(r) in testing whether this plan satisfies the coverage requirements of Code section 410(b)? **22a**		X
b	If a is " Yes," enter the total number of separate lines of business claimed by the employer . . . . . . ▶ _ _ _ _ _ _ _ _		
c	Does the plan consist of more than one part that is mandatorily disaggregated under Proposed Income Tax Regulations 1.410(b)-7(c)? **22c**		X
d	In testing whether this plan satisfies the coverage and discrimination tests of Code sections 410(b) and 401(a), does the employer aggregate plans? **22d**		X
e	Does the employer restructure the plan into component plans to satisfy the coverage and discrimination tests of Code sections 410(b) and 401(a)(4)? **22e**		X
	IF YOU ANSWERED a, c, or e "YES," DO NOT COMPLETE THE REST OF QUESTION 22 AND SEE INSTRUCTIONS FOR INFORMATION TO BE FURNISHED.		
f	If you meet either of the following exceptions; check the applicable box to tell which exception you meet and do NOT complete the rest of question 22:		
	(1) ☐ No highly compensated employee benefited under the plan at any time during the plan year;		
	(2) ☐ This is a collectively bargained plan that benefits only employees covered under a collective bargaining agreement, and no more than 2 percent of the employees who are covered under the collectively bargained agreement are professional employees.		
g	Did any leased employee perform services for the employer at any time during the plan year? **22g**		X

		Number
h	Total number of employees of the employer. Employer includes entities aggregated with the employer under Code sections 414(b), (c), or (m). The number of employees includes leased employees and self-employed individuals. **22h**	9
I	What is the total number of employees excludable under the plan because of: (1) failure to meet requirements for minimum age and years of service; (2) coverage under a collective bargaining agreement; (3) nonresident aliens who receive no earned income from U.S. sources; and (4) the 500 hours of service/last day rule? **22I**	0
J	Enter the number of nonexcludable employees (subtract line I from line h) **22J**	9
k	Do 100 percent of the nonexcludable employees entered on line I benefit under the plan? . . . . Yes ☒ No ☐		
	If line **k** is "Yes," do NOT complete lines 22I through 22o.		
l	What is the number of nonexcludable employees (line J) who are highly compensated employees? **22I**	
m	What is the number of nonexcludable employees who benefit under the plan? **22m**	
n	What is the number of employees entered on line m who are highly compensated employees? **22n**	
o	This plan satisfies the coverage requirements on the basis of (check one):		
	(1) ☐ The average benefits test		
	(2) ☐ The ratio percentage test -- enter value ▶		

36-3328521

Form 5500-C/R (1990)   Page **5**

			Yes	No
23a	Is it intended that this plan qualify under Code section 401(a)?	23a	X	
	If "Yes," complete **b** and **c** .			
b	Enter the date of the most recent IRS determination letter ▶ Month __3__ Year __88__			
c	Is a determination letter request pending with IRS?	23c	X	
24a	If this is a plan with Employee Stock Ownership features, was a current appraisal of the value of the stock made immediately before any contribution of stock or the purchase of the stock by the trust for the plan year covered by this return/report? . .	24a		
b	If **a** is "Yes," was the appraisal made by an unrelated third party?	24b		
c	If dividends paid on employer securities held by the ESOP were used to make payments on ESOP loans, enter the amount of the dividends used to make the payments . . . . ▶ 24c			
25	Does the plan provide for permitted disparity, see Code sections 401(a)(5) and 401(l)?	25		X
26	Does the employer/sponsor listed in 1a of this form maintain other qualified pension benefit plans?	26		X
	If "Yes," enter the total number of plans including this plan ▶			

27 If this plan is an adoption of a master, prototype or regional prototype plan, indicate which type by checking the appropriate box:

a ☐ Master **b** ☐ Prototype **c** ☒ Regional prototype

28a Is the plan covered under the Pension Benefit Guaranty Corporation termination insurance program?   ☐ Yes ☒ No ☐ Not determined

b If **a** is "Yes" or "Not determined," enter the employer identification number and the plan number used to identify it.

Employer identification number ▶ Plan number ▶

29 The following applies to item 29: (i) you may **NOT** use "N/A" in response to any line item and (ii) if "Yes" is checked you must enter a dollar amount in the amount column. During the plan year:

			Yes	No	Amount
a	Was this plan covered by a fidelity bond?	29a	X		25,000
b	Enter the name of the surety company Faithful Fidelity Company				
c	Was there any loss to the plan, whether or not reimbursed, caused by fraud or dishonesty?	29c		X	
d	Was there any sale, exchange, or lease of any property between the plan and the employer, any fiduciary, any of the five most highly paid employees of the employer, any owner of a 10% or more interest in the employer, or relatives of any such persons?	29d		X	
e	Was there any loan or extension of credit by the plan to the employer, any fiduciary, any of the five most highly paid employees of the employer, any owner of a 10% or more interest in the employer, or relatives of any such persons?	29e		X	
f	Did the plan acquire or hold any employer security or employer real property?	29f		X	
g	Has the plan granted an extension on any delinquent loan owed to the plan?	29g		X	
h	Has the employer owed contributions to the plan which are more than 3 months overdue?	29h		X	
i	Were any loans by the plan or fixed income obligations due the plan classified as uncollectable or in default as of the close of the plan year?	29i		X	
j	Has any plan fiduciary had a financial interest in excess of 10% in any party providing services to the plan or received anything of value from any such party?	29j		X	
k	Did the plan at any time hold 20% or more of its assets in any single security, debt, mortgage, parcel of real estate, or partnership/joint venture interests?	29k		X	
l	Did the plan at any time engage in any transaction or series of related transactions involving 20% or more of the current value of plan assets?	29l		X	
m	Were there any noncash contributions made to the plan whose value was set without an appraisal by an independent third party?	29m		X	
n	Were there any purchases of nonpublicly traded securities by the plan whose value was set without an appraisal by an independent third party?	29n		X	
o	Has the plan failed to provide any benefit when due under the terms of the plan because of insufficient assets?	22o		X	

30 Current value of plan assets and liabilities at the beginning and end of the plan year. Combine the value of plan assets held in more than one trust. Allocate the value of the plan's interest in a commingled trust containing the assets of more than one plan on a line-by-line basis unless the trust meets one of the specific exceptions described in the instructions. Do not enter the value of the portion of an insurance contract which guarantees during this plan year to pay a specific dollar benefit at a future date. **Round off amounts to the nearest dollar. Any other amounts are subject to rejection.**

Assets

			(a) Beginning of year	(b) End of year
a	Cash	30a		
b	Receivables	30b		
c	Investments:			
	(1) U.S. Government securities	30c(1)		
	(2) Corporate debt and equity instruments	30c(2)		
	(3) Real estate and mortgages (other than to participants)	30c(3)		
	(4) Loans to participants:			
	A Mortgages	(4)A		
	B Other	(4)B	4,156	6,260
	(5) Other	30c(5)	101,631	130,486
	(6) Total investments (add (1) through (5)) ►	30c(6)	105,787	136,746
d	Buildings and other property used in plan operations	30d		
e	Other assets	30e		
f	Total assets (add a, b, c,(6), d, and e) ►	30f	105,787	136,746

Liabilities

g	Payables	30g		
h	Acquisition indebtedness	30h		
i	Other liabilities	30i		
j	Total liabilities (add g through i) ►	30j	0	0
k	Net assets (f minus j) ►	30k	105,787	136,746

31 Plan income, expenses, and changes in net assets for the plan year. Include all income and expenses of the plan including any trust(s) or separately maintained fund(s) and payments/receipts to/from insurance carriers. **Round off amounts to nearest dollar. Any other amounts are subject to rejection.**

Income

			(a) Amount	(b) Total
a	Contributions received or receivable in cash from:			
	(1) Employer(s) (including contributions on behalf of self-employed individuals)	31a(1)	26,628	
	(2) Employees	31a(2)	0	
	(3) Others	31a(3)	0	
	(4) Add (1) through (3)	31a(4)	26,628	
b	Noncash contributions (enter total of a(4) and b in column (b))	31b	0	26,628
c	Earnings from investments (interest, dividends, rents, royalties)	31c		10,694
d	Net realized gain (loss) on sale or exchange of assets	31d		0
e	Other income (specify) ► _____	31e		0
f	Total income (add b through e) ►	31f		37,322

Expenses

g	Distribution of benefits and payments to provide benefits:			
	(1) Directly to participants or their beneficiaries	31g(1)	6,363	
	(2) Other	31g(2)		6,363
h	Administrative expenses (salaries, fees, commissions, insurance premiums)	31h		
i	Other expenses (specify) ► _____	31i		
j	Total expenses (add g through i) ►	31j		6,363
k	Net income (loss) (subtract j from f) ►	31k		30,959

SCHEDULE A (Form 5500)	Insurance Information	OMB No. 1210-0016

SCHEDULE A (Form 5500)

Department of the Treasury
Internal Revenue Service

Department of Labor
Pension and Welfare Benefits Administration

Pension Benefit Guaranty Corporation

Insurance Information

This schedule is required to be filed under section 104 of the Employee Retirement Income Security Act of 1974.

▶ File as an Attachment to Forms 5500 or 5500-C/R.

▶ Insurance companies are required to provide this information as per ERISA section 103(a)(2).

OMB No. 1210-0016

1990

This Form Is Open to Public Inspection

For calendar year 1990 or fiscal plan year beginning   1 / 1   ,1990 and ending   12 / 31   ,19 90

▶ Part I must be completed for all plans required to file this schedule.
▶ Part II must be completed for all insured pension plans.
▶ Part III must be completed for all insured welfare plans.

▶ Enter master trust or 103-12 IE name in place of "sponsor" and specify investment account or 103-12 IE in place of "plan" if filing with DOL for a master trust or 103-12 IE.

Name of plan sponsor as shown on line 1a of Form 5500 or 5500-C/R

Alpha Omega Organization

Employer identification number

23-9823600

Name of plan Alpha Omega Organization Retirement Savings Plan

Enter three-digit plan number ▶ 0 0 1

Part I   Summary of All Insurance Contracts Included in Parts II and III

Group all contracts in the same manner as in Parts II and III.

1 Check appropriate box: a ☐ Welfare plan b ☒ Pension plan c ☐ Combination pension and welfare plan

2 Coverage: (a) Name of insurance carrier	(b) Contract or identification number	(c) Approximate number of persons covered at end of policy or contract year	Policy or contract year (d) From	(e) To
Nationwide Life Insurance Company	CAP-91-543209	9	1/ 1/90	12/31/90

3 Insurance fees and commissions paid to agents and brokers:

(a) Contract or identification number	(b) Name and address of the agents or brokers to whom commissions or fees were paid	(c) Amount of commissions paid	(d) Fees paid Amount	Purpose
CAP-91-543209				
Total		0	0	

4 Premiums due and unpaid at end of the plan year ▶ $ 0 : Contract or identification number ▶ CAP-91-543209

Part II   Insured Pension Plans Provide information for each contract on a separate Part II. Where individual contracts are provided, the entire group of such individual contracts with each carrier may be treated as a unit for purposes of this report.

▶ Contract or identification number ▶

5 Contracts with allocated funds, for example, individual policies or group deferred annuity contracts:

  a State the basis of premium rates ▶
  b Total premiums paid to carrier . . . .
  c If the carrier, service or other organization incurred any specific costs in connection with the acquisition or retention of the contract or policy, other than reported in 3 above, enter amount . . . .
     Specify nature of costs ▶

6 Contracts with unallocated funds, for example, deposit administration or immediate participation guarantee contracts. Do not include portions of these contracts maintained in separate accounts:

a Balance at the end of the previous policy year	34,293
b Additions: (i) Contributions deposited during year 7,933	
(ii) Dividends and credits	
(iii) Interest credited during the year 3,249	
(iv) Transferred from separate account	
(v) Other (specify) ▶ Loan Repayments 254	
(vi) Total additions	11,436
c Total of balance and additions, add a and b (vi)	45,729
d Deductions:	
(i) Disbursed from fund to pay benefits or purchase annuities during year 2,311	
(ii) Administration charge made by carrier	
(iii) Transferred to separate account 1,090	
(iv) Other (specify) ▶ Loan Distribution 1,500	
(v) Total deductions	4,901
e Balance at end of current policy year, subtract d (v) from c	40,828
7 Separate accounts: Current value of plan's interest in separate accounts at year end	89,656

For Paperwork Reduction Act Notice, see page 1 of the instructions for Form 5500 or 5500-C/R.   Schedule A (Form 5500) 1990

Schedule A (Form 5500) 1990   Page 2

Part III Insured Welfare Plans

Provide information for each contract on a separate Part III. If more than one contract covers the same group of employees of the same employer(s) or members of the same employee organization(s), the information may be combined for reporting purposes if such contracts are experience-rated as a unit. Where individual contracts are provided, the entire group of such individual contracts with each carrier may be treated as a unit for purposes of this report.

8	(a) Contract or identification number	(b) Type of benefit	(c) List gross premium for each contract	(d) Premium rate or subscription charge

9 Experience-rated contracts: **a** Premiums: (i) Amount received . . . .

    (ii) Increase (decrease) in amount due but unpaid . . . .

    (iii) Increase (decrease) in unearned premium reserve . . . .

    (iv) Premiums earned, add (i) and (ii), and subtract (iii) . . . .

  b Benefit charges: (i) Claims paid . . . .

    (ii) Increase (decrease) in claim reserves . . . .

    (iii) Incurred claims, add (i) and (ii) . . . .

    (iv) Claims charged . . . .

  c Remainder of premium: (i) Retention charges (on an accrual basis)--

    (A) Commissions . . . .

    (B) Administrative service or other fees . . . .

    (C) Other specific acquisition costs . . . .

    (D) Other expenses . . . .

    (E) Taxes . . . .

    (F) Charges for risks or contingencies . . . .

    (G) Other retention charges . . . .

    (H) Total retention . . . .

    (ii) Dividends or retroactive rate refunds.   (These amounts were☐ paid in cash or ☐ credited.) . . . . .

  d Status of policyholder reserves at end of year: (i) Amount held to provide benefits after retirement . . . .

    (ii) Claim reserves. . . . .

    (iii) Other reserves . . . .

  e Dividends or retroactive rate refunds due (Do not include amount entered in **c** (ii).) . . . .

10 Nonexperience-rated contracts: **a** Total premiums or subscription charges paid to carrier . . . .

  b If the carrier, service, or other organization incurred any specific costs in connection with the acquisition or

  retention of the contract or policy, other than reported in 3 above, report amount . . . .

  Specify nature of costs ▶ _

If additional space is required for any item, attach additional sheets the same size as this form.

General Instructions

This schedule must be attached to Form 5500 or 5500-C/R for every defined benefit, defined contribution, and welfare benefit plan where any benefits under the plan are provided by an insurance company, insurance service, or other similar organization.

Specific Instructions

(References are to the line items on the form.)

Information entered on Schedule A (Form 5500) should pertain to contracts with policy or contract years ending with or within the plan year (for reporting purposes a year cannot exceed 12 months). **Exception:** If the insurance company maintains records on the basis of a plan year rather than a policy or contract year, the information entered on Schedule A (Form 5500) may pertain to the plan year instead of the policy or contract year.

Include only the contracts issued to the plan for which this is return/report is being filed.

Plans Participating in Master Trust(s) and 103-12 IEs-- See the Form 5500 or Form 5500-C/R instructions for "Reporting Requirements for Investment Arrangements Filing With DOL."

Line 2(c).-- Since the plan coverage may fluctuate during the year, the administrator should estimate the number of persons that were covered by the plan at the end of the policy or contract year.

Where contracts covering individual employees are grouped, entries should be determined as of the end of the plan year.

Lines 2(d) and (e).--Enter the beginning and ending dates of the policy year for each contract listed under column (b). Enter "N/A" in column (d) if separate contracts covering individual employees are grouped.

Line 3.--Report all sales commissions in column (c) regardless of the identity of the recipient. Do not report override commissions, salaries, bonuses, etc., paid to a general agent or manager for managing an agency, or for performing other administrative functions. Fees to be reported in column (d) represent payments by insurance carriers to agents and brokers for items other than commissions (e.g., service fees, consulting fees, and finders fees).

Note: For purposes of this item, commissions and fees include amounts paid by an insurance company on the basis of the aggregate value (e.g., policy amounts, premiums) of contracts or

policies (or classes thereof) placed or retained. The amount (or pro rata share of the total) of such commissions or fees attributable to the contract or policy placed with or retained by the plan must be reported in column (c) or (d), as appropriate.

Fees paid by insurance carriers to persons other than agents and brokers should be reported in Parts II and III on Schedule A (Form 5500) as acquisition costs, administrative charges, etc., as appropriate. For plans with 100 or more participants, fees paid by employee benefit plans to agents, brokers, and other persons are to be reported on Schedule C (Form 5500).

Line 5a.-- The rate information called for here may be furnished by attachment of appropriate schedules of current rates filed with appropriate state insurance departments or by a statement as to the basis of the rates.

Line 6.--Show deposit fund amounts rather than experience credit records when both are maintained.

Line 8(d).--The rate information called for here may be furnished by attachment of the appropriate schedules of current rates or by a statement as to the basis of the rates.

36-3328521

SCHEDULE P	**Annual Return of Fiduciary**	OMB No. 1210-0016
(Form 5500)	**of Employee Benefit Trust**	
	▶ File as an attachment to Form 5500, 5500-C/R, or 5500EZ.	**1990**
Department of the Treasury Internal Revenue Service	▶ For the Paperwork Reduction Notice, see page 1 of the Form 5500 Instructions.	

For trust calendar year 1990 or fiscal year beginning   1 / 1   , 1990, and ending   12 / 31   , 1990

P l e a s e   t y p e   o r   p r i n t

1 a Name of trustee or custodian
James Smith, Henry Jones, Mark Reilley

b Number, street, and room or suite no. (If a P.O. box, see the instructions for Form 5500, 5500-C/R, or 5500EZ.)
19 Harrison Street

c City or town, state and ZIP code
Philadelphia, PA 19111

2 Name of trust
Alpha Omega Organization Retirement Savings Trust

3 Name of plan if different from name of trust
Alpha Omega Organization Retirement Savings Plan

4 Have you furnished the participating employee benefit plan(s) with the trust financial information required to be reported by the plan(s)? . . . . ☒ Yes ☐ No

5 Enter the plan sponsor's employer identification number as shown on Form 5500, 5500-C/R, or 5500EZ. . . . . ▶ 23 9823600

Under penalties of perjury, I declare that I have examined this schedule, and to the best of my knowledge and belief, it is true, correct, and complete.

Signature of fiduciary ▶   Date ▶

Instructions

(Section references are to the Internal Revenue Code.)

A. Purpose of Form

You may use this schedule to satisfy the requirements under section 6033(a) for an annual information return from every section 401(a) organization exempt from tax under section 501(a).

The filing of this form will also start the running of the statute of limitations under section 6501(a) for any trust described in section 401(a), which is exempt from tax under section 501(a).

B. Who May File

(1) Every trustee of a trust described in section 401(a), which was created as part of an employee benefit plan.
(2) Every custodian of a custodial account described in section 401(f).

C. How To File

File Schedule P (Form 5500) for the trust year ending with or within any participating plan's plan year as an attachment to the Form 5500, 5500-C/R, or 5500EZ filed by the plan for that plan year.

Schedule P (Form 5500) may be filed only as an attachment to a Form 5500, 5500-C/R, or 5500EZ. A separately filed Schedule P (Form 5500) will not be accepted.

If the trust or custodial account is used by more that one plan, file only one Schedule P (Form 5500). It must be filed as an attachment to one of the participating plan's returns/reports. If a plan uses more than one trust or custodial account for its funds, file one Schedule P (Form 5500) for each trust or custodial account.

D. Signature

The fiduciary (trustee or custodian) must sign this schedule. If there is more than one fiduciary, one of them, authorized by the others, may sign.

E. Other Returns and Forms That May Be Required

(1) Form 990-T. — For trusts described in section 401(a), a tax is imposed on income derived from business that is unrelated to the purpose for which the trust received a tax exemption. Report such income and tax on **Form 990-T**, Exempt Organization Business Income Tax Return. (See sections 511 through 514 and related regulations.)

(2) Forms W-2P and 1099-R. — If you made payments or distributions to individual beneficiaries of a plan, report these payments on Forms W-2P or 1099-R. (See sections 6041 and 6047 and related regulations.)

(3) Forms 941 or 941E. — If you made payments or distributions to individual beneficiaries of a plan, you are required to withhold income tax from those payments unless the payee elects not to have the tax withheld. Report this withholding on Form 941 or 941E. (See Forms 941 or 941E and Circular E, Publication 15.)

36-3328521

Schedule P (Form 5500) 1990

§ B.10 —Summary Annual Report

The Summary Annual Report reflects the financial position of the plan for the plan year just completed. It should be reproduced and distributed to all plan participants no later than *September 30, 1991.*

SUMMARY ANNUAL REPORT FOR ALPHA OMEGA ORGANIZATION RETIREMENT SAVINGS PLAN

This is a summary of the annual report for Alpha Omega Organization Retirement Savings Plan, EIN 23-9823600, for January 1, 1990, through December 31, 1990. The annual report has been filed with the Internal Revenue Service, as required under the Employee Retirement Income Security Act of 1974 (ERISA).

BASIC FINANCIAL STATEMENT

Benefits under the plan are provided by a combination of trust and insurance. Plan expenses were $6,363.00. These expenses included $0.00 in administrative expenses and $6,363.00 in benefits paid to participants and beneficiaries, and $0.00 in other expenses. A total of 9 persons were participants in or beneficiaries of the plan at the end of the plan year, although not all of these persons had yet earned the right to receive benefits.

The value of plan assets, after subtracting liabilities of the plan, was $136,746.00 as of December 31, 1990, compared to $105,787.00 as of January 1, 1990. During the plan year the plan experienced an increase in its net assets of $30,959.00. This increase includes unrealized appreciation or depreciation in the value of plan assets; that is, the difference between the value of the plan's assets at the end of the year and the value of the assets at the beginning of the year or the cost of assets acquired during the year. The plan had total income of $37,322.00, including employer contributions of $26,628.00, employee contributions of $0.00, gains of $0.00 from the sale of assets, and earnings from investments of $10,694.00.

The plan has contract(s) with which allocate(s) funds toward individual and/or group policies or annuities. The total premiums paid for the plan year ending December 31, 1990, were $0.00.

YOUR RIGHTS TO ADDITIONAL INFORMATION

You have the right to receive a copy of the full annual report, or any part thereof, on request. The items listed below are included in that report:

1. an accountant's report;
2. assets held for investment;
3. insurance information including sales commissions paid by insurance carriers;

To obtain a copy of the full annual report, or any part thereof, write or call the office of Alpha Omega Organization, who is the plan administrator, 19 West Harrison Street, Philadelphia, PA 19111, (215) 420-8100. The charge to cover copying costs will be $1.00 for the full annual report, or $0.25 per page for any part thereof.

You also have the right to receive from the plan administrator, on request and at no charge, a statement of the assets and liabilities of the plan and accompanying notes, or a statement of income and expenses of the plan and accompanying notes, or both. If you request a copy of the full annual report from the plan administrator, these two statements and accompanying notes will be included as part of that report. The charge to cover copying costs given above does not include a charge for the copying of these portions of the report because these portions are furnished without charge.

You also have the legally protected right to examine the annual report at the main office of the plan, 19 West Harrison Street, Philadelphia, PA 19111, and at the U.S. Department of Labor in Washington, D.C., or to obtain a copy from the U.S. Department of Labor upon payment of copying costs. Requests to the Department should be addressed to: Public Disclosure Room, N4677, Pension and Welfare Benefit Programs, Department of Labor, 200 Constitution Avenue, N.W., Washington, D.C. 20216.

§ B.11 —Employee Benefit Statements

ALPHA OMEGA ORGANIZATION
RETIREMENT SAVINGS PLAN
VALUATION DATE: 12/31/90

EMPLOYEE: Dennis A. Adams
#1   **
            * STATEMENT FOR THE PERIOD 01/01/90 THROUGH 12/31/90 *
            ****

SOURCE OF FUNDS	BEGINNING BALANCE as of 01/01/90	CONTRIBUTIONS	GAIN/LOSS	FORFEITURES	DISTRIBUTIONS & ADJUSTMENTS	ENDING BALANCE as of 12/31/90
SALARY REDUCTION ACCOUNT(S)						
1) FIXED RETURN	5,875.72	1,344.00	581.43	0.00	0.00	7,801.15
2) BALANCED	3,925.83	2,688.00	491.15	0.00	0.00	7,104.98
3) GROWTH	4,541.80	1,344.00	542.75	0.00	0.00	6,428.55
4) GLOBAL	3,362.45	1,344.00	309.44	0.00	0.00	5,015.89
SUBTOTALS:	$17,705.80	$6,720.00	$1,924.77	$0.00	$0.00	$26,350.57
MATCHING ACCOUNT(S)						
1) FIXED RETURN	2,801.25	576.00	274.33	97.62	0.00	3,749.20
2) BALANCED	1,825.63	1,152.00	223.83	195.24	0.00	3,396.70
3) GROWTH	2,132.97	576.00	252.02	97.62	0.00	3,058.61
4) GLOBAL	1,542.62	576.00	140.41	97.62	0.00	2,356.65
SUBTOTALS:	$8,302.47	$2,880.00	$890.59	$488.10	$0.00	$12,561.16
TOTALS:	$26,008.27	$9,600.00	$2,815.36	$488.10	$0.00	$38,911.73

YOU ARE 100.0% VESTED IN YOUR EMPLOYER MATCHING ACCOUNT(S).
YOU ARE 100% VESTED IN ALL OTHER ACCOUNT(S).

****

SUMMARY OF ACCOUNT FROM INCEPTION TO 12/31/90

ACCOUNT	CONTRIBUTIONS	EARNINGS	FORFEITURES	DISTRIBUTIONS & ADJUSTMENTS
SALARY REDUCTION	22,080.00	4,270.57	0.00	0.00
MATCHING	10,080.00	1,993.06	488.10	0.00
TOTALS:	$32,160.00	$6,263.63	$488.10	$0.00

Average Yields For The Plan Year Ending December 31,1990

Retirement Fund	Average Yield
Fixed Return Fund	8.88%
Balanced Fund	9.32%
Growth Fund	10.41%
Global Fund	7.67%

ALPHA OMEGA ORGANIZATION
RETIREMENT SAVINGS PLAN
VALUATION DATE: 12/31/90

EMPLOYEE: Mary R. Brown
#2   **
           * STATEMENT FOR THE PERIOD 01/01/90 THROUGH 12/31/90 *
           ****

SOURCE OF FUNDS	BEGINNING BALANCE as of 01/01/90	CONTRIBUTIONS	GAIN/LOSS	FORFEITURES	DISTRIBUTIONS & ADJUSTMENTS	ENDING BALANCE as of 12/31/90
SALARY REDUCTION ACCOUNT(S)						
1) FIXED RETURN	1,836.15	450.00	183.03	0.00	0.00	2,469.18
2) BALANCED	1,226.82	450.00	135.31	0.00	0.00	1,812.13
3) GROWTH	1,419.32	450.00	171.17	0.00	0.00	2,040.49
4) GLOBAL	1,050.77	450.00	97.85	0.00	0.00	1,598.62
SUBTOTALS:	$5,533.06	$1,800.00	$587.36	$0.00	$0.00	$7,920.42
MATCHING ACCOUNT(S)						
1) FIXED RETURN	875.38	225.00	87.72	38.13	0.00	1,226.23
2) BALANCED	570.51	225.00	63.66	38.13	0.00	897.30
3) GROWTH	666.56	225.00	81.10	38.13	0.00	1,010.79
4) GLOBAL	482.07	225.00	45.60	38.14	0.00	790.81
SUBTOTALS:	$2,594.52	$900.00	$278.08	$152.53	$0.00	$3,925.13
TOTALS:	$8,127.58	$2,700.00	$865.44	$152.53	$0.00	$11,845.55

YOU ARE 100.0% VESTED IN YOUR EMPLOYER MATCHING ACCOUNT(S).
YOU ARE 100% VESTED IN ALL OTHER ACCOUNT(S).

****

SUMMARY OF ACCOUNT FROM INCEPTION TO 12/31/90

ACCOUNT	CONTRIBUTIONS	EARNINGS	FORFEITURES	DISTRIBUTIONS & ADJUSTMENTS
SALARY REDUCTION	6,600.00	1,320.42	0.00	0.00
MATCHING	3,150.00	622.60	152.53	0.00
TOTALS:	$9,750.00	$1,943.02	$152.53	$0.00

Average Yields For The Plan Year Ending December 31, 1990

Retirement Fund	Average Yield
Fixed Return Fund	8.88%
Balanced Fund	9.32%
Growth Fund	10.41%
Global Fund	7.67%

ALPHA OMEGA ORGANIZATION
RETIREMENT SAVINGS PLAN
VALUATION DATE: 12/31/90

EMPLOYEE: Deborah S. Carter
#3   ***
             * STATEMENT FOR THE PERIOD 01/01/90 THROUGH 12/31/90 *
             ****

SOURCE OF FUNDS	BEGINNING BALANCE as of 01/01/90	CONTRIBUTIONS	GAIN/LOSS	FORFEITURES	DISTRIBUTIONS & ADJUSTMENTS	ENDING BALANCE as of 12/31/90
SALARY REDUCTION ACCOUNT(S)						
1) FIXED RETURN	1,762.71	432.00	175.71	0.00	0.00	2,370.42
2) BALANCED	1,177.74	216.00	119.83	0.00	0.00	1,513.57
3) GROWTH	1,362.54	129.60	148.59	0.00	0.00	1,640.73
4) GLOBAL	1,008.73	86.40	80.68	0.00	0.00	1,175.81
SUBTOTALS:	$5,311.72	$864.00	$524.81	$0.00	$0.00	$6,700.53
MATCHING ACCOUNT(S)						
1) FIXED RETURN	840.38	216.00	84.22	36.61	0.00	1,177.21
2) BALANCED	547.69	108.00	56.08	18.30	0.00	730.07
3) GROWTH	639.89	64.80	69.99	10.98	0.00	785.66
4) GLOBAL	462.79	43.20	37.15	7.32	0.00	550.46
SUBTOTALS:	$2,490.75	$432.00	$247.44	$73.21	$0.00	$3,243.40
TOTALS:	$7,802.47	$1,296.00	$772.25	$73.21	$0.00	$9,943.93

YOU ARE 100.0% VESTED IN YOUR EMPLOYER MATCHING ACCOUNT(S).
YOU ARE 100% VESTED IN ALL OTHER ACCOUNT(S).

****

SUMMARY OF ACCOUNT FROM INCEPTION TO 12/31/90

ACCOUNT	CONTRIBUTIONS	EARNINGS	FORFEITURES	DISTRIBUTIONS & ADJUSTMENTS
SALARY REDUCTION	5,472.00	1,228.53	0.00	0.00
MATCHING	2,592.00	578.19	73.21	0.00
TOTALS:	$8,064.00	$1,806.72	$73.21	$0.00

Average Yields For The Plan Year Ending December 31,1990

Retirement Fund	Average Yield
Fixed Return Fund	8.88%
Balanced Fund	9.32%
Growth Fund	10.41%
Global Fund	7.67%

ALPHA OMEGA ORGANIZATION
RETIREMENT SAVINGS PLAN
VALUATION DATE: 12/31/90

EMPLOYEE: Robert F. Doyle
#4   ***

* STATEMENT FOR THE PERIOD 01/01/90 THROUGH 12/31/90 *
****

SOURCE OF FUNDS	BEGINNING BALANCE as of 01/01/90	CONTRIBUTIONS	GAIN/LOSS	FORFEITURES	DISTRIBUTIONS & ADJUSTMENTS	ENDING BALANCE as of 12/31/90
SALARY REDUCTION ACCOUNT(S)						
1) FIXED RETURN	1,468.92	600.00	90.48	0.00	-1,500.00	659.40
2) BALANCED	981.46	120.00	83.08	0.00	-300.00	884.54
3) GROWTH	1,135.46	120.00	108.83	0.00	-300.00	1,064.29
4) GLOBAL	840.61	360.00	43.77	0.00	-900.00	344.38
5) LOAN	0.00	0.00	0.00	0.00	3,000.00	3,000.00
SUBTOTALS:	$4,426.45	$1,200.00	$326.16	$0.00	$0.00	$5,952.61
MATCHING ACCOUNT(S)						
1) FIXED RETURN	700.31	300.00	75.51	50.85	0.00	1,126.67
2) BALANCED	456.41	60.00	45.33	10.17	0.00	571.91
3) GROWTH	533.24	60.00	58.63	10.17	0.00	662.04
4) GLOBAL	385.66	180.00	36.48	30.50	0.00	632.64
SUBTOTALS:	$2,075.62	$600.00	$215.95	$101.69	$0.00	$2,993.26
TOTALS:	$6,502.07	$1,800.00	$542.11	$101.69	$0.00	$8,945.87

YOU ARE 100.0% VESTED IN YOUR EMPLOYER MATCHING ACCOUNT(S).
YOU ARE 100% VESTED IN ALL OTHER ACCOUNT(S).

****

SUMMARY OF ACCOUNT FROM INCEPTION TO 12/31/90

ACCOUNT	CONTRIBUTIONS	EARNINGS	FORFEITURES	DISTRIBUTIONS & ADJUSTMENTS
SALARY REDUCTION	5,040.00	912.61	0.00	0.00
MATCHING	2,400.00	491.57	101.69	0.00
TOTALS:	$7,440.00	$1,404.18	$101.69	$0.00

Average Yields For The Plan Year Ending December 31,1990

Retirement Fund	Average Yield
Fixed Return Fund	8.88%
Balanced Fund	9.32%
Growth Fund	10.41%
Global Fund	7.67%

ALPHA OMEGA ORGANIZATION
RETIREMENT SAVINGS PLAN
VALUATION DATE: 12/31/90

EMPLOYEE: Paul D. Earley
#5   **
              * STATEMENT FOR THE PERIOD 01/01/90 THROUGH 12/31/90 *
              ****

SOURCE OF FUNDS	BEGINNING BALANCE as of 01/01/90	CONTRIBUTIONS	GAIN/LOSS	FORFEITURES	DISTRIBUTIONS & ADJUSTMENTS	ENDING BALANCE as of 12/31/90
SALARY REDUCTION ACCOUNT(S)						
1) FIXED RETURN	1,101.71	0.00	97.83	0.00	-1,199.54	0.00
2) BALANCED	852.60	0.00	79.46	0.00	-932.06	0.00
3) GROWTH	855.49	0.00	89.06	0.00	-944.55	0.00
4) GLOBAL	858.38	0.00	65.84	0.00	-924.22	0.00
SUBTOTALS:	$3,668.18	$0.00	$332.19	$0.00	-$4,000.37	$0.00
MATCHING ACCOUNT(S)						
1) FIXED RETURN	508.16	0.00	45.12	-442.62	-110.66	0.00
2) BALANCED	383.40	0.00	35.73	-335.30	-83.83	0.00
3) GROWTH	384.63	0.00	40.04	-339.74	-84.93	0.00
4) GLOBAL	385.88	0.00	29.60	-332.39	-83.09	0.00
SUBTOTALS:	$1,662.07	$0.00	$150.49	-$1,450.05	-$362.51	$0.00
TOTALS:	$5,330.25	$0.00	$482.68	-$1,450.05	-$4,362.88	$0.00

TOTAL VESTED PAYMENT: $4,362.88

****

SUMMARY OF ACCOUNT FROM INCEPTION TO 12/31/90

ACCOUNT	CONTRIBUTIONS	EARNINGS	FORFEITURES	DISTRIBUTIONS & ADJUSTMENTS
SALARY REDUCTION	3,300.00	700.37	0.00	-4,000.37
MATCHING	1,500.00	312.56	-1,450.05	-362.51
TOTALS:	$4,800.00	$1,012.93	-$1,450.05	-$4,362.88

Average Yields For The Plan Year Ending December 31,1990

Retirement Fund	Average Yield
Fixed Return Fund	8.88%
Balanced Fund	9.32%
Growth Fund	10.41%
Global Fund	7.67%

```
                          ALPHA OMEGA ORGANIZATION
                          RETIREMENT SAVINGS PLAN
                          VALUATION DATE: 12/31/90

    EMPLOYEE:        William A. Finch
    #6               ********************************************************
                     * STATEMENT FOR THE PERIOD 01/01/90 THROUGH 12/31/90 *
                     ********************************************************
```

SOURCE OF FUNDS	BEGINNING BALANCE as of 01/01/90	CONTRIBUTIONS	GAIN/LOSS	FORFEITURES	DISTRIBUTIONS & ADJUSTMENTS	ENDING BALANCE as of 12/31/90
SALARY REDUCTION ACCOUNT(S)						
1) FIXED RETURN	2,937.86	480.00	250.02	0.00	-724.63	2,943.25
2) BALANCED	1,962.91	480.00	216.98	0.00	250.32	2,910.21
3) GROWTH	2,270.91	480.00	258.38	0.00	-57.68	2,951.61
4) GLOBAL	1,681.22	480.00	167.76	0.00	531.99	2,860.97
SUBTOTALS:	$8,852.90	$1,920.00	$893.14	$0.00	$0.00	$11,666.04
MATCHING ACCOUNT(S)						
1) FIXED RETURN	1,400.61	240.00	118.92	40.68	-362.80	1,437.41
2) BALANCED	912.82	240.00	102.08	40.68	124.99	1,420.57
3) GROWTH	1,066.49	240.00	122.02	40.68	-28.68	1,440.51
4) GLOBAL	771.31	240.00	78.58	40.66	266.49	1,397.04
SUBTOTALS:	$4,151.23	$960.00	$421.60	$162.70	$0.00	$5,695.53
TOTALS:	$13,004.13	$2,880.00	$1,314.74	$162.70	$0.00	$17,361.57

```
          YOU ARE 100.0% VESTED IN YOUR EMPLOYER MATCHING ACCOUNT(S).
          YOU ARE 100% VESTED IN ALL OTHER ACCOUNT(S).

*********************************************************************************************************

                       SUMMARY OF ACCOUNT FROM INCEPTION TO 12/31/90
```

ACCOUNT	CONTRIBUTIONS	EARNINGS	FORFEITURES	DISTRIBUTIONS & ADJUSTMENTS
SALARY REDUCTION	9,600.00	2,066.04	0.00	0.00
MATCHING	4,560.00	972.83	162.70	0.00
TOTALS:	$14,160.00	$3,038.87	$162.70	$0.00

```
              Average Yields For The Plan Year Ending December 31,1990
              Retirement Fund                     Average Yield
              Fixed Return Fund                       8.88%
              Balanced Fund                           9.32%
              Growth Fund                            10.41%
              Global Fund                             7.67%
```

ALPHA OMEGA ORGANIZATION
RETIREMENT SAVINGS PLAN
VALUATION DATE: 12/31/90

EMPLOYEE: Theresa M. Gallagher
#7   ***
     * STATEMENT FOR THE PERIOD 01/01/90 THROUGH 12/31/90 *
     ****

SOURCE OF FUNDS	BEGINNING BALANCE as of 01/01/90	CONTRIBUTIONS	GAIN/LOSS	FORFEITURES	DISTRIBUTIONS & ADJUSTMENTS	ENDING BALANCE as of 12/31/90
SALARY REDUCTION ACCOUNT(S)						
1) FIXED RETURN	0.00	259.20	11.51	0.00	0.00	270.71
2) BALANCED	0.00	129.60	6.04	0.00	0.00	135.64
3) GROWTH	0.00	129.60	6.75	0.00	0.00	136.35
4) GLOBAL	0.00	129.60	4.97	0.00	0.00	134.57
SUBTOTALS:	$0.00	$648.00	$29.27	$0.00	$0.00	$677.27
MATCHING ACCOUNT(S)						
1) FIXED RETURN	0.00	129.60	5.75	21.96	0.00	157.31
2) BALANCED	0.00	64.80	3.02	10.98	0.00	78.80
3) GROWTH	0.00	64.80	3.37	10.98	0.00	79.15
4) GLOBAL	0.00	64.80	2.49	10.99	0.00	78.28
SUBTOTALS:	$0.00	$324.00	$14.63	$54.91	$0.00	$393.54
TOTALS:	$0.00	$972.00	$43.90	$54.91	$0.00	$1,070.81

YOU ARE 20.0% VESTED IN YOUR EMPLOYER MATCHING ACCOUNT(S).
YOU ARE 100% VESTED IN ALL OTHER ACCOUNT(S).

****

SUMMARY OF ACCOUNT FROM INCEPTION TO 12/31/90

ACCOUNT	CONTRIBUTIONS	EARNINGS	FORFEITURES	DISTRIBUTIONS & ADJUSTMENTS
SALARY REDUCTION	648.00	29.27	0.00	0.00
MATCHING	324.00	14.63	54.91	0.00
TOTALS:	$972.00	$43.90	$54.91	$0.00

Average Yields For The Plan Year Ending December 31,1990

Retirement Fund	Average Yield
Fixed Return Fund	8.88%
Balanced Fund	9.32%
Growth Fund	10.41%
Global Fund	7.67%

```
                              ALPHA OMEGA ORGANIZATION
                               RETIREMENT SAVINGS PLAN
                              VALUATION DATE: 12/31/90
      EMPLOYEE:      Arthur W. Hamilton
      #8             *******************************************************
                     * STATEMENT FOR THE PERIOD 01/01/90 THROUGH 12/31/90 *
                     *******************************************************
```

SOURCE OF FUNDS	BEGINNING BALANCE as of 01/01/90	CONTRIBUTIONS	GAIN/LOSS	FORFEITURES	DISTRIBUTIONS & ADJUSTMENTS	ENDING BALANCE as of 12/31/90
SALARY REDUCTION ACCOUNT(S)						
1) FIXED RETURN	2,106.63	288.00	211.16	0.00	254.54	2,860.33
2) BALANCED	716.07	432.00	104.66	0.00	381.81	1,634.54
3) GROWTH	608.25	576.00	119.80	0.00	509.08	1,813.13
4) GLOBAL	1,265.80	144.00	107.49	0.00	127.27	1,644.56
5) LOAN	4,156.15	0.00	376.58	0.00	-1,272.70	3,260.03
SUBTOTALS:	$8,852.90	$1,440.00	$919.69	$0.00	$0.00	$11,212.59
MATCHING ACCOUNT(S)						
1) FIXED RETURN	1,400.61	144.00	130.77	24.40	0.00	1,699.78
2) BALANCED	912.82	216.00	95.14	36.61	0.00	1,260.57
3) GROWTH	1,066.49	288.00	126.01	48.81	0.00	1,529.31
4) GLOBAL	771.31	72.00	61.92	12.20	0.00	917.43
SUBTOTALS:	$4,151.23	$720.00	$413.84	$122.02	$0.00	$5,407.09
TOTALS:	$13,004.13	$2,160.00	$1,333.53	$122.02	$0.00	$16,619.68

```
        YOU ARE 100.0% VESTED IN YOUR EMPLOYER MATCHING ACCOUNT(S).
        YOU ARE 100% VESTED IN ALL OTHER ACCOUNT(S).
```

****

```
                    SUMMARY OF ACCOUNT FROM INCEPTION TO 12/31/90
```

ACCOUNT	CONTRIBUTIONS	EARNINGS	FORFEITURES	DISTRIBUTIONS & ADJUSTMENTS
SALARY REDUCTION	9,120.00	2,092.59	0.00	0.00
MATCHING	4,320.00	965.07	122.02	0.00
TOTALS:	$13,440.00	$3,057.66	$122.02	$0.00

```
        Average Yields For The Plan Year Ending December 31,1990
        Retirement Fund                   Average Yield
        Fixed Return Fund                     8.88%
        Balanced Fund                         9.32%
        Growth Fund                          10.41%
        Global Fund                           7.67%
```

ALPHA OMEGA ORGANIZATION
RETIREMENT SAVINGS PLAN
VALUATION DATE: 12/31/90

EMPLOYEE: Martin D. Ingles
#9   **
              * STATEMENT FOR THE PERIOD 01/01/90 THROUGH 12/31/90 *
              ****

SOURCE OF FUNDS	BEGINNING BALANCE as of 01/01/90	CONTRIBUTIONS	GAIN/LOSS	FORFEITURES	DISTRIBUTIONS & ADJUSTMENTS	ENDING BALANCE as of 12/31/90
SALARY REDUCTION ACCOUNT(S)						
1) FIXED RETURN	2,203.40	540.00	175.24	0.00	-1,000.00	1,918.64
2) BALANCED	1,472.18	162.00	130.78	0.00	-300.00	1,464.96
3) GROWTH	1,703.18	108.00	172.51	0.00	-200.00	1,783.69
4) GLOBAL	1,260.92	270.00	87.89	0.00	-500.00	1,118.81
SUBTOTALS:	$6,639.68	$1,080.00	$566.42	$0.00	-$2,000.00	$6,286.10
MATCHING ACCOUNT(S)						
1) FIXED RETURN	1,050.47	270.00	105.27	45.76	0.00	1,471.50
2) BALANCED	684.61	81.00	67.58	13.73	0.00	846.92
3) GROWTH	799.86	54.00	86.08	9.15	0.00	949.09
4) GLOBAL	578.48	135.00	49.55	22.88	0.00	785.91
SUBTOTALS:	$3,113.42	$540.00	$308.48	$91.52	$0.00	$4,053.42
TOTALS:	$9,753.10	$1,620.00	$874.90	$91.52	-$2,000.00	$10,339.52

YOU ARE 100.0% VESTED IN YOUR EMPLOYER MATCHING ACCOUNT(S).
YOU ARE 100% VESTED IN ALL OTHER ACCOUNT(S).

****

SUMMARY OF ACCOUNT FROM INCEPTION TO 12/31/90

ACCOUNT	CONTRIBUTIONS	EARNINGS	FORFEITURES	DISTRIBUTIONS & ADJUSTMENTS
SALARY REDUCTION	6,840.00	1,446.10	0.00	-2,000.00
MATCHING	3,240.00	721.90	91.52	0.00
TOTALS:	$10,080.00	$2,168.00	$91.52	-$2,000.00

Average Yields For The Plan Year Ending December 31,1990

Retirement Fund	Average Yield
Fixed Return Fund	8.88%
Balanced Fund	9.32%
Growth Fund	10.41%
Global Fund	7.67%

ALPHA OMEGA ORGANIZATION
RETIREMENT SAVINGS PLAN
VALUATION DATE: 12/31/90

EMPLOYEE: Regina S. Jackson
#10   ***
           * STATEMENT FOR THE PERIOD 01/01/90 THROUGH 12/31/90 *
           ****

SOURCE OF FUNDS	BEGINNING BALANCE as of 01/01/90	CONTRIBUTIONS	GAIN/LOSS	FORFEITURES	DISTRIBUTIONS & ADJUSTMENTS	ENDING BALANCE as of 12/31/90
SALARY REDUCTION ACCOUNT(S)						
1) FIXED RETURN	3,672.32	960.00	368.73	0.00	0.00	5,001.05
2) BALANCED	2,453.64	480.00	251.05	0.00	0.00	3,184.69
3) GROWTH	2,838.64	480.00	320.49	0.00	0.00	3,639.13
4) GLOBAL	2,101.53	480.00	179.60	0.00	0.00	2,761.13
SUBTOTALS:	$11,066.13	$2,400.00	$1,119.87	$0.00	$0.00	$14,586.00
MATCHING ACCOUNT(S)						
1) FIXED RETURN	1,750.77	480.00	176.78	81.35	0.00	2,488.90
2) BALANCED	1,141.02	240.00	117.53	40.67	0.00	1,539.22
3) GROWTH	1,333.10	240.00	151.27	40.67	0.00	1,765.04
4) GLOBAL	964.14	240.00	83.15	40.68	0.00	1,327.97
SUBTOTALS:	$5,189.03	$1,200.00	$528.73	$203.37	$0.00	$7,121.13
TOTALS:	$16,255.16	$3,600.00	$1,648.60	$203.37	$0.00	$21,707.13

YOU ARE 100.0% VESTED IN YOUR EMPLOYER MATCHING ACCOUNT(S).
YOU ARE 100% VESTED IN ALL OTHER ACCOUNT(S).

****

SUMMARY OF ACCOUNT FROM INCEPTION TO 12/31/90

ACCOUNT	CONTRIBUTIONS	EARNINGS	FORFEITURES	DISTRIBUTIONS & ADJUSTMENTS
SALARY REDUCTION	12,000.00	2,586.00	0.00	0.00
MATCHING	5,700.00	1,217.76	203.37	0.00
TOTALS:	$17,700.00	$3,803.76	$203.37	$0.00

Average Yields For The Plan Year Ending December 31,1990

Retirement Fund	Average Yield
Fixed Return Fund	8.88%
Balanced Fund	9.32%
Growth Fund	10.41%
Global Fund	7.67%

§ B.12   Loan Documents

§ B.13   —Participant Loans
Procedural Checklist

1. *Documents*

_____ Complete loan application.

_____ Execute promissory note.

_____ Pledge and Assignment.

_____ If the loan is to be for more than five years, evidence of purpose satisfactory to the administrator is attached to the loan application.

_____ Payroll withholding authorization.

2. *Calculation of Maximum Permissible Loan*

Worksheet attached showing maximum loan permissible under the Plan. The maximum permissible loan under the Plan is $_____. The loan applied for _____ does ___X___ does not exceed the maximum amount permissible under the Plan.

3. *Administrative Action*

(a) _____ The loan has been:

_____ granted.

_____ denied.

(b) _____ The administrator has notified payroll service of deduction.

(c) _____ Cancelled note delivered to borrower upon satisfaction of loan.

4. *Terms of the Loan*

(a) Principal Amount: $_____.

(b) Term: _____ months. Final payment due: _____/_____/_____.

(c) Interest rate: _____% per annum, compounded _____.

(d) Periodic Payment: $_____ each _____.

§ B.14   —Maximum Amount of
Loan Worksheet

There are several limitations on the amount a Participant under the Plan can borrow from the Plan. For the purpose of applying these limitations, all loans for a Participant under the Plan are treated as a single loan.

A. First Limitation Calculation

    1. Enter the highest outstanding balance of loans from the plan during the 1-year period ending on the day before the date on which the new or additional loan is to be made. $_____

    2. Enter the outstanding balance of loans from the plan on the date on which the new or additional loan is to be made. $_____

    3. Subtract amount on line 2 from amount on line 1. $_____

    4. Subtract amount on line 3 from $50,000. $_____

B. Second Limitation Calculation

    1. Enter the present Account Balance under the plan. $_____

    2. Multiply the amount on line 1 by 0.50. $_____

    3. Enter amount on line 2. $_____

C. Third Limitation Calculation

    1. Enter the lower of the amount on line A4 (First Limitation Calculation) or the amount on line B3 (Second Limitation Calculation). $_____

    2. Enter the total of all loans outstanding at the time of the new or additional loan. $_____

    3. Subtract the amount on line 2 (if any) from the amount on line 1. $_____

THE AMOUNT ON LINE C3 IS THE MAXIMUM NEW OR ADDITIONAL LOAN THAT CAN BE PERMITTED AT THIS TIME.

§ B.15 —Application for Participant Loan

Participant's Name: _____Doyle_____ _____Robert_____ _____Francis_____
                                Last   First   Middle

Address: 1201 Capital Street   Xenia   OH   43002
               Street   City   State   Zip Code

Telephone: Home: (614) 828-9812   Office: (614) 302-8122

Date of Birth: August 7, 1954   Loan Amount Requested: $ 3,000

Marital Status: Married   Desired Date of Loan: November 30, 1990

Desired Loan Term: <u>60 months</u> (60 months maximum unless the loan is for the purpose of acquisition of principal residence for the Participant).

The loan _____ is <u>X</u> is not for the purpose of acquiring the principal residence of the Participant.

Repayment will be by payroll withholding in equal amounts over the term of the loan.

_____

Participant's Signature

_____

FOR PLAN ADMINISTRATOR'S USE ONLY

Loan Granted in Amount of $_____

Date of Loan: _____

Interest Rate: _____

Loan Denied _____

§ B.16 —Promissory Note

STATE OF_____ Ohio_____

COUNTY OF___ Summitt_____

<u>Robert F. Doyle</u> $ _____ 3,000 _____

Participant   Amount of Note

<u>1201 Capital Street</u>

<u>Xenia, OH 43002</u>   <u>November 30, 1990</u>

Address   Date of Note

FOR VALUE RECEIVED, the undersigned (the Borrower) promises to pay to the order of the Alpha Omega Retirement Savings Plan (the "Plan"), the sum of

_____ Three Thousand _____ DOLLARS ($ 3,000 _____),

plus interest at the rate of _10.50_ % said principal and interest thereon to be paid in the following manner:

__130__ equal and consecutive monthly installments of $__29.71____ commencing _____ January 1, 1991 _____ . This note may be prepaid without premium or penalty. Payment will be made by payroll deduction.

Any holder hereof may declare all amounts due hereunder to be immediately due and payable whenever the holder deems itself insecure or upon the default in any payment hereunder, or upon the Borrower's failure to comply with the terms hereof, or upon the Borrower's insolvency, bankruptcy, death or incompetency. After maturity, this note will bear interest at the highest legal rate. The Borrower (1) promises to pay all costs of collection, including a reasonable attorney's fee, upon any default hereunder, whether in connection with collection, trial, appeal or otherwise; and (2) waives presentment, demand, notice or dishonor and protest.

This loan is secured by the Borrower's Irrevocable Pledge and Assignment of the Borrower's vested interest in the Plan, a copy of which is provided with this note. The security interest created by the security agreement, if any, extends to all other and future obligations of the Borrower.

If the interest rate shown on the face of this note shall exceed the rate permitted by law, the rate will be reduced by the amount necessary to comply with the law. Any sum previously collected in excess of the legal limit will be used to reduce the principal amount due or refunded to the borrower.

Each borrower shall be jointly and severally liable and each borrower, co-borrower and guarantor of this note consents to renewals, replacements and extension of time for payment hereof before, at or after maturity, consents to the acceptance of security or substituted security for this note and waives demand and protest and the right to assert any statute of limitations.

Dated this _____ 30th _____ day of _____ November _____ , 19 ___ 90 ___ .

_____   _____
          WITNESS   BORROWER

§ B.17 —Irrevocable Pledge and Assignment

In consideration of a loan to me of $3,000, by the Alpha Omega Organization Retirement Savings Plan (the "Plan"), as evidenced by a copy of the Promissory Note attached to this pledge, I hereby irrevocably pledge and assign to the Trustees of the Plan, or to their successor or successors, my vested interest, at any time existing under the Plan, which may be necessary to satisfy the loan which is the subject of this pledge, any unpaid interest on such loan, all attorneys' fees necessary for collection of this obligation and all costs of collection. Failure by me to repay this loan when due or to pay any installment or interest when due shall authorize the Trustees to foreclose on any property or to bring a lawsuit to collect the outstanding indebtedness and interest on the indebtedness.

Should my employment terminate with Alpha Omega Organization for any reason while this obligation is unpaid and under circumstances in which the Trustees would ordinarily make a distribution from the Plan to me or to my named beneficiary, I authorize the Trustees to reduce the amount otherwise distributable to me or to my named beneficiary, by this outstanding indebtedness, together with any accrued interest due on the indebtedness.

This Irrevocable Pledge and Assignment shall bind my heirs, personal representatives or other legal representatives.

Dated this _____30th_____ day of _____November_____, 19____90____ .

_____   _____
        WITNESS   BORROWER

§ B.18 —Payroll Withholding Authorization

I, Robert F. Doyle, do hereby authorize and request that my employer, Alpha Omega Organization and any successor thereto (the "Employer") withhold from my compensation and pay directly to the Trustee under the Alpha Omega Organization Retirement Savings Plan ("the Plan") amounts sufficient to timely discharge my obligations under all promissory notes and other evidences of indebtedness that I have delivered or may hereafter deliver to the Trustee. The authorization and request contained herein shall expire upon the earlier of (1) the date on which the Employer receives from the said Trustee written notice of satisfaction by me (or on my behalf) of my obligations to the Plan to repay all indebtedness thereto and to pay all interest due in respect of such indebtedness, or (2) the date on which the Employer pays over to the Trustee the balance due of all principal amounts and all accrued interest in respect to all such indebtedness.

Date: ____November 30, 1990____ By: _____
                                            BORROWER

Social Security Number: 188-33-4102

§ B.19 —Spouse's Consent to Waiver of Benefits

Participant: ___Robert F. Doyle_____

Spouse: _____Mary L. Doyle_____

I hereby consent to the designation by my spouse of the Beneficiary elected on the Benefit Election Form as indicated above to receive benefits payable under the Alpha Omega Organization Retirement Savings Plan (the "Plan") reason of my spouse's death. These benefits may be paid in any form permitted under the Plan to my spouse's designated Beneficiary.

In granting this consent, I understand that I am waiving (giving up) any right I might have to any benefit under the Plan in the event of my spouse's death, except to the extent that my spouse may name me specifically as a Beneficiary herein. I also understand that, had I not granted this consent, I would have had a right protected by law (subject to the provisions of any applicable qualified domestic relations order in favor of another person) to benefits payable in the event of the death of my spouse if my spouse dies while married to me.

This consent and waiver is my free and voluntary act. I understand that I CAN NOT REVOKE this consent, and that, by executing this consent, I am voluntarily relinquishing my right to limit this consent to a specific form of benefits.

Retirement Committee
(Plan Administrator)

By _____   By _____
          Signature   Signature

Title _____   _____
                                           Date

§ **B.20** —**Amortization Schedule**

Robert F. Doyle

PRINCIPAL = $3,000.00   INTEREST RATE = 10.5%   2 WEEK PERIODS = 130

Period		Principal	Interest	Payment	Balance
1	1	17.59	12.12	29.71	2,982.41
2	2	17.67	12.04	29.71	2,964.74
3	3	17.74	11.97	29.71	2,947.00
4	4	17.81	11.90	29.71	2,929.19
5	5	17.88	11.83	29.71	2,911.31
6	6	17.95	11.76	29.71	2,893.36
7	7	18.03	11.68	29.71	2,875.33
8	8	18.10	11.61	29.71	2,857.23
9	9	18.17	11.54	29.71	2,839.06
10	10	18.24	11.47	29.71	2,820.82
11	11	18.32	11.39	29.71	2,802.50
12	12	18.39	11.32	29.71	2,784.11
13	13	18.47	11.24	29.71	2,765.64
14	14	18.54	11.17	29.71	2,747.10
15	15	18.62	11.09	29.71	2,728.48
16	16	18.69	11.02	29.71	2,709.79
17	17	18.77	10.94	29.71	2,691.02
18	18	18.84	10.87	29.71	2,672.18
19	19	18.92	10.79	29.71	2,653.26
20	20	18.99	10.72	29.71	2,634.27
21	21	19.07	10.64	29.71	2,615.20
22	22	19.15	10.56	29.71	2,596.05
23	23	19.23	10.48	29.71	2,576.82
24	24	19.30	10.41	29.71	2,557.52
25	25	19.38	10.33	29.71	2,538.14
26	26	19.46	10.25	29.71	2,518.68
YEAR	1	$481.32	$291.14	$772.46	
27	1	19.54	10.17	29.71	2,499.14
28	2	19.62	10.09	29.71	2,479.52
29	3	19.70	10.01	29.71	2,459.82
30	4	19.78	9.93	29.71	2,440.04
31	5	19.86	9.85	29.71	2,420.18
32	6	19.94	9.77	29.71	2,400.24
33	7	20.02	9.69	29.71	2,380.22
34	8	20.10	9.61	29.71	2,360.12
35	9	20.18	9.53	29.71	2,339.94
36	10	20.26	9.45	29.71	2,319.68
37	11	20.34	9.37	29.71	2,299.34
38	12	20.42	9.29	29.71	2,278.92
39	13	20.51	9.20	29.71	2,258.41
40	14	20.59	9.12	29.71	2,237.82
41	15	20.67	9.04	29.71	2,217.15
42	16	20.76	8.95	29.71	2,196.39
43	17	20.84	8.87	29.71	2,175.55

Period		Principal	Interest	Payment	Balance
44	18	20.92	8.79	29.71	2,154.63
45	19	21.01	8.70	29.71	2,133.62
46	20	21.09	8.62	29.71	2,112.53
47	21	21.18	8.53	29.71	2,091.35
48	22	21.26	8.45	29.71	2,070.09
49	23	21.35	8.36	29.71	2,048.74
50	24	21.44	8.27	29.71	2,027.30
51	25	21.52	8.19	29.71	2,005.78
52	26	21.61	8.10	29.71	1,984.17
YEAR	2	$534.51	$237.95	$772.46	
53	1	21.70	8.01	29.71	1,962.47
54	2	21.78	7.93	29.71	1,940.69
55	3	21.87	7.84	29.71	1,918.82
56	4	21.96	7.75	29.71	1,896.86
57	5	22.05	7.66	29.71	1,874.81
58	6	22.14	7.57	29.71	1,852.67
59	7	22.23	7.48	29.71	1,830.44
60	8	22.32	7.39	29.71	1,808.12
61	9	22.41	7.30	29.71	1,785.71
62	10	22.50	7.21	29.71	1,763.21
63	11	22.59	7.12	29.71	1,740.62
64	12	22.68	7.03	29.71	1,717.94
65	13	22.77	6.94	29.71	1,695.17
66	14	22.86	6.85	29.71	1,672.31
67	15	22.96	6.75	29.71	1,649.35
68	16	23.05	6.66	29.71	1,626.30
69	17	23.14	6.57	29.71	1,603.16
70	18	23.24	6.47	29.71	1,579.92
71	19	23.33	6.38	29.71	1,556.59
72	20	23.42	6.29	29.71	1,533.17
73	21	23.52	6.19	29.71	1,509.65
74	22	23.61	6.10	29.71	1,486.04
75	23	23.71	6.00	29.71	1,462.33
76	24	23.80	5.91	29.71	1,438.53
77	25	23.90	5.81	29.71	1,414.63
78	26	24.00	5.71	29.71	1,390.63
YEAR	3	$593.54	$178.92	$772.46	
79	1	24.09	5.62	29.71	1,366.54
80	2	24.19	5.52	29.71	1,342.35
81	3	24.29	5.42	29.71	1,318.06
82	4	24.39	5.32	29.71	1,293.67
83	5	24.49	5.22	29.71	1,269.18
84	6	24.58	5.13	29.71	1,244.60
85	7	24.68	5.03	29.71	1,219.92
86	8	24.78	4.93	29.71	1,195.14
87	9	24.88	4.83	29.71	1,170.26

Period		Principal	Interest	Payment	Balance
88	10	24.98	4.73	29.71	1,145.28
89	11	25.08	4.63	29.71	1,120.20
90	12	25.19	4.52	29.71	1,095.01
91	13	25.29	4.42	29.71	1,069.72
92	14	25.39	4.32	29.71	1,044.33
93	15	25.49	4.22	29.71	1,018.84
94	16	25.60	4.11	29.71	993.24
95	17	25.70	4.01	29.71	967.54
96	18	25.80	3.91	29.71	941.74
97	19	25.91	3.80	29.71	915.83
98	20	26.01	3.70	29.71	889.82
99	21	26.12	3.59	29.71	863.70
100	22	26.22	3.49	29.71	837.48
101	23	26.33	3.38	29.71	811.15
102	24	26.43	3.28	29.71	784.72
103	25	26.54	3.17	29.71	758.18
104	26	26.65	3.06	29.71	731.53
YEAR	4	$659.10	$113.36	$772.46	
105	1	26.76	2.95	29.71	704.77
106	2	26.86	2.85	29.71	677.91
107	3	26.97	2.74	29.71	650.94
108	4	27.08	2.63	29.71	623.86
109	5	27.19	2.52	29.71	596.67
110	6	27.30	2.41	29.71	569.37
111	7	27.41	2.30	29.71	541.96
112	8	27.52	2.19	29.71	514.44
113	9	27.63	2.08	29.71	486.81
114	10	27.74	1.97	29.71	459.07
115	11	27.86	1.85	29.71	431.21
116	12	27.97	1.74	29.71	403.24
117	13	28.08	1.63	29.71	375.16
118	14	28.19	1.52	29.71	346.97
119	15	28.31	1.40	29.71	318.66
120	16	28.42	1.29	29.71	290.24
121	17	28.54	1.17	29.71	261.70
122	18	28.65	1.06	29.71	233.05
123	19	28.77	0.94	29.71	204.28
124	20	28.89	0.82	29.71	175.39
125	21	29.00	0.71	29.71	146.39
126	22	29.12	0.59	29.71	117.27
127	23	29.24	0.47	29.71	88.03
128	24	29.35	0.36	29.71	58.68
129	25	29.47	0.24	29.71	29.21
130	26	29.21	0.12	29.33	0.00
YEAR	5	$731.53	$40.55	$772.08	
TOTAL		$3,000.00	$861.92	$3,861.92	

§ B.21   Hardship Withdrawal Documents

§ B.22   —Procedural Checklist

Date	Item

1. _____ Notice of Hardship Withdrawal Received. (HSWIA)

2. _____ Application for Hardship Withdrawal Received. (HSWIB)

Request for Hardship Withdrawal Received. (HSWIC)

Notice of Withholding Received. (HSWID)

a. _____ Returned for completion.

b. _____ Verified as complete.

3. _____ Participant Eligibility for Distribution Verified. (See HSWIA & HSWIC)

4. _____ Hardship Requirement satisfied.

5. _____ Participant Loan Balance Cleared.

6. _____ Qualified Domestic Relations Order File Cleared.

7. _____ Benefit Check Ordered _____.

8. _____ Delivered _____.

9. _____ Section 402(f) Lump Sum Distribution Notice Delivered. (LSDNOT 1 & 2)

10. _____ Receipt of Payment Filed. (HSWIE)

§ B.23   —Notice of Hardship Withdrawal

Alpha Omega Organization Retirement Savings Plan provides that you may withdraw Pre-Tax Contributions if you have an immediate financial need. Withdrawals are limited to Pre-Tax Contributions and pre-1989 earnings on this account. You may not withdraw earnings on contributions credited to your Salary Reduction Account after January 1, 1989.

An immediate financial need can arise for one of the following reasons:

(1) medical expenses which you, your spouse or dependents incur. These must be expenses described in Section 213 of the Internal Revenue Code;

(2) to purchase your principal residence;

(3) to pay tuition for the next semester or quarter of post-secondary education for you, your spouse, children or dependents; or

(4) to prevent your eviction from your principal residence or the foreclosure on your principal residence.

Also, in order to qualify for a withdrawal, you must have no other resources or savings to take care of the immediate financial need. Under special rules permitted by the IRS you will be considered not to have sufficient resources to meet the immediate financial need, but only if:

(1) the hardship distribution we make to you is not in excess of the immediate financial need including any amounts necessary to pay any federal, state, or local income taxes or penalties reasonably anticipated to result from the distribution;

(2) you have already obtained all distributions (other than a hardship distribution) and non-taxable loans available from any plan we maintain;

(3) you agree not to make salary reduction and voluntary contributions to the plan and all other plans maintained by the Employer for a 12-month period after you receive the hardship distribution

(4) you agree to reduce the amount of salary reduction contributions for the calendar year following the calendar year in which you receive the hardship distribution by the amount of salary reduction contributions which you made in the year you received the hardship distribution; and

(5) you agree to continue to make any loan payments currently through payroll deduction for the remainder of the loan.

The entire amount you withdraw will generally be subject to current Federal income taxation. If you are under age $59\frac{1}{2}$ at the time of the distribution, there may also be an additional income tax because of your age at the time of distribution. You should consult your personal tax adviser as to the tax consequences of any distribution you contemplate before filing the application.

If you wish to apply for a hardship distribution, you should fill out an application which the Administrator will provide. Return the application to the Administrator, Mr. Michael Salamon.

Retirement Committee   Participant

§ B.24 —Application for Hardship Withdrawal from Participant's Employee Salary

Participant's Name: ___Martin D. Ingles___

Address: ___140 Plymouth Drive___

City: ___Sharon___ State: ___PA___ Zip Code: ___31021___

Date of Birth: 09/30/58 Social Security Number: 401 – 28 – 3806

I hereby request that there be distributed to me from my Salary Reduction account under the Alpha Omega Organization Retirement Savings Plan (the "Plan"), the amount indicated below. I understand that this distribution may be in whole or in part subject to Federal income tax, and that if I am under age 59½ at the time of the distribution, any portion of the distribution which is subject to Federal income tax may be subject to an additional penalty income tax associated with "premature distributions."

Distribution requested:

[   ] Maximum amount available.

[X] $ ___2,000___ .

_____	_____
Date	Participant
_____	_____
Date	Retirement Committee

§ B.25 Savings Account

§ B.26 —Request for Hardship Withdrawal

Participant: ___Martin D. Ingles___ Birth Date: ___September 30, 1958___

Social Security #: 401-28-3806 Employment Date: February 8, 1980

Participation Date: ___January 1, 1987___

I understand that, according to the terms of the plan, I may request a withdrawal in cases of financial hardship. I understand that I can only withdraw Pre-Tax Contributions and pre-1989 earnings on the account,

Salary Reduction Contributions and earnings thereon only as of January 1, 1989.

I understand that the plan must strictly adhere to the IRS rules on hardship withdrawals, which state that such a withdrawal is allowable only to meet specifically defined immediate and heavy financial needs, for which funds are not reasonably available to me from other sources.

The following expenses will be deemed to constitute an immediate and heavy financial need:

(1) Medical expenses incurred by the employee, the employee's spouse or dependents;

(2) The cost of purchasing a principal residence for the employee (excluding mortgage payments thereon);

(3) The cost of tuition for the next 12 months of post-secondary education for the employee, the employee's spouse or dependents (excluding room, board, books, fees or other expenses); or

(4) The amount needed to prevent the eviction of the employee from his principal residence or foreclosure of a mortgage on the principal residence.

In accordance with those rules, I am hereby requesting a hardship withdrawal of $_____.

The reason I need this withdrawal is: _____

_____

(Please describe why the funds are needed)

_____   _____

Date   Participant's Signature

The Administrative Committee has considered this hardship withdrawal request:

( ) Request for hardship withdrawal is APPROVED.
    The Trustee is authorized to make the distribution.

( ) Request for hardship withdrawal is DENIED.

_____   _____

Date   Retirement Committee

§ B.27   Benefits Payment Documents

§ B.28   —Spouse's Consent to Waiver of Benefits

Participant	Martin D. Ingles
Spouse	Sara L. Ingles

I hereby consent to the withdrawn by my spouse of the amount indicated on the Application for Hardship Withdrawal Form by the Alpha Omega Organization Retirement Savings Plan (the "Plan"). This loan may be made as permitted under the Plan.

In granting this consent, I understand that I am waiving (giving up) any right I might have to any benefit under the Plan in the event of my spouse's death, except to the extent that my spouse may name me specifically as a Beneficiary herein. I also understand that, had I not granted this consent, I would have had a right protected by law (subject to the provisions of any applicable qualified domestic relations order in favor of another person) to benefits payable in the event of the death of my spouse if my spouse dies while married to me.

This consent and waiver is my free and voluntary act. I understand that I CAN NOT REVOKE this consent, and that, by executing this consent, I am voluntarily relinquishing my right to limit this consent to a specific form of benefits.

Retirement Committee
(Plan Administrator)

By _____   By _____
            Signature   Signature

Title _____   _____
                                                              Date

§ B.29   —Notice of Withholding on Plan Distributions

The benefit payments you receive from the above named Plan whether they be in the form of a lump sum payment or periodic payments will be subject to Federal income tax withholding unless you elect not to have withholding apply. Withholding will only apply to the portion of your benefit that is already included in your income subject to Federal income tax and will be like wage withholding. Thus, there will be no withholding on the return of your own after tax contributions to the Plan, if applicable.

You may elect to have or to not have withholding apply to your benefit payments by returning the signed and dated election to Alpha Omega Organization Retirement Savings Plan.

For periodic payments only, your election will remain in effect until you revoke it. You may revoke your election and make a new election at any time and as often as you wish by obtaining a new election form, and returning it to the above address signed and dated. Any election will be effective no later than the first day of each quarter of the Plan year after it is received, so long as it is received at least 30 days before that date.

If you do not return the election prior to the date a benefit is to be paid, Federal income tax will be withheld from the taxable portion of your benefit payments as if you were a married individual claiming three withholding allowances.

* * *

As a Participant or Former Participant in the above named Plan, I have received notification and understand the income tax withholding options I may elect.

( ) I DO NOT want to have Federal income tax withheld from my benefit distribution.

( ) I DO want to have Federal income tax withheld from my benefit distribution.

I understand that even if I elect not to have payments withheld that I am still liable for payment of Federal income tax on the taxable portion of my benefit payments. I am also aware that I may be subject to tax penalties under the estimated tax payment rules if my payments of estimated tax and withholding, if any, are not adequate.

_____   _____
        Date   Participant's Signature

§ B.30   —Application for Benefits Payable as a Single Sum

Participant: Paul D. Early   Social Security Number: 178-93-1002

Vested Percentage: 100%   Single Sum Benefit: $4,362.88

Date of Employment: September 8, 1986

Date of Termination: December 30, 1989

Application for Benefits and Consent to Distribution. I hereby request and consent to the distribution to me of my entire vested interest in the

Alpha Omega Organization Retirement Savings Plan (the "Plan"). I understand that upon receipt of this distribution, I shall have no further interest in the Plan and/or the corresponding Trust or any assets held by any funding agent of the Plan. I request that the distribution be made as a single sum in lieu of all other forms of benefits which may be offered under the Plan.

Domestic Relations Order Certification. I hereby certify that I alone am entitled to receive the benefit for which application is made and that no other person has a right to any part of that benefit. I further certify that there does not exist any court order or court-approved settlement pursuant to which any other party (such as, for example, a spouse, a former spouse, a child or other dependent) has an interest in or a right to any part of that benefit.

Receipt. I hereby acknowledge receipt of the sum of $4,362.88, representing my entire vested interest in the Plan and its Trust.

Release. In consideration of payment to me of the amount specified which is incorporated herein by this reference, I do hereby release, remise, and forever discharge, on my own behalf and on behalf of my heirs, assigns, personal representatives, and other beneficiaries, Alpha Omega Organization and its subsidiaries and related corporations (together the "Sponsor"), the officers and directors of the Sponsor, and each of them; the Trustees of the Plan and Trust, and each of them; the Plan Administrator (and if the Plan Administrator is a committee, each member of that committee), from all claims, actions, causes of action, suits, accounts, or demands, in law or in equity, which against the said Sponsor, officers, directors, trustees, Plan Administrator, or any of them, I have had, now have, or which I, my heirs, assigns, personal representatives, or beneficiaries shall or may have for any cause or thing whatsoever, especially in connection with benefits under the said Plan and Trust.

Federal Income Tax Withholding: I elect the following with regard to withholding of Federal Income Tax for my benefit distribution. (Check One)

_____ Do Not Withhold Federal Income Tax from my distribution.

_____ Withhold Federal Income Tax of $200 from my distribution so that my net distribution is $4,162.88.

Retirement Committee
(Plan Administrator)

By: _____   _____
                                                                    Participant's Signature

Title: _____   _____
                                                                            Date

§ B.31 —Notice of Withholding

The distributions you receive from the Alpha Omega Organization Retirement Savings Plan are subject to federal income tax withholding unless you elect not to have withholding apply. Withholding will only apply to the portion of your distribution that is includable in your income for federal income tax purposes.

You may elect not to have withholding apply to your distribution by signing and dating the election and returning it.

If you do not return the election, your distribution may be delayed. If you do not respond by the date your distribution is scheduled to be made, federal income tax will be withheld from the taxable portion of your distribution.

If you elect not to have withholding apply to your distribution, or if you do not have enough federal income tax withheld from your distribution, you may be responsible for payment of estimated tax. You may incur penalties under the estimated tax payment rules if your withholding and estimated tax payments are not sufficient. You have the right to revoke any election to waive federal income tax withholding at any time prior to the date on which the payment to which the election applies is made. Revocation must be in writing and delivered to the Plan Administrator. Any election hereunder remains in effect until revoked.

§ B.32 —Notice to Recipients of a Lump-Sum Distribution

Special Tax Rules

The Internal Revenue Code provides several complex rules relating to the taxation of the amounts you received in this distribution. This notice merely summarizes these rules. You should promptly consult a tax advisor in deciding what course to follow with respect to this distribution.

Rollovers

The Internal Revenue Code permits you to avoid current taxation on any portion of the taxable amount of an eligible distribution by rolling over that portion into another qualified employer retirement plan that accepts rollover contributions or into an individual retirement arrangement (IRA). A tax-free rollover is accomplished by transferring the amount you are rolling over to the new plan or IRA not later than 60 days after you receive the amount from this plan and notifying the trustee or issuer of the new plan or IRA that you are making a rollover contribution. If you receive a series of distributions within a single year that would be treated as a lump sum distribution. The 60-day period does not expire until 60 days after the day you receive the last distribution in the series.

Not all plan distributions are eligible to be rolled over. A distribution must be either a "qualified total distribution" or a "partial distribution" in order to be rolled over. In general, a qualified total distribution is either a lump sum distribution or a distribution because of a plan termination. Generally, lump sum distribution (as defined in Sec. 402(e) of the Internal Revenue Code) means a distribution (after five or more years of participation in the plan) of the entire amount in the plan (account balance) within one taxable year that is made because of an employee's death or separation from service or after an employee is disabled or reaches age 59½. A rollover of a partial distribution to an IRA may be made only if the distribution is an amount equal to at least 50% of an employee's account balance and the partial distribution was made due to the death or disability of the employee or on account of the employee's separation from service. A rollover of any portion of a partial distribution may disqualify a subsequent distribution from the same type of plan from five-year averaging (described below). There are specific and technical qualifications and requirements set forth in Sec. 402 of the Internal Revenue Code that must be satisfied in order for your plan distribution to be eligible to be rolled over.

Five-Year Averaging and Capital Gains Treatment

If your distribution qualifies under Sec. 402(e) of the Internal Revenue Code as a lump sum distribution, and no part of your distribution is rolled over, you may be able to elect to have the distribution taxed under special five-year averaging rules rather than having the entire amount of the distribution taxed as ordinary income. Use of the five-year averaging rules may reduce the amount of income tax you will be required to pay on account of this distribution. Five-year averaging may not be elected unless the employee has participated for any part of at least five years in the plan that made the distribution and unless the employee has attained age 59½ at the time of the distribution. An employee may elect five-year averaging only once.

Under the law prior to 1987, the pre-1974 portion of a lump sum distribution was eligible for capital gains treatment, with the remainder taxed either at ordinary income rates or under ten-year averaging provisions. Beginning in 1987 the special capital gains rules for the pre-1974 portion of a lump sum distribution are eliminated. However, a special transition rule allows limited use of capital gains treatment between 1987 and 1991.

An employee who attained age 50 before January 1, 1986 may elect to have his or her lump sum distribution taxed under a special rule. Under that rule, the pre-1974 portion of a lump sum distribution is taxed at a 20% tax rate; the remainder of the lump sum distribution may be taxed either at ordinary income rates, under five-year averaging provisions, or under special ten-year averaging provisions. Alternatively, the entire distribution could be taxed under five-year or ten-year averaging provisions. If ten-year averaging is elected, 1986 tax rates will be used to compute the tax on the distribution subject to the ten-year averaging provisions. Finally, an employee may elect to receive the special tax treatment described in this paragraph even if such employee has not yet attained age 59^1/$_2$.

Additional Taxes May Apply on Early Withdrawals

If you choose to take your distribution immediately in a lump sum, a 10-percent excise tax may apply in addition to ordinary income tax. The 10-percent penalty tax is imposed on distributions prior to attainment of age 59^1/$_2$. However, the additional tax will not apply to distributions in the event of death or disability. Also, this tax will not apply to employees who separated from service after the attainment of age 55.

The provisions relative to the additional tax on early withdrawals are effective for taxable years beginning after December 31, 1986.

§ B.33   —Spouse's Consent to Benefit Election Other Than a Qualified Joint and Survivor Annuity

Participant _____ Paul D. Early _____

Spouse _____ Martha F. Early _____

I hereby consent to the election by the Participant to decline coverage under the Qualified Joint and Survivor Annuity form of benefits offered by the Alpha Omega Organization Retirement Savings Plan. I understand that, but for this waiver, should the Participant die during my lifetime, I would be entitled to receive a surviving spouse's benefit commencing upon the Participant's death, continuing thereafter for the remainder of my life. I have been provided with all information that I may have requested as to the economic effect of my consent and waiver as provided in this instrument. I understand fully the consequences of this action on my part, and the loss of benefits that I may experience if I survive the Participant. I have participated in the Participant's decision to decline coverage under the Qualified Joint and Survivor Annuity form of benefit, and my action as set forth herein is voluntary and freely taken on my part.

This document does not constitute my consent to the naming of a person other than myself to receive any benefit payable by reason of the death of the Participant under the method of benefit payments he or she selects under the Plan.

Retirement Committee
(Plan Administrator)

By _____   By _____
                Signature   Signature
Title _____   _____
                                                           Date

§ B.34 —Explanation of the Qualified Joint and Survivor Annuity

Explanation of the Benefit

A Qualified Joint and Survivor Annuity is an arrangement providing monthly benefit payments for the life of the Participant (who is called the "primary annuitant"). If the primary annuitant was married at his or her annuity starting date, and is survived by the person who was his or her spouse as of that annuity starting date (the date when benefits are first paid under the annuity), monthly benefits will continue after the death of the primary annuitant to the surviving spouse (called the "contingent annuitant") for the remainder of the contingent annuitant's life. The contingent annuitant's monthly benefit will not be less than 50%, nor more than 100% (as elected by the participant), of the monthly benefit that is payable to the primary annuitant during the primary annuitant's lifetime. Under the Plan, the contingent annuitant's benefit can be set at 50%, 66²/₃% or 100% of the primary annuitant's reduced benefit.

Election Privilege

Under the Plan, if the Participant is married at his benefit commencement date and does not elect otherwise, the benefit he receives will be in the form of a Qualified Joint and Survivor Annuity, providing a surviving spouse's (contingent annuitant's) benefit. The Participant will decide how large the surviving spouse's benefit will be (50%, 66²/₃% or 100%) in relation to the Participant's lifetime monthly benefit. If the Participant does not elect a surviving spouse's benefit of more than 50% of the Participant's benefit, the surviving spouse's benefit will be automatically set at 50% of the Participant's benefit.

If benefits under the Plan are payable as a Qualified Joint and Survivor Annuity with spousal protection, the Participant's monthly benefit will be the reduced actuarial equivalent of his accrued benefit in the normal form under the Plan. The Qualified Joint and Survivor Annuity will have the same lump-sum dollar value or cost to the Plan as a Normal Form benefit, but monthly payments will be smaller than Normal Form benefit monthly payments because, while Normal Form payments always stop at the death of the Participant, the Qualified Joint and Survivor Annuity benefit payments will extend beyond the Participant's lifetime if the Participant's spouse survives the Participant. The greater the actuarial likelihood that benefits will be payable after the death of the Participant, the greater the amount of the contingent annuitant monthly payment, the greater the cost of the survivor's benefit protection, and therefore, the smaller the number of dollars that can be applied to the provision of lifetime benefits for the Participant. The Participant may elect to provide a surviving spouse's monthly benefit greater than 50% of the Participant's benefit (but the survivor's benefit may never exceed 100% of the Participant's monthly benefit), with the additional cost of the larger spousal benefit having the effect of reducing the Participant's lifetime benefit.

The Participant may also elect to decline the Qualified Joint and Survivor Annuity form of benefits in favor of any other available form of benefit of comparable value under the Plan. However, any such election to decline coverage under the Qualified Joint and Survivor Annuity must be consented to by the Participant's spouse, in the manner described below.

The Participant's election period, during which he or she can elect to decline the Qualified Joint and Survivor Annuity form of benefits, shall be the 90-day period immediately preceding his or her benefit commencement date or annuity starting date, except that if the Participant requests in writing from the Plan Administrator specific information on the financial effect of accepting or declining the Qualified Joint and Survivor Annuity form of benefits, the 90-day period will not be deemed to start running until the Plan Administrator provides the requested information. All elections must be in writing and can not be changed after the annuity starting date (the benefit commencement date). If a Participant begins to receive benefits in the form of a Qualified Joint and Survivor Annuity, and then survives his or her spouse, there is no change in the amount of the Participant's monthly benefit payable during the Participant's lifetime, and benefit payments stop at the Participant's death.

Spousal Consent Requirement

Any election by the Participant to decline the Qualified Joint and Survivor Annuity form of benefits must be consented to in writing by the

Participant's spouse. The consent must be witnessed by a representative of the Plan or by a notary public, must evidence understanding by the consenting spouse of the effect of such election and consent, and must become irrevocable as of the annuity starting date. If the election by the Participant of an alternate form of benefits would result in the payment of benefits after the Participant's death to persons other than his or her spouse, a separate or additional written consent by such spouse may be required in which the designation of non-spousal beneficiaries is approved.

Effect of Election

If a Participant makes an election to waive coverage under the Qualified Joint and Survivor Annuity form of benefits, the benefit, if any, payable after his or her death will be as provided under the form of benefit elected by the Participant. Under such circumstances, there may be no death benefit payable, there may be a benefit payable which expires before the death of the beneficiary, or there may be payable a death benefit which is smaller than, or payable for a shorter period than, the benefit that would have been payable under a Qualified Joint and Survivor Annuity. Moreover, any such benefit as may be so payable may be payable to a party other than the Participant's spouse. If the Participant makes (with spousal consent) an election to decline coverage under a Qualified Joint and Survivor Annuity and thereafter revokes the election (or his or her spouse revokes consent to that election), which revocation must occur prior to the Participant's benefit commencement date, the Participant's benefit will once again become payable in the form of a Qualified Joint and Survivor Annuity without again securing spousal consent to the new election.

NONQUALIFIED DEFERRED COMPENSATION: SAMPLE DOCUMENTS

§ C.1 Sample Plan Agreement

The plan document represented is a sample nonqualified deferred compensation plan which is intended to be an "unfunded top-hat" plan for purposes of ERISA. In this plan, no funds are being set aside from which to pay benefits. In other words, benefits are paid out of the general assets of the Company.

Sample, Inc.

Executive Deferred Compensation Plan

Article 1. Establishment and Eligibility

1.1 Effective January 1, 1992, Sample, Inc. (Company) hereby establishes the Sample, Inc. Management Deferred Compensation Plan (Plan). Its purpose is to provide certain employees employed by Sample, Inc. with the opportunity to defer the bonus and/or base salary otherwise payable to the employees by the Company.

1.2 The Company shall determine which employees of the Company shall be eligible to defer base salary or bonuses under this Plan. Employees will be eligible only if they are eligible under the terms of their written employment contract.

1.3 Each eligible employee shall be entitled to make an irrevocable election to defer either base salary or bonuses under the terms of this Plan. An eligible employee who makes such an election, shall be identified as a Participant of the Plan.

1.4 A Participant may elect to make an irrevocable election to defer the base salary and/or bonus otherwise payable to him for the following calendar year on an election form at any time up to December 31. The Participant may defer 5%, 10%, 15%, 20% or 25% of his or her base salary and/or bonus for such period.

Article 2. Separate Bookkeeping Accounts

2.1 A separate account shall be established and maintained for each Participant, which account shall reflect the base salary and/or bonus deferred pursuant hereto, and specified in the applicable election from, by such Participant, and all interest credited thereto from time to time. Each Participant's account balance shall be credited quarterly with interest as of the end of each calendar quarter. In the event of a Participant's account balance is distributed other than at the end of any calendar quarter, he shall be credited with interest thereon from the end of the immediately preceding calendar quarter to the date of distribution. No interest shall be credited to a Participant's account after the distribution of such Participant's account balance. Interest to be credited for any period shall be at a rate equal to the average annual return experience in the Sample, Inc. Defined Benefit Pension Plan for the previous calendar year.

Article 3. Distributions.

3.1 Any and all payments made to the Participant pursuant to the Plan shall be made only from the general assets of the Company. All accounts under the Plan shall be for bookkeeping purposes only and shall not represent a claim against specific assets of the Company.

3.2 No distribution of a Participant's base salary and/or bonus deferred pursuant hereto, or of any interest credited thereon, may be made except as provided in this Article. Subject to the provisions of 3.1, base salary and/or bonus deferred pursuant hereto, shall be payable only in cash, in a lump sum, at the time selected by the Participant in accordance with Section (B) above.

3.3 If any Participant dies before receiving all amounts credited to his account, the unpaid amount in the Participant's account shall be paid to the Participant's surviving spouse or if the Participant has no surviving spouse, the Participant's estate, with that payment to be made at the time selected by the Participant in accordance with Section 3.2 above.

3.4 Notwithstanding the above, any amounts payable hereunder to any person who is under legal disability or who, in the judgment of the Company, is unable to properly manage his financial affairs may be paid to the legal representative of such person. Any such payment shall be deemed to be payment for such person's account and shall be a complete discharge of all liability of the Company with respect to the amount so paid.

3.5 This Plan is intended to qualify xxx(Top hat plan).

Article 4. Administration.

4.1 The Administrator of this Plan shall be the Human Resources Committee except as otherwise determined by such Board of Directors. Such Committee shall have authority to adopt rules and regulations for carrying out the plan and to interpret, construe and implement the provisions hereof. Any decision or interpretation of any provision of the Plan adopted by such Board shall be final and conclusive. A Participant who is also a member xxx.

4.2 All expense of administering the Plan shall be borne by the Company and no part thereof shall be charged against any Participant's account or any amounts distributable hereunder.

Article 5. Amendment and Termination.

The Plan may, at any time or from time to time, be amended, modified or terminated by the Company. However, no amendment, modification or termination of the Plan shall, without the consent of a Participant, adversely affect such Participant's rights with respect to amounts then accrued in his account.

Article 6. Miscellaneous.

6.1 The amount of each Member's base salary and/or bonus which he elects to defer under the Plan shall not be deemed to be compensation for the purpose of calculating the amount of Member's benefits or contributions under a pension plan or retirement plan (qualified under Section 401(a) of the Internal Revenue Code), the amount of life insurance payable under an insurance plan established or maintained by the Company, or the amount of any disability payments payable under any disability plan established or maintained by the Company, except to the extent specifically provided in any such plan.

6.2 Establishment of the Plan shall not be construed as giving any Participant the right to be retained in the Company's service or employ or the right to receive any benefits not specifically provided in the Plan. All base salary and/or bonus deferred or otherwise held for the account of a Participant under the Plan shall remain the sole property of the Company, subject to the claims of its general creditors and available for its use for whatever purposes are desired. With respect to amounts deferred or otherwise held for the account of a Participant, the Participant is merely a general creditor of the Company; and the obligation of the Company hereunder is purely contractual and shall not be funded or secured in any way.

6.3 The rights of a Participant to the payment of deferred compensation as provided in the Plan shall not be assigned, transferred, pledged or encumbered or be subject in any manner to alienation or anticipant. No

Participant may borrow against his account. No account shall be subject in any manner to anticipation, alienation, sale, transfer, assignment, pledge, encumbrance, charge, garnishment, execution or levy of any kind, whether voluntary or involuntary, including but not limited to any liability which is for alimony or other payments for the sopor of a spouse or former spouse, or for any other relative of any Participant.

6.4   Except to the extent superseded by federal law, the laws of the State of Arkansas shall be controlling in all matters relating to the Plan, including construction and performance hereof.

§ C.2   Sample Rabbi Trust Agreement

PREAMBLE

The Sample, Inc. (Company) has entered into employment agreements with specific employees (Executives) pursuant to which, among other things, the Executives have elected to defer receipt of either regular salary or bonuses. In connection therewith, the Company desires to set aside funds in order to provide for the payment of the deferred amounts to the Executive and to establish an irrevocable trust (Trust), the asset of which will be subject to the claims of its creditors and which is designed to qualify as a grantor trust for Federal income tax purposes, and the Trustee is willing to serve as the trustee of the Trust, on the terms and conditions hereinafter set forth.

SECTION 1. General Duties

1.1   The Company has paid the sum of _____ to the Trustee to be held in the Trust as specified in this Agreement. Such sum and the interest earned thereon and proceed derived therefrom are hereinafter referred to as the "Trust Fund."

1.2   The Trustee shall invest the Trust Fund in any or all of the following types of investments: United States Treasury bills, other short-term government and agency obligations, certificates of deposit, commercial paper, money-market instruments, savings accounts and other deposits with a financial institutions. The Company shall direct the Trustee in the manner in which the Trust Fund shall be invested.

1.3   The assets of the Trust shall at all times be subject to the claims of the Company's general creditors, whether currently existing or hereafter arising. If at any time the Company is unable to pay its debts as they mature or is subject to a pending proceeding as a debtor under the Bankruptcy Code, then the President or any Vice President of the Company shall notify the Trustee of such fact and the Trustee shall hold the assets of the Trust in trust for the benefit of the general creditors of the Company and shall deliver any Trust assets to satisfy such claims as a court of competent jurisdiction may direct.

SECTION 2. Administration of the Trust

2.1 Persons dealing with the Trustee shall be under no obligation to see to the proper application of any money paid or property delivered to the Trustee or to inquire into the Trustee's authority as to any transaction.

2.2 The Trustee shall be indemnified by the Company from and against any and all liability or expense, including all expenses reasonably incurred by the Trustee in its own defense if the Company fails to provide such defense, arising out of any investment or disbursement of any part of the Trust Fund made by the Trustee in accordance with this Agreement or any action or inaction with respect to the Trust. Subject to the foregoing, the Trustee shall not be indemnified against any liability or expense for any action or inaction taken or omitted by the Trustee which, under the circumstances, the Trustee knows constitutes a violation of law or a breach of its fiduciary duties.

2.3 In addition to and not by way of limitation of any other powers conferred upon trustees by law or conferred upon the Trustee by the term of this Agreement, the Trustee is authorized and empowered in its discretion:

(a) to make, execute, acknowledge, and deliver any and all instruments required in connection with any transaction it enters into pursuant to the provisions hereof;

(b) to do all acts, whether or not expressly authorized hereby, which it may deem necessary or proper for the protection of the property held hereunder;

(c) to employ, at the expense of the Company, agents, accountants and counsel, and to rely upon information and advice furnished by them;

(d) subject to Section 3.1 hereof, to file and all tax returns with respect to the Trust, to pay any and all of such tax liabilities, and to satisfy any and all tax reporting and withholding requirements with respect to the Trust as may be prescribed from time to time by law; and

(e) in any case in which the Trustee is authorized or required pursuant to the provisions of this Agreement to make any payment or distribution in its absolute discretion in kind or in money or partly in kind and partly in money, to make such payment or distribution and, for the purposes of any such payment or distribution, the judgment of the Trustee concerning the propriety thereof and the relative values of the property involved therein, shall be conclusive and binding upon all persons who might then or thereafter have any claim or interest under this Agreement.

2.3   The Trustee shall keep full accounts of all investment, receipts and disbursements and other transactions hereunder. The Trustee's financial statements, books, accounts and records with respect to the Trust shall be open to inspection by the Company and the Executive and their respective representatives upon reasonable notice at all reasonable times during business hours of the Trustee.

2.4   The Trustee shall render to the Company monthly statements of its receipts and disbursements as Trustee hereunder. If within ten days after receipt of the account or any amended account the Company has not signed and returned a counterpart to the Trustee, nor filed with the Trustee notice of any objection to any act or transaction of the Trustee, the account or amended account shall become an account stated as between the Trustee and the Company. If the Company is satisfied with the account or the account becomes adjusted to it's satisfaction, the Company shall in writing filed with the Trustee signify its approval of the account, and it shall become an account stated as between the Trustee and the Company.

2.5   When an account becomes an account stated, such account shall be finally settled, and the Trustee shall be completely discharged and released, as if such account had been settled and allowed by a judgment or decree of a court of competent jurisdiction in an action or proceeding in which the Trustee, the Company, the Executive and all persons having or claiming to have any interest in the Trust Fund were parties.

2.6   The Trustee, the Company and the Executive shall have the right to apply at any time to a court of competent jurisdiction for judicial settlement of any account of the Trustee not previously settled as hereinabove provided. In any such action or proceeding it shall be necessary to join as parties thereto only the Trustee, the Company and the Executive (although the Trustee may also join other parties as it deems appropriate), and any judgment or decree entered therein shall be conclusive.

2.7   The interests of all persons in the Trust Fund shall be determined in accordance with the terms of this Agreement. To protect the Trust Fund from any expense which might otherwise be incurred, it is imposed as a condition for the securing of any interest in the Trust Fund, and it is hereby agreed, that no other person may institute or maintain any action or proceeding against the Trustee or the Trust or join in any such action or proceeding unless such person shall have obtained (a) written authorization by the Company, (b) a judgment of a court of competent jurisdiction that, in refusing such authorization, the Company has acted fraudulently or in bad faith, or (c) the written consent of the Execute. Except as otherwise provided in Section 2.5 and this Section 2.6, in any action or proceeding affecting the Trust the only necessary parties shall be the Company, the Executive and the Trustee, and no other person shall be entitled to any notice or process.

SECTION 3. Taxes, Compensation of Trustee and Expenses of
                  Administration

3.1 All taxes arising from any Trust Fund distribution which are required to be withheld and deposited with or for the benefit of the applicable taxing authority, including, but not limited to, United States federal income tax, all applicable state and city income taxes, FICA taxes and state disability insurance taxes (hereinafter collectively referred to as "withholding taxes") shall be computed and paid or deposited by the Trustee solely out of the Trust Fund. The Trustee shall prepare and file all tax returns required with respect to the Trust Funds, including, but not limited to, IRS Form 1041 and all information returns (such as Forms W-2 or 1099 -MISC). Any taxes on the Trust Fund or the income thereof or which the Trustee is required to pay with respect to the interest of any person therein shall be paid by the Trustee from the Trust Fund.

3.2 The Trustee shall be paid a fair and just compensation as agreed between the Company and the Trustee for its reasonable expenses of management and administration of the Trust, including reasonable compensation of counsel and any agents engaged by the Trustee to assist it in such management and administration. All expenses of managing and administering the Trust, including, without limitation, the compensation of the Trustee, accounting and legal fees and expenses, and any other expenses related to the administration of the Trust, shall be payable to the Trustee the Trust Fund.

SECTION 4. For Protection of Trustee

4.1 The Trustee may rely upon any certificate, notice of direction purporting to have been signed on behalf of the Company which the Trustee believes to have been signed by the Company or the person or persons authorized to act for the Company. The Trustee may rely upon any certificate, notice or direction of the Company which the Trustee believes to have been signed by a duly authorized officer or agent of the Company.

4.2 The Trustee may consult with any legal counsel, including counsel to the Company, with respect to the construction of this Agreement, its duties hereunder, or any act which it proposes to take or omit and shall not be liable for any action taken or omitted in good faith pursuant to such advice.

4.3   Fiduciary Responsibility

   (a) The Trustee shall carry out its duties hereunder and shall use the care, skill, prudence and diligence under the circumstances then prevailing that prudent person acting in a like capacity and familiar with such matters should use in the conduct of an enterprise of like character and with like aims; provided, however, that the Trustee shall not be liable for any loss sustained by the Trust Fund by reason of the purchase, retention, sale or exchange of any investment in good faith or in accordance with the provisions of this Agreement.

   (b) The Trustee's duties and obligations shall be limited to those expressly imposed upon it by this Agreement, notwithstanding any reference to the Employment Agreement.

4.4   The assets of the Trust shall remain solely those of the Company, and the Executive shall have no right, title or interest in the Trust assets. The trust is not intended to serve as security for the payment of amounts owed to the Executive under the Employment Agreement if the Company or its successor is insolvent. Neither the Company nor the Trustee shall create a security interest in the assets of the Trust in favor of the Execute or any creditor of the Company.

SECTION 5. Resignation and Removal of Trustee

5.1   The Trustee may resign at any time by filing with the Company its written resignation. Such resignation shall take effect 60 days from the date of such filing or upon appointment of a successor pursuant to Section 5.3, whichever shall first occur.

5.2   The Company may remove the Trustee at any time by delivering to the Trustee a written notice of its removal and an appointment of a successor pursuant to Section 5.3. Such removal shall not take effect prior to 30 days from such delivery unless the Trustee agrees to an earlier effective date.

5.3   The appointment of a successor to the Trustee shall take effect upon delivery to the Trustee of (a) an instrument in writing appointing such successor executed by the Company and (b) an acceptance in writing executed by such successor, both acknowledged in the same form as this Agreement. All of the provisions set forth herein with respect to the Trustee shall relate to each successor with the same force and effect as if such successor had been originally named as a Trustee hereunder. If resignation pursuant to Section 5.1, the Trustee or the Company may apply to any court of competent jurisdiction for appointment of a successor.

5.4 Upon the resignation or removal of the Trustee and the appointment of a successor, and after the final account of the Trust has been settled as provided in Article 2, the Trustee shall transfer and deliver the Trust Fund to such successor.

SECTION 6. Payment and Termination of Trust; No Revocation

6.1 The Trustee shall pay the Trust Fund to the Executive at such time or times and in the manner provided in the Deferral Notice and as otherwise provided in this Agreement. If the Executive is deceased at any time when payments form the Trust Fund are to be made to him, such payments shall be made to the Executive's beneficiaries or estate. The Trust shall terminate upon the payment of all of the Trust Fund in accordance with this Section 6.1.

6.2 This Agreement shall be irrevocable and may not be amended or terminated by the Grantor in whole or in part; provided, however, that (a) the Trust may be amended with the express written consent of a majority of the individuals who are beneficiaries on the date such amendment or termination is proposed and (b) the Trust may be amended as necessary either to obtain a favorable ruling form the Internal Revenue Service with respect to the tax consequences of the establishment and settlement of the Trust, or to make non-substantive changes which have no effect on the amount of any Beneficiary's benefits, the time or receipt of benefits, the identity of any recipient of benefits, or the reversion of any assets to the Grantor prior to the Trustee's satisfaction of all of its obligations hereunder.

SECTION 7. Miscellaneous

7.1 This Agreement and the Trust created hereby shall be construed and regulated by the laws of the State of Hawaii, except as otherwise provided by Federal law.

7.2 The titles of Articles and headings of Sections in this Agreement are placed herein for convenience of reference only and, in case of conflict, text of this Agreement, rather than such titles or headings, shall control.

7.3 The Trust hereby created has been established to pay the obligations of the Company, is subject to the rights of the general creditors of the Company and is intended to be (a) classified as a grantor trust as defined in Section 671 et seq. of the Internal Revenue Code of 1986, as amended, and (b) classified as a component of a "plan which is unfunded and is maintained by an employer primarily for the purpose of providing deferred compensation for a select group of management or highly-compensated employees" under Section 201(2), 301(a)(3), and 401(a)(1) of the Employee Retirement Income Security Act of 1974, as amended. Accordingly, all provisions of this Agreement shall be interpreted in a manner that satisfies the requirements that must be met in order that the Trust be so classified.

7.4   All notices, claims, certificates, requests, demands and other communications hereunder all shall be in writing and shall be deemed to have been duly given, delivered and received if personally delivered or if sent by nationally-recognized overnight courier, by telecopy, or by registered or certified mail, return receipt requested and postage prepaid, addressed as follows:

    (a) if to the Trustee, to: _____

    (b) if to the Company, to: _____

or to such other address as the party to whom notice is to be given may have furnished to the other party in writing in accordance herewith. Any such notice or communication shall be deemed to have been received (i) in the case of personal delivery, on the date of such delivery, (ii) in the case of nationally, recognized overnight courier, on the next business day after the date when sent, (iii) in the case of telecopy transmission, when received, and (iv) in the case of mailing, on the fifth business day following that on which the piece of mail containing such communication is posted.

7.5   Entire Agreement; Amendments. This Agreement (together with the other writings referred to herein) contains the entire agreement between the parties with respect to the subject mater hereof and supersedes all prior agreements or understandings between the parties with respect thereto. This Agreement may be amended only by an agreement in writing signed by the parties.

IN WITNESS WHEREOF, the parties have caused this Agreement to be executed as of the date first above written.

§ C.3 Sample Simplified Reporting Statement to U.S. Department of Labor

Dated ——————, 19——

Top Hat Plan Exemption
Pension and Welfare Benefits Administration
Room N-5644
U.S. Department of Labor
200 Constitution Avenue, N.W.
Washington, D.C. 20210

Re: *Alternative Reporting and Disclosure Statement for an Unfunded Deferred Compensation Plan*

Dear Department of Labor:

In compliance with the requirements of the alternative method of reporting and disclosure under Part 1 of Title I of the Employee Retirement Income Security Act of 1974 for unfunded or insured pension plans for a select group of management or highly compensated employees, specified in Department of Labor Regulations, 29 C.F.R. Sec. 2520.104-23, the following information is provided by the undersigned employer.

Name of Employer: Sample, Inc.
Address: 14 E. Drydock Road
                               Anywhere, US
Employer Identification Number: 99-99999999

Sample, Inc. maintains one non-qualified deferred compensation plan primarily for the purpose of providing deferred compensation for a select group of management or highly compensated employees. The name of the Plan is the Sample, Inc. Savings Plan. The Plan benefits 8 participants.

Sample, Inc.

By: ————————————————
         Plan Administrator

SALARY DEFERRAL SEP: SAMPLE DOCUMENTS

§ D.1   Form 5305: Individual Retirement Trust Account

Form **5305** (Rev. December 1987) Department of the Treasury Internal Revenue Service	**Individual Retirement Trust Account** (Under Section 408(a) of the Internal Revenue Code)	**Do NOT File** **with Internal** **Revenue Service**

State of ▶ _____ } SS   ☐ Amendment

County of ▶ _____

Grantor's name _____ Grantor's date of birth _____

Grantor's social security number _____ Grantor's address _____

Trustee's name _____ Trustee's address or principal place of business _____

The Grantor whose name appears above is establishing an individual retirement account (under section 408(a) of the Internal Revenue Code) to provide for his or her retirement and for the support of his or her beneficiaries after death.

The Trustee named above has given the Grantor the disclosure statement required under the Income Tax Regulations under section 408(i) of the Code.

The Grantor has assigned the trust _____ dollars ($ _____) in cash.

The Grantor and the Trustee make the following agreement:

Article I

The Trustee may accept additional cash contributions on behalf of the Grantor for a tax year of the Grantor. The total cash contributions are limited to $2,000 for the tax year unless the contribution is a rollover contribution described in section 402(a)(5), 402(a)(7), 403(a)(4), 403(b)(8), 408(d)(3), of the Code or an employer contribution to a simplified employee pension plan as described in section 408(k).

Article II

The Grantor's interest in the balance in the trust account is nonforfeitable.

Article III

1. No part of the trust funds may be invested in life insurance contracts, nor may the assets of the trust account be commingled with other property except in a common trust fund or common investment fund (within the meaning of section 408(a)(5) of the Code).

2. No part of the trust funds may be invested in collectibles (within the meaning of section 408(m) of the Code).

Article IV

1. The Grantor's entire interest in the trust account must be or begin to be, distributed by the Grantor's required beginning date, the April 1 following the calendar year end in which the Grantor reaches age 70 ½. By that date, the Grantor may elect, in a manner acceptable to the trustee, to have the balance in the trust account distributed in:

   (a) A single sum payment.

   (b) An annuity contract that provides equal or substantially equal monthly, quarterly, or annual payments over the life of the Grantor. The payments must begin by April 1 following the calendar year in which the Grantor reaches age 70 ½.

   (c) An annuity contract that provides equal or substantially equal monthly, quarterly, or annual payments over the joint and last survivor lives of the Grantor and his or her designated beneficiary. The payments must begin by the April 1 following the calendar year in which the Grantor reaches age 70 ½.

   (d) Equal or substantially equal annual payments over a specified period that may not be longer than the Grantor's life expectancy.

   (e) Equal or substantially equal annual payments over a specified period that may not be longer than the joint life and last survivor expectancy of the Grantor and his or her designated beneficiary.

   Even if distributions have begun to be made under option (d) or (e), the Grantor may receive a distribution of the balance in the trust account at any time by giving written notice to the trustee. If the Grantor does not choose any of the methods of distribution described above by the April 1 following the calendar year in which he or she reaches age 70 ½, distribution will be made on that date by a single sum payment. If the Grantor elects as a means of distribution (b) or (c) above, the annuity contract must satisfy the requirements of section 408(b)(1), (3), and (4) of the Code. If the Grantor elects as a means of distribution (d) or (e) above, the annual payment required to be made by the December 31 of the year following the year the Grantor reached age 70½. Annual payments for subsequent years, including the year the Grantor's required beginning date is for the calendar year the Grantor reached age 70½. Annual payments for subsequent years, including the year the Grantor's required beginning date occurs, must by made by December 31 of that year.

2. If the Grantor dies before his or her entire interest is distributed to him or her, the entire remaining interest will be distributed as follows:

   (a) If the Grantor dies on or after the Grantor's required beginning date, distribution must continue to be made in accordance with paragraph 1.

   (b) If the Grantor dies before the Grantor's required beginning date, the entire remaining interest will, at the election of the beneficiary or beneficiaries, either

   (i) Be distributed by the December 31 of the year containing the fifth anniversary of the Grantor's death, or

   (ii) Be distributed in equal or substantially equal payments over the life or life expectancy of the designated beneficiary or beneficiaries.

   The election of either (i) or (ii) must be made by December 31 of the year following the year of the Grantor's death. If the beneficiary or beneficiaries do not elect either of the distribution options described in (i) and (ii), distribution will be made in accordance with (ii) if the beneficiary is the Grantor's surviving spouse, and in accordance with (i) if the beneficiary or beneficiaries are or include anyone other than the surviving spouse. In the case of distributions under (ii), distributions must commence by the December 31 of the year following the year of the Grantor's death. If the Grantor's spouse is the beneficiary, distributions need not commence until the December 31 of the year the Grantor would have attained age 70 ½, if later.

   (c) If the Grantor dies before his or her entire interest has been distributed and if the beneficiary is other than the surviving spouse, no additional cash contributions or rollover contributions may be accepted in the account.

Form **5305** (Rev. 12-87)

5305.1

3. In the case of distribution over life expectancy in equal or substantially equal annual payments, to determine the minimum annual payment for each year, divide the Grantor's entire interest in the trust as of the close of business on December 31 of the preceding year by the life expectancy of the Grantor (or the joint life and last survivor expectancy of the Grantor and the Grantor's designated beneficiary, or the life expectancy of the designated beneficiary, whichever applies). In the case of distributions under paragraph (1), determine the initial life expectancy (or joint life and last survivor expectancy) using the attained ages of the Grantor and designated beneficiary as of their birthdays in the year the Grantor reaches age 70 ½. In the case of distribution in accordance with paragraph (2)(b)(ii), determine life expectancy using the attained age of the designated beneficiary as of the beneficiary's birthday in the year distributions are required to commence. Unless the Grantor (or spouse) elects not to have life expectancy recalculated, the Grantor's life expectancy (and the life expectancy of the Grantor's spouse, if applicable) will be recalculated annually using their attained ages as of their birthdays in the year for which the minimum annual payment is being determined. The life expectancy of the designated beneficiary (other than the spouse) will not be recalculated. The minimum annual payment may be made in a series of installments (e.g., monthly, quarterly, etc.) as long as the total payments for the year made by the date required are not less than the minimum amounts required.

Article V

Unless the Grantor dies, is disabled (as defined in section 72(m) of the Code), or reaches age 59½ before any amount is distributed from the trust account, the Trustee must receive from the Grantor a statement explaining how he or she intends to dispose of the amount distributed.

Article VI

1. The Grantor agrees to provide the Trustee with information necessary for the Trustee to prepare any reports required under section 408(i) of the Code and related regulations.

2. The Trustee agrees to submit reports to the Internal Revenue Service and the Grantor as prescribed by the Internal Revenue Service.

Article VII

Notwithstanding any other articles which may be added or incorporated, the provisions of Articles I through III and this sentence will be controlling. Any additional articles that are not consistent with section 408(a) of the Code and related regulations will be invalid.

Article VIII

This agreement will be amended from time to time to comply with the provisions of the Code and related regulations. Other amendments may be made with the consent of the persons whose signatures appear below.

Note: *The following space (Article IX) may be used for any other provisions you wish to add. If you do not wish to add any other provisions, draw a line through this space. If you add provisions, they must comply with applicable requirements of State law and the Internal Revenue Code.*

Article IX

Grantor's signature ....

Trustee's signature ....

Date ....

Witness ....
(Use only if signature of the Grantor or the Trustee is required to be witnessed.)

Instructions

(Section references are to the Internal Revenue Code unless otherwise noted.)

Purpose of Form

This model trust may be used by an individual who wishes to adopt an individual retirement account under section 408(a). When fully executed by the Grantor and the Trustee not later than the time prescribed by law for filing the Federal income tax return for the Grantor's tax year (not including any extensions thereof), an individual will have an individual retirement account (IRA) trust which meets the requirements of section 408(a). This trust must be created in the United States for the exclusive benefit of the Grantor or his/her beneficiaries.

Definitions

Trustee.—The trustee must be a bank or savings and loan association, as defined in section 408(n), or other person who has the approval of the Internal Revenue Service to act as trustee.

Grantor.—The grantor is the person who establishes the trust account.

IRA for Non-Working Spouse

Contributions to an IRA trust account for a non-working spouse must be made to a separate IRA trust account established by the non-working spouse.

This form may be used to establish the IRA trust for the non-working spouse.

An employee's social security number will serve as the identification number of his or her individual retirement account. An employer identification number is only required for each participant-directed individual retirement account. An employer identification number is required for a common fund created for individual retirement accounts.

For more information, get a copy of the required disclosure statement from your trustee or get Publication 590, Individual Retirement Arrangements (IRAs).

Specific Instructions

Article IV.—Distributions made under this Article may be made in a single sum, periodic payment, or a combination of both. The distribution option should be reviewed in the year the Grantor reaches age 70½ to make sure the requirements of section 408(a)(6) have been met.

Article IX.—This Article and any that follow it may incorporate additional provisions that are agreed upon by the grantor and trustee to complete the agreement. These may include, for example: definitions, investment powers, voting rights, exculpatory provisions, amendment and termination, removal of trustee, trustee's fees, state law requirements, beginning date of distributions, accepting only cash, treatment of excess contributions, prohibited transactions with the grantor, etc. Use additional pages if necessary and attach them to this form.

Note: *This form may be reproduced and reduced in size for adoption to passbook or card purposes.*

5305.2

§ D.2   Form 5305-A: Individual Retirement Custodial Account

| Form **5305-A** (Rev. December 1987) Department of the Treasury Internal Revenue Service | **Individual Retirement Custodial Account** (Under Section 408(a) of the Internal Revenue Code) | Do NOT File with Internal Revenue Service |

State of ▶ .... } SS ☐ Amendment

County of ▶ ....

Depositor's name .... Depositor's date of birth ....

Depositor's social security number .... Depositor's address ....

Custodian's name .... Custodian's address or principal place of business ....

The Depositor whose name appears above is establishing an individual retirement account (under section 408(a) of the Internal Revenue Code) to provide for his or her retirement and for the support of his or her beneficiaries after death.

The Custodian named above has given the Depositor the disclosure statement required under the Income Tax Regulations under section 408(i) of the Code.

The Depositor assigned the custodial account .... dollars ($ ....) in cash.

The Depositor and the Custodian make the following agreement:

Article I

The Custodian may accept additional cash contributions on behalf of the Depositor for a tax year of the Depositor. The total cash contributions are limited to $2,000 for the tax year unless the contribution is a rollover contribution described in section 402(a)(5), 402(a)(7), 403(a)(4), 403(b)(8), 408(d)(3) of the Code or an employer contribution to a simplified employee pension plan as described in section 408(k).

Article II

The Depositor's interest in the balance in the custodial account is nonforfeitable.

Article III

1. No part of the custodial funds may be invested in life insurance contracts, nor may the assets of the custodial account be commingled with other property except in a common trust fund or common investment fund (within the meaning of section 408(a)(5) of the Code).

2. No part of the custodial funds may be invested in collectibles (within the meaning of section 408(m) of the Code).

Article IV

1. The Depositor's entire interest in the custodial account must be or begin to be, distributed by the Depositor's required beginning date, the April 1 following the calendar year end in which the Depositor reaches age 70½. By that date, the Depositor may elect, in a manner acceptable to the Custodian, to have the balance in the custodial account distributed in:

(a) A single sum payment.

(b) An annuity contract that provides equal or substantially equal monthly, quarterly, or annual payments over the life of the Depositor. The payments must begin by April 1 following the calendar year in which the Depositor reaches age 70½.

(c) An annuity contract that provides equal or substantially equal monthly, quarterly, or annual payments over the joint and last survivor lives of the Depositor and his or her designated beneficiary. The payments must begin by the April 1 following the calendar year in which the Depositor reaches age 70½.

(d) Equal or substantially equal annual payments over a specified period that may not be longer than the Depositor's life expectancy.

(e) Equal or substantially equal annual payments over a specified period that may not be longer than the joint life and last survivor expectancy of the Depositor and his or her designated beneficiary.

Even if distributions have begun to be made under option (d) or (e), the Depositor may receive a distribution of the balance in the custodial account at any time by giving written notice to the Custodian. If the Depositor does not choose any of the methods of distribution described above by the April 1 following the calendar year in which he or she reaches age 70½, distribution to the Depositor will be made on that date by a single sum payment. If the Depositor elects as a means of distribution (b) or (c) above, the annuity contract must satisfy the requirements of section 408(b)(1), (3), and (4) of the Code. If the Depositor elects as a means of distribution (d) or (e) above, the annual payment required to be made by the Depositor's required beginning date is for the calendar year the Depositor reached age 70½. Annual payments for subsequent years, including the year the Depositor's required beginning date occurs, must by made by December 31 of that year.

2. If the Depositor dies before his or her entire interest is distributed to him or her, the entire remaining interest will be distributed as follows:

(a) If the Depositor dies on or after the Depositor's required beginning date, distribution must continue to be made in accordance with paragraph 1.

(b) If the Depositor dies before the Depositor's required beginning date, the entire remaining interest will, at the election of the beneficiary or beneficiaries, either

(i) Be distributed by the December 31 of the year containing the fifth anniversary of the Depositor's death, or

(ii) Be distributed in equal or substantially equal payments over the life or life expectancy of the designated beneficiary or beneficiaries.

The election of either (i) or (ii) must be made by December 31 of the year following the year of the Depositor's death. If the beneficiary or beneficiaries do not elect either of the distribution options described in (i) and (ii), distribution will be made in accordance with (ii) if the beneficiary is the Depositor's surviving spouse and in accordance with (i) if the beneficiary or beneficiaries are or include anyone other than the surviving spouse. In the case of distributions under (ii), distributions must commence by December 31 of the year following the year of the Depositor's death. If the Depositor's spouse is the beneficiary, distributions need not commence until December 31 of the year the Depositor would have attained age 70½, if later.

(c) If the Depositor dies before his or her entire interest has been distributed and if the beneficiary is other than the surviving spouse, no additional cash contributions or rollover contributions may be accepted in the account.

Form 5305 A (Rev. 12 87) Page **2**

3. In the case of distribution over life expectancy in equal or substantially equal annual payments, to determine the minimum annual payment for each year, divide the Depositor's entire interest in the Custodial account as of the close of business on December 31 of the preceding year by the life expectancy of the Depositor (or the joint life and last survivor expectancy of the Depositor and the Depositor's designated beneficiary, or the life expectancy of the designated beneficiary, whichever applies). In the case of distributions under paragraph (1), determine the initial life expectancy (or joint life and last survivor expectancy) using the attained ages of the Depositor and designated beneficiary as of their birthdays in the year the Depositor reaches age 70½. In the case of distribution in accordance with paragraph (2)(b)(ii), determine life expectancy using the attained age of the designated beneficiary as of the beneficiary's birthday in the year distributions are required to commence. Unless the Depositor (or spouse) elects not to have life expectancy recalculated, the Depositor's life expectancy (and the life expectancy of the Depositor's spouse, if applicable) will be recalculated annually using their attained ages as of their birthdays in the year for which the minimum annual payment is being determined. The life expectancy of the designated beneficiary (other than the spouse) will not be recalculated. The minimum annual payment may be made in a series of installments (e.g., monthly, quarterly, etc.) as long as the total payments for the year made by the date required are not less than the minimum amounts required.

Article V

Unless the Depositor dies, is disabled (as defined in section 72(m) of the Code), or reaches age 59½ before any amount is distributed from the custodial account, the Custodian must receive from the Depositor a statement explaining how he or she intends to dispose of the amount distributed.

Article VI

1. The Depositor agrees to provide the Custodian with information necessary for the Custodian to prepare any reports required under section 408(i) of the Code and related regulations.
2. The Custodian agrees to submit reports to the Internal Revenue Service and the Depositor prescribed by the Internal Revenue Service.

Article VII

Notwithstanding any other articles which may be added or incorporated, the provisions of Articles I through III and this sentence will be controlling. Any additional articles that are not consistent with section 408(a) of the Code and related regulations will be invalid.

Article VIII

This agreement will be amended from time to time to comply with the provisions of the Code and related regulations. Other amendments may be made with the consent of the persons whose signatures appear below.

Note: *The following space (Article IX) may be used for any other provisions you wish to add. If you do not wish to add any other provisions, draw a line through this space. If you add provisions, they must comply with applicable requirements of State law and the Internal Revenue Code.*

Article IX

Depositor's signature _____

Custodian's signature _____

Date _____

Witness _____

(Use only if signature of the Depositor or the Custodian is required to be witnessed.)

Instructions

(Section references are to the Internal Revenue Code unless otherwise noted.)

Purpose of Form

This model custodial account may be used by an individual who wishes to adopt an individual retirement account under section 408(a). When fully executed by the Depositor and the Custodian not later than the time prescribed by law for filing the Federal income tax return for the Depositor's tax year (not including any extensions thereof), an individual will have an individual retirement account (IRA) custodial account which meets the requirements of section 408(a). This account must be created in the United States for the exclusive benefit of the Depositor or his/her beneficiaries.

Definitions

Custodian.—The custodian must be a bank or savings and loan association, as defined in section 408(n), or other person who has the approval of the Internal Revenue Service to act as custodian.

Depositor.—The depositor is the person who establishes the custodial account.

IRA for Non-Working Spouse

Contributions to an IRA custodial account for a non-working spouse must be made to a separate IRA custodial account established by the non-working spouse.

This form may be used to establish the IRA custodial account for the non-working spouse.

An employee's social security number will serve as the identification number of his or her individual retirement account. An employer identification number is only required for each participant-directed individual retirement account. An employer identification number is required for a common fund created for individual retirement accounts.

For more information, get a copy of the required disclosure statement from your custodian or get **Publication 590**, Individual Retirement Arrangements (IRAs).

Specific Instructions

Article IV.—Distributions made under this Article may be made in a single sum, periodic payment, or a combination of both. The distribution option should be reviewed in the year the Depositor reaches age 70½ to make sure the requirements of section 408(a)(6) have been met.

Article IX.—This Article and any that follow it may incorporate additional provisions that are agreed upon by the depositor and custodian to complete the agreement. These may include, for example, definitions, investment powers, voting rights, exculpatory provisions, amendment and termination, removal of custodian, custodian's fees, state law requirements, beginning date of distributions, accepting only cash, treatment of excess contributions, prohibited transactions with the depositor, etc. Use additional pages if necessary and attach them to this form.

Note: *This form may be reproduced and reduced in size for adoption to passbook or card purposes.*

§ D.3   Form 5305A-SEP: Salary Reduction Simplified Employee Pension

Form **5305A-SEP** (Rev. September 1990) Department of the Treasury Internal Revenue Service	**Salary Reduction and Other Elective Simplified Employee Pension-Individual Retirement Accounts Contribution Agreement** (Under Section 408(k) of the Internal Revenue Code)	OMB No. 1545-1012 Expires: 3-31-93 **Do NOT File with Internal Revenue Service**

Caution: *This form may only be used if the three conditions found at Article III, items E, F, and G are met.*

_____ establishes the following arrangement under the terms of section
_____(Business name—employer)_____
408(k) of The Internal Revenue Code and the instructions to this form.

Article I—Eligibility Requirements

Provided the requirements of Article III are met, the employer agrees to permit elective deferrals to be made in each calendar year to the Individual Retirement Accounts or Individual Retirement Annuities (IRA), established by or on behalf of all employees who are at least _____ years old (see instructions) and have performed services for the employer in at least _____years (see instructions) of the immediately preceding 5 years. This ☐ includes   ☐ does not include employees covered under a collective bargaining agreement and ☐ includes ☐ does not include employees whose total compensation during the year is less than $300 (as adjusted annually per section 408(k)(8)).

Article II—Elective Deferrals

A. Salary Reduction Option. A participant may elect to have his or her compensation reduced by the following percentage or amount per pay period, as designated in writing to the employer (check appropriate box, or boxes, and fill in the blanks):

1. ☐ An amount not in excess of _____ % (enter a specified percent of 15% or less) of a participant's compensation.
2. ☐ An amount not in excess of $ _____ (not to exceed $7,000 per year as adjusted per Code section 415(d)).

B. Cash Bonus Option. A participant may base elective deferrals on bonuses that, at the participant's election, may be contributed to the SEP or received by the participant in cash during the calendar year. Check here ☐ if such elective deferrals may be made to this SEP.

Article III—SEP Requirements

The employer agrees that each employee's elective deferrals to this SEP will:

A. Be based only on the first $200,000 of compensation (as adjusted annually per Code section 408(k)(8)).

B. Be limited annually to the lesser of:

1. 15% of compensation (see instructions for Article III); **or**
2. $7,000 (as adjusted annually per Code section 415(d)).

Amounts in excess of these limits will be treated as excess SEP deferrals.

C. Be further reduced, as necessary in accordance with Code section 415, if the employer also maintains a SEP to which non-elective SEP employer contributions are made for a calendar year.

D. Be paid to the employee's IRA trustee, custodian, or insurance company (for an annuity contract) or, if necessary, an IRA established for an employee by an employer.

E. Be made only if at least 50% of the employer's employees eligible to participate elect to have amounts contributed to the SEP.

F. Be made only if the employer had 25 or fewer employees eligible to participate at all times during the prior calendar year.

G. Be adjusted only if deferrals to this SEP for any calendar year do not meet the "ADP" requirements described in the instructions on page 3.

Article IV—Excess SEP Contributions

The employer agrees to notify each employee by March 15 of each year of any excess SEP contributions to the employee's SEP-IRA for the preceding calendar year.

Article V—Top-heavy Requirements

A. Unless paragraph B below is checked, the minimum top-heavy contribution for each year must be allocated to the SEP-IRA of each non-key employee eligible to participate in this SEP in accordance with Code section 416. This allocation may not be less than the smaller of: (1) 3% of the non-key employee's compensation; **or** (2) the largest percentage of elective deferrals, as a percentage of the first $200,000 of the key employee's compensation, deferred by any key employee for that year.

B. ☐ The top-heavy requirements of section 416 will be satisfied through contributions to this employer's non-elective SEP-IRA.

_____   _____
Signature of employer   Date

_____
By

Form **5305A-SEP** (Rev. 9-90)

Instructions for the Employer

(Section references are to the Internal Revenue Code, unless otherwise noted.)

Paperwork Reduction Act Notice.—The Paperwork Reduction Act of 1980 says we must tell you why we are collecting this information, how it is to be used, and whether you must give it to us. The information is used to determine if you are entitled to a deduction for contributions made to a SEP. Completion of this form is required only if you want to establish a Model Elective SEP.

The time needed to complete and file this form will vary depending on individual circumstances. The estimated average time is:

Recordkeeping . . . . 40 min.
**Learning about the
law or the form** . . . . 54 min.
**Preparing the form,
copying, assembling, and
sending the form to IRS** . . . . 20 min.

If you have comments concerning the accuracy of these time estimates or suggestions for making this form more simple, we would be happy to hear from you. You can write to both the **Internal Revenue Service**, Washington, DC 20224, Attention: IRS Reports Clearance Officer, T:FP; and the **Office of Management and Budget**, Paperwork Reduction Project (1545-1012), Washington, DC 20503.

Purpose of Form.—Form 5305A-SEP (model elective SEP) is used by an employer to permit employees to make elective deferrals to a Simplified Employee Pension (SEP) described in section 408(k). This form is NOT to be filed with IRS.

What is a SEP?—A SEP is a plan that provides an employer with a simplified way to enhance the employee's retirement income. Under an elective SEP, employees may choose whether or not to make elective deferrals to the SEP. The employer puts the amounts deferred by employees directly into an IRA set up by the individual employee with a bank, insurance company, or other qualified financial institution. When using this form to establish a SEP, the IRA established by or on behalf of an employee must be a model IRA or a master or prototype IRA for which IRS has issued a favorable opinion letter. Making the agreement on Form 5305A-SEP does not establish an employer IRA as described under section 408(c).

This form may NOT be used by an employer who:

1. Currently maintains any other qualified retirement plan. This does not prevent an employer from also maintaining a Model SEP (Form 5305-SEP) or other SEP to which either elective or non-elective contributions are made.

2. Has maintained in the past a defined benefit plan, even if now terminated.

3. Has any eligible employees by or for whom IRAs have not been established.

4. Has only highly compensated employees.

5. Is a member of one of the groups described in the Specific Instructions for Article III, G, 2 below, UNLESS all eligible employees of all the members of such

groups, trades, or businesses are eligible to make elective deferrals to this SEP, and PROVIDED that in the prior calendar year there were never more than 25 employees eligible to participate in this SEP, in total, of all the members of such groups, trades, or businesses.

6. Is a state or local government or a tax-exempt organization.

This form should be used only if the employer intends to permit elective deferrals to a SEP. If the employer wishes to establish a SEP to which non-elective employer contributions may be made, Form 5305-SEP or a non-model SEP should be used instead of, or in addition to, this form.

Making the Agreement.—This agreement is considered made when:

1. IRAs have been established by or for all of your eligible employees;

2. You have completed all blanks on the agreement form without modification; **and**

3. You have given all your eligible employees copies of the agreement form, instructions, and questions and answers.

Keep the agreement form with your records; do NOT file it with IRS.

Currently, employers who have established a SEP using this agreement and have provided each participant with a copy of this form, including the questions and answers, are not required to file the annual information returns, Form 5500, 5500-C/R, or 5500EZ for the SEP.

Deducting Contributions.—You may deduct contributions made by the due date of the employer's tax return, and extensions thereof, to a SEP subject to the limitations of section 404(h). This SEP is maintained on a calendar year basis, and contributions to the SEP are deductible for your taxable year with or within which the calendar year ends.

However, please see the Actual Deferral Percentage worksheet on page 6.

Specific Instructions

Article I.—Eligibility Requirements

Any employee who is at least 21 years old and has performed "service" for you in at least 3 years of the immediately preceding 5 years must be permitted to participate in the SEP. However, you may establish less restrictive eligibility requirements if you choose. Service is any work performed for you for any period of time, however short. Further, if you are a member of one of the groups described in Article III, G, 2 below, service includes any work performed for any period of time for any other member of such group, trades, or businesses. Generally, to make the agreement, all eligible employees, including leased employees within the meaning of section 414(n) of the affiliated employer must be permitted to make elective deferrals to the SEP. However, employees covered under a collective bargaining agreement and certain nonresident aliens may be excluded if section 410(b)(3)(A) or 410(b)(3)(C) applies to them. Employees whose total compensation for the year is less than $300 also may be excluded.

Article II.—Elective Deferrals

You may permit your employees to make elective deferrals through salary reduction or on the basis of bonuses that, at the participant's option, may be contributed to the SEP or received by the participant in cash during the calendar year.

You are responsible for telling your employees how they may make, change, or terminate elective deferrals based on either salary reduction or cash bonuses. You must also provide a form on which they may make their deferral elections. (This requirement may be satisfied by use of the model form provided on page 5 or by use of a form setting forth, in a manner calculated to be understood by the average plan participant, the information contained in the "Model SEP Deferral Form.") No deferral election may be made with respect to compensation already received.

Article III.—SEP Requirements

A. Elective deferrals may not be based on more than $200,000 of compensation, as adjusted per section 408(k)(8) for cost of living changes. Compensation is the employee's compensation from the employer (figured without including the SEP-IRA contributions) and includes:

● Amounts received for personal services actually performed (see section 1.219-1(c) of the Income Tax Regulations), **and**

● Earned income defined under section 401(c)(2).

Note: *The deferral limit of 15% of compensation (less employer SEP-IRA contributions) is computed using the following formula: (compensation including employer SEP-IRA contribution + 115%) × .15 = 15% of compensation limitation.*

B. The maximum limit on the amount of compensation an employee may elect to defer under a SEP for a calendar year is the lesser of:

● 15% of the employee's compensation; or
● $7,000, adjusted as explained below.

Amounts deferred for a year in excess of $7,000 as adjusted are considered excess deferrals and are subject to the consequences described below.

The $7,000 limit on the amount an employee may elect to defer in each year applies to the total elective deferrals the employee makes for the year under the following arrangements:

1. Elective SEPs under section 408(k)(6);
2. Cash or deferred arrangements under section 401(k); and
3. Salary reduction arrangements under section 403(b).

Thus, the employee may have excess deferrals even if the amount deferred under this SEP does not exceed $7,000.

The $7,000 limit will be indexed according to the cost of living. In addition, the limit may be increased to $9,500 if the employee makes elective deferrals to a salary reduction arrangement under section 403(b).

If an employee who elects to defer compensation under this SEP has made excess deferrals for a year, he or she must withdraw those excess deferrals by April 15 following the year of the deferral. Excess deferrals not withdrawn by April 15 following the year of the deferral may also be subject, when withdrawn, to the 10% tax on early distributions under section 72(t).

C. If you also maintain a Model SEP or any other SEP to which you make non-elective contributions, contributions to the two SEPs together may not exceed the lesser of $30,000 or 15% of compensation for any employee. If these limits are exceeded on behalf of any employee for a particular calendar year, that employee's elective deferrals for that year must be reduced to the extent of the excess.

E. and F. Each of these calculations is made after first excluding employees who do not meet the eligibility requirements of Article I, including employees covered under a collective bargaining agreement and nonresident aliens.

F. New employers who had no employees during the prior calendar year will meet this requirement if they have 25 or fewer employees throughout the first 30 days that the employer is in existence.

G. Actual Deferral Percentage (ADP) Requirements. An excess SEP contribution for the calendar year is the amount of each highly compensated employee's elective deferrals that exceeds the ADP for a calendar year. To meet the ADP requirements for a calendar year, the following test must be satisfied. The ADP of any "highly compensated employee" eligible to participate in this SEP may not be more than the product obtained by multiplying the average of the ADPs for that year of all non-highly compensated employees eligible to participate by 1.25. Only elective deferrals count for this test; non-elective SEP contributions may not be included.

For purposes of making this computation, the calculation of a highly compensated employee's ADP is made on the basis of the entire "affiliated employer." The determination of the number and identity of highly compensated employees is also made on the basis of the affiliated employer.

In addition, for purposes of determining the ADP of a highly compensated individual, the elective deferrals and compensation of the employee will also include the elective deferrals and compensation of any "family member." This special rule applies, however, only if the highly compensated employee is a 5% owner and is one of a group of the ten most highly compensated employees. The elective deferrals and compensation of family members used in this special rule do not count in computing the ADP of individuals who do not fall into this group.

The following definitions apply for purposes of this ADP computation:

1. ADP—the ratio of an employee's elective deferrals for a calendar year to the employee's compensation (as defined in III A. above) for that year. The ADP of an employee who is eligible to make an elective deferral, but who does not make a deferral during the year, is zero.

2. Affiliated employer—the employer and any member of an affiliated service group (as described in section 414(m)), a controlled group of corporations (as described in section 414(b)) or trades or businesses as described in section 414(c),

10/22/90

or any other entity required to be aggregated with the employer under section 414(o).

3. Family member—an individual who is related to a highly compensated individual as a spouse, or as a lineal ascendant, such as a parent or grandparent, or a descendent such as a child or grandchild, or spouse of either of those.

4. Highly compensated individual—an individual who (as described in section 414(q)) during the current or preceding calendar year:
(i) was a 5% or more owner;
(ii) received compensation in excess of $75,000;
(iii) received compensation in excess of $50,000 and was in the top-paid group (the top 20% of employees, by compensation); **or**
(iv) was an officer and received compensation in excess of 50% of the section 415 dollar limit for defined contribution plans. (No more than 3 employees need be taken into account under this rule. At least one officer, the highest-paid officer if no one else meets this test, however, must be taken into account.)

A worksheet to calculate the ADP test and excess SEP contributions is provided on page 6.

Article IV.—Excess SEP Contributions

A. As stated above, a worksheet to calculate excess SEP contributions is provided on page 6 of this booklet. This worksheet should be used to determine the amount of excess SEP contributions to be reported to employees with respect to a calendar year. The employer is responsible for notifying each employee by March 15 of the amount, if any, of any excess SEP contributions to that employee's SEP-IRA for the preceding calendar year. If you do not notify any of your employees by March 15, you must pay a tax equal to 10% of the excess SEP contributions for the preceding calendar year. If you fail to notify your employees by December 31 of the calendar year following the year of the excess SEP contributions, your SEP no longer will be considered to meet the requirements of section 408(k)(6). This means that the earnings on the SEP are subject to tax immediately, that no more deferrals can be made under the SEP, and that deferrals of all employees in the uncorrected excess are includible in their income in that year.

Your notification to each affected employee of the excess SEP contributions must specifically state in a manner calculated to be understood by the average plan participant: (i) the amount of the excess contributions attributable to that employee's elective deferrals; (ii) the calendar year for which the excess contributions were made; (iii) that the excess contributions are includible in the affected employee's gross income for the specified calendar year; and (iv) that failure to withdraw the excess contributions and income attributable thereto by the due date (plus extensions) for filing the affected employee's tax return for the preceding

calendar year may result in significant penalties, with a reference to Question 6 of Form 5305A-SEP for further information concerning possible penalties. If you wish, you may use the model form we have included for this purpose on page 5 following the "Model Elective SEP Deferral Form." If you already have issued W-2s to your employees by the time of the notification of the excess SEP contributions, you must also inform the affected employees any required forms that reflect the fact that excess SEP contributions must be included in an employee's taxable income.

Example: Employee "A," a highly-compensated employee of employer "X," elects to defer $4,000 for calendar year 1987 to his SEP-IRA. A's compensation for 1987, excluding his SEP contribution, was $60,000. On January 15, 1988, X issues to A a W-2 stating that A's taxable income for 1987 was $60,000.

In February of 1988, X calculates the ADP test for 1987 for the SEP and discovers that A's maximum permissible SEP-IRA contribution for 1987 was $3,500. A is the only employee of X with excess SEP contributions. Therefore, on February 20, 1988, X notifies A that A had an excess SEP contribution of $500 for 1987. In addition, X issues the required form to A on that date that specifies that A's corrected taxable income for 1987 was $60,500. X is not liable for the 10% tax on excess SEP-IRA contributions because he notified A of the excess SEP-IRA contributions by March 15, 1988.

To avoid excess SEP contributions with respect to which you must notify employees you may want to institute a mechanism that would monitor elective deferrals on a continuing basis throughout the calendar year to insure that the deferrals comply with the limits as they are paid into each employee's SEP-IRA.

Article V.—Top-heavy Requirements

A. For purposes of determining whether a plan is top-heavy under section 416, elective deferrals are considered employer contributions. Elective deferrals may not be used, however, to satisfy the minimum contribution requirement under section 416. Thus, in any year in which a key employee makes an elective deferral, this Model SEP is deemed top-heavy for purposes of section 416 and the employer is required to make the minimum contribution to the SEP-IRA of each non-key employee eligible to participate in the SEP.

A key employee under section 416(i)(1) is any employee or former employee (and the beneficiaries of these employees) who, at any time during the "determination period," was:

1. an officer of the employer (if the employee's compensation exceeds 50% of the limit under section 415(c)(1)(A));

2. an owner of one of the ten largest interests in the employer (if the employee's compensation exceeds 100% of the limit under section 415(c)(1)(A));

3. a 5% or more owner of the employer; **or**

5305A-SEP.3

4. a 1% owner of the employer (if the employee has compensation in excess of $150,000).

The "determination period" is the current calendar year and the four preceding years.

B. The employer may satisfy the minimum contribution requirement of section 416 by making the required contributions through a non-elective SEP.

Information for the Employee

The following information explains what a Simplified Employee Pension plan is, how contributions are made, and how to treat these contributions for tax purposes.

Please read the questions and answers carefully. For more specific information, also see the agreement form and instructions to your employer on this form.

Questions and Answers

1. Q. What is a Simplified Employee Pension, or SEP?

A. A SEP is a retirement income arrangement. In this particular "elective" SEP, you may choose to defer compensation to your own Individual Retirement Account/Annuity (IRA). These elective deferrals may be based either on a salary reduction arrangement or on bonuses that, at your election, may be contributed to your IRA or received by you in cash. This type of elective SEP is available only to an employer with 25 or fewer eligible employees.

Your employer will provide you with a copy of the agreement containing eligibility requirements and a description of the basis upon which contributions may be made to your IRA.

All amounts contributed to your IRA belong to you, even after you separate from service with that employer.

2. Q. Must I make elective deferrals to an IRA?

A. No. However, if more than half of the eligible employees choose not to make elective deferrals in a particular year, then no employee may participate in an elective SEP of that employer for the year.

3. Q. How much may I elect to defer to my SEP-IRA in a particular year?

A. The amount that may be deferred to this SEP for any year is limited to the lesser of:

(1) 15% of compensation; **or**

(2) $7,000 (as adjusted for increases in the cost of living).

These limits may be reduced if your employer also maintains a SEP to which non-elective contributions are made. In that case, total contributions on your behalf to both SEPs may not exceed the lesser of $30,000 or 15% of your compensation. If these limits are exceeded, the amount you may elect to contribute to this SEP for the year will be correspondingly reduced.

The $7,000 is an overall cap on the maximum amount you may defer in each calendar year to all elective SEPs and cash-or-deferred arrangements under section 401(k), regardless of how many employers you may have worked for during the year.

The $7,000 will be indexed according to the cost of living and is increased to $9,500 (more in some cases) if you make salary reduction contributions under a section 403(b) arrangement of another employer.

If you are a highly compensated employee there may be a further limit on the amount you may contribute to a SEP-IRA for a particular year. This limit is calculated by your employer and is based on a special kind of non-discrimination test known as an ADP test. This test is based on a mathematical formula that limits the percentage of pay that highly compensated employees may elect to defer to a SEP-IRA. As discussed below, your employer will notify you if you have exceeded the ADP limits.

4. Q. How do I treat elective deferrals for tax purposes?

A. The amount you elect to defer to your SEP-IRA is excludible from your gross income, subject to the limitations discussed above, and is not includible as taxable wages on your Form W-2. These amounts are treated as amounts subject to FICA taxes.

5. Q. How will I know if too much is contributed to my SEP-IRA in one year?

A. There are two different ways in which you may contribute too much to your SEP-IRA. One way is to make "excess elective deferrals," i.e., exceed the $7,000 limitation described above. The second way is to make "excess SEP contributions," i.e., violate the "ADP" test, as discussed above. You are responsible for calculating whether or not you have exceeded the $7,000 limitation. Your employer is responsible for determining whether you have made any excess SEP contributions.

Your employer is required to notify you by March 15 if you have made any excess SEP contributions for the preceding calendar year. Your employer will notify you of an excess SEP contribution by providing you with any required form for the preceding calendar year.

6. Q. What must I do about excess deferrals to avoid adverse tax consequences?

A. Excess deferrals are includible in your gross income in the year of the deferral. You should withdraw excess deferrals under this SEP and any income allocable to the excess deferrals from your SEP-IRA by April 15. These amounts cannot be transferred or rolled over to another SEP-IRA.

If you fail to withdraw your excess deferrals and any income allocable thereto by April 15 of the following year, your excess deferrals will be subject to a 6% excise tax for each year they remain in the SEP-IRA.

If you have both excess deferrals and excess SEP contributions (as described in 6a below), the amount of excess deferrals you withdraw by April 15 will reduce your excess SEP contributions.

6a. Q: What must I do about excess SEP contributions to avoid adverse tax consequences?

A. Excess SEP contributions are includible in your gross income in the year of the deferral. You should withdraw excess SEP contributions for a calendar year and

any income allocable to the excess SEP contributions by the due date (including extensions) for filing your income tax return for the year. These amounts cannot be transferred or rolled over to another SEP-IRA.

If you fail to withdraw your excess SEP contributions and income allocable thereto by the due date (including extensions) for filing your income tax return, your excess SEP contributions will be subject to a 6% excise tax for each year they remain in the SEP-IRA.

7. Q. Can I reduce excess elective deferrals or excess SEP contributions by rolling over or transferring amounts from my SEP-IRA to another IRA?

A. No. Excess elective deferrals or excess SEP contributions may be reduced only by a distribution to you. Excess amounts rolled over or transferred to another IRA will be includible in income and subject to the penalties discussed above.

8. Q. How do I know how much income is allocable to my excess elective deferrals or any excess SEP contributions?

A. The rules for determining and allocating income to excess elective deferrals or SEP contributions are the same as those governing regular IRA contributions. The trustee or custodian of your SEP-IRA may be able to inform you of the amount of income allocable to your excess amounts.

9. Q. May I also contribute to my IRA if I am a participant in a SEP?

A. Yes. You may still contribute the lesser of $2,000 or 100% of compensation to an IRA. However, the amount that is deductible is subject to various limitations. See Publication 590 for more specific information.

10. Q. Are there any restrictions on the IRA I select to deposit my SEP contributions in?

A. Under the Model Elective SEP that is approved by IRS, contributions must be made either to a Model IRA that is executed on an IRS form or a master or prototype IRA for which IRS has issued a favorable opinion letter.

11. Q. Can I move funds from my SEP-IRA to another tax-sheltered IRA?

A. Yes but see below. It is permissible for you to withdraw, or receive, funds from your SEP-IRA, and no more than 60 days later, place such funds in another IRA or SEP-IRA. This is called a "rollover" and may not be done without penalty more frequently than at one-year intervals. However, there are no restrictions on the number of times you may make "transfers" if you arrange to have such funds transferred between the trustees, so that you never have possession.

12. Q. What happens if I withdraw my elective deferrals to my SEP-IRA?

A. If you don't want to leave the money in the IRA, you may withdraw it at any time, but any amount withdrawn is includible in your income. Also, if withdrawals occur before you are 59½, and not on account of death or disability, you may be subject to a 10% penalty tax. (As discussed above, different rules apply to the removal of excess amounts contributed to your SEP-IRA.)

13. Q. What happens if I transfer or distribute contributions from my SEP before the ADP test described in Question 3 has been satisfied.

A. If you make a transfer or a distribution from your SEP before the nondiscrimination test has been satisfied, the distribution will be subject to regular income tax as provided in section 72 and the additional 10% tax on early distributions in section 72(t).

14. Q. May I participate in a SEP even though I'm covered by another plan?

A. An employer may adopt this IRS Model Elective SEP (Form 5305A-SEP) and at the same time maintain an IRS Model SEP (Form 5305-SEP) or other non-elective SEP. However, an employer may not adopt this IRS Model Elective SEP if the employer maintains any qualified retirement plan or has ever maintained a qualified defined benefit plan. If you work for several employers, however, you may be covered by a SEP of one employer and a different SEP or pension or profit-sharing plan of another employer.

You should remember, however, as discussed in Question 3 above, that your elective deferrals to all plans or arrangements, even if maintained by unrelated employers, are subject to a $7,000 limit (more if one is a section 403(b) annuity). If you participate in two arrangements that permit elective deferrals, you should take care that this limit is not exceeded for any calendar year.

15. Q. Do I need to file any additional forms with IRS because I participate in a SEP?

A. No.

16. Q. Is my employer required to provide me with information about SEP-IRAs and the SEP agreement?

A. Yes. Your employer must provide you with a copy of the executed SEP agreement (Form 5305A-SEP), these Questions and Answers, the form used by the employee to defer amounts to the SEP, the notice of excess SEP contributions, if applicable, and a statement each year showing any contribution to your SEP-IRA.

17. Q. Is the financial institution where my IRA is established also required to provide me with information?

A. Yes. It must provide you with a disclosure statement that contains the following items of information in plain, nontechnical language:

(1) the statutory requirements that relate to your IRA;

(2) the tax consequences that follow the exercise of various options and what those options are;

(3) participation eligibility rules, and rules on the deductibility and nondeductibility of retirement savings;

(4) the circumstances and procedures under which you may revoke your IRA, including the name, address, and telephone number of the person designated to receive

notice of revocation (this explanation must be prominently displayed at the beginning of the disclosure statement);

(5) explanations of when penalties may be assessed against you because of specified prohibited or penalized activities concerning your IRA; and

(6) financial disclosure information which:

(a) either projects value growth rates of your IRA under various contribution and retirement schedules, or describes the method of computing and allocating annual earnings and charges which may be assessed;

(b) describes whether, and for what period, the growth projections for the plan are guaranteed, or a statement of earnings rate and terms on which these projections are based; and

(c) states the sales commission to be charged in each year expressed as a percentage of $1,000.

See **Publication 590,** Individual Retirement Arrangements (IRAs), available at most IRS offices, for a more complete explanation of the disclosure requirements.

In addition to this disclosure statement, the financial institution is required to provide you with a financial statement each year. It may be necessary to retain and refer to statements for more than one year to evaluate the investment performance of the IRA and in order that you will know how to report IRA distributions for tax purposes.

Model Elective SEP Deferral Form

I. Salary reduction deferral

Subject to the requirements of the Model Elective SEP of _____ , I authorize the following amount or percentage of my
(insert name of employer)
compensation to be withheld from each of my paychecks and contributed to my SEP-IRA:

(a) _____ percent of my salary (not in excess of 15%); or **(b)** _____ dollar amount.

This salary reduction authorization shall remain in effect until I give a written modification or termination of its terms to my employer.

II. Cash bonus deferral

Subject to the requirements of the Model Elective SEP of _____ , I authorize the following amount to be contributed to my
(insert name of employer)
SEP-IRA rather than being paid to me in cash: _____ dollar amount.

III. Amount of deferral

I understand that the total amount I defer in any calendar year to this SEP may not exceed the lesser of: **(a)** 15% of my compensation; or **(b)** $7,000 (as adjusted per Code section 415(d)).

IV. Commencement of deferral

The deferral election specified in either I. or II. above shall not become effective before: _____
(Specify a date no earlier than the next payday beginning after this authorization.)   (Month, Day, Year)

Signature ▶ _____   Date ▶ _____

Notification of Excess SEP Contributions

To: _____
(Name of employee)

Our calculations indicate that the elective deferrals you made to your SEP-IRA for calendar year _____ exceed the maximum permissible limits under section 408(k)(6) of the Internal Revenue Code. You made excess SEP contributions of $_____ for that year.

These excess SEP contributions are includible in your gross income for the calendar year specified above.

These excess SEP contributions must be distributed from your IRA by the due date (plus extensions) for filing your tax return for the preceding calendar year (normally April 15th) in order to avoid significant penalties. Income allocable to the excess amounts must be withdrawn at the same time and is includible in income along with the excess contributions. Excess contributions left in your SEP-IRA account after that time are subject to a 6% excise tax.

Signature ▶ _____   Date ▶ _____

Elective SEP Actual Deferred Percentage Worksheet

a Employee Name	b Status H = Highly compensated F = Family 0 = Other	c Compensation (Including compensation from related employers and compensation of family.)	d Deferrals (Add all SEP defer- rals; add deferrals of family to HCE*)	e Ratio (if family member enter N.A. - otherwise d ÷ c)	f Permitted ratio (for HCE* only from below)	g Permitted amount (for HCE* only) c X f	h Excess (for HCE* only) d minus g
1.							
2.							
3.							
4.							
5.							
6.							
7.							
8.							
9.							
10.							
11.							
12.							
13.							
14.							
15.							
16.							
17.							
18.							
19.							
20.							
21.							
22.							
23.							
24.							
25.							

Permitted Ratio Computation for column f:

A. Enter the total of all the ratios of the employees marked as "-0-" in column b _____

B. Divide line A by the number of employees marked as "-0-" in column b _____

C. Permitted ratio—Multiply line B by 1.25 and enter the permitted ratio here _____

* Highly compensated employee

INDEX